A Small Town Goes To War:

Histories of the World War II Veterans of Independence, Wisconsin

Michael Lyga

DEDICATION

This work is dedicated to the more than 280 men and women of the Independence, Wisconsin, "trade area" who served their country and their Community during the days of World War II. It is especially dedicated to those who gave their lives at such a young age for an ideal.

What you did mattered, and always will.

Honor Roll

Pvt. Ralph Sylla – died in training, Texas, October 17, 1942

Ensign Jerome Sobota – killed in action, South Pacific, July 18, 1943

Pfc Willis Cripps – died while on duty, England, December 23, 1943

Pfc Glen Rustad – killed in action, Italy, June 8, 1944

Pfc Elmo Berg – killed in action, France, June 11, 1944

Pfc Owen Carlson – killed in action, France, September 5, 1944

Pfc Ralph Sluga – killed in action, Belgium, January 14, 1945

Staff Sergeant Adelbert Bautch – killed in action, Luxembourg, January 20, 1945

Pfc Louis Bisek – killed in action, Luzon, April 1945

ACKNOWLEDGEMENTS

This project could not have happened if it hadn't been for the surviving veterans who so willingly described their experiences orally and in writing and provided personal materials to me. I know for some it was very difficult and painful to relive those days. I am indebted to the families of veterans who entrusted to me such valuable personal materials as they did in order to help me write a memorial to them – their father, mother, grandfather, grandmother, brother, sister, uncle, or aunt. A big "thank you" goes to the Independence Public Library for making its microfilm of the Independence *News-Wave* of the period available to me. To my cousin, Steve Johnson, who volunteered his time to reproduce all the photos included here, the "faces to the stories" help give the stories meaning. Ed Myers worked with ads and other graphics published in the *News-Wave*. World War II veterans George Michel of the 392nd Bomb Group and Chan Rogers and F. A. Rogers, both of the 103rd Infantry Division, were very helpful in tracking down details regarding biographies. My aunt, Pelchie Hotchkiss, whose husband's biography is included here, and Dan Halama of Independence were great sources of family-relationship information. Tim Kornowski, an Ashwaubenon High School student at the time this document was originally assembled, did several illustrations that are included herewith. Thank you for your help! And to all the people who encouraged me to complete, as another cousin called it, this "honorable endeavour," thank you, one and all.

I would be remiss if I did not acknowledge the work of Glenn Kirkpatrick, publisher of the Independence *News-Wave* during the war years, who, knowingly or not, preserved much of the history of Independence's war veterans by asking for and publishing numerous letters from the men and women in the service.

IMPORTANT AUTHOR'S NOTE – Please read.

This document was first compiled in the late 1990's. When completed, the author did exactly what should be done with computer-generated data – perform a backup. And, then it happened – my computer suffered a hard-drive crash! So, I purchased a new computer, but when the backup was installed, it was found that the disks were blank! Fortunately, all was not lost as I also had a hardcopy backup from which this published document was made. There are flaws, the most obvious being the right margins are not justified. I hope the reader would find that, and any other errors, to be a minor distraction and instead find the stories of the veterans to be of the most interest.

Like any historical document, this one is accurate only to the degree of the accuracy of the documents made available to the author, whether personal, military, or published. An attempt was made to utilize only reputable references and all information was thoroughly researched. Only verified information is presented and any speculation (which is at a minimum) is identified as such.

Michael Lyga
September 20, 2012

Table of Contents

Introduction (found in both volumes)   VII
Prelude to War (found in both volumes)   XI
Maps   XIV

The Biographies:

            * denotes oral history   + denotes written history

Austin, Waldo	3	Leque, Carl "Ole"	98
Baecker, Margaret *	5	Libowski, Joseph	100
Baecker, Walter	7	Lucente, John *	106
Bautch, Adelbert A.	10	Lyga, Edmund J. *	107
Bautch, Edmund	12	Markham, George F.	115
Bautch, Ernest P.	15	Markham, Richard "Dick"	121
Bautch, Roman T.	17	Marsolek, Marcel "Zeke" M. +	124
Bisek, Benedict	18	Marsolek, Michael W.	130
Bisek, Emil	20	Matchey, Ladislaus "Laddie *	131
Bisek, Frank	20	Maule, Edward J.	133
Bisek, Louis	22	Mish, Peter "Pete" P. *	134
Blaha, Everette "Blaze" *	23	Mlynek, Joseph "Chester" C.	136
Carlson, Owen K.	27	Nogosek, Adolph A. *	137
Cilley, Gordon D.	29	Olson, Afner H.	139
Cripps, Willis R.	31	Pampuch, Marcel	140
Dejno, Verna "Veronica" +	32	Pampuch, Paul J. *	142
Edmundson, Jesse	33	Pape, Allen C.	144
Gamroth, Henry "Hank"	36	Pieterick, Gerald "Bud" J.	145
Gasatis, Ben	42	Pieterick, Ray *	149
Gunem, Lester	45	Ressel, Stanley A.	160
Hendrickson, Glen F.	46	Rustad, Glen H.	161
Hotchkiss, Addison	50	Sather, George R.	163
Insteness, Glenn	52	Sather, Norval M.	164
Isaacs, Bernie +	53	Sather, Oscar W.	166
Jaszewski, John J.	55	Schneider, Benedict "Junior" V. *	167
Jaszewski, Joseph "Jazzy"	58	Schneider, George	170
Jaszewski, Nicholas B.	63	Skroch, Adrian	172
Jonietz, Ralph J. +	66	Skroch, Albert	173
Kampa, Lawrence "Laury" *	68	Skroch, Edward I.	175
Kampa, Louis P.	69	Skroch, Dr. Eugene E. +	177
Karasch, Apolinary "A.J." +	70	Skroch, Simon "Bob" R.	178
Karasch, Vincent *	73	Skroch, Peter	180
Killian, Eugene	73	Slaby, Peter	183
Klick, Raymond S.	74	Sluga, Clarence P. *	184
Klimek, Ralph S.	76	Sluga, Ralph R.	187
Kloss, Alex E.	82	Smick, Dominic A.	189
Kloss, Bennie	83	Smick, Thomas George	191
Kulig, Alphonse "Al" *	85	Smieja, Rudolph "Rudy" R.	195
Kulig, Arthur "Art" A.	88	Smieja, Vitus *	197
Kulig, Benedict "Bennie"	92	Sobota, Jerome J.	199
Kulig, Bernard "Bernie" J. *	96	Sobota, Roman "Butch" A.	202
Kulig, Edward J. *	97	Sobotta, Emil	205

Sobotta, Ernest "Sheeney" P. *   208
Sobotta, Paul P.   212
Sonsalla, Adolph   214
Sprecher, Drexel A.   216
Suchla, Edmund A.   225
Sura, Clarence   227
Sura, Dominic   233
Sura, Henry   234
Sura, Lawrence L.   235

Sura, Leonard   236
Sylla, Leonard L.   237
Sylla, Ralph   240
Tubbs, Lon F., Jr. +   240
Voss, Joseph J. *   241
Warner, Raymond R.   243
Weier, Clarence "Jack" J. +   250
Weier, Raymond *   256

Glimpses of 176 Other Veterans   259

Independence's Women Who Served   320

Bibliography   329

Index of Independence Names   334

Biographies and Photos Added at a Later Date:

Olson, Elmer Lester *   340
Wicka, Robert *   342
Jonietz, Ralph (photo)   345
Klimek, Ralph (photo)   346
Pampuch, Alfred *   347
Weier, Raymond (photo)   350
Isaacs, Jerome *   351
Gamroth, George R.   359
Kuka, Joseph E.   359
Pape, Earl   360
Stendahl, Ivan C.   361
Sylla, John P.   361
Thalacker, Lloyd   362
Wilczek, Joseph A.   362
Sluga, Clarence (photo)   363
Bautch Brothers (photo)   363
Bisek, Frank (photos)   364
Sobota, Roman (photo)   365
Gierok, Ignatius (photo)   365
Gamroth, Ben (photo)   366
Maloney, Calvin (photo)   366
Kampa, Paul (photo)   367
Kampa, Bennie (photo)   367
Bisek, Emil (photo)   368
Bisek, Benedict (photo)   368

INTRODUCTION

As a boy growing up in Independence, Wisconsin, a small rural community in Trempealeau County located in the west-central part of the state, I came to know and interact, as did all the youngsters, with many of the adults living there. With a population of approximately 1,000 people, it was easy to know many of its residents. I learned about World War II at an early age and by fifth grade was reading about the battles fought in Europe and the Pacific and the heroes those battles created, created most often out of necessity, by that global conflict. I remember being fascinated by the people and events, and this period in history left an indelible impression on my adolescent, teenage, and young adult life. I knew that my father, Edmund J. Lyga, had participated in the war in some capacity, though I did not understand to what extent beyond the fact that he was an artilleryman. He didn't talk about it much, nor did the others, because I didn't have the slightest idea that within my midst were so many men and women who, mostly in their late teens and twenties, went to war in those days of the early 1940's, leaving their homes, families, and way of life, and fighting to preserve what they held dear from the tyranny of Hitler, Mussolini, and Tojo.

During the summer of 1997, I finally asked by dad to provide me a written account of his travels while in the service. From his rather sketchy information, I was able to piece together a record of his draft, early training, and involvement in the Pacific Theater battles for Saipan, Leyte, and Okinawa. I was amazed at the information that was available involving his 531st Field Artillery Battalion, XXIV Corps, and the actions it had participated in. I was able to locate photos of his unit in action during the "Battle of Okinawa," film of his unit in action on Saipan, and numerous written references. One of the documents I found was an order issued by General Ushijima, Japanese commander on Okinawa, for his troops to "wipe out the enemy artillery on Keise Shima" that was so severely hampering Japanese movements on the main island. That was my dad's artillery he ordered to be wiped out, and fortunately on April 6, 1945, the Japanese were discovered approaching the little sand spit on which the big 155-mm "Long Toms" of the 531st Field Artillery had been placed.

While pouring through books and other records in an attempt to piece together dad's story, I came across a time-worn copy of the *Independence News-Wave*, the town's weekly newspaper, dated November 30, 1944, that my mother had saved. It was the "Special Serviceman's Edition," and it was filled with many special greetings from families and businesses "back home" that a committee of townspeople had accumulated and sent to Independence's men and women serving around the world. What astonished me was the list included in that edition entitled the "Honor Roll," identifying those men and women known to have been in the service by that time. The list consisted of 240 names, all of whom had an Independence mailing address. When I showed it to my dad, he was taken completely by surprise as well at the number of names listed and stated he never knew so many had been in the service during the war. He offhandedly remarked that it would be nice if someone recorded their World War II histories before they were all forgotten. And thus this project began.

As research and writing progressed, the format of the project finally began to take shape. Originally, the stories of the people who served were to be the main focus of this project, and I had decided early on to compile and write as many biographies of the veterans as possible. Regardless of whether they were in the front lines or remained in the States throughout the war, everyone in the service had a job to do, and it was these stories that I very much wanted to preserve. Many never talked about their experiences, and after hearing and learning of their stories, it is very understandable why. Many aren't even aware today, more than 50 years after the war, of what their friends and relatives -- their comrades -- did and endured.

I began asking surviving veterans and the families of deceased veterans whether they would be willing to either orally recount their stories or provide copies of records they possessed regarding their service years. The response I received was beyond my expectations as a number of Independence's World War II veterans allowed me to interview them while others forwarded from all parts of the country copies of discharge papers, diaries, newspaper articles, photographs, and other artifacts describing their actions and those of their units. Family members searched for records of deceased veterans, forwarding what they had or could still locate. Sometimes I was provided with a very detailed record of a service man or woman's wartime history and at other times only a few pieces of information came into my possession.

I found another important source of biographical information to be the weekly issues of the *Independence News-Wave*, which had fortunately been preserved on microfilm and stored in the Independence Public Library. Glenn Kirkpatrick, publisher during the war years, did a magnificent job of keeping people informed of the whereabouts and activities of the men and women in the service, doing this within the bounds placed upon him by wartime censorship.

The biographies presented here vary in length and some are not as complete as they should be, however, despite the wealth of information published in the *News-Wave*. Though some families during the war were very open with letters received from their son or daughter, many others kept what they viewed as their family affairs private. Often, though, if I was able to learn a few dates, places, and unit assignments through the means described here, I was able to trace a veteran quite thoroughly by consulting other sources of record such as those listed in the bibliography to this project. But not in all cases, or even enough cases, was I able to put all the pieces of the puzzle together.

As work progressed and time passed, however, I began to realize that this was not only a story about those who served in the military during World War II. It also was a story about the service men and women's family and friends who remained in Independence, worrying and wondering about their safety. The story really was about Independence itself, and thus the second part of the project emerged.

When I learned that all issues of the weekly *News-Wave* published during the war years had been preserved on microfilm and stored at the Independence Public Library, I reviewed several of them and found that these newspapers were a treasure trove of information describing what life was like on the "home front" during the war. Independence became a part of the war effort by participating in defense initiatives such as rationing programs, providing a civilian defense network, producing tens of thousands of surgical dressings, and collecting tons of scrap materials. Residents were urged to buy war bonds and contribute more of their limited dollars towards Red Cross and USO efforts, and did just that. Children even contributed by producing cards, place settings, and other items to be used by those away from home, making their lives a little more enjoyable during holidays.

Lists of Trempealeau County's draftees, including those from Independence, appeared regularly. And through it all, life had to continue for those remaining at home. Business had to be attended to, students produced plays at the high school and competed in basketball and baseball games against other area schools, and people celebrated marriages and mourned those residents who passed away. But there were other, more ominous pieces of information appearing in the newspaper, as well. It was interesting to note the names of the high school's basketball players in December, 1941, or its graduates in May, 1942, and realize what many of these "boys," and some "girls," would soon be doing, where they would be going, and how their lives would be so drastically changed.

The *News-Wave* contained quite a record of the people of the Independence area, both those in the service and those at home. Like most small town newspapers of the time, the *News-Wave* published all sorts of items about its residents. Unlike today, the 1940's were a time of not-so-instant news and, for many, a time of limited movement and contact with others in their community. The *News-Wave* was the "bugle" that informed everyone of everything, from the latest sales in the local retail stores to items of a more personal nature, such as who had just undergone a tonsilectomy during the past week and who had traveled to Eau Claire to visit relatives for the day.

As the war progressed and the men and women overseas mailed letters home, many of these, at the request of Mr. Kirkpatrick, were delivered by proud parents to the *News-Wave* office for publication. To them it was their way of letting everyone know what their sons and daughters were doing and how they were coping. These letters offered incredible insights into the lives of those in the service, providing valuable information to me, and in several cases even serving as biographies by themselves. They described the sights observed, the duties undertaken, and often, the fears and hardships encountered. They informed parents of their safe arrival at their destination and of meeting with a brother or fellow Independence resident aboard ship, in camp, or on some remote Pacific island. Often, they asked their parents not to worry about them but to pray for them nonetheless.

Life in Independence in the 1940's, a community consisting largely of Polish Catholics as well as Lutherans and Methodists, revolved around its churches, and the letters home frequently included statements of faith assuring parents of their writers' attendance at Mass and of their receiving the Sacraments, or explaining why they couldn't due to the circumstances of time and place.

On occasion, however, the letters received from the front or from Washington, D. C., were not so pleasant, informing families and friends of their son's being killed, wounded, or listed as missing in action or as a prisoner of war. The publication of these letters allowed a family's pain to be shared by the entire community. All published letters, whether to families or the *News-Wave* itself, are a vital part of this project.

As I was compiling the weekly reviews of life back home and finally reaching the end of the war in September, 1945, many stories began appearing regarding the return home of the service men and women. I decided not to include these reports from the weekly review because all of this information was contained in the individual biographies. But something struck me as I scrolled through the weekly notes and more and more names were appearing on my computer screen, and it became nearly overwhelming to review so many of their histories once again, to revisit their family's obvious joy, and their joy, at being reunited at home once again, and then by a push of a button, to delete them from my screen. There were so very many names, and as I read them all in such a comparatively short time, I finally realized just what this small town in West-central Wisconsin had done to help preserve what we all cherish, and often take for granted, so much. I believed as I was nearing completion of this project that I was beginning to understand what was happening to them at their time in history, and to me as I tried to uncover and record their histories for history's sake. But I now realized as I scrolled through and deleted their names just how symbolic pushing that "Delete" button on the computer was, as it signified that they really were all passing into history. I realized just how easy it would have been for all of it to have been lost, and how important for all of us that it is not.

Another thing that struck me as I prepared biographies and selected photographs of the veterans for inclusion in this project was how young they all were. They were America's youth of that day, and they were asked to leave their youth behind in Independence and risk their lives in an endeavor that must have simply frightened so many of them. And they persevered. Some did not come home. Some left a physical or psychological part of themselves -- of their youth -- on the beaches, in the seas, in the mountains, on the fields of battle. Their lives changed forever. But they also changed the course of history as participants of the defining event of the Twentieth Century. They made the history of the world and they are the history of Independence. I am proud to have had the good fortune of growing up in the town they made. And I personally want them all to know, I am in awe of what you accomplished during those terrible years. We cannot, as your descendents, possibly do enough to honor and recognize what you did. All we can say is, "Thank you," and assure you it will not be forgotten.

IX

NBC news anchor Tom Brokaw recently published a book honoring those of the World War II generation, stating that they are "The Greatest Generation." I will for the rest of my life argue with anyone who says they are not.

Mike Lyga
November 11, 1999

Prelude to War

When the Japanese launched their surprise attack upon the American Naval forces at Pearl Harbor on the Hawaiian Islands on December 7, 1941, the United States was thrust into a global conflict that would be, before its conclusion, of immense proportions. Many Americans, however, have a misconception that with that "dastardly act," as President Franklin Roosevelt declared it to be, World War II actually began. True, America entered the conflict at that time, but the preludes to World War II had already been developing for many years. When on September 1, 1939, Germany invaded Poland, the war actually commenced in Europe, but Germany had been preparing for it for nearly two decades. And by 1939, Asia had already been experiencing war for two decades as Japan had rampaged its way through China, Manchuria, and Micronesia as part of its plan of conquest. The seeds of war, it seems, the ideas of conquest and glory, had actually been planted early in the Twentieth Century, both in Europe and the Pacific.

In Europe, Adolph Hitler assumed power in Germany in 1933 and immediately began building his armed forces. This was done in festering response to the Versailles Treaty of 1919, following the conclusion of World War I, when the victorious French and British dictated terms to the vanquished Germans that were so harsh that they ensured Germany's suffering for many years to come. Hitler became very embittered by the actions of the victors, seeing them as a concerted effort to destroy his beloved Germany, and he vowed to force changes that would bring Germany once again to what he saw as her rightful place of power -- her rightful destiny. He did this by any means necessary, by first eliminating all opposition within Germany, then by lies and treachery in obtaining treaties with her neighbors, and finally by all-out war.

When Hitler unleashed his powerful military forces upon Poland, Britain and France, holding mutual defense treaties with the Poles, rushed to its defense by declaring war on Germany. But this did little to slow the German juggernaut, the German "blitzkrieg." Belgium, Holland, and France all fell in rapid succession and Germany was soon poised to attack England itself.

The German military build up began to alarm the United States as early as 1935. Still arguably isolationist and neutral as far as foreign policy was concerned, America nonetheless began focusing more and more attention on the disturbing events unfolding in Europe. When Germany overran her neighbors, Roosevelt felt America had no choice but to increase industrial production in order to keep Britain from falling as well.

By 1940, Britain was in a desperate situation when Roosevelt discovered loopholes in laws that allowed the United States to transfer large quantities of World War I equipment overseas. With this, 50 old destroyers and many aircraft quickly found their way to England. In exchange, the United States received 99 year leases on naval and air bases in the Caribbean and Newfoundland. In 1940, Congress quietly appropriated $17-billion to begin a rearmament program. That September, Congress approved the first peacetime draft, and in December of that year, Roosevelt proposed the Lend-Lease Act, which Congress approved in March, 1941. These actions set the course for an American confrontation with Germany.

In the Pacific, America's troubles with Japan can be traced even further back, to the turn of the century. At that time, American politicians such as Theodore Roosevelt and certain business concerns had definite imperialistic tendencies. Even before the Spanish-American War began, Commodore George Dewey, commander of the Asiatic Fleet, had been given orders to proceed to the Philippines as soon as he received word that hostilities with Spain had begun. His orders were to destroy the small, outmanned, and outdated Spanish fleet stationed in Manila and occupy the Philippines. And though this was to be done supposedly to free the Filipinos from Spanish domination, once the Spanish-American War ended, America simply continued its occupation of the island nation.

Even earlier than this, however, Japan was already exhibiting expansionist desires of its own. It built a powerful navy in the 1890's and easily defeated China in the Sino-Japanese Conflict of 1894, forcing China to cede Formosa and the Liaotung Peninsula which contained the important harbor of Port Arthur. This angered the Russians who then gained the cooperation of France and Germany to force Japan out of the peninsula. Somewhere around this time, it is believed the Japanese began viewing western countries, including the United States simply by default, as their enemies.

In early 1904, Japan attacked the Russian occupiers of Korea and Manchuria. In 1905, following massive land and sea loses and growing unrest at home, the Russians succumbed. Korea was recognized as a Japanese protectorate, Japan gained control of the southern half of Sakholin Island, and also regained the Liaotung Peninsula. By 1910, Japan totally controlled Korea and by 1931, Manchuria was considered a Japanese protectorate as well.

The Russo-Japanese War gave rise to the myth of Japanese military invincibility among many of its senior officers and political leaders. Japan was becoming increasingly more powerful and prosperous as raw materials flowed from Korea and Manchuria to bolster its industrial base. But with this increasing power also developed a growing influence of the Japanese army in political affairs, both domestic and foreign.

Taking advantage of a treaty with Britain at the onset of World War I, Japan quickly occupied German holdings in the Pacific. At the Versailles peace conference following the end of World War I, Japan succeeded in having its new territories recognized as its own. But in the years that followed, Japan felt she had been severely slighted by various western political actions, though the western nations felt Japan had been treated fairly throughout.

In the early 1920's Japan gained a major foothold in the islands of Micronesia. Though outward appearances pointed to an economic rather than military interest driving its presence there, the construction of a major naval base at Truk began throwing up red flags to a number of western observers. By now in Japan, right wing extremists in the military felt that Japan's future was tied to its expanding control over Asia, and they were exerting more and more influence over national policies. Eventually, those policies were changed to include a provision calling for the military to take control over the government if the country ever was at war. When in September, 1931, the Japanese army invaded Manchuria and declared war on China, the ultraconservative military, mostly army men, did just that, setting the stage for the December 7, 1941 surprise attack of Pearl Harbor.

The attack in Manchuria began a succession of Japanese aggressive acts in Asia. During this time, its militarists worked incessantly at gaining and consolidating power. They killed anyone who got in their way or opposed them, including their own top government officials such as Prime Minister Tsuyoshi Inukai and his finance minister. The army minister was killed and they attempted to kill the succeeding prime minister. Even American Ambassador Joseph Grew was targeted but escaped unhurt. By killing Grew, the militarists actually hoped to start a war with America, this as early as 1936.

On July 7, 1937, the Japanese army provoked a clash with Chinese troops on the Marco Polo Bridge near Peiping, China. What followed quickly proved that China's huge army was no match for the skillfully trained Japanese soldiers, who quickly overran large tracts of territory.

As the city of Nanking fell under siege in December, 1937, an American gunboat, the *U. S. S. Panay*, one of five such U. S. Navy boats stationed on the Yangtze River, was dispatched to evacuate American diplomats and Standard Oil Company employees from the city. Though she plainly flew the American flag, Japanese shore batteries and aircraft showed no hesitation in firing on her. She was forced to be abandoned and three oil barges she was escorting were sunk. Three Americans were killed and eleven wounded in the attack. And though there was no doubt the attacking Japanese knew the *Panay* was an American vessel, when the American government protested and condemned the unprovoked attack, the Japanese simply insisted they had made a mistake, saying they thought the boat was Chinese. In a surprising turn of events, however, Roosevelt's government did nothing more than demand an apology for the aggressive act and accept the Japanese explanation. The Japanese, hoping the event would draw America into a war, were seriously disappointed and surprised at the American response.

When Nanking fell in 1938, Japanese officers allowed their men to run wild, and the horrors that followed came to be known as the "Rape of Nanking." For more than a month, Japanese troops raped and murdered, and when it was over, more than a quarter of a million innocent Chinese had been slaughtered.

There were numerous Americans in China at the time of this atrocity, many of them serving as missionaries, and stories soon found their way back to the United States. The Japanese had attacked defenseless cities with a vengeance, and wantonly bombed churches, hospitals, and schools.

The United States, despite the attack on its ship and nationals, tried desperately to resolve the war between Japan and China, but to no avail. A conference in Brussels, Belgium, not attended by the Japanese, asked the warring parties to cease their hostilites and offered ways of mediating a settlement. The Japanese rejected the ideas outright. America then began directing more economic aid to the Chinese in the hope of stemming Japanese aggression. Finally on July 25, 1940, over the objections of Ambassador Grew who feared it would cause the Japanese to invade the Dutch East Indies and Malaya in order to obtain its needed raw materials, Roosevelt banned the export of oil, scrap metals, and, five days later, the sale of aviation gasoline outside the Western Hemisphere. Though not publicly aimed at the Japanese, these actions nonetheless were the first steps toward an outright embargo of trade with Japan.

But despite all of these signals of impending danger in the Pacific, America seemed, for the most part, fixated on events taking place in Europe, no doubt because of the incredible speed with which Germany was overrunning country after country. With her attention turned to the east and her focus on assisting England in her lonely stand against Hitler, America virtually ignored Japan. And on December 7, 1941, at a place many Americans knew little about, Japan sneaked in the back door while no one was watching, and nearly destroyed a great nation.

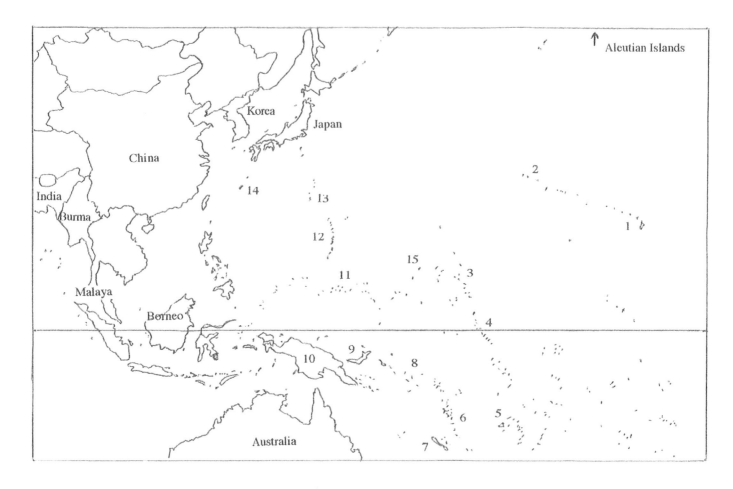

Figure 1: General Map of the Pacific Theater of Operations, with key locations identified.

KEY:
1 - Hawaiian Islands
2 - Midway Islands
3 - Marshall Islands (Kwajalein)
4 - Gilbert Islands (Tarawa)
5 - Fiji Islands
6 - New Hebrides
7 - New Caledonia
8 - Solomon Islands (Guadalcanal)
        Rendova, New Georgia, Bougainville)

9 - New Britain (Rabaul)
10 - New Guinea (Biak Island)
11 - Caroline Islands (Truk)
12 - Marianas Islands (Saipan, Tinian, Guam)
13 - Volcano Islands (Iwo Jima)
14 - Ryukyus Islands (Okinawa, Ie Shima)
15 - Eniwetok

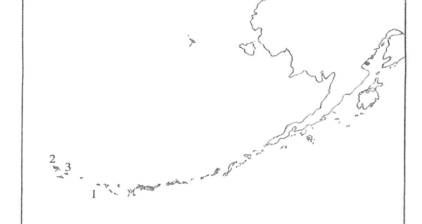

Figure 2: Alaska, with key locations identified.

KEY:
1 - Kiska Island
2 - Attu Island
3 - Shemya Island

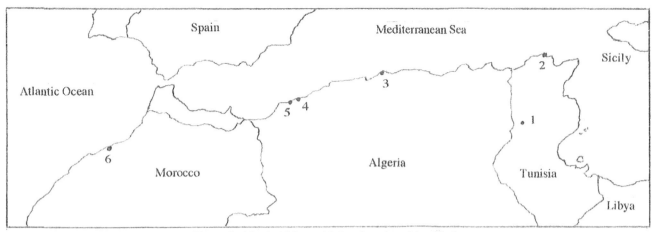

Figure 3: North Africa, with key locations identified.

KEY:
1 - Kasserine   4 - Arzew
2 - Bizerte   5 - Oran
3 - Algiers   6 - Casablanca

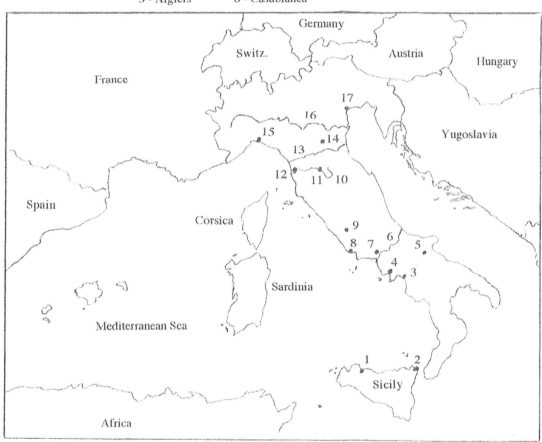

Figure 4: Sicily and Italy, with key locations identified.

KEY:
1 - Palermo   7 - Cassino   13 - *Gustav Line*
2 - Messina   8 - Anzio   14 - Bologna
3 - Salerno   9 - Rome   15 - Genoa
4 - Naples   10 - Arno River   16 - Po River
5 - Foggia   11 - Florence   17 - Venice
6 - *Gothic Line* 12 - Pisa

XV

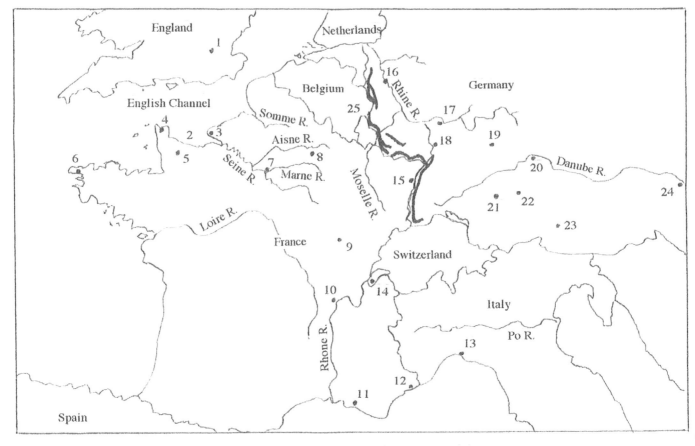

Figure 5: Generalized Map of the European Theater of Operations, with key locations identified.

KEY:
1 - London
2 - The Beaches of June 6, 1944
3 - Le Havre
4 - Cherbourg
5 - St. Lo
6 - Brest
7 - Paris
8 - Rheims
9 - Dijon
10 - Lyons

11 - Marseilles
12 - Nice
13 - Genoa
14 - Geneva
15 - Strasbourg
16 - Cologne
17 - Frankfurt-am-Main
18 - Mannheim
19 - Nuremberg
20 - Regensberg

21 - Landsberg
22 - Munich
23 - Berchtesgarden
24 - Vienna
25 - Ardennes Forest

Heavy Dark Lines - *West Wall*
      (*Siegfried Line*)

The Biographies

WALDO O. AUSTIN
UNITED STATES ARMY

Waldo Austin entered the United States Army on October 27, 1942, and was sent to Camp Adair and Camp White, Oregon, where the 91st Infantry Division,[1] the famous "Powder River Division," had been activated in August of that year. After its organization and initial training were completed, the Division staged at Camp Patrick Henry, Virginia, on March 30, 1944 and embarked from the Hampton Roads Port of Embarkation on April 14, 1944. It began arriving in North Africa on April 21 and received amphibious training at Arzew and Renan before crossing the Mediterranean Sea where it landed across the Anzio beaches in Italy by echelon beginning June 19, 1944. By July 13, 1944, the entire Division had been committed to combat as it attacked toward Arno; the evacuated town was entered the following day.

Waldo, a radio operator with Cannon Company of the 362nd Infantry Regiment, crossed the Era River near Capannoli on July 17, 1944 and reached the Arno River at Pontedera on July 21-22. There, the entire Division was involved in clearing the lightly-held area of enemy troops. The 91st then took up defensive positions along the Arno until August 18, 1944, when it was relieved and moved for training near Certaldo.

The Division moved back to the line on September 9, 1944, crossed the Sieve River the following day, and went on the attack at Mt. Calvi, Monticelli, and Altuzzo along the *Gothic Line* on September 12. The 362nd Infantry found itself in heavy combat on September 14, 1944, as it assaulted Mt. Calvi. It then fought its way through the Futa Pass, took the Antitank Ditch below St. Lucia on September 16, and captured St. Lucia itself by September 21, 1944.

When on September 15, 1944, communications directing artillery fire were disrupted by German shelling, Waldo volunteered to move forward and spot for his gun batteries. For his actions that day, Waldo was decorated with the Bronze Star by Major General William Livesay, commanding the 91st Infantry Division. A photo of Waldo being decorated by General Livesay appeared in the July 12, 1945 *News-Wave*, and is interesting because it appears to have been autographed by the General, who signed, "W. Livesay, Major General, USA." The commendation that accompanied the photo described Waldo's actions:

> Commendation for Meritorious Service: To whom it may concern, Waldo O. Austin is hereby officially commended for outstanding performance of duty. Citation: Waldo O. Austin, (36274508), Private First Class, Infantry, United States Army. For outstanding performance of duty on 15 September 1944, on Mt. Calvi, Italy. When communications between his company gun batteries and the fire direction center were destroyed by enemy fire, Private First Class Austin voluntarily set up his radio on the exposed slope of a hill to make contact necessary for important fire missions. Despite heavy shelling by enemy artillery and mortars, some shells bursting as close as 25 yards from him, Private First Class Austin maintained the connection with the fire direction center. The courage and devotion to duty exhibited by Private First Class Austin were responsible for valuable assitance given to attacking troops and brought relief from heavy enemy fire. His action brought great credit on himself and the Armed Forces of the United States. Entered military service from Independence, Wisconsin."
> Signed Wm. G. Livesay, Major General of the U. S. Army, Commanding.

Following the *Gothic Line* fighting of mid-September, 1944, the 91st Infantry Division continued its push through Italy, taking Loiano on October 5, fighting the "Battle for Livergnano Escarpment" the second week of October, and taking Livergnano itself on October 14, 1944. It then was relieved for rehabilitation and defensive purposes until January 24, 1945.

The Division next relieved the 34th Infantry Division in its line on February 13, 1945 in

---

[1] The 91st Infantry Division lost 1,400 men killed and 6,748 wounded, with 175 of those dying from their wounds, during its three campaigns in Italy.

Pfc. Waldo Austin being decorated with the Bronze Star by Major General William Livesay, commanding, 91st Infantry Division.

the Idice Valley region, where it was then once again relieved on March 20, 1945, for the purpose of preparing for a new offensive.

On April 5, 1945, the 91st Infantry again relieved the 34th Infantry Division along Highway 65 and began its attack up the highway on April 12. By the next day, its four objectives of Mt. Adone, Mt. Posigliano, Pianoro, and Mt. Arnigo, had all been taken. Without hesitating, the Division quickly began advancing toward Bologna, and on April 24, 1945, the 362nd Infantry crossed the Po River at Sermide. Then, after turning northeast, Cerea was taken on April 25, 1945, and the Adige River was crossed the next day. By April 30, 1945, the 91st Infantry found itself south of Venice, where it was located when German forces in Italy surrendered on May 2.

It has not been verified whether Waldo remained with the 91st Infantry Division through the cessation of hostilities on May 2, but most probably he did as the *News-Wave* later reported it had learned Waldo was the recipient of a Distinguished Unit Citation, bestowed upon the 91st Infantry for its valiant drive through the Po Valley. The commendation read:

> Division commendation: Headquarters II Corps, APO 19, U.S. Army, 91st Infantry Divsion is hereby commended. For heroic achievement on the field of battle. In a sustained drive unsurpassed in modern warfare, the 91st Infantry Division in eighteen days breached the defenses before Bologna, destroyed the enemy in the Po Valley, and forced the surrender of his beaten, demoralized, and disorganized troops in the Alps.
>
> Signed Geoffry Keyes, Lt. General, USA Commanding.

Pfc. Waldo Austin was discharged from the United States Army the last week of December 1945, at Camp McCoy, Wisconsin. Besides his Bronze Star and Distinguished Unit Citation bar, he wore three bronze battle stars on his European-African-Middle Eastern Theater Ribbon for his participation in the Rome-Arno, North Apennines, and Po Valley campaigns, three overseas service bars, the Good Conduct Medal, and the Combat Infantryman's Badge.

On January 25, 1945, the *News-Wave* published a short V-Mail it had received from Waldo, who acknowledged receipt of the "Special Serviceman's Edition" of the paper, something he, like so many other Independence-area servicemen, appreciated greatly:

> Italy
> January 6, 1945

4

Dear "Kirk":

　　　　Received the Special Servicemen's Edition of the News-Wave between Christmas and New Years. So now I'll drop you a few lines to let you know that I appreciated it very much and was very happy to receive it. I receive the regular edition about a month behind time, but its still pretty good to read, because time doesn't matter much over here.

　　　　Well, there isn't much news from here now, only we have quite a bit of snow at present. Wishing everyone lots of luck and happiness all the New Year through. Also hope we get our job done over here.

　　　　　　　Sincerely,
　　　　　　　Waldo O. Austin

Sources: Independence News-Wave; Book (Stanton)

MARGARET "MARGE" BAECKER
UNITED STATES ARMY NURSES CORPS

Margaret Walker was originally from Elroy, Wisconsin. She met Walt Baecker following the war, they were married, and subsequently made their home in Independence.

Following her high school graduation in Elroy, Wisconsin, Marge Baecker entered the nursing program at St. Francis Hospital in La Crosse, Wisconsin, in 1939. She graduated as a registered nurse in 1942 and became employed at Columbia Hospital, Milwaukee, Wisconsin, serving in the obstetrics department from November 1, 1942 until April 22, 1943. She then joined the Army Nursing Corps, was called to active duty on May 25, 1943 and reported to Lovell General Hospital at Fort Devens, Massachusetts, three days later for assignment to the Army's 298th General Hospital.

On June 19, 1943, Marge was transferred to Camp Shanks near Orangeburg, New York, from where she left three days later "to comply with movement orders." She arrived in England on July 6, 1943 with the 298th General Hospital and was temporarily stationed with her unit in Bristol, England. While there, Marge herself was hospitalized from November 6-13, 1943, and again from November 23-29, 1943, due to a bout with bronchitis.

In May 1944, 298th General Hospital personnel began preparations for transport to France in anticipation of an upcoming, hopefully successful, Normandy invasion. Several movements were made, all per secret movement orders, and various clothing articles, including combat jackets and trousers, were issued the medical staff. On July 12, 1944, the 298th General Hospital relocated to its marshaling area from where it embarked for France on July 15, 1944. It arrived in Cherbourg, France, the following day and quickly undertook its mission of treating the wounded.

As the Allied forces moved through France and entered Belgium, the 298th General Hospital was alerted to move to Liege, Belgium. It left Cherbourg on October 28, 1944 and arrived in its new location on November 1, 1944. While in Liege, Marge was promoted to First Lieutenant on May 1, 1945. Stationed primarily with the 298th General Hospital, she remained in Europe until September 12, 1945, when she was ordered to Camp Phillip Morris in Le Harve, France, for shipment to the United States. She arrived in Le Harve on September 13, 1945, embarked on September 23, 1945, and arrived in the United States on October 1, 1945.

Upon reporting to Fort Sheridan, Illinois, Marge was granted a 45-day leave in order to recuperate from the incredible strain of treating physically and emotionally wounded soldiers in the European Theater. Following this furlough, Marge next reported to Percy Jones General Hospital, Battle Creek, Michigan, on November 23, 1945, where she served until January 4, 1946, again caring for the many wounded who had been transported home. On January 6, 1946, she reported to the Station Hospital at Camp McCoy, Wisconsin, and served there until May 2, 1947. Effective May 1, 1947, Marge was promoted to the rank of Captain and placed on 60-day terminal leave prior to her separation from the Army, which occurred on June 30, 1947, at the Camp McCoy Separation Center.

Marge had participated in the Normandy, Northern France, and Rhineland campaigns while serving in the European Theater, and in recognition of that was awarded the European-African-Middle Eastern Theater Ribbon with three bronze service stars. She also was awarded the American Theater Ribbon and World War II Victory Medal. The 298th General Hospital, in which Marge served, was awarded the Meritorious Unit Citation.

Sources: Marge Baecker personal papers; Bob, Bill, and Nick Baecker, sons and grandson, respectively.

The ensuing edited narrative was prepared following a short interview with Marge at Tri-County Memorial Hospital Nursing Home in Whitehall, Wisconsin, on August 4, 1998.

I graduated from St. Francis School of Nursing in La Crosse, Wisconsin, and was awarded my cap as a registered nurse. Esther Skroch of Independence, Phyllis Boland of Arcadia, and I all graduated together from St. Francis. The three of us worked in Milwaukee together for close to a year, then all joined the Army Nursing Corps at the same time. This was in either 1942 or 1943.

I was a 1st Lieutenant when I went overseas to England. Shortly following D-Day, June 6, 1944, I crossed the channel from England and landed in France. I was stationed in Cherbourg, France, at the 298th General Hospital. In fact, Esther, Phyllis, and I were all stationed there. We pretty much traveled everywhere together, it seems.

At the 298th, all levels of severity of wounds came through, both physical and mental. I did the psychological nursing. There were more cases of mental trauma than you can imagine, men who wouldn't speak or sleep or would constantly rock back and forth. There were a lot of nightmares, bad memories being relived in their minds. About three-fourths of my time in Europe was spent at the 298th.

Following my tour there, I returned to the States and was given a one month leave. Then I reported to Camp McCoy, Wisconsin, where a lot of wounded were returning. Then sometime later, with the war over, I was given my discharge. I was a Captain at that time.

I saw a lot of things while in the Nursing Corps during the war. Anyone who has never been in combat can never imagine what those boys went through, as well as what the medical personnel caring for them experienced. War is a horrible, horrible thing.

WALTER BAECKER
UNITED STATES ARMY

Walt Baecker, originally from the Waumandee area near Independence, met Margaret "Marge" Walker of Elroy, Wisconsin, following the war. They were married and made their home in Independence. Marge was a combat nurse with the 298th General Hospital, serving two years and three months in the European Theater of Operations. Her biography can be found on the pages immediately preceeding Walt's biography.

Walt Baecker was drafted into the United States Army on November 26, 1941. On the bus heading to Fort Sheridan, Illinois, he met Bennie Kulig of Independence, and the two men would travel together in the 2d Armored "Hell on Wheels" Division[1] to North Africa and through Sicily and Western Europe.

From Fort Sheridan, Walt was sent to Fort Knox, Kentucky, for basic training, and while he was there, the Japanese attacked Pearl Harbor. He then traveled to Fort Benning, Georgia, and was assigned to Company A, 66th Armored Regiment, 2d Armored Division, where he would serve as a member of a light tank crew. The Division's commander at that time was General George S. Patton, Jr., the famous Third Army commander in Europe following D-Day.

On November 11, 1942, Walt and 2d Armored left Fort Dix, New Jersey, under the command of Brigadier General Alan Kingman, sailing for North Africa where he landed at Casablanca on December 24, 1942. Casablanca had been surrendered by the Axis on November 11, 1942 following Patton's threat to send tanks into the city. Though the 2d Armored Division did not actually participate in the Tunisian campaign while in Africa, it did spend several months training there, including undergoing full scale rehearsals of assault landings from convoys.

Combat Command A, of which Walt's 66th Armored Regiment was a part, boarded invasion craft at Bizerte, Tunis, on July 5, 1943 for the assault on Sicily that was scheduled to begin the night of July 9-10. Designated as "Floating Reserve" of the 3rd Infantry Division (reinforced) for the operation, it debarked landing craft over a period of several days before leading the drive on Palermo beginning July 22, 1943. The city was occupied on July 23.

Following the Sicily campaign, 2d Armored sailed for England on November 11, 1943, landing two weeks later and traveling to Tidworth Barracks in Salisbury Plain, about a hundred miles west of London. The Division's activities on Sicily had drawn the attention of such notables as Prime Minister Winston Churchill, Supreme Allied Commander General Dwight Eisenhower, and British commanders Field Marshall

---

[1] 981 men of the 2d Armored Division were killed in combat during its European Theater campaigns. Another 4,557 were wounded, of which 202 died of their wounds.

Montgomery and Air Marshall Tedder, all of whom visited the Division. Additionally, Combat Command A conducted tank warfare and tactics exercises for the world press during this time, as well.

2d Armored embarked from England aboard LST's and LCI's on June 8, 1944, heading for the Normandy coast upon which Allied forces had landed just two days earlier. Combat Command A, under the command of General Maurice Rose, landed on Omaha Beach on June 9, 1944, took up positions near Carentan, France, and quickly attacked a large group of German tanks, taking them entirely by surprise. The Division then continued driving through France, entering Belgium on September 2, 1944; a month later it was breaching the Siegfried Line in Germany.

On October 12, 1944, while in action in the Roer Valley of Germany, Walt found his flank under heavy attack by enemy artillery and mortars. He left his tank, climbed a tree, and directed American artillery fire, enabling his comrades to silence the German guns. For this action, Walt was awarded the Silver Star for bravery in action. The citation in part read, "he saved many lives, and his courage, fortitude and aggressive leadership were an inspiration to all his men."

On December 16, 1944, Hitler launched his Ardennes Counteroffensive, resulting in what is better known to Americans as the "Battle of the Bulge." In response, Patton hurled his armor, led by the 2d Armored Division, into the battle in an attempt to halt the German advance. By this time, Staff Sergeant Baecker was a platoon leader, taking command of five tanks when no officer was present. In one action in early January 1945, three tanks of Company E had been knocked out, leaving several men pinned down, and some of them wounded. Walt told his captain he would get the men out, so, taking five men with him, including his three crew members, his tank made its way toward a burning tank near which two wounded soldiers were located. After his tank became stuck in a creek and came under enemy fire, he and two others crawled the rest of the way. Two of the three men from the burning tank were wounded, one missing his lower leg and the other having lost a lot of blood. But, half crawling and half walking, they finally made it back to their own tanks where the two wounded men were taken to the rear for medical treatment. His commanding officer told Walt, "Nice going, sergeant." But as cold and wet as he was, all Walt wanted was some hot coffee.

When the Germans were driven from the area, Walt made it back to his tank, still stuck in the creek, and found the enemy had stolen the Christmas packages he and his crew had just received.

For his actions in saving his wounded comrades that day, Walt was awarded the Distinguished Service Cross,[2] with the citation reading as follows:

> Award of Distinguished Service Cross. By direction of the President the Distinguished Service Cross is awarded to Staff Sergeant Walter J. Baecker. For extraordinary heroism in connection with military operations in Belgium on 4 January 1945. Although realizing the danger involved, Sergeant Baecker volunteered to assist in the evacuation of two seriously wounded men. Silhouetted against two burning tanks, Sergeant Baecker and his companions were under continuous enemy artillery, mortar and small arms fire till they reached the wounded men. They placed the men on litters, carried them up a steep hill, still under enemy fire, and placed them on a tank which evacuated them. While under constant enemy shelling, Sergeant Baecker never faltered and his courage and willingness was an inspiration to the men of his organization. The extraordinary heroism and courageous actions of Sergeant Baecker reflect great credit upon himself and are in keeping with the highest traditions of the military service.
>
> By command of Lieutenant General Simpson.

Both wounded men carried out by Sergeant Baecker lived.

---

[2] Only 23 men of the 2nd Armored Division were decorated with the Distinguished Service Cross during its campaigns in the European Theater during World War II.

Walt and his tank company reached the Rhine River in March, 1945. At that time he was offered a choice of a furlough home or commission to Second Lieutenant; he opted for the furlough. On his last day in action, a Panzer anti-tank grenade exploded nearby, knocking off his helmet and causing a concussion. But this did not delay him from his well-earned trip home.

As a member of the 2d Armored Division, Walt had participated in the Algeria-French Morocco, Sicily, Normandy, Northern France, Ardennes-Alsace, and Rhineland campaigns, leaving Europe at the start of the Central Europe campaign. Only the Congressional Medal of Honor ranks higher than Walt's Distinguished Service Cross as a decoration for bravery while in action against the enemy. The Silver Star ranks immediately below the Distinguished Service Cross.

On December 28, 1944, the *News-Wave* described an article that earlier had appeared in the *St. Paul Dispatch*. Written by Alton Smalley, a correspondent traveling with the 2d Armored Division in Germany, the article mentioned Walt during an attack on German positions in the area of Puffendorf, Germany. The *News-Wave's* article read:

"'Keep on a'goin', keep on a'goin',' radioed the platoon leader, Staff Sgt. Walter Baecker of Independence, Wis., and Pvt. Robert Peterson of St. Paul kept 'on a'goin' in his light tank, kept 'on a'goin" principally for the reason that he couldn't go back and didn't dare sit still."

The correspondent heard the story a few hours after Sgt. Baecker and Pvt. Peterson had come out of the line for a rest in one of the houses occupied by their regiment in a captured front line German town.

"Peterson was a light tank commander during the above incident but has been transferred to a medium Sherman when I saw him in the German town," the correspondent continued. "Attacking German positions in the vicinity of Puffendorf, Peterson's little "Honey' tank was 'on the point,' in other words, was leading the battalion. Honeys have one 37 mm gun and three 30 caliber machine guns, one of them an anti-aircraft weapon in an open turret.

"'All my guns were out,' Peterson explained as we sat in the kitchen of the German house. 'And I discovered that my tank had turned into one of those Patton tanks -- just goes forward, never backward. The reverse wouldn't work. Then I got my order's from Baecker to keep on a'goin'. Well, I sure didn't stop. I couldn't go backward. The Germans were firing 40 mm stuff and if I had stopped I would have been out of luck. So I made a wide arc into the German fire and out again and went back. The Germans didn't hit us.'

"Baecker (son of Philip Baecker of Independence) asserts the 30 caliber anti-aircraft gun is the best weapon on the light tank. 'You got to stand up to shoot the thing, but it's worth it,' he said. . .

"Baecker told me tanks of his outfit, Company A, Second Battalion, were the first tanks to go ashore in Africa. The battalion is a unit of the 66th Armored regiment, the oldest tank regiment in the United States Army. The regiment stems from the (not readable in the article) Tank Regiment of World War I."

Sources: Bennie Kulig personal papers; Eau Claire Leader-Telegram; Arcadia News-Leader;
Books (Stanton) (St. John)

A Quote From History. . .

"As I am enlisting in the Navy, I offer for sale my traps, fishing tackle, rifle and other items."
Joseph Libowski
United States Navy
"Local Items" ad in Independence News-Wave, September 1942.

Killed in Action

ADELBERT A. BAUTCH
UNITED STATES ARMY

Adelbert Bautch was born on April 16, 1919, the son of Mr. and Mrs. Paul Bautch, on a farm in the township of Hale four miles north of Whitehall, Wisconsin. Following employment with Briggs and Stratton in Milwaukee, he was inducted into the United States Army from Trempealeau County on April 7, 1941. He underwent basic training at Fort Custer, Michigan, and then underwent additional infantry training. As a member of the 5th Division[1] (redesignated the 5th Infantry Division on May 25, 1943), Adelbert may have participated in the VII Corps Tennessee Maneuvers beginning May 29, 1941, and probably participated in the Arkansas and Louisiana Maneuvers of August and September, respectively. Following these exercises, the Division returned to Fort Custer on October 3, 1941, where it continued its training. Though the bulk of the Division departed the New York Port of Embarkation for Iceland towards the end of April 1942, Adelbert's unit apparently sailed earlier, as a letter to his parents was published in the April 16, 1942 edition of the *News-Wave* indicating his safe arrival in Iceland:

We reached Iceland safely and I must say I was glad to set foot on solid ground again. For a time, I thought the 2nd Infantry (Ed. - one of three regiments of the 5th Division) had joined the navy.

The trip across the ocean was quite an experience. We were able to miss all the subs so they can't be so thickly planted, or perhaps we out-witted them.

Iceland is not at all what I thought it was. Trees are quite scarce and the farms are small. Each farmer has a few sheep, a cow, and a couple of mountain ponies. I certainly would hate to try my hand at driving a car here. They have cars with right hand drives and drive on the left side of the road.

There are some hot springs here. In fact, there is one about the size of Elk Creek right near our camp. The water in the creek is warm enough for bathing. The language they speak here is Norwegian, and some Danish As for food, what we get here is mostly dried, dehydrated or canned, and we get all our milk from the states.

Greet everyone for me, and please have my News-Wave sent here, because it is sure good to get the news from home.

The May 21, 1942, issue of the *News-Wave* carried a short note from Adelbert stating he was still in Iceland and had received five issues of the paper. He also wrote:

This is a very interesting place if one could write about it. We have to be very careful what we say, because the censors are very strict. The days are getting longer. It is now 9:30 and still daylight.

Expecting a German attack on Iceland, the 5th Infantry's objectives included guarding long stretches of beaches, building camps, unloading ships, and manning observation posts. It also

---

1 The 5th Infantry Division suffered 2,298 killed in action and 9,549 wounded, with 358 of those dying from their wounds, while in action in Europe.

10

undertook training exercises, though these were by necessity limited due to the lack of large scale training areas. Its winter combat training, however, which included learning to ski, later proved invaluable to the men of the 5th Infantry in France.

In early August 1943, the newly-redesignated 5th Infantry Division relocated to England in anticipation of the invasion of the continent that all knew was coming. Stationed at the Tidworth Garrison facilities, the men began physical and weapons training in earnest, as well as manning defensive positions along the English coast. After moving to Northern Ireland in October 1943, the individual training continued but additional specific training was undertaken in such areas as river crossing, attacking a fortified position, and other exercises requiring the coordination of large groups of men under battle conditions. It was during this time that the Army issued a press release received by the *News-Wave* and reported in its March 30, 1944 issue, stating that Corporal Lester Ulberg and Corporal Adelbert Bautch, "two well-known boys, now in service, have a 'secret weapon' which they are quite certain will do away with anything that Hitler can use to overcome their strength. These are the weapons: Their own endurance and inventiveness, coupled with the intense training they are getting. Both boys are infantrymen, and the item was reported through headquarters of the European Theater of Operation."

By May 1944, the 5th Infantry Division was ready to cross the channel, the call for which came at midnight on June 29. Troopships were boarded and on July 9, 1944, the men began setting foot on Utah Beach along the Normandy coast. Initially, the 5th Infantry was assigned to First Army and assumed defensive positions from the 1st Infantry Division near Caumont. On July 26, 1944, it attacked and took Vidouville, and was advancing to the Torigny-sur-Vire-- Caumont Road when it was reassembled and assigned to Third Army on August 1, 1944. A week later it began its offensive toward Nantes, taking Angers and Chartes by August 18, 1944. It then crossed the Seine River at Montereau on August 24, 1944, took Rheims on August 30, and established a bridgehead across the Meuse at Verdun the next day.

On September 7, 1944, the 5th Infantry opened its attack on Metz, one of the most heavily fortified cities in Europe. Inching forward through withering German artillery fire and infantry counterattacks, the Division suffered very heavy casualties and withdrew to rest on October 12, 1944. On November 12, 1944, the Division resumed its attack, and one by one the forts guarding Metz, including the incredibly fortified Fort Driant, fell. On December 6, 1944, the last German fortification at Metz surrendered and the Division was once again withdrawn to reorganize and rest.

But its rest period didn't last long. Following the German's Ardennes Counteroffensive, which began December 16, 1944, the 5th Infantry Division was quickly mobilized to relieve the battered 95th Infantry Division at the Saarlautern bridgehead. Attacking on December 18, 1944, the Division began pecking away at the southern flank of the "bulge" created by the German breakout and by January 1, 1945, was poised along the Sauer River ready to cross and attack to the north. With temperatures in the teens and 12 inches of snow on the ground on January 18, 1945, assault boats made the crossing in front of the initially surprised enemy, with the 2nd Infantry Regiment crossing west of Diekirch, Luxembourg, and the 10th Infantry Regiment to Diekirch's east. Once across, the 1st Battalion, 2nd Infantry, immediately pushed northward along a north-south section of the Sauer while the Regiment's 2nd Battalion swung behind Diekirch to cut off any escape routes. The 3rd Battalion, 2nd Infantry, then took the city while the 2nd Battalion, 10th Infantry, also began swinging behind Diekirch. By nightfall of January 18, 1945, the 2nd and 10th Infantry Regiments had pushed forward in a bridgehead more than a mile deep and five miles wide.

Though an article in the *News-Wave* dated August 16, 1945 stated Staff Sergeant Adelbert Bautch was with "Headquarters Company, 1st Battalion, 2nd Regiment, 5th Infantry Division," this is probably not entirely correct, and his actual assignment could not be verified beyond doubt. Due to events of January 20, 1945 and known records, it is possible he was with either the 2nd or 10th Infantry Regiment. It is more probable he was attached to Headquarters Company, 5th Infantry Division, however, which was formed with an original cadre that included men from 1st Battalion, 2nd Regiment. Regardless, on January 20, 1945, in the drive north from Diekirch,

11

Luxembourg, Adelbert was with a group of men laying road signs to guide the oncoming infantry. The truck he was riding moved too far ahead of the infantry and attempted to turn around in the road. While backing onto the road shoulder, a land mine was struck and Adelbert, riding on the side rail, was killed.

Adelbert Bautch had two brothers also serving in the European Theater of Operations -- Anselm, with a bomber squadron stationed in England, and Edmund, a staff sergeant with the 3rd Armored Division. In January 1944, while on furlough in England, Adelbert went to London where he accidentally ran into his brother, Edmund, at a service center. They promptly contacted Anselm, whose commanding officer then granted him leave so he might meet with his brothers. A photo of the three brothers in London was sent to their parents, Mr. and Mrs. Paul N. Bautch, who subsequently delivered it to the *News-Wave* for publication in its November 30, 1944 edition.

Following the war and before returning home from Europe in early August 1945, Edmund visited Adelbert's grave in the military cemetery at Hamm, Germany. Edmund stated in a *News-Wave* article of August 16, 1945 that he was happy for his own sake and that of his parents that he was able to visit Adelbert's grave site, and indicated the cemetery was well-cared for and guarded around the clock.

A requiem mass was held at Ss. Peter & Paul's Catholic Church, Independence, on February 19, 1945 in memory of Adelbert Bautch. Msgr. L. J. Kufel officiated with assistance from Rev. Francis Przybylski, and the Sura-Wiersgalla American Legion Post 186 attended as a body. On September 13, 1948, a reburial service was held for Adelbert at the Church following a request by his family that his remains be returned from overseas.

This photo taken of the three Bautch brothers -- Anselm, Adelbert, and Edmund -- while on leave together in England in January 1944, was sent by the boys to their parents, Mr. and Mrs. Paul N. Bautch.

Sources: Independence News-Wave; Book (Fifth Division Historical Section)

EDMUND BAUTCH
UNITED STATES ARMY

Edmund Bautch was inducted into the United States Army in June 1941. Following basic training, he began armored training at Camp Polk, Louisiana, was assigned duty with the 32nd Armored

Regiment (Light), 3rd Armored Division,[1] which was stationed at Camp Polk at the time, and soon became leader of a half-track platoon carrying assault guns. While at Camp Polk, Edmund was promoted to sergeant on February 22, 1942.

Redesignated on January 1, 1942 as the 32nd Armored Regiment, Edmund's unit transferred with 3rd Armored to Indio, California, on July 26, 1942, where it began intensive desert training during the Desert Training Center II Armored Corps California Maneuvers. The Regiment was relocated to Camp Pickett, Virginia, on November 9, 1942, and Indiantown Gap Military Reservation, Pennsylvania, on January 17, 1943. The entire 3rd Armored Division departed the New York Port of Embarkation on September 5, 1943, and arrived in England on September 16, 1943.

By January 1944, Edmund was a platoon sergeant with Headquarters Company, 1st Battalion, as 3rd Armored continued its training in preparation for the inevitable invasion of the continent yet to come. But despite the emphasis on training, soldiers were at times granted leave, and Edmund was fortunate in seeing Anselm, one of his two brothers also stationed in England, several times while off-duty. Late in January 1944, when on leave in London, Anselm and Edmund happened to meet at an Army service center. They immediately contacted their third brother, Adelbert, whose commanding officer granted him leave so he could visit with them. On January 24, 1944, a cable was sent by Edmund to the brothers' parents, Mr. and Mrs. Paul Bautch, informing them that the three had been together in London. A photograph of the three brothers taken during that meeting, published in the *Eau Claire Telegram*, and in the *Independence News-Wave* on November 30, 1944, later arrived at the Bautch home along with a description of their meeting. But this was the last time Edmund, Anselm, and Adelbert would be together because on January 20, 1945, Adelbert was killed in action while his 5th Infantry Division was racing through Luxembourg.

On June 23, 1944, the 3rd Armored Division landed on the Normandy beaches in France, and by June 29, Edmund found himself in combat with his armored mortar platoon as 3rd Armored attacked the Villiers-Fossard salient northeast of St. Lo. The Division moved through France and by August 13, 1944 was swinging around Domfront attempting to close the Falaise Gap, which would have encircled as many as 250,000 German soldiers. For some reason, however, probably the belief that Germany was finished along that part of the front, the order was not given by Allied headquarters to complete the operation -- in fact, General Patton had been ordered to halt his encircling advance -- and the bulk of the German *Seventh Army* and *Fifth Panzer Army* were able to escape.

Two weeks later, 3rd Armored crossed the Seine River below Paris, crossed the Marne River near Meaux, France, and continued pursuing the disorganized, retreating German armies. By September 12, 1944, it found itself poised along the *West Wall*, Hitler's name for the Siegfried

---

[1] 3rd Armored Division suffered 1,810 killed and 6,963 wounded, with 316 of those dying from their wounds, during its five campaigns in the ETO.

Line, at Schmidthof. After passing through the fortifications between Roetgen and Rott, Germany, the troops reached a second zone of *West Wall* pillboxes and tank traps where a large number of American tanks were lost in the Battle of Geisberg Hill on September 16, 1944. With Geisberg Hill taken, Weissenberg Hill and Muensterbusch Hill were assaulted next.

The city of Stolberg, Germany, was taken on September 22, 1944, but when 3rd Armored's Combat Command B found itself being encircled by the Germans, the advance through the *West Wall* was halted in order to help Combat Command B withdraw its forces from Donnerberg. Following this, the Division then continued its attack through the Lousberg Heights and cut the Aachen-Laurensberg Highway by October 28, 1944. On November 18, 1944, 3rd Armored suffered heavy tank losses once again at Hastenrath and Scherpenseel before taking the towns and moving on through a minefield to take Huecheln on November 24.

It was for actions during the period of August 14 through October 22, 1944, when the 3rd Armored Division was involved in very bitter and continuous combat, that Edmund was awarded his first of two Bronze Stars. He also was awarded the Purple Heart for an ear wound he received from a sniper as he was leaving an observation post near Stolberg. On November 7, 1944, he wrote the following letter to his parents in which he informed them of his 3rd Armored Division's spearheading the American drive into Germany. It was published in the December 28, 1944, edition of the *News-Wave*:

> Dear Folks:
>
> Hope I haven't caused you any unnecessary worries through lack of writing but things happen sometimes that we have no control over, and it's just one of those things.
>
> You may have been wondering where I am at and all that; you may have had some idea about it from what the papers and radio news had to say. I can tell you now that we are in Germany and have been here for sometime and that is about all that can be said on that now. However, you are going to hear more, and I am sure a lot more, about our outfit that you ever did before. At least for a while you will, and we are going to get the credit due us and some of our hard work and fighting will be made known to the public. It is going to be hard for some people to believe some of these things, but we are the ones that cracked the biggest and stiffest part of the enemy's force in and through France, also Belgium, and first inside of the German border. Though I am letting my modesty get away from me there still is a lot more to be said about what we have done and been through.
>
> Have you wondered why other divisions were heard about and getting a lot of publicity and never a word about ours? There was good reason for that and it may account for some of our success. Ever hear of the Ghost force sometime ago? I would like to have you show that to Uncle Joe as I am sure that some of these places were his hunting ground in the first war. I would send him one but don't have enough of them. Also tell him that some of the scars from those days are still there, even some of the trenches and a lot of shell fragments are still lying around.
>
> You may be getting some pictures. They were taken in England on the fourth day of a seven-day, day and night, problem for my platoon. We thought at the time that it was a rough deal. Am enclosing a part of the "Stars and Stripes" for you . I am very well.
>
> Bye for now. Best of luck and God bless you all.
>
> Ed.

3rd Armored next attacked along the west bank of the Roer River beginning on December 10, 1944. When the German Ardennes Counteroffensive began on December 16, 1944, the combat commands of 3rd Armored were moved in to reinforce other units that were being hard hit by the German advance. A more than month-long period of heavy combat then occurred with both gains and losses being registered throughout the lines. But the German advance was eventually halted and the American forces went on the offensive once again. Grandmenil was taken at Christmas, and this was followed by an assault and seizure of Sadzot. On January 12, 1945, Bihain was attacked, a week later the Ourthe River was reached, and on January 22, 1945, Bouvy and Beho were in American hands.

3rd Armored's next attack began on February 26, 1945 as it moved out of the Elle River bridgehead toward Stommeln. It reached the Rhine River at Roggendorf and Worringen, Germany, on March 4, 1945, and for the next three days was involved in the Battle for Cologne. It crossed the Rhine again on March 23, 1945, quickly resumed its advance, and reached Marburg, Germany, on March 28. Following the Battle of Paderborn[2] on March 31-April 1, 1945, it next closed the Ruhr Pocket where it helped trap 372,000 German soldiers. It then continued eastward, liberating prisoner of war camps and the large concentration camp at Nordhausen. By April 21, 1945, it was fighting the Battle for Dessau before being relieved along the Mulde River on April 25, 1945. 3rd Armored was in the area of Dessau when Germany formally surrendered on May 7, 1945.

For his actions during the drive from the Ruhr Pocket to Dessau, Edmund was awarded an Oak Leaf Cluster in lieu of his second Bronze Star.

By late July, 1945, it was apparent Edmund would be returning to the United States, but before he left, he was able to visit the grave of his brother, Staff Sergeant Adelbert, in Hamm, Germany. In an August 16, 1945 *News-Wave* article announcing his return to Independence, Edmund stated that he was happy for his own sake and that of his parents to have visited the cemetery. For the two remaining brothers, however, the photograph taken in London would be a bittersweet reminder of a happier time.

By the end of the war, Edmund was wearing five battle stars on his European-African-Middle Eastern Campaign Ribbon, along with his Purple Heart and Bronze Star with Oak Leaf Cluster.

---

[2] It was at Paderborn where the highly respected commander of the 3rd Armored Division, Major General Maurice Rose, was killed in action. General Rose was the man who brought national attention to Bennie Kulig outside Palermo, Sicily, in 1943 (see Bennie Kulig biography).

Sources: Independence News-Wave; Book (Stanton)

ERNEST P. BAUTCH
UNITED STATES ARMY

Ernest Bautch was inducted into the United States Army on March 16, 1943. Following basic training, he was assigned to the 1st Battalion, 36th Armored Infantry Regiment, 3rd Armored Division,[1] that departed the New York Port of Embarkation on August 27, 1943 and arrived in England on September 16. On June 25, 1944, the 3rd Armored Division landed in Normandy and began its advance inland.

3rd Armored's initial combat occurred in the Villiers-Fossard salient northeast of St. Lo beginning on June 29, 1944. In mid-August 1944, the Division was in position to pinch off the Falaise Gap that would have trapped as many as 250,000 German soldiers. But the order to complete the operation never came from Allied Headquarters, so the Germans escaped to face 3rd Armored again at later dates.

The Division passed south of Paris, France, on August 25, 1944 and continued to press forward against a disorganized enemy. By September 12, 1944, it had reached the *West Wall* at Schmidthof and the following day attacked the German fortifications in the area of Roetgen, Germany. The next day, it had reached the outskirts of Aachen and then suffered heavy tank

---

[1] The 3rd Armored Division lost 1,810 men killed in action and 6,963 wounded, of which 316 died of their wounds, during its five campaigns in the European Theater.

15

losses in the Battle of Geisberg Hill while attempting to breach another line of *West Wall* defenses. Ground was won and lost over a period of several days until Stolberg, Germany, was finally taken on September 22, 1944. When at this time 3rd Armored's Combat Command B found itself in danger of being cut off, the rest of the Division halted its advance and aided in CCB's withdrawal from Donnerberg, Germany, before resuming its attack towards the Roer River.

With the start of the German Ardennes Counteroffensive of December 16, 1944, 3rd Armored was rushed to shore up positions in danger of collapsing in front of the enemy onslaught. But by January 3, 1945, 3rd Armored was on the offensive once again and by January 19, 1945, had reached the Ourthe River.

By February 26, 1945, 3rd Armored was attacking out of bridgeheads over the Elle River at Glesch and Paffendorf, Germany. It reached the Rhine River on March 4, 1945 and fought in the "Battle for Cologne" beginning the next day, after which the newly-liberated residents of Cologne threw a party for the men of the 3rd Armored and 104th Infantry Divisions. It reached Marburg on March 28, 1945 and helped trap 372,000 German troops in the Ruhr Pocket on March 31-April 1, 1945. Then, after crossing the Weser and Mulde Rivers, it fought the "Battle for Dessau" on April 21-23, 1945 before being relieved for rehabilitation. 3rd Armored was in the Dessau area when hostilities ceased on May 7, 1945.

In a letter to his parents, Mr. and Mrs. John C. Bautch, dated March 11, 1945, Ernest sent the Army's announcement of his unit's receiving the highest possible decoration, the Distinguished Unit Citation, one of two such awards it earned during the war:

> With the Third Armored Division -- Amid the mud, rubble and destruction of German soil, A and C companies, 36th Armored Regiment, recently were awarded battle honors entitling them to wear the Distinguished Unit Badge.

Several days later, news reports in the United States announced that 3rd Armored's popular commander, Major General Maurice Rose, had been killed in action in Germany. General Rose had helped bring notoriety to Bennie Kulig and Independence during the 1943 Sicily campaign through an article in LIFE magazine which detailed Kulig's role in knocking out a German heavy gun that was blocking the way for General Patton's entrance into Palermo.

At the close of the war, a letter was received by Ernest's parents, subsequently published in the *News-Wave,* in which he gave a short account of his European campaign, plus mentioned the German sniper's rifle he had sent to his father along with two officer's knives, one of which had a Swastika engraved on the heel and pommel of the blade:

Klien Welzheim, Germany
Dear Mom and Dad,

Have a little spare time so will drop a few lines at the least. I can't figure out this mail rightly. Maybe your letters will come in one bunch. I hope!

Have been in three armies since VE-Day, the first, ninth and now, the Seventh. It shouldn't be hard to figure what that means. The seventh is staying here. So you see it may be a long time before I can come home. Please do not worry over it. The only thing wrong is that I'll be an old man before I get home. Ha, ha!

I can now tell you a little about our last campaign of the war. Our last battle was fought at Dessau, just below Berlin. At that time the Russians were only 5,000 yards away from us. I fought in Normandy, Northern France, Germany, the Rhine campaign and the Belgian Bulge. All of this entitles me to wear five campaign stars, two Presidential Unit citations, the Meritorious Service medal, the Combat Infantrymans badge, the ETO ribbon, and the Good Conduct ribbon. Just think, I came through all of this without a single scratch. Hard to believe isn't it? Many times I thought I would be a dead duck. The closest call I had was when a mortar shell landed about six feet from me. All it did was knock me over and shake me up a bit. Another time I was out setting booby traps, and accidentally tripped on one of the wires I had hooked. It went off right in front of me. So, you see, it's all God's will. By the way, Dad, did you get the sniper's rifle with the telescope, and the two officers knives that I sent you? The rifle is just like

16

new.

     How are the kids? I suppose they're grown up now. Tell them "hi" from me. Tell all the relatives hello from me also.

     Will close for now hoping to hear from you soon. So long, and please do not worry.

       Your son,

       Ernest

Besides the two Distinguished Unit Citations earned during his 22 months and five campaigns in Europe, Ernest also earned the right to wear the Meritorious Service Medal, Combat Infantryman's Badge, the European-African-Middle Eastern Ribbon with five battle stars, Good Conduct Medal, and World War II Victory Medal. He was discharged from the Army at Fort Sheridan, Illinois, as a Corporal on December 6, 1945.

No photo.
Sources: Independence News-Wave; Book (Stanton)

ROMAN T. BAUTCH
UNITED STATES ARMY AIR CORPS

Roman Bautch enlisted in the United States Army Air Corps sometime prior to the Japanese attack on Pearl Harbor. He went through more than two years of training and was awarded his wings in late 1943. Following a furlough spent visiting with his parents, Mr. and Mrs. Frank J. Bautch, in late November 1943, Roman traveled to an air base at Marfa, Texas, though it is not known whether he remained there for any amount of time or was transferred to another location. By the end of 1944, however, he was a Staff Sergeant and Flight Engineer aboard a B-25 bomber stationed at Greenville, South Carolina.

Roman's squadron left for the China-Burma-India Theater sometime in early 1945, probably February or March. Stationed in Yanghi, China, Roman's squadron flew 23 combat missions up to the end of the war, accumulating a total of 87 combat hours. It flew missions over Canton, China; Hanoi, French Indo-China; the Yellow River area; and Hong Kong harbor, among others. In a *News-Wave* article published November 22, 1945 regarding Roman's service years, he indicated that throughout his eight months in the CBI Theater, he never happened across anyone from the Independence area.

In that same article, Roman described how American servicemen were housed by the Chinese government for one dollar per day. He said they were served rice daily with, it seems, no variation in the recipes. Vegetables, other than a few cucumbers and sweet corn, were rare additions to their diet, and meat was extremely scarce except for the occasional old water buffalo that was no longer useful for work.

Servicemen were housed in mud huts, four to a room, that seemed to "melt away" when heavy rains occurred. Wooden furnishings were rare and highly prized by the Chinese because it was so difficult to construct tables and chairs due to the primitive methods of harvesting trees and cutting lumber. Roman reported that any damage done to furnishings by Americans resulted in heavy fines being placed upon the servicemen. Most Chinese were illiterate, he found, but hard workers in the fields and rice paddies.

Roman said the Red Cross served doughnuts and coffee at a service center on the base, the doughnuts made of rice flour, and, when not on duty, the servicemen engaged in various sports, with softball being the favorite. He said the service center provided up to two shows per week, which, he indicated, were a real treat for everyone.

When the war ended, Roman's squadron eventually returned to the United States. On

17

November 1, 1945, he received his discharge at Camp McCoy, Wisconsin. He was wearing three service stars in recognition of his participation in the China Defensive, China Offensive, and Central Burma campaigns.

No photo.
Sources: Independence News-Wave; Book (Stanton)

BENEDICT BISEK
UNITED STATES ARMY

One of four brothers who served during World War II, Benedict Bisek was inducted the same day as his brother, Emil. They both began their service careers with the Arcadia, Wisconsin, National Guard unit on October 15, 1940, but this didn't last long as on that same day both entered active duty. He and Emil attended basic training together at Camp Beauregard and Camp Livingston, Louisiana, and Camp Blanding in Florida. An interesting article regarding Benedict and Emil appeared in the March 18, 1943 *News-Wave*, one that appears to have been published in a military newsletter or newspaper in England. (See page 19.) It was sent to Benedict's aunt by their cousin, also serving in England.

Early August 1942 found Benedict with the 107th Ordnance Company stationed at Dilworth, North Carolina. On November 24, 1942, he left for the European Theater of Operations, arriving in England on November 30. He spent the next 21 months in the ETO with the 107th Ordnance Company, MM (Motor Mechanized).

Prior to D-Day, the assignment given Benedict and other mechanics stationed in England was to devise ways of weatherproofing the heavy equipment slated to land with the invasion force in Normandy in early June 1944. Their waterproofing experiments proved successful and Benedict was decorated with the Bronze Star for his personal efforts by Colonel J. B. Medaris, First Army Ordnance Officer. A photograph of the medal being pinned on his uniform appeared in the March 8, 1945 *News-Wave*.

On August 28, 1944, the 107th Ordnance crossed the English Channel and landed in France. Through the course of the rest of the war, Benedict participated in the Northern France, Ardennes, Rhineland, and Central Europe campaigns, earning him four bronze battle stars on his European-African-Middle Eastern Theater Ribbon. At war's end, he also wore five overseas service stripes, the Good Conduct Medal, and the American Defense Service Ribbon.

Benedict left the European Theater on June 23, 1945 aboard a plane flying from Paris to Presque Isle, Maine, in 24 hours with only one stop in the Azores. He was discharged as a Technical Sergeant Third Grade on June 29, 1945 at Fort Sheridan, Illinois, and reverted to National Guard status.

It is not clear when he may have learned of his brother, Louis', death on Luzon, Philippine Islands, in April 1945.

Source: Independence News-Wave

Staff Sergeant Benedict Bisek being decorated with a Bronze Star by Colonel J. B. Medaris, 1st Army Ordnance Officer.

Bisek Brothers Reverse Old War Story
Never Separated In Army

Here is a story I'm sure folks back home will enjoy reading. This was received by Miss Martha Bisek, Independence, from her nephew, Andrew Gawel, who is stationed somewhere in England.

(A U. S. Ordnance Deport, England). The story about brothers in the army usually is that one goes to Australia and the other to Iceland.

Here are two guys who haven't been separated from the day they got in. Staff Sgt. Emil Bisek, 28, and Staff Sgt. Benedict Bisek, 26, joined the U. S. Army together at Arcadia, Wis. Instead of Emil going to San Diego, California, and Benedict to Bangor, Me., as frequently happens with brothers, both went to a camp in Louisiana for training. Both became M. P.'s there the same day and neither had to arrest the other during their seven months "swinging the stick." So good was their conduct in fact, that both were promoted on the same day. Neither ever has had a chance to "pull rank" on the other. Each became a Specialist Fifth Class on July 1, 1941. In August 1942, they became T/4's the same day.

On another pleasant day in September 1942, each became a T/3, which rank each still holds.

Formerly farm hands from Independence, they became expert Ordnance mechanics and came overseas in the same company, on the same boat, in the same room.

Both are single, but neither expects to stay that way.

"You can't marry the same girl," they were warned.

"No, but we can find a coupla sisters."

They are stationed somewhere in England and are still together.

- Published *Independence News-Wave*, March 18, 1943

EMIL BISEK
UNITED STATES ARMY

Emil Bisek joined the Arcadia, Wisconsin, National Guard unit, the 32nd Military Police, on October 15, 1940. with his younger brother, Benedict. That same day the unit went to active duty status, taking the Bisek's with it. His story is basically the same as Benedict's, with the two attending basic training together, being trained as artillery mechanics together, reverting to the 107th Ordnance Company, MM (Motor Mechanized) together, traveling overseas to England where they served together, and participating in the same campaigns together. They were decorated identically, although it is not clear whether Emil received a Bronze Star as Benedict had for the D-Day waterproofing operation he was involved with, as it is not indicated on his military separation record. Additionally, the brothers were promoted at the same time, with both attaining the rank of Technical Sergeant Third Grade by September 1942.

The only notable difference in the brothers' records is that Emil left the European Theater for home in September 1945, arrived in the States on September 20, and was discharged with the rank of Staff Sergeant on October 4, 1945 at Fort Sheridan, Illinois.

The March 1, 1945, *News-Wave* carried the news that Staff Sergeant Bisek was serving with the Ninth U. S. Army in Germany and had been receiving the newspaper and other mail quite regularly, and that he was always happy to hear from people back home. He expressed great surprise at seeing his mother's photograph in the "Special Serviceman's Edition" of November 30, 1945, and commented on the photos of the corn husker and new tractors that appeared in that edition. (See article in *Special Stories* in Volume II of this document.)

It should be noted that the 107th Ordnance Company, MM, received the Meritorious Unit Citation for its outstanding performance against the enemy.

No photo.
Source: Independence News-Wave

FRANK J. BISEK
UNITED STATES ARMY

Frank Bisek, one of four sons of Mrs. Agnes Bisek and the late John Bisek to serve during World War II, was inducted into the United States Army and entered active service on March 20, 1942. at Eau Claire, Wisconsin. Following basic training, Frank was sent to Fort Knox, Kentucky, where on April 17, 1943, he completed specialized training as a tank mechanic. He became a tank driver and mechanic, assigned to Company A, 708th Amphibian Tank Battalion. On December 24, 1943, Frank's unit left the San Francisco Port of Embarkation, arriving in Hawaii on December 31, 1943. While in Hawaii, the 708th was attached to the Army's 7th Infantry Division and given orders to support the invasion of Kwajalein in the Marshall Islands that was scheduled for February 1, 1943. Capture of the Marshall's would allow American aircraft to strike deeply into Japanese-held territory in the Pacific. Kwajalein Island, the largest coral atoll in the world, was the main target of this operation.

Within hours of the 7th Infantry's first wave landing on Kwajalein, Frank's 708th Amphibian Tank Battalion began arriving on the beach. It quickly joined with the infantry units and began systematically eliminating Japanese positions. By February 4, 1943, action had been reduced to mop-up operations, and when it was all over the Japanese had lost 7,800 men. In contrast, American forces suffered 1,954 casualties with only 372 of these killed. According to one reputable source (Stanton), following the occupation of Kwajalein, the 708th Amphibian Tank Battalion was reorganized and redesignated as the 708th Amphibian Tractor Battalion. But other official Army accounts of later campaigns continued to call Frank's unit the 708th Amphibian Tank Battalion. The reason for this confusion is unclear.

On February 17, 1943, Frank and his unit arrived on Majuro Island, just south of Kwajalein. Majuro had already been taken without opposition by the 27th Infantry Division's 106th Infantry Regiment and its large lagoon was being utilized as a major assembly point for units boarding ships. Frank then left Majuro and the Marshall Islands, arriving back in Hawaii on March 14, 1944. The next nearly eleven months were spent in training exercises on the Hawaiian Islands.

By February 1945, much of the Philippine Islands was back in American and Filipino hands. On February 25, 1945, Frank's 708th arrived in the Southern Philippines and, though this is not entirely clear, probably landed in support of the 41st Infantry Division's 186th Regimental Combat Team in its assault on Palawan Island, a long island immediately west of the main Philippine group. However, his unit remained in the Philippines for only about one month before it was loaded aboard ship and sent to the Ryukyu Islands to participate in the invasion of Okinawa and other islands in the group. There it was kept busy, with elements of the 708th landing on Yakabi Shima, Aka Shima, and Zamami Shima, islands of the Kerema Retto group southwest of Okinawa, on March 26, 1945. The next day saw other elements of the 708th land on Amura Shima, Kuba Shima, and Tokashika Shima of the Keremas. On March 31, 1945, the 708th aided the landing of the 420th Field Artillery Group, which included Lieutenant Ed J. Lyga's 531st Field Artillery Battalion, on Keise Shima, an island eight miles from Okinawa's landing beaches. It was from Keise Shima that the big 155-mm "Long Toms" were to support the main invasion scheduled for the next day, April 1, 1945.

On April 16, 1945, closely following the first waves of the 77th Infantry Division, the 708th Amphibian Tank Battalion next assaulted the beaches of Ie Shima, an island off Okinawa's northwest coast, where it encountered stiff opposition from the Japanese defenders. Frank was on Ie Shima when famed war correspondent Ernie Pyle was killed by an enemy machine gun burst.

Four days after Ie Shima was declared secured, and following very intense fighting there, the 708th landed on Okinawa itself on April 25, 1945, again in support of the 77th Infantry Division's attack. The battle for Okinawa continued through June, with hostilities declared officially over on June 22, 1945. Following this, the 708th, minus Company C which remained on Okinawa, again boarded ship for the Philippines, arriving there on July 17, 1945. Here they aided in mop-up operations on Cebu Island. It was on Cebu in early August, 1945, where the men of the 708th Amphibian Tank Battalion learned the war against Japan had ended.

Frank left the Philippines for the United States on November 13, 1945, arriving two weeks later. He had participated in the Eastern Mandates, Southern Philippines, Ryukyus, and Western Pacific campaigns, earning four bronze battle stars on his Asiatic-Pacific Theater Ribbon. He also had earned three Overseas Service Bars and the Good Conduct Medal. His 708th Amphibian Tank Battalion had been awarded a Distinguished Unit Citation with one Bronze Cluster for outstanding unit action against the enemy, though it is unclear which campaign this was for. On December 9, 1945, Frank received his separation from the United States Army at Camp McCoy, Wisconsin.

No photo.
Source: Alphonse Bisek, brother; Book (Stanton)

A Quote From History. . .

"I get plenty to eat, and a place to sleep -- what more would a person want."
    Bennie J. Kampa
    United States Army
    From a letter home, July 20, 1943

LOUIS P. BISEK
UNITED STATES ARMY

The youngest of four sons of Mrs. Agnes Bisek to join the United States Army during World War II, Louis Bisek entered the service on September 10, 1941. He attended basic training in California, after which he remained in various California camps for about the next two years. In early August 1942, Louis was stationed with Battery C, 216th Coast Artillery, near San Francisco, probably guarding the port there.

On September 10, 1943, the 216th Coast Artillery was redesignated as four separate antiaircraft artillery units in the 216th Antiaircraft Artillery Group. It moved to Camp Haan, California, on April 15, 1944, and then was later transferred to Camp Howze, Texas, on November 18, 1944. At Camp Howze the 216th AAA Group was inactivated and its personnel transferred to other units. This, as it turned out, would prove to be a fateful turn of events in the life of Louis Bisek.

In the "Special Serviceman's Edition" of the *Independence News-Wave* published on November 30, 1945, Louis' mother had placed an ad expressing to her four sons just how proud she was of them (see article in *Special Stories* section of Volume II of this document). Though she knew her sons were or could be placed in danger, she couldn't know at that time that she wouldn't see Louis again.

Louis embarked for overseas duty as an infantry replacement in December, 1944, arriving in the Philippine Islands where he was assigned to the 2nd Battalion, 126th Infantry Regiment, 32nd Infantry Division.[1] The 32nd Infantry Division, and probably Corporal Bisek, landed with the main invasion force on Luzon, Philippine Islands, on January 27, 1945, and began its push towards Manila. The famous bloody "Battle for Villa Verde Trail" was fought from February 6-22, 1945, in which the "Red Arrow" men repulsed numerous fanatical Japanese counterattacks. Battles were fought at Salacsac Pass and through the Arboredo and Ambayang Valleys in March, 1945, before mop-up operations began in the Villa Verde Trail region. It was here, during mop-up along the Villa Verde Trail, when on April 25, 1945, Louis Bisek was killed in action. He was 26 years old.

The May 17, 1945, edition of the *Independence News-Wave* carried the news that Mrs.

---

[1] The 32nd Infantry Division, the famed "Red Arrow Division" consisting originally of Michigan and Wisconsin National Guardsmen, was already a veteran division of the New Guinea and Southern Philippines (Leyte) campaigns by the time Louis joined it. It lost 1,613 men killed and 5,627 wounded, with 372 of those dying from their wounds, by war's end.

Agnes Bisek had been informed of her son's death. The telegram from the War Department simply said:

Secretary of War desires to express his deep regret that your son, Cpl Louis P. Bisek, was killed in action on Luzon 25 of April, 1945. Letter of confirmation follows.

That same article stated that Louis' last letter to his mother had been dated April 17, 1945, and in it Louis had informed her that he was serving in the 2nd Battalion of the 126th Infantry. For some unknown reason, no additional mention was made in the article of any memorial service to be held in respect for Louis. In fact, nothing is noted again in the paper regarding Louis until April 25, 1946, the one-year anniversary of this death, when a memorial service was held at 9:00 A. M. at Ss. Peter and Paul's Catholic Church. In the announcement of the service scheduled for that same day, it stated the Rt. Rev. Msgr. L. J. Kufel would offer the Requiem High Mass, assisted by the Rev. Francis Przybylski, and that the American Legion Sura-Wiersgalla Post No. 186 would be in charge of the service at the serviceman's plot of ground. All members of Post 186 plus others who served in World War II were urged to attend in full uniform.

The following week's *News-Wave* carried a short review of the memorial service held the previous week for Louis. Veterans of both World War I and World War II did attend in very large numbers and the Legion presented the flag to Louis' mother following the church service. Louis' three brothers, Emil, Frank, and Benedict, all of whom had also served in the United States Army during World War II, were reported to have been in attendance, as well.

Louis Bisek was the final Independence resident to give his life during the greatest conflict the world has ever known.

Sources: Independence News-Wave; Book (Stanton)

EVERETTE BLAHA
UNITED STATES ARMY

The following narrative was written following an interview with Everette Blaha at his home in rural Independence on July 9, 1998.

I was living in Milwaukee when I was inducted into the Army on March 9, 1943. I went to Fort Sheridan, Illinois, to enter active duty and then went to Camp Roberts in California for basic training. Along the way at a depot in Spur, Texas, the train stopped for a while and we got to talking with four girls through the train windows. We got their names -- actually one of the other guys got their names -- and then we went on our way. While at Camp Roberts, the actor Gabby Hayes came to camp with a USO show and I had my picture taken with him. I also volunteered for parachute training while I was there so after basic I went to Fort Benning, Georgia, for parachute school. After we were parachute certified, we went by troop train back to Camp Roberts.

We boarded ship in California and sailed to Australia to join the 503rd Parachute Infantry Regiment that was already in Port Moresby, New Guinea, and seeing action. From Port Moresby we went to Hollandia on the north coast of New Guinea. At Hollandia my regiment boarded a plane and we jumped on Noemfoor Island. On the Noemfoor jump, I busted up my knee some and was given the Purple Heart.

We landed on Leyte by landing craft later in November and then participated in the Mindoro invasion, again by landing craft. But when we were to hit Corregidor, the regiment was

Left: Everette Blaha with famed Hollywood actor Gabby Hayes at Camp Roberts, California.
Right: Everette in the Philippine Islands.

scheduled to jump. Mine was the last battalion scheduled but at the last minute they decided to put us on landing craft and we went ashore the next day. That landing was something because the Navy landing craft guys wouldn't get close enough to the beach. Instead they dropped us off in deep water. I was in neck deep and the Japanese were shooting at us. I pulled a dead guy to shore. Some of the guys who did jump, though, missed their jump spot and were captured. I remember hearing one guy screaming as he was being tortured. The next day his body was thrown out where we could see it. When we got to it, we found bamboo driven under all of his finger and toe nails, his tongue was cut out, and his ears cut off.

On Corregidor, the Japanese banzaied regularly and we were so tired. Also, our regiment had a colonel as commanding officer instead of a general that usually is in command of a unit that big. Because of that, we couldn't get the supplies we needed because the colonel didn't have as much clout as a general, I guess. Our regiment became known as "Colonel Jones and the 3000 Thieves." That was one way to get some of the supplies we needed. Actually, though, MacArthur did a helluva good job because so much equipment and supplies were going to Europe.

Corregidor was one helluva fight. I remember on February 26 we were camped on a place called Monkey Point. Fortunately that morning we kind of spread out because it turned out we were right on top of a Jap ammo dump, and they blew it. A 30-ton tank was thrown 50 yards. Company A had 140 men the night before. After this they had 2 officers and 42 men left in condition to fight.

It got so bad that I reached a point where I didn't care if the Japs had killed me. It was a sickening place to be. One day, I remembered those four girls at the Texas train depot, so I found the guy who had their addresses and wrote one of them a letter in which I told her about how I didn't care anymore. I got a letter back from her, and you know what, that is what kept me going. I got letters from her regularly after that and she could really write well. She became my inspiration to stay alive.

A few years ago, I started looking for her. Her name was Shirley Powell from Spur, Texas. In 1993, I found her. She and her family were no longer in Spur but they were still in Texas, and our families have corresponded since. If not for her letters when I was in that jungle, I

24

The massive Japanese ammo dump explosion of February 24, 1945, on Corregidor's Monkey Point killed and wounded 200 American troops. It was so powerful, it threw a 30-ton tank 50 yards.

would have given up for sure.

One guy in our unit, though, was so convinced that he would be killed that he asked to be 1st Scout on our patrols, and he was killed. His name was Rufus McCall.

One day I was out on patrol and when I got back I was told Alex Kloss had stopped by the company. It was too bad I missed him.

I was wounded on Corregidor, too, and still have a piece of a Jap grenade in my finger. Actually, I was wounded a couple other times as well, but I didn't even bother reporting it so I didn't get Purple Hearts for those times, just for Noemfoor and this one time on Corregidor.

From Corregidor we landed on Negros Island. This was a tough one, too. One time I was really scared because we had a lieutenant who had just learned his brother had been killed, and he was so mad, he was going to clean out the whole Jap army by himself. He made some mistakes and all of a sudden the Japs had us surrounded. We escaped by climbing down a cliff by some vines.

Just before the war ended, we were sent out to find the Japs. We didn't have any trouble following them. We didn't have much in the way of supplies with us and were told they would be airdropped to us. Well, they were airdropped, but they were airdropped to the Japanese! We had to then scavenge for food and ate whatever we could find. Headquarters told us they couldn't drop anything more than they already had.

One day a bunch of us were going up a little hillside when we found out the war was over, and we really were excited. But then some Japs started showing themselves and we got back to business again. It turned out they heard the war was over, too, and they were surrendering. We were so lucky it ended when it did because we were told there were several thousand Japs on this half-mile of hillside, and there were only 50 of us. We would have been wiped out for sure.

We were sent to Cebu and another island for a while to help out there, but eventually found ourselves on Luzon. I was attached to Company H of the 124th Infantry Regiment, left Luzon on October 29, 1945, and headed home. We finally reached San Francisco on December 14, 1945.

25

We didn't make any stops as I recall, it was just a "slow boat from China."

I was separated from the Army at Camp McCoy here in Wisconsin on December 23, 1945. I remember a WAC gave me just enough clothes to get home. Our regiment still holds a reunion every year. There are three guys from Osseo who were in the Regiment with me.

You know, I got a million dollars worth of experience during that time and in that jungle, but I wouldn't take a million to go through it again.

Everette Blaha participated in the New Guinea, South Philippines, and Luzon campaigns. Besides his two Purple Hearts, he was awarded a Bronze Star for actions on Corregidor, the Asiatic Pacific Theater Service Medal, Philippine Liberation Medal, Distinguished Unit Citation with Bronze Arrowhead, and Good Conduct Medal. His rank at war's end was Tech Sergeant.

He had left California aboard ship on September 20, 1943, arriving in Australia on October 7, 1943. His Noemfoor parachute jump was made on July 3, 1944. The 503rd Parachute Infantry Regiment landed on Leyte by landing craft on November 19, 1944, and invaded Mindoro on December 15, 1944. Though the 2nd and 3rd Battalions parachuted onto Corregidor Island on February 16, 1945, Everette's 1st Battalion reinforced them by landing craft the following day. The Regiment arrived on Negros Island on April 7, 1945, and from April 9-July 1, 1945, it was attached to the 40th Infantry Division. Following heavy combat, especially throughout May, 1945, the Regiment assumed mop-up responsibilities on Negros.

When Everette injured his knee while jumping on Noemfoor, the 503rd had originally been the reserve force for the operation. However, when a captured Japanese soldier told his American captors that 3,000 troops had recently landed to reinforce the garrison already numbering 3,000, expedition commander Major General Edwin Patrick asked for and received reinforcements from Lieutenant General Walter Krueger, commander of Alamo Force which was assaulting New Guinea. Though this information later proved to be false, Everette's 503rd from Hollandia and the 24th Infantry Division's 34th Infantry Regiment from Biak were brought into action. 1,424 paratroopers of the 503rd, including Everette, dropped from very low level on July 3-4, 1944. Their target was the Kamiri airfield and many of the troops, nine percent of the 503rd's force, in fact, were injured when they landed on parked heavy equipment, rocks, and tree stumps.

By February 24, 1945, American forces controlled all of Corregidor except for a final 3,000 yards. The ammo dump explosion of February 26, 1945, was the last of several suicide acts by the Japanese. Besides killing and wounding 200 American soldiers, it also killed more than 200 Japanese. Only 20 Japanese soldiers surrendered on Corregidor. On March 2, 1945, the 503rd Parachute Infantry Regiment's commander, Colonel George Jones, formally presented "Fortress Corregidor" to Supreme Commander General Douglas MacArthur.

Everette's copy of the *News-Wave's* "Special Serviceman's Edition" finally caught up with him in the Philippines. On April 3, 1945, he wrote a short letter to Glenn Kirkpatrick, thanking everyone involved with producing the November 30, 1944 issue. Kirkpatrick published the letter on April 19, 1945:

> Dear Kirk:
> Received the Servicemen's Edition of the News-Wave a while back, so I'm taking the first opportunity to write and thank you for it. It sure made me feel good to see some of the old places and folks back there. It makes a guy feel good to see all the people backing us up, and doing a wonderful job on the home front.
> I don't get much time to write around here. They've kept me pretty busy since I've been here. They always find something for us to do.
> I guess I'll have to sign off for now, so I wish to thank you again for the edition. Hope to see you in the near future.
> "Blaze"

When the war ended and Everette was on Negros Island, he was fortunate the group of enemy soldiers in front of his small unit of 50 men had heard the surrender news from Japanese sources and decided to surrender themselves. As many as 6,000 Japanese continued fighting on the island, however, many through September, 1945, before they became convinced the war was really over.

Sources: Books (Flanagan) (Stanton); Independence News-Wave

Killed in Action

OWEN K. CARLSON
UNITED STATES ARMY

Owen Carlson was the son of Mr. and Mrs. Carl "Charley" Carlson. He was born on January 21, 1919, attended the rural schools in the Chimney Rock area north of Independence, and was confirmed in the Chimney Rock Lutheran Church. At the age of 21, he enlisted in the Civilian Conservation Corps at Camp Ettrick and remained there until the camp closed. On July 31, 1942, Owen entered the United States Army.

He was immediately sent to Camp Forrest near Tullahoma,Tennessee, for basic training where that July the 80th Division, redesignated one month later as the 80th Infantry Division, had been activated.[1] While at Camp Forrest, the Division participated in the Second Army No. 2

Tennessee Maneuvers beginning June 23, 1943, moved to Camp Phillips near Salina, Kansas, on September 8, 1943, and finally to the southwest for the Desert Training Center No. 4 California Maueuvers on December 9, 1943.

On March 20, 1944, the 80th Infantry Division arrived at Fort Dix, New Jersey, staged at Camp Kilmer, New Jersey, beginning June 23, 1944, and sailed from the New York Port of Embarkation on July 1, 1944. The convoy carrying Owen and his Division landed in England on July 7, 1944, after which Owen wrote to his parents informing them of his safe arrival. The 80th then quickly went about the business of preparing men and equipment for transport across the English Channel to France. After landing across Utah Beach in Normandy on August 3, 1944, and moving inland, Owen sent another letter to his parents telling them that he was seeing action in France.

The 80th Infantry Division's initial assignment was that of mopping up the area around Le Mans, after which it moved to assist in the famous Battle for Falaise Gap where it took the towns of Le-Bourg-St. Leonard and Argentan by August 20, 1944. It then followed the 4th Armored Division across the Meuse River at Commercy,

---

[1] The 80th Infantry Division lost 3,038 men killed in action and another 12,484 wounded, with 442 of those dying from their wounds, during its four campaigns in Europe during World War II.

France, on September 1, 1944, and moved forward to the Moselle River at Toul, France. While forcing a crossing of the Moselle against strong German opposition, Pfc. Owen Carlson was killed in action on September 5, 1944, at the age of 25.

The War Department telegram notifying Mr. and Mrs. Carlson of their son's death arrived on September 20, 1944. Besides his parents, he left a brother, Hiram, at home, and two sisters, Mrs. Broadus (Alpha) Girtman and Clarice, at home.

On October 15, 1944, a memorial service was conducted at Chimney Rock Lutheran Church in honor of Owen Carlson. Following a prelude performed by William Olson, the colors of the United States were presented by uniformed members of the Sura-Wiersgalla American Legion Post 186. The Reverend H. A. Wichmann then gave an invocation, and a vocal solo was performed by Martin R. Olson. After the red star in front of Owen's name on the church's service flag was replaced by a gold star, the Legion honor guard solomnly led Owen's family and friends to the church cemetery where several songs were sung and the Reverend O. G. Birkeland, American Legion State Chaplain, dedicated the plot of ground in his memory. The American flag was then presented to Owen's mother by Legion Commander Henry Helgeson and taps, played by Alan Hanson, concluded the ceremony.

With his death, Owen left friends in England as well as in the Independence area. In the short time he was in England, he had apparently met a young woman, Margaret Kent of Macclerfield, England, and quickly befriended her and her parents, visiting them as often as possible. One year after Owen's death, his parents received the following remembrance from the Kent's, which was published in the September 6, 1945, edition of the *News-Wave*:

> In loving memory of dear Owen, killed in action, France, Sept. 5, 1944.
> No morning dawns, no night returns
> But what I think of you.
> And always in my heart you live anew.
> The happy hours we spent,
> The dreams we shared,
> The joys we might have known
> Had you been spared.
> And so you live
> Though death decree we part,
> Not just today
> But forever in our hearts.
> Sadly missed by Margaret. Ever remembered by Mr. and Mrs. Kent, Macclerfield, England.

One year later, in the September 12, 1946, edition of the *News-Wave*, another remembrance appeared, having been sent to Owen's family by the Kent's, who requested it be published:

> In our home, there stands a picture
> More precious than silver or gold.
> It's a picture of Dear Owen
> Whose memory will never grow old.
> Always remembered by Mr. and Mrs. Kent
> And sadly missed by Margaret.
> Macclerfield, England

With that remembrance, a letter from Mrs. Kent to Mrs. Carlson also contained information regarding life in England following the war, parts of which read:

They are making a film in Macclerfield called 'So Well Remembered,' starting with the 1914-18 war and ending with the last war. It will be released in about nine months.

Here's the way rationing is over here -- one egg and one shilling's worth of meat per person a week. Two ounces of butter, four ounces of margarine, one-half pound of sugar, four ounces of cheeses, one-fourth pound of bacon per person per month.

Clothing is 48 coupons per person a year, as follows: 1 pair stockings, 1-1/2 coupons; 2-piece undies, 8 coupons; a coat, 18 coupons; a frock, 7 coupons; pair of shoes, 7 coupons; a vest, 1 coupon; a girdle, 3 coupons, and a sweater, 5 coupons.

With World War II more than a year in the past and America entering a period of massive prosperity and growth, the people of England were still experiencing great hardships. But because of the sacrifice of Owen Carlson and so many young Americans like him, England was still free.

Sources: Independence News-Wave; Book (Stanton)

GORDON D. CILLEY
UNITED STATES ARMY

Gordon Cilley enlisted in the United States Army in November, 1940, and following basic training was attached to the 6th Division which was stationed at Fort Snelling, Minnesota. In August 1941, the Division participated in the Arkansas Maneuvers, and then moved on to the Louisiana Maneuvers the following month. On October 10, 1941, the Division arrived at Fort Leonard

Wood, Missouri, where it was redesignated as the 6th Motorized Division on April 9, 1942. It participated in the I Corps Tennessee Maneuvers in September 1942 before arriving back at Fort Leonard Wood in November of that year.

Training never seemed to end for the 6th Motorized. On November 29, 1942, it arrived at Camp Young, California, for the Desert Training Center No. 1 IV Armored Corps Maneuvers, an exercise that lasted until February 22, 1943. Then it moved to Camp San Luis Obispo, California, where it was once again redesignated, this time as the 6th Infantry Division,[1] on May 21, 1943.

Gordon was a machine gunner with the Service Battery, 80th Field Artillery Battalion, 6th Infantry Division, when most of the Division sailed from the San Francisco Port of Embarkation for Hawaii on July 21, 1943. Gordon's artillery battalion, however, did not leave the States until September 20, 1943, upon which time it rejoined the rest of the Division on the Hawaiian Islands.

---

[1] The 6th Infantry Division lost 410 men killed and 1,957 wounded, 104 of which died from their wounds, during its campaigns in the Pacific.

The entire Division began leaving for Milne Bay, New Guinea, on January 26, 1944. In early June 1944, the 6th Infantry Division was moved piecemeal to the Hollandia-Aitape area of New Guinea, where on June 20, 1944, its 20th Infantry Regiment began an attack. By July 12, 1944, despite fanatical Japanese counterattacks throughout, the Division had secured the area around Maffin Bay.

In a surprise move against the Japanese, and with no pre-landing bombardment, the Division's 1st Infantry assaulted Sansapor, East Indies, on July 30, 1944, while it's 63rd Infantry landed on the undefended Middleburg and Amsterdam Islands. Sansapor was taken fairly easily, and the Division garrisoned it until December 1944.

On January 9, 1945, the 6th Infantry landed at Lingayen Gulf on Luzon, Philippine Islands, where it immediately began chasing the Japanese through the Cabaruan Hills. Then, after a short holding action, the Division again attacked beginning January 17, 1945, with the 20th Infantry continuing to push through the Cabaruan Hills while the 63rd Infantry attacked and took Blue Ridge near Amlang. The 1st Infantry took San Jose on February 4, 1945, opening the way to the Cagayan Valley, and by mid-February 1945, the Division had divided Japanese forces into two groups and began eliminating the enemy on southern Luzon.

On February 24, 1945, north of Manila, as the 20th and 63rd Infantry Regiments began a push on Japanese defenses known as the "Shimbu Line," the enemy's resistance began to suddenly stiffen, and the 1st Infantry was called in to reinforce in the center of the Division's line. The 63rd Infantry was thrown off the newly-won Mt. Pacawagan on February 27, 1945, and the 1st Infantry had to withdraw following unsuccessful efforts to take Mt. Mataba the same day. The Division didn't renew its attack in that area until March 8, 1945, at which time it met surprisingly little resistance.

On February 28, 1945, as the 80th Artillery Battalion was protecting the withdrawal of the infantry, the Japanese began shelling its positions. An enemy 105-mm shell exploded near Pfc. Cilley, shrapnel from which wounded him very severely in both legs. He was evacuated to an aid station and then was sent to a surgical hospital serving the combat area.

On March 21, 1945, Gordon's parents, Mr. and Mrs. William H. Cilley, received a War Department telegram informing them of his having been wounded. But they were already aware of this as the day before they had received a letter from the 80th Field Artillery's commanding officer, Captain Donald S. Brown. The letter from Captain Brown appeared in the *News-Wave* on March 29, 1945, along with a brief review of Gordon's Army history. It reflects on the impression Gordon had made on the men of his unit:

> Philippine Islands
> 7 March, 1945
> Dear Mr. Cilley:
> Your son, Pfc. Gordon Cilley, is at the present time in a surgical hospital awaiting evacuation to the better conditions available in the rear areas. He was severely wounded in the left leg by a fragment from a 105 mm shell that fell in the service battery area the morning of February 28, 1945.
> I have had only one opportunity to see Gordon since he was taken to the hospital but a number of men in the battery base have had a chance to stop and see him and they all join me in assurances that your son is well out of danger, making good progress, and is in good spirits.
> The loss of your son is a serious one to this organization. Besides being a fine soldier, he is exceptionally well liked by the men in the battery and I know you would feel proud of their confidence in his judgement (sic) and skill as a machine gunner on the perimeter guard at night.
> He asked me to write to you and assure you that he is receiving the best of care and will write when he reaches a large hospital with a permanent address.
> Sincerely yours,
> Donald S. Brown
> Capt., 80th F. A.
> Commanding

Gordon's left leg was badly damaged in the attack and required amputation. He was then transferred to the 44th General Hospital on Leyte, Philippine Islands, where he was awarded the Purple Heart. According to a short article in the May 17, 1945 *News-Wave*, he sent the medal to his parents with a letter dated March 30, 1945 in which he told them he was doing well and was scheduled to return to a hospital in the States. On April 11, 1945, Gordon left the Philippines aboard a hospital ship that arrived in the States on May 13, 1945. By May 29, 1945, he was hospitalized at the Percy Jones Hospital Center, Battle Creek, Michigan, where he remained until receiving a furlough in November, 1945 and traveling to Independence to visit his parents.

Gordon returned to Battle Creek following his furlough for further hospitalization and received an honorable medical discharge there on December 12, 1945. He had participated in the Central Pacific, New Guinea, and Luzon campaigns and had been awarded, together with his Purple Heart, the Asiatic-Pacific Theater Medal with three bronze battle stars, the Philippine Liberation Medal with one bronze star, and the American Theater, American Defense, Good Conduct, and Victory Medals.

But Gordon's story doesn't end here. World War II changed the lives of so many young men in so many different ways, and continued doing so even after the final battles were won. The loss of his leg prevented him from continuing with his pre-war occupation as a construction worker, and he therefore received training as a linotype operator instead. He then was employed for two-and-a-half years with the *Lewiston Journal*, Lewiston, Minnesota, all the while requiring regular medical checkups at a Veteran's Administration rehabilitation center in Minneapolis. One day in April, 1952, while driving to Minneapolis for an appointment at the center, Gordon lost control of his vehicle eight miles west of Hastings, Minnesota, crashed, and died later that night. Funeral services were held at the Independence Lutheran Church. He was 33 years old.

Sources: Mrs. Audrey Lee, sister; Independence News-Wave; newspaper article, unknown origin; Book (Stanton)

WILLIS R. CRIPPS
UNITED STATES ARMY

Died on Duty

Willis Cripps was born on September 10, 1917 in the Town of Burnside. He spent his early years in Independence and then worked for Adolph Passon and Pietrek Brothers until entering the service on January 8, 1942. He received his basic training at Tucson, Arizona, and Camp Pendleton, Virginia. In September 1942, Willis was sent to England as part of the American force preparing for the D-Day invasion of June 6, 1944.

Serving with the Quartermaster Corps, Private First Class Willis was either loading or unloading supplies from a train on December 23, 1943, when an accident occurred and Willis was killed. He was 26 years old at the time and engaged to an English girl, Joan Lee, of Shrewsbury.

On January 20, 1944, the *News-Wave* published a letter from Norval Sather to his parents, Mr. and Mrs. Helmer Sather, in which he states, "Oh, yes, I met that Cripps boy that went in the Army with Ervin over here. He's been here 14 months now. Sure felt good to see someone from home." Norval apparently didn't know that Willis had died since their meeting.

Interred temporarily in Brookwood Military Cemetery in the British Isles, Willis' remains were returned following the war at the request of his parents, Mr. and Mrs. Ralph Cripps. Arriving in Independence on July 27, 1948, his casket was accompanied by a uniformed Army escort from the Chicago Distribution Center of the American Graves Registration Division. Services were held on July 29, 1948 at Wiemer Funeral Chapel and the American Legion Post 186 conducted the military service at Greenwood Cemetery, Independence.

Pallbearers were Alfred Pampuch, Jesse Edmundson, Vitus and Rudy Smieja, Dallas Wiltsey, and Oliver Rustad. Color Bearers were Roman Slaby and Hillary "Jack" Halama while the Color Guard consisted of Herman Bautch and LaVerne Pientok. The Legion Firing Squad was composed of Gerald "Bud" Pieterick, Lester Gunem, Ben Kulig, Vincent Karasch, Earl Hutchins, Mike Marsolek, Ed. J. Lyga, and Ray Smieja.

Willis was survived by his parents; three sisters, Ruth, Maureen, and Peggy; and two brothers, Charles and Sammy.

No photo.
Source: Independence News-Wave

VERNA "VERONICA" DEJNO
UNITED STATES ARMY NURSES CORPS

Verna "Veronica" Dejno was a registered nurse at Mother Cabrini Hospital in Chicago, Illinois, early in the war. Initially, she had received general nurse's training, but in October, 1943, she applied for the Nurses Cadet training program. Graduating from the program in June 1944, she became a reserve nurse and awaited her appointment to a duty assignment.

Besides Veronica, Mr. and Mrs. John Dejno had three other daughters serve as nurses during World War II -- Eleanor, Mary, and Pat as a Nurse Cadet -- as well as two sons, Alphonse, with Eighth Air Force in Europe, and John, who entered the Army late in the war and served with the Army of Occupation in Japan.

The following edited narrative is taken from a letter received from Veronica regarding her service years:

I joined the Army in 1944 and served during World War II from late 1944 through the end of the war, and into 1946. I spent my time in Camp McCoy, Wisconsin, and Brooks General Hospital in Texas. The returning casualties from the European Theater were arriving in droves and we were busy. I was slated to go to Japan to join the Army of Occupation but I chose instead to leave the Army. As all officers who requested to leave the service, I was put under reserve status and remained as such until 1948. Then we were given the choice of staying in the reserves or going to active reserve or inactive reserve. I chose to be placed in the inactive bracket, and as things would have it, during the Korean fracas, instead of calling the actives, the inactive reserves were called for some reason, so I was again given orders to report. Though I was granted two extensions thanks to my chief nurse at Hines Veteran's Hospital, where I was working, and the fact that I was attending night school at De Paul University in Chicago, I eventually had to report in November 1951. In December 1951, I was shipped to Korea where I remained until April, 1953.

A Quote From History...

"Well, one of those bears came after us and I had to shoot him!"
  Dominic Sura
  United States Army
  From an interview, August 3, 1998, describing an incident
    on Kodiak Island, Alaska.

32

Verna "Veronica" Dejno with her parents, Mr. and Mrs. John Dejno, outside their home.

JESSE EDMUNDSON
UNITED STATES ARMY

Jesse Edmundson left Independence on March 20, 1942 for Eau Claire, Wisconsin, where he was inducted into the United States Army. He completed basic training at Camp Chaffee, Arkansas, and participated in the Louisiana Maneuvers in August 1942. He then transferred to Needles, California, where he received desert training under General George S. Patton. He was stationed at Camp Cooke, located about 65 miles from Santa Barbara, attended radio school there, and became a tank commander with Headquarter's Company, 6th Armored Division.[1] Jesse's wife, Marge, was then living in Santa Barbara when one day Jesse came home and announced he had been granted a furlough and wished to leave Santa Barbara and visit Independence. They traveled to Independence even though Marge would have preferred staying in Santa Barbara. What Jesse hadn't told her was that he and his 6th Armored Division had orders for overseas shipment. From Independence, Jesse would be going to New York, and then to Europe.

By February 3, 1944, the 6th Armored Division was staging at Camp Shanks, New York, and on February 11, 1944 it sailed from the New York Port of Embarkation. It arrived in England on February 23, 1944 where it resumed its training in anticipation of landing in France. On July 19, 1944, Jesse and 6th Armored landed across Utah Beach in Normandy, France, and began moving inland. By July 27, 1944, the Division found itself in action against the German army near Le Bingard. Two days later it crossed the Sienne River near Pont de la Roche, quickly overran Granville, and then moved through Avranches where it relieved the 4th Infantry Division. On August 1, 1944, the Division moved into Brittany and by August 7, 1944 was approaching Brest. It destroyed a large German force at Plouvien over the next two days before continuing its drive between Orleans and Auxerre. On November 9, 1944, the Division crossed the Seille River. After experiencing very intense fighting in the Remering area in late November, it was relieved on December 2, 1944 and maintained defensive positions near Saarbruecken for the next three weeks.

---

[1] The 6th Armored Division suffered 833 killed in action during its tour of duty in Europe. Another 3,666 men were wounded, of which 156 later died of their wounds.

Following the German's Ardennes Counteroffensive of December 16, 1944, the 6th Armored Division was sent south of the Sauer River between Ettelbruck and Mostroff where it assumed responsibility for that area on December 27, 1944. It was involved in heavy fighting east of Bastogne beginning December 31, 1944. and was forced to withdraw, but it counterattacked nine days later and recovered the ground it had lost. It then pushed on for the next month, at times experiencing fierce opposition during house-to-house fighting as it passed through small cities and towns.

On February 20, 1945, 6th Armored attacked Hitler's vaunted *West Wall*, reached its objective of Muxerath on February 24, 1945, and then moved to a new zone west of the Pruem River where it relieved the 90th Infantry Division. It crossed the Rhine River into Germany at Oppenheim on March 25, 1945, then crossed the Main River and attacked towards Frankfurt. By April 4, 1945, it had crossed the Fulda River and encircled Mulhausen, and within a few days was again pressing its attack forward. It crossed the Saale River southwest of Naumberg on April 11, 1945, and reached the Zwick Mulde River at Rochlitz three days later. There it turned over its bridgehead to the 76th Infantry Division and was maintaining defensive positions in the area when Germany surrendered on May 7, 1945.

Though the Division arrived back in New York on September 18, 1945, where it was inactivated on that same date at Camp Shanks, New York, Jesse didn't leave Europe until September 24, 1945, arriving back in the United States aboard the *U. S. S. Argentina* on October 1, 1945. He was discharged from the United States Army on October 8, 1945.

As a Medium Tank Commander with the 6th Armored Division in Europe, Jesse held the rank of Sergeant. He had participated in the Normandy, Northern France, Rhineland, Ardennes-Alsace, and Central Europe campaigns. He had been awarded the Purple Heart for injuries received in combat,[2] as well as the Bronze Star, European-African-Middle Eastern Theater Ribbon with one Silver Battle Star, Good Conduct Medal, and three Overseas Service Bars. His Bronze Star citation reads:

> For heroic service in connection with military operations in France, Belgium, Luxembourg and Germany during the period 1 Aug 1944 to 1 April 1945. As a gunner he has consistently demonstrated outstanding courage and valor in the face of heavy enemy fire. Entered the military service from Wisconsin.

In a conversation with Jesse's widow, Marge, in June 1998, it was quite apparent she was very proud of Jesse's accomplishments during the war, though she indicated he never spoke about it.

"Jesse idolized General Grow.[3] He was the General's barber and cut his hair often. In high school, Jess had worked in Albert Fellenz' barber shop in what is now Marc Mish's shop. The General was bald and one day when Jess was cutting his hair, he couldn't help but ask him, 'Sir, would you like a little bit off the top today?' He said the General began laughing quite heartily at that question. This was the only thing Jesse ever told me about his time in the Army. He simply would not tell me anything.

"When the war was over, I didn't know Jesse was returning home. When he got to La Crosse, he started hitchhiking and was picked up by George Knudtson of Elk Creek. When they got to Elk Creek, Jesse said he would hitchhike the last five miles to Independence but George insisted on taking him all the way home. He was in the house when I got home that day.

"Jesse had shrapnel in his neck and behind his ear. Dr. Meyer found it one time when Jesse went in for a checkup. All of his papers were lost on the way to Fort Sheridan so he had no record of this injury. Lon Tubbs, the Veteran's Service agent in Whitehall, recommended Jesse apply for a disability because of the shrapnel, but because his papers were lost, he had no proof he

---

[2] The date, location, and circumstances regarding Jesse's wounds are unknown.

[3] Major General Robert W. Grow became commander of the 6th Armored Division, in May, 1943. He remained with the Division until July, 1945.

had been wounded. Jess had to get letters from guys he served with who knew about the incident.

"One day during the war, a letter arrived from Jesse, and I was surprised to find his wedding ring enclosed. In the letter, though, he explained that he had slipped off his tank because of the heavy dew that was on it and the ring got caught on a hook. He had to have his finger cut open in order to get it released."

Jesse Edmundson. The photo below also depicts a tank used in training while in the United States.

35

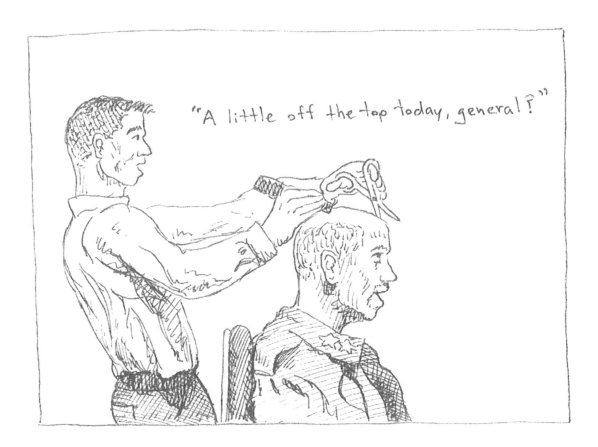

Sources: Mrs. Marge Edmundson, wife; Book (Stanton)

HENRY "HANK" GAMROTH
UNITED STATES ARMY

Henry "Hank" Gamroth enlisted in the United States Army on February 7, 1939 at Fort Snelling, Minnesota. Following basic training, Hank received specialized training, qualifying as an Expert Bayonet in October 1939. Assigned to Company K, 3rd Battalion, 89th Infantry Regiment, he was then sent to Bermuda where he spent 16 months guarding Antilles Command positions. On June 2, 1942, Hank was promoted to Sergeant. He returned to the States in September 1943 and subsequently joined the 503rd Paratroop Infantry Regiment at Fort Benning, Georgia. While making his third training jump from a 300-foot tower, Hank injured his back and sprained an ankle. Following recovery from these injuries, he was transferred to the 77th Infantry Division,[1] where he joined Company B of the 307th Infantry Regiment. On March 24, 1944, he left San Francisco with the Division for Oahu, Hawaii, arriving on March 30 for three months of amphibious and jungle training.

Leaving Hawaii in July 1944, the 77th Infantry Division sailed to Eniwetok Island in the

---

[1] The 77th Infantry Division lost 1,449 killed during its Pacific Theater campaigns. Additionally, 5,935 were wounded, of which 401 died of their wounds.

36

Marshall Islands group, and from there to Guam. United States Marines had hit the beaches of Guam on June 21, 1944 and the 77th Infantry was being sent in to reinforce them. On July 27, 1944, Hank's 307th Infantry Regiment began moving toward Mount Tenjo, two miles inland from Apra Harbor. The Division then formed the right wing of the advance to clear the northern third of the island. Following the securing of the island, the 77th was engaged in mop-up operations until November 3, 1944, when it left Guam.

The 77th Infantry Division arrived at Leyte Island in the Philippines on November 23, 1944 and landed unopposed at Deposito on the west side of the Island on December 7. The 307th Infantry, with the 306th, took Ormoc on December 10, 1944, after which the 77th Infantry's commander, Major General Andrew Bruce, notified Sixth U. S. Army's commander, Lieutenant

General Walter Krueger, of its capture with the simple message, "Have rolled two sevens in Ormoc."

The 307th then struck northward to take Valencia and its airfield on December 16-17, 1944. Following heavy combat, Libongao was taken on December 20, 1944. The Division remained in combat until February 9, 1945, at one point liberating 15,000 Filipino prisoners.

The 77th Infantry Division was next sent to the Ryukyus Islands. On March 26, 1945, Hank's 307th Infantry landed on Yakabit Island, part of the Kerama Retto group of islands southwest of Okinawa. It was on the various islands of the Kerama group where the 77th discovered more than 500 Japanese suicide boats.

Next, within days following the April 1, 1945 invasion of Okinawa itself, the 307th followed the rest of the 77th Infantry onto Ie Shima, a large island off Okinawa's northwest coast. Ie Shima was taken by April 21, 1945, but not until famed war correspondent, and the 77th's buddy, Ernie Pyle, was killed.

The 307th Infantry landed next on the secured Hagushi Beaches of Okinawa on April 27, 1945. On April 30, 1945, the 77th relieved the 96th Infantry Division as it was about to attack the Maeda Escarpment, a rocky ridge that topped out 500 feet above sea level. It was at the Battle of the Maeda Escarpment early in May 1945, that Staff Sergeant Hank Gamroth found himself embroiled in one of the most brutal battles of the Pacific War, was wounded, and then pulled to safety by one of the most famous citizen soldiers of the war, Congressional Medal of Honor recipient Desmond Doss. As Hank recalled in a newspaper interview following the war (unknown source, unknown date), "From Ie Shima, which is only about two miles from Okinawa, we were ordered to relieve the 96th Division on Okinawa. Until then, we soldiers thought that the battles we had fought were like hell. Okinawa, to our surprise, was like many 'hells' put together. My Company went on line with full strength at 11 A. M., but very few of us remained alive by nightfall."

Upon entering the lines at the base of the Maeda Escarpment, the men of the 307th Infantry immediately entered battle. On May 2, Hank heard the tapping sound of a Japanese grenade near him. He was just able to issue a warning to his two foxhole mates when the grenade exploded, killing the other two and somehow leaving Hank without a scratch.

The next day, using cargo nets and ladders, the 307th attempted to scale the wall of the escarpment, during which it came under murderous Japanese mortar fire and grenades. As Hank was climbing a net, a mortar shell exploded nearby, knocking him off the net to the ground 25 feet below. He had suffered a completely fractured fibula and tibia of the right leg. But potentially even more serious was his landing in front of a cave from which he could hear Japanese voices. He readied a grenade, just in case, but it wasn't long before another American was kneeling over him. It was his Company B medic, Desmond Doss, who rendered first aid and carried him to safety.

Hank was subsequently transferred to a Fleet hospital ship and then to a hospital in the Marianas Islands. From there, due to the severity of his wound, he was transferred to a hospital in the States on May 18, 1945.

Company B, 307th Infantry - Hank's Company - scaled the Maeda Escarpment at this point using the cargo nets shown. In a letter to his sister, Mary, Hank informed her that he was one of only two men from his squad of 12 that survived the attack. The soldier at the top of the cliff is Desmond Doss, the Congressional Medal of Honor recipient who saved Hank's life on May 3, 1945.

On Memorial Day, 1987, Hank was reading an article carried by the Associated Press about Desmond Doss, who had been awarded the Congressional Medal of Honor for actions taken while on Okinawa and serving with the 77th Infantry Division. Doss, a Seventh-Day Adventist, was a conscientious objector to war and refused to touch a weapon due to his religious convictions. Instead, he entered the service as a medic. On Okinawa, he was with the 77th Infantry Division's 307th Infantry, Company B -- Hank Gamroth's Company -- where he is

38

credited with pulling at least 75 wounded soldiers to safety from April 30 to May 21, 1945, all the while under enemy fire. It was while reading the newspaper description of Doss's actions of early May 1945, that Hank realized the article was describing his own rescue by Doss. This Gamroth-Doss connection was publicized in several newspapers, leading Hank to contact Doss by telephone at his home in Rising Fawn, Georgia. Because Doss was completely deaf, they communicated through Doss' wife.

At the time this story was made public in 1987, Hank was quoted as saying, "I can't figure that guy out. The lead was flying. He was bending over and treating the wounded."

Hank wrote several letters to his mother, Mrs. Anna Gamroth, from overseas that were published in the Independence *News-Wave*. The following came from Guam in 1944, where Hank tasted combat for the first time:

Dear Mother,

I am writing this letter and you don't know how lucky I am to be alive. I have been in the battle of Guam in the Marianas Islands and I sure thank God for it as I prayed and somebody else must have prayed for me also.

You wouldn't believe how horrible war is and what a soldier has to go through. Right now I am in a foxhole writing this letter with flies and mosquitoes by the millions covered by dead Japs and other things. I had a swell trip coming over here. We stayed at the Marshall Islands which interested me. The natives over here are sure glad that we Yanks came back to take the island back, as you know the Japs took Guam away from us once.

This will be all for now as I don't have much time to write. Tell everybody hello from me.

Your loving son,
Hank

From Leyte in the Philippine Islands, Hank wrote the following letter home:

Dear Mother,

I don't have time to write much as I am in battle on Leyte Island in the Philippines. The going is tough with lots of lead flying. I hope God stays with me as he has helped me so far. There is artillery fire over my head right now, so I'm in a hurry.

I'm writing this in a trench so I hope nothing goes wrong with this letter. We got the Japs on the run and we won't stop until every one of those yellow bastards is killed. They sure are mean to our soldiers when they capture them.

I haven't received any packages yet and don't expect them until next Christmas or probably they're sunk some place.

Don't worry about me mother, only pray hard.

Your loving son,
Henry

On January 2, 1945, Hank wrote a letter addressed to his mother, his sister, Clara, and a nephew, Roland Gamroth, from whom he had received a letter. The introduction to the letter in the February 8, 1945 *News-Wave* noted that Hank weighed 190 pounds when he had left the states:

Dearest Roland and Mother:

I got your letter Roland and I sure was glad to hear from you. I am on Leyte Island mopping up the Japs, the yellow murdering **!**!*!*. I am resting a little bit now, and I am not up to the front at present and have time to write.

You should have seen me when we were fighting. I didn't shave or wash for fourteen days. I looked like a jungle beast. I have a sword as a souvenir that I have taken from a dead Japanese officer that we bumped off. I will bring that back for you.

39

I know God has been with me, as I sure had some close shaves. The going is tough up here but these Japs are getting what they asked for. We are killing them just like rabbits.

I did not get any of the packages yet, but I do not worry about that, only that I am glad to be alive. Clara, I received that scapular you sent me and I have it on my rosary around my neck. This war has changed me in the way of religion and many of the other soldiers too. I know God has been with me all the time, and I hope He will continue to be with me.

Clara, you will have to cook me some good dumplings when I get back. I will buy a hog and will I ever eat. I weight 140 pounds now. This war is a terrible thing, and I will never forget what I have seen. These Philippine Islands aren't much, and I do not think are worth fighting for. I have a little shack built and it is made of cocoanut leaves. You should see it. A Philippine built it for me for a package of cigarettes. The Philippines took a beating from the Japs when they were here.

I am in a good outfit with a bunch of tough guys. We sure gave the Japs a shellacking. Tokyo Rose, propaganda broadcaster, said that Japan was willing to sacrifice a million troops to knock off my outfit. It was just the other way around. The war is hell and believe me it is cold murder. You will not believe what I have to tell you when I get back to the God Blessed U. S. A. Write again as I sure am lonesome.

Goodbye,
Henry

Following his being wounded on Okinawa, Hank wrote this V-Mail from a hospital in the Marianas, again to his mother:

Dear Mother and Rest:

I have a little bad news for you. I was wounded on Okinawa but am getting along alright so don't worry about me. I am in a hospital in the Mariana Islands and am getting the best of care. I think I will be in the hospital a long time, but I will be okay. I'm hoping to come to the USA when I get a little better, so maybe I will see you sometime in the near future. The war over here is like a bunch of hells put together. I hope everybody is fine. I think I am very lucky the way I am and that I didn't get killed. I can't explain to you where I am wounded but you will find out sometime. Has the War Department notified you? Goodbye and don't worry.

> Your loving son,
> Henry

The previous V-Mail was followed shortly by another that read:

Dear Mother:

Just a line to let you know I am getting along okay. I am now back in the Hawaiian Islands in a hospital and I am getting the best of care. I sure got a long plane ride and I was sure glad to get back on the ground. I am in a nice hospital and everything sees to look good around here. I am writing this laying down so you will have to excuse me if I don't write much. I will be alright but it will take some time. I was hit with a Jap shell which landed close to me. Say, mother, I think you will get some of my stuff from Okinawa such as souvenirs and my wrist watch, as I told them to send them to you. Again I say I'm thankful to be alive, as it certainly was awful. Tell everybody hello from me. I don't need anything as I get plenty to eat and everybody is good to me. Goodbye mother.

> Your loving son,
> Henry.

Upon his arrival back in the States, Hank wrote a letter to his sister, Mrs. Peter Maule, from Fitzsimmons General Hospital in Denver, Colorado, where he was convalescing. He describes his injury and trip back to the States, and alludes to combat in the Pacific. The letter was dated July 9, 1945 and was published in the July 19, 1945 *News-Wave*:

Dear Mary,

I owe you several letters so will answer now. I am up on crutches now and am sitting up writing this to you. I have a walking cast so I don't think it will be long before I get a convalescent furlough.

You wanted to know how badly I was hurt. My leg is broken above the ankle about eight inches and then I have a bone cracked just below the knee cap. I have an aluminum plate put in my leg as the bones weren't growing together.

I had a nice trip coming over. I came all the way from Guam to here by plane. I stayed in Pearl Harbor a month and also in California one week. Stopped in Ogden, Utah, for a day and I had the Red Cross try to find Millard and Esther but I guess they were gone. I never thought I would see this God-given country again for, Mary, I tell you it was just awful. Especially, Ie Shima and Okinawa. I figured on going to Tokyo but I guess my luck didn't hold out. Now, I think I've done my share in getting the yellow men. The boys from Europe will find out that they are fighting a tougher war and a meaner soldier than a German when they come to the Pacific.

I hope Bennie comes back okay but he is not in the infantry. And he is not in the front lines, and, too, the only thing he has to fear is planes.

On Okinawa I started off with 12 men in my squad and when I got hit it was just me and another guy left and the rest of them were done for and they were such good boys, too. I will tell you more, Mary, when I see you. I could keep on writing all day about this horrible war and would never finish.

Sure will be glad to see you all again for we fellows sometime cried wondering if we would ever see our folks and the other ones back home.

The weather is fine and everything loods good. This is a big hospital and we get good care.

Good-bye for now.

> Your brother,
> Henry

While at Fitzsimmons, Hank received his Purple Heart during ceremonies conducted September 14, 1945 by Brigadier General Omar H. Quade.

Staff Sergeant Henry D. Gamroth received his Honorable Discharge and Separation from the Army on November 17, 1945, at Fitzsimmons General Hospital, Denver, Colorado. For his years in the service, Hank was awarded the Purple Heart for injuries received May 3, 1945, the Bronze Star, Good Conduct Medal, Philippine Liberation Ribbon with one battle star and one arrowhead, American Defense Service Medal, Victory Ribbon, Asiatic-Pacific Theater Ribbon, and the American Theater Medal.

Sources: Mrs. Henry Gamroth; Independence News-Wave; Books (Stanton) (Appleman, et al)

BEN A. GASATIS
UNITED STATES NAVY

Ben Gasatis enlisted in the United States Navy on December 18, 1934 following his graduation from Independence High School. He underwent basic training at Norfolk, Virginia. His first duty assignment was aboard the *U. S. S. Idaho* (BB-42), a 624-foot long battleship commissioned in 1919. He probably joined the crew of the *Idaho* in April 1935, at her home port of San Pedro, California, to where she had returned from a shakedown cruise following a year's reconstruction at Norfolk Navy Yard.

It appears Ben transferred to the *U. S. S. Chicago* (CA-29), sometime after October 1, 1940, while both *Idaho* and *Chicago* were based at Pearl Harbor. The *Chicago* was a cruiser in the Northampton Class, 600 feet long and carrying a crew of 621 sailors. She was armed with nine eight-inch and four five-inch guns plus six 21-inch torpedo tubes.

When the Japanese attacked Pearl Harbor on December 7, 1941, *Chicago* was at sea with Task Force 12 conducting training exercises and developing tactics and cruising formations in response to the growing Japanese threat in the Pacific. When word of the attack reached the Task Force, the ships began searching an area south of the Hawaiian Islands for the Japanese fleet. But without finding it, Task Force 12 returned to Pearl on December 12, 1941. Two days later, *Chicago* left Pearl with Task Force 11 for two weeks of additional patrol duty.

On February 2, 1942 *Chicago* left Pearl Harbor once again, this time to join a newly formed task force that during the months of March and April, 1942, supported attacks on Japanese-held Lae and Salamaua, New Guinea. It also provided cover for American troops landing on New Caledonia.

On May 1, 1942 she joined the aircraft carrier *U. S. S. Yorktown* (CV-5) as she attacked Tulagi in the Solomon Islands. *Chicago* then sailed with a support group to intercept a Japanese force heading for Port Moresby, New Guinea, on May 7, 1942, where she suffered several casualties from Japanese strafing the following day. The enemy force was turned back by the American warships.

Chicago supported America's first offensive in the Pacific, at Guadalcanal, beginning August 7, 1942. On August 9, she participated in the "Battle of Savo Island" where she was struck by a Japanese torpedo but continued fighting until contact with the enemy was lost. She then headed to Noumea, New Caledonia, and from there to Sydney, Australia, for repairs before arriving in San Francisco, California, on October 13, 1942.

Departing San Francisco in early January 1943, *Chicago* escorted a convoy from Noumea to Guadalcanal beginning January 27, 1943. As the ships approached Guadalcanal the night of January 29, Japanese aircraft attacked in what has become known as the "Battle of Rennell Island." When *Chicago* became silhouetted by two burning enemy planes, two Japanese torpedoes were put into her side, causing severe flooding, loss of power, and a serious list. The list and damage were controlled, however, and the cruiser *U. S. S. Louisville* (CA-28) began taking *Chicago* in tow. The next morning, following relief towing by a tug, Japanese aircraft attacked again, hitting *Chicago* with four more torpedoes. This time she quickly sank, leaving many of her crew, including Ben Gasatis, swimming for their lives.

In the March 4, 1943 edition of the *News-Wave*, it was reported that Ben's parents, Mr. and Mrs. August Gasatis, had received a cable from Ben upon his arrival in San Diego, California, informing them of his having been aboard *Chicago* when it was sunk, but also assuring them that he was safe and uninjured. The March 18, 1943 *News-Wave* contained a letter written by Ben on March 2, 1943 from his Portland, Oregon, home where he was on leave with his wife and son. In it he described his ordeal while aboard the *Chicago*:

> Hello Mom. I'm home with the Mrs. and little Benny. I arrived last night. Well, Mom, I'm glad to be here and luck(y), also. I guess you got my telegram that I arrived in San Diego. I'm getting a good stay home this time -- 31 days in all. I'm going to San Francisco March 30 where I'll go to school in landing surface Diesel barges. That's all I am permitted to say in a letter. It's a new thing. I'm glad I didn't get another ship at the east coast like most of the other guys did. This leave is a real one, and we deserve it after going through all that hell. I guess you read in the papers all about the sinking of the ship. It would take a lot of writing to tell all about it, so I'll just mention the highlights.
>
> First, I came out without a scratch. I was shaken up a little. I lost my best friend. He's missing in one of the six torpedo hits that we took. I went over the side into the water with what I had on, including my life belt, and I lost everything I had on the ship. I got a nice bag of clothes, $130, from the Government. The Red Cross Veterans of Foreign Wars gave us a lot of stuff, so I've plenty again.
>
> I was in the water an hour and a half before I was picked up. If it wasn't so cold this time of year,[1] I would bring the wife and little Benny. Well, Mom, I hope everything is o. k. with you and Dad. I'm fine. So long for this time.

After Ben attended the school in San Francisco mentioned in his letter, he was assigned duty aboard the *U. S. S. Ashland*, (LSD-1), probably near the time she was commissioned in early June 1943. An LSD, or Landing Ship, Dock, transported smaller landing craft containing tanks, cargo, or troops to be put ashore during amphibious landings. The *Ashland* was 457 feet long, displaced 9,375 tons loaded, and had a top speed of 15.4 knots. 326 men served aboard

U. S. S. Chicago, cruiser of the Northhampton Class, torpedoed and sunk by the Japanese the night of January 29, 1943.

---

[1] Ben undoubtedly was describing late winter in Wisconsin at this point.

her.

Following two months of training, amphibious craft and personnel were loaded aboard *Ashland* at San Diego, California, and she sailed on August 11, 1943, arriving at Pearl Harbor on August 19. There she loaded more cargo before proceeding to Baker Island on August 25. Returning to Pearl on September 27, 1943, she sailed again on October 19, 1943 loaded with Army troops to join Task Force 53 and participate in amphibious exercises in the Gilbert Islands area.

Ashland returned to Pearl Harbor on December 7, 1943, where she underwent repairs before participating in additional amphibious training exercises off Maui, Hawaiian Islands. She took part in the Kwajalein invasion from February 1-5, 1944, and then after embarking troops and equipment at Roi and Namur, proceeded to Eniwetok to participate in the assault there. Beginning on February 17, 1944, *Ashland* served as a repair vessel in Eniwetok harbor before leaving for Pearl on February 29.

On April 1, 1944, *Ashland* arrived in San Francisco. It is probable, though not certain, that Ben was detached from her at this time as the May 4, 1944, edition of the *News-Wave* reported that he and his family had been in Independence visiting his parents for the first time in five years. It is also not certain when Ben was commissioned an Ensign in the United States Navy, but this same article identified him as such and indicated that Ben's next assignment would be that of Engineering Officer aboard a new cruiser at Newport News, Virginia.

The light cruiser *U. S. S. Duluth*, (CL-87), was a 610-foot long ship of the Cleveland Class. Commissioned September 18, 1944 at Newport News, the same day Ben joined her crew, she had a compliment of 992 men and was armed with twelve six-inch and twelve five-inch guns. *Duluth* served as a training cruiser at Newport, Rhode Island, from December 14, 1944 to March 2, 1945. A letter dated December 15, 1944 and sent to Glenn Kirkpatrick, editor of the *News-Wave*, identified Ben as being stationed aboard the *Duluth*, expressed his appreciation for the "Special Servicemen's Edition" of November 30, 1944, and indicated he was looking forward to the end of the war:

> U. S. S. Duluth (CL87)
> December 15, 1944
> Dear Mr. Kirkpatrick:
> I received your very interesting News-Wave and enjoyed it very much. Although I've forgotten a good many of the people whose names appear in the paper, I nevertheless racked my brain trying to recollect their faces. I must say, I spent some time, day dreaming or bringing back old memories, which really does a person good; sort of rests the mind. Being that I'm an engineering officer in charge of a division aboard my new home, the cruiser Duluth, I'm kept pretty busy.
> I was surprised to know that there were so many in the service from Independence. I didn't think there were that many. Yes, indeed, it will be one happy day when everybody returns home and can live the rest of their life in peace with their loved ones.
> So I'll close this short note, wishing you kind people a Merry Christmas and a Happy New Year, and that come next holiday season, the boys and girls will be back with their folks; that the News-Wave will still be in commission for a long, long time afterward to serve these same boys and girls with the news of happenings in and around Independence as it did when they left their homes.
> Thanks again!
> Ben A. Gasatis
> Ensign U. S. N.

On April 7, 1945, *Duluth* left the east coast of the United States and sailed for the Pacific, arriving at Pearl Harbor on April 29. She left Pearl on May 8, 1945, and joined the 5th Fleet on May 27. When the fleet was struck by a powerful typhoon on June 5, 1945, *Duluth* suffered bow damage severe enough to warrant her heading to Guam for repairs. But by July 21, 1945, she had rejoined Task Force 38 and participated in screening operations for the final air strikes on the

Japanese homeland. As occupation forces began arriving in Japan following her surrender, *Duluth* served as radar picket with Task Force 38 until September 16, 1945 when she proudly entered Tokyo Bay as part of the occupation force.

Ben, now a Lieutenant, Junior Grade, wrote his parents from Tokyo Bay, the letter appearing in the *News-Wave* on October 11, 1945, and describing what he saw while ashore in Japan:

> USS Duluth (CL87)
> Tokyo Bay, Japan
> Dear Folks,
> Well, I finally got there. It took a long, hard row, but I came and saw, and believe my own eyes. I went to Tokyo and Yokohama yesterday and in riding the train one hour from the Port of Yokohama to Tokyo, as far as I could see, on either side of the tracks for miles and miles, I saw nothing but rubble, broken brick and burned walls from the bombing, and boy! how those Japs held out as long as they did is beyond me.
> I saw the Emperor's grounds with a high wall around his palace and a body of water around it. Saw the Japs continually go up a quarter of a mile hill to this high wall, beyond which is the Mikado's palace. They would kneel down and bow low. We also saw there those who were with instruments playing music which supposedly drove away the evil spirits, or something to that effect. One and a half miles down town in the heart of Tokyo when the people pass they remove their hats and bow to the Americans.
> A few of us who went up there were amused at the way people have a totally blank expression; something like the bomb victims I see in service. I guess it is from that continuous bombing day and night.
> The trains are loaded by the thousands with baggage and all, going somewhere, but evidently not knowing where.
> Not much food. A bar of candy or cigarettes, or something to eat, goes farther than money.
> I was in the Imperial hotel where MacArthur had headquarters. Today I had charge of a bunch of mugs off the ship with several other officers and took them out to Yokasticks (Ed. - ?) City for liberty.
> Am sending this letter in a souvenir envelope celebrating one year of the commissioning of the USS Duluth. Also am sending a little for your scrap book.
> Your son, Ben

On October 1, 1945, *Duluth* left the western Pacific for the United States, arriving at Seattle, Washington, on October 19. Ben remained with her until November 25, 1945, at which time he departed for, ironically, Chicago, Illinois, where he received his discharge from the United States Navy on November 29, 1945 at Great Lakes Naval Station. Lt. (j. g.) Gasatis had participated in eleven engagements in the Pacific Theater and was wearing the American Defense Medal, American Theater Medal, Good Conduct Medal, Asiatic-Pacific Theater Medal, and World War II Victory Medal.

No photo.
Sources: Independence News-Wave; Internet

LESTER GUNEM
UNITED STATES ARMY

It is not known when Lester Gunem joined the United States Army, where he completed basic training, or when and where he was discharged. In fact, his biography will seem quite impersonal because of this. However, Lester served with the 338th Infantry Regiment, known as the "Old Timers," of the 85th Infantry Division[1] during World War II, a unit with a storied history as it fought through the Rome-Arno, North Apennines, and Po Valley campaigns in Italy. The 338th's, and therefore his, story is presented here.

The 338th Infantry was activated with the 85th Infantry Division on May 15, 1942. at Camp Shelby, Mississippi. It participated in various maneuvers in Louisianna and California through the summer of 1943. The Division then transferred to Fort Dix, New Jersey, on October 7, 1943, staged at Camp Patrick Henry, Virginia, on December 18, 1943, and departed the Hampton Roads Port of Embarkation on December 24, 1943.

Arriving in North Africa on January 2, 1944, the 85th Infantry Division underwent extensive training at Port-aux-Poules from February 1 - March 23, 1944, before leaving for Italy, where it landed at Naples. The 338th Infantry went ashore on March 27, 1944, held defensive positions along the *Gustav Line* until late April. 1944, and then launched an attack of its own on May 11, 1944. During this assault, Lester's 338th Infantry took Cave d'Argilla and Hill 131, and had reached the intersection of Highway 7 and Ausonia Road by May 15, 1944. The 338th then took Formia in mid-May 1944, before landing by landing craft at Sperlonga, fighting through a railway tunnel, and moving towards Mt. Leano.

After the Division crossed the Amaseno River on May 25, 1944, it attacked once again, with the 337th and 338th Infantry's assaulting Mt. Artemisio and capturing the town of Lariano. Bloody battles were fought against the vaunted *Herman Goering Division* along the *Velietri-Valmontone Line* before the Division found itself speeding up Via Tuscolana through Rome on June 5, 1944. It was relieved at the Viterbo River on June 10, 1944, rehabilitated, and sent back into action in mid-August to relieve the *New Zealand 2nd Division* and, two days later, the 91st Infantry Division near Fucecchio.

The 85th Infantry Division experienced another bloody battle as it attacked the Il Giogo Pass of the *Gothic Line* on September 13, 1944. During this time, the 338th Infantry fought and won the "Battle for Mt. Altuzzo."

After the Division broke through the *Gothic Line* in mid-September 1944, it experienced numerous battles for various hills, mountains, and villages, and on October 24, 1944 found itself at Mt. Mezzano overlooking the Po Valley.

Placed in defensive positions through November 22, 1944, the 85th Infantry was then relieved for rehabilitation the next day. It then entered the Po Valley campaign where it first relieved the *British 1st Division*. On April 17, 1945, it relieved the 1st Armored Division and began an ever-quickening advance as the German army before it began to collapse. On April 26, 1945, the Division crossed the Adige River near Verona and soon after began clearing the Piave Valley of remaining German troops. On May 2, 1945, German forces in Italy formally surrendered.

---

[1] The 85th Infantry Division suffered 1,561 killed and 6,314 wounded, with 175 of these dying from their wounds during World War II.

No photo.
Sources: Independence News-Wave; Book (Stanton)

GLEN F. HENDRICKSON
UNITED STATES NAVY

It took a special breed of man to serve in submarines during wartime. Cramped quarters and stale air were the norm, while the uncertain, but very real, threats of enemy mines, depth charges, and aircraft could be terrifying to even the strongest among them.

Glen Hendrickson enlisted in the United States Navy at La Crosse, Wisconsin, on November 20, 1942, and entered active service that same day. In May 1943, he visited his parents as a Seaman Second Class based at Great Lakes Naval Station, Illinois, and was quoted in the *News-Wave* as stating about Navy life: "It's great, if you have what it takes."

When he graduated from the Service School at Great Lakes on May 31, 1943, Glen was promoted to Electrician's Mate Third Class. He then reported to the Navy's submarine school based at New London, Connecticut, completed basic submarine training in early September 1943, and thus earned the right to wear the twin dolphin insignia of the submarine service. However, he still had to prove he was fully qualified for submarine service by passing a battery of physical, mental, and psychological tests.

The *U. S. S. Perch*, (SS-313), was the second submarine to carry that name in World War II, the first having been lost on March 3, 1942 during the Navy's early desperate attempt to slow the Japanese advance across the Pacific. SS-313, of the Balao Class, was 311 feet long and carried a crew of 66. Commissioned on January 7, 1944, she was armed with one five-inch gun, one 40-mm machine gun, and ten 21-inch torpedo tubes. Having fully qualified for submarine service, Glen was assigned duty aboard the *Perch* probably at the time of her commissioning.

Following her shakedown, *Perch* left Groton, Connecticut, on February 19, 1944, and sailed to Key West, Florida, where she was assigned to the Fleet Sound School for a period of time. She later sailed for Hawaii, arriving at Pearl Harbor on April 3, 1944.

Forming a wolf pack with submarines *Peto* (SS-265) and *Picuda* (SS-382), *Perch* left Pearl on April 29, 1944 and headed for the South China Sea. On May 24, she fired four torpedoes at a medium-sized Japanese tanker, but because of a counterattack by the tanker's escort, sinking was not confirmed. During this counterattack, *Perch* suffered damage to both high pressure air compressors when her pump room was flooded, so she then set a course to the Marshall Islands for repairs, arriving at Majuro on June 4, 1944. While waiting for repairs to be completed there, Glen wrote to his parents, Mr. and Mrs. Ole Hendrickson, the letter appearing in the *News-Wave* on July 6, 1944:

U. S. S. Perch
June 18, 1944
Dearest Mother and Dad:

Something tells me it's time to write you another letter. As usual there is very little to write about, but will try to make some sort of a letter.

I'm feeling quite well and have had a pretty nice time the past two weeks. Although there was plenty to do I still found plenty time for things I've always wanted to see. Many people will never have a chance to see the outer world which is so much different than our way of life. Most of the boys prefer being back in the States and of course that's only natural.

This morning I attended church services and did the same last Sunday. They aren't elaborate chapels like in the States but guide one through the dark days ahead. Worship can be followed wherever one is if he has the right way of living in him.

I just wonder what the home town will be like when all the boys return. That will be the day!

Will close for this time. Don't worry if there is a long period of time before you get another letter. I'll be where it's impossible to send mail. So long for now. Hope this finds you all well.

Love to all,
Glen

The place from "where it's impossible to send mail" was Surigao Strait near the Philippine Islands to where *Perch* sailed on June 27, 1944. There, she sank a Japanese trawler with surface gunfire before returning to Pearl again on August 26, 1944.

Perch's third war patrol began when she left Pearl on September 19, 1944 to join submarines *Croaker* (SS-246) and *Escolar* (SS-294) near Midway Island. On September 23, 1944, the three submarines met and sailed together, their mission to search the waters of the East

China and Yellow Seas for enemy shipping. The patrol resulted in *Perch* unsuccessfully attacking a heavily escorted transport, but no other ships were sighted. During this patrol, the subs also performed lifeguard duty for damaged B-29's attacking the Japanese home island of Honshu.

On the day *Perch* left Midway, Glen penned another letter, this one to Glen Kirkpatrick of the *News-Wave*:

> September 23, 1944
> Dear Editor:
>
> It's been quite some time since I've read the home town paper, and I am curious as to what's going on. Letters of course keep me in contact with the news at home, but it's impossible to write everything in a letter, so enclosed is the amount for a year's subscription to your paper.
>
> My Navy career thus far has accounted for most of my travels and different places I have been. Some of them have been interesting and educational, partly due to the fact that I'm on submarines. In order to safeguard our military security it is impossible to give my location.
>
> Other than longing to have this war over, as so many others do, I'm getting along quite well. According to the Allies rapid advances the termination of part of it shouldn't be far off.
>
> Will close hoping this finds you in good health and happiness. I'll be looking forward to your interesting weekly issues.
> Sincerely,
> Glen F. Hendrickson, Em 2/c

On October 17, 1944, *Perch* heard from *Escolar* for the last time. Her reported position and intended destination, coupled with captured Japanese records, would indicate she possibly struck a mine. As this patrol came to a close, *Perch* headed for Saipan to refuel before sailing to Brisbane, Australia, where she joined Submarines, Southwest Pacific Fleet.

Her next war patrol began when she left Brisbane on December 19, 1944. She patrolled off Hainan, China, then Singapore and in the Balabac Straits off Borneo, without sighting any enemy ships. She arrived in Fremantle, Australia, on February 15, 1945.

Perch departed Fremantle on March 12, 1945 on a special mission carrying eleven Australian commandos bound for Balikpapan, Borneo. On the night of March 20, 1945, several of these men were put ashore to make a reconnaissance of the beach and surrounding area. When *Perch* came close ashore two nights later to disembark the remaining commandos, a Japanese coastal freighter entered the area and threatened to cut off her return to open water. She then engaged the freighter with surface fire, causing it to burst into towering flames before sinking. With her mission completed, she returned to Fremantle once again.

Departing Fremantle on April 15, 1945 on her sixth war patrol, *Perch* traveled to the Java Sea where she again searched for enemy shipping to attack. At about the same time she made contact with a two-ship convoy, the convoy's escort discovered her and initiated a two-hour-long depth charge attack that caused serious damage throughout the boat. But the damage was contained and repaired quickly after the attack ended and *Perch* continued its patrol off Hainan, China, before returning to Pearl Harbor on June 5, 1945. Six days later, she left Pearl for duty in the "Lifeguard League" off Japan, again searching for and rescuing downed airmen. On August 13, 1945, she rescued a Navy fighter pilot just two miles off the Japanese coast, then fired several five-inch shells into Japanese fishing boats and buildings along the beach before heading to the open sea once again. Later that day, another pilot from the same fighter squadron was rescued five miles off shore. When Japan surrendered on August 15, 1945, *Perch* returned to Pearl Harbor, arriving there on August 30.

Glen Hendrickson, Electrician's Mate First Class, and the *U. S. S. Perch* arrived at Hunter's Point near San Francisco, California, on September 8, 1945. The September 13, 1945 issue of the *News-Wave* mentioned he had again remitted for another year's subscription and was quoted as writing, probably from Pearl Harbor:

> The best news to date is the ending of the long and struggling war we've all been waiting for. I

guess every peaceful minded citizen cannot help but rejoice over the outcome. I sure would like to be back in the States for V-J Day, but I'm sure it will be impossible. I do hope to get a leave in the near future.

The short article also noted that Glen was serving aboard the *U. S. S. Perch* and that he would have several interesting stories to tell upon his return to Independence.

It is not certain when Glen left the submarine service of the United States Navy, but the *U. S. S. Perch* remained in active service for most of the next 25 years before being struck from the Navy List of Ships on January 1, 1971.

Sources: Independence News-Wave; Internet

The Independence Veterans Memorial was established in conjunction with this record being initially completed in 2000. Located in Independence High School, it can be seen during any public event. It currently consists of two large and one small display case of artifacts, a *Hallway of Heroes* housing 66 frames of photos and biographies, and 15 individual cases containing uniforms. Its purpose is to identify and recognize the hundreds of military veterans of the Independence area going back to the 1850's. All artifacts have a direct connection with an Independence veteran.

ADDISON HOTCHKISS
UNITED STATES ARMY

Addison Hotchkiss was 30 years old when he was inducted into the United States Army on January 8, 1943. He entered active service on January 15, 1943, at Fort Sheridan, Illinois. Following basic training, he received training as a crane operator, and was stationed near Cleveland, Ohio, as a Tech 4 with the 106th Ordnance Company. On October 13, 1943, Addison left the United States via ship, arriving in North Africa on November 2, 1943.

After only three weeks in North Africa, Addison again boarded ship, this time bound for India where he was to join the 77th Ordnance Base Depot in the China-Burma-India Theater. There, his unit would organize an assembly plant in Bombay, India, where planes, tanks, jeeps, and other military equipment arriving from the United States would receive final assembly before being delivered to the CBI front.

Sailing aboard a troopship of Convoy KMF 26, Addison left Oran, Algeria, destined for Bombay, India, on November 23, 1943. Just three days out to sea, near Bizerte, Algeria, the convoy was attacked by German bombers. The British troop transport *HMT Rohna*, part of the convoy and sailing near Addison's transport, was attacked by a single Heinkel 177 bomber carrying a secret HS-293 "glider bomb." Operated through manipulation of a joystick control box, the HS-293 was guided to its target and in essence was one of the world's first guided missles. The Heinkel's bomb was expertly directed into the *Rohna's* port side where it exploded, tearing a hole through the ship. The *Rohna* sank quickly, resulting in the deaths of 1,015 of the 1,988 American soldiers aboard as well as members of the British crew and Red Cross personnel. The 853rd Engineer Aviation Battalion alone lost 491 officers and men. What Addison had actually witnessed was the second greatest naval loss of U. S. troops in World War II, accounting for nearly one-third of the total lost during the sea war with Germany and Italy. However, this incident was kept from the American public due to its enormity, and families were simply informed their sons and husbands had been killed in action. Upon reaching Bombay, Addison was a crane operator for the next 11 months, until July, 1944.

At the time of the attack on Pearl Harbor, the Japanese were already moving quickly through Southeast Asia and China, a region rich in minerals and oil. The Allies had established a command in the theater in an effort to slow the Japanese advance, but bickering among the various commands caused ineffectiveness and led to a loss of morale among the troops, especially those assigned to the dense jungles of the region. Despite this, the Allied presence in the region, though probably having little direct effect on the rest of the war in the Pacific, did keep Japanese troops occupied that otherwise could have been used to reinforce other areas of the Pacific Theater.

The Burma Road was China's last important supply link with the Allies, but it had been broken when the Japanese occupied Burma in May 1942. Thereafter, supplies to the Chinese had to be flown by American transport planes 500 miles over the Himalaya Mountains, an assignment known to the airmen as "flying the Hump." In December 1942, the Allies began construction of a road leading from Ledo, India, across northern Burma to join the Burma Road. The Japanese were pushed back far enough in 1944 to allow completion of this new road, and on February 4, 1944, the first Allied truck convoy traveled over the Ledo Road, later renamed the "Stilwell Highway" in honor of General "Vinegar" Joe Stilwell, Allied commander in the CBI Theater. This Ledo-Burma Road connection thus allowed the Allies to transport the supplies needed in their attempt to dislodge the Japanese from the region, and because of it, the Japanese were withdrawing from south and central China by the spring of 1945.

Addison was transferred in July 1944, to the Ledo-Burma Road complex to help establish service stations for the convoys transporting men and supplies. As a Technical Sergeant, Motor Inspector, he inspected vehicles, stopping them on the road and spot checking them to assure the equipment was in proper working condition to complete the journey along the twisting and turning, mountainous road. There were a number of times when the Japanese, despite retreating, bombed his area in an attempt to disrupt transport over the Road.

While stationed in Calcutta, India, Addison was delivering supplies to a point 300 miles distant when, while driving through a village, he heard someone call his name. When Addison stopped his truck, he found it was Pvt. Eugene Killian of Independence, and they were able to spend some time catching up on events.

The June 14, 1945 edition of the *News-Wave* included a short article regarding Addison and the "Wisconsin Club," which was comprised of soldiers from Wisconsin stationed in Calcutta. In honor of the state's 97th birthday, 1,029 members of the one-year-old organization held a party. Representing 221 communities of Wisconsin, members of the group included Brigadier General Clarence C. Fenn of Antigo, who was the theater's judge advocate. It was also announced the group had applied to the State of Wisconsin for a charter as a non-political, non-partisan veteran's organization following the war.

In the November 1, 1945 *News-Wave*, people were informed that Addison had been among 61 servicemen from Wisconsin feted at a state party hosted by the American Red Cross' "60 Club" in Calcutta. The men enjoyed dinner, a stage show, and -- something quite rare in India -- ice cream! All 61 men were introduced from the stage after which several community reunions then ensued.

Addison remained in his ordnance capacity in India until December 7, 1945, at which time he began his trip back to the United States. His transport docked on January 3, 1946, and Addison was separated from the United States Army at Fort Sheridan, Illinois, on January 10, 1946 while attached to the 146 Ordnance Company. He had been awarded the World War II Victory Medal, Asiatic-Pacific Theater Ribbon, four Overseas Service Bars, one Service Stripe, and the Good Conduct Medal. Following completion of his tour of duty, a Meritorious Service Unit Plaque was awarded by the Commanding General, United States Forces, India-Burma Theater, to Headquarters and Headquarters Detachment, 77th Ordnance Base Depot, Base Section, India-Burma Theater "for meritorious service during the period 1 November 1944 to 31 October 1945."

Sources: Mrs. Addison Hotchkiss; Todd Wiench, grandson; Book (VFW Magazine)

A Quote From History. . .

"Most of our infantrymen boarded the *S. S. Leopoldville*."
    Jack Weier
    United States Army
    From a letter, January 1999 describing the sinking of a ship carrying his 66th Infantry
        Division to France. Leopoldville was sunk by a torpedo, resulting in 800 dead.

GLENN F. INSTENESS
UNITED STATES ARMY

Glenn Insteness entered the United States Army on October 28, 1941, completed basic training at Camp Wolters, Texas, and then departed for Alaska on April 17, 1942. He was stationed on the Aleutian Islands for 26 months, spending time at Adak, Umnak, and Cold Harbor along with fellow Independence natives Simon "Bob" Skroch and Sidney Solfest.

Following this duty on the bleak Aleutian landscape, he returned to the States where he trained for six months before leaving for England on Thanksgiving Day, November 22, 1944. After one month in the area of Bournemouth, England, Glenn, now with the 76th Infantry Division, crossed the channel to Le Havre, France, on January 12, 1945, and quickly moved to help with mop-up operations following the Battle of the Bulge.[1]

On January 22, 1945, the 76th Infantry Division relieved the 87th Infantry Division along the Sauer and Moselle Rivers near Echternach, Luxembourg. Across the icy-watered Sauer, the men of the 76th Infantry were looking at Germany, and their first attack would be directly into the concrete pillboxes, barbed wire, and mine fields of the *West Wall*, the formidable defensive positions known better to the Americans as the Siegfried Line.

The 76th Infantry Division crossed the Sauer River on February 7, 1945, and after battling through the *West Wall*, took Ernzen with the 5th Infantry Division by February 14, 1945. It next crossed the Pruem River on February 24-25, 1945, after which it began moving toward Trier, Germany. It neutralized enemy resistance in the area from Karl to Wittlich, Germany, along the Klein Kyll and Lieser Rivers, and then relieved the 2nd Cavalry Group along the Rhine River on March 21, 1945. After engineers selected a likely crossing place on the Rhine, elements of the 76th Infantry Division quickly made their way to the other side beginning early on March 28, 1945. By March 29, 1945, they had reached Kamberg where house-to-house fighting took place against a fanatical group of German officer candidates. The message "Kamberg cleared of enemy" was signaled back to headquarters the morning of April 1, 1945.

The American troops were moving very rapidly by this time. A bridgehead was won at Niederhone on April 5, 1945. and, following closely behind the 6th Armored Division, the 76th Infantry found itself near Buttstaedt on April 11, 1945. Zeitz fell on April 15, 1945 to the Division's 417th Infantry Regiment while the 304th Infantry moved on Altenburg. The Division then moved up to take over the Mulde River bridgehead established by 6th Armored, and remained in this area of Chemnitz, Germany, near the Czech border until the war ended on May 7, 1945.

Glenn remained in Germany with the Army of Occupation until August, 1945, at which time he boarded ship for the return home. He arrived at Camp McCoy on September 19, 1945, where he was stationed until his discharge on October 4, 1945.

---

[1] The 76th Infantry "Onaway" Division lost 433 men killed and 1,811 wounded, of which 90 died of their wounds, during its Ardennes-Alsace, Rhineland, and Central Europe campaigns.

No photo.
Sources: Independence News-Wave; Books (Stanton) (76th Infantry Division)

BERNIE ISAACS
UNITED STATES NAVY

The following edited biography is based upon letters received from Bernie Isaacs in 1998 in which he detailed his military experiences during World War II:

After I graduated from Independence High School in 1939, I spent two years at Eau Claire State Teacher's College in Eau Claire, Wisconsin. Following that, I took a year off to raise some money for my last two years of college. When the war broke out, I was living at the YMCA in Eau Claire and employed at Sterling Pulp and Paper Company. Then, on July 8, 1942, I enlisted in the United States Navy. I was sent to Great Lakes Naval Station in Chicago, Illinois, where they discovered that one of my jobs at Sterling had been lab testing and first aid. So, consequently, I was put in the Medical Corps. I never had to attend basic training because of that.

On September 15, 1942, I was sent to the University of Wisconsin Naval Radio School in Madison, Wisconsin, but my assignment again was medical, something I never really wanted. I didn't receive any radio training while in Madison, but it was great duty on the campus.

While I was at Madison, one of my superiors said to me one day, "I know you really don't like the medical duty. I'm going to try to get you assigned to Gene Tunney's Chief Petty Officer Training at Bainbridge, Maryland." My transfer was accepted. The Gene Tunney Physical Education School trained athletes as basic trainers of naval recruits. My new title was "Chief Petty Officer, Athletic Specialist."

On July 19, 1943, I returned to Great Lakes to indoctrinate and train black recruits in the about-to-be desegregated Navy. I later was selected as one of thirteen Chief Petty Officers to train qualified recruits to become the first black Naval officers. A book, *The Golden Thirteen*,[1] was written describing what turned out to be a pretty significant event. There were thirteen officer candidates selected from our trainees. My candidate was Graham E. Martin who had graduated from the University of Indiana where he had been an outstanding football player. Graham and the other candidates later were commissioned as Naval officers.

When the program was completed, we must have done a good job because we were rewarded with our choice of duty. I selected Officer's Training School and was sent to Columbia University in New York City on March 6, 1944. It was a four month accelerated course after which I was commissioned as an Ensign with a specialty in Navigation. I had hopes of seeing some action, and action I got!

I was sent to San Francisco on July 12, 1944, for overseas assignment. On August 10, I went to Pearl Harbor, Hawaii, and was assigned to LCI(L)-1022. LCI(L) stands for Landing Craft Infantry (Large). It is the smallest ocean-going craft in the Navy with a top speed of eleven knots, or approximately twelve miles per hour, and is equipped with four 40-mm anti-aircraft guns. It is flat-bottomed, 110 feet long, and 30 feet wide at its beam, with two side ramps that are lowered to disembark soldiers during invasions. The ship is equipped to carry 200 soldiers who go down the ramps and onto the beach. Its crew consists of five officers and 25 enlisted men. After disembarking the troops, we would pull away from the beach by drawing up the rear anchor

---

[1] *The Golden Thirteen: Recollections of the First Black Naval Officers*, edited by Paul Stillwell, Director of History at the Naval Institute, and published in 1993 by the United States Naval Institute, is an oral history of the memories of the eight surviving members of the Golden Thirteen. On page 16 of the book, Bernie's trainee, Graham E. Martin, states, without naming Bernie or any other trainer, that they "had a white chief petty officer in charge of the company. He was very sympathetic and helpful. The race thing never came up, but I don't think he was in any way prejudiced." Though only one of these original black Naval officers remained in the Navy after the war, all of them made their marks in significant post-war careers, among them an engineer, teacher, justice of a state appellate court, and attorney. The desegregation of the Navy's officer corps, of course, paved the way for General Colin Powell's eventual appointment as Chairman of the Joint Chiefs of Staff.

Bernie Isaacs. In the photo above,
Bernie is pictured with the Company of
black Naval personnel from which the
first black Naval officers were selected.

which had been dropped for disembarkation.

On November 9, 1944, I was reassigned to LCI(L)-965 as Navigator, and promoted to Lieutenant, j.g. (Ed. - junior grade). We were part of the Seventh Fleet under General Douglas MacArthur and headed for the Philippines. The beach at Leyte Island was already quite secure when we arrived three days after the battleships, cruisers, and destroyers had neutralized the Japanese Navy in the area. On December 8, 1945, we were assigned to invade Ormoc on the back side of Leyte. This was to be a battle royal because the Japanese Air Force apparently decided that this might be their last stand of consequence in the Philippines.

There was a lot of support for our invasion at Ormoc and we had a ringside seat for two days of kamikaze attacks on the large ships of our Navy. I witnessed some 75 to 100 of these missions which probably was the end of their strength in that region. I never felt very much danger because they seemed to be after the big ships. But it was a tremendous show. Thereafter, we made invasion trips to other islands, but the resistance was limited. We helped secure Cebu, Luzon, Mindanao, Mindoro, Corregidor, Masbate, and Panay.

In August 1945, we were ordered to gather at Leyte with other elements of the Navy in preparation for the invasion of Japan. That's when the news came of the tremendous atomic explosions in Japan and the sudden end of the war. Every ship in the harbor shot off all the live ammunition and pyrotechnics they could muster. It was a colorful display. All of the beer and alcohol being saved for shore picnics or medicinal use disappeared that night. What a great party!

With the war ended, we thought we were going home, but soon learned that orders had been received sending us to Shanghai, China, to transport the Chinese Nationalists to Formosa in order to rescue them from being run into the sea by the Communist Army. It was now October, 1945, and by this time, I was the ship's Captain as our Captain had qualified for return to the

54

States. When the Formosa duty ended, we headed back to the United States via Guam, Hawaii, and San Diego. At twelve miles per hour, it took us over three months.

After arriving in San Diego, I turned the ship's command over to our Executive Officer who finished the trip through the Panama Canal to Florida where the ship was to be decommissioned and mothballed.

I was now a Lieutenant. Mimi and I were married in Cleveland, Ohio, on March 31, 1946, shortly after my discharge from the Navy. We returned to Madison, Wisconsin, where I enrolled under the G. I. Bill at the University of Wisconsin to complete work toward my Bachelor of Business Administration degree.

JOHN J. JASZEWSKI
UNITED STATES ARMY

John Jaszewski joined the United States Army on March 3, 1941. By April 1942, the *News-Wave* reported that he was stationed at Fort Cooke, Nebraska, though the accurracy of this is questionable as Fort Cooke was located in California. In the Army, he was assigned duty with an ordnance motor transport company. His unit and responsibilities are best described by John himself in two lengthy letters he sent to Glenn Kirkpatrick at the *News-Wave* while he was in Europe.

From "Somewhere in Belgium," the first letter is dated January 15, 1945. and appeared in the *News-Wave* on February 22, 1945. Besides giving a good description of his duties in Europe, it leaves a little mystery that remains unsolved. What *did* happen on November 11, 1944 that John could not write about but "maybe some day I'll tell about it"?

Dear Friend Kirk:

I've been trying to write a few words to you folks for a long time, but something always happens, and there it is all over again. Last night I received the special edition of the "good old News-Wave": and was that ever a treat to me! Sure was good to see all those pictures and those familiar faces again. Hope they are still there when I get back 'cause I take on where I left off when I left the old town four years ago. That is, there abouts. But, wherever I'll make my home, I'll never forget good old Independence.

Maybe I should mention a little about the situation around here. Well, since the invasion of Normandy and Cherbourg we've swept through quite well, then when we started on "Der Deutchland" something happened, which you folks no doubt have heard, and the Christmas Eve, just passed, I will never forget. It was like a nightmare, as was the night of the great invasion at the early hours of the morning of June 6, 1944. At this writing the situation is somewhat improved, and we are nearly at normal production capacity.

The outfit I'm with, and have been since I entered the service March 3, 1941, is the Ordnance of the Motor Transport Co. And since landing at Normandy, till the present time, our men have put thousands of vehicles back on their six drivers. We deal with the repair of all and any type of wheeled vehicle the army has, from the quarter ton Jeep to the twelve and fourteen ton Prime Mover. Occasionally a half track or light tank comes in for an over-haul job. Oh, yes, we have serviced a couple of our Recon. planes too. That is, a valve grinding job, for the Taylor Cubs, or, as we call it, the "flying Jeep."

All in all we have a job to do seven days a week, and it sure keeps us out of mischief. Our sleeping quarters are not too bad now, but a few months ago, those fox holes were getting too deep for us, and too much water came in so we had to move to higher ground, where we are ever since.

The weather is just like back home now and plenty of snow. The days are getting longer right along, too, and soon it will be more like spring.

I've made another jump in rating too since we are here in Belgium. I'm now a Staff Sergeant; got that on November 11, 1944. Maybe on that day something happened here. It did. But I will not mention

55

it for military reasons. Maybe some day I'll tell about it.

Well, folks, I guess this article will about cover a page, so will sign off "pronto." Besides, it is a little late and I need some sleep. In fact my flash light is growing dim and so with it, I'll close.

As ever, your friend

John Jaszewski

P. S. I want to thank you once again for the News-Wave. I certainly appreciate every thing that's in it. I want to mention about my brother, Nicky. He's somewhere in France and I hear from him quite often, although I can't go to see him at the present time. I've seen my cousin, Wally Rebarchek of Milwaukee, several times here, as we are close by. Haven't run into anyone else from around Independence as yet.

The war in Europe was over for nearly one month when Sgt. Jaszewski penned the following letter to "Kirk" at the *News-Wave* from "Longway, France, near Luxemberg (sic)." Dated "Wednesday, June 6, 1945, or D-Day plus 365," he describes in it his experiences with buzz bombs and the tragedy that has come to be known as "the Holocaust." It was published on June 21, 1945:

Dear Kirk:

On this day we soldiers of the U. S. Army can have a rest. So, I'm going to take this opportunity to write a few lines to you folks, and, if you find it interesting enough, you may publish it in the News-Wave.

Well, on this day, one year ago was one of the most tragic in the history of World War II. Thousands of our soldiers were mowed down like weeds, by German 88's, and machine gun fire. The Jerries apparently were having maneuvers at the Normandy coast, at the time of the invasion. The combat engineers had landed after clearing mines in the channel and the beaches, but were stopped somewhere along their path. Fresh troops were pouring in, along side of tanks, preceded by our mighty air power of eleven thousand bombers and fighters. The picture which followed cannot be visualized and painted unless the artist was there to see it went on. It was a day long to be remembered by many who were fortunate to see it through. Those who were wounded and recovered later, are back home now. And the war for (once??) did not last very long, when they hit the beach. Perhaps a couple of hours or less. Now, then, I should say a few words about the 3534 Ord. (and?) A.M. Co.

Back in England we were alerted long before D-Day. We got our orders to move up to the Southhampton coast. We got there, and somewhere along the line, something went wrong and we stayed there through D-Day, and a month or so after. Instead, another Ord. Co. had been called and landed on the Normandy Coast, on D plus 1. They never got inland very far as Jerries were plentiful, and their maneuvers were at their peak then. Our Co. got called later, and we landed on August 1, 1944. By that time it was still hot, as we operated shops only three miles from the front. St. Lo had been already taken, or leveled up, I should say, and the front was spreading fast along the southern and southwestern coast. We dug Fox holes and dodged a lot of straffing from Jerry planes. Well, everything was going fine, through Paris and on up to the Siegried Line. There we stopped. We moved into Liege, Belgium, on September 23, 1944. Our shops and sleeping quarters were at a large steel factory. We operated from 18 to 20 hours every day, seven days a week, turning out 30 to 35 vehicles per day, and some vehicles were reconditioned thoroughly, when completed. (Including changing engines in some)

Then came the break through on December 16, 1944. We've survived a lot of buzz bombs during the time. Buzz bombs is what we called Hitler's Secret Weapon V1 to V2's. On Christmas Eve, Jerry planes came over and straffed three hospitals, which were set up within a block or two from our set-up. The 28th Gen., the 76th Gen. and the 16th Gen. hospitals. We heard women, men and children screaming and moaning. We were called to help protect these hospitals and had twelve machine guns (50 calibre) mounted on our wreckers and G.M.C. trucks, and set them up around them. A German prison of War Camp, with a couple hundred Jerries in it, was situated about two blocks from us, and there, too, we had plenty of fire power, in case they had funny ideas. We had a machine gun spaced every five yards and two men to each gun, with a finger on the trigger, ready for any riot which we had expected to take place. This went on all Christmas Eve, and during the following day. Then, we had to move on the opposite side of the Muese River. The Jerries were only 20 miles from Liege. We moved back some but not too far. We

56

had set up shops at a factory, four miles from Liege, Belgium. To us it was called Buzz Bomb Alley because that's where they were falling. We had our chow hall set up at one end of the huge building, and one night just about supper time, one of those bombs hit about 25 feet from the place. Our good supper was gone, and so we ended up with a box of K-rations. We also had four wounded boys. The following day, another one had struck within 20 feet from us. Here's where it got one of our boys. He was blown to bits. The third bomb which landed so close to us in the two days, hit our gas supply dump, on the far end of the factory, which was about 50 yards away. But by that time, one of our Lts. who is always full of the devil, comes out and sings, "Come out, come out, where ever you are", and we all "came out" from our hiding places, and joined in with him. Thereafter for our safety, we all took off upon hearing the least noise that sounded like the bomb. It was very nerve-wracking 'cause one never knew where and when the bombs would hit.

We survived those bombs, and from there on in, we started again, on the Jerries trail, and finally crossed the Rhine, and on up to near Lepzig (Ed. - Leipzig), Germany where we stayed for a couple of weeks, after the final collapse of Germany. But we are still here. We left Germany about a week ago, and are now in France. Our mission from now on is to get a certain quota of vehicles reconditioned, and getting them ready for shipment to the Pacific theatre. Our quota is supposed to be 1200 per month. These vehicles will be coming in from Italy and all over the European theatre. We came to an eight hour day, six day a week basis now. But, as for me, I'm going on my fifth year in this man's army, and I've collected 87 points. So, I'm sweating out my discharge at this time.

I've been with the First Army back in England, and I still am now. But we were changed over to the third battalion since the end of this war. That is, in three different ones. Right now, we are with a battalion which is a part of the 9th army. We are the only Co. of Ord. personnel in this battalion (of three or four such Co's.) and we are still in the First Army. Oh, well, I'm still sweating it out. Two weeks ago one of our boys left the Co. He had a 115 points. Now, there's but two of us left with 87 and 93 points. We still hope to be home soon.

Well, sir, I could keep writing on different subjects, but I'm not much good on my vocabulary. I've seen a lot of ghastly things when we got the other side of the Rhine, such as the brutal murders in forced labor camps. One of our boys took pictures of some of the sights, one of them in particular. One which we've all seen. Men and women and children, some dead, some half-dead, all purely naked, piled up like cord wood, and left to either get burned or just left there, I don't know how. Apparently the Nazis hadn't had time to dispose of these bodies before the Americans came in on them. This was not the only thing we saw . We've seen a lot of other things, too. But I won't mention them right now. I guess I had better taper off here, so, till next time, I am as ever,

Your friend,
John Jaszewski

It is not certain when John left Europe on his return trip home, nor where or when he was discharged from the Army.

No photo.
Source: Independence News-Wave

A Quote From History. . .

"A guy near me was killed by a direct hit from a mortar. That was my first taste of combat."
Clarence Sluga
United States Army
From an interview of June 23, 1998 describing the Battle of the Bulge when, on his first day in the lines, 27 of the 38 men in his unit were either killed or wounded.

JOSEPH J. JASZEWSKI
UNITED STATES ARMY

The story of Joseph Jaszewski, "Jazzy Joe" as he was known by his many friends in Independence, is one of untold hardship and a simple desire to survive during a march over the Owen Stanley Mountains of New Guinea.

Joe was inducted into the United States Army on July 17, 1941. He was sent to Camp Grant in Rockford, Illinois, which was a medical replacement unit training center, then later was transferred to Camp Lee, Virginia, where he received further Medical Corps training. From Camp Lee, Joe was sent to Fort Bragg, North Carolina, and served as a battery aide with field artillery. In February 1942, he was ordered to report to Fort George G. Meade, Maryland, where he joined the 28th Surgical Hospital and prepared for overseas shipment. From Fort Dix, New Jersey, Joe finally embarked on March 1, 1942 on a tedious 41-day journey to Australia.

Four-and-a-half months after his arrival in Australia, Joe and his unit were attached to the 32nd Infantry Division, the "Red Arrow Division," which had been undergoing jungle warfare training at Camp Cable near Brisbane.[1] With the 32nd Infantry, Joe was to see duty with the 19th Portable Hospital, 107th Medical Battalion.

New Guinea, already under Japanese attack for several months before Joe reached

Australia, was simply a stepping stone for the Japanese in their conquest of the Southwest Pacific. Since Australia was the headquarters of Allied defenses in the region, it was imperative that the enemy not be allowed to invade the continent. General Douglas MacArthur therefore hastily prepared a defense of the Port Moresby, New Guinea, area. Both the 32nd, under Major General Edwin F. Harding, and 41st Infantry Divisions had just recently arrived in Australia, so while the Americans were receiving additional training, Australian troops were quickly dispatched to Port Moresby. From there, the Australians seemed to at least slow the Japanese advance, and MacArthur then developed a plan to use an American regimental combat team in a flanking movement, thus forcing the enemy to withdraw to the north of the island or risk being trapped.

Major General, soon to be promoted to Lieutenant General, Robert L. Eichelberger, in command of I Corps, decided the 32nd Infantry would be sent to Port Moresby ahead of the 41st, for no other reason than the 32nd's Camp Cable was inferior to the 41st's camp at Rockhampton and therefore the 32nd would have to be moved anyway, and despite the fact the 32nd had not yet been adequately trained for jungle warfare. The 32nd's 126th Infantry Regiment was deemed to be the best trained and led of the Division's three regiments. It therefore was selected for the flanking maneuver. On September 15, 1942, the first American troops to set foot on New Guinea left Brisbane for Port Moresby. Referred to as "the spearhead of the spearhead of the spearhead" by General Harding, this group consisted of the 126th Infantry's Company E, a

---

[1] The 32nd Infantry Division lost 1,613 killed and 5,627 wounded, of which 372 died of their wounds, during its three campaigns in the Pacific.

medical officer and four aid men, and an attached platoon of Company A, 114th Engineer Combat Battalion, a total of 172 men. Joe Jaszewski remained in Brisbane with the rest of the 126th Infantry, leaving by ship three days later and arriving in Port Moresby on September 28. MacArthur's plan called for a three-prong advance with the Buna-Gona area the objective. One prong had troops following the Kokoda Trail, another would see troops move northwest along the coast from Milne Bay in the southeastern corner of New Guinea, and the third would consist of a drive through Kapa Kapa and Jaure. The initial goal would be to consolidate forces along the Kumusi River and Owalama Divide, and then drive toward Buna. Joe's story involves the march on Jaure.

After an advance party under Captain William F. Boice reached Jaure on October 4, 1942, General Harding received permission to move a larger advance group forward with orders to prepare air drop sites at Laruni and Jaure and to build up food and other supplies dropped there for later use by the main force. Selected for this duty was an echelon of the 2d Battalion, 126th Infantry Regiment. Attached to the 2d Battalion echelon were the regimental Antitank and Cannon companies acting as riflemen, and a small medical detachment. These 250 troops, with 100 native bearers, were under the command of Captain Alfred Medendorp. They began their march to Jaure on October 6, 1942, with their first goal that of joining up with the 45 men of Boice's Company E at Nepeana.

Because they were heavily burdened with equipment and not well-conditioned for jungle marching, Medendorp's group had a difficult time that first day on the trail. General Harding gave permission to lighten their packs, including cutting down on ammunition, and the second day went better. By the fourth day, however, most of the bearers had deserted the group and the men were forced to carry the additional supplies and equipment. They reached Laruni on October 13, 1942 and began developing a dropping zone on October 14. That same day the main 2d Battalion force, under battalion commander Lieutenant Colonel Henry A. Geerds, began leaving Kalikodobu for Jaure at the rate of one company per day. Attached to this main force was a platoon of the 114th Engineer Battalion and the 25 men and four officers of the 19th Portable Hospital, Joe's unit.

The trek to Jaure was much more difficult for the main 2d Battalion than it had been for the advance force as it began raining heavily as they left Kalikodobu, and not abating in the least for the next five days and nights. The men were drenched and miserable throughout, and because of the incessant rains, the 9,000-foot high Owen Stanley Divide at Mount Suwemalla became a nightmare. The trail was extremely narrow with no place to bivouac on either side, forcing the troops to travel in single file. They tripped over vines and roots, slogged through knee-deep mud, and had to ford streams that instantly became raging floods. To climb the steep ridges, the men used their hands and knees, or cut "steps" into the rock with axes. One "razorback" ridge was followed by another and what required eight hours to climb often took as little as forty minutes to descend as they slipped, stumbled, and fell often 2,000 feet or more. Four or five of these ridges meant a day's march though the horizontal distance covered was a matter of only a few miles. To rest, men would simply hang on to vines in order to keep from slipping down the mountainside.

Though much personal equipment, such as gas masks, helmets, mess kits, and heavy weapons had been left behind due to Boice and Medendorp's experiences, the troops were soon discarding other gear as well. Toilet articles, raincoats, shelter-halves, mosquito nets, blankets, and other items began littering the trail. Now the men would not only be cold and wet at night as well as during the day, but they would also become constant targets of every insect and parasite in the jungle. Because they were poorly fed, with much of the air-dropped canned food being damaged and its contents spoiling, acute diarrhea and dysentery began taking their toll. The lack of bowel control became so bad that many men simply cut holes in the seat of their pants.

Through this all, the medical personnel took care of the injured and sick. There was no way to simply send them back to their embarkation point so they did what they could to help them continue their march. Though many of the sick simply wanted to quit and die in the jungle, many undoubtedly owe their lives to the men of the 19th Portable Hospital, including Pfc. Joe Jaszewski. They picked up the ill and injured, they cared for them, and they moved them forward, despite their being as ill and miserable as their patients. As 2d Battalion's Sergeant Paul Lutjens

The soldiers sent to stop the Japanese advance on New Guinea suffered unspeakable hardships as they trekked over the Owen Stanley Mountains.

wrote in his diary, "Our strength is about gone. Most of us have dysentery. Boys are falling out and dropping back with fever. Continual downpour of rain. It's hard to cook our rice and tea. Bully beef makes us sick. We seem to climb straight up for hours, then down again. God, will it never end?"

Though it didn't really come to an end for some time for the 126th Infantry Regiment, Colonel Geerds' "mountaineers" finally did begin arriving in Jaure on October 25, 1942. Their clothing was in tatters and their shoes moldy and worn out, and Geerds himself had suffered a heart attack on the trail and had to be evacuated back to Port Moresby.

The 2d Battalion plus attached troops was the only unit to cross the Owen Stanley's, or "Ghost Mountain"[2] as it was called by the troops who traversed the divide, on foot. While they were enroute, General Harding was made aware of another passage much more suitable for marching troops, and it wasn't long before several airstrips were constructed to accomodate C-47's carrying the rest of the 126th Infantry. With November 15, 1942 selected as the date of attack towards Buna, General MacArthur himself flew into Port Moresby on November 6 to direct the operation.

Conditions didn't improve much for Captain Boice's command or for the 126th Infantry as a whole. Boice's men, still in search of good air-drop grounds between Jaure and Natunga, were

[2] The Owen Stanley's were called "Ghost Mountain" by the troops because they often were shrouded in fog, low hanging clouds, that lent the already dangerous situation an even more eery appearance. Joe and the other men of the 2d Battalion plus attached units were the first white people to cross the Owen Stanley Mountains on foot since 1917.

60

starving on a diet of bananas and papayas. On November 5, 1942, while himself aboard a plane trying to get food to his beleagured men, 126th Infantry Regiment commander Colonel Lawrence Quinn was killed when his plane crashed. Quinn was General Eichelberger's best regimental commander and it was a stunning blow to the General, as well as to the exhausted, sick, and starving men of his Regiment.

Despite all the hardships, the 32nd Infantry Division continued its three-pronged assault toward Buna, eventually linking with the Australians and ending the Buna-Sanananda campaign in January, 1943. It was relieved beginning January 25, 1943, by the 41st Infantry Division, and began a month-long exodus back to Australia. The 32nd Infantry, plus the 41st Infantry's 163d Infantry Regiment, which had also participated in the campaign, suffered 2,868 battle-related casualties by that time. But the cost to the Americans due to a lack of adequate training, poor food and medical supplies, disease and parasites, and the horrible conditions of fighting in the jungle of New Guinea, was devastating. Because there were practically no replacements, some units became basically non-existent. As General Eichelberger wrote to General MacArthur, "Regiments here soon have the strength of battalions and a little later are not much more than companies."

When the 32nd Infantry Division had first entered the combat zone, its total strength numbered 10,825 men. By the time it was relieved in January 1943, it had suffered an incredible 9,688 casualties, of which 7,125 were caused by sickness -- malaria, dysentery, dengue fever, and typhus -- an astounding 90-percent casualty rate. Of the Division's three regiments, the 126th Infantry Regiment suffered the most. It consisted of 131 officers and 3,040 enlisted men when it began its action, and on January 22, 1943, the day the Regiment was evacuated by plane to Port Moresby, there were 32 officers and 579 enlisted men left. For all practical purposes, the 126th Infantry Regiment no longer existed.

Joe was evacuated on January 22, as well, one of 20 officers and 141 enlisted men remaining from the 196 attached divisional troops that had entered the zone with the combat teams. In such bad condition was the 32nd Infantry Division following its return to Australia that it did not enter combat again until October 1943, when it once again participated in the New Guinea campaign. While in Australia, Joe's unit operated a hospital train for four months. When it returned to New Guinea, his unit traveled up the entire northern coast with the Division. He and his hospital unit spent a brief time on the Admiralty Islands, then landed on Leyte of the Philippine Islands on October 20, 1944 with General MacArthur's main invasion force. There the 32nd Infantry Division was involved in the bloody battles of Corkscrew Ridge and Breakneck Ridge, among others. From Leyte, the 32nd Infantry traveled to Luzon in the Philippines where it engaged the Japanese in the "Battle of Manila," the "Battle for Villa Verde Trail," and several other major battles. The Division was on Luzon when the war ended.

Following the surrender of Japan, the 32nd Infantry Division moved to Japan on October 14, 1945, where it remained as part of the Army of Occupation until February 28, 1946. Though Joe was with the Division through the Leyte campaign, he did not accompany the Army of Occupation to Japan. Instead, after serving more than 34 months overseas, he parted with the 32nd Infantry on December 7, 1944 and arrived back in the United States on December 25, 1944, whereupon he spent a 21-day furlough in Independence. In an interview with the *News-Wave* while on furlough, Joe briefly recounted his travels in the Southwest Pacific, but did not discuss any of the horrors he had seen in New Guinea. He summarized his story by simply stating, "I believe I've seen enough to last me the rest of my living days."

Following his time at home, Joe reported back to active duty in Miami, Florida, from where he was assigned to the Mayo General Hospital in Galesburg, Illinois.

Tech 5 Joseph Jaszewski was separated from the United States Army on August 21, 1945, at Fort Sheridan, Illinois, after having participated in the Papuan New Guinea and Southern Philippines Liberation campaigns. He had been awarded the American Service Ribbon, American Theater Ribbon, Asiatic-Pacific Theater Ribbon with three bronze battle stars, Philippine Liberation Ribbon, five Overseas Service Bars, one Service Stripe, and the Good Conduct Medal. His unit had also been awarded a Distinguished Unit Citation which allowed him to wear the Distinguished Unit Badge.

Joe's widow, Marie, states that Joe seldom said much about his time in combat, but he did relate a few experiences to her. In one instance, as Joe and his comrades were resting one evening, there was a rustling in the brush nearby. The Americans promptly opened fire in the direction of the noise, thinking it possibly had been caused by Japanese troops. Upon inspection, however, they found they had killed a wild boar. This animal provided an immediate opportunity to eat fresh meat rather than the usually spoiled canned food they had been consuming, and a fire was quickly made in such a way so as to conceal it from the Japanese. The pig was roasted throughout the night, but in the morning the men found the meat to be so tough they could not eat it, and all of their excitement over the possibility of fresh food turned to bitter disappointment.

Another time, Joe was rendering aid to a soldier who had suffered a severe abdominal wound. The next day, when the soldier asked Joe whether he had been dreaming when he recalled seeing his intestines lying outside his body, Joe told him he most certainly must have been. However, the soldier's "dream" in fact was reality as Joe and others had cleaned his internal organs before replacing them in his abdominal cavity and closing his wound. Joe did not say whether this soldier survived his ordeal in the jungle of New Guinea.

And finally, one of the other few things Joe ever mentioned to Marie about his incredible experience in New Guinea was that his flight back over the Owen Stanley Mountains was a lot easier than his long walk.

On February 2, 1945, the *News-Wave* reported Corporal Jaszewski had spent a 21-day furlough in Independence, during which time he gave the following account of his experiences to the newspaper. It is a summary of his experiences as described in his biography:

> Here's a little of the life I spent in the past three and a half years.
>
> I left for the army in July, 1941. My first camp to start life was at Camp Grant, Illinois. From there a transfer was made to Camp Lee, Virginia, where I received my training in the Medical Corps. Upon completion of my basic training I was sent to Fort Bragg, North Carolina, where my work was to serve as a Battery Aidman with a Field Artillery outfit.
>
> In February of 1942 I received orders to report at Ft. George G. Meade, Maryland. There joined the 28th Surgical Hospital, now changed to the 360th Station Hospital, where preparations were being made for overseas service. Then from there our unit was sent to Ft. Dix, New Jersey, and on the first day of March, 1942, we embarked for a long and tedious trip.
>
> After spending forty-one days on water we arrived in Australia.
>
> After spending four and a half months in that country, we were attached to the 32nd Division which fought it first battle -- Buna in New Guinea.
>
> After a few months of fighting, and after the objective was taken, we again returned to Australia where my hospital unit operated a Hospital Train. We once more returned to New Guinea after four months of Train work.
>
> From then on we traveled up along the whole coast of New Guinea until preparations were made for the Philippine invasion. We then went to the Admiralty Islands and from there onto the last objective, the Philippines.
>
> Yes, I went in there the 20th of October last year, with the first forces to hit that country. It was a swell show, all in our favor. That's something I'll never forget as long as I live. I believe I've seen enough to last me the rest of my living days.
>
> Where I'll go after my return to Miami, Florida, I can't say because I don't know, but wherever it may be, I'm sure I'll do my part.

Sources: Marie Jaszewski, wife; Independence News-Wave; Books (Stanton) (Milner)

NICHOLAS B. JASZEWSKI
UNITED STATES ARMY

Nick Jaszewski had completed three years of pre-medicine and two years of medical school at Marquette University, Milwaukee, Wisconsin, when he enlisted in the United States Army on September 20, 1943. He entered active service ten days later and attended Medical Department Basic Training, though the location of this training is unknown. Having been previously trained in pathology, anatomy, biochemistry, bacteriology, pharmocology, and other aspects of medicine, Nick was then sent to the Medical Department Technician School at Lawson General Hospital, Atlanta, Georgia, for 16 weeks where he learned to apply his knowledge to military situations. Lawson was an amputation center where casualties from all fronts were brought. He was a Private First Class, Clerk General until June 1944, when he was promoted to Technician 4th Grade and became a Medical Laboratory Technician. Prior to his embarking for Europe, there is evidence that he was stationed at Camp Grant, near Rockford, Illinois, which was a Medical Replacement Unit Training Center.

On October 12, 1944, Nick left the United States bound for France where he was assigned to the 196th General Hospital. While there, he was in charge of a blood bank, his duties including drawing, processing, and transfusing blood, as well as testing blood for various diseases. He also assisted at autopsies and did work in the pathology, serology, bacteriology, hematology, and chemistry departments of the hospital. A photograph taken in March 1945 places Nick in Carentan, France, a small city of 4,000 that was a major target of the Allied invasion of Normandy in June 1944.

Nick Jaszewski, center, with buddies Milt Cornwell, left, of Hudson, Wisconsin, and John McLaughlin, right, taken somewhere in France.

On March 1, 1945, Nick, who obviously had a real sense of history, wrote a lengthy letter to his mother in which he vividly described a trip to Mont-Saint Michel. The *News-Wave* introduced the letter, which it published on April 5, 1945, by stating, "It (Mont-Saint Michel) is a village of Brittany on an island in the Bay of Cancole and has a population of 2,700. The island is now connected with the mainland by a causeway. The abbey was later a fortress and afterward part of it a prison and is one of the most picturesque and curious monuments of the middle ages. Low tide recedes there for seven miles. Cpl. Jaszewski's letter will tell in detail about this historic spot. It is as follows:"

Hello Mom and Home --

Haven't heard from you in ages. Mom -- last letter I got was dated 12 Jan., and I got it about a month ago. I've managed to write to you once or twice per week so far, but chances are I'll be forced to slow down for a while -- you know why.

Must tell you about my trip to the historic La Mont St. Michael last Sunday.

Chapter 1 -- Departure and Arrival

Some 40 of our officers and men (39 men and one officer) assembled in front of the detachment area early Sunday morning and after a roll call, typical army fashion, packed into two "6x6" carryalls and a jeep, which comprised our convoy, and when I say "packed" I mean just that because when you consider that besides 20 men, each truck had to pack the noon lunch for its men, you realize we must have been packed pretty tight in that 6x6. But we didn't mind it one bit for we were at last going to visit a spot in France about which we had read in McMaster's History way back in the grades. The trip to the Mont was for the most part uneventful, except for getting lost in a few towns, only because we chose the wrong street at a crossroad, and also the numerous effects of the invasion last June -- craters, wrecked buildings and smashed Nazi tanks. But when we approached the vicinity of the sea shore we were able to see the Mont glistening in the bright rays of the early morning sun, its abbey bedecked summit looking very much like a dream castle in fairyland. The closer we came, the more massive and majestic the Mont became and it seemed to cast its ancient spell upon our excited, curiosity crazed minds. Finally we had passed the narrow isthmus which connects the Mont with the mainland of France at low tide, and were just outside of the wall of Mont St. Michel.

Chapter II -- The Wall and the Village

Almost immediately we were ushered to a tunnel which led us through the 15 ft. thick, ancient stone wall which surrounds the rock -- permit me to deviate a second here to explain the wall. In ancient times, every little hamlet, every castle, every stronghold was protected by a rampart. So, too, was and is, Mont. St. Michel. Its particular wall is some 30 feet thick and is wide enough on top for 5 men to walk comfortably abreast, as you see by the picture I am enclosing. Its top edge seems to be picketed. This, I suppose, was for added protection. Now back to my story. Our duck walk through the wall, for we had to crouch low to pass through the tunnel, led us right into the center of a neat little old French Hamlet with its one street so narrow and crooked we knew it could be no other place but France. Especially since the street was typically cobblestone. The street winds its way up the Mont terminating in a series of steps leading to the front entrance of the Abbey on the summit of the Mont. It is lined on either side by hotels, and curio shops. We passed these by rather hurriedly as we were mostly interested in the tour of the Abbey and prison.

Chapter III - La Abbe De Mont St. Michel

We were met at the entrance of the Abbey by a French woman who was to be our guide. First she told us to look back at the street below us and explained that the spot we came through the tunnel was some 220 ft. below. Now she said to look at the statue of St. Michael perched atop the steeple of the Abbey. This she said was 450 ft. above the ground. With this awe inspiring message she took a huge key and unlocked a massive wooden door which brought us directly into the main hall of the Abbey in which she pointed out four distinct types of Ancient Architecture. There were numerous Niches, where I suppose, altars had been placed and Masses celebrated. This scene made us feel as though suddenly time had moved backwards and we were living in the 12th Century, visiting the Abbey with King Louis XI for the Abbey is now some 700 years old, having been built during the 13th century. Indeed, it put us in the proper mood to continue the tour. Next the guide took out another huge key and opened another heavy wooden door. We walked down a short flight of steps and emerged into another massive room whose extremely high ceiling was supported by thick stone pillars. This, the guide explained, was the Monks dining room and unlike other parts of the building, was unrestored, the same since 12 hundred 30. Connected with the room was a veranda where the Monks used to spend many an hour watching the angry ocean lash at the rock some 250 ft. below. I suppose many a famous Monk, possibly even a few Saints, had stood on the same spot that we now were on. We were unfortunate in one thing. The tide was low and the ocean didn't come up to the rocks. After a few moments of silent meditation here we visited two more dining halls and a huge kitchen, passed through the "Tunnel of Pillars" and came onto a huge tread wheel placed just inside a panel of the thick wall, the ledge of which was connected to a steep incline stretching all the way to the

64

bottom of the Mont. This wheel was run by six men who pulled two tons of provisions up the incline daily in times when the Abbey flourished. Almost unbelievable, but nevertheless true. From here we were led into the Monk's library which now serves as the Abbey's museum. The murals decorating its walls are as impressive as they are ancient, giving an excellent picture of 13th century art. In the museum cases we beheld such sacred objects as rosaries, medals, crucifixes, soles of famous Monks sandals, manuscripts and old prayer books found in the Abbey at various times. This concluded the tour of the Abbey and we were turned over to another guide.

Chapter IV -- La Prison De Monte St. Michel

For some reason, perhaps because of the eeriness of our next tour or woman-power shortages, our next guide was a man. He led us down seemingly endless flights of stairs until we finally came into a dingy dungeon -- the prison of the mont -- where political prisoners were kept. The first thing to meet our awe popping eyes was a group of wax figures representing the Norman invasion of 800 A. D., for it was right at the base of the Mont that the Normans struck. They looked so real we almost expected to hear the shouts of the men. The French, you know, are noted for the exactness of their wax models. In the next cell stood St. Michael for whom the Mont and Abbey were named. He, too, looked real even down to a two days growth of beard. In his hand he clutched a crucifix, which is a real relic of St. Mike. The next cell held King Louis XI and his courtiers all as lifelike as the others. Next was St. Aubert who had the vision to build the Abbey. His figure is in the kneeling position and his face is perfectly beautiful. Now come the political prisoners, each chained down in his own four ft. cell, one hunched over, a gory look in his face; another reading a book; a third lying in agony, rats having chewed one-half his body away, just as they found him one morning, and in a pit a mass of human bones -- some still chained to the wall and others crumbling away. This dungeon with its realistic gruesomeness was by itself worth the trip here. Now we were led up a series of steps to a brighter room which contained things as Napoleon's sword, the flags of Louis XVI and XV, ancient guns, watches and pictures, an old French chest with nine locks all turned by one key, etc. Our tour of the museum ended with a view of the Mont through an old submarine periscope taken off a French vessel of the 1888 model.

Chapter V -- French Wine and Beer

Now we felt free to roam the village until time came to go home. We stopped into a cafe and had beer -- almost as good as American, too. Next we shopped around the souvenirs and then had some wine in a hotel lobby overlooking the sea. All that was lacking was a juke box, but perhaps that would have broken the spell cast upon us by the antiquity of the Mont.

The trip home was uneventful, but as we left the Mont behind we felt we had seen something great. We had lived with King Louis XI; we had made the pilgrimage to the Shrine of St. Michael along with Charlamagne; we had meditated and prayed with the Monks; we had condemned prisoners who had dared to defy the law. Soon the spires of the Abbey had vanished into the golden rays of a setting sun -- melted away like the fairy castle we had first seen. We reached camp at a reasonable hour with a full and satisfied feeling.

Well, Mom, that's it. Miss you all very much. Write often. Work is going alright. I'm really well, happy and healthy. Got a letter from Wally. He's still in Belgium. Say hello to everybody.

Be good. God Bless you and keep you.

Love,
Nicky

While in the service, Nick received the American Theater Service Medal, European-African-Middle Eastern Service Medal, two Overseas Service Bars, and Good Conduct Medal. He arrived back in the United States on January 1, 1946, and received his separation from the Army on April 6, 1946 at the Camp McCoy, Wisconsin, Separation Center.

Sources: Bernadine Jaszewski, wife; Maria Jaszewski, daughter; Independence News-Wave

RALPH J. JONIETZ
UNITED STATES ARMY

The following narrative is taken from a letter received from Ralph J. Jonietz in 1998 regarding his military service during World War II.

I was inducted into the Army in Whitehall, Wisconsin, on April 24, 1944. My basic training was at Camp Hood, Texas, during that summer, and I could never imagine that it could get so hot! I was designated as an infantry replacement and joined Company I, 3rd Battalion, 397th Regiment, 100th Division,[1] in November 1944. I don't remember the exact date. I went overseas on the *S. S. Thomas H. Barry*, landing in France on Omaha Beach. This was actually several months after the Overlord (Ed. - D-Day) landing occurred.

Near the village of Ingwiller, France, on Hill 296, I was wounded by shrapnel in the shoulder.[2] This was on December 2, 1944. When I got hurt, I crawled down the hill until I reached a foxhole at the base of the hill. I don't know how long I had been in this foxhole when a jeep came along and took me to the battalion aid station. From there I went to the 116th Evacuation Hospital where I had surgery to remove the shrapnel and reset the shoulder. They were unsuccessful in removing the shrapnel so I was transported to the 36th General Hospital in Dijon, France, where I again had surgery to remove the piece. Again they were unsuccessful. In fact, the shrapnel was never removed.

One day a nurse came by and told me that I was going home to a hospital in Wisconsin to try yet again to remove the shrapnel. I was very happy. I went to the 43rd General Hospital in Marseilles, France, to await a ship to take me home. While there, I was passing through a ward one day when I saw someone I knew. It was Leonard Nysven, who had gone into the service with me. He was going home, too. He pulled back the covers to show me his missing leg.

Eventually my orders were changed, however, and I did not go home. I was very disappointed with this at the time. It turned out fine, though, as I went to a stockade as a prison guard at the 19th Replacement Depot in Etampes, France. I really did not like being a prison guard so when I heard that there was an opening as a clerk typist, I applied and got the assignment.

While at Etampes, we slept in six-man tents. One morning, about 2:00 A. M., someone woke me up. It was Everett Bautch, known back home as "Iky." I don't know how he ever found me. I got a leave and we spent some time together.

The complete stockade was eventually moved to the Paris Detention Barracks and became part of the 787th Military Police Battalion. As I had been a clerk typist at Etampes, I was given the job of typing court orders.

At the time the war ended, I had a European-African-Middle Eastern Theater Ribbon with one battle star for the Rhineland campaign, a Combat Infantry Badge, the Purple Heart, and a Bronze Star. I probably should have had an oak leaf cluster with the Purple Heart because I had a bullet crease my lower lip earlier on the same day I received the shrapnel wound. But I was so

---

[1] The 100th Infantry Division suffered 883 killed and 3,539 wounded, of which another 101 died from their wounds, during its European Theater campaigns.

[2] The 100th Infantry Division had landed at Marseilles, France, on October 20, 1944, entering combat at St. Remy in the Vosges Mountains on November 1, 1944. After relieving the 45th Infantry Division, it attacked on November 12, 1944, with Ralph's 397th Infantry Regiment and the 399th Infantry crossing the Meuthe River at Baccarat in a flanking maneuver. A German counterattack was repulsed on November 13, 1944, and Raon-l'Etape was taken on November 18, 1944 after the 397th overcame the Quarry Strongpoint. After taking Moyonmoutier and St. Blaise, the Vosges advance was halted on November 26, 1944. The Division then relieved the 44th Infantry Division near Saarebourg on November 27, 1944. Ralph was wounded one day before the Division began its push on Bitche.

glad to get out of there that I wasn't thinking of anyoak leaf cluster!

I came home aboard the *S. S. Mexico* in May, 1946, as a Private First Class and received my discharge at Camp McCoy, Wisconsin.

On February 15, 1945, an article in the *News-Wave* reported Ralph had recently been able to use his right arm to write a short letter to editor Glenn Kirkpatrick. However, it stated it would be some time before the injured arm would be healed completely. The letter was dated January 1, 1945 from France, and seems to be referring to Ralph's having received the "Special Serviceman's Edition" of the paper while recovering from his wounds of December 2, 1944:

Dear Mr. Kirkpatrick:

I am writing you this letter to thank you for the News-Wave that I received this morning. It was the first one I've received since I've been in France and it sure is good to know what the people at home are doing. Keep them coming.

I also see that Stanley Ressel is in a hospital in England. It was a surprise to me because we were in the same camps together in the States and came over here together. It's quite a coincidence because I'm in a hospital, too, only I'm still here in France.

We have below zero weather here with plenty of snow. Haven't been to any French cities as yet. All I've seen of France is mud and cold. I really don't care much about visiting Paris and other places. All I'm waiting for is to get back to good old Independence.

Ralph Jonietz

Ralph remained in Europe with the Army of Occupation following the war. On December 27, 1945, the *News-Wave* published a letter he had written from Etampes, France, on December 8, 1945 -- his 21st birthday, it seems -- that described his dislike for his current duties:

Dear Mom, Pop and Roger:

Well, here I am 21 and still over here. I sure do hope that I don't have to spend another birghday or Christmas over here. I and a bunch of the fellows here went to town last night but didn't do much celebrating because it was too cold. We have a GI club here and that's where we went. They only sell American beer and Coca Cola there. They had the orchestra play happy birthday for me. I thought it was very nice of the fellows. I got a hand from the crowd and had to get up and take a bow.

Today we had another attempted escape, but guards stopped them before they got away. I wish that they would have shot them because it's just on account of them that we have to be over here and the guys that we're getting in here now are all ex-criminals in civilian life. They're no good, none of them.

I'm OK so don't worry about me. I'm still at the same old job. Boy, I'd really hate to be out in that cold on guard.

Here's some poetry for you.

AMERICAN MOTHERS
America's mothers are brave and true,
America's mothers are strong.
They are the red, white, the blue,
They are the nation's song.
Red for the blood of America's pride,
Flowing in tireless veins.
Working for victory, side by side,
Turning the wheels and cranes.
White for the uniform on the field,
White by the hospital bed,
Healing the warrior on his shield,
Whispering prayers for the dead.

Blue for the stars the banners unfold,
        When sons and daughters are gone,
Blue for the stars that turn to gold,
        In the mist of a silent dawn.
They are the women who gave us birth,
        And the women who bear our sons,
Sharing our destiny over the earth,
        Guiding our souls and our guns.
They are the song of the liberty bell,
        Answering America's call,
They re the women we love so well,
        God bless and protect them all.

Well, today is Sunday the 9th. I didn't get to finish the letter yesterday so I will today. There isn't much more news. I am in the office all today as there isn't much to do except answer phone calls. Today is visitors' day here so there will be a lot of French women coming in to see the prisoners. How do you like that ? The prisoners can have visitors come to see them and we can't. If there would be anybody come to see us they send them away. The other day, too, the prisoners had ice cream with their meal and we didn't. In fact, the prisoners are treated better all the way around than we are.

It's another cold day here. It snowed a little last night but not much. I guess that will be all for this time: more next.

        All my love,
        Your son and brother,
        Ralph

Photo received following initial publication can be found on page 347 of this volume.
Sources: Independence News-Wave; Book (Stanton)

LAWRENCE "LAURY" J. KAMPA
UNITED STATES ARMY AIR CORPS

This edited narrative was written following an interview with Laury Kampa at his Independence home on July 13, 1998.

I enlisted in the Army Air Corps on February 11, 1944 while I was still in high school. I graduated that spring and was finally called to active duty on August 3, 1944 at Fort Sheridan, Illinois. Then I went by train to Sheppard Field, Texas, for basic training. I actually wanted to be an aircraft navigator but apparently they didn't need any at the time so I attended radio school at Truax Field in Madison, Wisconsin. I specialized in radio communications as a radio mechanic. From Madison, I went to Scott Field, Illinois, then back to Sheppard Field where, after sitting around camp for awhile, they sent us on a bivouac. We realized later why it happened this way -- dropping the A-bomb on Japan changed the whole picture.

I finally received orders for overseas so I traveled to Camp Shanks, New York. On November 5, 1945, I headed for Europe aboard the *U. S. S. George Washington.* I learned sometime afterward that the *George Washington* burned while at Newport News, Virginia.

We arrived in Europe on November 15, 1945, landing at Le Havre, France, where I was attached to Det. 313, 763 AAF B(ase) U(nit) (133rd AACS Sq.), which was an Army Airways Communication System unit. We stayed for a time at the famous Chateau-Thierry. Then we traveled by train to Frankfurt, Germany, where we saw a lot of damage along the way. It seemed like everything was destroyed. From then on, I was assigned to the 762nd AAF Base Unit, headquartered at Bad Soden, where two of us maintained a range station up in the mountains until it was time to go home.

I went back to France, to Camp Phillip Morris, but it was filled up, so we were sent to stay in a hotel in Paris, where we had good time for six days. Then I boarded a Liberty Ship on June 15, 1946 and headed back to Camp Kilmer, New Jersey. We landed there on June 23, were processed at Camp Kilmer, New Jersey, and then traveled to Fort Sheridan where on June 29, 1946 I was separated from the Army Air Corps and came home.

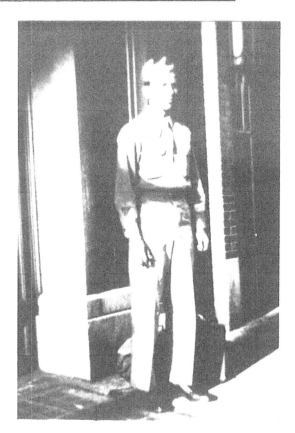

Lawrence "Laury" Kampa

Louis P. Kampa

LOUIS P. KAMPA
UNITED STATES ARMY

Louis Kampa was inducted into the United States Army on June 18, 1941 and entered active service that same day in Milwaukee, Wisconsin. Following basic training, he was attached to a heavy artillery gun crew and sent to the Pacific Theater in October 1941. In the December 11, 1941 edition of the *News-Wave*, Louis was reportedly stationed in the Aleutian Islands. Though it is unclear whether he served there throughout his time in the Pacific, it is known that he didn't return to the United States until March 1, 1944. On February 18, 1945, Louis left the States once again, this time for the European Theater, where he remained until September 10, 1945.

In both the Pacific and European Theaters, Louis served as a member of an eight-inch howitzer gun crew. He was trained to set horizontal angles for the gun, manipulate the traverse wheel, place the gun on target, make changes in deflection as directed, and transfer fire to other targets. He also was responsible for inspecting, cleaning, oiling, and making minor repairs and adjustments to the guns. Additionally, he became familiar with tactical employment of the howitzer, as well.

In Europe, Louis landed in Italy on March 1, 1945, where he was assigned to one of the 88th Infantry Division's artillery battalions,[1] though exactly which one is unclear. The 88th Infantry launched its attack on the Bologna, Italy, area on April 15, 1945, fighting the "Battle for Mount Monterumici" the following two days. By April 23, 1945, it had reached the Po River near Carbonarai, in the process capturing large numbers of German troops before they could cross the river and escape. Crossing the Po River on April 24, 1945, the Division then captured Verona and Vicenza, from where it continued its advance by crossing the Brenta River on April 30, 1945. It was racing towards Innsbruck, Austria, via the Dolomite Alps when the German Army in Italy surrendered on May 2, 1945.

Louis participated in the North Appenines campaign while in Italy and was awarded the European-African-Middle Eastern Theater Ribbon with a bronze battle star for that campaign. He also was awarded the American Defense Service Ribbon, five Overseas Service Bars, one Service Stripe, and the Good Conduct Medal. He arrived back in the United States on September 30, 1945, as a Private First Class and member of Company B, 351st Infantry Regiment, and was separated from the Army on October 13, 1945, at the Fort Sheridan, Illinois, Separation Center.

---

[1] The 88th Infantry Division, which included Louis' artillery unit, suffered 2,298 killed and 9,225 wounded, of which 258 died of their wounds, during World War II.

Sources: Vitus Kampa, nephew; Book (Stanton)

APOLINARY J. KARASCH
UNITED STATES ARMY

Apolinary "A. J." Karasch was inducted into the United States Army on August 13, 1942. From Fort Sheridan, Illinois, he was sent to Warner Robbins Army Air Corps Training Center for basic training in the Army Air Corps. Following basic, he was stationed with the South Eastern Training Command, which covered states from east of the Mississippi River to the Atlantic Ocean. With the Command, he was stationed at a major headquarters of the 384th Air Service Group.

He remained with the 384th until receiving orders for overseas shipment, at which time he traveled to Texas in the fall of 1944 to prepare for departure. He left the States by ship, crossed the Pacific, and traveled along the north coast of New Guinea before arriving at Tacloban, Leyte Island, Phillippine Islands. A. J. served in an Army Class B Finance Office on Leyte where he was in charge of three other men; his duties involved readying payrolls and ensuring the troops received their pay. But he also at times took his turn with guard duty, household and mess hall duties, and church duties, as well.

On March 8, 1945, the *News-Wave* published a letter received by A. J.'s parents, Mr. and Mrs. John Karasch, that he had written on February 5, 1945, describing his first few days on the Philippine Islands. At this time, A. J. held the rank of Staff Sergeant:

Hello to all:
I finally have found a little spare time to be able to write a letter. I know you have been wondering what has happened since you haven't heard from me for some time. But it takes a little time before one gets settled.

70

We landed several days ago and have been very busy ever since getting things in order and set up. When we got off our trucks it was pouring rain. There was mud almost ankle deep everywhere and in some places, a lot deeper. Fortunately it isn't raining and we were able to set up our pup tents. We got some sticks, bamboo poles, leaves, and grass together in one pile on the ground and that was our mattress. Over that we set up our pup tents. They are our bedroom, living room, dining room and guest room. The tent leaked the first night but we took care of that the next day. We are supposed to get large tents any time, but the way things look we don't know when we will get them. We are still eating K-rations but we will have warm meals as soon as the kitchen is set up.

We find the place very interesting, although there is a lot of work. It has been awful hot during the day but it cools off nicely at night. It's liable to rain most anytime. We get some every day. The place is very green since they have so much rain. The place is full of cocoanut trees and we have all the cocoanut we want. The people are very friendly and most of them speak English - not too good but one can get along well with them. They are very poor. The army hires many of them and pays a common laborer 63 cents for an eight-hour day of labor and a meal of rice. They are much smaller than we are and think that we just roll in money. Most of their clothes were given to them by the soldiers. The Japs, when they left, took practically everything they had. Their houses, what we have seen where we are, are of bamboo poles and cocoanut leaves. But, poor as they are, they keep themselves very clean. I can't understand how they can do it, but they sure do. For plowing they use a water buffalo and everything else. It looks very much like an ox but it's a lot smaller. There are Japs buried everywhere in the area where we are.

Most of the people are Catholic, but I haven't had a chance to go and see their church. We went past it and it is very large.

I am sending some money which was used here when the Japanese were here. A Philippino dollar is worth two of ours. There isn't any place to spend very much money, so the less one has the better off he is.

I have received all of your letters up to January 15. It's better to send regular letters than V-mail.

We could use some of that cold weather you are having. We can walk around in shorts all day - it's warm enough. At night we have to have something on for the mosquitoes are very bad. We sleep under nets.

I hope that you all are feeling as good as I am.

Bye,
"Paul"

Sometime late in the war, A. J. was sent to the island of Mindoro in the Philippines on temporary duty and he was there when the war ended. He then returned to his unit on Leyte where he remained until being transferred to Kyushi, Japan, as part of the Army of Occupation within a few days after peace was declared. At one point, he was sent from Japan to Okinawa, where he was caught in a powerful typhoon that he described as "a frightening experience," before returning once again to Japan.

In early 1946, A. J. left Japan aboard a troopship headed for San Francisco, California. From there he traveled by troop train to Camp McCoy, Wisconsin, where he was separated from the Army on February 8, 1946. He had spent 4 years, 6 months in the service, all of it in the Army Air Corps Finance Section. He earned the Asiatic-Pacific Campaign Medal, American Campaign Medal, Good Conduct Medal, Philippine Presidential Citation Medal, Philippine Liberation Medal, World War II Victory Medal, and Japan Army of Occupation Medal.

Following the war, A. J. remained with the Air Force Reserve and Wisconsin Army National Guard, serving with the 32nd "Red Arrow" Infantry Division's Quartermaster and Field Artillery branches. In 1960, he was recalled to active duty in connection with the Berlin Crisis. In 1974, he retired from the military while holding the rank of Major.

Sources: Personal letter; Independence News-Wave

Top: A. J. Karasch, left, in front of tent.
Right: A. J. Karasch, sitting on rock on the
right, in front of a shot-up building in
Kanoya, Japan, 1945.

Left: Vince Karasch.
Below: Vince Karasch aboard U. S. S. Stevens
during trip home from Italy, December, 1944.
He is standing prominently just below center.

The Karasch Brothers

VINCENT KARASCH
UNITED STATES ARMY

The following narrative was prepared from an interview with Vince Karasch at his home in Independence on July 10, 1998, and through notes provided by him.

I was drafted on June 16, 1945 through the induction center in Milwaukee, Wisconsin. That was following my junior year in high school. I received my shots, my G. I. haircut, and was issued my military clothing, and then boarded a troop train to the infantry training center at Fort McClellan, Alabama. I began my basic training on June 24, 1945. Weston Cooke of Lookout was in basic training with me.

I was a private in Company D, 27th Battalion, following completion of my 17 weeks of basic. I was promoted to Private First Class and sent home on leave for 11 days. Because my father was very ill at the time, I received a 10-day extension of my leave.

On December 1, 1945, I left for Naples, Italy, arriving there on December 11, 1945. I was assigned to the 337th Quartermaster's Depot Company at Tombolo, Italy, which is midway between Leghorn and Pisa. My duties included the shipping of rations to various army camps in Europe. Because I was in the occupation forces, I received the European Theater Operations Medal and the World War II Victory Medal.

While I was having coffee and a doughnut in a Red Cross club on a Sunday afternoon in January 1946, Roman "Cooky" Kuka walked in. We saw each other every other weekend after that. I spent a 10-day leave in Switzerland in June 1946, traveling through Lugano, Lucerne, Bern, Lausanne, and Lake Geneva.

I was boarding the Liberty Ship *U. S. S. Stevens* for home when I spotted Ralph Sobota leaving the ship. He was arriving to spend his service time in Italy. For my trip home, the *Stevens* had 1,175 men aboard. When they announced they were taking photos of the men aboard, I got myself into a good spot where I would recognize myself. Of course, everyone was dressed alike and I would have never been able to pick myself out otherwise. Sure enough, when I got my photos, I could see myself easily in one of them!

I left Livorno, Italy, on December 11, 1946 and arrived in New York Harbor on December 24, 1946, at 4:00 P. M., Christmas Eve. We were sent to Camp Kilmer, New York. But Roman Kuka's ship arrived at 5:00 P. M. that day so those guys had to spend Christmas Eve aboard ship. His Liberty Ship, the *U. S. S. Newbern*, brought 1,228 men home from Leghorn, Italy.

From Camp Kilmer we were sent by troop train to the Separation Center at Fort Sheridan, Illinois. I received my discharge from the Army on January 29, 1947 as a Tech 4. I then completed my high school education with the senior class of 1947.

EUGENE A. KILLIAN
UNITED STATES ARMY

Eugene Killian entered service with the United States Army on March 9, 1943 and was sent for his basic training to Camp Roberts, a large infantry and field artillery replacement training center near San Miguel, California. On April 8, 1943, a brief note appeared in the *News-Wave* concerning a letter received by his parents. In it, Eugene stated that he was beginning basic training, that he liked army life, and that meals were "just as good as at home."

In July 1943, Eugene was sent to India, arriving September 10, 1943, where he was stationed for a year at Ramghar. Since his job involved training Chinese soldiers in the use of vehicles and other equipment, he first attended classes to learn the difficult Chinese language. From Ramghar, Eugene was transferred to Kunming, China, and this was followed by a transfer to Chanyi, China, where he again trained Chinese recruits while serving with the 3428th Ordnance Company.

The November 9, 1944 *News-Wave* announced Eugene had been promoted to the rank of Tech 5 for his excellent work in Hihar Province, India, where he was teaching American combat methods to the Chinese.

On October 4, 1945, the *News-Wave* carried the news that Eugene had been wounded in action in the China-Burma-India Theater. An article regarding his discharge, appearing January 24, 1946, stated that he was hospitalized in Kunming, China, for two months before returning to the United States aboard a plane that seems to have made many stops along its circuitous route. Mitchano, Burma; Calcutta, Agrar and Karachi, India; Oran, Persia; Cairo, Egypt; Tripoli and Casablanca, North Africa; the Azores, Bermuda; and finally, Miami Beach, Florida, were all identified as points where the plane touched down. From Miami Beach, Eugene was transported to O'Riley General Hospital in Springfield, Missouri, where he received additional hospital care for another month before traveling to Fort Custer, Michigan. He also spent a 40-day furlough at home with his parents following his return to the States.

The *News-Wave* of December 13, 1945 announced that Eugene had been discharged on December 4, 1945 at Fort Custer. Again it was mentioned he had been wounded in the China-Burma-India Theater.

In the January 24, 1946 article, it states that Eugene had run into Addison Hotchkiss of Independence while in India.

No photo.
Source: Independence News-Wave

RAYMOND S. KLICK
UNITED STATES ARMY

Ray Klick was inducted into the United States Army on May 15, 1942 in Milwaukee, Wisconsin, as part of Trempealeau County's May selective service quota, and entered active service that same day. It is not clear where he underwent basic training, but it probably was at Camp Shelby, Mississippi, where the 85th Division was being formed. Following his three months of basic training, he was promoted to Private First Class and began training as a light truck driver. He also qualified in the use of several different weapons, earning an expert's badge with the .30-caliber light machine gun, sharpshooter's badge with the submachine gun, and marksman's badge with a rifle. On August 1, 1942, the 85th Division was redesignated as the 85th Infantry Division,[1] and Ray was assigned duty with the Division's 85th Reconnaissance Troop, Mechanized, also known as a Cavalry Recon Troop.

On April 6, 1943, the 85th Infantry Division began moving to the Louisiana Maneuver Area where it participated in the Third Army's No. 2 Louisiana Maneuvers. It then moved to Camp Young, California, on June 23, 1943, where it took part in the Desert Training Center No. 3 California Maneuvers. Following that exercise, the Division traveled to Fort Dix, New Jersey, on October 7, 1943, then staged at Camp Patrick Henry, Virginia, on December 18, 1943, where it

---

[1] The 85th Infantry Division suffered 1,561 killed and 6,314 wounded, of which 175 died from their wounds, during its three campaigns in Italy.

prepared for overseas shipment. With transports loaded, the Division began departing the Hampton Roads Port of Embarkation for North Africa on December 24, 1943, arriving at Casablanca, Morocco, beginning January 2, 1944. Ray's personnel records indicate that he, probably with his Recon Troop, left Hampton Roads on December 29, 1943, and arrived in Casablanca on January 7, 1944.

The 85th Infantry Division underwent amphibious training at Port aux Poules in North Africa from February 1 through March 23, 1944. It then embarked for Italy, landing at Naples over a twelve day period beginning March 15, 1944. By April 10, 1944, the Division was in the line west of Minturno where it held defensive positions for a month north of the Garigliano River and in front of the *Gustav Line*.[2] On May 11, 1944, it began its attack. Through the rest of that month, the 85th Infantry Division took mountain positions and villages held by strong German forces, encountering heavy fighting throughout, and suffering a few setbacks and many casualties. On May 24, 1944, the Division's 337th Infantry Regiment entered the evacuated city of Terracina following extensive combat, thereby opening the road to the Anzio beachhead. From here, the Division pursued the retreating Germans into the hills west of Priverno, and by the end of May had relieved the Anzio-battered 3rd Infantry Division which was then assigned as the garrison force in Rome following the Allied occupation of that city.

Without hesitating, the 85th Infantry continued its attack on May 31, 1944, breaching the Mt. Artemisio and town of Lariano defenses. With its forward drive in high gear, the Division sped along Via Tuscolana, passed through Rome on June 5, 1944, and reached the Viterbo River where it was relieved on June 10, 1944. Following a well-deserved rest, it then took over the Arno River Line, relieved the *New Zealand 2nd Division* near Montelupo on August 16, 1944, and joined with the 91st Infantry Division south of Fucecchio on August 18, 1944.

On September 13, 1944, the 85th Infantry began its attack on the Il Giogo Pass of the *Gothic Line*.[3] Numerous battles ensued to take individual mountains where the Germans had emplaced their artillery, but on September 18, 1944, the *Gothic Line* was broken and the Germans began hastily retreating. They were pursued into the adjacent valleys, across the Santerno River and beyond, where more towns and mountain defenses were overcome by the American army despite rainy, muddy conditions, occasional heavily entrenched German opposition, and counterattacks. On October 24, 1944, the 85th Infantry Division reached Mt. Mezzano overlooking the Po Valley. Two days later it halted its offensive and was given defensive duties near Pizzano for nearly a month beginning October 27, 1944. On November 23, 1944, it was relieved for rehabilitation before entering into the Po Valley offensive.

During the time of January 9-17, 1945, the 85th Infantry Division relieved the *British 1st Division* in the Mt. Grande area. On March 18, 1945, it was placed in reserve status, and then relieved the American 1st Armored Division on April 17, 1945. It attacked toward Gesso and reached the outskirts of Bologna, Italy, on April 20, 1945. As German resistance collapsed in the Po Valley, the Division moved quickly, crossing the Panaro River at Camposanto on April 22, 1945 over a bridge left intact by the retreating Germans. Reaching the Po River at Quingentole, it easily established a bridgehead there on April 23-24, 1945. It then crossed the Adige River near Verona, Italy, on April 26, 1945, and five days later began clearing the Piave Valley of Germans. Hostilities ended for the 85th Infantry Division on May 2, 1945, when the German army in Italy surrendered.

During the 85th Infantry Division's drive through Italy, Ray served ably with his 85th Cavalry Recon Troop. He drove trucks up to 2-1/2 ton capacity, as well as jeeps when necessary. The trucks he drove carried a variety of cargos -- ammunition, personnel, and other supplies -- of

---

[2] The *Gustav Line* was the name given to the formidable barrier of defense offered by the Italian Alps as they stretched across Italy from Tyrrhenian to the Adriatic Sea.

[3] The *Gothic Line* was a 150-mile defensive line along the northern Apennines Mountains extending across Italy from Pesaro on the Adriatic Coast west to the mountains north of Pisa. Consisting of a massive collection of concrete defensive emplacements and bunkers, tank traps, embedded steel turrets, barbed wire, and mines, it formed a serious threat to the American's entry into the Po Valley.

up to five tons at times. He was also familiar with the function and repair of those vehicles, as were all drivers, so that the flow of men and materiels could continue unabated.

The 85th Infantry Division left Italy in August, 1945, but a month earlier Ray had been assigned as a liaison agent in Italy and therefore remained in the country until October 22, 1945. On that day his transport pulled out of an Italian port, arriving at the Hampton Roads Port of Embarkation on November 3, 1945. Six days later, on November 9, 1945, Ray was separated from the United States Army at the Camp Grant, Illinois, Separation Center. During his nearly three-and-a-half years in the service, Ray had participated in the Rome-Arno, Northern Apennines, and Po Valley campaigns. He was awarded the American Campaign Medal, European-African-Middle Eastern Theater Ribbon with three bronze battle stars, one Service Stripe, three Overseas Service Bars, the Good Conduct Medal, and World War II Victory Medal.

No photo.
Sources: Mrs. Raymond Klick; Book (Stanton)

RALPH S. KLIMEK
UNITED STATES ARMY

Ralph Klimek entered the United States Army on March 21, 1943 following a year in the Civilian Conservation Corps at Hixton, Wisconsin. He received his basic training at Camp Roberts, San Miguel, California, and then spent time at Camp Stoneman, near Pittsburg, California. Following this training, he received a short furlough and was soon after sent to the Southwest Pacific.

In early March 1942, the Japanese had captured Rangoon, the heart of Burma in the China-Burma-India Theater, as well as the vital Burma Road. General Joseph Stilwell, commander of Allied forces in Burma, led the mixed force of American, British, and Chinese out of the jungles and eventually found his way to India from where he vowed to retake Burma. For their part, the Japanese were determined to hold Burma with its wealth of raw materials and stationed five divisions there, including the battle-tested *18th Division*, the conquerors of Singapore and Malaya. Within a year, General Stilwell was ready to begin what many considered an impossible task by carving roads out of the jungle and inserting special espionage, sabotage, and intelligence units. British Major General Orde Wingate led penetration units, the famed Chindits, in probes against the Japanese forces, at the same time experimenting with radio-directed air drops of supplies.

In May 1943, President Franklin Roosevelt and British Prime Minister Winston Churchill decided the European Theater would take precedence and agreed to keep the Japanese guessing in the Pacific by initiating small-scale actions throughout the region, thus buying the time necessary to build for a full-scale assault. At the Quadrant Conference in Quebec, Canada, in August 1943, Roosevelt and Churchill decided the Americans would form an all-volunteer force modeled after the Chindit brigade whose mission would be to penetrate and operate deep inside the Japanese lines in Burma. The plan was code-named "Galahad."

Within weeks a Presidential call for volunteers was made on bases throughout the country, in the Caribbean, and in the Pacific and Southwest Pacific regions. The directive from the War Department requesting volunteers informed all who heard it that this would be "a dangerous and hazardous mission." Approximately 2,900 men responded to the call.

Camp Stoneman was the gathering point for the San Francisco Port of Embarkation to the Pacific and since Ralph Klimek was in California, and specifically Camp Stoneman, when this unit was being formed, it is probable he volunteered for the unit at that time and probably was aboard the *S. S. Lurline* when it departed San Francisco on September 21, 1943. The men didn't know where they were going and they hadn't been told about "Galahad." The whole operation was so highly classified the *Lurline* didn't even have escort, instead sailing completely alone with two battalions of men who didn't have any idea what they were getting into.

At Noumea, New Caledonia, the *Lurline* picked up 650 additional men, most of whom were veterans of Guadalcanal and New Guinea, and another 270 were boarded at Brisbane, Australia. Now, with the equivalent of three battalions aboard ship, the *Lurline* headed toward Bombay, India. Along the way, copies of a pamphlet entitled "Long-Range Penetration Units" was distributed to the men based upon General Wingate's experiences with his Chindits, and they were also informed that India was their destination..

The men of the still nameless unit disembarked at Bombay on October 13, 1943. and were transported to a British camp at Deolali where they received three weeks of training. They then traveled to central India for two months of very intensive training. During this time, many men, most veterans of other Pacific campaigns, had to be treated for malaria, which slowed and complicated the complex problem of organizing them into a very special fighting force. But the training continued nonetheless, with the men undergoing an increasingly strenuous physical conditioning program, studying Chindit methods, and meeting and learning to work with the famed tribal fighting men of Burma, the Gurkhas. Each of the three battalions was formed into two combat teams, and each of these was trained to function independently of the others.

Up to this point, the unit had been under the able command of Colonel Charles N. Hunter, whose job it had been to assemble, transport, and begin training the volunteer force in India. But now, as that training continued, the unit's field commander arrived, selected by General Stilwell because Stilwell knew he could delegate authority to him and he would get the job done. Brigadier General Frank D. Merrill, who had served as General MacArthur's intelligence officer after being stranded in Burma following the attack on Pearl Harbor, had become General Stilwell's aide in India. Now he was being entrusted with a secretive and very special unit of highly trained jungle fighters whose mission, though they would be totally outnumbered, would be to work with the Chinese and Burmese tribesmen and drive the Japanese out of Burma.

On October 3, 1943, the unit finally was given a name by the Department of the Army. When the men were informed of it, many did a double-take -- the 5307th Composite Unit (Provisional), was not something that easily slid off their tongues. But they would soon become known, because of their exploits, as something much easier to remember.. They would become known simply as "Merrill's Maurauders," the men who traveled a thousand miles through hell on foot, and in so doing, made history.

By early January 1944, the 5307th was declared ready for its mission. It made a 1,000 mile journey by train and boat to Ledo, India, over a span of three weeks, then walked the last 150 miles in ten days. This got them in top condition again following the relative inactivity of the previous three weeks and gave the pack troops a chance to become more familiar with the pack animals -- the mules -- that would carry much of the men's supplies. The men also became more acclimated to the terrain and climate and got to know the tribal Kachins, a primitive people who hated the Japanese because of atrocities committed upon them; many Kachins served as guides for the Americans and fought bravely alongside them.

The Marauders were involved in three missions in Burma, and during them fought five major battles and 30 minor skirmishes with the Japanese, all of this besides the numerous firefights involving small patrols and ambushes.

Their first mission took place from February 24 to March 7, 1944, during which they traveled from Ningbyen to Walawbum with orders to set up a roadblock on the Kamaing Road near Walawbum and attack a Japanese forward command post that Stilwell's intelligence officers believed was just north of the village. Relying almost solely on air supply drops, the combat teams worked their way about 20 miles behind the Japanese lines, occasionally encountering small groups of the enemy moving between the front lines and rear positions.

By March 3, 1944, however, when the Japanese realized there were American soldiers nearby, they began probing into the jungle in an effort to determine just what they were up against.

On March 3, most encounters were between small groups, but by the next morning larger groups of Japanese had begun mounting organized attacks on the Americans, and by 11:00 A.M. on March 4, all Marauder units had come under attack. Despite this Japanese resistance, however, the Marauders had blocked the Kamaing Road and two other trails, and had tapped into the enemy's telephone line running from the front lines to headquarters.

The next two days saw fierce fighting, often at close range, as the Japanese brought more and more troops in from their front lines. The Marauders endured artillery and mortar fire as well as fanatical charges by numerous Japanese. They, in turn, had no tanks or artillery to counter with, and had to rely solely on their relatively light weapons, foxholes, and determination.

On March 7, 1944, the Chinese *38th Division* arrived and by that evening the Japanese had been forced to retreat to the south. Eight Mauraders were dead, another 37 wounded, and 109 were down with various illnesses; 800 Japanese bodies were counted. A short runway quickly materialized from the jungle and small planes began arriving to carry out the wounded and seriously ill, often one at a time, which undoubtedly saved the lives of many men who otherwise would have been forced to remain in the jungle.

With the Hukawng Valley under American control, General Stilwell turned his attention to the next valley to the south, the Mogaung Valley, and the Marauders second mission was soon underway. Stilwell's plan, which both General Merrill and Colonel Hunter opposed, was to send the Chinese *22nd Division* into the valley to push the Japanese further south. In the meantime, the Marauders and units of the Chinese *38th Division*, in two columns and over two separate routes, would again move through enemy lines to encircle the Japanese east of the Kamaing Road. The trip through the jungle was expected to take two weeks and it required that both columns arrive at their targets on the same day so as to divide the attention of the overwhelmingly superior Japanese forces. If the Japanese could face only one column at a time, the operation could be a disaster for the Allies. The unknowns of traveling through jungle for that length of time, plus the difficulties the Chinese seemed to have in keeping to timetables, is what bothered Merrill and Hunter, and, as it turned out, justifiably so.

All three Marauder battalions began moving out toward their objectives on March 12, 1944. The 2nd and 3rd Battalions reached their target on March 24, 1944, four days ahead of schedule, and struck at the Kamaing Road at Inkangahtawng. The 1st Battalion had a much more difficult time on its march and eventually left the trail and simply hacked its way through the jungle, enduring mosquitos and an even more bothersome pest -- leeches that attached themselves, opened lesions, and then injected an anticoagulant that caused bleeding sometimes lasting several days after the parasite was removed.

But the 1st Battalion reached its objective undetected, and on March 28, 1944 launched a surprise attack at 3:00 A. M. against the several hundred Japanese holding Shaduzup. The Japanese were completely surprised and believed the American force was much larger than it actually was, but by 7:00 A. M. they had reorganized and launched a counterattack. Despite heavy and accurate shelling by Japanese 77- and 150-mm guns, the Marauders held their positions until the Chinese entered the battle and began pushing the Japanese back further to the south. The exhausted 1st Battalion had suffered eight men killed and 35 wounded.

Also on March 28, General Merrill suffered a heart attack. Found lying in a path at the Galahad Hsamsh-Ingyang headquarters, he refused to be evacuated until all wounded had first been taken out. Colonel Hunter assumed command of Galahad that day and on March 31, Merrill was flown out to a hospital from where he continued working to support his men, even arranging for two 75-mm pack howitzers to be airdropped complete with instructions on how to assemble them.

The 2nd and 3rd Battalions had a much more difficult time achieving their objective than did the 1st, however. Because they had arrived early, they faced overwhelming Japanese forces in their efforts to establish a roadblock at Inkangahtawng. With enemy attacks becoming stronger, the 2nd Battalion was forced to withdraw from its position and began a desperate retreat under heavy fire to Nhpum Ga, where General Stilwell had ordered a stand to be made. The exhausted Marauders beat the fresh Japanese to Nhpum Ga, carrying their wounded with them and guiding their pack animals, and immediately dug in. The 3rd Battalion established a perimeter about five miles from the 2nd.

Within two days, the 2nd Battalion was surrounded and soon ran out of drinking water, precipitating the use of stagnant water for the next ten days despite the certainty of the water being laden with disease-bearing parasites. The 3rd Battalion made repeated attempts at reaching the 2nd but was beaten back each time by the Japanese.

Because of the possibility of losing both the 2nd and 3rd Battalions, an ordered was issued to the 1st Battalion to attempt a rescue as quickly as possible. Following a four day march, mostly uphill, the 800 men reached Nhpum Ga late in the afternoon of April 7 following an arduous night march through dense jungle. They were bloodied and dirtied, exhausted both physically and emotionally, and as many as a third of them suffered from dysentery. But they turned the tide, and by noon on Easter Sunday, April 9, 1944, the 2nd Battalion had been rescued and the Japanese were retreating once again. 57 Marauders were killed at Nhpum Ga alone, with another 302 wounded and 379 needing hospital care for dysentery and malaria.

For the next two weeks, the Marauders remained in the Nhpum Ga area for rest and rehabilitation; they were simply too exhausted to walk anywhere else. It was an uneasy time, with occasional skirmishes with the Japanese in the jungle and the constant stench of death in the air. For the first time in two months, the Marauders received mail, a simple affair that raised morale enormously, and were allowed to write two V-mails each. However, no mention of where they were, what they were engaged in, or what unit they were in could be made, this, of course, due to wartime censorship regulations, but also because of the still top-secret nature of the 5307th Composite Unit (Provisional).

During the previous 80 days, the Marauders had marched 500 miles over exceptionally difficult terrain, living only on "K" rations,[1] and had endured an onslaught of mosquitos that caused illness and leeches that left what were called "Naga sores," not to mention the Japanese. What they didn't know was that their most difficult assignment still lay ahead.

By late April. 1944, the Japanese were being pressured throughout northern Burma. The Marauders, Chinese, and General Wingate's unit had regained much territory previously held by the enemy and were pushing for more. The only supply route left to the Japanese was up the Irrawaddy River, and General Stilwell had his sights set on cutting this as well. Once again, the Marauders would be used in an encircling operation in a direct attack at Myitkyina, 170 miles southeast of Ledo, an important point in the navigation of the Irrawaddy and site of a primary Japanese airstrip that the Allies wanted badly.

To date, the Marauders had lost about 700 men killed, wounded, and ill, and with no replacements available, it was decided to add Kachin and Chinese troops in order to bring the number of troops available for the operation to 7,000. The 2nd Battalion, having lost a large number of their men, underwent a major reorganization while the other battalions simply had men added to their various combat teams.

The Marauders themselves were not pleased with the addition of the unreliable Chinese as they began moving out toward their objective on April 28, 1944. It was going to be a long 65-mile journey through the jungle for men not adequately recovered from the previous operation, but the word of General Merrill that following this assignment the 5307th would be moved to India for a long rest was enough to move them once again.

The march to Myitkyina almost immediately ran into problems as the trail over the 6,000-foot high Kumon Range was completely grown over. Additionally, the monsoon season had begun a month earlier that expected. Air drops of supplies had to be aborted, the heat was stifling, and pack animals often lost their footing and fell to the valleys below. These animals often carried ammunition and weapons that would be needed at Myitkyina. At one point, a 12- or 13-year-old Kachin boy acting as a guide was bitten by a poisonous snake, an event that, had he died, would

---

[1] One of the army field rations issued to troops in the field when other rations are not available. It provides the soldier with three meals consisting of highly concentrated or dehydrated portions of meat, beverage, candy, etc.

have left the unit he was leading basically lost in the jungle. Two officers spent two hours sucking poison from the boy's badly swollen foot and by the next day he was well enough to ride Colonel Hunter's horse and continue leading the troops.

The Marauders reached their objective on May 16, 1944 and prepared to attack the Japanese-held airfield at 1:00 A. M. the next morning. When the attack began, the Japanese were completely surprised and by noon the village of Pamati, the ferry on the Irrawaddy, and the airfield all had been taken.

But then things began going wrong. Japanese strength had been misjudged, Chinese forces got mixed up several times and fired upon themselves, forced marches had to be ordered, food and rest was inadequate, and the men ran out of ammunition. Coupled with the poor physical condition of the Marauders who were now more exhausted than ever, it soon became apparent the men would have to begin defensive operations instead of continuing with their offensive mission. When the Japanese began overrunning Allied positions, a call was made to Marauders previously sent to the rear area for medical reasons to report if at all possible. As many as 400 of these men were flown in to Myitkyina, where as many as a quarter of these, when they arrived, were judged unfit for duty and sent right back out.

It now became apparent that the remainder of Galahad Force could not continue as an effective fighting force. The 2nd Battalion took a beating at Charpate, north of the airstrip, on May 17, 1944, when attacked by a relatively small group of Japanese. The 2nd's commander, Colonel McGee, lost consciousness three times during the battle simply due to fatigue and had to be removed to an aid station, while other men actually fell asleep during the attack. When the Japanese were beaten off, Colonel McGee asked that the 2nd Battalion be relieved as soon as possible. By June 1, 1944, 679 men had been evacuated to hospitals in the rear.

Allied reinforcements then began arriving to help with the taking of Myitkyina itself. About 200 men of the 1st Battalion also participated in this action and the village fell on August 3, 1944. Then these men, too, were flown out of Myitkyina to the 20th General Hospital.

For their efforts regarding the Myitkyina operation, the 5307th Composite Unit (Provisional) was awarded the Distinguished Unit Citation, the highest award given a unit for its actions in combat. It reads:

> After a series of successful engagements in the Hukawng and Mogaung Valleys of North Burma, in March and April 1944, the unit was called on to lead a march over jungle trails through extremely difficult mountain terrain against stubborn resistance in a surprise attack on Myitkyina. The unit proved equal to its task and after a brilliant operation on May 17, 1944, seized the airfield at Myitkyina, an objective of great tactical importance in the campaign, and assisted in the capture of the town of Myitkyina on Aug. 3, 1944.

On August 10, 1944, the 5307th Composite Unit (Provisional) was disbanded, its men for the most part no longer able to fight effectively. New United States Army regulations stated that any soldier serving overseas for two straight years would be sent home. This meant the entire rosters of the 2nd and 3rd Battalions were soon on their way back to the United States. Some of these men were hospitalized further while many others were reassigned, including to units stationed in Europe where a number of them died in the "Battle of the Bulge."

Most of the men of the 1st Battalion, however, were flown to India where they became part of the new 475th Infantry Regiment of the 5332nd Brigade (Provisional), soon to become known as "MARS Task Force." MARS Task Force would take the place of the 5307th in Burma and on October 15, 1944, it opened its offensive to clear northern Burma of Japanese and open a supply route to China. Working closely with the Chinese, the 475th found itself in combat near Tonk-wa, Burma, by December 9, 1944, where it had to repel several strong Japanese counterattacks.

A month later, following a march to Central Burma, the 475th caught the Japanese in a surprise attack along the Burma Road, 30 miles below its junction with the Ledo Road. More than 700 enemy troops were trapped and killed there from January 19 to February 5, 1945, culminating with the "Battle for Loi-kang Ridge," a Japanese stronghold, on February 3-4, 1945. Following this battle, MARS Task Force commander, Brigadier General John P. Willey, stated, "I feel very proud to command a unit of this calibre."

In April, 1945, the 475th entered China where it was inactivated on July 1, 1945.

It is uncertain as to just how Ralph fared as a member of Merrill's Marauders, whether he had been wounded or stricken by disease, or whether he participated in all actions of the 5307th. It is not certain which unit he was in, as well, but since he was transferred to the 475th in India, it is most probable that he was in the 1st Battalion rather than the 2nd or 3rd whose men all were rotated to the States following the Myitkyina operation. An article in the March 5, 1945 issue of the *Independence News-Wave*, probably a Department of the Army release, identified Ralph as being a member of MARS Task Force following service with Merrill's Marauders in Burma. It briefly described the hardships the men endured as well as the taking of the Myitkyina airstrip, and then further described actions of MARS Task Force at Tonk-wa and Loi-kang.

A July 12, 1945 *News-Wave* article announced Ralph's return to Independence on furlough. It seems he arrived in Milwaukee, the home of his brother Clifford, at the same time another brother, Pfc. George, also arrived on leave after serving with the Eighth Air Force in England. The article again described some of the actions experienced by Ralph as a member of Merrill's Marauders and MARS Task Force.

Also described in this article was the fact that Ralph had run into several men from the Independence area while overseas. One time, while swimming in India, he heard someone calling to him who turned out to be Clyde Kapas of Osseo. Others identified as "men whom he knew and that were with him" included Harold Christianson and Norman Moe of Whitehall, Wisconsin, and Laverne Larson of Hixton, Wisconsin. Ralph indicated that Moe had been wounded and removed to a hospital and was therefore no longer with the unit at the time he left the Theater. Whether these men were actually with Merrill's Marauders or not is not confirmed.

Ralph Klimek was discharged from the United States Army at Camp Hood, Texas, in November 1945, after marching up to a thousand miles through hell. Besides the Distinguished Unit Citation, one account, though unsubstantiated, states that all men of the 5307th Composite Unit (Provisional) had been awarded the Bronze Star, the 5307th being the only unit ever to be so honored.

No photo.
Sources: Independence News-Wave; Internet; Book (Legacy of Merrill's Mauraders)

A Quote From History. . .

"We then loaded ship and headed for the U. S. A. We went under the Golden Gate Bridge on Thanksgiving Day, 1945. . . When I got back to Independence and walked into my dad's store, my mother walked in shortly after. She was awfully glad to see me and I was awfully glad to see her."
  Edmund J. Lyga
  United States Army
  Describing his return home following three campaigns in the Pacific Theater.

ALEX E. KLOSS
UNITED STATES ARMY

Alex Kloss was inducted into the United States Army on January 9, 1942, and entered active service that same day at Fort Sheridan, Illinois. Having had civilian experience as a bulldozer operator for Trempealeau County prior to entering the service, Alex was sent to Engineering Basic Training for three months at Fort Leonard Wood, Missouri. The commanding officer at this engineer replacement training center was Brigadier General U. S. Grant, III, grandson of Civil War General and later President Ulysses S. Grant.

Following basic training, Alex arrived at Vancouver Barracks, Vancouver, Washington, assigned to Company B of the newly-formed 340th Engineer General Service Regiment. On April 18, 1942, he and the Regiment boarded a train for Seattle, Washington, where it then boarded the *U. S. S. St. Mihiel* bound for Skagway, Alaska. Arriving there on April 22, 1942, the Regiment remained in Skagway for a month as supplies and equipment were delivered. Following the Japanese attack on Dutch Harbor and Kiska in the Aleutian Islands of Alaska, the Regiment organized the defense of Skagway and its important harbor.

On May 22, 1942, the 340th Engineers left Skagway for its original assignment, the construction of a 220-mile section of the Al-Can Highway. By June 18, 1942, following train and barge transport and a 75-mile overland march through grueling, mostly unmarked swamps, most of the Regiment had arrived at Morley Bay where work commenced immediately. Due to a lack of necessary equipment, only 10 miles of the highway were completed in the first month. But in the next two months, the 340th Engineers constructed an amazing 210 miles of highway through the desolate Alaskan wilderness, eventually meeting with the 35th Engineer Regiment which was working toward them. Following initial construction of the highway, the 340th maintained and improved the road surface, constructed permanent bridges over three rivers, and built rest camps. For its extraordinary efforts in constructing its portion of the Al-Can Highway, the men of the 340th Engineers were honored with a Distinguished Unit Citation for "meritorious conduct in the construction of 127 miles of road over most varied and difficult terrain, a daily rate of 4.9 miles."

In February 1943, Alex was one of 95 enlisted men and four officers who formed a cadre sent to Fort Lewis, Washington, to organize new engineer combat battalions. On March 5, 1943, however, he was ordered back to the 340th in Canada where he continued aiding the construction of highway infrastructure until August 22, 1943, upon which time he again traveled back to the United States.

On February 27, 1944, Alex embarked from the Portland, Oregon, Port of Embarkation aboard the U. S. Motorship *Pennant*. Following refueling at San Pedro, California, the *Pennant* sailed alone with no protective escort for a then-secret destination. After 37 days at sea and a short, three day stopover at Townsville, Australia, the *Pennant* finally reached Darwin, Australia on April 4, 1944. The Regiment immediately began construction of hangars, taxiways, and other facilities to accomodate the arrival and stationing of a B-29 bomb group. While in Darwin, the 340th Engineer General Service Regiment was officially reorganized and Alex became a member of the Headquarters and Service Company, 340th Engineer Construction Battalion.

Leaving Australia, Alex arrived at Hollandia, New Guinea, on August 26, 1944, where his new unit established a camp on Hill 600 during a typical tropical downpour. The Battalion's time at Hollandia was spent in preparation for the invasion of Morotai Island.

Departing Hollandia via LST on September 4, 1944, the 340th practiced landing operations for three days at Wakde Island. Then on D-Day, September 15, 1944, it landed on Morotai Island. Most of the Battalion's time there was spent constructing roads, piers, and other buildings, but it also experienced regular Japanese bombing raids. It prepared for the invasion of Luzon of the Philippine Islands while on Morotai, as well, and by December 26, 1944, two LST's and one AK ship had been loaded as the Battalion joined the 900-ship convoy heading to Lingayen Gulf. After landing on Luzon on January 9, 1945, the Battalion spent ten months building every sort of structure from bridges to roads to buildings. It also removed booby traps and hunted for

Japanese snipers and infiltrators.

Alex was on Luzon preparing for the invasion of the Japanese mainland when the war in the Pacific ended, but he remained there until November, 1945, when he received orders to board a ship for home. He arrived back in the United States on November 24, 1945, and on December 6, 1945, was separated from the Army at Camp McCoy, Wisconsin, as a Technician Third Grade.

Throughout his time in Alaska, Canada, and the Southwest Pacific, Alex drove heavy trucks, bulldozers, road graders, and other heavy equipment. He also made repairs on equipment when necessary. He had been awarded the Distinguished Unit Badge for his Regiment's work on the Al-Can Highway, the American Theater Service Ribbon, Asiatic-Pacific Theater Service Ribbon, Philippine Liberation Ribbon with one bronze star, six Overseas Service Bars, and Good Conduct Medal, and had participated in the New Guinea and Luzon campaigns.

Sources: Don Kloss, brother; Unit documents

Kloss brothers Alex, left, and Bennie, above.

BENNIE KLOSS
UNITED STATES ARMY

Bennie Kloss was inducted into the United States Army on March 3, 1941 in Milwaukee, Wisconsin, and entered active service on that same date. Following basic training, Bennie received additional training as a Cannoneer (Medium). He then was ordered for overseas shipment and left San Francisco on December 5, 1941. But just two days later, the Japanese attacked Pearl Harbor, and Bennie's ship was returned to the United States. He then was assigned to Battery C, 205th Field Artillery Battalion, 41st Infantry Division, upon its formation in February 1942.[1] The 205th Field Artillery Battalion consisted of 105-mm tractor-drawn howitzers. Bennie departed the San Francisco Port of Embarkation with the 41st Division's artillery on April 22, 1942, arriving in Australia on May 14, 1942. The Division first trained at Camp Seymour, then moved to Rockhampton, Australia, for intensive training that began on July 19, 1942.

Following behind the 41st Infantry Division's move to New Guinea, which began in December 1942, Bennie's 205th Field Artillery landed as the 41st Division was relieving the exhausted troops of the 7th and 32nd Infantry Divisions along the Gona-Sanananda front. By then, all that was left of the Japanese forces on New Guinea's northern coast were fragmented units at the mouths of the Kumusi and Mambare Rivers. And though it took until August, 1943 to totally eliminate these pockets of resistance, the Japanese in this part of New Guinea had already been effectively crushed.

In early October, 1943, the 41st Infantry Division was removed to Australia for rehabilitation and additional training. Then it once again was sent to New Guinea, where its infantry regiments were handed separate assignments. The 163rd Infantry Regiment assaulted Wapil on April 22, 1944, and then took Aitape, Rohn Point, and Kamti Village by April 24, 1944. The 162nd and 186th Infantry Regiments, meanwhile, landed as Task Force RECKLESS at Humboldt Bay on April 22, 1944, and took the airdromes at Hollandia and Sentani. Bennie landed at Hollandia on D-Day of the assault there. The 162nd and 186th were then relieved by the 24th Infantry Division for rehabilitation at Hollekang on May 6, 1944. The 163rd remained in action, however, and landed at Arara, New Guinea, on May 17, 1944. It secured the Arara and Toem area, then crossed to assault the caves and pillboxes on Wakde Island, taking it on May 18-20, 1944.

Bennie's 205th Field Artillery Battalion next landed on Biak Island off New Guinea in support of the 162nd Infantry Regiment on May 28, 1944. In his words, "Biak was a tough one." The Japanese put up a fanatical struggle, occupying numerous caves throughout the island, and on June 12, 1944, the entire 41st Infantry had to be committed in order to overcome their resistance. On June 30, 1944, one gun from Bennie's Battery C -- a battery consisted of four guns -- was sent to a position near Mokmer village from which it fired about 800 smoke and high explosive shells directly into nearby caves. Whether this was Bennie's gun, however, is unknown.

Biak was taken, but mop-up continued until late August, 1944. At the end of January, 1945, the 41st Infantry's components began leaving Biak, heading for Mindoro in the Philippine Islands.

Bennie's 205th Field Artillery Battalion arrived on Mindoro on February 9, 1945. The Division entered combat on February 28, 1945, when its 186th Infantry Regiment assaulted Palawan Island. The entire Division was committed to recapturing Mindanao on March 10, 1945, during which the 205th Field Artillery Battalion was involved in combat around the village of Zamboango for about a month. Bennie was then transported with the rest of his unit cross-country by truck convoy to Davao on the other side of the island. A beachhead had been secured there but fighting was still in progress. Following three weeks of combat at Davao, he returned to Zamboango where a garrison camp had been established.

At Zamboango upon the war's end, Bennie was replaced on the point system and left the Philippines as a Technical Sergeant Fourth Class on August 13, 1945, arriving back in the United States on September 5, 1945. He had participated in the New Guinea and Southern Philippines campaigns and been awarded the Asiatic-Pacific Theater Service Medal, American Defense Service Medal with star, Philippine Liberation Ribbon with one bronze star, six Overseas Service Bars, and the Good Conduct Medal. During his three years, four months in the service, Bennie was first a cannoneer in the 205th Field Artillery Battalion, then later received additional training and served

---

[1] The 41st Division had 743 of its men killed and 3,504 wounded, with 217 of those dying of their wounds, during its two campaigns.

as a motor mechanic and artillery mechanic, repairing and servicing motor vehicles and the 105-mm howitzers in his battalion. He received his discharge from the Army on September 12, 1945 at Camp McCoy, Wisconsin.

Sources: Bennie Kloss personal papers; Books (Stanton) (Smith)

ALPHONSE "AL" KULIG
UNITED STATES NAVY

The following narrative was prepared following an interview with Al Kulig at his Independence home on July 9, 1998.

I was inducted into the service in Whitehall, Wisconsin, sometime around March 3, 1943. Ed Skroch and I then went to the Plankington Building in Milwaukee where we were told we had a choice of service branch to enter. We both selected the Navy because we figured at least we would have a place to eat and sleep while aboard ship.

I then went to the Naval Training Center in Farragut, Idaho, for basic training. This was a

new base and there was still a lot of construction going on when I got there. Supposedly, Eleanor Roosevelt had flown over the area once and commented it looked like a good place to put a training camp, so they did!

After six weeks of basic, I became a Seaman 1st Class, then was given a series of tests to see what specialty area I would be trained in. One other guy from the camp and I were sent to radar school at Point Loma near San Diego, California. We actually stayed at Camp Pendleton, which was nearby, because Point Loma was locked up tight for security reasons. We went to class during the day, left everything there overnight, and picked up where we left off the next day. I saw Vitus Smieja while I was at Camp Pendleton.

Next I was sent to Port Hueneme, which was near Oxnard and Ventura, California. The Navy was forming Argus Units there and I was put into Argus Unit 15. For several weeks there, we trained to set up land-based radar. We got pretty good at it. They set up trials to see how quickly we could become operational by landing us on San Clemente Island, and we got to where we could do it in one hour.

In early fall of 1943, our unit was sent to Hawaii where we were stationed at

85

the Barber's Point Naval Air Station on Oahu. Here it was practice and practice and practice and practice, and we became a crack unit.

One day I was playing catch behind the barracks when a scout from the St. Louis Browns baseball team walked over. He had been watching me throw and apparently thought I threw a pretty good ball. He asked if I had ever thought about playing professional baseball and I responded that that had always been a dream of mine. He said it was against regulations to sign servicemen but that the Browns would contact me after the war. They did and I played a while with their Wausau, Wisconsin, farm team after returning home.

Another day I was walking along the beach near the Station when I spotted Ed Lyga from a distance. I was running toward him when I stumbled on a rock and cut my big toe pretty bad. That didn't stop me from running, though, as I was happy to see someone from home. But when I reached Ed, he seemed cold and didn't talk much at all. I couldn't figure that out but afterwards I learned he had written to his mother about seeing me, who then told my mother that when he saw my foot bleeding so badly, he almost fainted. So that explained why he didn't seem as excited to see me as I was to see him!

I found out later, also, how our mothers -- Ed's and mine -- learned that we were in Hawaii. In that same letter to his mother, Ed said we were in a place that means "small" in Polish. The Polish word "mali" means "small," and is pronounced the same as is the island of "Maui."

After eight months on Oahu, we were ready for the combat area and, though we weren't told where we were going, were sent to the Marianas. The Argus Units arrived off Saipan aboard ship, and after two days, some of our radar guys followed the Marines in and set up their equipment. Once they were in total operation, our radar could pick up Jap raids from 70 to 120 miles away, depending on the altitude their planes were flying at. Some of those Jap planes never knew what hit them. I saw a lot of the "Marianas Turkey Shoot"[1] while aboard ship. There were so many tracers going through the air at those Jap planes, I don't know how anyone could've gotten through!

I landed on Tinian Island after it was taken. We called Tinian "Coral Base." The island was mostly all coral so we had to revet sandbags around our radar. Basically, we were set up above ground.

While on duty one day, I spotted incoming planes that had to be Japanese. I called out, "Got 'em at Angels 28!" This meant they were coming in from the north at 28,000 feet. Well, an officer didn't believe they could be that high so he ordered our fighters to "Angels 18," 18,000 feet up. When the pilots couldn't find them, they were sent 3,000 feet higher, then another 3,000 feet, and then higher still. Finally when the fighters were at 25,000 feet, one of the pilots called out, "Tally-ho! Tally-ho! Got 'em at Angels 28!" They were right where I had spotted them! During times when our planes attacked Jap planes, we could always hear the pilots giving directions and warnings. We could also hear the guns being fired at times, as well.

Eventually, we put B-29's on Tinian's big airfield. These planes flew at really high altitudes, and back then they didn't know much about the jet stream. This would sometimes mess up the navigators and those big planes sometimes were as much as a hundred miles off course while returning to Tinian. We could see they were off course on our radar screens so we would

---

[1] In response to the American invasion of the island of Saipan on June 16, 1945, Japanese Admiral Ozawa converged two large battle groups onto the Marianas. On the morning of June 19, 1945, he launched his first airstrikes against the American forces. Though the Americans didn't know from where they were coming, they nonetheless knew the enemy planes were approaching because a Japanese scout plane flying above the American fleet was sending instructions as to where to attack. The Americans were listening to every word and fighter aircraft were launched from aircraft carriers to meet them. By this time of the war, Japan was relying on mostly inexperienced pilots and the American planes and ships shot them down almost at will. Of the 373 aircraft launched by Ozawa that day, 240 were shot down, another 50 or so were destroyed near Guam, and another approximately 25 were lost to other causes -- a total of 315 aircraft lost in one day! Not one hit was made on an American carrier and damage to American forces as a whole was very slight. American pilots dubbed this event "the Great Marianas Turkey Shoot."

send the Combat Air Patrol fighters up to lead them back home.

One time I saw a plane on my screen that was losing altitude and finally it just disappeared entirely. Our planes had emergency IFF (Identification Friend or Foe) radios so I watched real closely to see whether this might be one of our planes ditching into the sea. Suddenly one pip, and only one, showed on the screen, so I noted the coordinates, the information was turned over to a sea rescue unit, and they rescued a whole B-29 crew. I'm pretty proud of having done that.

After Tinian was secure, the Army relieved our radar unit and I flew back to Pearl Harbor where the unit was broken up. I went back to school on Oahu where I got pretty high grades and was kept there as a radar instructor. Dick Markham came through our course at one time, as did a British Admiral.

With new ships coming into Pearl regularly, instructors were put aboard them to train their personnel. I was assigned to the aircraft carrier *U. S. S. Antietem*, which was then sent to join Admiral Halsey's 3rd Fleet. This is when I crossed the International Date Line seven times in one day! The ship was training in the launching and recovering of aircraft and turned into the wind a number of times, and we happened to cross the Date Line back and forth during these exercises.

Early in the war, the Japs had taken Wake Island from us, but when our forces began moving across the Pacific, we bypassed it and left their garrison stranded. Whenever our ships passed by Wake, though, we would launch an air attack on them. When I was aboard the *Antietem*, the carrier had its planes ready to launch a raid when we received word that Japan had surrendered. Needless to say, there was a lot of cheering and celebrating at that! I attended a Thanksgiving Mass on the deck of the carrier.

Following the surrender, the *Antietem* was ordered to Tokyo Harbor to participate in the surrender ceremony. But we had developed mechanical problems that forced us to turn back to Guam and I missed out on seeing all of that.

From Guam, the ship was ordered to join Admiral Spruance's 7th Fleet. When we arrived at Okinawa, I had enough points to go home so I got off and waited for a flight to Pearl. I finally was able to get aboard a C-54, a big four-engine plane. We were quite a ways from Pearl when one of those engines caught fire. They were able to extinguish the fire with the plane's automatic fire control system, but it was still scary! We landed on Johnson Island, south of Hawaii, and I took a destroyer to Pearl. I was just glad to get back!

I traveled back to San Francisco aboard the *U. S. S. Saratoga*, which was stripped down to haul personnel home, in October 1945. Then I took a train to Great Lakes Naval Station at Chicago, Illinois. From there I had a 30-day leave, and went home to Independence. Following the leave, I went back to Great Lakes where I was discharged on December 1, 1945.

Radioman Second Class Al Kulig sent the following letter to the people of Independence, written January 10, 1945, from Hawaii, after receiving the "Special Serviceman's Edition" of the *Independence News-Wave*:

Dear Kirk and All Folks at Home:

Received your most wonderful Christmas issue of the News-Wave on the 6th of January. Despite its late arrival, I still enjoyed it very much. It probably would have taken longer, but I met it over half the way.

I wish to express my thanks to everybody back home who helped make it such a success. I am sure everyone else in the service feels the same. I sure was surprised at the honor roll. So many are in the service. I never covered a paper so thorough before in my life, I don't believe. I got so interested that I nearly missed my next class.

I am now in Hawaii, attending Radar school for several weeks. From there, that's my question too. Right now I feel rather happy because we just finished the most rugged test in my life. That's one!

Was rather surprised to read about so many fellows from home being at places that I was at, and didn't even know it. Have been right along with Lt. Ed. Lyga, but somehow, for various reasons, we couldn't meet.

I suppose, naturally, you'd like to know what I think of Hawaii. Well, I'll give it to you straight.

Unless you are a civilian and on a honeymoon or something, it's rotten. It's so filled with servicemen! People waiting on a serviceman aren't courteous a bit. No matter where you go you have to wait in long lines. As far as sceneries, its O. K., but I have seen better ones elsewhere. The climate couldn't be better.

Upon returning here we spent a week of recuperation at the Royal Hawaiian Hotel. It formerly was a hotel for big shots and movie stars, but now it was presented to the navy for men who need rest. That's the only nice thing about Honolulu. We were free to do what we wanted during the stay. Now we're back on the job.

I must say that I miss Independence very much and will be longing for the days when I'll be back there.

Incidentally, I just missed going to the States by two hours. The rest of my unit practically is back by now. I can't quite see the day yet. I know that a lot more guys would like to go back and can't, but its just one of those things.

Guess this will be all, so the Best Wishes to everyone and once again, Thanks a Lot!

Sincerely,

A. A. Kulig

Source: Independence News-Wave

ARTHUR A. KULIG
UNITED STATES ARMY

Art Kulig enlisted in the United States Army on October 5, 1942 in Milwaukee, Wisconsin, and entered active duty that same day. He traveled to Camp McQuaide near Watsonville, California, where he underwent basic training at the Coastal Artillery Replacement Training Center. During his 13 weeks in California, Art received rifle training at Fort Ord near Monterrey as well as 155-mm howitzer training at Camp McQuaide. In a letter to his sister, Carrie, and her husband, Frank, dated November 14, 1942, he stated that he had seen "more in this month-and-a-half than I did in my whole 20 years." He went on to say that there were men in the camp from the entire country, and that "some of them sure talk funny. . . I noticed easterners, southerners, and westerners. There is one guy here who came from Germany about six years ago and you should hear him talk."

A month later, in a letter dated December 13, 1942, Art described his rifle training:

I will be getting a medal for qualifying in 30-30 rifle shooting. I got a score of 143 out of a possible 200 points. This isn't so good but it is a lot better than some guys got. You have to get 134 points in order to get a medal. We shoot at targets 200 yards away and when you look at the bull's eye through the sight it looks like the eraser on a pencil, about the size of a marble. Boy, my shoulder was sore from shooting. Those guns kick about like a 12-gauge shotgun. We shot 10 shots standing, 5 kneeling, and 5 sitting. Standing is the worst, it really is hard to hold 16 pounds of rifle steady.

He wished Carrie and Frank a "Happy New Year" in a letter dated January 1, 1943, but indicated that though he had received "about 20 Christmas cards," Christmas and New Year's didn't mean much to him that year:

I was going to go New Year's Eve with Dominic Sura, but he had to get ready for shipment, and he left today. He didn't know where, he said he heard north, so I don't know. I think I will be leaving in another week or so, too. I'd just as soon go. I am getting sick of this camp. I've got a cold now and it seems like I will never get rid of it here in these damp nights.

88

Art Kulig. The photo above was taken with his parents, Joseph and Petronella Kulig, on October 1, 1942, just four days before Art enlisted in the Army.

Following basic training, Art was sent to Camp Stoneman near Pittsburg, California, the staging area for the San Francisco Port of Embarkation. He spent several weeks at Camp Stoneman during which time he was able to visit San Francisco and California's redwood forest. On March 19, 1943 he wrote his sister and her husband informing them of his new address and that he had run into another Independence resident:

> The other night I was in the Post Exchange and I met Ed Lyga there. He's a second Lt. in the Field Artillery. I talked with him for a while and he said he's been in the Army over two years and been all over the U.S. and that's the first time he met somebody from his home town. He just came to this camp, too, and he figures on going across. He said that he didn't think I would go across yet.

Ed apparently wasn't in on actual troop shipment plans because within a few days, Art was transferred once again, this time to the Los Angeles Port of Embarkation staging area known as Camp Anza. During his two weeks at Camp Anza, Art was reassigned from Coast Artillery to Special Service Engineers as a tractor and truck driver, boarded a troopship destined for Wellington, New Zealand, and sailed on March 30, 1943. The ship remained in Wellington two days, only long enough to refuel, and then continued its journey to Melbourne, Australia. Upon arrival in Melbourne, the 8,000 troops disembarked and marched in a column two miles long to a camp where they remained for only three days. Art then once again boarded ship and sailed for Bombay, India. There the troops left the American troopship and walked about a mile in 100-degree-plus heat, all the while carrying their barracks bag, rifle, and full field pack. They then boarded an English troopship where they soon discovered the food to be bad. Following what Art described many years later as a "near mutiny," the Indian cooks were replaced with Americans and the men spent nearly half a day throwing all the spoiling goat's meat overboard into the bay of

Bombay. He marveled at the size of the fish that were surfacing to eat the meat.

Finally, however, Art's journey to his final destination, Basra, Iraq, began, and after 10 days at sea, he arrived there on May 22, 1943. The next day he wrote a letter to his parents, which the *News-Wave* published on June 17, 1943:

> Dear Folks:
>
> I received your first letter today. It was dated April 16th. It was the first letter I got from you since I left for overseas. I sure was glad to get it even if it was so old. I am now in Iran, a country near Persia. The people are just like they picture them in the Bible in the time of Christ, nothing but old ragged clothes wrapped around them. Some of the natives bring out black goats and a bunch of burrows to a pasture near the camp every morning. The camp I came to is a lot better than I expected. We are now in big tents with a nice cot to sleep in, with a mosquito bar over it. The flies and mosquitoes are really bad out here. The weather is really warm. In the daytime it gets to be about 20 degrees higher than it ever was in Wisconsin. All I do is walk guard 24 hours on and 24 off. It's warm here but I'd rather take the heat than duck bullets. Space is running short. Don't worry about me. Notice my APO No. is changed.
> So Long,
> Arthur

Stationed at Khorramshahr, Iran,[1] Art served with Company C, 363rd Engineers Special Service Regiment. Initially, his unit constructed roads, churches, barracks, and other facilities to accomodate the increasing number of Allied troops in the area. The port of Basra then began receiving large quantities of equipment which were being sent to the Russians fighting the Germans on the Eastern Front. A letter dated June 13, 1943 indicated Art had met "a Sergeant Olson from Taylor, Wis., one guy from Wausau and another from Stevens Point." He went on to describe some of the Iranian wildlife, as well:

> The jackals and hyenas really howl around here in the night. Couple guys got young jackals for pets. One guy has got a pet monkey. He really is a comical one. There also are a lot of date trees around here, but I guess they just finished blooming now and I never had dates yet. The natives sell them but I never got a chance to buy yet.

On August 16, 1943, he informed Carrie and Frank that he had been promoted to Private First Class and was now earning $64.80 per month, which was an increase of $4.80 per month.

He wrote his sister and her husband again on November 21, 1943 about a chance meeting with yet another Independence native:

> I went to the show last nite and I sat down right in back of Vincent Reck. The folks wrote and told me he was here but I never met him before. It sure was funny, he lives right across the road from me and I walked past his barracks lots of times and I never seen him. I guess in Army clothes everybody looks alike from a distance. He came here about three weeks after I did, he's in the 385th Port Battalion. He must have been in Camp Stoneman when I was there. He left from San Francisco and I left from Los Angeles. I sure was glad to see somebody I knew at home. He's got a baby girl nine months old he's never seen. He showed me her picture.

For 21 months, Art was stationed in Iran, a place he didn't really mind except for the incredibly hot weather where one "couldn't be outside at all in the afternoon." On May 18, 1944 he informed Carrie and Frank that "up here there isn't anything new. I have been on an eight day sight-seeing tour to Esfahan, about (censored) miles from here. Was a pretty nice place and was supposed to be the most beautiful city in the world at one time. All of the old palaces and mosques are really pretty." In the same letter, he announced "they started selling ice cream in the Post

---

[1] The Basra and Khorramshar region is at the northernmost tip of the Persian Gulf at the confluence of the famed Tigris and Euphrates Rivers.

Exchange about a week ago. Us engineers built a Coca-Cola and ice cream plant combined. Didn't have any coke yet as the plant isn't quite finished." He expressed concern about how "the folks will make it this summer" with the usual farm chores needing to be done and less help available due to his being in the service, brother Ralph undergoing serious surgery, and sister Pat entering nursing school. He also told Carrie and Frank that he "was to the recreation center in Tehran, the capital of Iran. Had a hell of a time. Spent plenty of money but it may never happen again so what's the difference." He said beer was "$1.20 a bottle" and that he "saw the king's palace and the hotel the President slept in when he was there. The city has a lot of nice buildings but there are too many dumpy ones to call the city beautiful. It was nice compared to the other places I saw in Iran, though."

Another letter dated July 27, 1944 reflected on a soldier from Independence, Glen Rustad, who had been killed in action:

> Got a letter from Angie today dated July 12th with all the latest. Another Independence boy lost in action, the Rustad boy that's married to Sarah Smieja. I bet there will be a lot more of them when this is over with.

In that same letter, Art was finally able to inform his family of the fact that he was stationed near "Khorramshahr, if you can pronounce that. It's a little dumpy village about thirty miles west of Basrah."[2]

On January 26, 1945 Art left Iran and sailed through the Suez Canal, "which is only wide enough for one ship with places made for two to meet." During the next eight days at sea, Art's troopship stopped in Port Said, Egypt, Corsica, and Augustine, Sicily. In Sicily, the men remained aboard ship and "a lot of Italians came up in row boats selling things like oranges and guitars. We could get a good guitar for a carton of cigarettes."

The ship landed in Marseilles, France, on February 17, 1945, where the men stayed in pup tents for two weeks. Reassigned to the infantry because the war in the German homeland was taking its toll on the American troops, Art began undergoing infantry basic training at Compiegne, France. He later was sent to Toul, France, 30 miles from Nancy, where he remained one month. From Toul, Art and seven other soldiers were sent to Dijon, France, where they were placed in charge of 250 German prisoners being transported by train to Morhange, France. As the war in Europe was reaching its end, Art was again transferred, this time to the 334th Engineer Special Service Regiment, and traveled with it to Mannheim, Germany. He was in Mannheim when hostilities ceased. Though Art had experienced the destruction caused by the war in France, he was amazed at the condition of Germany. Mannheim, he wrote many years later, was "nothing but piles of bricks."

When Art was reassigned yet again, he thought it was for a trip back to the United States. He was sent to Marseilles where he boarded ship and sailed on July 14, 1945. The men aboard, however, soon learned they were being sent to the Pacific Theater. After passing through the Panama Canal, they arrived in the Marshall Islands on August 14, 1945 where they refueled and then continued on to the Caroline Islands. At the Carolines, Art spent some pass time on Mog-Mog, an American base in the island group. They were enroute to Okinawa when word was received of Japan's surrender. The men celebrated, or as Art put it: "Talk about some whooping on board ship!"

Art remained on Okinawa for the next three months, but with the war over, there was a lot of leisure time and "all I did was swim and eat." On September 27, 1945, he wrote that he was stationed "about three miles southwest of Naha. . . There aren't any people living in it because it's entirely wrecked. In the week and a half I have been here I haven't seen a native of any kind. I did see a lot of dead Japs though, a couple or three hundred, still lying where they were killed, clothes and all. . . We are stationed practically right on the beach and we can go swimming every

---

2 Khorramshahr is about that distance from Basra, but to the east, not the west as Art had written in his letter.

morning and evening when the tide is in. It's nice and warm, too." He stated there were not many duties to perform, "putting up a few tents and today I am on K.P. We have guard duty as there are quite a few Japs still hiding in caves and they like to come in the night and steal food. They also tossed a hand grenade in another outfit's tent and hurt a few of the boys badly. Outside of that it's a great life but I am afraid this life will get old in a hurry as the time goes so darn slow." He wrote of his hope of being home for Christmas, but "I think I would settle for being at home for Easter. Well, here's hoping you're both well. As for me I couldn't be much better except that I am unhappy in the service."

Art left the Southwest Pacific on December 1, 1945 and arrived in Seattle, Washington, on December 20, 1945. He traveled immediately to Camp McCoy, Wisconsin, where he received his discharge from the Army on December 26, 1945. He had not been home since the day he entered the service in 1942 as a 20-year-old. During his time in the service, Art had earned the European-African-Middle Eastern Theater Service Ribbon, Asiatic-Pacific Theater Service Ribbon, five Overseas Service Bars, and Good Conduct Medal.

Sources: Carrie Prokop, sister; Independence News-Wave

BENEDICT "BENNIE" KULIG
UNITED STATES ARMY

On November 27, 1941, at the age of 21, Benedict Kulig volunteered for and entered the United States Army at Fort Sheridan, Illinois. He received training as a light artillery gun crewman at Fort Knox, Kentucky, and Fort Benning, Georgia, where he also received specialized tank training. At Fort Benning, Bennie was assigned to the Reconnaissance Company of the 66th Armored Regiment, 2d Armored Division.[1] At the time, 2d Armored was under the command of Major General George S. Patton, Jr., and during maneuvers conducted in 1941 had earned the nickname "Hell On Wheels."

On the bus ride to Fort Sheridan, Bennie met Walt Baecker who had recently been drafted. Walt had also been assigned to 2d Armored's 66th Armored Regiment, in Company A, and the two traveled together throughout the Division's campaigns, and both returned home in early 1945.

Bennie boarded ship in New York on December 12, 1942 and arrived in North Africa on December 24, 1942. North Africa had been invaded by the Allies in "Operation Torch" on November 8, 1942, and the city of Casablanca, where he landed, had just been captured. Bennie arrived just in time to receive a significant honor as he was one of 11 soldiers called to stand in review for President Franklin Roosevelt when he visited the area.

On July 5, 1943, Bennie and 2d Armored boarded invasion craft at Bizerte, Tunis, and headed for Sicily, landing there on July 10, 1943. It was in Sicily where Bennie had the first of three vehicles shot out from under him when an enemy shell knocked out the radiator and front tire of a half-track named "Ripper" that he and his crew were riding.

It was also in Sicily where Bennie brought himself and his home town of Independence to national prominence. As Combat Command A, of which he was a part, reached the outskirts of Palermo, a surrendering German soldier told the Americans that the German's had one of their powerful 88-mm guns guarding the entrance to the city, just around a curve in the road. Brigadier General Maurice Rose, in command of Combat Command A, was under pressure from General

---

[1] 981 members of the 2d Armored Division were killed in action during World War II. Another 4,557 were wounded, of which 202 died of their wounds.

Top photos: In a letter from England to Mr. and Mrs. Aloysie Halama in March 1944, Bennie informed them of a chance meeting with Edward Maule. The photo at the top left was taken at that time, with Edward on the left and Bennie on the right. Fifty years later, during a Memorial Day service in Independence, Edward and Bennie were photographed together once again. Note the similarities in their poses!

Photo on left: Photograph of Bennie taken in 1993 holding a framed photo of himself from the war years, his two Purple Hearts, and other medals. Photo courtesy of *Eau Claire Leader-Telegram*.

93

Patton to enter Palermo as rapidly as possible, and soon responded by flanking the enemy position with infantry. Then Corporal Kulig's halftrack, mounted with a 75-mm cannon, was ordered to the front of the column.

General Rose, standing next to Bennie's gun, ordered him and his crew to "Get it!" With that, rifle fire commenced from the infantrymen and Bennie's crew swung its gun around the corner. All of this sudden activity confused and stunned the Germans for an instant, which was just long enough for the gun crew to go into action. Bennie fired once to find his range, the gun was reloaded, and he quickly fired again. This second shot scored a direct hit on the big gun, destroying it. As the German gun crew began scattering, Bennie swung his gun over slightly and fired two more rounds rapidly. With these he blew up the German gun's camoflaged ammunition dump. Eleven Germans and four Italians operating the gun were captured.

In his book, *War As I Knew It*, General Patton later recalled the incident allowing for the capture of Palermo, stating, "This act was as lucky as it was heroic."

The August 9, 1943 issue of LIFE Magazine carried an article entitled, *Adventure in Sicily* by Jack Belden. Belden, who was on the scene when this action occurred, described the incident and identified Bennie as the gunner who knocked out the German "88," as well as his being from Independence, Wisconsin. This, along with a byline carried across the Associated Press wire, brought the story of Cpl. Bennie Kulig and his hometown to national attention.

On October 14, 1943, the *News-Wave* published a short letter Bennie had written to his brother, Clifford, who had apparently informed him of the LIFE Magazine article:

> Received your letter some time ago and just getting around to answer it now. How is everybody making their way out there? I am still plugging along, taking things as they come and it seems to be going o. k.
>
> That news about me smashing that 88 sure got home fast but I know it got knocked out faster. We got a few clippings here from different states, so it did really get around. We were getting into something like that nearly every day. Hope I can tell you the real story on it some day. There is a lot that never was mentioned in those clippings.
>
> That's about all I have to write about for this time, so tell everybody hello from me, and write soon. The mail gets here slowly, but it has a long way to travel.

Following his promotion to Sergeant, 2d Armored returned to England for training. Because it was the only American armored division in England to have seen combat to that point, the 2d drew the personal attention of such figures as Prime Minister Winston Churchill and Supreme Allied Commander General Dwight Eisenhower, as well as British General Montgomery and Air Marshall Tedder. In March 1944, Combat Command A demonstrated tank warfare and tactics to several dozen world press representatives.

While in England, Bennie wrote the following letter to Mr. and Mrs. Aloysie Halama, which the *News-Wave* published on March 30, 1944. In it, he described his meeting up with two other men from Independence:

> Hello Everybody:
>
> Guess that you are waiting for an answer to a few of the letters you sent to me. Well, there's not much news here. Everything's fine; just got thru with my wash so that's one job that's done for a week. It's after eleven o'clock now and here I am still sitting around writing. Got to bed kinda late the last two nights. Edward Maule was over to see me and I talked him into staying a couple of nights, so we really had a swell visit; a good time and a lot to talk over.
>
> I was in London for a couple of days. Met Chester Mlynek and a few guys from Arcadia that I know. Sure is good to run into some old friends like that. They were glad to see me and I was glad to see them. Chester wants me to stay with him and his wife some weekend. I didn't have time enough to meet his wife. If I had met Chester a day earlier I would have spent the night with him, but I had to get back, too.
>
> Will write more later. This V-mail is short at one end. Best regards to all.

As Ever,
Ben

    Three days after the Normandy invasion of June 6, 1944, Bennie Kulig and the 2d Armored Division landed on Omaha Beach. He and his division participated in the St. Lo breakthrough which cut off German armies in Western France and allowed the Allies to enter Paris. Now assigned to a Sherman tank, Bennie was riding point outside the French town of Vire in August when his tank was hit and virtually split in half near the turret by a German shell. The tank was damaged beyond repair and Bennie was slightly wounded, for which he was awarded the first of two Purple Hearts he was to receive by war's end.

    In September 1944, he entered Belgium. His unit was holding a position along the Roer River north of Aachen in December when the Germans launched their Ardennes counteroffensive that came to be known as the "Battle of the Bulge." General Patton, in typical fashion, told Eisenhower he could move 2d Armored into position to counter the German advance in two days. Eisenhower scoffed at this pronouncement, but Patton had the entire Division packed up and marching in three hours, and had his armor in action nearly 100 miles distant in one day. Bennie's 66th Recon was involved in heavy fighting during the "Battle of the Bulge," which was Germany's last effort to push the Allies back to the sea. During this time, 2d Armored knocked out over 400 German tanks, virtually wiping out the *2nd Panzer Division* in what Lieutenant General Courtney Hodges, commanding First U. S. Army, called "an outstanding and distinguished feat of arms."

    During a lull in combat, Bennie wrote a letter to his brother, Clifford, informing him of 2d Armored's progress. Clifford delivered the letter to the *News-Wave*, which published it on November 30, 1944:

> September 23, 1944
> Hi Cliff:
>   It's great time that I sat down to do a little writing again. The mail is coming here O. K., only we are kept busy most of the time and when we have a few minutes to ourselves, there's work to do around, so just excuse me for not writing more often and one day I might be able to give you the whole story on France, Belgium, Holland, or the Netherlands. Right now we're giving them hell in their own country, which is Germany itself, and getting them from all angles.
>   Everything is fine and I am also O. K. The going gets a little rough -- tough at times, but this is war. How is your tractor now? Guess you must be working day and night now. How about trading? Ha! Well, space is getting short now, so I will close for this time, hoping you're all in the best of health out there, and keep dropping a line as usual. Tell Rosemary to write, also.
>   As Ever,
>   Brother Ben

    During a night manuever on December 27, 1944, and while Bennie was out of the tank, his tank struck a land mine. The force of the explosion blew off his helmet and caused a concussion and bleeding from both ears. This earned Sgt. Kulig a three week stay in a hospital, and his second Purple Heart.

    While he was in the hospital, Bennie's tank was repaired and, following recovery and at his request, he rejoined his unit, remaining with it until it crossed the Rhine River. There, his name was drawn from a helmet, and Bennie received a 45-day furlough home. On March 24, 1945, he left Europe aboard ship after nearly two-and-a-half years in the European Theater. Just three days after he arrived home in Independence, on May 8, 1945, Bennie's tour of duty ended with the declaration of V-E Day.

    On June 28, 1945, Bennie Kulig was separated from the United States Army at Fort Sheridan, Illinois, where his enlistment began. He had participated in the Sicilian, Normandy, Northern France, Ardennes, Rhineland, and Central Europe campaigns. He had been awarded the following decorations and medals: Two Purple Hearts, the Good Conduct Medal, American

Defense Service Ribbon, American Campaign Medal, European-African-Middle Eastern Theatre Ribbon with one silver battle star and one bronze battle star, World War II Victory Medal, Belgian Fourragere, Honorable Service Lapel Button WWII, and four Overseas Service Bars.

Sources: Bennie Kulig personal papers; Eau Claire Leader-Telegram; Books (Stanton) (St. John)

BERNARD J. KULIG
UNITED STATES ARMY

The following edited narrative was written following an interview with Bernie Kulig conducted on June 24, 1998, at the Independence Public Library.

I was in the National Guard at Arcadia when I was 16 or 17 years old. I graduated from high school in 1939. The Guard was mobilized in 1940 and I left the unit on August 24, 1941. I wasn't 21 yet on December 7 when Pearl Harbor was attacked.

On October 6, 1942, I was drafted into the Army. I was put into Coast Artillery and trained on big guns. From basic training I was sent to Fort Miles, Delaware, where we guarded the entrance to Delaware Bay. We had 21-inch guns and checked all incoming ships. It was here where I was promoted to sergeant.

I was ordered for overseas training when the "Battle of the Bulge" occurred. I was sent to Fort Ord, California, and was told to prepare for arctic shipment. I didn't know if I was going to Alaska or where. I was designated as a "supernumerary," which meant if someone didn't show up for some reason at the embarkation ship, I would take a place. Everyone showed up for the arctic ship, however, so I didn't go there.

Then I was told to prepare for tropical shipment. This time I did board a Liberty ship and headed for the Philippines, though we weren't told that was where we were going. We had destroyer escorts leading the convoy checking for mines.

The Japs had a tendency to hit at dawn or early morning, so at those times all the troops were on deck with very specific orders in case the ship was hit and we had to abandon it. It was during this trip when I heard President Roosevelt had died.

It was May. 1945, when we arrived at Leyte designated basically as replacements where needed. We landed at Tacloban where MacArthur had landed in October. There was already a monument erected noting his return to the Philippines as he had promised he would. Our tents were set up nearby the monument. I ran into Ollie Symiczek about this time.

I started helping in a dentist's office and when I requested it, that was made my permanent duty station. A bunch of us were at an outdoor theater when the movie was stopped and an announcement made of the Japanese surrender. Everyone cheered![1]

I left Leyte on New Year's Eve, 1945 for the States. At this time I ran into Bennie Kloss. We were all rushed into loading aboard the aircraft carrier *U. S. S. BonHomme Richard* due to an approaching typhoon. The first night out the water was really rough and I thought the ship was going to break in half. We weren't supposed to do this but I sneaked up on deck once during the storm. The deck of the carrier must have been 100 feet above the surface and yet the waves were crashing over it. It was really rough!

During the trip home I developed hepatitis. I boarded a train for Fort Sheridan and went on sick call early in the trip. The doctor put me on an ambulance at Bakersfield, California, where I spent a few days in the hospital. Then I was transferred to a Pasadena, California, hospital and from there I was sent to Bushnell General Hospital in Brigham City, Utah, where they had a whole ward of hepatitis patients. They were using some new techniques for treatment there at Bushnell. I was treated from January 16, 1946 through May 24, 1946. On May 24, I received my separation from the Army at the Fort Douglas, Utah, Separation Center.[2]

---

[1] Not mentioned by Bernie during this interview was the fact that while on Leyte, he continued pursuing his interest in athletics, becoming the star pitcher of his league-leading team, the Cardinals.

[2] Following his time in the service, Bernie was awarded the American Theater Service Ribbon, Asiatic-Pacific Theater Service Ribbon, Philippine Liberation Service Riboon with one bronze star, World War II Victory Medal, and Good Conduct Medal.

Source: Independence News-Wave

EDWARD J. KULIG
UNITED STATES NAVY

The following edited narrative was written following an interview with Ed J. Kulig at his home in Independence on July 13, 1998.

I was practicing law in Lancaster, Wisconsin, when the Japanese attacked Pearl Harbor. In February, 1942, I traveled from Lancaster to Des Moines, Iowa, and enlisted in the U. S. Navy. Then I was given two weeks to clear up my business in Lancaster before reporting to the Great Lakes Naval Station near Chicago. I spent only three days there, never saw boot camp, and went straight to duty. I was shipped to the U. S. Naval Prison in Portsmouth, New Hampshire, where I was put in charge of personnel recreation. I finally received all of my Naval clothing at Portsmouth.

I only spent about 30 days at the Naval Prison because of an incident that occurred there. I was on duty at the gate when a vehicle carrying the Secretary of the Navy arrived and wanted to pass through. I couldn't give the vehicle clearance due to my orders and even pulled my weapon at one point. They wanted to enter and I had no authority to let anyone through the gates without proper authorization. I didn't recognize the Secretary even though others in the vehicle said it was him. Finally, another officer arrived and told me to allow them entrance.

Because of this, I was called into the office of a Captain who was looking over my file. He asked me what I thought I was doing at the gate and I told him that I was simply following my orders. Then he asked whether I could speak Polish to which I responded that I could. After a few additional questions, I was for all practical purposes given a commission as an Ensign on the spot and told to report to the Office of Naval Procurement in Washington, D. C. For the next nine or ten months I did background checks on officer candidates from New York and Pennsylvania,

working out of Pittsburgh, Pennsylvania. One area in my district, around Coalport, Pennsylvania, was a heavy Polish-speaking area, and that turned out to be the reason I was asked whether I spoke the language. I was also put in charge of any military funerals in the area, as well.

Next I was transferred to Commander All Forces Aruba-Curacao, known as CAFAC, in the Carribean. I was promoted to Lieutenant junior grade, and remained there until the end of the war. Following the war, I was involved with the decommissioning of Camp Parera, a CAFAC base, then was sent to the Naval base in Puerto Rico. I remained there until February 1946, when I received my discharge at Great Lakes Naval Station in Chicago.

I said earlier that I never went to basic training of any kind, which I suppose was pretty unusual for new recruits. I never attended any specialized schools, either, while in the service. This was probably because of my law background and the type of job the Navy assigned to me. I was always involved with duties that required legal training.

CARL "OLE" LEQUE
UNITED STATES ARMY

Carl "Ole" Leque entered the service with the United States Army sometime in October 1942, though it is not certain exactly when as there are conflicting dates in the various *News-Wave* reports regarding him. He received his basic training at Camp Adair, Oregon, from where he was then sent to Camp White, Oregon, to join the 91st Infantry Division.[1] The Division staged at Camp Patrick Henry, Virginia, beginning the end of March 1944, and departed the Hampton Roads Port of Embarkation in mid-April. Sailing directly to North Africa, Ole and his unit landed in Oran on May 1, 1944, where the Division underwent extensive training at Arzew and Renan.

Beginning June 1, 1944, the 91st Infantry Division began landing in Italy. From all indications, Ole was attached to the 91st Infantry Division's 361st Infantry Regiment, landing at Anzio and moving up along the coast to join the 1st Armored Division which temporarily took control of the 361st Infantry for the drive on Rome. On June 25, 1944, while facing weakened but crack German units, Ole was captured and became a prisoner of war.

---

[1] The 91st Infantry Division, nicknamed "Powder River," suffered 1,400 killed in action and another 6,748 wounded, 175 of whom died from their wounds.

Soon after, Ole's mother, Mrs. Arthur Leque, received word that her son had been missing in action since June 25, 1944 in Italy. Several weeks later a second telegram arrived from the War Department stating simply:

> Report just received through the International Red Cross states that your son, Pvt. Ole C. Leque, is a prisoner of war of the German government. Letter of information follows from Provost Marshal General.
> Signed, Adjutant General

On October 16, 1944, Mrs. Leque received a letter through the Red Cross dated August 12, 1944 from her son in the German prisoner of war camp, Stalag 2B:

> Dear Mother,
> How are you all? I am fine. Doing something every day. I don't have any news, but will write a few lines. Last year at this time I was home having lots of fun. Hope it will soon be over. They are good to us here. I am sure glad of that. How is Lyle? Is he still in the same place? Well, guess I will close for this time. With best wishes and good luck to you all. Will write again when I can. Be good.
> Ole

In May, 1945, a War Department telegram informed Mrs. Leque of Ole's liberation:

> The Secretary of War desires to inform you that your son, Pvt. Ole C. Leque returned to military control May 4, 1945.
> Signed, J. A. Vilo, The Adjutant General

This telegram was followed shortly by a letter from Ole himself, informing his mother he was free once again. The letter was published in the June 21, 1945 edition of the *News-Wave*:

> Dear Mother and All:
> How are you all? I am fine. I should have written before. I am back with the U. S. Army. Have been back since May 3rd. I am in the hospital with trench foot, but am getting better now. It sure takes a long time to get well, though.
> I was so run down when I got here, but I will soon be home and I hear I will get a 60-day furlough. That sure will be nice. I am in France now. It is very nice here.
> Well, think I will close for this time with best wishes and good luck to you all.
> Love,
> Ole

Ole remained hospitalized in France for nearly two months before boarding a plane and arriving at Presque Isle, Maine, on June 22, 1945. Upon reporting to Mayo General Hospital in Galesburg, Illinois, he was granted a 30-day furlough which he spent at home. He then returned to Mayo General for two months of additional hospitalization before receiving another 30-day furlough. Following this furlough, Ole reported to Fort Custer, Michigan, where he received a medical discharge on October 11, 1945.

Following his return from Europe, Ole reported that upon his capture he and other prisoners were marched on foot for eight days, during which time they were given little food or water. They then had been ordered into railroad boxcars for transport to their prisoner of war camp when, while climbing into a boxcar, Ole's hand was stepped on by another prisoner, causing severe injury to a finger. The journey by rail ended at Stalag 2B in East Prussia where Ole was to remain for the duration of the war, with badly overcrowded quarters and treatment at the hands of the German guards that at times, he reported, was quite inhumane. Ole and the other prisoners were simply forced to wait for their liberation, which finally came on May 3, 1945, with the arrival of the United States Army's 7th Armored Division.

Sources: Independence News-Wave; Books (Stanton) (Starr)

JOSEPH LIBOWSKI
UNITED STATES NAVY

Joe Libowski enlisted in the United States Navy on September 18, 1942 at La Crosse, Wisconsin. A day earlier, the *News-Wave* announced he would be enlisting and stated, "Joseph is only 19, but is anxious to get in the scrap against the Nazis and Japs, and isn't waiting for the draft." Joe must have thought he would be gone a while because, before leaving Independence, he placed a small ad in the "Local Items" section of the *News-Wave* stating simply and to the point:

> As I am enlisting in the Navy, I offer for sale my traps, fishing tackle, rifle and other items.
> Joseph Libowski

Joe was sent to San Diego, California, for basic training, after which he was transferred to the University of Oklahoma at Norman, Oklahoma, on October 29, 1942 for training in aviation mechanics. There he studied mechanical drawing, blue print reading, mathematics, and signaling. The November 12, 1942 issue of the *News-Wave* contained a small article announcing that the paper's editor, Glenn Kirkpatrick, had received money from Joe for a subscription to the "good old *News-Wave*." In an accompanying letter, Joe said he liked Norman as the climate and farms "reminds me a lot of Wisconsin. This camp is still being built. Rather a dirty place here as the mud is ankle deep, the same as country roads in Wisconsin in the spring."

By the following summer, Joe had completed his training at Norman, had enjoyed a leave at home, and was back at Norman awaiting a duty assignment. He wrote the *News-Wave* again in late May, apparently finding life in the Navy agreeable:

> Am sorry that I missed you the last time I was home but hope to see you in the near future. The eastern and southern parts of the state are having bad floods, but so far we've been lucky. The closest the flood came to us was 50 miles. Am sitting in the USO waiting for my date to come. The USO club is a very fine place. We have all sorts of recreation and entertainment. We are having a dance here tonight and 500 Tulsa girls are coming to relieve the woman shortage. Greetings to all friends in Independence.

Joe's next letter to Kirkpatrick, dated February 20, 1943, appeared in the March 4, 1943 issue of the *News-Wave*. By then, he had completed his aviation mechanics schooling and on the date of the letter had been issued orders assigning him as a Seaman Guard at his Norman, Oklahoma, camp, guard duty being an assignment the camp commander no doubt saw as an area needing upgrading, what with the arrival of 3,500 WAVES! He also, as he often did in his letters, expressed his appreciation for receiving regular news from home through the *News-Wave*:

> February 20, 1943
> Dear "Kirk',
> 　　Well, here I am again. It's been some time since I wrote to you so I guess it would do no harm to write again.
> 　　Well "Kirk", my school days are over again. I finished with Aviation Machinist Mate School last Wednesday. As much as I liked the courses at school I'm still glad it's over with. They kept us pretty busy during our term, but it didn't hurt any of us.
> 　　I want to take time now to ask you to transfer my paper to Barracks 73 of the same base. Our

100

base in now under a new name. It was the wish of the Captain that it be called Naval Air Technical Training Center.

I have been receiving the News-Wave regularly and I wish to thank you very much. It really feels good to lie down and read what the folks are doing back home.

At present my duties are of a Seaman Guard. I was transferred to my new duties today. As far as I know they will consist of keeping law and order at this base.

Some time ago we were fortunate enough to have 3,500 Waves sent to this base. Since then more and more are coming day after day. The sailors, including myself, welcomed them heartily. It seems good to see a Wave now and then just to break the monotony of seeing sailors all day.

Well, "Kirk", I must bring this letter to a close so just keep sending the News-Wave and I'll keep reading it.

> Sincerely,
> Joseph J. Libowski, Sea 2/c
> N. A. T. T. C., Barracks 73
> Norman, Oklahoma

A year after arriving in Norman, Joe sent the following letter to the *News-Wave*, renewing his subscription once again, describing how the camp had grown in that one year, and informing Kirkpatrick that he had come across others from the Independence area. It seems time was passing quickly for the young seaman, who now was a base police officer:

Norman, Oklahoma
October 30, 1943
Dear "Kirk":

Well, "Kirk", I noticed today that my subscription to the News-Wave is just about to run out so I'll have to take these measures and have it renewed.

I've enjoyed every issue of the paper and hope I can keep on enjoying it. It's good to sit down and enjoy reading what the folks are doing back home. It sort of helps us boys that are away from home for a short time to keep up on the things that are going on back home.

Well "Kirk", one year ago yesterday I came to this base. It was just an open field then with only one building. This was one wing of the four mess halls we have now. We had to sleep in the mess hall during the night and eat in it during the day. Yes, it was a rugged place then but is has developed into a large sized city in the past year. Many more buildings sprung up since then and many improvements have been made by the boys here.

It doesn't seem like I have spent a year on this base or have served the past fourteen months in the U. S. Navy. The time has passed by fast and I hope the time between War and Peace will speed by just as fast so our boys can come to a peace loving world like the one they are fighting for.

We have had a taste of winter already. We haven't had any snow as yet but the weather has been very cold.

I have met up with several boys from around home. Vilas Briggs, who is in the Marines and is stationed here along with Dallas Erickson from Whitehall who is also in the "Leatherneck" service, and Clemence Schneider who is stationed at Tinker Field has come in contact with me.

My duties for the past six months have been that of a Police Petty Officer. We have our regular detail here on the base which consists of keeping law and order on the base.

Well "Kirk", the time is drawing near towards "taps" so I must bring this letter to a close.

Oh, yes, one more thing -- I am sending money for the renewal of my subscription of the News-Wave so that's taken care of for a while again.

Tell all my friends hello from me and I hope to see them soon.

> Joseph Libowski

Joe's next published letter was written while at sea. It is not certain when he was transferred from Norman to duty aboard the *U. S. S. Aylwin* (DD-355), but it most likely occurred in December 1943, after *Aylwin* had returned from the Pacific while escorting the battleships *Maryland* (BB-46), *Tennessee* (BB-43), and *Colorado* (BB-45). The letter, dated May 7, 1944, appeared in the June 8, 1944 issue of the *News-Wave*. In it, Joe again mentioned the *News-Wave*, obviously an important part of his Navy life, and made reference to action he apparently was seeing:

> May 7, 1944
> Dear "Kirk":
>
> It's been some time now since I've written to you, so I am taking this opportunity to do it now. One's time is sorta rationed out here so we just have to make the most of every minute we have.
>
> So far since I've left the "States" I've gotten a few additions (Ed. - editions) of the News-Wave. It takes them a long time to get here but considering the length of its travel they are getting here in rather good time. My last issue I received was the March 9 issue I believe. I guess the rest of them will catch up to me sooner or later.
>
> It seems funny to think that winter back there is almost over. You see since I've left the states I haven't witnessed a cold day. Every day out here is wonderful (with a few exceptions) with a nice hot sun shining. I've gotten so tan since I've been out here I could almost pass for an Indian. So far I've rather enjoyed my trip out here with a few exceptions. Some of the days I wouldn't want to witness again.
>
> Well, "Kirk", I want to take this time and thank you for sending me the News-Wave as it really is a treat to read what is happening in your "home town." Thanks a million and keep them coming.
>
> Joseph J. Libowski

The *U. S. S. Aylwin* was the third naval ship to wear that name. She had been commissioned on March 1, 1935 at the Philadelphia Navy Yard. For her shakedown cruise, *Aylwin* was sent on a tour of European countries where such notables as Belgium's King Leopold III and Queen Astrid inspected her. For the next several years, *Aylwin* underwent extensive training exercises in both the Atlantic and Pacific, as well as serving as a search and rescue vessel on several occasions. As war approached in 1941, she served as escort to ships delivering planes and other materiels to Hawaii.

On March 17, 1941, *Aylwin* was severely damaged when struck by another destroyer while on night exercises. With her bow nearly severed, an immense fire ensued, and men from several ships came aboard in an effort to stem the blaze. Eventually, with temporary repairs made at sea, *Aylwin* was taken in tow to Pearl Harbor where she remained in drydock until November 1941.

On the morning of December 7, 1941, *Aylwin* was berthed with other destroyers of her squadron in Pearl Harbor as Japanese planes began their attack of America's Pacific naval force. Though half of her crew, including all senior officers, were ashore on liberty and leave that morning, the men aboard soon were operating her machine guns and lighting her main boilers. Within half an hour, the destroyers received orders to get underway out of the harbor, and shortly after a near miss from a Japanese bomb, *Aylwin* was headed for the channel.

The ship was now under the command of four young ensigns, the senior of which, Ensign Caplan, had been at sea for only eight months. As *Aylwin* made for the channel, her men kept up their fire at the Japanese aircraft and may have been responsible for shooting down as many as three. As she was steaming at full speed out of the harbor, her men noticed a surprising sight, that of a motor launch speeding toward them. Aboard the launch was her captain, Lieutenant Commander Robert H. Rodgers, and other officers, making a valiant but vain effort in trying to catch up. *Aylwin* had been ordered to make haste to the open sea and Ensign Caplan was doing all he could to do just that and save the ship from the Japanese.

Once clear of Pearl Harbor, Ensign Caplan took *Aylwin* on patrol duty for the next day. On December 12, 1941, Lieutenant Commander Rodgers heaped praise upon his half-a-crew that may have saved his ship and had special praise for the actions of Ensign Caplan.

Following the attack on Pearl Harbor, *Aylwin* saw considerable action in the Pacific. She was with the task force sent to relieve Wake Island, an action aborted due to the increased Japanese naval force around Wake. She then carried evacuees from Pearl to San Francisco, underwent repairs, and escorted a convoy back to Pearl. She was a part of Task Force 11 sent to raid the giant Japanese base at Rabaul, and when the American force was discovered and attacked by Japanese aircraft, was credited with shooting down two of the enemy planes. She was involved in the "Battle of Coral Sea" beginning May 7, 1942, and on May 28, 1942, screened for carriers *Enterprise* (CV-6), *Hornet* (CV-8), and *Yorktown* (CV-5), as they sailed to set a trap for the Japanese fleet north of Midway Island, an action historians say turned the tide of the war in America's favor. She screened for carriers delivering planes to support the Marines on Guadalcanal and in May, 1943, supported operations in the Aleutian Islands. In December, 1943, *Aylwin* and the *U. S. S. Bailey* (DD-492) escorted the battleships *Maryland*, *Tennessee*, and *Colorado*, from Pearl to San Francisco, arriving there safely on December 21, 1943.

As stated previously, it is probable, though not confirmed, that Joe Libowski joined the crew of the *U. S. S. Aylwin* after she arrived on the west coast that December of 1943. If so, he and his ship later left San Diego, where she had picked up a convoy of LST's (Landing Ship, Tank) and motor minesweepers headed for Hawaii. From Hawaii, she sailed to the Marshall Islands, and then left the Marshall's to participate in the softening up of Japanese defenses on Parry Island in the Eniwetok Atoll on February 21, 1944. By mid-March 1944, *Aylwin* was assigned to Task Group 58.2 which included the carriers *Bunker Hill* (CV-17), *Hornet, Monterey* (CVL-26), and *Cabot* (CVL-23), screening for them as they struck Japanese positions in the Central Pacific. She then screened for the same Task Group 58.2 as its carrier planes attacked Japanese installations in support of the landings at Aitape, Tanahmerah Bay, and Humboldt Bay, New Guinea, as well as supporting the paratroop drop at Hollandia airfield in which Everette Blaha participated (see Blaha biography).

On June 6, 1944, *Aylwin* left Majuro, where she had received minor repairs, and sailed toward the Marianas Islands as part of the powerful Task Force 58. There she initially screened carriers as their planes attacked the Japanese in preparation for the June 15, 1944 landings on Saipan. Then she herself shelled the northern coast of Saipan on June 13, 1944, following which she next served as an antisubmarine screen for battleships in the area. After returning to and resuming screening duties for her carriers, *Aylwin* received orders to rescue several downed airmen, which she did successfully.

On June 17, 1944, *Aylwin* left her carriers to screen for transports, and because of this, missed the "Battle of the Philippine Sea" where Japanese carrier-based airpower was basically eliminated as a future fighting force.

Following repairs and replenishment of supplies at Eniwetok, *Aylwin* left with Task Force 58 for Guam, the next island scheduled for invasion. She screened once again for her big sisters as they pounded enemy positions throughout the island, then covered underwater demolition teams in relief of *U. S. S. Dale* (DD-353) by carrying out harassing fire from off Asan Beach. The bombardment group then turned its fire on nearby Rota Island before *Aylwin* left the area on July 30, 1944 for Eniwetok. She had received orders to return to Bremerton, Washington, for an overhaul, arriving there on August 17, 1944, after a short stop at Pearl Harbor.

Considering his correspondence relationship with the *News-Wave*, it is probable that Joe did not spend any leave time he may have had in Independence during this overhaul period, as there is no mention of this in the paper from the time of his ship's arrival in the States in August through several weeks following *Aylwin's* subsequent departure for Hawaii on October 11, 1944.

After training off Hawaii in early November 1944, *Aylwin* left for the western Pacific in the company of several cruisers and destroyers, reaching Ulithi on November 21 before heading to the Philippines the first week of December in support of operations there. As part of Task Force 38 undergoing refueling out to sea on December 17, 1944, the weather took a sudden turn for the worse as a typhoon surprised the American ships, leaving many improperly ballasted with depleted fuel tanks. With all ammunition and other equipment stored below deck, *Aylwin* began riding out the storm.

At 2:45 A. M. on December 18, *Aylwin* lost electrical power and steering control. She quickly shifted to hand steering and attempted to rejoin the other ships. But the wind and waves were so severe that control could not be maintained, and she was soon at the mercy of the storm.

Suddenly, *Aylwin* found herself rolling seriously to port,[1] a roll that didn't stop until she was at an angle of 70-degrees. As she slowly righted herself, her captain, Lieutenant Commander Rogers, ordered to get her underway, but he quickly learned that any forward movement caused the ship to roll even more. After a second 70-degree roll, the ship only righted herself to 60-degrees, and *Aylwin's* survival was becoming doubtful. If she went under, the entire crew would be lost as she was buttoned up tight and non-essential crew members were lashed in their bunks. It was shortly after noon on the 18th when two men, including the chief engineer, were swept overboard, neither to be seen again.

At 1:30 P. M., the engine room ventilators ceased functioning, and when the engine room temperature rose to 180-degrees, it had to be abandoned. *Aylwin* continued her rolling and for the next six hours she simply hung on. And if things were not already bad enough, she also sprung a leak in the engine room that before coming under control caused additional stability problems due to the sloshing water.

Eventually, however, the storm passed on and *Aylwin* found herself still afloat. But three other destroyers, *Hull* (DD-350), *Spence* (DD-512), and *Monaghan* (DD-354) were lost, with the loss of 440 of their combined complements of 533 men. 17 other ships suffered damage due to the storm, as well.

Aylwin was repaired at Ulithi following the storm. During that time, Joe wrote another letter to "Kirk" at the *News-Wave* in which he let everyone know how much he appreciated the "Special Serviceman's Edition" of the paper and mentioned seeing men from the Independence area:

> January 5, 1945
> Dear "Kirk":
>
> Received your Servicemen's edition of the News-Wave yesterday and I want to take this opportunity to thank you and the other parties responsible who helped to make it possible. It really was swell of you folks to think of us at this time. Some of the photos and views of the old places in town really brought back some very pleasant memories. I had no idea one can forget so many people and places in so short a time. James Everson of Whitehall and I both enjoyed reading the paper as it refreshed our memories in many ways.
>
> Had an opportunity to run across Cliff Hanson of Whitehall and Clarence Maule. Cliff is on one of the Destroyer's Tenders here and Clarence is on a "Tin Can" as I am. Was swell seeing them both again as it has been some time since we have seen each other. Seeing someone you know out here is really a treat.
>
> By now I suppose you people have had a taste of winter. Well I guess it's time for it to set in since it is the first of January already. How would you like to trade some nice warm sunshine for a few days of winter? I've had my fill of this warm weather and I could really enjoy a few days of winter for a change. Haven't seen any snow for three years now so hope before long I will be seeing it again.
>
> My time is drawing to a close now "Kirk," so once again I want to thank you all for the swell papers and I hope you folks had a very Happy Christmas, and wish you all a very Happy New Year.
> Joe

When repairs at Ulithi were completed, *Aylwin* continued screening operations as part of Task Group 50.8 in preparation for the invasion of Iwo Jima. On February 23-24, 1945, she fired 330 five-inch rounds in close support of the Marines advancing to the north end of the island. She then headed back to Ulithi.

During the early stages of the Okinawa operation, *Aylwin* screened for supply ships between Ulithi and Kerama Retto, a group of small islands southwest of Okinawa that served as a supply base for General Simon Bolivar Buckner's Tenth U. S. Army. She survived another, less severe, typhoon on June 5, 1945, and then aided the *U. S. S. Pittsburgh* (CA-72), which had lost

---

1 "Port" is to the left while "starboard" is to the right of a ship.

its bow in the storm, before heading to Guam for her own repairs.

On July 10, 1945, *Aylwin* escorted a 41-ship convoy safely to Okinawa, after which she returned another convoy to Ulithi. She then was sent on picket station around Okinawa on August 3, 1945 to protect the larger ships from kamikaze attacks. But the next morning she received orders that hurried her away from picket duty and in search of survivors from the torpedoed *U. S. S. Indianapolis* (CA-35). *Indianapolis* had delivered components of the atomic bombs used on Hiroshima and Nagasaki to Saipan and then was on its way to the Philippines when sunk by a Japanese submarine. Unfortunately, no one on the Philippines thought her being overdue was cause for concern, and by the time a search was ordered, many of the *Indianapolis'* survivors had either drown or been killed by sharks. Though there were survivors, by the time *Aylwin* arrived on the scene, she found only three bodies, which were identified and buried at sea, two empty rubber rafts, and an empty floater net. In the early morning of August 6, 1945, *Aylwin* called off her search and headed back to Ulithi.

After escorting a convoy of troopships to the Marianas, *Aylwin* was anchored in Apra Harbor at Saipan when word was received of Japan's surrender on August 15, 1945. She sailed to Hawaii, where she embarked officers and men headed for the west coast, and then, after dropping off her passengers at San Diego, sailed on September 11, 1945 for the Panama Canal and the east coast of the United States. On September 19, 1945, Joe wrote the following letter to Kirkpatrick at the *News-Wave*, which published it on October 4, 1945, describing the typhoons he had experienced, among other things:

U. S. S. AYLWIN (DD-355)
September 19, 1945
Canal Zone
Dear "Kirk":

Been trying to get this letter written ever since we left San Diego but our work here in the office has piled up on us so it wasn't until today that we really succeeded in finishing it up.

First of all, "Kirk", before I go any further, I want you to change my address for the News-Wave to F.P.O. New York, N. Y., instead of F.P.O San Francisco. Our address changed while we were in San Diego so I wish you would send my papers to that address.

Yes, we finally came back to the States after a year of Pacific duty. This past year has been none too jolly for any of us out there. We moved faster and farther this last year, so consequently we ran into that much more trouble. This ship never missed out on a thing but seemed like each battle took its quota of men.

The Japs were not the only things we had trouble with out here. Last December we ran into one of the tropical typhoons. In this storm two of our squadron of "Cans" were lost. How we managed to survive is still a mystery to me. During this storm we rolled as much as 70 degrees and many times our smoke stacks were dipping water. In June we were unfortunate enough to hit another of those storms but luckily this one was not as severe as the first.

I myself would be willing to meet the whole Jap fleet and fight it out with them rather than fight one of these storms where all you can do is hang on and hope she pulls through. We managed to survive both of them along with all the other trouble we had so I'm very thankful for that.

The occupation of Japan, according to all indications, is coming along better than it was expected. This ship was to take part in the occupation but it had to return to port for repairs from damages received at sea a few weeks before. Would have liked to have been a part of that force after taking part in all the other events out here, but it's good to be back in the States just the same. Personally, I'm rather glad we didn't.

Right now we are in Panama. Arrived here today from San Diego. Our destination is New York Navy Yards and then for some well earned leave. Plan on being in that community soon so I hope my plans for the future aren't interrupted. Will be grand to be back there again after being gone for so long.

Well, "Kirk", my time is growing rather short so I'll have to be closing. Hope before very long I'll be able to see all the folks there again.

Sincerely,
Joe

It was not determined when Joe left the United States Navy. But the *U. S. S. Aylwin* didn't last long following the war. After reaching the New York Naval Yard on October 16, 1945, *Aylwin* was struck from the Navy list of active ships on November 1, and then sold for scrap.

The *U. S. S. Aylwin* received 13 battle stars for her participation in World War II in the Pacific, a good number of those earned while Joe Libowski was aboard.

Sources: Independence News-Wave; Internet

JOHN LUCENTE
UNITED STATES ARMY

The following narrative was written following an interview with John Lucente on November 8, 1998 at his home in Independence, Wisconsin. John was originally from Cumberland, Wisconsin. In the fall of 1946, John began his teaching career at Independence High School and he and his wife have lived in Independence since.

John Lucente, on left.

On January 3, 1942, not long after the bombing of Pearl Harbor, I enlisted in the Army at Fort Snelling, Minnesota. I was sent to Camp Grant, Illinois, for basic training, then to Camp Cooke, California, for training as a medical lab technician in a hospital there. I stayed in California until December 1942, when I was accepted into infantry officer candidate training. I left for Fort Benning, Georgia, in January 1943, where I completed the officer training course but was not commissioned at the time.

In May 1943, I was sent overseas where I was assigned to the 16th Station Hospital near London, England. I served there as a medical lab technician until September 1944. During this time, the Germans were hitting London with their V-2 rockets. I didn't know what the first one was when I saw it. I heard this strange sound, looked up, and saw this big cigar-shaped object flying through the air. I saw a number of them. They made a lot of noise, then went quiet when their motor shut down, and this was always followed by a hell of an explosion. One of them hit near us and killed 65 of our troops, and another broke windows in our hospital, but no one was injured.

Then the 16th Station Hospital was moved to France where we set up near St. Cheron. We weren't too far from the "Battle of the Bulge" and received a lot of casualties during that time.

Then, around Christmas the weather cleared and things started changing. A lot of planes passed overhead in big groups and the ground troops started pushing the Germans back. One day, General Patton showed up at the hospital as his son had been wounded and was at the 16th for medical attention.

106

In January 1945, I was accepted into infantry officer candidate school in France and was commissioned a Second Lieutenant in May 1945. I was immediately assigned to the 63rd Infantry Division[1] as an infantry platoon officer. Following the end of the war, the 63rd Division was assigned to Army of Occupation duty. We moved from town to town, never staying anywhere more than one or two weeks. We primarily had patrol duty and basically everything went well, except for the occasional fanatic that had to be dealt with. I remember shortly after arriving at the 63rd that we stopped one Sunday in a town that had a Catholic Church. We were able to go to church but had to carry our loaded weapons due to potential problems that still existed with the German population. It sure seemed strange to have a loaded weapon in church!

I remained in this capacity with the 63rd until the end of July or early August 1945, when I was ordered back to the States for a 30-day leave. Then I was supposed to be sent to the Pacific Theater. But I hadn't even reached Cherbourg, France, yet to embark to the States when word came through that Japan had surrendered. So, a whole group of officers, including myself, was held back and we were reassigned to various units in the area. I was assigned to the 787th Military Police Battalion that was operating in and around Paris, and remained with them until December 1945, when I was ordered once again to the States. This time I did go, however.

When I arrived home, I requested to be put in the Army Reserve and then joined the Wisconsin National Guard. I remained with the 128th Infantry, 32nd Infantry Division, until 1966 when I retired as a Major, completing 23 years of military service.

---

[1] The 63rd Infantry Division arrived in France in December 1944. In late April 1945, it was withdrawn from the line and assigned security duty from the Rhine River to Darmstadt and Wurzburg on a line to Stuttgart and Speyer. While in Europe, the Division lost 861 men killed and 3,326 wounded, of which 113 died of their wounds.

Source: Book (Stanton)

EDMUND J. LYGA
UNITED STATES ARMY

The following edited narrative is from extensive interviews and discussions with my father, Ed J. Lyga, at various times during 1997-98. It is supported by official Battalion records.

I was drafted on June 17, 1941 and had a physical in Milwaukee on June 18. My trip from Whitehall to Milwaukee was by bus; all other traveling while in the Army was done by train. From Milwaukee, I was sent to Camp Polk, Louisiana, and put in Battery A of one of the 3rd Armored Division's artillery battalions. Battery A was made up of four 75-mm guns mounted on half-tracks. Six months after arriving at Camp Polk, the Japanese attacked Pearl Harbor.

Following the attack on Pearl Harbor, I was sent to a small arms school at Fort Knox, Kentucky, for six weeks. Then I went back to Camp Polk where I was promoted to staff sergeant. From Camp Polk I moved to Camp Young in the Mohave Desert to train for fighting in Africa. The overall commander of this training was General George Patton, the famous Third Army commander in Europe following D-Day. He addressed the troops on several occasions regarding tactics before and after our "red army" vs. "blue army" scrimmages.

One day, General Patton told us that in combat there would be times when we would feel like throwing down our weapon and running. He said something like, "When this happens, just think of your mother and yell 'Mother! Mother! Mother!' Then take up your weapon and go after them!"

Around November 1, 1942, I went to Officer Candidate School at Fort Sill, Oklahoma. I

107

made Second Lieutenant on February 1, 1943. After a ten day furlough, I went to Camp Stoneman at Pittsburg, California, which as I remember was close to San Francisco. There I awaited orders to be sent to the Pacific Theater. About May 1, I went under the Golden Gate Bridge on my way to Hawaii. At this time I was not attached to an outfit yet; we were just a bunch of officers aboard ship. Our orders would come when we arrived in Hawaii.

I stayed on Oahu for a few days before being sent to the island of Maui, where I was put in the 225th Field Artillery Battalion to protect the island in case of a Japanese attack. At this time I was the executive officer under Captain Charlie Cameron. We were dug in a few miles south of Wailuku with our howitzers covering the waters of Maalaea Bay. The guns were 155-mm that could shoot about 10 miles. We had an observation post on the shores of the bay but about the only excitement called in was when a few whales came into the bay.

About the time I made First Lieutenant, I was given a battery of four 75-mm guns located on top of Mt. Haleakala, near the crater. This place gave a beautiful view of the ocean and when the volcano on Hawaii acted up, we could see it.

While on Maui, we were sent to the 55th Coast Artillery to help change it from Coast to Field Artillery. This was a change from 155-mm howitzer guns to 155-mm "Long Toms," and we later were redesignated as the 531st Field Artillery Battalion. This ended up being a good move because the "Long Toms" were big, heavy guns that put us a long way from the front lines.

The change of Coast Artillery to Field Artillery was mostly a matter of the commands given to the gunners to change the direction and elevation of the barrel to hit the target. In Coast Artillery, both the person directing the guns and the gunners can see the target or ship in their sights. In Field Artillery, the people at the gun very seldom see what they are shooting at. An officer well out in front of the guns and overlooking the target area, called the forward observer, finds the target and gives the commands to the guns to hit the target.

Before this can be done the four guns in a battery are first set so all barrels are parallel. This is done with an instrument called an "aiming circle" that has a magnetic compass marked off in mils. There are 6400 mils in a circle and 0 mils is true north. When guns are parallel, each gunner sets a stake about 150 feet in front of the gun. The gun sight, which swivels, is then set on 0 mils and the sight is turned to see the stake in front of the gun. This is the gunner's aiming point. All movements of the barrel left and right are then made while aiming at the stake.

The guns are now ready to fire but the forward observer has to know where the round will hit. To do this, he selects a permanent target in enemy territory, estimates the distance from the guns to the target, called the aiming point, and then gives the direction in mils to the executive officer at the guns. Let's say the target is directly east of the guns. The direction would then be 1600 mils. 1600 mils is set on the gun sight and the gun is turned until the sight is on the stake. The distance is given in meters which is converted into mils for the elevation of the barrel. The commands from the executive officer go something like this:

"Cannoneers post;
Guns adjust;
Shell H E;
Charge normal;
Base deflection 1600;
Elevation 254."

"Shell H E" means high explosive and "charge normal" means one bag of powder. There is a super charge of two bags of powder.

From these commands, the sight is set, the gun is loaded, and the sight set on the stake. The gunner then yells "Ready," and the executive officer's response is "Fire!" At this, only Number One gun fires, but the other three guns were following all the commands as well so the barrels all stay parallel.

The forward observer then must spot the burst and estimate how far right or left, over or short, the round hit from the target point in meters. This distance is changed to mils, the sight is

Ed Lyga during training in the United States.

The real reason Ed joined the Army -- someone told him the fishing was good in the big pond off Hawaii!

1st Lt. Ed Lyga's 531st Field Artillery Battalion, XXIV Corps Artillery, setting up a 155-mm "Long Tom" on one of the Keise Islands off Okinawa, March 31, 1945. By this time, Ed had been attached to Battalion Headquarters as Assistant S-2 (Assistant Intelligence Officer).

adjusted, and the gun fired again. Adjustments are made until the forward observer feels he is within 50 meters of the target. Because all guns followed the commands, if all guns fired, the bursts should land like this:

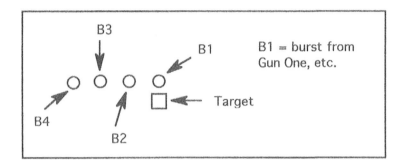

From this point on, all shifts to an enemy target are made in relation to the target from the aiming point.

Once the guns were adjusted on the target, a command similar to, "Three rounds, fire when ready!" would be given. Now all four guns would fire based upon the adjustments they all made following number one gun.

The first part of June 1944, we loaded ship and headed for the island of Saipan, which was held by the Japanese. We were attached to the 27th Infantry Division that landed on Saipan June 16. The 27th was under the command of Army Major General Ralph Smith, but in overall command of the operation was Marine Major General Holland "Howling Mad" Smith. He had two Marine divisions and the Army's 27th Division under him.

On the way to Saipan, I met a ship's officer that I knew at school in River Falls. He was the one who told me about a friend from Independence, Jerome Sobota, who also went to River Falls. Jerome was a naval officer whose ship was torpedoed by the Japanese and he went down with his ship. Only three people lived to tell about it.[1]

At about 5:30 A.M., on June 16, the first wave of Marines hit the beaches of Saipan. The beach was about 200 yards deep and the first wave caught hell, mostly from enemy artillery and mortar fire. The Marines who first landed really caught it from the Japs. There were already so many casualties by the time the artillery officers hit the beach that evening. There was a doctor who came ashore with us that night. Within a few days he had a breakdown and had to be shipped out.

The artillery officers hit the beach south of Charan Kanoa about 6:00 P. M., when the front lines were about 150 yards from the beach. One thing we were told before landing on Saipan was that the Japs would target the officers, trying to cause confusion among the troops. When the artillery officers landed the evening of the invasion, there was a private with us who was carrying a big garbage can. I remembered what we had been told about officers being targets so I grabbed one side of the garbage can from the private, saying something like, "Here, I'll help you." Actually, I was thinking "I think I'm going to try to be a private for awhile."

Our guns were transported to the beach in landing craft. When the craft hit the beach a large door in front of the ship opened down so you could drive out onto the beach. The 155-mm guns were pulled by half-track cats. I spent that first night in a Jap ammo dump that had been blown up. I didn't sleep because of the gun fire and the sky full of flares all night long. The next morning our skin was red and itching, probably from chemicals in the soil.

In the morning, our Battalion commander and I took off toward the southern coast of Saipan to find a gun position. I remember crossing a small railroad track. This is when I saw my

---

[1] More than 40 crewmen of *LST-342* actually survived the torpedo attack of July 18, 1943.

first dead Marine, a big blond-haired kid, and an old Japanese couple, also dead. I picked up the Marine's rifle and carried it with me, just in case. We found a good position about 400 yards from the ocean shore from which we could set the guns pointing at the island of Tinian, about 6,000 yards to the south. Our orders were to place Battery B, of which I was Executive Officer, facing toward Tinian just in case the Japs would start firing from Tinian to Saipan. My battery used an enemy coast artillery position on Agingan Point and facing Tinian for our observation post. This was a good safe place because the coast gun emplacement was completely covered with thick concrete with an opening about three feet high and 18 feet long for the gun barrel. Also by the gun we had big, powerful field glasses.

Next, we lay the four guns by firing on a prominent target on Tinian. I had selected three Japanese guns that were apparently out of order with their barrels pointing straight up. They maybe were 37-mm anti-aircraft guns. Using these guns, we then could shift to other targets. These three guns were near the coast of Tinian and as we faced them I remember there were cliffs to the left of them as well as a big cave that we could easily see.

The first night at the guns proved to be exciting. At about midnight all hell broke out at number one gun. It lasted just a few seconds. When I went there to check, no one really knew what had happened. Everyone just started to fight or scream. I checked to see if all were present and discovered one man was missing. He was found the next morning about 100 yards from the gun, dead. The only explanation was that this guy had a bad nightmare and woke up fighting and hollering thinking Japs were in the gun pit. Somehow, he got stabbed.

Early in the battle, a friend of mine, Lieutenant Floyd Doty from Texas, was at an observation post about a half mile down the beach on Cape Obiam Point when General "Howling Mad" Smith, the Marine, came to my observation post. It was then that two fighter planes went in strafing the big cave we could see on Tinian. General Smith thought the Japs were firing back at the first plane so he wanted to talk to someone at the other o. p. and find out what he could see. When I told my friend General Smith wanted to talk to him, he thought I was trying to pull something on him and I could not convince him otherwise. Well, I don't have to tell you it didn't take long and General Smith was howling! My friend later received an Article 15, a reprimand, because of this. I actually think tracers from the second plane were richocheting back up toward the lead plane, making it look like someone was firing from the cave.

After things in our area were pretty quiet, I and others from the other observation post decided to have a look around. Our Cape Obiam o. p. was about 300 yards from the big coral cliff you see in the paper clippings. We heard about the civilians jumping off into the water committing suicide so we went there to have a look.[2] On the side of the cliff facing the other observation post were two caves. We went in front of the caves to have a look. That evening someone brought a 37-mm anti-tank gun and shot into the caves, then left.

Late that night, my friend and five others at that o. p. were half asleep when they heard noise. They challenged it, "Who goes there?", and everything went quiet. It turned out to be a large group of Japs that apparently was in the caves. Not knowing what to expect, the people at the o. p. took off for their gun position. No one was hurt but Captain Brewster said it was the first time he ran 100 yards in 10 seconds and came in last. Another guy in our unit was crawling on his hands and knees and when he looked to his right, a Jap was also crawling on his hands and knees. Our guy said that when he spotted the Jap, he dove into some sugar cane and stayed there the rest of the night.

A few nights later a few rounds of small artillery hit our position. One round landed under the barrel of number one gun. No one was hit, just one tire was out. We figured the Japs got one of the three guns we used as our aiming point on Tinian working. We fired a few rounds and ended that. This ended our excitement at the guns but things were not yet over with. It was estimated that there were about 3,000 enemy soldiers left when the 27th Division had them ready to be pushed into the sea. Then they started their banzai attack and killed a large number of

---

2 These supposed suicide cliffs on the south end of Saipan were probably only rumored or fact that became confused as the actual suicide cliffs made famous during the battle were on the north end of the island.

Americans before they were stopped.

On Saipan, another unit was camped about 200 yards from our area. After things were pretty well over with, a Jap plane flying about 300 feet high opened up on our neighbors with machine guns loaded with tracers. Those on the ground fired back with tracers. It was something to see but I was glad I was not on the receiving side. The plane crashed and killed several Americans.

When things were quiet, some of the artillerymen would go out souvenir hunting. One time, three guys from another unit near us lowered themselves down a cliff by rope. Some Japs came out of the caves there and killed one of them. The other two made it back to their unit and reported what had happened. When our soldiers returned to that area, they found the Japs were gone. But they had eaten part of the soldier they had killed.

One of the things I remember most is the 27th Division cemetery that was placed between our battery and the beach.[3] I remember the smell. One day I walked down to the 27th Division cemetery, which wasn't too far from our gun position. As I began walking back, there was some gunfire and bullets passed pretty near me. I don't think it would have been Americans doing the shooting.

By the time Saipan was secured, the U. S. suffered about 14,000 casualties. After Saipan, a few of our men landed on Tinian, which did not amount to much. A big air field was then built on Tinian for the big planes that eventually took off with the atomic bomb.

In November 1944, we left Saipan and later landed on the east shore of the island of Leyte in the Philippines. Our artillery was attached to the 77th Division there.[4] We landed at a place called Terragona which was just south of the Dulag landing beaches. MacArthur had things under control by the time we got there. We positioned our battery's guns along a nice beach, pointing them out to sea, and I don't believe we did any firing except to establish an aiming point. One day, however, we saw a kamikaze dive into one of our ships. It didn't sink right away and they were able to keep it about a quarter afloat. We were told the ship was carrying ammunition and guns. We didn't see any of the sailors swimming from the ship so they must have gotten it under control.

After a short while we loaded ship again and went around Leyte, landing near Ormoc on the west side of the island. This was some time in December 1944. Here, too, we set up the guns facing the ocean and except for establishing an aiming point by firing on Ponson Island, didn't do any firing on Leyte itself.

In the bay out from our guns, either the Japs or the local people had placed large pieces of wood that crossed one another above the water. They were maybe part of the Jap defense against boats coming to shore. I used to row out to them once in a while and fish along the wood logs. Once I cut a long bamboo stick and made a fish trap that I hung from one of those logs. Then I'd go out there and lift the trap to see whether I had caught anything. When we left Leyte, I just left the trap out there. I also remember tossing grenades into the water and when the fish would float to the surface the natives went after them.

One of the things I remember most from Leyte was when we went to the little island of Ponson, just southwest of Ormoc. There we heard of the Japs rounding up all the civilians and putting them in a church. Then they machine-gunned them.

I never did figure out why, but one night I was put on a PT boat to patrol the waters around the many islands, looking for Japs that were moving from island to island. When the captain decided to go up a river on the island Negros, it was scary. That PT boat was mostly made of plywood and I was thinking what a Jap 50-caliber machine gun could do to it.

---

3 The 27th Infantry Division had 1,053 killed during the Battle for Saipan. Another 2,617 were wounded and more than half of those never returned to duty.

4 Of the 15,584 U. S. Army casualties incurred during the liberation of Leyte, the 77th Infantry Division suffered 2,226 -- 499 killed, 1,723 wounded, and 4 missing.

112

I spent Christmas 1944 on Leyte.

In late March, 1944, we were off for the island of Okinawa. Again, we were attached to the 77th Division.[5] On Easter Saturday, March 31, we landed on a small sand island of about four acres, 6,000 yards off of Okinawa, called Keise Shima. It was a beautiful, sunny, quiet day. We were still unloading after dark when the first enemy artillery shell hit this little island and we found out what it was like to be under artillery fire. A truck driver with a load of 155-mm shells stopped near where I had my foxhole. He jumped out of his truck and I called him into my foxhole. It's the first time I remember shivering and sweating at the same time. I'm sure my foxhole partner was doing the same thing. We were lucky the Japs were using small artillery because if big guns had been used, they probably would have done a lot of damage. The island was small and really had no cover. The next day when our guns were in position, we did very little firing.[6]

On Keise Shima, there was a covered shelter dug for the officers to enter when we were fired upon by the Japs. At the time we landed, there was a colonel with us -- an older Army guy -- and he would get real nervous when we were being shelled. In the shelter he would take his handgun out and pace back and forth. I was more afraid of him than the shelling, I think! He didn't stay with us for too long.[7]

Most of our firing was done on Saturday nights, when we were being fired at. Our fire didn't do much good because we caught it the next five Saturdays and one Friday. We had no way of knowing where this Jap gun was located and mostly went by sound. We came to believe it was in a cave, pushed out, fired a few rounds, and pulled back in.

One night the Japs landed an amphibious tank and a few swimmers on our small island, but didn't do much.[8] We could see one of the Japs on the island next to ours where another "Long Tom" battery was positioned. An American plane flew over and it looked like grenades were dropped. Anyway, they must have gotten him because we didn't see him again. Three of our guys in a machine gun position were killed, though, before this incident was over. We lost one man throughout all of the shellings we received. I was on graves detail when this happened. I remember going up to the guy and he was all worked up because one of his fingers was missing. But he had been hit real bad in the stomach, too, and he died a short time later.[9]

While in the Pacific Theater, many of the American troops listened to Tokyo Rose, the propagandist who had been born in the United States and went back to Japan when the war began. She played American dance-type music and told sad stories about all the troops being away from

---

[5] On Okinawa, the 77th Infantry Division lost 1,018 men killed, 3,968 wounded, 40 missing, and had an additional 2,100 non-battle casualties. The Tenth U. S. Army suffered a total of 65,631 casualties, with 39,420 being battle-related.

[6] Ed Lyga was attached to Battalion Headquarters during the Okinawa campaign as Assistant S-2 (intelligence officer). According to official records, the 531st Field Artillery Battalion was credited with eliminating 13 enemy gun positions on April 1, 1945, the day of the invasion.

[7] Battalion records show the commanding officer of the 420th Field Artillery Group, of which the 531st Field Artillery Battalion was a part, Colonel Lucas, left for the United States early in July 1945. Records also show Lt. Colonel Alonzo C. Hyde, commanding officer of the 531st FA Battalion, received orders on July 14, 1945, transferring him "for purpose of returning to mainland for readjustment."

[8] This occurred on the night of April 6, 1945. The raid was ordered specifically by the Japanese commander on Okinawa, Lt. General Mitsuru Ushijima, to "wipe out the enemy artillery on Keise Shima," because of its continual harassing fire. Ushijima's senior staff officer, Colonel Hiromichi Yahara, the only high-ranking Japanese survivor of the battle, wrote many years later that as he, Ushijima, and Chief of Staff Lt. General Isamu Cho stood on Mount Shuri on March 31, 1945, they were all shocked by the view of American personnel unloading heavy guns on Keise Shima. Ushijima, as with other senior officers, never dreamed this would happen.

[9] Battalion records indicate this was probably Pfc. William E. Morrow, Headquarters Battery.

113

their wives and girlfriends. We all knew her job was to damage our morale and didn't pay much attention to her stories. But she was the best entertainment we had!

The next day following the raid on Keise Shima by the Japs, we were listening to Tokyo Rose and suddenly she was talking about us. She reported the raid had occurred on Keise Shima and that all the artillerymen had been wiped out. That was news to us!

After several weeks on Keise Shima, we moved our guns to the main island of Okinawa. We set them up inland a ways and every morning I and three or four others had to check the area around our guns looking for Japanese infiltrators. One time I looked into a pile of sticks set up like a teepee and found a dead civilian sitting in it. Another time I tossed a smoke grenade into a pit that had been covered over to conceal it. Three civilians came out and the hair on one of them was smoking.

One day after we took the guns from Keise Shima to Okinawa itself, a colonel ordered us to move one of the guns to a big ridge. The problem was the Japs were watching the ridge and when our men broke the skyline, they would be fired upon. Well, the colonel didn't tell us about that, or he didn't know, and when we broke that skyline, they really opened up on us from another ridge that paralleled the one we were on. That colonel was the first one out of there! We eventually did get our gun back off the ridge, though.[10]

On June 21, 1945, Okinawa was secured.

We were eventually ordered to load ship to go back to the Philippines to join the 8th Army which was getting ready to invade Japan. While loading ship, the first atomic bomb went off. The second was dropped while we were at sea. We heard it was over and there was a lot of cheering. We all knew what it would be like to go into Japan.

We went on to the island of Luzon and stayed there until November 20, 1945. It was just killing time. I went to Manila several times and did a lot of swimming. We then loaded ship and headed for the U. S. A. We went under the Golden Gate Bridge on Thanksgiving Day 1945.

From a camp near San Francisco, I boarded a train and got off at Camp McCoy, Wisconsin. When I got back to Independence and walked into my dad's store, my mother walked in shortly after. She was awfully glad to see me and I was awfully glad to see her!

As an officer, I did not get my discharge until three months after getting home, in March 1946.

---

[10] Battalion records indicate this incident occurred on May 11, 1945, and was intended to support the 307th Infantry's assault of the Shuri Defense Line.

Sources: Independence News-Wave; Books (Crowl) (Appleman) (Cannon) (Stanton); 531st Field Artillery Battalion records

A Quoto From History. . .

"The celebration was dampened by the fact that our squadron had lost that day two of its best pilots. . ."
George Markham
United States Navy
Letter to parents, August 28, 1945, describing how he, as Combat Information Officer of VF-24 aboard the U. S. S. Belleau Wood, felt upon hearing news of Japan's surrender.

114

GEORGE F. MARKHAM
UNITED STATES NAVY

George Markham was commissioned an Ensign in the United States Navy in June, 1942. He was stationed at the United States Naval Air Station at Quonset Point, Rhode Island, in August 1942, where he received training in intelligence. By May 1943, he had been promoted to Lieutenant junior grade and stationed at Bennett Field, New York.

The keel of the escort aircraft carrier *U. S. S. Belleau Wood* (CVL-24), was originally scheduled to be that of the light cruiser *U. S. S. New Haven* (CL-76) in August, 1941, but within months was converted because of a need for fast, light aircraft carriers. When commissioned at Camden, New Jersey, on March 31, 1943, as an Independence Class carrier, she was 622 feet long and carried a crew of 1,569 officers and men. She spent time in Chesapeake Bay and adjoining waters where, because she was a new type of carrier, she was thoroughly tested before making her way to Norfolk Naval Base, Virginia, for final alterations. She then sailed to Annapolis, Maryland, where she was inspected by top naval brass and hosted hundreds of midshipmen from the Naval Academy who came aboard to learn about the new fast carrier. She then returned to Norfolk, received her squadron of aircraft, and departed for a shakedown cruise in the Caribbean.

George was assigned as combat information officer for Fighter Squadron 24, one of four such squadrons aboard the *Belleau Wood*. While in the Caribbean, he, his pilots, and their crews worked incessantly at becoming a competent combat force as the carrier was being hurried for duty in the Pacific Theater. Following this training, *Belleau Wood* was then ordered to the Pacific in July, 1943. She passed through the Panama Canal on July 26, 1943, before reaching Pearl Harbor on August 9.

On August 25, 1943, *Belleau Wood*, the *U. S. S. Princeton* (CVL-23), and other vessels left Pearl Harbor for Baker Island southwest of Pearl. This island was deemed invaluable as a fighter base to lessen the threat of Japanese raids coming from Tarawa and Makin Islands. Though the Japanese were not known to have a force on Baker Island, the aircraft of *Belleau Wood* and *Princeton* flew continual air cover for the landing on September 1, 1943, and to everyone's surprise, the Japanese did not try to prevent American occupation of the island. *Belleau Wood* crossed the equator 32 times while it circled Baker Island in support of the landing and occupation.

Although Fighter Squadron 24 did not enter into any combat during the Baker Island operation, the invasion of Tarawa on September 18, 1943 was a different matter. Here, the pilots gained invaluable experience in striking Japanese facilities, machine gun positions, fuel dumps, and anti-aircraft and shore defenses. Late in the afternoon of September 18, *Belleau Wood* returned to Pearl Harbor with her pilots having combat experience under their belts.

On September 29, 1943, *Belleau Wood* again left Pearl, this time in the company of five other carriers for a strike against Wake Island. For two days, October 5-6, 1943, the carrier planes and warships pounded the Japanese on Wake, and following the operation, Commander-in-Chief, Pacific Fleet, Admiral Chester W. Nimitz sent a message to the ships and crews of Task Force 14, stating, "The thorough job done on Wake by planes and ships of your task force will have results reaching far beyond the heavy damage inflicted."

Upon returning to Pearl Harbor on October 11, 1943, George's brother, Dick, stationed at the time in Hawaii, happened to see *Belleau Wood* steaming into port. He soon was able to contact George and the two spent two days together ashore.

Once resupplied and refueled, however, *Belleau Wood* left Pearl on November 10, 1943 as part of Task Force 50 heading for the Gilbert Islands where Tarawa was slated for assault by a Marine amphibious force. The American planes and ships found the enemy heavily entrenched and resisting fiercely on the islands of the group as they struck Japanese airfields, radio installations, pillboxes, and ammunition and fuel dumps. Enemy aircraft attacked the ships regularly, and one time *Belleau Wood* narrowly averted being struck by a torpedo dropped by a

Japanese torpedo bomber. But though at times the outcome of the land battle hung in the balance, the Japanese forces in the Gilbert Islands were eventually broken by the end of November, 1943.

Following a return to Pearl on December 10, 1943, *Belleau Wood* next participated in the invasions of Makin Island and Kwajalein in the Marshall Island group, this time accompanied by large carriers such as the *U. S. S. Enterprise* of Rear Admiral Marc Mitschner's powerful Task Force 58. On January 29, 1944, *Belleau Wood's* aircraft were sent to neutralize the airfield on Taroa and harass shipping in the vicinity before moving to Kwajalein the next day. By February 4, Kwajalein was in American hands and the Task Force anchored at Majuro Atoll for a short rest.

After leaving Majuro, *Belleau Wood*, still with Task Force 58, then participated in the raids on Truk, Saipan, and Tinian in February 1944. Truk was a huge Japanese naval installation comparable in importance to that of Pearl Harbor to the Americans, and it was heavily defended. Air battles began at dawn on February 16, 1944, and by mid-afternoon more than 200 Japanese planes had been destroyed. Eventually, however, Truk was bypassed in favor of other targets, but by knocking out Japan's air power in the region, the subsequent landings on Eniwetok Atoll the following day met with less opposition.

Following refueling at sea, *Belleau Wood* sailed directly to its next objective, the Marianas Islands. Raids to determine enemy strength were conducted on Tinian, Rota, and Guam, as well as the main island fortification of Saipan, where invasion was scheduled for June 1944. Here, too, as at Truk, the Task Force faced large numbers of Japanese planes. On February 22, 1944 alone, carrier-based planes destroyed 200 enemy aircraft while losing 45 of their own.

Belleau Wood next sailed to Espiritu Santo, New Hebrides, on March 7, 1944, where a task force was assembling for a strike in the Western Carolines. On March 15, 1944, the huge armada of ships headed for Palau where 31 Japanese ships were sunk, 18 others damaged, and over 200 planes destroyed. *Belleau Wood*, in a task group centered around four carriers, arrived after the action had begun, but her pilots still shot down three Japanese planes and sunk a medium freighter and minelayer. Her planes were involved in destroying a weather station on Ngulu Island on March 31, 1944, sinking a cargo ship at Ulithi, and shooting down two enemy planes only 22 miles distant from her. Next, her aircraft destroyed seven Japanese planes on Woleai Island and strafed numerous enemy installations there. She then spent a week resting at Majuro.

Belleau Wood's next assignment was that of supporting the landings at Hollandia, New Guinea, where her planes raided the Sawar airfield and Wakde Island from April 22-24, 1944, and destroyed enemy installations in both locations. Once northern New Guinea was secured, the task force sailed again, raiding Truk and totally eliminating Japanese air power in the area, and then raiding Ponape in the Carolines on May 1, 1944 before arriving at Kwajalein Atoll.

In June 1944, *Belleau Wood* was one of 15 carriers in Task Force 58 under the command of Admiral Raymond Spruance that headed for the Marianas Islands. On June 11, 1944, she launched her first airstrike against Japanese targets in the islands, shooting down four enemy planes over Guam. The following day, her aircraft continued their attack at Guam and Rota before moving further north with the task force on June 13 and raiding the Bonin Islands and islands in the Iwo Jima group.

During this operation, the Japanese launched a major air attack against Task Force 58, which proved disastrous to their ever-dwindling air forces. 360 Japanese aircraft were shot down by American ships and planes in what officially is known as the "Battle of the Philippine Sea," but what the Americans who fought in it soon dubbed the "Marianas Turkey Shoot." Besides claiming their share of Japanese planes, *Belleau Wood's* aircraft also received full credit for sinking the Japanese aircraft carrier *Hiyo*, one of only a few instances during World War II where American carrier-based planes, even those from the large Essex Class carriers with three times the number of planes stationed on *Belleau Wood*, accomplished this feat.

Belleau Wood spent the remainder of June 1944, covering operations in the Marianas, as well as raiding Iwo Jima once again, before receiving orders to proceed to Pearl Harbor for overhaul, her first since leaving the United States one year earlier.

At Pearl, George again met with his brother Dick, who had arrived in Pearl aboard the *U. S. S. Independence* on July 4, 1944. He then left *Belleau Wood* on furlough and traveled to

Independence to visit with his parents, Attorney and Mrs. John A. Markham. Upon his arrival in San Diego, California, George received a letter of commendation for distinguished service as combat information officer for Fighter Squadron 24 from Rear Admiral William K. Harrill, Commander, Fleet Air, West Coast, at special award ceremonies held at the U. S. Naval Air Station there. The commendation covered the time of August, 1943 to July, 1944 and stated in part:

> In the 24 major air operations in which this squadron participated against the enemy, he assembled and disseminated to the pilots all information relative to the target objectives. On at least one occasion it was due to his quick action and good judgment that a pilot of his squadron was rescued from enemy held waters.

An article describing the award ceremony, with a photograph of George receiving the commendation from Rear Admiral Harrill, appeared in the October 19, 1944 *News-Wave*.

George Markham being congratualated by Rear Admiral William K. Harrill upon receiving his commendation for distinguished service while aboard the *U. S. S. Belleau Wood*.

An extensive article appeared in the *Independence News-Wave* on July 27, 1944, courtesy of the *Winona Republican-Herald* where George had worked for a short time as a reporter prior to the war. In it, he described the Japanese fortifications on Guam as seen through the photos taken by his pilots. He was quoted as stating, "The pictures showed heavy fortifications, including many pillboxes, gun placements and barriers to landing forces. Of course, many of these have been destroyed by bombing and shelling since the aerial survey of the 32-mile long island, containing 225 square miles of surface, was made." In regards to the sinking of the Japanese carrier *Hiyo* in the Philippine Sea, George was quoted as saying, "Three of our planes made direct hits on the carrier and one was shot down. Two of the men from this plane were rescued the following day, 350 miles from the fleet. They had on only their 'Mae West' lifesaving belts as they floated in the ocean. They saw the Jap carrier burning and were nearly run over by a Jap battleship." He further indicated that a major number of downed pilots are rescued, though some spent a considerable amount of time in their rafts waiting to be located and picked up.

In the article, George said the most exciting time was during the "Battle of the Philippine Sea" when three Japanese torpedo bombers broke through the American air defenses and had to be shot down by his carrier's guns. "I was watching the show from the flight deck," he was quoted as saying. "The third plane came over 20 feet above, burning furiously that the heat of the flames hit me in the face. It's dead pilot could be seen hanging limp in the cockpit. It missed the carrier deck by a few feet, plunging into the sea behind us."

As for American newspaper coverage of the action in the Pacific, George said, "The figures on planes shot down and our losses are correct. The day-by-day story of action tells what is actually happening. The figure of 402 Jap planes being shot down to our loss of 27 in the Saipan fight was correct." He further assured the people back home that wounded Americans were receiving the best of care, with hospital ships providing immediate medical aid and the most seriously wounded being flown to Pearl Harbor.

George stated that he was looking for big news out of the Guam and Philippine Islands areas soon and that the superiority of the American planes over those of the Japanese was being demonstrated regularly. The Japanese planes did not carry protective armor for their pilots and the Japanese pilots did not work as a team as did the American pilots, who demonstrated "marvelous teamwork."

Following his 21-day leave, George reported to Quonset Point, Rhode Island, for additional training at the Naval Officers Training School, already wearing five campaign ribbons from his time aboard the *U. S. S. Belleau Wood*.[1] He then reported for duty aboard the *U. S. S. Ticonderoga* (CV-14), an 888-foot-long fleet carrier of the Essex Class that carried a crew of 3,448 and more than 80 aircraft. Newly commissioned on May 8, 1944, *Ticonderoga* left Norfolk, Virginia, on July 30, 1944, and arrived at San Diego, California, on September 5, where she loaded provisions, fuel, aviation gas, and 77 of her aircraft. It is unclear as to when George joined the crew of *Ticonderoga*, but he was aboard when she sailed for Hawaii on September 19, 1944, again serving as a combat information officer.

While remaining at Pearl Harbor for nearly a month following her arrival there, *Ticonderoga* and the *U. S. S. Carina* (AK-74) conducted experiments in transferring aviation bombs from cargo ship to aircraft carrier while underway. *Ticonderoga* also practiced various drills and procedures such as day and night landing operations and antiaircraft defense drills, all in preparation for her entry into combat. She then left Pearl on October 18, 1944, arriving at Ulithi in the Western Carolines on October 29 where she joined Task Force 38.

On November 2, 1944, Task Force 38 headed to the Philippines where the aircraft of *Ticonderoga* provided air support for the Leyte operation and also launched air strikes in the Luzon area, destroying enemy aircraft both in the air and on the ground in preparation for the amphibious landing there. The Japanese, however, retaliated on November 5, 1944, when a large number of kamikaze planes struck the task force. With two planes crashing into the *U. S. S. Lexington* (CV-16), the unscathed *Ticonderoga* continued its attack by striking at Japanese airfields on Luzon the next day where her pilots claimed they destroyed 35 enemy planes.

Following refueling and the loading of replacement aircraft at sea, *Ticonderoga* returned to the Philippines, where on November 11, 1944, aircraft of Task Force 38 attacked and destroyed a large enemy force about to enter Leyte's Ormoc Bay. The planes destroyed all the approaching enemy transports and four of the seven escorting destroyers. Over the next two days, more attacks were launched against targets on Luzon as well as Japanese ships in the area, and the carrier-based planes accounted for the sinking of the cruiser *Kiso*, four destroyers, and seven merchant ships. Task Force 38 then sailed for Ulithi where it took on provisions, arms, and fuel.

Returning once again to the Philippines, *Ticonderoga's* pilots continued mounting an impressive score, sinking the cruisers *Kumano* and *Yasoshima* and several other smaller ships on November 25, 1944, plus destroying more than two dozen aircraft both in the air and on the ground. That same day, the Japanese launched a large attack that included torpedos, bombs, and

---

[1] The *U. S. S. Belleau Wood* continued in action following George's departure, participating in the Philippine Islands campaigns where on October 30, 1944, she was struck by a kamikaze, killing 92 of her crew. Following repairs at San Francisco, California, *Belleau Wood* returned to the Pacific Theater and participated in the Iwo Jima and Okinawa campaigns, as well as conducting raids on the Japanese homeland. Besides her twelve battle stars, the *U. S. S. Belleau Wood* was awarded the Presidential Unit Citation, the highest decoration awarded a naval combat unit.

suicide planes. The *U. S. S. Essex* (CV-9), *Ticonderoga's* sister ship, was hit by a kamikaze and would have been struck a second time if not for *Ticonderoga's* gunners splashing the plane just short of the burning *Essex*. Later that afternoon, aircraft from *Essex* and the *U. S. S. Intrepid* (CV-11), also badly damaged, landed on *Ticonderoga*, after which Task Force 38 headed quickly for Ulithi.

December 11, 1944 found Task Force 38 returning to the Philippines where it again attacked enemy airfields and other installations for three days before heading out to sea for refueling. In a surprising turn of events, the task force sailed directly into a violent typhoon that had not been forecast, and though *Ticonderoga* and the other carriers managed to survive with little damage done to them, the storm did cause the loss of three destroyers and over 800 sailors. The task force then retired to Ulithi where repairs were made until the end of December, 1944. During the first week of January 1945, the carriers again hit Luzon before heading north to cover Japanese airfields in the Ryukyus Islands as the Luzon landing was taking place on January 9. Bad weather, however, forced *Ticonderoga* and Task Group 38.3 away from the Ryukyus and into rejoining the rest of Task Force 38 in attacking targets on and around Formosa instead. On January 12, 1945 the task force's 850 aircraft sank an incredible 44 enemy ships before moving on in search of targets along the Chinese coast toward Hong Kong.

Following its sortie off China, Task Force 38 then headed northeast again, sailing through the Luzon Strait in the early morning hours of January 21, 1945. Just after noon that day, the Japanese attacked and quickly hit the *U. S. S. Langley* (CVL-27) in a glide-bombing attack. Within seconds after that, a kamikaze broke out of the clouds above *Ticonderoga* and crashed through her flight deck, its bomb exploding just above her hanger deck and killing and injuring dozens of men. As fueled American planes began exploding below deck, *Ticonderoga's* crew fought to keep the damage from getting out of hand. In an incredible display of command, the stricken ship's captain, Captain Dixie Kiefer, immediately changed course to keep the wind from fanning the already huge fire. He then ordered magazines flooded to prevent additional explosions, using this flooding to also stabilize the ship's starboard list. When he ordered flooding continued to intentionally cause a 10-degree list to port, most of the fire was neatly dumped overboard, allowing firefighters and aircraft crews to extinguish the remaining flames.

Now, however, *Ticonderoga* was a marked ship and other kamikazes began targeting her. The first three suicide planes to attack were destroyed, but a fourth managed to slip through the wall of shells directed at it to crash into the carrier's starboard side near the command island. Another 100 men were killed or wounded, including Captain Kiefer. Heroic firefighting saved the ship, however, and she was able to leave the area under her own power without experiencing further kamikaze attacks.

Arriving at Ulithi on January 24, 1945, *Ticonderoga's* wounded were moved to the hospital ship *U. S. S. Samaritan* (AH-10), her surviving aircraft were transferred to the *U. S. S. Hancock* (CV-19), and passengers heading home were boarded. *Ticonderoga* left Ulithi on January 28, and after a brief stop at Pearl Harbor, arrived for repairs at Puget Sound Navy Yard, Washington, on February 15,1945. It is believed George was not among those injured during the kamikaze attack and that he remained aboard for the trip to Washington, even though his fighter squadron was detached at Ulithi.

When repairs were completed, *Ticonderoga* left Puget Sound on April 20, 1945 bound for Hawaii, where she welcomed Air Group 87 aboard and began training exercises in preparation for a return to combat. On May 22, 1945 she arrived at Ulithi and joined Task Group 58.4, a part of the Fast Carrier Task Force. For the next 20 days, *Ticonderoga's* aircraft struck airfields on the Japanese home island of Kyushu in an effort to destroy the kamikazes threatening American forces on Okinawa. She was forced into riding out another typhoon, which she did with minimal damage, on June 4-5, 1945, and the following day her pilots shot down three kamikazes headed for Okinawa. On June 13, 1945 *Ticonderoga* arrived at Leyte for two weeks of rest and resupply, and it was there that George and his brother Dick were able to spend time together once again.

Ticonderoga then departed Leyte with Task Force 38 to resume raids on Japan. But a damaged reduction gear forced her to Apra Harbor at Guam where she remained until June 19, 1945, for repairs before rejoining the task force. By this time, not much was left of the Japanese fleet and there was virtually no air cover protecting its few remaining warships. On June 24, 1945, planes from Task Force 38 found and sank three battleships -- *Ise*, *Hyuga*, and *Haruna* -- as well as the escort carrier *Kaiyo* and two heavy cruisers, and four days later, an aircraft carrier, three cruisers, a destroyer, and a submarine were sunk at the Kure Naval Base. Then, Honshu and Hokkaido Islands were struck on August 9-10, 1945, where in one instance a major kamikaze buildup planned to hit the B-29 base in the Marianas Islands was thwarted.

On August 6, 1945, an atomic bomb was dropped on Hiroshima, Japan, followed by another on Nagasaki three days later. On August 16, 1945, *Ticonderoga* had just launched a strike, this one against Tokyo, when word was received of the Japanese surrender. And though her crew remained at full combat readiness, her aircraft were now diverted for another purpose, this being the location of prisoner of war camps so that food and other supplies could be air-dropped to the men held in them.

On September 6, 1945, the *U. S. S. Ticonderoga* entered Tokyo Bay where she embarked passengers for the trip home. In her first two such trips, more than a thousand soldiers and sailors were delivered to Alameda, California, and Tacoma, Washington. After she left Tacoma for Alemeda on October 29, 1945, following her second trip, the aircraft of Air Group 87 were transferred to airfields ashore and *Ticonderoga* then readied herself to bring troops home from Pacific bases in what became known as "Magic Carpet" voyages.

It is not clear as to when George left the *U. S. S. Ticonderoga*, but it may have been following the transfer of her aircraft. In any event, he arrived in Independence as a Lieutenant Commander to visit with his parents in early November, 1945, before traveling to Boston, Massachusetts, where he received his discharge from the United States Navy on November 15, 1945. He had been in the service for 39 months, 22 of which he served as an officer aboard two of the truly great fighting ships of World War II, the *U. S. S. Belleau Wood* and the *U. S. S. Ticonderoga*.

On August 28, 1945, George wrote the following letter to his parents. It appeared in the October 11, 1945, edition of the *News-Wave* and included his impressions of the B-29 base on Guam, the reaction aboard ship towards Japan's surrender and how that day two of his pilots were lost, speculation of his return home, and even a political commentary:

Dear Mother and Dad -

It seems a long time since I last wrote, and I feel very guilty about it. For a long time, we had no opportunity to get mail off, and, of course, received none. Finally, when things relaxed, I was just swamped with reports, etc., which had to get out to higher echelons as soon as possible. They are not all done yet but I am far enough ahead of the yeomen now so that I can take time out this evening and write a few letters. I don't know when this will get on its way to you, but mail service is getting better now. So much has happened since I last wrote that I hardly know where to commence. As I guess I told you before, if Dick hasn't by now, we spent some time at anchor in San Pedro Bay off Leyte and Samar in late June after the first operation. We sailed with the rest of the task force but the ship developed engine trouble and we had to put in for repairs at Guam. We were there about two weeks because repair parts had to be flown in from the States. I stayed aboard the ship most of the time, although the pilots were at an attractive rest camp on the other side of the island from Apra harbor. I met a number of friends there and also had a chance to visit the big B-29 base and to sit in on a briefing for one of their raids on a Japanese city. A lot of the officers from the B-29 fields also came down and visited the ship. It was interesting to drive around the place and see at first hand the places I had briefed the old squadron on in our attacks on the island when held by the enemy. You have undoubtedly seen stories and pictures about the tremendous construction job which has been done on the island. It was quite spectacular to see at night when (since work continued at night) the superhighways over the island were filled with moving vehicles, all with their lights on. It looked like a superhighway on Saturday night around Boston or New York. The harbor was all lit up, of course, also.

As you can imagine, there was tremendous rejoicing aboard the ship when the news first came that

Japan had accepted the Potsdam ultimatum. The celebration was dampened by the fact that our squadron had lost that day two of its best pilots in strikes over enemy bases. The news was also rather discouraging on the next and succeeding day, when the feeling was pretty general that Japan was not acting like a defeated nation and that her keeping the emperor did not sound like unconditional surrender. I am very afraid of that situation and am of the belief that no sound democratic movement will take control in that country until the emperor and the emperor divinity myth are eradicated. Powerful anit-Soviet and imperialistic forces in our country are becoming bolder and attempting to influence adversely our foreign policy. We are really on trial in Asia, and we will be held responsible by the millions of people there for the acts of our allies, as well as ourselves. We have got to keep our eyes open and make intelligent responses to state department policies. Russia seems to be going at least half way in seeking satisfactory adjustment of conflicts existing among various interests in east Asia, and we must develop a realistic, democratic policy to compete. We have a fine start in the Philippines, but that is not enough.

Enough of that. When am I coming home? I don't know yet, but would assume that it might be well within a couple of months. Everything is pretty much up in the air yet. The Navy has set up a point system for discharge, which as it stands just now means I would not be able to get out of the navy for about two years yet even though on state-wide duty. However, that is certain to be modified, and I don't think it will take long once I am back in the states.

I am enclosing a page of Liberty magazine (June 18) which I hope you will save. It shows Gene Strouse at the bedside of his crew member seriously burned in tossing out that incendiary bomb over Japan.

I knew the officer or one of them who was in charge of filming "Fighting Lady" but Mrs. Hicks was probably referring to the photographer (or one of them) who took some of the pictures. The man I knew was a Lt. Dwight Long. Charles Melby's ship was with us a number of times, but I had no chance to see him. Hope Dick is back by now. I have heard from him a couple of times but didn't answer.

All for now. My love to you all.

> Your affectionate son,
> George

Sources: Independence News-Wave; Books (Karig series) (Morison) (Boyne)

RICHARD "DICK" MARKHAM
UNITED STATES NAVY

It isn't clear when Richard "Dick" Markham joined the United States Navy but a brief article in the February 11, 1943, *Independence News-Wave* announced his parents had been informed that he had been commissioned an officer and was ordered to report to the University of Arizona for further training. By June of that year, he had completed his training and had been granted leave, at which time Dick, with his wife and young son, visited Independence. He then spent several weeks at Camp Huenema, north of Los Angeles, California, attached to Argus Unit No. 17, an advanced radar unit that would prove to be of great value in the Pacific as the war progressed. He remained there until shipping out to Hawaii in September or early October, 1943.

On October 11, 1943, shortly after his arrival in Hawaii, Dick saw an aircraft carrier entering Pearl Harbor, and it didn't take him long to recognize it was the *U. S. S. Belleau Wood* (CVL-24), aboard which his brother, George, was serving as combat information officer of Fighter Squadron 24. Once *Belleau Wood* was secured in port, Dick made contact with George and the brothers were able to spend two days together ashore. Dick then resumed training with his Argus Unit as George returned to his ship.

Built upon a hull originally scheduled to be the cruiser *U. S. S. Amsterdam* (CL-59), the first of what became an entirely new class of aircraft carriers was commissioned on January 14, 1943, at Camden, New Jersey, as the *U. S. S. Independence* (CV-22). Following her shakedown

121

cruise in the Caribbean, *Independence* arrived at Pearl Harbor in July, 1943, where she was redesignated on July 15 as CVL-22, indicating a light carrier in contrast to a fleet carrier of the CV-designation. Following two weeks of intensive training, she quickly joined a task force on a raid of the Japanese facilities on Marcus Island. Conducted on September 1, 1943, the raid was a huge success as the aircraft from the carrier group destroyed 70-percent of the enemy installations on the island.

Independence participated in raids on enemy-held Wake Island and the huge base at Rabaul during the next six weeks. In mid-November, 1943, she headed for the Gilbert Islands where her aircraft softened up Tarawa in advance of the Marine amphibious landing there. While engaged in this operation on November 20, 1943, Japanese torpedo planes attacked, and though six were shot down, one torpedo found its mark, seriously damaging *Independence*. Following emergency repairs, she headed for San Francisco for permanent repairs and the addition of an additional aircraft catapult.

Dick probably began duty aboard the *U. S. S. Independence* immediately following the carrier's return to Pearl Harbor on July 3, 1944, as a note in the July 20, 1944 edition of the *News-Wave* indicated he was aboard the ship when he once again met with his brother, George, on July 4. George's ship had just returned to Pearl following its participation in the Marianas Islands campaign.

Independence then began training in the pioneering work of night carrier operations, a task in which Dick's expertise as a radar officer would play a crucial role. She continued this training through late August, 1944 out of Eniwetok before sailing with Task Force 38 on August 29 to participate in the Palaus operation, the purpose of which was to secure bases for the assault on the Philippine Islands scheduled for October. During this operation, she provided night reconnaissance and night combat air patrol.

In September, 1944, *Independence* and the rest of Task Force 38 shifted its attention to the Philippines, regularly striking Japanese installations throughout the islands. In early October, the Task Force left the Philippines for resupply at Ulithi, following which it quickly set sail for Okinawa, striking there, at Formosa, and the Philippines, and exhibiting a mobility that demonstrated just why Task Force 38 was called a "fast carrier task force." During this time, *Independence* successfully repelled enemy air attacks during the day and provided defensive cover and reconnaissance at night.

By the third week of October, 1944, it was becoming apparent the Japanese were attempting to break the American foothold on Leyte Island in the Philippines by sending in a major part of their fleet. On October 24, 1944, when Japanese Admiral Kurita's force was located in the Sibuyan Sea, the American carriers launched a series of attacks, sinking the giant Japanese battleship *Musashi* and damaging or disabling other ships, including a cruiser.

That same evening, Admiral Halsey decided to head his Task Force 38 northward in search of the enemy carrier group commanded by Admiral Ozawa. It was night search planes from *Independence* that spotted the Japanese force and shadowed it until a massive attack could be launched the morning of October 26, 1944. The result of the attacks was that all four Japanese carriers were sunk, thus ending the "Battle of Leyte Gulf." As for the *U. S. S. Independence* in this action, with its night operations capacity and probably Dick Markham as a radar officer aboard her, she had contributed highly to the development of night operations by aircraft carriers, thus saving many American lives because, coupled with major victories in Suriago Strait and in the "Battle Off Samar," the threat of the Japanese Navy had been effectively neutralized for the remainder of the war.

Independence and Task Force 38, which Dick's brother George's new carrier, *U. S. S. Ticonderoga* (CV-14),[1] joined on November 2, 1944, resumed its operations over the Philippines

---

[1] It is not known whether Dick was aware of George's new assignment aboard *Ticonderoga*, in light of the fact that he probably knew the *U. S. S. Belleau Wood*, also in Task Force 38 and Dick's previous ship, had been seriously damaged by a kamikaze on October 30, 1944 off the Philippines, resulting in 92 of her crew being killed. George had left *Belleau Wood* prior to this incident.

with *Independence* providing search planes and night fighter protection. *Independence* then spent five days in November, 1944, at Ulithi for rest and resupply, after which she continued operating in the area of the Philippines until late December.

In early January, 1945, *Independence's* task force supported the landings on Luzon, Philippine Islands, and followed that with a trip through the South China Sea, attacking Japanese air bases on Formosa, Indo-China, and China. The carrier force then returned to the Philippines where in Luzon Strait on January 21, 1945, the *U. S. S. Ticonderoga*, brother George's ship, was severely damaged by a kamikaze, killing 100 men. George, fortunately, was not injured in the incident. On January 30, 1945, *Independence* sailed to Pearl Harbor for repairs.

March 30, 1945 found aircraft from the *U. S. S. Independence* and other carriers beginning their pre-invasion attacks of Japanese installations on Okinawa. During the days following the landing, her pilots shot down numerous Japanese planes which were desperately trying to fend off the American assault. On June 10, 1945, *Independence* left the waters of Okinawa and sailed for Leyte, Philippine Islands, for rest and resupply. It was probably in mid-June when Dick's parents received a letter describing an interesting experience Dick had while at sea. A portion of the letter appeared in the June 28, 1945 issue of the *News-Wave* as follows:

> I got back to the ship yesterday. I was over on a Destroyer for five days as a Fighter Director. It was very interesting. It was quite an experience being transferred at sea from one ship to another while traveling along at 20 miles per hour. The ships get about 100 feet apart and then throw a line over, pulling a heavy line over with it. On this line is a coupling and pulley holding a chair to which is attached a second line. This chair, with me in it, is then pulled across the intervening water.
>
> We expect to have a couple of weeks rest now and expect to be able to see George again. It will be interesting to see a place which was so close last fall (Ed. - probably referring to the Philippines). George's ship is of the Essex Class and within sight of our ship.

Leaving the Philippines following her rest period at Leyte, *Independence* next headed for Japan itself, where the continual attacks by her planes and those of other carriers undoubtedly affected Japanese morale on the home islands. When the war ended on August 15, 1945, her aircraft turned their attention to locating prisoner of war camps and flying cover for Allied occupation troops before departing Tokyo on September 22, 1945, bound for San Francisco.

It was probably sometime immediately following the end of the war that Dick received leave and flew back to the United States. The September 6, 1945, *News-Wave* announced that Dick, a Lieutenant (junior grade), his wife and son, had arrived for a visit in Independence following Dick's 18 months aboard the *U. S. S. Independence*.

Following this leave, Dick reported to St. Simon Island, Georgia, where he joined the staff of the Navy's radar school. But like the uncertainties surrounding his entrance into the Navy, details regarding Dick's departure from the Navy are also unclear. However, after he left the Navy, he did spend six years in private legal practice in Independence, then returned to active duty once again and was stationed in the Judge Advocates Office in the Pentagon, Washington, D. C.

The *U. S. S. Independence* received eight battle stars for her participation in World War II. She then was selected for a rather inglorious duty, that of a target vessel for the Bikini Island atomic bomb tests in 1946. Though she was only one-half mile from ground zero for the July 1 explosion, she did not sink, so she was targeted again during another explosion on July 25, 1946. Her hulk, now highly radioactive, was later taken to Pearl Harbor, and then San Francisco, for various tests. Finally, she was sunk off the coast of California on January 29, 1951 during weapons tests.

No Photo.
Sources: Independence News-Wave; Internet

MARCEL M. "ZEKE" MARSOLEK
UNITED STATES ARMY AIR CORPS

The following edited narrative was prepared from a personal military history written by Marcel Marsolek on September 24, 1997, and from additional notes supplied by him.

I was inducted into the Army on March 9, 1943 in Milwaukee, Wisconsin, from where I was transported to Fort Sheridan, Illinois. From there I was transported to Fort Jackson, South Carolina, and assigned to the Defense Platoon of Division Headquarters, 106th Infantry Division. I went through basic training and then applied for the Army Specialized Training Program (ASTP). In August 1943 I was sent to Clemson University in South Carolina to take the ASTP qualification tests. I did qualify and was then sent to the University of Georgia in Athens in time for the fall semester which began in September 1943 and ran through December 1943. While at the University of Georgia, I was sent to the hospital at Fort McPherson in Atlanta, Georgia, for nasal surgery to repair a football injury and also to correct a deviated septum. Following the surgery, I was transferred to Georgia Tech in Atlanta in January 1944. While there, I applied for Air Cadet Training and was sent to Greensboro, North Carolina, in February 1944. I did not qualify for pilot training and was sent to Buckley Field, Colorado, to be trained as an Armorer. When I got to Buckley Field I learned the Armorer program was shut down, so next I was sent to Lowery Field, Colorado. At Lowery, I went through the Armorer course and then the Remote Turret Mechanized Gunner School. I completed the B-17 Armament School and then progressed to B-29 Central Fire Control School. Upon completion of the Central Fire Control (CFC) course, I was classified a CFC Gunner for the B-29 heavy bomber and became an aircraft gun commander. In November 1944, the CFC class graduates were sent to Lincoln, Nebraska, for assignment to a B-29 combat crew.

In December 1944, our crew was sent to Peyote, Texas, for flight training. However, upon our arrival there we were sent almost immediately to Clovis, New Mexico, where we did go through a combat flight training program. While at Clovis, I received a gash on my lip while on a training flight to Galveston, Texas, and required suturing on the field by a medic. When we completed combat flight training at Clovis, our crew was sent to Kearney, Nebraska, on March 19, 1945. There we picked up our B-29 to fly overseas. We were sent to Mather Field, California, on March 30, 1945, then flew to Oahu, Hawaiian Islands, on April 6, 1945. Two days later we flew to Kwajalein Atoll and then landed on Saipan on April 10, 1945. They kept our aircraft on Saipan and transported us to Guam via Air Transport Command. On April 12, 1945, our crew was assigned to an aircraft of the 43rd Bombardment Squadron, 29th Bombardment Group, 314th Bombardment Wing. From then through June 10, 1945, our crew completed twelve combat missions.

While on Guam, Clarence Mlynek from Independence located me. We met a couple of times and looked for Ben V. Schneider, Jr., also from Independence. Clarence was in a Signal Corps outfit and "Junior" was an officer in the Marines. Both saw much rougher duty than I. They were on the ground around the clock, day after day, with the mud, bugs, and snipers. We fly boys were rather insulated from those ravages. Other than the few minutes through flak and fighter passes, we were dry inside the plane and had beds to sleep on. We did not locate "Junior," however. I would have liked seeing him to thank him and the Marines for taking Iwo Jima. It saved about 20,000 B-29 crewmen who made emergency landings there. We used it five times ourselves!

Not all of our flights were against the enemy, however. One Sunday afternoon in May 1945, as we lay around in the Quonset, the bullhorn blared out, "Anderson's crew report to your aircraft prepared to fly!" When we returned from our flight, the other two crews of enlisted men in our hut were curious about our "call out." This is where, without batting an eyebrow, our tail gunner, Jack Snipes, spoke up with his usual flair for rhyme and poetry. He told a little story about "Andy's crew. . . the hottest bunch that ever flew," which he ended, "In case you're tired and want to hit the sack, I'll skip the details of the flight out and back. But to cut you in on this deal, we flew the Colonel and his date to Harmon Field." Needless to say, he received a rousing applause from the guys, and maybe it was only a coincidence, but in about a month our crew was picked to go back to the States to Lead Crew School for special training at Edwards Air Force Base near Muroc, California. We spent about a month there and often wondered why we were selected to go. Maybe it was a pay-off or maybe it was a case of hiding the evidence for a while! We returned to Guam in early August 1945, before the A-bomb was dropped, and resumed combat duty once again.

In November 1945, the relocation program began and our aircraft commander, co-pilot, navigator, radar observer, flight engineer, and radio operator were assigned to fly a plane full of "high point" troops back stateside. The bombardier and the four of us gunners were left behind. We were assigned as instructors for the new incoming replacement crews. From time to time, as various men were rotated stateside, we would fill in temporarily at other jobs until a permanent man was in place. Once I filled in a couple of days in the mail room. I wasn't reclassified as a postal clerk but stayed on flying status and still had to go up to check out the new crews.

During this period of November 1945 to February 1946 I was experiencing periods of high fever and was told I had contracted dengue fever. Following my discharge in April 1946, I had a relapse but have not suffered any further bouts since.

In February, 1946, I was sent to Saipan to board the *U. S. S. Sitka* (APA- 113) for my return to the States. We docked at San Pedro, California, and from there I was sent to Camp McCoy, Wisconsin, where I was discharged on March 1, 1946.

It is often said that the United States is a melting pot of humanity with its diverse races and nationalities. Well, our crew also was a melting pot, representing all parts of America, and I would like them remembered here:

Pilot H. W. "Andy" Anderson, Idaho, 26 years of age;
Co-Pilot H. M. "Mac" Price, Little Rock, AR, 23;
Navigator Louis "Lou" Galezewski, South Bend, IN, 24;
Radar Operator Harold Salmonowitz, "Jr.", New York, NY, 22;
Bombardier Thomas Wheeker, Detroit, MI, 25;
Flight Engineer Dan Breaux, Monroe, LA, 25;
Right Blister Gunner J. C. "Kris" Lingerfelt, Morganton, NC, 19;
Left Blister Gunner David Levinson, Fairmont, NC, 19;
Tail Gunner Jack Snipes, Morganton, NC, 19;
Radio Operator John "J. J." VonUtter, Connecticut, 25;
I was a 22-year-old Central Fire Control Gunner.

Marcel wrote a letter home on March 23, 1943 from South Carolina, that was published on April 1, 1943 in the *News-Wave*. In it he gave a brief description of life in his camp:

Dear Folks and All:

Well, I'm finally assigned to my company and finally found out where I'm at. Boy, our bunch sure was split up. I don't believe there are two fellows left together.

When we left Fort Sheridan last Saturday at 5:30 p.m. there still was Jack DeBow, Floren Hegge and myself together. We left Sherman Erickson there. Oh, yes, by the way, I met Clarence Gamroth there. He has been there since October and is to be shipped for his basic training Wednesday.

There is plenty I could write and tell you about the trip and camp, but as you know, there is a war on and we are not supposed to write about such things. But I can say that now I have been in St. Louis, Mo., Cairo, Ill., Nashville, Tenn., and Atlanta, Georgia, and we are only six miles from Columbia, South Carolina, the state capital. It is quite a large city but we were told it wasn't a very good place to go to and anyway, right here at the post we have a large theatre, service club, 3 p. x.'s near my barracks, so we are sitting pretty. We have baseball, football and softball.

The crew of Captain Holly Anderson's B-29.
Front row, left to right: David Breaux, Flight Engineer; Lucas, extra radio operator on special mission to locate missing General Harmon; Harold Salmonowitz, radar observer; John Von Utter, radio operator; Jack Snipes, tail gunner; David Levinson, right blister gunner.
Back row, left to right: Louis Galazewski, navigator; Herbert Price, co-pilot; J. C. Lingenfelt, left blister gunner; Thomas Wheeler, bombardier; H. W. Anderson, aircraft commander and pilot; Marcel "Zeke" Marsolek, central fire control operator.

Damage done to Marcel's B-29 during a mission over Japan. At left is Captain H. W. Anderson, aircraft commander; at right is Master Sergeant Daniel Breaux, flight engineer.

126

Old "You Hoo!" Lear is our general. Everybody knows he's tough. Hope I never run across him, for a while anyway. I think I got quite a break because of the 600 that left Ft. Sheridan, only five of us were attached to the Division Headquarters Company. I think I'll like it here. Our basic training does not start until about the 29th. Until then we just drill around here each day.

Say, when you get Blazes' (Ed. - Everett Blaha) address send it to me and send him mine, as we know not of each other's whereabouts.

The meals here so far are good -- plenty of milk, butter, meat, cheese, beans, cabbage, bread, potatoes and eggs. What more can one expect.

Well, I'll have to quit for tonight so as to get through before lights are turned out at 9:30 p. m. So good bye to you all. I remain your son and brother,

Marce

While overseas, Marcel maintained records of his missions as the Central Fire Control man in Captain Holly W. Anderson's crew of B-29 #44-69885. The following is a copy of that record:

Formation Nomenclature:

```
          1
       3  2
   7          4
 9 8         6 5
   11         10
```

Note: This scheme will aid in identifying the position of Zeke's aircraft during the various missions described below.

4-19-45 Milkrun over Rota. Checking out problem with bomb bay doors. 3 hrs. 5 min., 15k[1] altitude.

4-27-45 Daylight to Kushira Airfield on Kyushu. Formation all fouled up. Flew #4 in lead flight. No opposition. Bombed at 16 k by radar. Bombs away 11:10. Bombed alternate target Kokubu on Kyushu. Saw 23 P-51's. Flight 16 hr 7 min.

4-29-45 Daylight to Kushira Airfield on Kyushu. Fair formation, flew lead #7 of low flight. Meager flak, two fighters attacked us. Chris (Cpl. James C. Lingerfelt), Dave (Cpl. Levinson), and Jack (Cpl. Snipes) fired.[2] Bombed visual from 17.5 k at 9:55. Flight 15 hr 15 min.

5-3-45 Daylight on Tachiari Airfield. Long bomb run, fair formation, flew #3 of lead flight. Heavy flak and aggressive fighters, about 30, Nicks and Tonys. Took a direct flak hit in our lower aft turret. Knocked out copilot's controls, no rudder control, all radios out, oxygen out, 3 of 4 guns in upper forward exploded. (Lt.) Wheeker and I each claimed fighters. Jack (Cpl. Snipes) was out for a short time from concussion. Bombed from 18 k. B(ombs) away at 16:08.
Flight 16 hrs 50 min landed on Iwo Jima. Plane had rear section replaced on Iwo.

5-11-45 Daylight raid on Kobe airplane factory. Good formation, flew #3 of lead. Five passes by fighters, moderate flak, took some damage, flew back on only #1 and #2 (engines). #4 feathered, #3 no power.[3] Lead bombardier had his radar man take over on bomb run because of cloud cover, radar man wasn't fully prepared and so bombs landed in hills north of city. Take off 2:50 from Guam. Bombs away 11:05 from 19.5 k. Flight 15:25.

5-14-45 Daylight Nagoya City fire raid. Fair formation, #3 of high flight. Moderate flak, a few holes. Take off 12:55, bombs away 10:52 from 18.5 k. Flight 16 hrs.

5-17-45 Night raid on Nagoya Mitsubishi plant. Bombs away 4:05 from 7.9 k, rest of formation

[1] The letter "k" represents 1,000 feet. Therefore, 15k equals 15,000 feet altitude.

[2] By the time Captain Anderson and his crew returned to Muroc, California, in June. 1945, Lingerfelt and Snipes had been promoted to Staff Sergeant and Levinson to Sergeant. From a letter from Marsolek.

[3] Zeke indicated that #3 engine lost turbo over target but the plane was still able to operate at reduced power. From a letter.

at 14 k. Screwed up timing of ETA. Aft bomb bay doors stuck, I went out got them open. Light flak, mostly auto weapons. About 20 search lights picked us up. Junior (Lt. Salmonowitz) threw out chaff.[4] Flew through heavy smoke and heavy turbulence. Took off 8:05, landed 16 hrs 5 min later. Had no bomb bay tanks, air speed over target 300.

5-23-45 Night raid on Tokyo City. Bombs away 3:04 from 14 k. 12 bombs hung up, I kicked them loose. A few lights picked us up but not long. Junior dumped window, air speed on run 290. Saw a couple balls of fire. Only a few holes. Had to land at Iwo, ran out of gas, no bomb bay tanks. Flight 18:20.

5-26-45 Night on Tokyo. Bombs away 12:47 from 12.8 k. Search lights had us about 7 min off and on. Air speed 280+. Heavy flak and auto weapons. Buddied a damaged 29 back to Saipan. Major Thacker. They lost #1 and #4. We took a little flak in tail section. Dave (Cpl. Levinson) and Tom (Lt. Wheeker) sick, replaced by Sam (Carter) in tail and Lt. Morrison for Tom. Flying time 16 hr. 55 min.

5-29-45 Yokohama day raid. Not too good a formation. Bombs away 11:07 from 19.5 k. Accurate flak, took a hit in #1. A Nick (Japanese aircraft) hit our tail section with a 20 mm. Jack (Cpl. Snipes) scratched. Saw a 29 spin in from 11 k ft., also a P-51 ditched, pilot bailed out, radioed position. We later lost #4 and landed at Tinian. Tough mission, 8 out of 9 of our planes were hit. Flying time 16 hr 40 min. Saw one Jap fighter go down.

6-5-45 Kobe day raid. Good formation. Flew #5. B(ombs) away 9:07 from 13 k. Accurate and intense flak, took hits in #s 1-2-4, damage in tail section damaged fuel line to #4. Took 14 aggressive fighter passes. Flying time 15:12 Lower aft turret out of order.[5]

6-7-45 Osaka Arsenal. Not too good formation.

6-10-45 Tachikawa day raid, good formation, flew #9. Bombs away 8:54 from 21 k ft. Moderate accurate flak, 19 fighters, not aggressive. Oil leaks from #s 1-2-3. Flying time 14:50. Had 9 holes in plane.

6-11-45 Left Guam for Lead Crew training at Edwards A. F. Base at Muroc, California.

8-4-45 Returned to Guam

8-27-45 Went to Iwo to fly navigational escort for P-51 fighters.

8-31-45 Flew to Tokyo, photo mission. Flew down at around 600 ft. Saw Tokyo, Kawasaki, and Yokohama.

9-9-45 Returned to Guam from Iwo.

9-16-45 Flew group formation for General Twinning's departure from area.

9-30-45 Flew a display of force over Korea. Flying time 17 hr 50 min. We were the lead of a 10 plane formation, over several cities at 8 k ft. Were first to return.

10-8-45 Flew search mission for General Harmon's missing plane. No results.

10-10-45 Again flew search for General Harmon's plane. Again no results.

10-14-45 Flew relief mission from Guam to Saipan to Okinawa. A typhoon about leveled most buildings on Okinawa.

10-16-45 Returned to Guam.

Marcel left the service in 1946. During the 29th Bomb Group's time in the Asiatic-Pacific Theater, it was awarded two Distinguished Unit Citations. One of the citiations was awarded while Marcel was a member of the Group, which allowed him to wear the Distinguished Unit Bar. This was for actions against the enemy from June 19-26, 1945, when the 29th BG destroyed high-priority industrial and military targets while being attacked by enemy fighter and ground fire. Additionally, Marcel was awarded the Air Medal with Cluster, the Asiatic-Pacific Theater Service Medal with Bronze Service Star, American Theater Medal, one Overseas Service Bar, and Good Conduct Medal.

---

[4] The "chaff" referred to in the entry of 5-17-45 and the "window" referred to in the entry of 5-23-45 were terms used by air crews for radar counter measures. Tin foil was dumped from the planes in order to jam and therefore confuse enemy radar-controlled searchlights and anti-aircraft guns. From a letter.

[5] The cause of this problem was identified as a flak hit. From a letter.

Photos taken of the Tokyo, Japan, area by Marcel Marsolek's B-29 about the time the war ended.

Destroyed oil refinery.

An undamaged civic building.

Sources: Marcel Marsolek personal papers; Independence News-Wave

MICHAEL W. MARSOLEK
UNITED STATES ARMY

Mike Marsolek entered the service with the United States Army on January 9, 1942 at Fort Sheridan, Illinois. Nine days later he arrived at Fort Francis C. Warren, Wyoming, where he underwent basic training as a member of Company K. Following completion of basic training, Mike was sent to Fort Bliss, Texas, where he was assigned to the 854th Ordnance H(eavy) M(aintenance) Company. He was promoted to Technician Fourth Grade on July 1, 1942 while serving with Company F of the 52nd Ordnance Maintenance Regiment (HM). He was later transferred to the 124th Ordnance M(edium) M(aintenance) Company, which had been activated at Camp Claiborne, Louisiana, on February 10, 1943. When the Louisiana Manuevers began on July 12, 1943, Mike was assigned to a unit that maintained 3,500 vehicles during the exercises. At this time, and throughout his military service, Mike was a cook, baker, and meat cutter; on his shift he served as first cook.

Mike's company moved to Camp Swift, Texas, in January 1944, where on March 8, 1944, the company was reorganized and redesignated as the 124th Ordnance (HM) Company. While at Camp Swift, the 124th helped organize and prepare the 102nd Infantry Division and 10th Mountain Division for overseas shipment.

On November 4, 1944, Mike and his unit left Camp Swift for Camp Kilmer, New Jersey, where they themselves prepared for overseas shipment. Boarding the former British Raider *HMS Carnarvon Castle* on November 22, 1944, they sailed the following day in a 50-ship convoy headed for Southhampton, England. They experienced a submarine alert on December 3, 1944, but nothing came of it, and the convoy began debarking the next day in Southhampton.

Arriving at Ordnance Depot 0-640 in Tidworth, Hampshire, England, the men of the 124th Ordnance found wooden double-decked frame beds with chicken wire for springs and canvas bags filled with hay for mattresses. The weather they encountered was much different from what they had experienced in Texas, as well. It was cold, often raining and foggy, and mud was everywhere. They immediately set to work in a series of details and assignments, but many of the men still found time to see some of the historic cities of England, including Bath, Hornemouth, Stratford- on-Avon, and London.

On February 18, 1945, the 124th Ordnance (HM) Company left Tidworth and drove to Camp C-13 near Hursley, England. Ten days later, it moved to Camp C-5, located near Winchester. Here it prepared for overseas shipment once again, but this time to the mainland of Europe.

Boarding the *HMS Empire Rapier* on March 11, 1945, Mike and his Company arrived in Le Harve, France, two days later. The Company traveled to Valenciennces, France, then to Namur, Belgium, and into Germany through the ruined city of Aachen. It was here the Company entered the combat zone, where it remained until the end of the war. Its first base of operations was established at Dulken, Germany, on March 20, 1945.

On April 5, 1945 Mike's Company left Dulken, making the first of five moves that month. It traveled through Munster, Walendorf, Bielefeld, and Cunrau, and arrived at Rohstorf, Germany, on April 28, 1945. It had crossed the Rhine River on April 5, 1945 and the Weser

River on April 16, 1945.

Almost immediately upon arriving in Cunrau, an alert was sounded because a large unit of German tanks had completely surrounded the area from Klotze to beyond Cunrau. This happened because the rapidly advancing Allied army had bypassed a pocket of woods that was concealing the German armored units. The Company's security plan went into effect immediately, but elements of the Allied Ninth Army quickly eliminated the German positions.

During its time in Germany, Mike's 124th Ordnance (MM) Company received a commendation from the commanding officer, 16th Ordnance Company, for the excellent work it had done while working with the 16th Ordnance for about one month. Because the units were often moving, most areas were unsuitable for ordnance work and conditions were often cramped, but despite this and the supply section's continually having difficulty obtaining the parts necessary for ordnance work, the 124th's primary mission was still accomplished.

The 124th Ordnance left Rohstorf on May 8, 1945, and relocated at Zarrentin, Germany. It was here the Company learned Germany had surrendered, and it wasn't long before two barrels of wine -- 400 gallons! -- were liberated for an impromtu celebration!

On May 17, 1945, the Company moved to Hillerleben, Germany, where a remarkable amount of work was accomplished. On June 12, 1945, it moved 240 miles to Laubach, Germany, and it was here that the men of the 124th Ordnance (MM) Company learned on June 25 that they were being sent home.

The Company arrived at Camp Twenty Grand on July 6, 1945, where it remained for two weeks. Then, following a last minute 24-hour delay at Camp Twenty Grand, it arrived in Le Harve, boarded the converted cargo ship *U. S. S. Biensville* on July 22, 1945, and sailed for the United States. When the *Biensville* arrived in Boston on July 31, 1945, the Company traveled to Camp Myles Standish near the city where the men were given a 30-day furlough. During this time, Japan surrendered, so following their furlough, the Company's men boarded trains and headed for Camp Chaffee, Arkansas. It was at Camp Joseph T. Robinson in Little Rock, Arkansas, that Mike received his discharge from the Army on November 16, 1945.

Sources: Mike Marsolek personal papers; Unit records

LADISLAUS "LADDIE" MATCHEY
UNITED STATES MARINES

The following edited narrative is from an interview with Laddie Matchey recorded on June 22, 1998, at his home in rural Independence.

I enlisted in the Marines on September 22, 1943, but was kept on a waiting list until March 1944. I was 17 years old when I enlisted. When I was finally called, I went to the Camp San Diego Recruiting Station. From there, I went to Camp Pendleton where I received basic infantry training. This camp was in the Sierra Madre Mountains and it seemed like we were fighting fires every day that were caused by our tracer bullets.

I spent time in other camps as well, one being at Capistrano, where the swallows fly, and another being Camp Elliot in California. We were always taken to these camps by trucks.

Sometime in 1944, I don't remember the actual date, we boarded a troopship, the *U. S. S. General E. T. Collins*, and sailed out into the Pacific. We stopped overnight to let off a thousand sailors in Hawaii. We later stopped in the Marshall Islands, Kwajalein, and Eniwetok. At Eniwetok we were all allowed to get off ship for the day but had to be back aboard at night.

131

We didn't know where we were going at all. It was a big secret all along the way. We couldn't keep a diary or anything -- that was a court-martial offense! We had been designated as the 3rd Replacement Draft and would be attached where needed. Finally we were told we were near Saipan. I don't know why it took so long to get there, though we were zig-zagging all the way and made those few stops. We spent 37 days aboard ship from the time we left California to when we arrived at Saipan.

At Saipan, we didn't join a division. In fact, after we landed there, we turned right around after three or four hours when they called us back to the ship. We went back on a Higgins boat. There was still some fighting going on there but the main battle was over.

Then we landed on Tinian, another island just below Saipan. On my 18th birthday there was an air raid and the flares and tracers lit up the sky like fireworks. It made a nice birthday party!

Tinian was already secured but there were air raids now and then. I was taken out of infantry and assigned to the 14th and 12th Antiaircraft units, though I wasn't officially a part of those groups.

Most of the time there I was assigned to security on the airfield perimeter. There were no B-29's there yet, but there were a lot of fighter planes. This is the airfield from where the *Enola Gay* eventually took off carrying the first atomic bomb.

At Tinian we were holding a few POW's and I spent time guarding them when they were in work parties, usually 10 or 12 in a group. They weren't any problem and they really enjoyed the food! I think they were glad to eat!

We left Tinian after a month or two and went to Guam. Here I joined another antiaircraft unit, the 9th, for guard duty. We had some 40-mm guns but mostly 50-calibers. I was on Guam until 1946 because when I enlisted it was for the duration of the war plus six months, and they kept me for the six months!

From Guam we sometimes boarded destroyer escorts to patrol around the islands. We also guarded ships docked there when we had nothing else to do. We always had to man our guns but one guy from each gun would be taken for these patrols and guard duties.

There were three airfields on Guam that we guarded. A lot of B-29's landed there after returning from bombing Tokyo. Some came in sideways and we even saw guys hanging out of them now and then. Quite a few of those planes crashed there.

We were happy when we heard the war was over but don't recall really hearing about the atomic bomb being dropped. They kept us pretty busy through all that time. We kept patrolling and manning the guns even after the surrender was signed on the *U. S. S. Missouri*. There were still a lot of Japanese in caves on the island who wouldn't surrender. One even held out until just a few years ago!

Through all of this I was a private until President Roosevelt issued an order saying anyone who had been a private for 18 months was automatically made a Private First Class. This was in 1945, sometime just before he died. We were also on standby for Okinawa just in case we were needed, but nothing came of that. I finally got home in 1946.

In November 1944 Laddie sent a letter home to his mother from the Marianas Islands that was published in the "Special Serviceman's Edition" of the *News-Wave* on November 30, 1944:

132

Dear Mom:

Well, here I am again. Way out in the Pacific, in the Marianas Islands. But I can't tell you just where. Just heard about the farm two weeks ago. Sure is too bad. Did you have an auction in September? I hope you didn't sell out the farm. I want to try to help you. Did the tractor and binder sell well?

If you sold out where are you going to move?

I got out of the infantry now and am in the Anti-aircraft. Sure am glad I got out of the infantry.

We've got a nice place here, but it rains nearly all the time, and when it doesn't rain it is awfully hot. Will probably go to church today. Well, I'll close now and try to get there for sure as we have to go on trucks to church. It's about three miles from here.

Write and tell Verna to write.

With love,

Laddie

Source: Independence News-Wave

EDWARD J. MAULE
UNITED STATES ARMY

Edward entered the United States Army on September 14, 1942. Following basic training, he was assigned duty as a cook with Company A, 112th Infantry Regiment, 28th Infantry Division.[1] At the time he joined the 28th Infantry, it had just completed training in the IV Corps Louisiana Maneuvers and had returned to Camp Livingston, Louisiana. The Division transferred to Camp Gordon Johnston, Florida, on January 23, 1943, and then to Camp Pickett, Virginia, on June 6, 1943, where it participated in the XIII Corps West Virginia-Norfolk Maneuvers in August-September, 1943.

On October 8, 1943 the 28th Infantry Division departed the Boston Port of Embarkation, arriving in England on October 18, 1943. It trained in Wales and Marlborough, England, for nine months before landing in Normandy, France, on July 22, 1944 where it immediately entered combat in the hedgerow country near St. Lo, France. On August 12, 1944. the 28th Infantry's commander, Major General Lloyd D. Brown, was killed in action.

The Division paraded through Paris, France, on August 29, 1944 before attacking once again northeast of the city. It entered Belgium on September 7, 1944 and Luxembourg the following day. It then crossed into Germany near Binsfeld on September 11, 1944, in the process capturing an important Our River bridge intact.

By mid-September 1944, the 28th Infantry had overcome strong German resistance along the *West Wall* near Grosskampenberg, passing through that defense line and continuing its offensive push. The 112th Infantry Regiment, with the 5th Armored Division, successfully repelled German counterattacks against the Wallendorf Bridgehead on September 19, 1944. The 28th Infantry Division then moved northward to continue assaulting *West Wall* fortifications.

In early November 1944, the Division attacked toward Schmidt, Germany, and soon found itself in the Huertgen Forest, the scene of one of the bloodiest battles of the war in Europe. Sustaining very heavy casualties, the 112th Infantry had to be pulled out of the line on November 14, 1944, with the 110th Infantry withdrawn three days later. On November 19, 1944 the battered 28th Infantry Division was relieved by the 8th Infantry Division and moved to the Our River in Luxembourg for defensive and rest purposes.

Barely recovered from its Huertgen Forest battle, and still resting in Luxembourg, the 28th

---

[1] The 28th Infantry Division suffered 2,316 killed and 9,609 wounded, of which 367 died of their wounds, during its four European Theater campaigns.

Infantry was hit by the full fury of the German Ardennes counteroffensive on December 16, 1944. It was forced out of Wiltz, Luxembourg, on December 19, 1944, and many small units were forced to find their own way back to friendly lines. On December 23, 1944, the 112th Infantry had to abandon St. Vith as it and other Division units were being pushed hard by the Germans. On January 1, 1945, the 28th Infantry was relieved by the fresh 17th Airborne Division near Neufchateau and moved to defensive positions along the Neuse River between Givet and Verdun.

On January 18, 1945 the 28th Infantry relieved the 3rd Infantry Division and prepared to take the offensive once again against the Colmar Pocket.[2] Attacking on February 1, 1945, it reached Colmar the next day only to see tanks of the 5th Armored Division rush by to enter the city first.

The 28th Infantry crossed the Rhine-Rhone Canal on February 6, 1945, after which it relieved the 2nd Infantry Division on February 20. It then began a push toward the Ahr River in early March, 1945, and found itself along the Rhine River within a couple days. On April 24, 1945 it relieved the 36th Infantry Division at Regierungsbezirk, Saarland, where it took responsibility for the military government of Saarland and surrounding region through the end of the war.

Edward arrived at Camp McCoy, Wisconsin, in August, 1945 as a Tech 5, and received his discharge on September 18, 1945. At the time he left Europe he was serving with Headquarters Company of the 112th Infantry. He had been awarded five battle stars for his European-African-Middle Eastern Theater Ribbon for his participation in the Normandy, Northern France, Rhineland, Ardennes-Alsace, and Central Europe campaigns, and had earned four service stripes, the Combat Infantryman Badge, and Good Conduct Medal.

---

2 The Colmar Pocket was the name given to a stubborn German bridgehead on the west side of the Rhine River that proved very difficult for General Jacob Dever's 6th U. S. Army Group to overcome.

Photo: Page 93.
Sources: Independence News-Wave; Book (Stanton)

PETER P. MISH
UNITED STATES ARMY

The following narrative was prepared following an interview with Pete Mish on July 13, 1998 at his home in Independence.

Before entering the Army, I was playing pro baseball as an outfielder for the St. Louis Browns farm team in Appleton, Wisconsin. But then I was drafted and had to leave the team. I was inducted on October 13, 1942 and entered active duty on October 27, 1942, at Fort Sheridan, Illinois. For basic training, I was sent to Camp White, Oregon.[1] We participated in Oregon Maneuvers, after which we were sent to Camp Adair, also in Oregon. I was there for quite awhile and was eventually promoted to Staff Sergeant, a non-commissioned officer, with qualifications in M-1 and .03 rifles. Sometime in early 1944, we boarded a train for Camp Patrick Henry, Virginia. There I boarded the Liberty Ship *U. S. S. Noah Webster* and left for overseas

---

1 At Camp White, the 91st Infantry Division had been activated on August 15, 1942. Pete, upon arriving at Camp White, was immediately assigned to the Division. The 91st Infantry Division, under Major General William G. Livesay, suffered 1,400 killed in action and 6,748 wounded, with 175 of those dying from their wounds, during its three campaigns in Italy.

Pete Mish, lower center, with other members of his company, taken during training in the United States prior to going overseas.

duty on April 21, 1944.

On May 10, 1944, I arrived in Oran in North Africa where we underwent beach training, supposedly for the Normandy invasion. But our orders were changed and we were sent instead to Italy, where we landed at Naples. We moved through Rome, which was declared an open city, and went into the mountains north of Rome. At Villa de Mezza I was wounded in the right hand, both legs, and the face by a grenade. The wounds were pretty bad but when I wrote home, I just said I was hit in the hand and one leg. I didn't want anybody to worry too much. I spent three months in the hospital recovering and had to go through a lot of rehabilitation for my knee, which kind of stiffened up a bit.

After my stay in the hospital, I wasn't allowed to go back to my combat unit because of my leg. Instead, I was reclassified and sent to clerical school at Pisa, Italy. For six weeks I studied clerical and administrative procedures and practices and when I was put back on active duty, it was at the 17th General Hospital in Italy. There I processed papers and made entries in enlisted personnel service records. I also typed orders and reports, answered correspondence, and kept files in order. Then I was transferred to the 300th General Hospital, also in Italy, where I did basically the same things as I did at the 17th. I spent about eight months on duty in the hospitals, into November, 1945.

On November 28, 1945, I boarded the aircraft carrier *U. S. S. Wasp* and headed home, arriving back in the States on December 4, 1945. On December 11, 1945, I received my discharge at Fort Sheridan, Illinois, and went home to Independence.

Pete's 91st Infantry Division began landing at Anzio, Italy, on June 1, 1944. His 363rd Infantry Regiment entered combat on July 4, 1944 during the attack on Hill 675. It took Mt. Vase northeast of Castellini on June 6, 1944, but withdrew due to a German counterattack the next day. The Division attacked toward the Arno River in mid-July, with the 363rd Infantry reaching Livorno on July 18, 1944 and entering Pisa on July 24, 1944.

Following nearly three weeks off the line for rest, the Division crossed the Sieve River on

135

September 10, 1944, attacking Mt. Calvi, Monticelli, and Altuzzo. It took Mt. Beni on September 25, 1944 and fought the Battle for Mt. Oggioli on September 27-28, 1944. On October 1, the day Pete was wounded, the Division had attacked toward Loiano, taking the town on October 5, 1944 following very heavy fighting.

The October 26, 1944 edition of the *News-Wave* carried the report that Pete's parents, Mr. and Mrs. Frank Mish, had received two verifications of his having been wounded. The article stated that shortly before supper on October 21, they had received a letter from Pete's comrades stating that he was unable to write because of injuries to his right leg and right arm. Shortly after eight o'clock that same evening a telegram from the War Department was delivered stating the same and that more details would arrive at a later date. In early November, they were informed that Pete's condition was improving, and on December 14, 1944 it was reported his parents had received his Purple Heart.

Staff Sergeant Pete Mish participated in the Rome-Arno and Northern Appennines campaigns. Besides receiving the Purple Heart for wounds suffered on October 1, 1944, he was also awarded the World War II Victory Medal, the American Theater Ribbon, the European-African-Middle Eastern Theater Ribbon with two bronze battle stars, three Overseas Service Bars, one Service Stripe, and the Good Conduct Medal.

Sources: Independence News-Wave; Book (Stanton)

JOSEPH "CHESTER" C. MLYNEK
UNITED STATES ARMY

Chester joined the National Guard Military Police Company at Arcadia, Wisconsin, on October 15, 1940. He received his basic training at Camp Livingston, Louisiana, before receiving specialty training as a mail clerk. He then left for England with the 32nd Military Police Company on February 19, 1942, arriving there on March 4, 1942, and joining Service Platoon No. 2, Headquarters Company, Headquarters Command, United Kingdom Base, London. In June 1942, Private First Class Mlynek was assigned as the regular Army mail clerk for the 32nd M. P. Company.

On December 10, 1942 Major Lorraine S. Fogarty, Postal Officer, Headquarters, Army Post Office 887, London, recommended a commendation be granted Pfc. Mlynek for "his sincere and whole-hearted interest in his work." Major Fogarty stated that though Chester's work was made exceptionally difficult due to the rapid transfer of personnel in and out of the unit, it was noted that he took the additional steps necessary in searching for and forwarding mail to the appropriate serviceman. It had also been brought to Major Fogarty's attention that Chester kept the best set of records for Registered and Insured mail and even prepared his own forms for tracking that mail. The recommendation was forwarded to Lieutenant Colonel C. W. Hoffman, Provost Marshall, London Base Command, who approved the commendation on December 12, 1942, and added his "own personal appreciation and congratulations upon the high manner of performance of a very difficult duty."

In April 1944, Chester was transferred to the Casual Center, Headquarters Detachment, Central Base Section, Services of Supply, European Theater of Operation, also based in London. During an inspection on May 6, 1944, Captain Patrick Angeline commended Chester on his personal appearance, something that was considered very important in this position of operating a casual billet that is similar to a hotel. He remained in this duty until returning to the States by air on June 30, 1945.

In a *News-Wave* article published on July 12, 1945, Chester described how he had slept in an air raid shelter for three months when the German bombing raids over London were at their worst. He also told how 140 men in a chemical warfare company attached to his headquarters had been killed from a direct hit by a German V-bomb. While in London, Chester said he happened to meet three Independence men -- Hillary Halama, Bennie Kulig, and Henry Sura.

On August 23, 1943, Chester married Rita Agnelli in London and they had a son, Ronald, while still in England. Chester arrived back in the United States on June 30, 1945, though his wife and son had to remain in England until transportation could be arranged.

Chester was discharged from active duty on July 6, 1945, at Fort Sheridan, Illinois, and reverted back to National Guard status. He earned six overseas service bars, the American Defense Ribbon, Good Conduct Medal, and European-African-Middle Eastern Theater Ribbon.

Sources: Joseph Mlynek personal papers; Independence News-Wave

ADOLPH A. NOGOSEK
UNITED STATES ARMY AIR FORCE

The following edited narrative was prepared following an interview with Adolph Nogosek at his home in Independence on August 2, 1998.

I was inducted into the United States Army on March 3, 1942, at Fort Sheridan, Illinois. After basic training I was assigned to the 3000th Army Air Force Base Unit in Los Angeles, California. This was the home of the Western Flying Training Command where somewhere around one-million men went through various types of flight training, from pilots to ground crew.

General Ralph P. Cousins was the commander of Western Flying Training Command. He was also in charge of a lot of the morale-building programs that came out of California. Then he was married on May 10, 1944. Well, I was originally assigned to the motor pool at the 3000th and one day an officer came in looking for a driver for General Cousins. Nobody in the motor pool wanted the job because all of us then, mostly privates, were afraid of driving generals around. Finally, I was simply told, "Adolph, you're the driver." So, I became a driver for the General's wife and his wife's maid. I took them around Beverly Hills, Santa Barbara, even Los Vegas, the Petrified Forest area, and Roswell, New Mexico. My home base through all of this was Santa Ana, so I would be flown back and forth now and then. While I was at Santa Ana, I learned that Larry Halama was also stationed there, but I never got to see him.

Later that year I requested to be relieved as the General's wife's driver and assigned overseas. On November 9, 1944, I received a commendation from the General for my work, plus was released for overseas duty. The General then had another driver, and he must not have been

Adolf Nogosek, with General Ralph Cousins' Cadillac.

too happy with him because before I could leave the country, my orders were changed and I became the General's personal driver. General Cousins said, "Adolph, you're my driver," and, you know, when a General says to do something, you'd better do it! I think they shot you if you didn't! So I never did get overseas.

My wife and I actually moved into the General's house. I was his chauffeur, butler, and handy man, while my wife became their maid. General Cousins and his wife threw a lot of parties for the Hollywood stars. You see, the General was in charge of producing a weekly radio show called "This Is The Army," and every week he would have a different guest celebrity on the show, all in order to boost morale among the civilians. I would have to pick up the celebrities and then drive them home or wherever they wanted to go after the show. I chauffeured for Bob Hope, Bing Crosby, Gene Autry, and Clark Gable, to name a few. Gene Autry was in the service, too, and was stationed at the same Santa Ana camp I had been at. I remember Bing Crosby's son, one of the young kids, opened a carton of milk in a restaurant one day with his thumb and splashed it all over.

Sometimes I would take the General to see the movie stars at the studio. He would go in the front door and I went in the kitchen. I usually could find something to eat and drink there. I always carried sidearms when driving the General.

I often worked with the General in his garden at home. We were both pretty relaxed when doing that. But when in uniform, and with other people around, we both had to be very business-like and follow proper decorum. And that's the way it had to be, considering his position.

138

I still have a lot of respect for General Cousins. He always treated me well. In 1950, we went to California to see him and his wife. A number of years later, I heard he died. I know he had heart problems, even during the war years.

I was separated from the Army on February 13, 1946, at the Army Air Force Separation Base at Santa Ana, California. For my time in the service, I received the American Theater Ribbon, World War II Victory Medal, and Good Conduct Medal.

On November 20, 1943, Adolph wrote the following letter to his brother, Simon, who then delivered it to the *News-Wave* for publication on December 12, 1943:

Dear Brother:

I guess I'll just sit down and answer your letter. I'm off duty for a few hours so I might as well do something.

Well, how is everybody around home? Just fine I hope. I'm just fine, too, only kept too busy. I guess you already know I have a different job. I'm still driving but now I'm driving for a Major General. And he really keeps me going day and night. I haven't had but one evening off for over two weeks. Last night I was lucky and he released me at nine. Other days it's always 10 or 11 or 12. But I do like this better than driving in the motor pool. I don't have to drive for anyone but him and he's usually gone 10 days out of every month when he flys, and when he's gone I don't have to do a thing. The last time he went out he was gone 14 days and I didn't do a thing for 14 days. I also don't have to live or eat on the post. I have my own private room in town and I only eat one meal a day in the mess hall and the other two I eat in restaurants.

I get $152.65 a month but I have to pay my own board and room out of that. I have a room in town and I pay $3.50 a week for it. But the board costs me quite a bit. If I was back home I could make pretty good money on that. But even at that I'll try and put $50.00 in the bank every month.

You ought to see the car I'm driving now. It's a great big Packard Clipper. It's really a honey. It makes me feel like I'm in civilian life again. Well, how is Eleanor? Fine, I hope. I suppose I'll be an uncle again pretty soon. I'm sorry but I just don't think I'll be there this time, but I plan on seeing you in about March. This time I hope I'll have more days up there. I'm going to try and catch a plane ride at least half ways. How is the weather up there now? I suppose colder than hell. It's pretty nice down here. But its cloudy today so we might get some rain before morning.

Yes, I finally got back from New Mexico. I flew back in a B-17. That was sure a nice trip. It took me three days to get there and I came back in five hours, so that was making pretty good time, don't you think? I won't tell you much about it now for it would be too much to write, but I'll tell you more on my next furlough.

Your brother,
Adolph

Source: Independence News-Wave

AFNER H. OLSON
UNITED STATES ARMY

Afner Olson entered the United States Army on February 20, 1941. In October, 1942, he was transferred to Camp Beale, California where the 13th Armored Division[1] had just been

[1] The 13th Armored Division lsot 214 men killed and 912 wounded, of which 39 died from their wounds, while in action in the European Theater of Operations.

activated. Afner served in 13th Armored's 67th Armored Infantry Battalion, Company B.

From September 15 through November 8, 1943, 13th Armored participated in the IV Corps Oregon No. 1 Maneuvers, after which it returned to Camp Beale. It later transferred to Camp Bowie, Texas, on December 18, 1943 before staging at Camp Kilmer, New Jersey, on January 14, 1945, and leaving for the European Theater from the New York Port of Embarkation on January 17, 1945.

13th Armored sailed directly to Le Havre, France, where it arrived on January 30, 1945 and immediately undertook occupation duty. On April 5, 1945 it was sent to Homberg, near Kassel, Germany, from where it was sent into combat against the Ruhr Pocket on April 8, 1945. In this two-week long battle, 18 Allied divisions had trapped 400,000 German troops that Hitler had ordered to remain in their positions to the last man in an effort to protect the important Ruhr Valley industrial area. When it was over, 317,000 Germans had surrendered.

At the Rhine River on April 18, 1945, 13th Armored was relieved by the 8th Infantry Division and began preparing for operations in Bavaria. Attacking out of Parsberg on April 27, 1945, it moved rapidly along the Danube River before reaching the Isar River at Platting on April 28, 1945. It had difficulties crossing the Isar River and was not able to take the Marktl Bridge near Eisenfelden intact. On May 2, 1945, however, 13th Armored's Combat Command A received the surrender of Braunau, the city of Hitler's birth. The Division was reassembling north of Inn, Bavaria, when the war in Europe ended on May 7,1945.

Afner arrived at Newport News, Virginia, with his 13th Armored Division on July 23, 1945, after which the Division reported to Camp Cooke, California. There, on October 20, 1945, Afner received his discharge with the rank of Sergeant.. He had earned the European-African-Middle Eastern Theater Ribbon with two bronze battle stars, American Defense Service Medal, and Good Conduct Medal.

In an article published in the *News-Wave* on January 3, 1946, Afner spoke highly of the treatment 13th Armored had been given while training in California. He stated the Division took the name "Adopted Sons of California" as the people of the state took a personal interest in the Division while it was stationed there. The men were shown every kind of hospitality, he said, as the residents had put on shows for them and organized tours of Hollywood for off-duty men.

No photo.
Sources: Independence News-Wave; Books (Stanton) (VFW)

MARCEL PAMPUCH
UNITED STATES ARMY

Marcel was inducted into the United States Army on March 29, 1942 in Milwaukee, Wisconsin. He was sent overseas in August 1943, where he joined the 3rd Infantry Division[1] following its Sicily campaign.

The 3rd Infantry Division landed at Salerno, Italy, nine days after the initial invasion of that country. Moving inland, it took Acerno on September 1943, and followed this with the capture of Avellino on September 30. After crossing the Volturno River on October 13, 1943, it captured Cisterna two days later. The Division then fought a fierce ten-day battle for the *Winter Line* beginning November 5, 1943.

On January 22, 1944 the 3rd Infantry assaulted Anzio at X-ray Red and Green beaches.

---

[1] The 3rd Infantry Division lost 4,922 men killed and 18,766 wounded, of which 636 died of their wounds. This is equivalent to suffering more than 150% casualties during its European Theater campaigns of World War II.

Though the Allies caught the Germans by surprise and suffered few casualties during the landing, the Germans quickly sealed off the beachhead and cornered the Allies into an area 11 miles long and seven miles deep stretching between the Anzio and Nettuno harbors. With eight German divisions in place and another five enroute, the Allies were destined to be stuck there for the next four months, always within range of heavy German artillery which regularly rained shells down on the men. One of the most deadly German guns was the Leopold Cannon, known as the "Anzio Express" and "Anzio Annie" by the troops. These were 280-mm railway guns that were capable of delivering 550-pound shells more than 30 miles. The Allies became very frustrated in their attempts at finding and destroying the guns as they could quickly be hidden in tunnels in the surrounding Alban Hills.

Within a few days of sealing off the beachhead, the German *Fourteenth Army* was ordered by Berlin to remove what it called the Allied "abcess" on the Italian coast. On February 3, 1944 a series of very strong German attacks began which at times threatened to push the Allied troops back into the sea. It was during these attacks when Marcel was seriously wounded on February 7, 1944, receiving three machine gun bullet holes to his right leg.[2]

Marcel and his sister, Theresa.

The March 30, 1944 edition of the *News-Wave* reported that Marcel's mother, Mrs. Paul Pampuch, had received notice of Marcel's wounds from the War Department on March 20, and that she learned he had been brought to the United States and was a patient at Stark Hospital in Charleston, South Carolina. The April 13, 1943 edition reported he had been transferred to Schick General Hospital at Clinton, Iowa, and that his mother and sister, with Mr. Anthony Wiench, had traveled by train to visit him. It was reported Marcel had sent word that he hoped to see his Independence friends in a few months.

On August 3, 1944 the *News-Wave* reported 21-year-old Marcel was home on a 21-day furlough and then would return to Clinton where he would undergo additional surgery on his leg.

Marcel was eventually discharged from the Army but continued having problems with his right leg due to the nerve damage it had sustained. Years later, he was forced to undergo amputation.

Marcel was awarded the Purple Heart, Good Conduct Medal, American Theater Medal, and European-North Africa-Middle East Ribbon. He had participated in the Naples-Foggia and Anzio campaigns, two of the 3rd Infantry Division's European Theater campaigns during World War II.

---

[2] By early March, 1944 the tide began to slowly turn at Anzio as Allied air command began attacking German positions. For the next two months, however, all the troops on the beachhead could do was keep their heads down. On May 23, 1944 Operation Shingle was launched and the Allies began their breakout. When it was over, Anzio had cost the U. S. Army 5,538 men killed in action and 14,838 wounded. 22 Medals of Honor were won by the men of Anzio, where Chaplain William Johnson of the 1st Special Service Force, and veteran of Anzio, uttered the famous words, "Surely all who have survived the assault on Anzio will go to heaven, since they have already served their time in hell."

Sources: Independence News-Wave; Books (Stanton) (VFW)

PAUL JOSEPH PAMPUCH
UNITED STATES ARMY

The following narrative was prepared from notes provided by Paul Pampuch and from an interview with him at his Custer, Wisconsin, home on October 10, 1998.

I was drafted on June 30, 1943 and entered the service with the Army in Milwaukee, Wisconsin. From there, I went to Camp Grant, Illinois, for processing. I spent 17 weeks in basic training at Fort Knox, Kentucky, where I was in the 3rd Armored Replacement Battalion, Company B. Then I was sent to Camp Chaffee, Arkansas, for eight months of advanced tank training. At Camp Chaffee, I was assigned to different battalions. My next stop was Camp Phillips, Kansas, where I went through one month of additional tank training, and from there I was sent to Fort Meade, Maryland, to be processed for overseas shipment. After arriving at Camp Shanks, New York, I boarded ship with a lot of other men who were in the replacement pool and we departed for Glasgow, Scotland.

It took four days to get to Glasgow, where we then boarded a train and transferred to Wells, England. But we hadn't been in Wells very long -- only three days -- when we were again loaded aboard ship and taken across the English Channel where we landed at Omaha Beach on the Normandy Coast of France. Once ashore, we were transferred by truck to the replacement pool center.

In July, 1944, I joined the 735th Tank Battalion, 5th Infantry Division, in the St. Lo area.[1] Then we began advancing through France. As the 5th Division was attacking the city of Metz, our tanks were traveling near a town called Pournoy[2] when we lost communications with battalion. The Germans were waiting for us in an ambush and as our tanks rolled by, they jumped out behind them with bazookas that they called "panzerfausts." We lost 24 of our 25 tanks that day and a lot of good guys were killed or captured. I ran all night to get out of there.

---

[1] The Fifth Infantry Division lost 2,298 men killed and 9,549 wounded, of which 358 died of their wounds, during its five campaigns in Europe during World War II.

142

We were near Aschaffenburg, Germany, in the Saar River Basin, when we were ordered to go north because of the German counteroffensive that started in December, 1944. Traveling by tank all night in blackout conditions was a nightmare. We traveled through Luxembourg and arrived south of Bastogne, Belgium, where we were engaged in the "Battle of the Bulge."

After the Germans were beaten back, we crossed the *Siegfried Line* and kept moving because the Germans were falling back now. In a few months, the war was over. We were bivouaced in a forested area at the time and one morning when I woke up, I found my knee had frozen. I couldn't straighten my leg. I was put on an airplane, a C-47, and transferred to either the 25th or 45th General Hospital in Liege, Belgium, where I remained for 45 days. After my leg recovered, I was released back to my battalion and then from there we were transferred to other outfits by the point system. As men were being sent home, some units were disbanded, so those of us remaining simply were moved into other units.

When I was in the States, I was a Private First Class, but by the end of the war had been promoted to Sergeant. My assistant tank driver was a barber back home, and one day while I was sitting by the tank getting a haircut, the company clerk handed me my sergeant's stripes and told me to sew them on.

In October, 1945, I was discharged. After 90 days in Milwaukee and Independence, though, I re-enlisted for three years with the idea that I was going back to Germany. But instead, the Army sent me to Korea for a year! When I got there, I questioned the battalion clerk why I was in Korea since I had enlisted for Germany and three days later I received shipping orders back to the United States. I landed at Fort Lawton, Washington, and transferred to Eustus, Virginia, but I didn't do much of anything there.

I noticed on my DD-214[3] that my MOS (Military Occupation Specialty) didn't identify that I had served in tanks, so I asked to have it changed to include #2736, medium tank crewman. When this was done, it didn't take long and I was on my way to Fort Knox, Kentucky, where I was assigned to Headquarters, 70th Medium Tank Battalion, and trained recruits and commanded a half-track platoon.

After this, though, I had had enough, and received a second discharge as a sergeant on October 8, 1948.

On March 1, 1945, the *Independence News-Wave* published a short letter written by Paul to its editor, Glenn Kirkpatrick, regarding the "Special Serviceman's Edition" he had received:

Dear Sir:
I had the pleasure today of receiving your wonderful copy of the News-Wave. It came a little late, but the way things have been happening around here the last few months it can hardly be helped. Even if it did come late it was real swell to get it after being out here for seven months.
My address has changed quite a bit since you sent the paper.
Right now I'm praying to meet up with my brother. He's over here somewhere close by. So far I haven't had a chance to get in touch with him.
Well, this is all the time I have left so will have to close for the night. Thanks again for the paper 'cause it sure is swell to read about your own people for a change.
Yours truly,
Paul

---

[2] Metz was the most heavily fortified city on the Western Front, ringed with numerous defensive castles and other fortifications. Some of the bloodiest fighting of World War II occurred during the siege of the city that began September 7, 1944.

[3] Form DD-214 was the paper record servicemen received at the time of discharge listing all pertinent personal information as well as identifying dates of movement, shots received, decorations earned, insurance information, etc.

On November 29, 1945, the *News-Wave* reported Paul's mother had received a telegram from him saying he had arrived safely in Boston and was homeward bound.

Sources: Independence News-Wave; Books (Stanton) (Fifth Division Historical Section)

ALLEN C. PAPE
UNITED STATES ARMY

Allen Pape joined the United States Army on February 9, 1942. He received his basic training at Camp Robinson, Arkansas, where he trained with Dominic Kampa, Raymond Sluga, Frank Sluga, Clifford Klink, Henry Misch, and others from the Independence area. He was separated from them, however, when he was sent to Camp Chaffee, Arkansas, to join the 87th Ordnance Company and undergo additional specialized training. From Camp Chaffee, Allen was next transferred to Fort Bragg, North Carolina, a field artillery replacement training center, and then traveled to Camp Kilmer, New Jersey, the staging area for the New York Port of Embarkation. It was from New York that he and his unit set sail for North Africa on November 2, 1942.

Landing at Casablanca, French Morocco, the 87th Ordnance began its duties in support of the 1st Armored Division.[1] The North African invasion, code-named "Operation Torch," was the first time most of the troops had experienced combat, for which they paid a high price as they soon went up against the battle-hardened veterans of German General Erwin Rommel's *Africa Korps*, culminating in the heavy losses suffered at the Kasserine Pass in February 1943. But the Americans learned quickly and by mid-March 1943, were on the attack once again. By May 9, 1943, the German forces in Tunisia began surrendering in large numbers.

Following Operation Torch, Allen and the 87th Ordnance departed for Sicily, arriving there on July 9, 1943 in support of the 45th Infantry Division.[2] The 87th Ordnance then followed the 45th Infantry into Italy, though the exact time of its arrival was not confirmed. It may have participated in the 45th's attack on Salerno, Italy, beginning on September 10, 1943, which resulted in a drive that took the Division north of the famed Monte Cassino area. It is also unclear, but probable, that Allen and his unit participated in the 45th's next campaign, the nearly disastrous landing at Anzio, Italy, on January 22, 1944, which saw the Americans desperately defending their tenuous beachhead for the next four months until the breakout of May 23, 1944. One thing that is certain, however, is that Allen did participate in the Rome-Arno campaign and had an opportunity to visit Rome during a rehabilitation period beginning in mid-June.

When the 45th Infantry Division was shipped out to participate in the invasion of southern France on August 15, 1944, the 87th Ordnance again followed. Pushing northward through France, the Division swung around Switzerland into Germany with General Patch's Seventh U. S. Army, reaching the *West Wall* in the Zweibruecken area on March 17, 1945. It fought the "Battle for Nuremberg" on April 16-20, 1945, and then led the way for the 20th Armored Division toward Munich. Exchanging places enroute with 20th Armored, the 45th Infantry followed it into Munich, where it remained in occupation until the war ended in Europe on May 7, 1945.

Throughout its campaigns, the 87th Ordnance deployed as a roving group of mechanics supporting artillery and armored units. When the big guns and tanks faltered, Allen and his unit

---

[1] 1st Armored Division saw 1,194 of its men killed in action during World War II. Another 5,168 were wounded, of whom 234 died.

[2] The 45th Infantry Division suffered 3,547 killed and 14,441 wounded, with 533 of those dying from their wounds, while in action in Sicily, Italy, France, and Germany.

repaired them. When nitrogen pressure equilibrators on the 155-mm guns and 8-inch howitzers needed to be repacked, the 87th did the job. During the winter of 1944-45 in the Alsace region, the 87th repaired 150 artillery pieces, though the heavy snow and bitter cold hindered work dramatically.

After two years, eleven months in the European Theater of Operations, Allen finally boarded ship for the United States having accumulated 108 service points. He traveled to Fort Sheridan, Illinois, where he was granted a discharge from the Army in October 1945 and immediately journeyed home to Independence. He had earned the European-African-Middle Eastern Theater Service Ribbon with one silver and one bronze battle star, representing the six campaigns he had participated in. He also wore a Bronze Service Arrowhead, five overseas service bars, one Service Stripe, and the Good Conduct Medal.

No photo.
Sources: Independence News-Wave; Book (Stanton)

GERALD "BUD" J. PIETERICK
UNITED STATES ARMY

Gerald "Bud" Pieterick was inducted into the United States Army on May 31, 1944 as an eighteen year-old fresh out of high school. He entered the service at Fort Sheridan, Illinois. Following basic training, Bud was quickly assigned to Company L, 242nd Infantry Regiment, 42nd Infantry Division.[1] On November 25, 1944 he departed from the New York Port of Embarkation for England. While at sea, he met up with Clarence Sluga, who was also going overseas.

Bud landed at Marseilles, France, on December 8-9, 1944 as part of an advance headquarters detachment organized as Task Force Linden. On Christmas Eve 1944 Task Force Linden entered combat near Strasbourg along the Rhine River in relief of the 36th Infantry Division. It was defending a 31-mile line when hit by a series of strong German counterattacks. Bud's 242nd Infantry lost Hatten on January 9, 1945 to one of these attacks, and within ten days, several more positions defended by the 242nd were overrun. It was during this time that Bud was captured by the Germans. He and the other prisoners were stripped of their clothing and interrogated in a cold, wet warehouse, later being given back only their overcoat and boots.

It was soon after Bud's capture that his brother Ray, serving with the 12th Armored Division, was in his unit's headquarters where he noticed a red circle around Bud's regiment on the operations map posted there. Ray knew that meant they were surrounded and probably captured. But Bud's prisoner status remained for only a short time as they were soon liberated by elements of 12th Armored.

Bud saw his brother Ray on Valentine's Day 1945. Following a day of training, he had returned to his tent to lie down on his bunk when he found Ray sitting there. He had been waiting for eight hours. Bud stayed with his brother that night and they talked until 2:00 A.M.

The end of January, 1945 found the 42nd Infantry Division pulled back to reserve status. But by mid-February, 1945, the entire Division was relieving the 45th Infantry Division and holding defensive positions near Haguenau, France, in the Hardt Mountains. On March 15, 1945 the Division attacked the *West Wall*, more commonly known as the Siegfried Line, at Baerenthal, France, and early in the action, Bud was wounded, taking shrapnel in his left arm below the elbow. The shrapnel was not removed.

The Division continued its push into Germany, encountering strong opposition at times,

---

[1] The 42nd Infantry Division suffered 553 killed and 2,212 wounded, of which 85 died from their wounds.

and crossed the Rhine River on March 31, 1945. On April 1, 1945 it followed the 12th Armored Division into Wertheim. Then the 242nd Infantry moved along the Main River while the Division's other regiments assaulted other positions. The Division as a whole attacked Schweinfurt with 12th Armored from April 8-12, 1945, then moved on to Fuerth where intense house-to-house fighting preceded its capture on April 19, 1945. Along with the 3rd and 45th Infantry Divisions, the 42nd attacked and took Nuremberg on April 20, 1945.

Being relieved at Nuremberg, the 42nd Infantry Division then moved south toward the Danube, this time preceding 12th Armored. Two regiments, including Bud's 242nd, attacked across the Danube at Donauwoerth and began a drive on Munich following behind the 20th Armored Division on April 28, 1945. With Munich taken on April 30, the 42nd crossed into Austria north of Salzburg on May 5, 1945. and was in the Salzburg area when the fighting officially ended on May 7, 1945.

Tech Sergeant Gerald "Bud" Pieterick left Europe on May 31, 1946, more than a year after hostilities there ended. He arrived back in the United States on June 11, 1946, having participated in the Rhineland and Central Europe campaigns as a platoon sergeant. Besides the Purple Heart for wounds received on March 15, 1945, Bud was awarded the European-African-Middle Eastern Theater Service Medal, the Army of Occupation Medal-Germany, and the Good Conduct Medal. He received his separation from the Army at Camp McCoy, Wisconsin, on June 17, 1946.

Bud, like his brother, Ray, was a writer of long letters home. He was very much aware of his surroundings and did a marvelous job of describing the sights to his family, Mr. and Mrs. Charlie Pieterick and brothers Gene and Alfred. His parents often gave the letters to the *Independence News-Wave*, where they were published:

November 1944
Dear Mom, Dad, and brothers:
>   The trip on the water was getting monotonous. The first two days I was so sea myself a sailor. On the ship they fed us two meals a day. They had what one would call a P. X. on the ship. One could buy candy bars - three for ten cents. Cigarettes were 50(cents) a carton.
>   I met Clarence Sluga on the ship and it sure felt good to meet someone you knew. By the way, you should have heard the orchestra from our outfit. Were they good! And I could go for a dance!
>   While aboard ship I listened to the Army-Navy football game and was very pleased with the results. Also heard the "Hit Parade."
>   I'm okay but very lonesome as I haven't received any mail for some time. Didn't finish your letter when I started, so will continue where I left off. I received my first batch of mail today! Boy! What a different feeling it puts into a guy. You can't realize what a little thing like a letter means to one so far away. Until this time, and that is about four weeks, I received only one letter from home.
>   Here in France one has to pay as high as $2 for a pack of cigarettes so who wants to pay such outrageous prices.
>   Gerald

Christmas Day, France
Dear Mom, Dad, and brothers:
>   It is Christmas day and I have a little spare time so I'm dropping you a few lines to let you know how I spent the day.
>   Christmas Eve I was on duty so that held me from midnight Mass. I went to town today and attended Mass this morning. It was wonderful to go into a civilian church. I also received Communion and offered it for you at home. They had three altars here, too, with services only at the main altar, and the one on the right held the crib. I looked at that, too, and it had white light bulbs around it. Mass was offered by our chaplain and the church was filled mainly with soldiers. Six altar boys were clad in red and white cassocks. The chaplain delivered the sermon. In this church is a large pipe organ, and a choir of young boys and girls sang. When they sang "Silent Night" the chills ran through me. It was sung in German. Then thoughts came to me of a year ago when I was home for Christmas, and only Ray was

gone. Now two of us are away and if this war keeps up much longer, Gene will be gone for the next year.

Received our P. X. rations today which consisted of three bars of candy and a pack of cigarettes. So you see they don't issue us much. Could you send me a box of sweets? As yet most of my mail hasn't caught up with me and I haven't received any News-Waves or packages since I left the states. To tell the truth, I haven't received very much mail. Just one letter from home since I have been in France. Sure hope my mail catches up soon.

I almost forgot, we had a Christmas dinner here too. Turkey topped the list. Also had asparagus, peas, fruit salad, coffee, raisin bread, fruit and candy. Sure was surprised to have such a meal out here.

Met Ernie Rogstad from Hixton out here. We had a swell time together visiting some of these old ruins out here.

Will be closing for today 'cause I have to go on with some more letters. May God Bless and protect you.

"Bud"

On February 19, 1945, Bud again wrote his parents and brothers from France, describing what he had recently experienced, including finding his brother, Ray, also with the Seventh U. S. Army, sitting on his bunk one night:

Dear Mom, Dad, and Brothers:

I am still on the so-called "rest period." I'm enjoying it very much while it lasts. I am feeling O. K. - wishing you all nothing less. The weather is starting to break, to which we have all looked forward to for a long time. I had a "pass" and I've seen the following places: Strasbourgh, Hagenau, Marseilles, and Nancy and a few others. Of all the cities I've seen I think Hagenau is the best. It has some buildings that have seen battle, but there still are a number of beautiful buildings without scars. The rest are quite battered.

We sleep in foxholes when out in the lines, otherwise we sleep in civilian homes. These houses are sure funny because they all seem to be joined together. One goes into the village and there is just one row of houses joined to the other on each side of the street. They also have living quarters above the stables. The odors from the stables are really strong. The boys are just having an argument as to which one is to get the wood and start the fire. The first Sergeant said he built the fire eight times today and the other Sergeant decided to move the stove to a sawmill because it takes so much wood. But, as a rule, we usually get along O. K.

I received your box of sweets and cookies on January 5 for which I am very grateful. Thanks a lot.

It was at a civilian church that I attended Holy Mass and received Communion.

We now know definitely that our Division is being mentioned in the newspapers. Clip out all you can and save it for me as some day I can look back to see what our outfit did in this world fracas. I sure did appreciate the Special Edition to the News-Wave. Thanks a lot.

I'll now tell you when and how Ray and I met. This happened on Valentine's Day. We were out training all day and I came in pretty well pooped out, so I was going to sit on my bunk and who do you suppose was sitting there? Yep! It was Ray. Boy! was I surprised. I almost jumped to the ceiling. Yes, he waited for me for about eight hours. He stayed with me over night and believe me it was two o'clock in the morning and neither of us was asleep. Yep! Same Ray as he was when back home.

I think I'll bring my letter to a close with hopes that the Almighty God will hear and answer our prayers and grant us our wishes. May God bless you all and keep you safe through this worldly fracas.

With all my love,
"Bud"

Three weeks after the war in Europe ended, Bud wrote additional letters to his parents, these dated May 26 and June 10, 1945. from Austria, and describing some of the sights he was seeing recently. Both were published on July 5, 1945:

Dear Mom, Dad, and All:

147

Received your letters and will answer them while the mood for writing keeps up. This is only my eighth letter tonight. Also received a ten-page letter from Ray. I don't know how he does it.

Mom, don't worry about our drinks. We get water from a place which is checked by our division. A bottle of champagne costs about 75 cents. The beer here is good. Americans manage the brewery here. Of course, passing through Germany, the civilians would give us bottles of schnapps. We had them take the first glass, then we took the bottle and kept moving to the next place. That's how we traveled all day and night.

Passing through Germany was like a picnic. We ate meals that the civilians had on the tables and were about to eat. After eating we kept right on our journey. At one place we came upon a nice big ham. We didn't stop to eat it but took it along to eat later. None of us starved. The little we did to the people didn't compare to what they did to us last winter in the Battle of the Bulge, which you read so much about. You never heard of our outfit being in it. I always like winter but after the last one. . . The snow was up to our belts; we waded through rivers, sleeping in fox holes with no blanket and most of our winter clothing and equipment was captured by the Germans. That's when the Jerries took all my personal belongings. I thank the good Lord and all of you for your prayers. That is what pulled me through to this day. That's why Ray and I didn't write for long times.

Dad, you want to know what happened to the Jerries. Well, they fought to the last man. We had them in the top of the Alp Mountains. They just couldn't go any further and were plenty tough at times. They still are surrendering.

Finally received my mail. About 75 letters and six packages. Don't think my morale isn't up! I can't express how happy I am tonight. Had a nice letter from Miss Hogue, Miss Benjamin and Miss Higgins (Ed. - teachers at Independence High School). I sure do appreciate them.

We look out through our windows and can see the Alp mountains. They are snow covered with beautiful blue lakes at the foot of them. Wish I had a film or two. I would like to take some pictures of different buildings and scenery. In our billet we have a radio, kitchen range, beds and what not. Sure make use of the radio.

Talk about refugees along the wayside. That's all one can see. I talked to some of them and they sure had tough times. Most of them are young boys and girls.

Lost all of my belongings again, while hospitalized.

Germany is a country much different than France. As far as a German city is compared with one in the States, there isn't much difference.

We pull a lot of guard duty and this outfit never stays longer than a week on one place.

Finally, Bud informs his parents of his having been captured by the Germans, and that he had visited the concentration camp at Dachau:

June 10, 1945

Folks, I must tell you that today I went skiing on the Alps. We take a car on a cable all the way up and ski down. Boy! It just takes one's breath away we go so fast. Yes, and we took our shirts off too. A lot of civilians go skiing in their bathing suits. We also had a snow ball fight. Then again we go swimming and fishing and sometimes boat riding on the lake.

Must tell you that I received mail from you within six days. That breaks the record.

The time that I lost all my personal belongings, well I might as well confess now, that I was in German hands for 15 hours. They were just ready to load up on troop wagons and haul us to the prisoner of war cage when our buddies came and rescued us. Don't think I wasn't scared. That is when one really starts to think and think fast. Oh, I thank God I got out of it. A lot of our buddies weren't as lucky. I went through several of those prison camps including Dachau camp. The things that I've seen there are just indescribable. One has to see things to believe. After seeing a few gruesome results of mistreatment, and such, I got so sick I couldn't eat for two days.

> With all my love,
> "Bud"

Source: Bob Pieterick, son; Independence News-Wave; Book (Stanton)

148

The Sons of Mr. and Mrs. Charles Pieterick

Sometime following the end of World War II, this photograph was taken of Charlie Pieterick, a veteran of World War I, and his four sons, with all five in their military uniforms. From Left: Gerald "Bud," 42nd Infantry Division; Eugene, who entered the Army in the summer of 1945; Ray, 12th Armored Division; Charlie; and Alfred, the youngest of the four brothers, who entered the service shortly after World War II ended.

RAY PIETERICK
UNITED STATES ARMY

The following account was written following an interview with Ray Pieterick at his Eau Claire, Wisconsin, home on July 9, 1998.

I was inducted into the Army in Milwaukee on October 16, 1942. They gave me two weeks to get things in order and then I reported for active duty at Fort Sheridan, Illinois, on October 30, 1942. Following basic training I was assigned to the 92nd Cavalry Reconnaissance Squadron (Mechanized) of the 12th Armored Division.[1] I was sent to the Division's communication school at Fort Campbell, Kentucky, and became an administrative

---

[1] The 12th Armored Division saw 214 of their members killed and another 912 wounded, with 39 of those dying from their wounds.

noncommissioned officer and radio operator.

On September 30, 1944, I left New York for England as part of a 202-ship convoy. I was aboard the *U. S. S. Thasker H. Bliss*, which was the convoy's flagship. We had several submarine alerts as we got closer to England and depth charges were dropped a few times by the ships protecting the convoy, but we made it okay. In England, we were transported to Tidworth Barracks where we underwent additional training.

I left England and arrived in Le Havre, France, on November 11, 1944. Our columns moved to a bivouac area first, then started moving forward once everything was ready. We traveled through Soissons on November 30, 1944, then Rheims. On December 7, 1944, we began fighting around Rohrbach-les-Bitche, and entered Uttweiller, Germany, on December 21, 1944. Though there was heavy fighting at times, these in general were smaller skirmishes. Then we were pulled back to Metz where we were ordered to remove all bumper insignia and patches. We were moved to the southern edge of the 3rd Army area and became known as Patton's "Mystery Division." We were in reserve because the Ardennes battle, the "Battle of the Bulge," was going pretty good for the Germans and we were now in a good position just in case we were needed there. The brass was hoping that our being there alone would divert the Germans away from Bastogne.[2]

The Division's first really heavy combat occurred around January 17, 1945, at Herrlisheim and Bischwiller. At Herrlisheim, our whole 43rd Tank Battalion was wiped out. It really was hell. There were a lot of little canals and other problems that caused our tanks to get bogged down. After the battle, we all felt pretty bad about damaging their beautiful church, but we had no choice. Before we left, the 12th Armored took up a collection so the townspeople could begin replacing the stained glass windows in that church. Herrlisheim became the Division's "sister city" from then on and we still help them out today when we have our annual reunions.

It was in January 1945 when I walked into headquarters one day, looked up at the operations map, and saw a big red circle around my brother Bud's unit of the 42nd Division. I knew right away that meant they were surrounded and probably captured by the Germans. It later turned out he had been captured, but they didn't keep him for too long as elements of our Division quickly liberated them.

We crossed the Rhine River at Worms on March 28, 1945. Engineers built a bailey bridge and we crossed at night with no lights. The next day the Division split in two, one group going towards Erbach, while the other, the one I was in, headed for Beerfelden. The two groups joined up again just before we entered Tauberbischofsheim on March 31, 1945. Tauberbischofsheim was like a county seat, it was a nice city, and it hadn't been destroyed like almost all the other cities we saw. On April 5, 1945, we pulled out of Kitzingen, heading south toward Austria. We bypassed several cities while moving pretty fast. One infantry battalion made 70 miles in one day and had to be halted because they were pretty much by themselves.

When we reached Donauworth, we backed up and crossed the Danube River at Dillingen into Austria on April 22, 1945. The Germans were ready to blow up the bridge there, however, and a couple guys risked their necks to crawl down and cut the detonating wires before it could be destroyed. It had taken the Division only 37 days to travel from the Rhine to Austria. We were the first division to cross the Danube and it didn't take long and some guys put up a sign saying, "You are crossing the Beautiful Danube thru courtesy of 12th Armored Division." When I visited Dillingen in 1971, a sign saying exactly that was still there!

---

[2] Bastogne was a key crossroads city surrounded by the Germans during their Ardennes Counteroffensive that began December 16, 1944. The 101st Airborne Division, the "Battered Bastards of Bastogne," courageously defended the city against overwhelming German forces and despite the inability of the Allies to reinforce or resupply them due to bad weather. When ordered to surrender by the German commander, the 101st Airborne assistant commander, Brigidier General Anthony McAuliffe, simply responded with the now-famous and resounding, "Nuts!" By January 8, 1945, Hitler ordered a withdrawel of his troops from "the Bulge," thereby admitting the counteroffensive had failed, and the American First Army liberated Bastogne.

On April 27, 1945, we liberated the Hurlach Lager No. 4 concentration camp at Landsberg, Germany. Jesus, I don't ever want to see that again! There were box cars with bodies loaded like cordwood.

After we left Landsberg, we entered Murnau on April 29, 1945. This was really beautiful country. Next was Wurm on April 30, 1945 and Bad Tolz on May 2, 1945, where we met some heavy resistance before the Germans there surrendered. On May 4, 1945, we were in Kufstein, Austria, when the Division was placed in reserve. We were in the area west of Berchtesgaden engaged in security duty when Germany surrendered on May 7, 1945.

At the time the war ended, I was one point short of a fast trip home, so I was transferred from 12th Armored to the 81st Recon of the 1st Armored Division for further duty during the occupation. I finally left Europe on March 3, 1946, and landed at Fort Dix, New Jersey on March 20, 1946. My first meal back in the States was steak and all the milk I wanted to drink! I was squadron sergeant major then so Sergeant Robert Novak and I were put in charge of 180 soldiers for the train trip to Camp McCoy, Wisconsin. We were in charge of everyone's records and there would be hell to pay if they were lost! So one of us had to always be right with those records at all times.

I was discharged at Camp McCoy on March 26, 1946, and went home.

During his years in the service, Ray wrote numerous long letters home, several of which were published in the *News-Wave*. The first one published, written while at Camp Campbell, Kentucky, on May 11, 1943, appeared in the May 27, 1943, edition. It was written basically to his younger brother, Alfred, though it is addressed to his mother, father, and brothers, Bud and Gene, as well:

Dear Mother, Dad, and Brothers:
Well, Alfred, I guess I owe you a letter so I might as well address it to you and answer dad's, mom's, and Bud's letter right in your letter.

First of all I am sending Mom a large photo taken at the P. X. I don't know if you all will like it or not. I don't like it as it looks very pale; there is no color in it.

I am getting along quite well these days. Everything is going good. I guess I caught another cold. My head feels terribly heavy again. I got soaked Sunday when I attended the Pontifical Military Mass on Mother's Day. It was held right out in the open field. That is a ceremony I'll never forget as long as I live. It certainly is a very impressive ceremony. Each Battalion of the 12th and 20th Armored Division marched in a group headed by the colors and color guard. We assembled around the temporary constructed Sanctuary in a fan-like shape. In the middle of the group was a large isle leading from the altar. The color bearers and color guards marched one behind the other and formed in front of the sanctuary. The master of ceremonies (a priest) explained throughout the mass the symbols of the mass to Christ's last supper. The speaker was a priest with a commission of Lt. Col. He is the head chaplain of the Armored Force. He gave a sermon about our mothers at home and that nothing is too good for them. Gee, when you scanned over the crowd of soldiers their heads were bowed and tears were running down their cheeks. The bishop of the Murfreesboro, Tennessee Diocese was the celebrant at the mass. He was assisted by a deacon and subdeacon.

There were about 10 priests attending and assisting at the mass besides all the mass servers. There was a choir of 50 girls from Nashville who sang at the mass. There were two bands from the division that played pieces also. At the elevation of the host and chalice a volley of ammunition was shot and the colors raised. At the same time the snare drum players played the drums which made the sound effect of a strong wind coming up. Gee, what a gang of boys who took communion. I went too and offered it up for you, Mom. Just during the distribution of communion it started to rain. Not a member of the crowd left though. They all braved the rain until the end of mass and the playing of the national anthem. They were going to have benediction too, but it was called off. After the mass the National Anthem was played and the colors raised while the men stood at attention and gave salute, and during the same time the bishop extended his arms to the crowd and gave them his blessing. That is all for that.

151

It is almost bed check so I'll have to cut this letter short. I'll answer the questions in my next letter. Write if you receive the picture O.K., and if you like it. May God Bless you all. Good night and sweet dreams.

With Love,
Your son and brother,
Ray

Ray's next published letter appeared in the November 25, 1943 *News-Wave*. It was dated November 16, 1943, from "Somewhere on the move:"

Dear Mom, Dad and Brothers:

Nothing else to do at this early hour in the morning, so I thought I'd drop you a line or two. Yes, I just got up in the middle of the night so if this letter sounds sort of droopy, well don't be surprised.

We have to maintain a 24-hour guard on this troop train, so I was lucky as usual to pull it in the middle of the night. My shift is from 2 until 4 in the morning. Each car has two guards posted, one at each end of the car. The reason is so that none of the fellows get off or no unauthorized person gets into the car.

We left Watertown, Tenn., yesterday at 11:30 a. m., and from what I understand we are only about 100 miles out of Nashville, which makes it a grand total of 145 miles we have covered in 15 hours. Not bad time, eh? It seems as though we are spending the biggest part of the time waiting to let other trains by either way. At present it is standing.

As is usual, we left Tennessee and the maneuver area in the rain. It just seems as though you can't leave or come into the states of Tennessee or Kentucky without it raining. When I came into Camp Campbell it was raining. When I left there for maneuvers it was raining. When we hit the Tennessee maneuver area it was raining too. To complete the picture it couldn't help but rain also when we left this area. It started to rain Monday night about 7 o'clock and it terminated at about 11 o'clock yesterday morning. Boy, what a mess we were in. We marched through muck and mire in the rain for approximately two miles from our bivouac area to the depot.

Sleeping is wonderful in the cars that we have, and then they are not the regular type Pullman cars. We are riding in a Tourist Sleeper and Observation car. Maybe it isn't the best car, but it has nice soft mattresses and it certainly is a treat to us after sleeping on the ground for about 12 weeks. I slept from 10 p. m. until 2 a. m. and I already feel as though I had gotten a good nights rest. Really, I don't know how to act, crawling into a bed with a mattress to stretch out on.

While riding these troop trains you have to make the best of it as far as amusement is concerned. Funny books and magazines are passed and exchanged with one another right down the aisle. Of course, as always in the army, you have your poker and crap games ranging from a nickel and dime limit to a limit of what is known as "The Sky is the Limit." A lot of "cabbage," meaning money, really passes back and forth through the games.

We get service deluxe in these cars on this trip, if we could only get out for these nine inning stretches. We are couped up in these cars as a farmer has his chickens couped up for the winter. We cannot as much as travel, or should I say wander, from car to car within this troop train. Everyone of us is assigned to a particular car and there we must stay throughout the entire trip.

We are due in Camp Barkeley, Texas, sometime Thursday afternoon, but at the rate this train is traveling we won't get there until sometime next week. So far the train has been averaging about 8 or 10 miles an hour. Oh what fun it is getting to be! I'd hate to travel this slow on my way home on a furlough.

Well, my shift on guard is about to terminate so I might just as well end this letter also, and thereby kill two birds with one stone.

Once again, goodbye, and best wishes. May God bless and protect you all through this worldly fracas.

With Love,
Your son and brother,
Ray

Once overseas, Ray continued his letter writing campaign. A fine description of England is offered in the following letter. Practically a course in English history, it is long, but it must have been very educational and insightful to those back home in 1944:

November 3, 1944
Somewhere in England
Dear Mom, Dad and Brothers:

I have a little time at present so I might as well utilize it and write you a letter for a change again. I am going to start this letter by describing the places of interest that I saw while I was in London. I took a sightseeing tour through London which cost me six shillings or the equivalent of $1.20 in American money. We took this tour in a taxi so we got to see the sights pretty well.

If I ever go back to London again I'd like to take another tour to some particular spot, such as the Tower of London and spend more time there and get more out of it. A tour as we took it is all right when time is very limited. The places that were the most interesting to me was Tower of London, St. Paul's Cathedral, London Bridge and Westminster Abbey. The architecture and beauty of the buildings is very amazing. One would think or rather one would wonder how the people in years gone by, with implements of the crudest nature, could ever build such massive structures.

I'll try and describe some of these places. As much as I can remember of what was told us. The first place I'll describe is Buckingham Palace for that was the first place I saw on the way in a taxi towards the Red Cross Club where we stayed. It is a very old building and is nothing more out of the ordinary than are the other buildings of London. A person would think that Buckingham Palace, the home of the King and Queen of England, would be a very beautiful and spacious place. We could not go inside the grounds because it is heavily guarded and we quite didn't merit the privilege of getting a pass to enter. The day we were at the place the Royalty of England was not home. You can tell this from outside the grounds because whenever they are home the King's and Queen's flag is always flying over the building. There are 200 rooms in that building all for themselves, their visitors and for the help I guess. The main entrance to the grounds has a large marble arch with a huge fountain just inside the gate. All around the grounds is a high picket fence as a means of protection against outsiders.

On the way in the taxi to the Red Cross we just got in on the tail end of their formal change of the guard and guard mount. It nowhere compares with the ceremonial affair of peace time. Of what I had seen of this guard mount I'll still take the formal guard mount that the United States Army has for its occasions. The King and Queen have an entire regiment of soldiers that are especially picked, who do nothing else but guard the home of the leaders of England. The guard is on duty 48 hours and off 48 hours.

The next place I visited was Hyde Park. To my notion it nowhere near compares to the parks of its size back home. This probably is due to the fact that war is so much closer here and help is scarce which deprives the parks of the beauty that could be theirs. The outside perimeter of this park is a large horse-racing track which is arched nearly all the way around by large trees. On one end of this park are a few of the self standing step-ladders from which on Sunday afternoons, ministers are preaching sermons, others are telling jokes, and still others asking questions of the people and answering them too. These ladders cannot be more than 15-or 20 feet apart and when all occupied there is a conglomeration of voices with one trying to outdo the other. When we saw this from a distance we thought it was a series of auctions all at once. English sense of humor is very odd in that it hasn't the spirit or that certain thing that we have to make it a joke or a humorous saying. Their sense of humor is very dry. You tell an Englishman one of our crazy jokes and he doesn't savvy. Too thick in the upper story I guess.

Another place that proved very interesting was the Tower of London. This place is a series of buildings joining one another over a very large area and surrounded by a very high wall. I guess it was a fortress in the centuries past. It is located on the river Thames (pronounced Tems). We also saw the room where Rudolph Hess was kept in confinement when he turned himself in to England. He is not there now and where he is now they do not know. The next time I go to London, if that chance comes, I want to spend quite some time and go through this place thoroughly.

Number 10 Downing Street is from the outside nothing better than a British home. For a place like this Britain's Prime Ministers are not lavishly quartered. There is only one guard who is stationed right at the entrance.

153

A place that really struck home while on this sightseeing tour was the out residential district. The taxi driver showed us one district, a residential district, with only a brewery as a commercial establishment, that had been bombed out for blocks and more blocks around. Not a building was standing in this area. A sight like this really makes a person stop and think. I sometimes wonder how the people at home would stand up under the strain that the Englishmen had to contend with during the 1940-41 blitz and the robot bombs. Late in the afternoon we took a subway out to one other district. We stopped in a "Pub" and became acquainted with a young couple who showed us a British home that only a week before had been standing. The English homes are continuous blocks of homes which are very similar to tenement houses in the large cities back home. Going back to this incident, this couple showed us a home that was struck by a flying bomb at about 4:15 in the evening when the people were just returning home from work and were preparing their evening meal. In this particular home 123 persons were killed and windows for blocks around were shattered. That same fateless evening another robot hit a hospital a block or so away and destroyed one entire wing of it. Bombs or no bombs the hospital is still operating.

Oh yes, I also had the privilege and honor to see Big Ben and also to set my wrist watch to the most correct time in the world. The dial on this clock looks pretty well weather beaten.

Another building is St. Paul's Cathedral, of superb structure and a significant building showing the art of the labor, patience and intelligence of the people years back. If I remember correctly it took 65 years to complete the building. This building had two direct hits and several other bombs were dropped on buildings and demolished those buildings surrounding the Cathedral. This place has one main chapel and two other smaller chapels all in the same building. One was directly hit by a 1200 pound bomb. It went through the roof, the concrete floor, which is about 18 inches thick, and clear through to the basement. This bomb was a dud, lucky thing. It tore a hole in the concrete floor to measure about five feet in diameter. The other bomb hit the rear of the cathedral and exploded but did little damage. All around the cathedral are statues of famous people with their cremated remains inside the statue or in the floor beneath. One statue was especially interesting, that of Lord Kirchner, a famous leader and warrior of World War I. The statue stands in a horizontal position in one little room. It was carved from one solid piece of Italian White Marble. It is a life size statue of Lord Kirchner in complete battle dress and carved to the last minute detail of his features, garment folds, etc. It took the man doing the carving 18 months to complete his work. Over the main door leading into the room where Kirchner's statue lies, are his battle colors hanging with no signs of wearing except for the accumulated dust. The cathedral itself is a massive structure with a very high dome in the center.

We also visited the building with the "whispering walls." Can't recall the name of the place, but two people can stand, one at either end of the building, whisper to each other, and their words are easily understood. What an amazement that was. We tried it and it worked to our astonishment.

We saw the Bank of England which is over all about four or five stories high and covers one complete block. What a place!

The place known universally as Scotland Yard, home of the British detectives, was also a part of our tour.

Westminster Abbey is quite a place too. In this place nearly every inch of the floor space has a lot containing the cremated remains of some notable scientist, poet, artist, law-maker, explorer and some of the nobility. The floor is literally covered with plaques dedicated to these people. That gave one a funny feeling to be walking right on top of their remains. There was one beautiful altar in there built entirely by a British king who was a faithful member of the English church. Today, the only time the altar is used is on the occasion of the kings and queens. Behind this altar is a chair that is used for these rare occasions. There is a legend connected with that chair. In it someplace is a very rare stone that has the power to bestow upon the person to be crowned the power to rule England and her territories successfully and if he or she are involved in any war during their reign, the stone has the power to give them victory in war. This memorable structure was hit by a bomb. One section of the Abbey is closed off to visitors because of fear that the roof or some of the loosened pillars may topple any moment. The loosened walls are strengthened by large iron beams bolted together.

We also saw Charles Dickens' curiosity shop. It stands to this day just as he had the place when he was living.

Lastly, I'm sure you heard of this place some time or other. Yes, it is Picadilly Circus. It is

154

something like 42nd Street and Broadway in New York City, only worse. Servicemen and women from all nations meet here besides plenty of others.

There is also the old English Bobby (English policeman) and the American M. P.'s. You really have plenty of both in and about London. From what I hear the Bobbys and the M. P.'s are nothing to fool with either, as it doesn't take long to get your name taken down and a report sent to your commanding officer.

I guess this letter has told you everything about my tour while in London, so I'll bring this letter to a close. Write soon. May God Bless and Protect You All.

With Love,
Ray

Fifteen days later, Ray was writing his family again, but this time from war-torn France:

November 18, 1944, France

Dear Mom, Dad, and brothers:

The biggest and most horrible looking sights are the bomb leveled homes, factories and business places of small towns as well as of the larger cities of France. Today I saw some craters that were approximately 20 feet in diameter and eight to 10 feet deep. Also on our journey today, we saw fields along the roads that had warning signs and white tape that designated that it was an area that contained mine fields. What amazed me is the large amount of Nazi and allied equipment strewn along the roads and about the fields. We saw everything from small caliber ammunition, clothing, etc. to heavy weapons and vehicles. It is not an uncommon sight to see weapons and vehicles blown to bits or burned. We are now bivouacked near a cemetery containing bodies of the Canadian and British forces and also of the Polish Division. In this cemetery is that same old sight as was seen throughout the last war. Yes, it is ""Unknown Soldier."

I wish I knew some French. Maybe I could get around a bit then. I was in a jewelry store yesterday looking at some silver and gold bracelets.. The exchange is an equal amount of silver or gold in exchange for the piece of jewelry whatever it is made of, plus a few Francs for the workmanship of the item.

I looked around in England for souvenirs or what there was and in France it still appears worse.

I am feeling exceptionally well. How is everybody at home. Yes, I am seeing a lot of things that I never dreamed of seeing before. Yes, I got to see London while I was there on a 48 hour pass. I got some postal cards while in London which cost me one shilling and six pence or 30 cents each. There are no such things as good photo shops, unless the dime store pictures which are not worth wasting money.

Will close this letter now. Love to you all.

Ray

Ray wrote again on Christmas Day 1944, finishing his letter several days later:

Christmas Day (1944)

Dear Mom, Dad and brothers:

Received about 20 letters the 23rd of December so while I have the chance today I'll answer the three that I received from you Mom. They were postmarked the 30th of September, 25th of September and 7th of September. They are old letters but still news to me.

We really had a swell Christmas eve when one considers the circumstances. These French people invited us all over last night and treated us to coffee and apple pie. After the treat we sang Christmas carols in English while they sang them in French. We also sang some of our old American folk songs and the National Anthem, and then they would sing their French songs. Oh, yes, they also treated us to apples and home grown walnuts.

Today the Division's Catholic Chaplain is going to hold Mass in this town. We told the French about it and invited them to go along with us. You should have seen them rejoice with happiness that they have a chance again to attend Holy Mass in peace. I also want to go to Confession and Holy Communion. I hope we have the chance to do so. These people it seems cannot do enough for us. They always keep asking us if they can do this or that.

December 29, 1944

      We moved again and this is the first chance I had to finish this letter to you. I might as well go at it tonight and get it out of the way.

      That postal card you sent was a beauty. We never had such a well-equipped Service Center as that one. I bet you had a wonderful time that day that you were serving coffee and cakes to the men. The nearest to this center is the main service club at Camp Campbell, Kentucky.

      From your last letter I think you are really having winter weather. We really are having very "nippy" weather these days. The ground is frozen so solidly that our tanks can go across the country without any difficulty. I'd rather have this cold weather, as is now, than the rain and mud we have been having in the past.

      Souvenirs are very hard to get. These towns we go through are regular ghost towns. I have a few pieces of English money, French and German money that I have put away in a little tobacco sack to send home as a souvenir some day.

      Send a box of sweets such as some hard home-baked cookies, mom.

      I heard from Bud. He is in southern France. He states that he had little use for the French language.

      May God bless and protect you as you go along. Write when time permits. Goodnight.

      Ray

On April 4, 1945 Ray wrote a letter home from "Somewhere in Germany" covering a wide range of subjects. It appeared in the *News-Wave* on May 3, 1945:

Dear Mom, dad, and brothers:

      Our mad dash across Germany has temporarily stopped so that gives us a little break again. Thank God for that. Going day and night without proper sleep, rest, eats and washing is no fun whatever. Adventures are plenty but we cannot mention much at the present. It would not pass the censors. A certain amount of time has to elapse before we can mention anything specifically. I imagine by this time you have a pretty good idea on what side of the water we are now on. The excursion west of the Rhine was quite some rat-race.

      We were going day and night. So whenever we halted, if we were not alert at our guns we tried to catch a wink or two of sleep. I received box number four on February 20, Easter Sunday.

      Sometime ago, before we pulled out of France, I was on a pass to Nancy. But it was Sunday so every place was closed. I picked out a poor day. Two other buddies went with me to Holy Mass in the largest Cathedral in Nancy. What a magnificent and large structure! I counted five altars. We just loafed around the city, then jumped on a street car with no definite spot in mind to go to. Wound up in the country and then the problem was to find our way back, but we made it in time to see a French movie.

      Gee, was I surprised to hear you say that you know all about Bud's and my outfit. I guess you can rest in peace since the radio and newspapers give all those details. All that news you wrote about that you hear over the radio is correct to the very last bit of it. I think I'll put a requisition to our S-3 to get a complete operations map, if you are keeping up with the situations.

      Before I go on with my letter I am going to answer all of your questions. I have received about 25 letters from different people and haven't had the chance to answer one of them.

      Remember that spiritual bouquet you sent out the 19th of March? I received it on Easter Sunday. Thank you a lot, mother, for all those prayers and Holy Communions that you offered up for my intention. Yes, I heard Mass on Palm Sunday in a Catholic church in Germany and it was celebrated by a German Catholic priest. I didn't get a chance to go to church during Holy Week or Easter Sunday. We were as busy as could be.

      Yes, Edward Maule is with the 28th Infantry Division. When we were fighting down in the Colmar pocket we fought right along with his outfit. At the time though I never knew he was in that outfit or I would have inquired about him. Did I ever tell you that some time ago I received a very long and interesting letter from Bennie Kulig? Was I ever surprised to hear from him. Say, whatever happened to

Roman Sosalla? Used to her from him very regularly and all of a sudden he stopped writing me.

I think you are mistaken in this mom. I don't think that Bud has seen more of France than what we have. We have been through France from North to South and from East to West. We had to travel back and forth in our vehicles when we fist arrived in France. We are doing the same over here now.

Say, dad, you should have been with us when we were making our push through the Rhine Valley. It was rough but we had fun also. Talk about wine cellars that we found in the cities and villages along the Rhine! I wouldn't be afraid to bet my last nickel that in one cellar we ran across there were 50,000 gallons of wine. There was wine in bottles and in at least 500 gallon vats dated way back to 1934. I took the measurements of one vat of wine and it was nine feet deep and seven feet across. What a time we had for a while there. In fact, there was too much of it for a while. It was a sour light wine, but very good and of course, it had its share of wallop too. Some of these wine cellars were two stories below the surface of the earth and ran sometimes for the length of a block and about 50 feet wide. They were really loaded with wine.

If you ever send peanuts do not send those that are in shells or in the cellophane bags. By the time they reach me they are very soggy. If you can get them sealed in cans then you may send me some. They are always fresh.

No mail that I receive from your side or from anyone back in the states is censored. It is only our mail that is censored. No, mother, if we fellows write to one another over here, it does not go to New York and then come back to the receiver.

I do not need any scapulas, rosaries or medals. I am now wearing a chain around my neck with some medals on it. I also received through a buddy of mine some medals from some nuns and a priest while we were still in France. They were some relics of St. Therese. I always wear the rosary in my pocket.

Yes, it was quite a treat to meet Bud, who still looks the same and is good as ever. Of course, that day I saw him he had just returned from a problem in the field so was dirty and dusty.

It is dinner time now so I'm going to bring this letter to a close. Read the newspapers and listen to the news broadcasts very carefully and I'm sure you will hear plenty about the 12th armored division. I can't tell you much of anything of our present operation and of the one that we just completed. I am feeling very well and enjoying everything. You need not worry about me in the least.

May God bless and protect you all at home. Write whenever time permits.

> With Love,
> Your son and brother,
> Ray

The same day the previous letter was published, Ray wrote another. Finally, the end of the war was very near for Ray and his 12th Armored Division, but before it ended, Ray witnessed the horrors of the concentration camps and Hitler's "Final Solution" regarding the Jews:

Germany, 3 May 1945
Dear Mom, Dad and Brothers:

It has been quite some time since the last time I wrote to you, so will try to write a decent letter.

I believe that our rat races have about come to an end. There isn't much more of Germany left that we can conquer. I hope that peace is here again and from all appearances it is except for small organized bands of soldiers here and there. Last night's news really built up that hope that it is finished. All German soldiers in Italy and Austria ceased fighting; Berlin has completely; Hitler has died or is on his dying bed. Our encounters with the enemy is very light and disorganized. The common German soldier (Wehrmacht) doesn't even put up a fight anymore. The only German units that put up any kind of stubborn resistance are the SS Troopers. I give the war in this theatre another week and it will be "Kaput". In the next couple of days we fellows sense something big is about to happen. Everything from "Der Fuhrer" on down.

Today is May 3 and it is snowing to beat the band. Yesterday morning the ground and trees were covered with a two-inch blanket of snow. That should give you a pretty good idea of where we are and the elevation also. This is the first time in my life that I recall snow falling so late in the year.

In this last big push that we have just completed, I've seen sights that are indescribable. In one town we liberated 69 American soldiers who were prisoners of war in Germany. They were so happy to see us come into the town that when our column of vehicles halted they ran out and kissed the vehicles. When we dismounted they grabbed our hands, shook them and hugged us from joy. They told us that their weekly package   from the American Red Cross is what kept them alive, because the food that they received was very little and what there was, wasn't very stable. There were 2,000 or more Polish and Jewish inmates of a prison camp the Germans tried to evacuate by trains. They were put in enclosed box cars just like hogs and then as the train started to move, the Germans machine-gunned them. We saw the train on the tracks and some of the box cars were opened and there with my own eyes I saw the dead bodies piled up in a heap, about half full in each car. On this station platform I saw a middle aged man on hands and knees trying to stand up. He would get into a squatted position and down on his face and stomach he would fall - simply too weak to stand. When I read this and that in the papers I thought it was all farce, but now that I have seen it all, I'll believe every word that anybody else has to say of the inhuman treatment of the German people. There are individual stories I've learned from these people, but I'll leave them for when I get home as I could write endlessly about them.

I am also a half-track driver now, besides the typist and clerk for the S-1 Section. Our regular driver is in the hospital. While doing so I had the privilege of driving on Hitler's network of roads which is called Autobahn. What a beautiful highway that was, with not a curve in it for miles. It really was a pleasure after all those cross-country jaunts we have been having.

Yes, Dad, we certainly are giving those Kraut eaters a round for their life. We always are the first to hit them, get them stirring up like a nest of bees and then the rest of the division comes along to clean them out with the doughboys. The Polish I learned at school and home is coming in mighty handy now, and I'm getting to speak the real good pure Polish, too, so that when I get home I'll be able to speak it like an "old timer." I've come in contact with a lot of Polish refugees and slave laborers.

We really are located in a beautiful spot. It is a palace which is owned by the Hapsburg family who are the royalties of Austria. The prince of this family owns 10 of them. There is the palace, servants quarters, green house, private swimming pools, different court yards, outside buildings and is joined by a very large forest which has bridal paths criss-crossing throughout it. When we are not on guard duty we participate in the sports program. Yes, the war here is over, but now the work begins as to taking care of all the people and odds and ends, and to indoctrinate into the "square headed" Germans how much better it is to live under peaceful conditions instead of warfare all the time.

(Ed. - At least this last paragraph must have been written at a later date.) It has been quite cold the last few days, with intermittent showers and drizzles throughout the day. It was good to hear of the German surrender. To us in the front lines it simply meant just another thing and we casually carried on. There was no alternative for us, but keep watch and guard for a possible flare-up. In that first push we captured Von Runstadt and many other high German officials. There were a lot of prisoner camps along the 7th Army front so we had to be very cautious. As far as we knew Hitler had one of his SS Trooper stooges shoot him in an underground tunnel in Berlin before the Russians captured him. Toward the final end he was going so crazy that not a person could reason with him anymore, not even his closely associated stenographer whom he had for years.

Well, I'll close for now. All my love.

Ray

Finally, on September 17, 1945, Ray wrote a letter from Gross Unstadt, Germany, that was published on November 1, 1945:

Dear Mom, Dad and Brothers:

Don't be surprised but here I finally come with a letter for a change. I suppose you were beginning to think just what has become of me. Well, to tell you the truth, I just haven't been in a letter-writing mood these days. There is nothing to write about because everything is the same day in and day out. I'm not alone in this as all the fellows are saying that it sure is getting very hard to write a decent letter these days.

First of all I must tell you that I made another advancement in this world and in this man's army. Yes, last Saturday I was promoted to the rank of Staff Sergeant. I am enclosing a copy of the Special Order

158

promoting me. I am now the Squadron Sergeant Major. Talk about responsibility with that job. The Adjutant wanted to promote me direct to Master Sergeant from T/4 but the Colonel objected to that. He says that for the time being I'll be promoted to S/Sgt and thus a month later be promoted to T/Sgt and then still a month later to Master Sergeant. I hope that I can make the grade. A Master Sergeant, and on top of it all, it is the highest rating that an enlisted man can get in the army before getting a commission. The Adjutant right now is working hard to promote me direct to a Master Sergeant from Staff Sergeant. I hope that it goes through.

Bud finally got a pass to come and see me. The only trouble was that it was so short. He had a total of four days. He arrived here Thursday noon and had to be back at his place Sunday noon. He just caught me in time because if he would have come Friday he would have missed me. The 15th of Sept. was the third anniversary of the 12th Armored Division so the Commanding General asked permission of the General of the Seventh Army if all former members of the 12th could get away from their organizations to come to this anniversary reunion. Friday morning we left in convoy at 9 o'clock for Heidensheim and arrived there at 3:30 in the afternoon. Man, what a trip. The trip to and back knocked the life out of me. It really was quite a lift to Bud because that saved him hitchhiking about 200 miles. He rode along with me. He stayed over night with me at the 92nd Cav. and got in on a little party also. When we got there he took a bath and cleaned up and by that time it was nearly time to eat supper. In the evening the 92nd had a party all in store for us. They had plenty to eat, drink, and the women for dancing. The dance lasted from 8 o'clock in the evening of Friday through 2 o'clock Saturday morning. I and Bud tied in with my old Polish buddie from the old outfit and boy what a time we had. They used a large tobacco warehouse as the place for the party and dancing. While sitting at our table the executive officer came over, sat down with us and began to shoot the breeze. Then the party really got started with him. He noticed that Bud was from the 42nd Inf. Div, so he asked him when and how he is getting back. When Bud told him that he was going to hitchhike in the morning from the 92nd the Major told me right away that I could get one of their jeeps and take him as far as I wanted to that Saturday.

It was about three o'clock in the morning before Bud and I got to bed. At seven o'clock we were again up and at 8 we were on our way towards Augsburg. We stopped at the American Red Cross Club and had some doughnuts and hot coffee. While sitting there at a table we got to talking with some other fellows and they asked me where we were heading for. I told him we were taking my brother the biggest share of his way to his outfit and after they found out where he lived they said they were going within 60 miles of his place. That really was a break for him. So away Bud went with these fellows and I turned around and headed back for the 92nd. I arrived in the area about 12:30, just in time to get in on the tailend of noon chow. That afternoon they were supposed to have a large street festival in Heidensheim but due to rain it had to be called off. A bunch of us fellows in order to keep the party going started a party of our own up in the castle taxis. Then again it was a rip roaring time. Saturday night I went to bed early because I was aware of the fact that I had a big trip staring me in the face Sunday. We arrived here at 6 o'clock that evening. Boy was I tired. Going back to the 12th Armored Division will certainly hold me for a long time.

You asked me how we all took VJ-Day. To us over here it was just another day. In fact, we never gave it a thought, because we still have this army of occupation staring us in the face. We saw our first combat on December 5, 1944 and finished up on VE-Day. I figure that if I get home by next July or August I'll be plenty lucky. I hope that it will be sooner.

Since I took over this new job my time is pretty well occupied and even occupied in the evenings because there is so much work to do. The job even keeps me agoing on Sundays and holidays. As far as magazines are concerned I have plenty to read for the time being. Bud is in the Third Army and I'm with the seventh. I am now with the 1st Armored Division.

I've been transferred to a different place as you will note by the change of address. Received a transfer from the 12th Armored to the 1st. Also have my old job back with this 0outfit, as typist and clerk in the S-1 section. Thank God for that.

We moved about 60 miles north of our old location. I like the set-up a whole lot better than what we had before. It's a fairly good-sized city and seems more civilized.

Well Mom, I guess that about takes care of all of your letters so I'll bring this letter to a quick finish. It is all ready way past midnight. May God bless and protect you all.

159

With Love,
Ray

Sources: Independence News-Wave; Book (Stanton)

STANLEY A. RESSEL
UNITED STATES ARMY

Stanley Ressel joined the United States Army on April 25, 1944, entering active service that same day at Fort Sheridan, Illinois. Upon completing basic training, he left for Europe on October 22, 1944 where, after arriving in England on November 4, 1944, he was assigned to the 26th Infantry Division[1] as an infantry replacement. It wasn't long and Stanley soon found himself in combat in France.

The 26th Infantry Division had taken Vic-sur-Seille with its bridges still intact about the time of Stanley's arrival. It then assaulted Hill 310, Rodalbe, the Berange Farm strongpoint, and the Koecking Ridge Forest. On November 19, 1944, the Division was halted by strong German opposition on the Dieuze-Benestroff line. The Germans quickly withdrew, however, and the 26th continued its forward push, taking Marimont and Dieuze on November 20, 1944. The following day, during a German attack near Albestroff, Stanley was wounded in his left leg when a German 88-mm shell burst in the trees above him. After lying in a ditch for some time, Stanley was evacuated to a field hospital.

Regulations stated that if a wounded soldier was hospitalized for 120 days, he earned a trip home. On Stanley's 119th day, however, he was discharged from the hospital, sent to England, and reassigned to Eighth Air Force. Initially he spent his time recovering further from his wounds and basically had no assignment other than an occasional K. P. and simple clean-up around the camp.

On August 1, 1945 Stanley left England bound for the States, arriving in New York on August 12, 1945. Following a furlough, he was sent to Drew Field, Florida, in October 1945, where he was assigned to the 301st Army Air Forces Base Unit and worked in the base shipping section as a dispatcher. There he kept records of troops being transported to the railroad station in town, dispatched trucks and buses transporting those troops, and maintained records of transportation availability.

On February 13, 1946 Stanley was separated from the Army at Camp Atterbury, Indiana. He had earned the American Theater Ribbon, European-African-Middle Eastern

---

[1] The 26th Infantry Division suffered 1,850 killed in action and 7,886 wounded, with 262 of those dying from their wounds.

Ribbon with four bronze stars, Good Conduct Medal, Victory Medal, and the Purple Heart for wounds received on November 21, 1944, in France.

In December, 1944, Stanley's parents, Mr. and Mrs. Clemence Ressel of Korpal Valley, received the following letter from Stanley regarding his having been wounded. It appeared in the *News-Wave*:

Dear Mother,

Only a few lines to tell you I'm in a hospital in France. I was wounded in my left leg. It isn't very bad. I'll be back on my feet before long. I no longer am with any of the boys from home. I know Hanson (Ed. - Ardell Hanson, Arcadia) was up on the front lines. I don't know about the others (Ed. - Ralph Jonietz, Leonard Sylla, Independence; Leonard Nysgen, Strum, men Stanley joined the army with the previous April), but I imagine they're there also. I've been given the Purple Heart.

It's a nice place where I'm at now. We sure have nice people taking care of us. We had turkey for Thanksgiving dinner. It is kind of hard writing in bed, so will sign off.

Don't worry about me, I'll be all right. I hope you can read this.

Your son,
Stanley

Sources: Stanley Ressel personal papers; Independence News-Wave; Book (Stanton).

GLEN H. RUSTAD
UNITED STATES ARMY

Glen Rustad, the son of Mr. and Mrs. Ole Howland, was born on May 15, 1919 in Buffalo County, Wisconsin. Prior to World War II, his family moved to Independence where he married the former Sarah Smieja. He was drafted on May 14, 1942 and attended basic training at Camp Shelby, Mississippi, where it appears he was nearly immediately assigned to the 85th Infantry Division,[1] a unit which had been activated at Camp Shelby that same month. The Division participated in the Third Army Louisiana Maneuvers beginning April 6, 1943, and then traveled to Camp Young, California, in June 1943 for the Desert Training Center Number 3 California Maneuvers. The Division transferred to Fort Dix, New Jersey, on October 7, 1943, began staging at Camp Patrick Henry, Virginia, on December 18, 1943, and left the Hampton Roads Port of Embarkation on December 24, 1943, bound for North Africa.

After arriving at Casablanca in North Africa on January 2, 1944, the 85th Infantry Division underwent extensive amphibious training at Port-aux-Poules for several weeks beginning February 1, 1944. It then boarded ships and landed at Naples, Italy, during March 15-27, 1944. Shortly after the Division entered combat on the Minturno-Castelforte front in late March and early April 1944, Glen was wounded. His mother received a letter from him in late June, dated May 1, 1944, informing her that he had been hospitalized for several weeks recovering from his wounds but was much improved and expected to rejoin his unit soon. Within only a few days of receiving this letter on July 2, 1944, however, Mrs. Howland received another short letter, this time from the War Department. Delivered to Mrs. Howland by the Trempealeau County Chapter of the American Red Cross, it informed her that her son, Glen, had been killed in action on June 8,

---

[1] The 85th Infantry Division lost 1,561 killed in action and 6,314 wounded, of which 175 died from their wounds.

1944 in Italy.

By the time Glen was killed, his 85th Infantry Division had, despite heavy opposition at times, moved through the *Gustav Line* and overcome German defenses at Cave d'Argilla, Hill 131, Formia, Castellonorato, and Terracina, allowing for the opening of the road to the Anzio beachhead. By late May, 1944, the Division was in pursuit of retreating German units west of Priverno and through Sezze. On May 31, 1944, the 85th Infantry Division attacked into the Loriano sector, taking Mount Artemisio, the town of Lariano, Mount Ceraso, Mount Fiori, and the town of Frascati all in a matter of four days.

Quickly moving along the *Via Tuscolana* highway, it entered and passed through Rome on June 5, 1944, and continued its drive toward the Viterbo River. It was somewhere in this area of the Viterbo where Glen was killed on June 8.

Though Ensign Jerome Sobota had been listed as missing in action in the Pacific in 1943, he had not yet been declared dead. Now Independence was about to experience something quite new and disturbing as the first memorial service for a soldier killed in action from the city was scheduled for July 16, 1944, at Independence Lutheran Church. Pastor O. G. Birkeland, who also was the District Chaplain of the American Legion, conducted the service before a large gathering of family, friends, and others simply wishing to pay their respects to the fallen 25-year-old, a ceremony marked by a strong reminder of the sacrifice made by so many like him -- a plain white cross in the front of the church over which had been placed a soldier's helmet.

Between an organ prelude played by Miss Lillian Garthus and a vocal duet sung by Mr. and Mrs. Philip Thomte of Whitehall, Wisconsin, fully-uniformed members of Sura-Wiersgalla Post 186 of the American Legion advanced the colors to the front of the church. Reverend Birkeland then addressed those in attendance with a sermon of the theme, "Are We Worth the Sacrifice?" in which he stressed the importance of obeying the laws of the United States and showing respect for our elected leaders and others in positions of authority. He also addressed the tendency of people to complain about the little inconveniences they were facing due to rationing, this at a time when the young men of the country "were bleeding and dying on the battlefields of this world."

Following additional musical selections, uniformed Independence Boy Scouts Alan Hanson and Donald Gunderson advanced the Honor Roll of the Church and Reverend Birkeland affixed a gold star beside the name of Pfc. Glen Rustad. The United States flag was then presented to Glen's widow, Sarah, and following a silent 30-second tribute, taps was sounded by Richard Holtan of Whitehall. The ceremony in memory of Glen Rustad then ended.

Glen left his wife, Sarah, and daughter, Diane, along with his mother, three brothers, Pvt. Oliver stationed in England, Walter and Myron, and a sister, Leone. On September 18, 1944 the Purple Heart awarded posthumously to Pfc. Glen Rustad was presented to his wife.

On July 8, 1948, it was reported by the *News-Wave* that the remains of Glen Rustad were being returned from overseas for final burial. It stated he had been interred in the Nettuno temporary military cemetery in Italy but that his return had been requested by his mother, Mrs.

Emma Howland.

Following his return on August 31, 1948, reburial services were held on September 2 at the Independence Lutheran Church, with the Reverend O. G. Birkeland officiating. Graveside services at Bethel Cemetery were conducted by the American Legion Post 186. Ray Pieterick, Henry Helgeson, Homer and Ernest Bidney, Eugene Pieterick, and Dominic Smick served as pallbearers. Color Bearers were Hillary "Jack" Halama and Vitus Smieja while the Color Guard consisted of Alfred Pientok and Ernest Sobotta.

Source: Independence News-Wave; Book (Stanton)

GEORGE R. SATHER
UNITED STATES ARMY

George Sather entered the United States Army on October 14, 1942 at Fort Sheridan, Illinois. Following his basic training, he was sent to Hawaii where he immediately joined the 40th Infantry Division[1] which at the time had defensive responsibilities on the outer Hawaiian Islands. Shortly after George arrived on the islands, the 40th Infantry Division was moved to northern Oahu, an assignment which lasted from mid-January until mid-October 1943. On October 17, 1943 it began two months of intensive jungle and amphibious training, and then left Hawaii on December 25, 1943.

Arriving on Guadalcanal on December 31, 1943, the 40th Infantry Division continued its

---

[1] The 40th Infantry Division lost 614 men killed and 2,407 wounded, with 134 of those dying from their wounds, during its time in the Pacific Theater of Operations.

jungle training and carried out combat patrols on a limited basis. It then was ordered to relieve the 1st Marine Division on New Britain Island. It arrived at Cape Gloucester in late April 1944 and continued operations there until it, too, was relieved on November 27, 1944. by the *Australian 5th Division*. The Division departed Borgen Bay, New Britain, the next day and sailed for the Philippine Islands via Huon Gulf, New Guinea, and Manus Island..

On January 9, 1945 the invasion of Luzon, Philippine Islands, the largest amphibious landing to date, began. The American XIV Corps, consisting of the 37th Infantry Division and George's 40th Infantry Division, approached the beach between Lingayen town and Dagupan during mid-morning against surprisingly light Japanese resistance. As George's landing craft ground to a halt and its front door lowered open, the troops began spilling out. George jumped from the craft and upon landing in the shallow water immediately felt a sharp pain in his back. He was helped ashore and tended to by medics who determined he had suffered a serious back injury. Though two *News-Wave* articles indicated he had been wounded, it has not been determined whether the injury was caused by enemy fire or by landing awkwardly in his jump from the landing craft. Regardless, he was removed from the beach with other wounded men to a ship which eventually delivered him to the 27th General Hospital in New Guinea. It was in New Guinea where he learned he had a fractured spine that necessitated his being placed in a body cast from his arms to just above his knees.

George's father, Peter L. Sather, received a telegram from the War Department on February 3, 1945 informing him of his son's having been "slightly wounded," but it wasn't until late February or early March when George's letter to his sister, Mrs. William Cilley, apprised the family of his condition.

When he returned to the States in March 1945, George was taken to Fletcher General Hospital in Cambridge, Ohio, where he continued to convalesce. By May, he was well enough to leave the hospital and spend time with his father and sister in Independence. He then returned to Ohio for more care and rehabilitation.

George Sather spent 27 months in the South Pacific with the United States Army. He received his discharge in August. 1945 with the rank of Technical Sergeant Fifth Class, and recovered enough from his injury to take employment in Milwaukee, Wisconsin, shortly after.

No photo.
Sources: Independence News-Wave; Book (Stanton)

NORVAL M. SATHER
UNITED STATES ARMY AIR FORCE

It is uncertain when Norval Sather entered the service. Following his initial basic training, however, he did undergo specialized training with the Army Air Force at Inglewood, California, and Grieger Field, Washington. He then trained further at the Great Falls, Montana, Army Air Base before being sent to England where he was assigned to an Eighth Air Force Bomber Station. While in England, Norval met up with Willis Cripps, an Independence man who was later killed in an accident while on duty with his quartermaster unit. A short letter received by Norval's parents, Mr. and Mrs. Helmer Sather, and published in the January 20, 1944 edition of the *News-Wave*, made mention of this and the fact that Cripps had been inducted into the service at the same time as Norval's brother, Ervin:

Dear Folks,
Will drop a few lines to let you know that I arrived safely here. Everything is fine so you don't have to worry about me. I'm somewhere in midland of England. It's pretty much the same as home here.

People are real friendly and all that. The weather is the worst thing to get used to . It's cold and foggy all the time. Wish I could tell you more about things here but it wouldn't get there.

Oh, yes, I met that Cripps boy that went in the army with Ervin over here. He's been here 14 months now. Sure felt good to see someone from home.

Will have to close, hoping this finds everyone fine at home and tell them all "hello." Bye for now and hope I hear from you soon.

Lots of Love.
Norval

As a crew maintenance chief of heavy bombers such as the B-24 "Liberator" and B-17 "Flying Fortress," Technical Sergeant Sather had the responsibility of ensuring the big planes could complete their frequent bombing runs over enemy territory and return their crews safely to their home base. In September 1944 his parents received word their son had been awarded a Bronze Star for his efforts, with the citation reading in part:

For meritorius achievement as crew maintenance chief of heavy bombardment aircraft in connection with military operations against the enemy in the European Theater of Operations from 29 January 1944 to 25 July 1944.

In November 1944, a letter dated October 9, 1944 from "somewhere in England" informed Norval's parents of an illness he was suffering from, possibly brought on by exhaustion, but that he considered himself lucky despite the prospect of another Christmas being spent overseas:

Dear Folks:

Will this evening try to answer your letter I received several days ago. Sure am glad to hear everything is O. K. at home. You sure don't write very often, but then, I guess you are writing at least three to my one, so I shouldn't have a word to say.

Just had an interruption on this letter. Couple of the boys came down to see me. Yes, I finally had to give up and go to the hospital for a few days. My throat is pretty bad and I had infection in my right hand. My hand is almost healed now. I guess I was just all washed out more than anything. You know you can even kill a good horse in time. I lost 15 pounds in the last three weeks, so I guess a little rest won't hurt me any. Sure does feel good to just rest like this. If my throat wasn't so sore, I'd really enjoy it. Please don't worry about anything, 'cause I'll be out again in a couple of days. Can't keep a good soldier down, you know. Or can you? I hope you can make this out, as my hand is pretty stiff yet. Kind of hard to steer the pen.

Well, it looks like another Christmas in England for us boys, huh? But I guess we're lucky considering what those boys are going through on the front line. Golly, this is sure getting to be a long war. It better end pretty soon or they'll be sending me home in first class style. Ha!

Well, folks, I guess I'll close now. My hand isn't very good at this work yet. Tell the kids to write me. Tell everyone hello and write real soon. Bye now.

Lots of love,
Norval

Unfortunately, no additional information regarding Norval's remaining time in the service was uncovered.

No photo.
Source: Independence News-Wave

OSCAR W. SATHER
UNITED STATES ARMY

Oscar Sather was inducted into the United States Army on December 19, 1942. He underwent basic training at Camp Wolters, an infantry replacement training center near Mineral Wells, Texas. He then was sent to the Shenandoah, Pennsylvania, replacement depot for two weeks before being ordered to Camp Stoneman, California, for shipment to the Pacific Theater of Operations. On June 1, 1943 Oscar embarked for Noumea, New Caledonia, a major American base 800 miles east of Australia, where he remained for four weeks awaiting assignment to an infantry division.

The 25th Infantry Division had seen combat during the Japanese attack on Pearl Harbor on December 7, 1941 and later landed on Guadalcanal, the first strike in America's offensive war which began in late December 1942. It was in July 1943, near the end of the Guadalcanal campaign, when Oscar joined Company I of the 25th Infantry Division's 27th Infantry Regiment.[1]

On August 1, 1943 Oscar's 27th Infantry landed on Sasavele Island during the New Georgia campaign. As the 25th Infantry Division's 161st Infantry aided the 37th Infantry Division in taking Munda, New Georgia, Oscar's 27th Infantry slogged through jungle and swamp in reaching Piru Plantation in order to attack and take Zieta on August 15, 1943. When the 27th, with the 37th Infantry Division's 145th Infantry Regiment, occupied Bairoko Harbor on August 25, 1943, New Georgia was declared secured.

The 27th Infantry Regiment was next sent to Arundel where it assisted the 43rd Infantry Division in its attack toward Stima Peninsula beginning September 17, 1943. When the Japanese abandoned Stima Peninsula on September 21, 1943, the Regiment was ordered to make an amphibious landing on Kolombangara, which it did unopposed on October 6, 1943. With this, the Central Solomons campaign ended.

In late November 1943, Oscar's unit left New Georgia for New Zealand via a short stop at Guadalcanal, arriving in New Zealand on December 5, 1943 where it remained for the next three months undergoing rehabilitation and training. With the cancellation of the New Britain operation, Oscar then traveled to New Caledonia where he trained further in anticipation of his division's next assignment.

On January 11, 1945 the 25th Infantry Division landed in the San Fabian area of Luzon, Philippine Islands, and five days later undertook the clearing of Japanese from the central Luzon Plain. With the taking of Umingan on February 2, 1945, Japanese forces on Luzon were cut in two.

Following reorganization at La Paz, the Division next attacked the Caraballo Mountains beginning February 21, 1945 by heading along Highway 5 toward Balete Pass. The 27th and 161st Infantry Regiments pushed up Highway 5 while the 35th Infantry Regiment moved along the Old Spanish Trail, with all three regiments facing strong Japanese opposition.

The Battle for Norton's Knob began on March 15, 1945, where the Division was stopped cold for ten days by the entrenched and determined Japanese. Finally, Putlan was taken on March 18, 1945, and a month later Kapintalan fell following fierce fighting by the 35th Infantry on Fishhook Ridge, the 161st Infantry on Crump Hill, and the 27th Infantry on Mt. Myoko.

The 25th Infantry Division next immediately drove on Balete Pass, encountering stiff resistance along the entire way. It wasn't until May 13, 1945 that the pass was taken following intense fighting for Kapintalan Ridge where the 27th and 35th Infantry Regiments found the Japanese concealed in numerous caves. Eventually, more than 200 caves were sealed by the advancing Americans, these becoming tombs for an uncounted number of Japanese soldiers.

The 27th Infantry captured Santa Fe on May 27, 1945, and following mop-up operations along Skyline Ridge and the Old Spanish Trail, it relieved the 37th Infantry Division and mopped

---

[1] The 25th Infantry Division lost 1,235 men killed and 4,190 wounded in action, with 262 of those dying from their wounds, during its four Pacific Theater campaigns.

up remaining Japanese along Highway 5. On June 30, 1945, the 25th Infantry Division was relieved by the 32nd Infantry Division and was stationed south of Tarlac undergoing rehabilitation when word was received of the Japanese surrender to end the war.

For Oscar's 25th Infantry Division, however, this didn't mean an immediate trip home. It was instead ordered to Japan where it served in the Army of Occupation from October 28, 1945 through 1946. Oscar traveled to Japan with his Regiment, but because of the points he had accumulated for his service in the Pacific, he earned a trip home by late 1945. In December of that year, Oscar set sail aboard the *U. S. S. General Mason* bound for Tacoma, Washington, but upon his arrival found he had to remain aboard the ship for eight additional days due to a lack of facilities in Tacoma. Once ashore, however, he left within a few days for Camp McCoy, Wisconsin, where he received his discharge on January 13, 1946 with the rank of Technical Sergeant Fifth Class.

Oscar had earned the Asiatic-Pacific Theater Service Medal with two battle stars for the Central Solomons and Luzon campaigns he had participated in with the 25th Infantry Division. He also wore the Philippine Liberation Ribbon with one battle star, five overseas service bars, combat infantryman's badge, World War II Victory Medal, and Good Conduct Medal.

No photo.
Sources: Independence News-Wave; Book (Stanton)

BENEDICT "BEN" V. SCHNEIDER
UNITED STATES MARINE CORPS

The following edited narrative was prepared following an interview with Ben Schneider conducted on June 23, 1998, at the home of Ernest Sobotta in Independence.

In December 1940 I enlisted in the Marines and spent the next six months in basic training at Quantico, Virginia. Following basic, I entered Officer Candidate School at Quantico and was commissioned a Lieutenant. I then was sent to Camp Lejune, North Carolina, to help organize the 1st Brigade of the 1st Marines.

In February 1942 I boarded ship and spent the next 41 days at sea heading to New Zealand. The ship we were on was a Norwegian luxury liner that hadn't yet been converted into a troop ship and there were six junior officers per stateroom. We spent the entire 41 days unescorted.

I was with the 1st Marines when we hit the beaches of Guadalcanal in August 1942.[1] It turned out that was the most miserable place I was at during the war and it wasn't just because the Japs were shooting at us. It seemed like we were always short of food and ammo and they couldn't get supplies into us because the Jap Navy was offshore. They sunk several of our ships the first night we were there.

Jap submarines were also out there. They stayed 7,000 feet from the beaches and would surface now and then. We could see them doing calisthenics on the deck and they knew we didn't

---

[1] Through December 10, 1942, the First Marine Division suffered more than 600 killed and 800 wounded during the campaign to take Guadalcanal. An additional 5,749 men contracted malaria, however, and other illnesses such as gastro-enteritis also took their toll. However, despite this, the lack of air and naval power, inadequate food and armament, and Japanese air, naval, and infantry attacks, the Division took and held an extremely valuable airfield it named Henderson Field. For its achievements on Guadalcanal, the 1st Marine Division was presented with a Presidential Unit Citation. Other American units had 691 killed during the same time period on Guadalcanal.

have any guns that could reach them.

We were shelled a lot on Guadalcanal. I remember one guy was on an old mattress when a big navy shell buried itself underneath him in the sand. After it exploded, we couldn't find him at first, then saw he was blown up into a tree. He wasn't even hurt!

I was promoted to Captain while at Guadalcanal. Then in January 1943 I went to Australia where I spent six or seven months in Brisbane and Melbourne. From Australia we went to New Britain where we landed with the main invasion force.[2] I remember a place called Pagoo-goo[3] where I think the rats were bigger than police dogs!

While the New Britain campaign was still going on, I was sent back to Quantico in the States to attend school. At Camp Legune I joined the 1st Brigade and headed back to the Pacific.

We were in floating reserve at Saipan, then went to Guadalcanal to form the 6th Marine Division. While there, I was promoted to Major and was the Executive Officer of the 3d Battalion during the invasion of Okinawa.[4]

On April 1, 1945 we landed on the beaches of Okinawa where our division first headed north up the island. About a month into it we were relieved by the Army's 27th Division, and we turned around and went to the southern part of the island, ending up in Naha. There the Division built a bridge and put up a sign stating, "This is the biggest damned bridge ever built by the Marines." A little later someone put up a little structure over a trickle of water with a sign saying, "This is the smallest damned bridge ever built by the Marines."

I left Okinawa on July 4 and headed to Guam to prepare for the invasion of Japan's home islands. That's where I was when the atomic bombs were dropped. Dropping those bombs was the best thing that could have happened because an awful lot of us would have been killed if we would have had to invade Japan itself.

---

[2] The 1st Marine Division landed at Cape Gloucester, New Britain, on December 26, 1943.

[3] Spelling may be incorrect.

[4] On Okinawa, Ben was the Executive Officer of the 3d Howitzer Battalion, 15th Marines, 6th Marine Division. His name appears in Appendix III: Command and Staff List of Marine Units on Okinawa, in *Okinawa: Victory in the Pacific* by Nichols and Shaw. The 3d Howitzer Battalion, 15th Marines lost 3 killed and 34 wounded during the Okinawa campaign.

Sources: Books (Miller, John) (Nichols and Shaw)

It didn't take long for America to begin raising the money needed to fight the war. Many newspaper ads urging people to purchase War Bonds were of a more comical nature early in the war, but this changed when the realities of the war became apparent.

GEORGE SCHNEIDER
UNITED STATES MARINE CORPS

George Schneider joined the United States Marine Corps towards the end of his second year at the University of Notre Dame in 1942. Following basic training, he was accepted into Officer's Training School at Quantico, Virginia, where he received his Second Lieutenant's bars on June 2, 1943. He later was sent to the Hawaiian Islands for further amphibious training. On December 1, 1944 George was promoted to First Lieutenant and then aided in the preparations being made at Pearl Harbor for the invasion of Iwo Jima.

Iwo Jima is a small, ham-shaped island 800 miles directly south of Japan. It is only four-and-a-half miles long and two-and-a-half miles at its widest point in the northeastern end. Dominating this desolate volcanic piece of nothing is Mount Suribachi, a 550-foot high peak located at the southern tip of the island. The American high command early in World War II saw Iwo as an emergency landing point for damaged bombers that already were planned to attack the Japanese mainland. It was a strategic location, and the Japanese knew it as they developed a complex and extremely effective defense of Iwo's beaches.

When the Marines shipped out of Hawaii on February 15, 1945, George first learned their destination was Iwo Jima. On the morning of February 19, 1945, George led his platoon of Company L, 3rd Battalion, 23rd Marine Regiment, 4th Marine Division, under the overall command of Major General Clifton Cates, onto the beaches of Iwo in one of the first waves of assault troops. Besides the Marines needing to deal with rough seas, the Japanese were pouring heavy fire onto the approaching LVT's loaded with troops, knocking out several before they could even reach the beach. Then, once ashore, Marines of the 4th Division faced not only intense enemy fire, but also soft volcanic sands that made the digging of foxholes nearly impossible.

Additionally, a series of high sand terraces caused by storms made movement inland slow and deadly. That morning, all regiments of the 4th Division suffered heavy casualties on the beach because of this combination of factors.

While pinned down on the beach, George and other commanders knew their men had to get out of the sand in order to gain shelter and survive the deadly accurate enemy fire. He coaxed them forward, and in so doing, probably saved the lives of a number of the men under his command. Movement inland was extremely slow that first day and casualties were mounting rapidly in all units along the two-mile beachhead. On February 20, 1945, the day following the invasion and while assaulting a Japanese pillbox, George himself was severely wounded by an exploding enemy mortar shell.

Being evacuated from the island onto a hospital ship, it was obvious George's leg was badly damaged. Because of the large number of such casualties, it was impossible for the doctors available to adequately treat them all, so many limbs were amputated in order to save the soldier's life. Thus,

George's leg was scheduled for amputation, with the surgery to take place the day following his arrival aboard the ship. In the meantime, however, a doctor passed by his bed and saw the name "Schneider" on his identification tag. He stopped and said to George, "I knew a wonderful nurse at the Mayo Clinic named Schneider. Romelle Schneider, it was, and she was a damned good nurse!" All George could say was, "That's my sister!" Following the initial surprise registered by both doctor and patient, the doctor began work on George's leg, and saved it from the following day's amputation. George was later presented with a Purple Heart for the wounds he had received.

In a letter home to his mother, Mrs. Agnes Schneider, George stated that though his face hadn't been hit, "a mortar shell exploded between my legs and completely severed the fibula (bone below the knee) in my right leg, also hitting the chest." He also reported that every friend he had in the 4th Marine Division was killed on Iwo Jima and that out of the 600 officers there, 300 were killed. He told her that before landing, he had estimated he had a 50/50 chance of surviving the battle. And he did survive, despite the fact the Marines suffered 3,000 casualties during those first two days on the beaches of Iwo Jima.[1]

For his actions of those two days, his only taste of combat in the entire war, First Lieutenant George Schneider was awarded the Bronze Star, for which the citation stated:

> For heroic achievement in connection with operations against the enemy while serving as a platoon leader of a rifle platoon in a Marine rifle company on IWO JIMA, VOLCANO ISLANDS, on 20 February, 1945. During an attack against an enemy fortified position on a ridge line where his platoon was held up, Lieutenant SCHNEIDER, exposing himself to enemy rifle, mortar, and artillery fire, moved forward of his own front lines to the ridge line, in order to observe enemy positions and to ascertain the enemy situation in an endeavor to coordinate all elements of his company in setting up a night action, he had set an example of courage and initiative for his men. Through his aggressiveness and leadership under the most difficult conditions, he was at all times an inspiration to his men. His daring movement to the observation point ahead of his own front lines contributed an invaluable service to his unit. His courage and conduct throughout the operation were in keeping with the highest traditions of the United States Naval Service.
>
> (Signed) C. B. Cates, Major General, U. S. Marine Corps.

George remained in the Marine Corps while he recuperated from his injuries, and received his honorable discharge on January 24, 1946.

---

[1] Overall, casualties in the Battle for Iwo Jima amounted to 4,900 Americans killed, 1,900 missing or later dying of their wounds, and an incredible 19,200 wounded. George's 4th Marine Division, as well as the 5th Marine Division, suffered an astounding 75-percent casualty rate in its infantry units. A total of 27 Congressional Medals of Honor were earned on Iwo, all for 10 square miles of volcanic ash and rock. This epic battle was memorialized in famed war correspondent Joe Rosenthal's photograph of the raising of the American flag on the summit of Mount Suribachi, a scene venerated in a National Monument in Washington, D. C.

Sources: Mrs. George (Fran) Schneider; Independence News-Wave; Book (Gailey)

A Quote From History. . .

". . . they rescued a whole B-29 crew. I'm pretty proud of having done that."
   Al Kulig
   United States Navy
   Interview of June 9, 1998, and describing his spotting "one pip' on
   his radar screen while on Tinian in the Marianas Islands.

ADRIAN SKROCH
UNITED STATES NAVY

Adrian Skroch had already completed a three-year hitch in the United States Navy before the Japanese attack on Pearl Harbor occurred, originally enlisting in August 1937 and serving aboard the battleship *U. S. S. Maryland* (BB-46). He reenlisted on January 23, 1942, after which he served aboard the *U. S. S. Courage* (PG-70) for about 20 months. The *Courage* was a British/Canadian-built corvette that the United States obtained from Britain at the start of the war. She was 205 feet long, had a top speed of 16-1/2 knots, and was manned by a crew of 80.

Sometime around August 1944 Adrian was transferred to the *U. S. S. Robert I. Paine* (DE-578), a newly commissioned destroyer escort named for a United States Marine killed on Tulagi in the Pacific on August 7, 1942 and awarded the Silver Star for heroism. Aboard the *Robert I. Paine*, Adrian served in the ship's office.

The *Robert I. Paine* was 306 feet long and carried a crew of 225 officers and men. Under the command of Lieutenant Commander Drayton Cochran, she completed her shakedown cruise off Bermuda in mid-April 1944, and immediately joined the Atlantic Fleet. Her first duty out of Brooklyn was to screen for the aircraft carriers *U. S. S. Ranger* (CV-4) and *U. S. S. Card* (CVE-11) as they transported aircraft and personnel to Casablanca in North Africa. The ships arrived off Casablanca on May 4, 1944, after which *Robert I. Paine* patrolled in nearby waters for several days before beginning the trip back to the United States.

On May 10, 1944 she received a change in orders and joined a hunter-killer group that included the escort carrier *U. S. S. Block Island* (CVE-21). The group returned to Casablanca on May 18, 1944, then left there on May 23 to undertake antisubmarine duties west of the Canary Islands and south of the Azores. On May 29, 1944, *Block Island* was sunk and the destroyer escort *U. S. S. Barr* (DE-576) badly damaged in a torpedo attack launched by the German U-boat *U-549*. The escorts immediately began search and rescue operations during which *Robert I. Paine* took on 279 survivors from *Block Island*. She then moved in to cover the damaged *Barr*. Other escorts located and sank the U-boat, and after search operations were called off the next day, the ships made their way back to Casablanca. On June 4, *Robert I. Paine* headed for Gibraltor where she met with a convoy that she helped escort to New York.

Following training in Casco Bay, Halifax, Canada, *Robert I. Paine* sailed from Hampton Roads, Virginia, on July 13, 1944 with UGS48, a slow convoy destined for Bizerte in North Africa. On July 31, 1944 her radar detected enemy planes shadowing the convoy and the next day she aided in beating off a German air attack. In late 1944, she escorted another convoy to Bizerte and then returned to Boston after which she underwent training before resuming antisubmarine activities ranging between Casco Bay and Argentia, Canada.

In February 1945, *Robert I. Paine* again was escorting convoys on the southern New England coast leg when she was attached to the 12th Fleet under the Royal Navy's Western Approaches Command. She arrived at Liverpool, England, for this duty on April 3, 1945 and from then until the end of the war escorted convoys on the eastern transatlantic convoy lanes.

172

On May 14, 1945, the war with Germany was already over and Adrian was aboard *Robert I. Paine* when she represented the United States Navy at the formal surrender of eight German U-boats. The boats were disarmed at a base in the north of Scotland and, guarded by British naval officers and men, skeleton crews of German seamen manned the boats as they were escorted to Londonderry Harbor in England. Word preceded their arrival there and large numbers of sailors, marines, and other military personnel lined the shores as the boats entered the harbor. Leading the way was the *H. M. S. Hesperus*, followed by the Canadian frigate *H. M. C. S. Thetford Mines* and the *U. S. S. Robert I. Paine*. Then came the U-boats, seven of them over 500 tons and the eighth at 750 tons, all of them rusty and battle scarred with unkempt and dirty crews. An article appearing in the June 7, 1945 *News-Wave* reported the Germans all appeared to be less than 25 years old but looked healthy and well fed. Some were reported as sulky, while others acted indifferent and some even cocky.

On June 1, 1945 *Robert I. Paine* arrived in New York Harbor and after a short time there continued on to Houston, Texas, where she was scheduled to be converted to a radar picket ship. Sometime following her arrival in Houston, Adrian, a Chief Yeoman, left the ship and traveled to Minneapolis, Minnesota, where he received his discharge on September 12, 1945. Seven days later, his wife, the former Sally Skroch of Independence, gave birth to a son at Whitehall Community Hospital.

The *U. S. S. Robert I. Paine* received one battle star for its service in the Atlantic during World War II.

Sources: Independence News-Wave; Internet

ALBERT SKROCH
UNITED STATES NAVY

Albert Skroch enlisted in the United States Navy in 1921, a full 20 years before the Japanese attack on Pearl Harbor that forced America's entry into World War II. By 1941, he had been married seven years and had a son, Clarence, and was serving aboard the destroyer *U. S. S. Peary* (DD-226). The *Peary* was an older ship in the Navy's service, having been launched on April 6, 1920 and commissioned October 22, 1920. She was named in honor of the famous Admiral Peary, whose expedition in 1909 was the first to reach the North Pole. Throughout her service, *Peary* was stationed in the Far East, patrolling with the Yangtze Patrol Force from 1923 to 1931 and making regular excursions into Chinese waters in support of American interests from 1931 until the outbreak of World War II. It is uncertain as to when Albert joined the crew of the *Peary* but he was aboard on December 7, 1941 when the Japanese launched their attack on the American fleet at Pearl.

In October 1941, *Peary* and the destroyer *Pillsbury* were involved in a collision. While at the Cavite Navy Yard, Philippine Islands, for repairs, her crew received word of the Japanese attack and learned America was at war. Two days later, on December 10, 1941, 50 Japanese twin-engine high level bombers, flying above the range of anti-aircraft fire, attacked Cavite and destroyed nearly the entire base. In this attack, *Peary* was hit by a bomb that damaged her superstructure and stack, killing eight of her crew. When a torpedo overhaul shop near the pier to which *Peary* was tied was set afire by bombs, and torpedoes began exploding, *Peary* found herself in serious danger that, if not for the quick actions of minesweeper *Whippoorwill* in towing her out and *Pillsbury* in extinguishing her fires, could have caused her to be lost. In this action, *Peary's* commanding officer, Commander H. H. Keith, was wounded and had to be evacuated from the ship, after which he was relieved by Commander J. M. Bermingham.

Peary left Cavite on December 26, 1941, and shortly after getting underway was subjected

173

to another Japanese raid. Several bombs were dropped near the ship but no damage was sustained. The following morning found *Peary* in Campomanes Bay of Negros Island, where she put in for the day. The crew feverishly attempted to camoflage her with green paint and palm fronds in an effort to conceal her from any Japanese planes that happened by. Their efforts were successful as five bombers passed overhead but apparently did not spot her. That night she set sail through the Celebes Sea toward Makassar Strait..

The next morning, however, December 28, 1941, *Peary* wasn't as fortunate as she was spotted by a lone four-engine Japanese bomber which shadowed her for several hours until three other bombers arrived in early afternoon. For the next two hours, *Peary* was attacked by these four bombers but was still able to evade the 500-pound bombs and four aerial torpedoes unleashed at her. The four torpedoes bracketed *Peary's* bow and stern, missing her by only a matter of yards. Following their attack, the bombers left.

January 1, 1942, found the *Peary* stationed at Darwin, Australia, where she operated primarily in anti-submarine action during January and into February. On February 19, 1942, beginning at 10:45 A. M., *Peary* became the focus of an intense attack by Japanese single-engine dive bombers as she attempted to shield the Australian hospital ship, *Manunda*, by laying down a smokescreen. The first bomb to strike her hit her fantail, and a second, an incendiary, exploded on the galley deck house. A third bomb did not explode, but a fourth set off the forward ammunition magazines while a fifth, another incendiary, exploded in the aft engine room. *Peary's* .30- and .50-caliber machine guns continued firing until the Japanese planes flew away, but by then *Peary* was mortally wounded. About 1:00 P. M., the *U. S. S. Peary* sank stern first, with a loss of 52 men killed and many wounded of its total complement of 101 sailors.[1] Only one officer survived.

Albert Skroch, machinist's mate first class, was one of the wounded sailors forced to swim with the few other survivors of the ship. The May 14, 1942, edition of the *Independence News-Wave* reported that Albert's parents, Mr. and Mrs. John C. Skroch, had been informed that Albert had been seriously injured, that he had suffered severe burns to his hands, with his right hand possibly permanently crippled, as well as shell shock. Following hospitalization overseas, Albert was transferred to the Naval hospital at Mare Island, California, in April, 1942. By August, he was recovered enough to be able to occasionally visit at the homes of friends, but he remained at the Mare Island hospital for some time receiving treatment for his injuries. In an article in the *Sonoma* (California) *Sentinel* in late summer, Albert was quoted as saying, "As soon as I recover, I am anxious to return to the Far East and help give those Jap rats a real drubbing."

It is uncertain whether Albert ever got that chance as no further information was found regarding his service career. He undoubtedly received the Purple Heart for wounds received, while the *U. S. S. Peary* received one battle star for its World War II service and was struck from the Navy's list of active ships on May 8, 1942.

---

[1] Another, later, report identified 80 killed and 13 wounded.

No photo.
Sources: Internet; Book (Karig and Kelley)

A Quote From History. . .

"With best wishes and good luck to you all."
    Carl "Ole" Leque
    United States Army
    Letter of August 12, 1944, to his mother while a POW in Stalag 2B.

EDWARD I. SKROCH
UNITED STATES ARMY

In the late 1930's, Ed Skroch was a member of the 32d Military Police Company of the Wisconsin National Guard, stationed at Arcadia, Wisconsin. On July 1, 1939, he left that unit. But with the arrival to America of World War II, Ed once again entered the service, this time with the United States Army, on September 14, 1942. He spent four months in basic training after which he received six months of additional training in automotive mechanics, a trade at which he worked for E. J. Passon in Independence prior to his call to active duty. Following this, he attended an Army Ordnance School at Camp Wheeler, Georgia, for twelve weeks.

Though the exact date is not clear, it appears Ed was then assigned to Headquarters Company, 2nd Battalion, 101st Infantry Regiment, 26th Infantry Division.[1] He probably was with the unit when the Division arrived at the Tennessee Maneuver Area on January 24, 1944 for the Second Army No. 5 Tennessee Maneuvers. Following completion of this training exercise, the 26th Infantry Division returned to Fort Jackson, South Carolina, on March 30, 1944, staged at Camp Shanks, New York, on August 20, 1944, and departed the New York Port of Embarkation on August 27, 1944.

Sgt. Ed Skroch, left, with
Lt. Phil Corey of Ohio.

The Division sailed directly to France, landing at Cherbourg and Utah Beach on September 7, 1944, where it relieved the 4th Infantry Division and held defensive positions in the Salonnes-Moncourt area of France. On November 8, 1944 the 26th Infantry Division began an offensive that quickly took Vic-sur-Seille and its bridges intact. Ed's 101st Infantry captured Hill 310 on November 11, while the Division's other two regiments successfully won their objectives, as well. As the 26th Infantry continued to push hard, the Germans offered strong opposition, but eventually were forced into retreating. Albestroff, an important crossroads town, finally was taken on November 23, 1944. The 101st Infantry Regiment then aided in the 4th Armored Division's attack east of the Sarre River, which resulted in savage house-to-house fighting lasting until December 4, 1944.

As the 26th Infantry Division was training replacements near Metz, France, the Germans launched their Ardennes counteroffensive on December 16, 1944. The Division was quickly mobilized and moved to Luxembourg within a few days where it attacked in the Rambrouch-Grosbous area before pushing on to the Wiltz River. The Wiltz was crossed, the city itself fell on January 22, 1945, and the 101st Infantry Regiment took Clerf along the Clerf River on January 25. The Division then was given defensive responsibilities in the area surrounding Saarlautern until March 6, 1945.

On March 13, 1945 the 26th Infantry Division attacked toward the Rhine River, reaching

---

[1] The 26th Infantry Division suffered 1,850 men killed and 7,886 wounded, of which 262 died from their wounds, during its European Theater campaigns of World War II.

it on March 21. It crossed the Rhine at Oppenheim on March 26, and, reinforced by tanks of the 4th Armored Division, took Hanau following heavy house-to-house fighting. The 101st Infantry took Fulda on April 2, 1945, and then relieved the 11th Armored Division which had led the American attack following the fall of Hanau.

On April 8, 1945, the 26th Infantry Division reached the Nahe River and linked once again with the 11th Armored Division. Following 11th Armored, the 26th Infantry crossed into Austria on May 1, 1945, assisted in the taking of Linz on May 4, and was pushing toward the Vlatava River southeast of Volary, Czechoslovakia, on May 7, 1945, when hostilities officially ceased.

Throughout the 26th Infantry Division's four campaigns in the European Theater -- Northern France, Rhineland, Ardennes-Alsace, and Central Europe -- Ed served as an Administrative Specialist with Headquarters Company, 2nd Battalion, 101st Infantry. As a motor transportation NCO (non-commissioned officer) and first sergeant of his infantry battalion, he supervised a variety of clerical and administrative functions necessary to insure the smooth operation of his unit. He supervised the preparation of reports, rosters, morning reports, sick reports, passes, furloughs, and other matters pertaining to personnel. He also supervised duties of 128 enlisted men.

The 26th Infantry Division remained in Europe with the Army of Occupation until being inactivated in Germany on December 29, 1945. Ed's 101st Infantry, however, left Europe earlier and arrived at the Boston Port of Embarkation on that date, after which it was immediately inactivated at Camp Myles Standish, Massachusetts. After having spent 16 months in the European Theater, Ed traveled to the Fort Sheridan, Illinois, Separation Center where he was separated from the United States Army on January 6, 1946.

On December 10, 1945, First Sergeant Edward I. Skroch received a Meritorious Commendation from Colonel Thomas A. Vetter, Commanding, 101st Infantry Regiment. It stated as follows:

> It is with deep regret that I bid farewell to my endeared assistant, First Sergeant Edward I. Skroch of Headquarters Company, 2nd Battalion, 101st Infantry. Sergeant Skroch had demonstrated his technical ability and efficiency in thoroughly and skillfully maintaining the most commendable and successful status of administration within his company. This administrative system, initiated through his conscientious and arduous efforts, distinctly marked the superior progress of this unit.
>
> His prompt, precise application to detail, utmost care and efficiency in drawing up and handling of the necessary administrative reports, with the same noteworthy calm and pleasant disposition under all conditions, denotes a high sense of responsibility for Headquarters Company and has supervised and maintained this system to a successful completion. The efficiency and success of his Company depended on his ability. Sergeant Skroch's efforts and untiring courage reflect a great credit upon himself and the Armed Forces of the United States Army.

A letter dated May 12, 1948 to Ed from the Adjutant General's Office of the War Department's Records and Administration Center, confirmed Ed's being awarded the Bronze Star for actions during the Northern France campaign:

> By direction of the President, under the provisions of Executive Order 9419, 4 February 1944 (Sec. II, WD Bul. 3, 1944) a Bronze Star Medal is awarded for exemplary conduct in ground combat against the armed enemy, to First Sergeant (then Sergeant) Edward I. Skroch, 36 261 840, 101st Infantry, during the Northern France Campaign in the European Theater of Operations.

One other note of interest regarding Ed's time in Europe is that, while serving with the U. S. occupation forces in the American Zone in Austria, Ed was granted a hunting permit on October 5, 1945. It is not know whether he was successful in his hunt.

Sources: Fay Skroch, daughter; Book (Stanton)

EUGENE E. SKROCH
UNITED STATES NAVAL RESERVE

The following narrative was prepared from a letter received from Dr. Eugene Skroch in January, 1999.

The background of my military service goes back to when I was a medical student, during which time the World War II hostilities began. Shortly after the war broke out, the Surgeon General of the United States felt that we would be of more benefit as physicians rather than in another role, so they established a program in which we could enlist as Ensign Cadets in the Navy and continue our medical education. There was no compensation for this and on May 10, 1943, I resigned from the program and was accepted into the Navy's V-12 program, which is the same as ASTP (Army Specialty Training Program) in the Army.

The nice part of the V-12 program was that all of our school expenses -- tuition and books -- were paid, plus I believe we received a compensation of $50 a month. The sad part was that I was almost finished with medical school, so on November 19, 1943, I was done with the program as well as medical school. I was then commissioned as a Lieutenant, junior grade (j.g.), in the Medical Corps of the United States Naval Reserve. The government then established what was called a "9-9-9" program, in which we would undergo nine months of internship, nine months of residency, and, if lucky enough, another nine months of residency. My nine months of internship were at Research Hospital in Kansas City, Missouri, and my first nine months of residency at the Mayo Clinic in Rochester, Minnesota. I was not lucky enough to get another nine months of residency, however, and was ordered to active duty instead.

I reported for active duty at the U. S. Naval Hospital in Seattle, Washington, on July 10, 1945. On July 25, I received orders to report for duty aboard *LST-117* at Coronado, California. So I left Seattle on July 27, 1945, arrived in San Diego, California, on July 29, and reported aboard *LST-117* the next day. Because it was scheduled to go to the western Pacific to participate in the invasion of Japan, our ship had been partially converted so it could land troops, tanks, and other equipment ashore and retrieve and treat casualties incurred during the landing. Fortunately, this never came about and on August 2, 1945 we sailed to San Francisco instead, arriving there on August 5. Then, of course, V-J Day occurred on August 14, 1945.

The next day, August 15, we sailed for Pearl Harbor and to this day I do not know why -- just typical government waste. We arrived at Pearl Harbor on August 25, 1945 and four days later I was detached from *LST-117* to await further orders. These arrived on September 19, 1945, when I was ordered to report to the destroyer *U. S. S. Charles S. Sperry* (DD-697), which was at Eniwetok. I left Pearl Harbor on September 22 via Naval Air Transport, and traveled to Eniwetok by way of Kwajalein.

On September 26, 1945 I reported aboard the *U. S. S. Sperry* only to find that the physician I was to replace had already been replaced. A few days later, on October 2, 1945, I received orders to report to another destroyer, the *U. S. S. John W. Weeks* (DD-701). My duties here were to serve as physician for four destroyers. By October 7, I was aboard and we left for Tokyo, Japan. The highlight of this trip was riding out a typhoon during which our destroyer was more of a submarine than a ship!

We arrived in Tokyo Bay on October 13, 1945, but left shortly after, on November 1, for Sasebo, Japan, which is on the west side of the island of Honshu. From there we sailed to Pusan, Korea, on November 7, 1945, but were back in Sasebo on November 12. On that day, I received orders to report to the aircraft carrier *U. S. S. Ticonderoga* (CV-14), back in the States. I detached from the *Sperry* on November 20, 1945, reported to the *U. S. S. Barber* (APD-57), and began the trip back to the United States. We arrived in San Diego, California, on December 13, 1945, and five days later I left for San Francisco where I spent the next month doing nothing but waiting for the *Ticonderoga* to arrive in port. Then I finally heard the *Ticonderoga* returned to Seattle instead, so on January 19, 1946, I left San Francisco to find my ship.

I reported aboard the Ticonderoga after arriving in Seattle on January 21, 1946, only to find out again that the physician I was to replace was already replaced, and that they had no place to send me for the time being! Finally, on March 30, 1946, I reported aboard the World War I vintage battleship, *U. S. S. Maryland*, where I remained until July 9, 1946, when I was sent home.

Now this must be the most boring story of one's military service you have ever read! As you can see, all I did was chase ships around the Pacific!

The total time I spent in the service was just a little over twelve months, so in 1954 I was drafted in a special physician's draft and reported to duty with the Navy once again. I reported first to Great Lakes Naval Training Center near Chicago on October 18, 1954, and from there was ordered on December 11 to report to the Hospital Ship Haven at Long Beach, California. While stationed there I did general surgery on troops in the area. Then, on June 30, 1955, I was transferred to the Naval Hospital at Camp Pendleton, Virginia, where I was assigned as a general surgeon to officer's dependents and wards. This was very similar to my post-service practice here in Madison, Wisconsin. I was finally separated from the service on April 6, 1956.

SIMON "BOB" R. SKROCH
UNITED STATES ARMY

Simon "Bob" Skroch was inducted into the United States Army on October 28, 1941, and entered active duty that same day at Fort Sheridan, Illinois. Following basic training, he received further training as a rifleman. On June 2, 1942 Bob left for the Aleutian Islands where American forces were facing a Japanese invasion and troop buildup. He arrived on the Aleutian's on June 16, 1942, and spent the next two years there. During that time, on January 4, 1944, he wrote a letter to the *News-Wave* thanking the American Legion Post 186 for sending servicemen a Christmas gift of cigarettes. The *News-Wave* published the letter on February 17, 1944:

Dear Friends:

Thanks very much for the cigarettes you sent to me. That is something a fellow can always use. It is nice to know that the folks at home still think of the boys who have left.

Everything is as well as can be expected. We don't have very much entertainment besides a movie now and then. A fellow can find something to pass away the time if there is any spare time to pass away. There is always plenty of books and magazines around.

This year we received a few bottles of beer for Christmas. Our New Year's supply is still in the messhall. It will be given out the first time the company is together as there is someone out working most every hour of the day and night.

The Thanksgiving, Christmas, and New Year's dinners consisted of roast turkey and all the trimmings. The meals never tasted as good as they would have if they would have been eaten at home, but under the circumstances were pretty good. The messhall was pretty quiet on those three days, whereas nearly everyone is talking on other days. Everyone was there in body but not in spirit.

It will be a happy day when we can return home to stay. I am sure everyone hopes that day isn't too far in the future.

Thanks again for the cigarettes, and keep the home fires burning.

Sincerely,

Bob

On May 13, 1944 Bob returned to the United States, and following a furlough was ordered to report to Camp Shelby, Mississippi. At Camp Shelby, he was assigned to the 385th Infantry Regiment, 76th Infantry Division,[1] which moved to Camp Miles Standish, Massachusetts, and departed for Europe on November 23, 1944, landing in England on December 5, 1944.

The 76th Infantry Division arrived at Le Havre, France, on January 12, 1945, and by January 23, 1945 was staged at Champlon, Belgium. Upon relieving the 87th Infantry Division along the Sauer and Moselle Rivers near Echternach, Luxembourg, on January 25, 1945, the 76th Infantry joined the attack on February 7, 1945 in the Weiterbach-Echternach area. It took Echternacherbruck and fought through Hitler's *West Wall* fortifications before Bob's 385th Infantry Regiment and the Division's 304th Infantry took the 800-foot high ground north of Minden, overcoming murderous fire from Germans entrenched in pillboxes throughout the hillsides. It was during this action that the 76th Infantry Division earned the reputation as "the greenest, yet the fastest moving and hardest hitting division participating in the assault."

The Division crossed the Pruem River on February 24-25, 1945. It attacked toward Trier on February 27, 1945 and captured Olk, Herforst, Grosslittgen, and Musweiler. The 385th Infantry, redesignated Task Force Onaway, also outflanked and captured the vaunted Katzenkopf fortress near Irrel. By March 14, 1945 the Division had reached the Klein Kyll and Lieser Rivers.

Bob Skroch, front row, far right.

After the 76th Infantry Division relieved the 2nd Cavalry Group along the Rhine River, its 385th and 417th Infantry Regiments crossed the Rhine on March 26-27, 1945 and engaged in house-to-house fighting at Kamberg, Germany. At Kamberg, the Americans were opposed by German officer candidates who temporarily stopped their advance with fierce close-quarter fighting. After eliminating this pocket of resistance, the Division finally reached the Wehre River and took the bridge at Niederhone on April 5, 1945. The 304th Infantry Regiment attacked Zeitz next after crossing the Wisse-Elster River on April 13, 1945, then was relieved by the 417th Infantry Regiment which took the city on April 15, 1945. The Division took over the 6th Armored Division's bridgehead across the Mulde River, and was defending that bridgehead near Chemnitz when Germany surrendered on May 7, 1945.

The 76th Infantry Division was inactivated on August 31, 1945, at which time Bob was attached to Company G, 410th Infantry Regiment, 103rd Infantry Division. On September 11, 1945 he left Europe with the 103rd and arrived back in New York on September 19, 1945. He

[1] The 76th Infantry Division lost 433 of its men killed in action while another 1,811 were wounded, with 90 of these dying from their wounds.

had participated in the Ardennes-Alsace, Rhineland, and Central Europe campaigns as a Private First Class and had been awarded his Combat Infantry Badge, the American Defense Service Ribbon, European-African-Middle Eastern Theater Ribbon with three bronze battle stars, Asiatic-Pacific Theater Ribbon with one bronze battle star, five Overseas Service Bars, one Service Stripe, and the Good Conduct Medal. On September 30, 1945 Bob received his discharge at the Army Separation Center at Fort Sheridan, Illinois.

Bob's son, Bill, remembers two stories his father told him regarding his tour of duty in Europe. In one instance, his unit was being shelled by German artillery, forcing them to take cover in a cellar of a French house. There they found a case of vermouth and Bob told Bill he could not touch vermouth for many years after that.

The other story was much more serious, however. Bob was watching an episode of the television series *Combat* during the 1960's when in the show an American soldier, startled by movement and noise, shot and killed a young French boy. Bob told his son he once saw a German soldier, startled in much the same manner, shoot and kill a young boy. The German, stunned by what he had just done, simply dropped his weapon and surrendered to Bob's unit.

Bob appears in a photograph in Berry Craig's book, *76th Infantry Division: Onaway*, which is a history of the Division.

Sources: Mrs. Bernice Skroch personal papers; Bill Skroch, son; Books (Craig) (Stanton)

A Quote From History. . .

"My nerves are sure shot."
    Ray Warner
    United States Army
    Journal entry, February 11, 1945, during the Battle of Manila.

PETER SKROCH
UNITED STATES NAVY RESERVE

The following narrative was written following an interview conducted with Peter Skroch on December 8, 1998 at his home in Oconto Falls, Wisconsin.

I was 16 or 17 years old when I joined the National Guard; I belonged to the 32nd Military Police Company, 32nd Division, in Arcadia, Wisconsin. After high school, I went on to school at River Falls State Teachers College in River Falls, Wisconsin. I attended drill there while school was in session and during the summer I went back to Arcadia and attended drill at Camp McCoy. In 1940 my unit was mobilized for active duty that was to last one year but since I had only three months left in the Guard, I could either go with the unit to Louisiana or stay in Arcadia and complete my time there. They told me that if I went to Louisiana, I would have to re-up for another three years, so I stayed behind and soon left the Guard.

I was in school at River Falls on December 7, 1941 when the Japanese attacked Pearl Harbor. In early 1942 I applied for and was accepted into the Navy's V-12 Reserve Officer Program. On June 1, 1943 I graduated from college. Just prior to graduating, I had received a letter asking whether I was interested in joining the V-5 program. This was the air cadet program and they were specifically looking for pilots for aircraft carrier duty. So, following graduation I went to Milwaukee to await acceptance into V-5. In Milwaukee, I had been working at Pabst

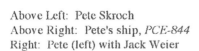

Above Left: Pete Skroch
Above Right: Pete's ship, *PCE-844*
Right: Pete (left) with Jack Weier

Brewing Company for four months when I finally received orders to report to V-5 at St. Olaf College in Northfield, Minnesota. It was there where I entered active duty on November 1, 1943. and began my pre-flight training.

From St. Olaf, I went to Minot, North Dakota, where I received 40 hours of actual flight training, 20 hours of which was solo. In all, I spent three months in V-5, receiving my basic training and flight training in light training planes. But then, because of the turn of events in the war, aircraft carrier production was cut back and the V-5 program was reduced by 50 percent in one day. No more carrier pilots were needed so I was reclassified back to V-12. On September 14, 1944 I graduated from Midshipman School at Navy Pier, Chicago, in the 20th Class, 31st Company, and was commissioned an Ensign in the Navy.

181

I was next sent to the Anti-Submarine Warfare School in Miami, Florida, where I underwent three months of training. I then was assigned to *PCE-844*, a Patrol Craft Escort 184 feet long with a 33-foot beam.[1] In January 1945 we embarked Key West, Florida, and sailed for the Pacific. Over the next several months, we spent time in New Guinea, Leyte, Manila, and Bornea. We spent lots of time in the Sulu Archipelago patrolling Makassar Strait between the South Philippines and Tawi-Tawi, the northernmost island of Bornea. At first we were assigned to the 7th Fleet but after several months in the Philippines, our ship was transferred to the 3rd Fleet. The 3rd Fleet stayed in the Philippines while the 7th Fleet participated in the Okinawa invasion.

We patrolled for several months but there weren't any Japanese ships that far south anymore. Before I got to the area, Jap subs were attacking our convoys, but they were all gone by the time I arrived. While on patrol duty, we usually spent two weeks patrolling followed by one week at anchor where we would line up with six or seven other ships like ours and be resupplied and refueled all at the same time. We also escorted convoys from New Guinea to Leyte for a while. There were usually 40 ships in each convoy and they left New Guinea every seven days. By this late in the war, the greatest danger to the convoys was from kamikazes. One time, the convoy that sailed immediately before us, and the one that followed us, were both hit by kamikazes, but I never actually saw any on that trip or any other.

As the war was drawing to a close, we were ordered to Batangus Harbor in the Philippines. This was the staging area for the invasion of Japan. All the troop ships were to sail from there so a lot of equipment was being stockpiled on the beaches. Three or four ships a day for several months were being unloaded and you never saw so much hardware in one place! And there were five other staging areas like this one! Our duty was to anchor in the harbor and direct ship traffic. As a ship entered or left the harbor, a coded message would come in identifying the ship and its destination or point of origin. As Assistant Communications Officer, I had to summarize all of this information each day.

I later became Communications Officer of *PCE-844* and was then in charge of the sonar and radio men. I had received sonar training while in Miami, at what was called "Ping School." The word "ping" was used to describe the sound made when a sound wave was bounced off another ship, such as a submarine, and then received by the electronic equipment we had on board. I had three sonar men in my sonar department and they manned the sonar in eight-hour shifts when we were on patrol. Sonar wasn't manned while we were anchored for refueling and resupply or while we were on harbor duty.

We had one radio technician and five radiomen aboard ship, also. The radiomen had to work at all times. We received a radio schedule every day and I was the one who read the encoded messages. I also had to encode the outgoing messages that were sent daily at midnight. We had machines called cryptographic aides to help encode and decode the messages. I was the custodian of the codes, which changed every month. While we were in Batangus Harbor, our Captain would send someone to Manila, about 90 miles overland, by truck to get the monthly codes. There were seven or eight truck convoys a day traveling this route with ten or twelve trucks and jeeps per convoy. There still were Jap snipers around, but we never encountered any the times I rode to Manila.

About the time the bomb was dropped on Hiroshima, *PCE-844* was assigned as a weather ship off the Philippines, monitoring the weather in preparation for the invasion of Japan. We released theodolite balloons with radio devices in them that would send us wind direction, wind speed, and air temperature at 1,500 feet, 3,000 feet, and one other altitude I don't remember. We worked with two other ships and we rotated duty stations, with two at sea monitoring the weather while the third ship was in harbor. We passed through quite a few storms, some typhoons, during which the men would have to strap themselves into their bunks. I remember I spent five days strapped in during one storm. The weather during this time was our worst enemy, it seemed.

One storm, at Latitude 13 North off the Philippines, was especially bad. It had winds of 150 miles per hour! The Captain of one of our sister ships forgot which way typhoons rotated in the northern hemisphere, turned the wrong way, and the ship capsized completely. But somehow it got reorganized and righted itself once again. We were called to search for survivors but by the time we got there they had already determined that amazingly no hands had been lost. Everyone was secured inside watertight compartments and this saved them. The ship was decommissioned, though, due to a sprung beam.

We were well-trained and well-equipped and had a very, very proud, confident crew. Three times we underwent target-training exercises where we "hunted" an American sub. The sonar department was busiest at times like these. We had to find the sub by "pinging," then I would plot a course using the dead-reckoning plotting table. When we arrived over the target, we dropped dummy depth charges on it. In all three exercises, the sub informed us by radio that we had scored a direct hit.

Only once while escorting a convoy did we get detached from the convoy to check on something suspicious. Sonar has a limited range, about a two-mile radius, so we began our search by sailing a one-mile square, then enlarging that to a two-mile square, then a three-mile square, and so on. We spent three days doing this but turned up nothing.

In April, 1946, *PCE-844* arrived in San Francisco. I was sent to the Great Lakes Naval Station in Illinois where, after two years and 10 months in the service, I was separated from the Navy. Then, following ten years in the active and inactive reserves, I received my discharge.

PETER SLABY
UNITED STATES NAVY

Peter Slaby owned and operated a shoe and harness shop in Arcadia in the early days of World War II. Married, he and his wife, Severine, had two sons. Early in December 1942, Pete sold his shop, retaining ownership of the machinery, and enlisted in the United States Navy on December 7, exactly one year following America's entry into the war.

Pete received his initial naval training at Great Lakes Naval Station near Chicago, Illinois, and from there was sent to gunnery school for another 14 weeks. He next reported to Norfolk, Virginia, where in December 1943 he was assigned to the *U. S. S. Algorma*, then designated AT-34, a tug that had been commissioned on May 15, 1920 at the New York Naval Yard in Brooklyn, New York.

Following her commissioning in 1920, *Algorma* spent a short time stationed at Norfolk before being ordered to sail through the Panama Canal to San Diego, California, where she arrived on March 29, 1922. Except for a two-plus-year period where she was placed out of commission, *Algorma* continued various towing duties through June 1941. One of her more meaningful assignments during these years was when she transported emergency supplies to earthquake victims in the Santa Barbara, California, area in late June 1925.

On July 14, 1941, *Algorma* arrived for her new assignment with the Atlantic Fleet. Once again, she performed various towing duties until being sent to the Caribbean in July 1942, to participate in fleet exercises by towing targets for ships and shore batteries. She also was involved in antisubmarine patrols and visited many of the Carribean ports before returning to Norfolk in December 1943.

It appears Pete may have joined the crew of *Algorma* on October 8, 1943, and if so, he would have spent some time in the Carribean. Following on overhaul at Norfolk, *Algorma* joined a convoy that sailed for England on January 25, 1944 and arrived at Falmouth, England, on February 15, 1944. She immediately undertook patrol, escort, and towing duties and then prepared to aid in the forthcoming invasion of Normandy. On May 15, 1944 *Algorma's* designation was changed to ATO-34, the "O" indicating "Old."

Following the Normandy invasion of June 6, 1944, *Algorma* assisted disabled vessels, carried out barge duty between Great Britain and France, and aided in salvage operations. From an article in the November 18, 1945 edition of the *Independence News-Wave*, it appears Pete manned *Algorma's* 20-mm machine gun, being called upon at times when German fighters and bombers appeared. It was reported that once, a 60'x120' concrete waterbreak being towed by *Algorma* was hit by a bomb and sunk. It was also reported that "the guns on his tugboat shot down many enemy planes," but this could not be confirmed.

With a battle star under her belt for the Normandy operation, *Algorma*, with Pete aboard, left Ireland on March 23, 1945 with a convoy headed for the United States. After arriving in New York on April 13, 1945 *Algorma* sailed to Norfolk for overhaul following which she received orders to proceed through the Panama Canal to San Francisco, a journey completed on August 25, 1945. Her assignment there once again was that of towing. But Pete didn't remain aboard long after *Algorma's* arrival in San Francisco, as he was discharged from the Navy with the rank of Gunner's Mate Second Class on September 25, 1945 at Shoemaker Naval Station, California. Following his discharge, Pete returned home where it was reported he was thinking of reopening his shop once again.

In the newspaper article describing Pete's service and discharge, it was indicated that he found shark to be very good eating. Because *Algorma* was towing a hotel ship and repair boat on the trip from Norfolk to California, they had to make regular stops for fuel and other supplies and Pete often found time during the nine-week trip to do a little fishing. Some of the sharks he caught were nine feet long!

The *News-Wave* article also stated that "the biggest boat he is ever going to get into again is a row boat for a fishing trip." Apparently, at 164 feet long, *Algorma* did not handle real well in rough water. But she was good enough to bring Peter Slaby home!

No Photo.
Sources: Independence News-Wave; Internet

CLARENCE P. SLUGA
UNITED STATES ARMY

Clarence Sluga was drafted into the United States Army on May 5, 1941. By the time the war ended, he had been awarded the Purple Heart for injuries received in combat, the European-African-Middle Eastern Theater Ribbon with three bronze battle stars, the American Theater Ribbon, and the World War II Victory Medal. This edited narrative is from an interview with Clarence at his Independence home on June 23, 1998.

I was drafted into the Army on May 5, 1941 and entered the service in Milwaukee, Wisconsin. For basic training, I went to Camp Davis, North Carolina, which was a new camp with no grass. I was put in Coast Artillery but training was in infantry. After basic training, we went to what was called "Carolina Maneuvers," and I was in the Blue Army during this training. After that was done, I was getting ready for a furlough, but then Pearl Harbor was bombed and all the furlough's were cancelled.

Next I was sent to Washington, D. C., where I spent two or three weeks. First I was at Camp Sims, which was right in the city. Then I went to Ocean View, Virginia, on Chesapeake Bay. I operated a decktor search light on coast security and our job was to challenge all the ships that tried to enter the Bay.

From Washington, I went by truck to Newport News, Virginia, where I boarded a train and headed for Seattle, Washington. It was quite a trip over the Rocky Mountains. We were in 13

184

cars -- Pullman, I think -- and to get over the mountains we were pulled by two large engines and pushed by one other. It took a long time to get over those mountains.

We were located first at Renton, Washington, about nine miles out of Seattle. But we did a lot of moving around. I remember Kent is a town that we spent time near, also. I was stationed around Seattle for about two years and again I operated a search light in an anti-aircraft unit. At one point I was stationed near the Boeing plant which was heavily guarded because of the airplanes they made there. I liked it in the Seattle area because the weather was usually pretty nice. And the "Battle of Seattle" wasn't too difficult on us, either!

Eventually, I was sent to Camp Gruber, Oklahoma, for infantry training. It was really hot here and I overheated once during a hike. There were guys dropping out one after the other. I wasn't going to, but it finally got to me. This was with the 42d Division, also known as the "Rainbow Division." At the same camp I ran into Bud Pieterick, who knew Louis Kampa was also there somewhere. So one day, Bud and I went over to see Louis.

We were finally sent to somewhere around New York to board ship for overseas duty. After only one or two days, we were loaded on the *U. S. S. William S. Black*, a Liberty ship, and left for Europe on November 25, 1944.

We arrived at Marseilles, France, on December 8. There I was taken out of the Rainbow Division and put in the 90th Division of Third Army.[1] I was in Company A of the 359th Infantry Battalion. We went by train and truck to a small town near the Saar River. We could see Germans across the river and a patrol of 13 of us were sent to capture one. I had a cold and was coughing so the Lieutenant told me to stay with the two or three rubber boats that we took across the river. We captured a German but it turned out he didn't know anything about anything. We didn't get our Combat Infantry Badge for this although we thought we were pretty damned close to the action. It was near here where some of the guys killed a cow and caught hell for it. We were supposed to leave stuff alone. I wasn't involved in that.

Next we were sent to the Ardennes by truck.[2] We walked up a hill into our first day of combat. There was a foot-and-a-half of snow on the ground and we saw dead Americans in foxholes. We could see a German tank shooting at us, point blank. One shell whizzed by me but didn't explode. It turned out we were on the wrong side of the hill. We didn't have any communication by phone or radio and were just in the wrong place. It was strange because at ground level it was clear but up above us a ways there was thick fog. When a mortar attack kept coming closer to us, we started moving back. A guy near me was killed by a direct hit from a mortar. This was my first taste of combat.

The next morning, only 11 of us were left of the 38 that went onto that hillside the day before. All the others had been killed or wounded. One vet of the fighting told me that was about as bad as it gets.

I asked Sergeant Franklin, who was from Chicago, if he was scared. He seemed so calm. He said he was as scared as anyone but what could you do about it.

Another guy in our unit was George Miller from Minnesota. He could talk German. One day we were just past the Siegfried Line when George, the Lieutenant, and I came up against a German pillbox. I was the BAR man -- Browning Automatic Rifle -- so was third in line as we approached that spot. They had these pillboxes all over the place along the Siegfried. They were really heavily fortified with concrete and it was tough getting the Germans out of them. Well, at this pillbox, George was told to try to talk the Germans out. It wasn't long and nine of them surrendered.

The next day we went up a road toward a building. It was snowing and the Lieutenant was shot in the forehead.

---

[1] From the day it landed in France to the end of hostilities in May, 1945, the 90th Division lost 3,342 men killed and had another 14,386 wounded. 588 of those died from their wounds.

[2] This is a reference to the German Ardennes Counteroffensive which began December 16, 1944. On December 19, 1944 the Division withdrew from its Dillingen Bridgehead and regrouped on the west bank of the Saar River for the next few days before attacking toward Doncels on January 9, 1945.

We stayed in that building upstairs above the cows for a couple days. At just about dusk one night I saw some movement on the horizon. We all got ready but then we heard American voices. It turned out to be 13 of our guys and they had 90 German prisoners. The funny thing was, our guys were completely lost. They didn't know where they were at all when the Germans surrendered. The Germans knew they were beaten and just gave up. So we sent our guys back in the right direction with their prisoners.[3]

Then we were put in reserve and thought we would get some rest, but that lasted just one day.

We crossed the Moselle River at a town that hadn't been damaged much.[4] There were Germans on the hill across the river and they opened up on us with heavy machine guns as we crossed.

It was about this time that I was hit in the foot. The Germans had their artillery shells set to explode in the trees above us. When they did this, even our foxholes didn't help much and a lot of guys got killed. Some shrapnel hit me. I was sent 50 miles to a field hospital where I stayed two days. The doctor said I could stay longer but I didn't. It took a whole week to get back to my unit by truck.

We soon came to another river that we started crossing by wading. Germans opened up on us with machine guns and rifles when we were in the water. The water was up over our knees and it was so cold. There was an artillery Captain with us and when our radioman was shot and killed and the radio destroyed, he got really mad! 13 of us were under a bridge. A guy next to me was hit in the leg and another guy was killed. We were in that ice cold water for three hours and the Lieutenant told us to keep moving our legs up and down to keep our circulation going. At dusk the Captain left first for the top of the hill, followed by the rest of us one at a time. One guy tripped a booby trap wire and was wounded.

We crossed the Rhine River on pontoons. Then we moved into Czechoslovakia. We were not too far into Czechoslovakia riding on tanks when a company runner came by and said the war was over.[5]

We stayed a few days in a small town. The Czechs were nice people. They even put on a parade for us!

Then we left Czechoslovakia and were stationed in Vielsig, Germany.[6] There was nothing smashed there and we stayed in a Catholic school for a period of time. One day three deer were brought in, though that was outlawed, and we had quite a dinner. I met a Sluga, a schoolteacher, who lived there. Another day we caught 90 trout by hand in a small stream.

Finally, we went to Amberg, Germany, where I had to wait my turn to go home. On October 15, 1945. I boarded the *U. S. S. George Washington* and got back to the United States on October 25. On October 31, 1945, I got out of the Army.

---

[3] In February 1945, the Germans were holding an area of very rugged terrain along the *West Wall* stretching 22 miles wide from near Habscheid to north of Wallendorf and 11 to 13 miles deep from the German frontier along the Our River to the Pruem River. This was known to the Americans as the "Vianden bulge." As the American divisions attacked the Vianden bulge, the Germans still manning pillboxes and other fortifications began retreating or surrendering. By February 22, it was apparent their defense was cracking as American units made advances of several miles. Clarence's reference is to a squad of Company A, 358th Infantry Regiment, that had captured the 90 Germans near Mauel. The prisoners were mostly artillerymen who were trying to hitch their horses to their artillery pieces and escape.

[4] The 90th Infantry Division crossed the Moselle River in the Kattenes-Moselkern area on March 14, 1945.

[5] The Rhine River was crossed on March 24, 1945. The Division entered Czechoslovakia at Prex on April 18, 1945. and advanced towards Prague. The tanks Clarence makes reference to were from the 4th Armored Division, sent through the 90th Infantry Division's lines by General Patton in the hope that General Eisenhower would approve a run to Prague. But approval never came as Germany officially surrendered and the war in Europe ended.

[6] Correct spelling of "Vielsig," Germany, could not be determined.

"We soon came to another river that we started crossing by wading. Germans
opened up on us with machine guns and rifles when we were in the water."

No Photo.
Source: Books (Stanton) (MacDonald)

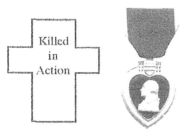

Killed
in
Action

RALPH R. SLUGA
UNITED STATES ARMY

On January 25, 1945 a brief "Local Items" note in the
Independence News-Wave reported a son had been born on January
20 to Ralph and Elizabeth Sluga at Community Hospital in
Whitehall. "The father, Pvt. Ralph Sluga, is somewhere in Belgium serving with an infantry
unit," it stated.

Only nine days after the birth of their son, Elizabeth received the telegram from the War
Department that so many wives, mothers, and girlfriends dreaded during the long years of World
War II.

Ralph Sluga was born January 2, 1921, the son of Mr. and Mrs. Eddie Sluga. As he was
growing up, he attended school in Elk Creek and Independence, and then helped on his father's
farm in Elk Creek and worked briefly at Land O'Lakes Creamery in Whitehall, Wisconsin, until he
entered the United States Army on June 29, 1944. He received his basic training at Camp
Wheeler, Georgia.

Ralph received a furlough home for Thanksgiving in 1944, which he spent with his wife

and parents. Upon his return to camp, his unit was informed they would soon be sent overseas. They were transferred to Fort George G. Meade, Maryland, from where they were shipped to England. Very soon after that, Ralph found himself as an infantry replacement with the 120th Infantry Regiment, 30th Infantry Division, and in the middle of the "Battle of the Bulge."

When the Germans launched their Ardennes counteroffensive on December 16, 1944, the 30th Infantry Division was quickly rushed to the Malmedy-Stavelot area the next day. It held at Stavelot as the Ambleve Bridge was destroyed by engineers in an effort to slow the enemy advance. It lost and then regained Stoumont from December 19-22, 1944. during very heavy fighting before clearing the area north of Ambleve between Stavelot and Trois Ponts. Then it launched its own attack on January 13, 1945. toward Malmedy. On January 14, 1945, only six days before the birth of his son, and without ever learning of it, Ralph was killed in action. An article in the *News-Wave's* February 1, 1945 edition stated his parents had not heard from him after he left the States and his wife had received only one letter from him, dated December 18, 1944, in which he indicated he was on the front lines and had not received any mail.

On that same February 1, 1945, and only four days after official notice of Ralph's death had been received, a letter arrived at the Eddie Sluga residence from their son. It had been written between Christmas Day and New Year's from "Somewhere in Belgium" and was published in the *News-Wave* on February 8, 1945:

> Dear Folks:
>
> Just a line to let you know where I am. How is everybody? I guess I am alright, ha! I slept out in the rain and snow last night.
>
> Norman Smith is still with me.
>
> I haven't received any mail for three weeks or more. Boy! Are we ever going! If we keep going the way we are, they will never catch up with us. I suppose you listen to the radio.
>
> Tell all the kids hello, and be sure you give Romelle my address.
>
> How was Santa Claus? Did he bring Bobby anything? He sure was good to me. I got a new rifle.
>
> I spent Christmas in a box car, and I wonder where I'll spend the New Year.
>
> Seen anything of Elizabeth lately?
>
> Well, so long for now, and the best of luck.
>
> > From your son and brother,
> > Ralph

Services were held at Ss. Peter and Paul's Catholic Church on February 27, 1945. for 24-year-old Ralph. The Right Reverend Monsignor Kufel officiated with the assistance of Father Przybylski, while the American Legion Post 186 attended in a body.

On March 9, 1945. Elizabeth Sluga received her husband's Purple Heart.

Upon his death, Ralph had been interred in the Malmedy, Belgium, temporary military cemetery. At the request of his wife and parents, the remains of Ralph Sluga were returned to Independence following the war, arriving with full military escort on July 29, 1945. Funeral services were held the following morning, July 30, 1945 at Ss. Peter and Paul's, again with Monsignor Kufel officiating. All places of business in Independence were closed during the time of the service in respect.

Pallbearers were Ernest Marsolek, George and Dominic Smick, Norman Smith, John Sylla, and Clarence Sluga. The Legion presided over the church cemetery service with Roman Slaby and Hillary "Jack" Halama the Color Bearers and Herman Bautch and LaVerne Pientok serving as Color Guard. The Legion Firing Squad consisted of Gerald "Bud" Pieterick, Lester Gunem, Ben Kulig, Vincent Karasch, Earl Hutchins, Mike Marsolek, Ed. J. Lyga, and Ray Smieja.

Besides his parents, Ralph was survived by three sisters, Romelle, Delores, and Betty Lou, and three brothers, George, Gerald, and Bobby.

And with his widow, Elizabeth, he left an infant son, Dennis Ralph Sluga.

Source: Mrs. Elizabeth Johnson, widow; Independence News-Wave

DOMINIC A. SMICK
UNITED STATES ARMY

Dominic Smick was inducted into the United States Army on April 8, 1941 in Milwaukee, Wisconsin, and entered active service on that same date. Following three months of basic training, he received five months of additional training as a Rifle Ammunition Bearer. Then, in December 1941, Dominic began training as a Quartermaster Supply Technician. On February 19, 1942 he left the United States via troopship and arrived in Iceland where he helped organize for the 5th Infantry Division's May 1942 arrival. Attached to the 5th Infantry's 2nd Infantry Regiment, Company H, he earned a commendation while in Iceland that stated as follows:

> That S/Sgt Dominic A Smith is an Iceland Veteran of the 5th Infantry Division, U. S. Army by virtue of his service in Co. H, 2nd Inf., in Iceland from 3 March 1942 to 19 Aug 1943. During this period, S/Sgt. Smick worked long, rigorous and lonely hours in discharging his duties to enable the division to fulfill the mission of guarding the wind-swept North Atlantic Island against German invasion, to keep the important Reyhjavik harbor and dockside functioning and moving supplies, and to help build the Air Transport Command's strategic bomber ferry point, Alceks Airfield on the Keflavik Peninsula. Having stood guard in dark and long hours, worked in all kinds of weather from blizzards in mountain passes to 90-mile-per-hour wind gales on the plains, endured endless nights in pyramidal tents and Quonset huts and withal trained for future combat, S/Sgt Smick has proved himself qualified as an Iceland Veteran.
> James H. Bennett, Commanding

The 5th Infantry Division left Iceland on August 5, 1943 and arrived in Northern Ireland four days later where it underwent additional training for the next eleven months. During his time in Iceland and Northern Ireland, Dominic carried out his Quartermaster Supply duties, a role he would fulfill throughout his European tour of duty. He handled the procurement, receipt, storage, issue, and salvage of all quartermaster supplies, edited requisitions and purchase orders, and wrote all survey and exchange reports. He also supervised two supply clerks.

On July 11, 1944 the 5th Infantry Division landed across Utah Beach in Normandy, France, after which it relieved the defensive positions of the 1st Infantry Division near Caumont,

France.[1] Within a month, however, the 5th Infantry was launching its own offensive toward Nantes. It crossed the Seine River at Montereau on August 24, 1944, claimed the city of Rheims on August 30, 1944, and began crossing the Meuse River at Verdun, the city made famous during World War I, the following day.

The 5th Infantry Division began attacking the heavily fortified city of Metz, France, on September 7, 1944, with Dominic's 2nd Infantry Regiment at the fore. 2nd Infantry's repeated frontal assaults of the city's outer fortifications resulted in the Division gaining a precarious but important bridgehead that allowed tanks to cross the Moselle River and continue the attack on September 8, 1944. Metz was a city designed to be defended through a series of forts, so the 5th Infantry Division set about the task of methodically eliminating German resistance one fort at a time. Its attack and the German counterattack of early October. 1944. cost the Division dearly and it was forced to withdraw for rest on October 12. One month later, it again entered the battle, with 2nd Infantry taking Ancerville while other regiments overcame other enemy strongholds. In early December. 1944. the final German positions around Metz surrendered to the Division.

When the German Ardennes counteroffensive began December 16, 1944, the 5th Infantry Division was sent to the Saarlautern Bridgehead where it relieved the 95th Infantry Division. It then slowly pushed forward, helping to reduce the German southern flank. After it was relieved on February 4, 1945, the 5th Infantry Division quickly launched another attack across the Sauer River near Echtenach on February 7, 1945, despite heavy German artillery shelling and a very strong river current. Three days later it was breaching the *West Wall* [2] and by February 19, 1945. had reached the Pruem River. Dominic's 2nd Infantry crossed the Pruem near Peffingen during the night of February 24-25, 1945. and the Division then began moving rapidly toward the Moselle River, bypassing German-held towns in the process. It reached the Moselle on March 10, 1945, crossed four days later with the 2nd Infantry again leading the way, and quickly moved to take Treis, Lutz, and Eveshausen. On March 22, 1945. the Division crossed the Rhine River at Oppenheim and Nierstein against light opposition, thus entering Germany.

By April 4, 1945, following the taking and securing of Frankfurt-am-Main, the Division was pressing forward, with the 2nd Infantry reaching the Rohr River on April 12, 1945. The Division had occupied the Westphalian region south of the Ruhr River when it was relieved by the 75th Infantry Division on April 24, 1945. It crossed into Czechoslovakia on May 1, 1945, and then into Austria, and was attacking areas across the Tepla River a few days later when Germany surrendered.

Though the 5th Infantry Division left Europe in July 1945. for home, Dominic remained until September 2, 1945. On that date, he boarded the *U. S. S. Oneida Victory* in Le Havre, France, and set sail the following day. Arriving in the United States on September 11, 1945, Dominic then traveled to Fort Sheridan, Illinois, where he was discharged from the Army on September 17, 1945. At that time he held the rank of Staff Sergeant and had participated in the Normandy, Northern France, Rhineland, Ardennes-Alsace, and Central Europe campaigns with the 5th Infantry Division. His "Enlisted Record and Report of Separation" indicates he was awarded the American Defense Service Medal, European-African-Middle Eastern Theater Ribbon with one silver battle star, seven Overseas Service Bars, one Service Stripe, and the Good Conduct Medal. Other documents and the remembrances of his son, Jeffrey, indicate he probably remained in the Army Reserve in some capacity until March 1, 1950. His "Transcript of Military Record" of that date states he had also been awarded the Bronze Star, though the circumstances for which this decoration was bestowed are unknown.

---

[1] During its campaigns through Europe, the 5th Infantry Division lost 2,298 men killed and 9,549 wounded, of which 358 died from their wounds.

[2] The *West Wall* was Hitler's name for the famed *Siegried Line*.

No photo.
Source: Jeffrey Smick, son; Book (Stanton) (5th Division Historical Section)

THOMAS GEORGE SMICK
UNITED STATES ARMY

When Thomas Smick -- George -- was inducted into the United States Army on August 8, 1941 in Milwaukee, Wisconsin, he was already 26 years old.

Following basic training at Fort Leonard Wood, Missouri, George joined Company C, 109th Engineer Combat Battalion, 34th Division. The 34th Division began leaving the United States through the New York Port of Embarkation on January 14, 1942. On February 1, 1942 the Division was redesignated as the 34th Infantry Division.[1] George left New York in February but en route off Iceland, his ship was torpedoed by a German U-boat and forced to return to the States. The rest of the Division, however, landed in Northern Ireland where it began undergoing amphibious training, though at that time it still had not been determined just where the first Allied thrusts against the Germans would be made. George's Company C, 109th Engineer Combat Battalion, left the New York Port of Embarkation once again on April 30, 1942 on the *U. S. S. Cathay*, part of an eight-ship convoy that began arriving in Northern Ireland on May 10, 1942.

At about this same time, Chief of Staff General George C. Marshall appointed newly-promoted Major General Dwight David Eisenhower as commander of the European Theater of Operations, headquarters of which would be based in England. Eisenhower and Marshall both wholeheartedly believed the Allies had to strike in France as early as 1943, but British Prime Minister Winston Churchill and Field Marshal Allan Brooke wanted to invade North Africa in the fall of 1942 instead. Because American forces were still being organized and were far from fighting strength, the British view prevailed. On November 8, 1942 Operation Torch was underway as American soldiers landed in Morocco and Algeria and British troops landed near Oran. This decision to attack North Africa first would dramatically affect George for more than the next two years.

The 168th Infantry Regiment landed west of Algiers on D-Day, November 8, 1942, while the rest of the 34th Infantry Division, including the 109th Engineer Combat Battalion, landed on January 3, 1943. The Division was moving inland with the 1st Armored Division when it came face-to-face with famed German armored commander, soon-to-be Field Marshal, Erwin Rommel. The two American divisions, constituting II Corps, had been told a German attack was probably going to take place, but far to their north. Instead, on February 13, 1943, Rommel's *Deutches Afrika Korps* launched its attack directly at them, and the Americans found themselves facing the battle-hardened *10th German Panzer Division*. As Rommel's armor moved quickly through the Faid Pass near Faid village, the Germans could soon see the village of Sidi Bou Zid 12 miles to the west as the German Luftwaffe began bombing the area where the Americans were establishing their defenses. The German armor was too powerful and moved too rapidly, and as American ranks broke, a general retreat began. Two groups of defenders were left to protect the American withdrawal, but they were soon surrounded and were then ordered to escape as best they could. This famous battle at the Kasserine Pass cost the Americans thousands killed and wounded, with 4,000 others taken prisoner by the end of the second day alone. On February 17, 1943 George was captured by the German army at Faid Pass and he would spend the rest of the war as a prisoner. In a War Claims Commission affidavit filed with Trempealeau County on November 29, 1948, George stated that

---

[1] The 34th Infantry Division suffered 2,866 killed and 11,545 wounded, of which 484 died of their wounds, during its North African and Italian campaigns.

he was held in captivity in the Faid Pass area for three or four days before being transported out of Africa. He said that during that entire time, he and other POW's were given only half a loaf of bread and water. Then for the next five or six days he was issued half a loaf of bread each day with water.

Sometime in late March 1943, George's parents, Louis and Anna Smick, received a Casualty Message telegram from the War Department. It stated:

> The Secretary of War expresses his deep regret that your son Technician Fifth Grade Thomas G Smick has this date been reported missing in action in North African area since February 17. Additional information will be sent you when received
>
> Echinette, Adjutant General

On April 6, 1943 American Red Cross Home Service Chairman Norman I. Gilbert, Blair, Wisconsin, wrote to the Midwestern Area American Red Cross office on behalf of George's parents in an effort to learn more regarding George's status. In the letter it was stated his parents had last heard from George on January 3 and that he was then in North Africa. Edith Barack of the Red Cross' Midwestern Area office responded on May 11, 1943, stating George was still listed as "missing," meaning he could have somehow become detached from his unit or been taken prisoner. She also stated, "We fully realize the anxiety of the Smick family at this time. However, we hope that when you (Ed. - meaning Mr. Gilbert) convey this information to them that you will also advise them that we hope that 'the missing status' may soon be reversed and their son located."

Within days of this, word was received via a War Department telegram that George had indeed been taken prisoner. The telegram stated:

> Report just received through the International Red Cross that your son Technician Fifth Grade Thomas G Smick is a prisoner of war of the German government. Letter of Information follows from Provost Marshal General.
>
> Albert H. Daves, Jr., Captain, A. G. Office

Miss Barack of the Red Cross again wrote Mr. Gilbert on July 12, 1943 indicating George was identified as POW #110092 and interned in Stalag 3B. Her letter gave instructions to be passed along to the Smick's for mailing packages and letters to George. Packages had to have proper labels which were furnished by the Provost Marshal General's office. Mail did not require any special labels as it went through regular mail channels, postage free, though it had not yet been determined whether letters were actually being received by the prisoners. Miss Barack warned the family to be careful regarding short-wave messages they may be informed of supposedly made by their son, but that most such messages were being verified as authentic, therefore relieving anxieties of families. Additionally, Miss Barack's letter informed the Smick's that books could be sent to George as long as they were wrapped and sent directly from the publisher or book dealer and not from the family itself. They were warned the German authorities would not permit books written by Jewish authors or emigrants of German-occupied territories and that American censors would not allow scientific or technical books be sent, presumably to avoid providing potentially useful information to the Germans.

In July 1943 George's mother, Anna, sent a standard food package through the Red Cross to George, who was now correctly identified as POW #110902 in Stalag 3B. The package cost $3.50 to send, which was apparently paid by a donor.

Miss Barack was again contacted on September 28, 1943 by Lon F. Tubbs, Home Service Chairman of Trempealeau County, stating that George's mother was concerned since they had received only one letter, in March, and had not heard from him since. Tubbs stated that Anna had been writing her son every week and was sending the maximum number of packages permitted, and was worried her "son may be sick or dead because she hasn't heard from him." He also expressed his frustration in not being able to help the Smick family more due to a lack of information. He finished his letter by stating, "This is the only prisoner of war from this county in the hands of the Germans that we know about and would like to know something definite with regard to his health and welfare."

Miss Barack responded to Tubbs that she had just received a letter giving information on Stalag 3B that stated, "The International Red Cross delegate visited this camp on May 12, 1943. It has only been opened since the end of March, 1943 and it is not yet possible to state the length of time mail takes from the United States to this camp." She felt the prisoners of the camp probably were being allowed to write the permitted number of letters but that "it is felt that non-receipt of mail is a problem of delivery caused by the overburdened transportation system and other exegencies (sic) of war." She also stated "the general condition of the camp in May was not very satisfactory but many improvements were being made. . . therefore, may we be very trite by saying 'no news is good news.' But seriously, you may assure the family that if there is a change in the status of their son other than a prisoner of war, they will be immediately notified by the War Department." A letter from Tubbs dated October 4, 1943 relayed this information to Mrs. Smick.

As time progressed, letters from George began arriving at the Smick residence. As a prisoner of war, he was allowed to send four cards and two letters each month, and he himself received over 200 letters during the time of his confinement. Two letters written by George were published in the April 6, 1944 edition of the *Independence News-Wave*:

November 15, 1943
Dear Mother and Dad:
        Have been receiving your letters quite steady and also some from the kids. Haven't heard from Deak and maybe never will.
        The weather is getting kind of chilly here, but one good thing we have plenty of clothes which we get from the American Red Cross. We also get a food parcel each week from the Red Cross. If it wasn't for that I don't know what a fellow would do.
        Got a letter from Verna Sura the other day, but won't be able to answer it for some time because we only get four cards and two letters per month, so can't write very many. Write often.
                Love, George

January 11, 1944
Dear Mother and Dad:
        Received your Christmas parcel last week. Everything arrived in good shape. I sure can use every bit of it, especially the woolen socks. I haven't gotten any letters the last two weeks, but maybe I shouldn't complain because I see by your letter that you received only one card from me. Seems funny because I write every week, either to you or the kids. We got some clothes today from the Red Cross, such as shirts, socks, scarfs, towels. In a day or so we will get the rest, so for the time being I am not short of clothes. Thank God that there is such a thing as the Red Cross.
        How is everyone around there? What is everyone busy with? Tell them all to write as often as possible.
                Love, George

Following his capture in North Africa, George and other prisoners were flown by transport to Sicily, then to Italy from where they were transported by train to Germany, arriving at Stalag 7A near Merseberg, Germany, about March 1, 1943.[2] Quarters in Stalag 7A consisted of heated barracks and rations consisted of 1/5 to 1/12 of a loaf of bread each day, although some days were skipped. Prisoners also received about one cupful of very weak soup, every third day they received a small portion of margarine, and once daily they were issued a simulated coffee or tea. During his short stay at Stalag 7A, George received one American Red Cross food package.

Within a few days, George was among a large group loaded aboard railroad cars that

---

[2] All references to travels as a POW and conditions encountered by George while interned in German POW camps are found in War Claims Commision affidavits filed by George following the war.

193

traveled off and on for the next 12 days to Stalag 3B. These trains were not marked as carrying POW's and occasionally were attacked by American fighter planes, though it appears George's train traveled unhindered during its journey. He arrived at Stalag 3B about March 15, 1943. This camp contained 8,000 POW's and was located near Furstenberg and Oder, Germany, on the Oder River about 25 miles southeast of Berlin. He was quartered in barracks once again, but the windows were broken out, and though they were issued six or seven small briquets daily, it was impossible to keep the barracks warm. Rations here were the same as at Stalag 7A. George did not receive any Red Cross food packages at Stalag 3B until August 1943, but then for the next year he received one weekly. After August 1944, Red Cross packages were no longer received by the prisoners.

George remained in Stalag 3B until January 10, 1945, at which time the prisoners were transferred again, this time on foot, to Stalag 3A near Luckenwald, Germany. This march took about one week during the entire time of which the prisoners were given a total of half a loaf of bread plus water. Arriving at Stalag 3A, George and the other prisoners found a tent camp with 400 men per tent, no bunks or beds other than the ground over which straw had been spread, and absolutely no heat. Food rations were the same as at the previous camps except they were no longer issued margarine. George received only four Red Cross food parcels during his three months at Stalag 3A.

Throughout his confinement in Germany, George was issued about a tablespoon of sugar on Sundays, though many Sundays were missed, and he did not receive any milk or milk substitutes from his captors. Often, the weak soup they were given was made from wormy peas or other ingredients not fit for human consumption. All in all, the prisoner's food ration was about one-fourth that of the German soldiers stationed at the camps.

Conditions at both Stalag 3B and 3A were quite deplorable. In order to stay warm, many of the prisoners remained in bed day and night, covered by just the one blanket the Germans issued each man. Around Christmas 1943, the prisoners each received two additional blankets from the Red Cross, making it easier to maintain warmth, but as the number of prisoners increased, the Germans took away two of the three blankets from each man, giving the new prisoners one blanket each. From around Christmas 1944 to April 15, 1945, the day the men of Stalag 3A were liberated, George only had one blanket.

At all three camps, very unsanitary conditions existed. Stalags 7A and 3B had only one toilet with 25 openings for every 1000 prisoners and the Germans did not do any sanitary cleaning, leaving this to the prisoners themselves. The tents of Stalag 7A had no ventilation, making the air within them very unhealthy. Drinking water was always in short supply with only one water tap available for more than 3,000 men. Additionally, the Germans at George's three camps did not provide any medical care, with the only medical supplies coming from the Red Cross and made available to the POW doctors. Infirmaries at all three camps could accomodate only 15 to 20 men at any given time and no hospital facilities were available for the prisoners.

George was fortunate in that he did not become ill while a prisoner of war until his last three weeks of confinement when he experienced severe diarrhea probably caused by the poor food. However, following the war, he experienced arthritis of both knees which grew progressively worse. This may have been due to prolonged exposure and the inadequate shelter and clothing he experienced throughout his ordeal. The only articles of clothing he ever received from the Germans were wooden clogs, and though he was not forced to do any work for the Germans, he did help erect shelters for other prisoners and unload Red Cross packages. During his 26 months of confinement, George lost 50 pounds.[3]

While imprisoned, George and the other prisoners were subjected to humiliation, generated by Reichsfuhrer Goebbels, from the civilian population. Additionally, barracks of men, or at times the entire camp, would be punished for various transgressions by forcing them to stand out in rainy or otherwise inclement weather for hours or entire nights. And because the camps were not marked in any way as housing POW's, there was always the threat of bombardment by Allied

---

[3] George weighed 166 pounds at the time he was inducted into the Army.

planes.

The morning of April 15, 1945, the men of Stalag 3A awoke to find their German captors and guards had evacuated the compound. Within a short while, Russian armored units arrived at the Stalag, putting an end to their nightmare. Because the Russians were an army on the move, however, the food situation did not improve for the liberated prisoners, but they now at least could search the surrounding area for what they could find. After two weeks of waiting, the American army arrived with trucks and transported George and other former prisoners to Hidburgshn, Germany, from where they traveled to Le Havre, France, to await shipment home.

By late May 1945 George was aboard ship and heading back to the United States. He arrived on June 3, 1945, whereupon he traveled home to visit with his parents. Prior to his discharge on September 5, 1945, George spent 11 days at an army-operated hotel in Miami, Florida, where he had opportunities to sightsee, deep sea fish, and enjoy other recreational activities. While there he met several of his comrades who had also been imprisoned with him. Shortly following his discharge, George received notice of his promotion from Technician Fifth Grade to Technician Fourth Grade.

George had participated in the Algeria-French Morocco and Tunisian campaigns, been a prisoner-of-war for 26 months, and been awarded the European-African-Middle Eastern Theater Service Medal, American Defense Service Medal, six Overseas Service Bars, four Discharge Emblems, and Good Conduct Medal.

Source: Jeffrey Smick, nephew, personal papers of George Smick; Independence News-Wave; Book (Stanton)

RUDOLPH "RUDY" R. SMIEJA
UNITED STATES NAVY

Rudy Smieja, right, with his brother, Vitus.

Rudy Smieja enlisted in the United States Navy on April 17, 1943. It is uncertain as to where he was stationed immediately following his initial training at Great Lakes Naval Station, Illinois. However, in early 1945, probably February, Rudy received orders to report to the *U. S. S. Strong* (DD-758), in California.

DD-758 was the second destroyer to bear the name *Strong* during World War II, the first having been sunk by the Japanese in 1943. It was an Allen M. Sumner Class destroyer designed as a result of a developing need for anti-aircraft warfare defenses. Displacing 2,200 tons, it had a length of 376'6", a beam of 40'10", and a top speed of 35 knots. Its complement of 345 men was protected by six five-inch and twelve 40mm guns, as well as ten 21-inch torpedoes. *Strong* was launched April 23, 1944 and commissioned on March 8, 1945.

The *Strong* began her shakedown cruise on March 27, 1945 in the San Diego Bay area. On May 31, 1945 she left for Pearl Harbor where her crew underwent training exercises off Oahu from June 6-20. On June 20, she left Hawaii to begin escort duty for convoys between the Marshall and Caroline Islands. Then from July 27 through August 31, 1945, the *Strong* escorted convoys and provided antisubmarine protection in the Ryukyu Islands (Okinawa) area. She entered Japanese home waters to patrol air-sea rescue stations on September 1, 1945 and served as courier between Wakayama, Nagoya, and

Yokosuka.

On December 5, 1945, more than three months following the end of the war, the *Strong* sailed from the western Pacific after receiving orders to join the Atlantic Fleet along the east coast of the United States. She passed through the Panama Canal on January 11, 1946, and arrived in New York four days later. Following a period of maintainence, the *Strong* cruised the northeast coast until April 29, 1946, when she arrived in Boston. It was sometime during this early period of 1946 when Rudy, having attained the rank of Yeoman Second Class, left the *U. S. S. Strong*, traveled to the U. S. Naval Personnel Separation Center at Great Lakes, Illinois, and was separated from the Navy on May 8, 1946. He had earned the Victory Medal, American Theater Campaign Medal, Asiatic-Pacific Theater Campaign Medal, and Good Conduct Medal.

The best review of Rudy's time in the Pacific is offered by Rudy himself in a letter written to this parents, Mr. and Mrs. Roman Smieja, following Japan's surrender. In it, he describes several of his duties as well as actions he was involved in while aboard the *U. S. S. Strong*. The letter was published in the September 27, 1945, edition of the *Independence News-Wave*:

Dear Mother, Dad and Wilfred:

Censorship was stopped aboard our ship yesterday morning and now we have the privilege of sealing our own letters before we drop them into the ship's mail box. We have all been waiting for this halt of censorship for a long time now, for we want to let the folks back home know where we are at.

Last week we were anchored in Buckner Bay at Okinawa for five days and while there I had the opportunity to go to Confession and receive Holy Communion aboard the USS Alaska. That was my first since I left the states in March and I believe it was my first opportunity also, so I didn't waste it.

Last week we were all hoping that we would be put on the list of ships that went to Japan for the signing of the peace treaty but I guess we were not wishing hard enough for we got another odd job. After those five days in port they sent us out to a picket station off Okinawa and we're still out here. I believe we're going back to Buckner Bay sometime Saturday and refuel and prepare to get on our way again, but I don't know where we will go and on what kind of duty. I hope it's with the Fifth Fleet.

At the time that the Japanese were officially offering to surrender, we were on a screening station about five miles off Okinawa. That night Okinawa really went wild for a while, after they heard the news, for their machine guns, anti-aircraft guns lighted the sky with millions of tracer bullets and search lights went wild lighting up the sky and falling on ships giving the Japs a chance to make sure baits of us. We were lucky that night for no planes ever came around.

After we left Pearl Harbor in the middle part of June we took twelve ship troop convoys to Eniwetok in the Marshall Islands. We spent four days there getting the ship ready for another voyage. Out of those four days I made liberty twice on a small island near the ship which was set up by the navy as a fleet recreation center. There I had my first swimming lesson in salt water and sure was fun. I believe I spent most of my four hours liberty in the water each time. Oh, yes, there I also had my first can of beer - Milwaukee's finest "Miller's High Life." The other two days I helped load supplies which were mostly fresh fruits, potatoes and ice cream powder.

Our next trip we made to Ulithi in the Caroline Islands with another big troop convoy and this trip lasted six days. It was a wonderful trip for the weather was perfect and the water smooth as glass. We spent about five days there loading supplies and getting everything ready for another trip. After leaving Ulithi we found that we were on our way to Okinawa with a large tanker. I don't know what was in the tanker but scuttlebutt at the time was that it was filled with high octane gas for the B-29's.

Well, according to the navy plan of demobilization on the point system, it looks as if I'll be in for a couple of years to come for I have only 25 points and one has to have 44 to get out. I imagine they will lower the points in a month or so, probably even change the system all around. They will have to do something because they plan on discharging over two million men within the next six months.

Well, I really didn't see very much of the war for I was in only seven air raids. In one of these raids, the USS Pennsylvania, a huge battlewagon, was hit by a co-aerial torpedo and put out of commission. At the time we were only a short distance away from her, so I guess we were lucky that night. The other raids were short, lasting only a couple of hours.

I'm beginning to get hungry, so I'll be closing with the wish that you are all feeling fine and in

196

the best of health.

Love, Rudy

Sources: Gary Smieja, son; Independence News-Wave; Internet

VITUS SMIEJA
UNITED STATES NAVY

The following edited narrative was prepared following an interview with Vitus Smieja that was conducted at the Independence home of Tony Sylla on August 4, 1998.

I was supposed to be drafted but beat them to the punch by enlisting in the Navy on August 11, 1942. I went to Great Lakes Naval Station in Chicago for basic training, then went to Treasure Island near San Francisco for three months of cooks and bakers school. After that I was sent to the San Diego Destroyer Base where I was put on the day crew. I helped cook for 21,000 men there for the next three or three-and-a-half years. Bill Brown from West Allis, Wisconsin, went through both Great Lakes and chef's school with me, then was assigned to the night crew at San Diego, as well. He got married out in California so one day I went to visit him at his trailer. There I met my wife who was living in the trailer next to the Brown's.

From California things got all fouled up. I was put aboard a Coast Guard ship bound for Leyte. I was just a passenger and didn't have any duties. I was supposed to be replacing somebody who was going home but all I did, it seemed, was transfer from one ship to another. Finally I was sent aboard the *U. S. S. Girard*, a mail boat that was sailing out to the fleet. When we got there, I rode a dolly on ropes from the *Girard* to the aircraft carrier *U. S. S. Bennington*. But this wasn't yet the end of my moving. I only stayed aboard that carrier overnight, was fed, and then got orders to board a destroyer that was going to take me to the battleship *U. S. S. Massachusetts*. When I got there, the chief said he didn't need me, that he only wanted the men who were already aboard. I told him, "Too bad, you've got me!"

This was toward the end of the war and we were already knocking on Japan's door. The *Massachusetts* was ordered to participate in the first night bombardment of Japan itself. But first we had to find the British fleet that had somehow gotten lost! Soon after our fleet found the British, the bombardment of the Japanese mainland began. The *Massachusetts* had orders to target an ammo dump, a piano factory that was making propellers, and a bridge.[1] My battle station was

---

[1] The "piano factory" targeted by the *U. S. S. Massachusetts* the night of July 28, 1945 was the Japan Musical Instrument Company located in Hamamatsu, an important port, rail, and industrial center 120 miles southwest of Tokyo. The ship's log noted, "The attack was not an advanced form of musical criticism but arose from the fact that the factory had been converted to the manufacture of aircraft propellers."

below one of the big 16-inch gun turrets but I went up on deck to see some of the action, and it was really something! We were told, "close eyes, close ears," just before our big guns fired because it was so blinding and deafening. Then I watched as the huge shells headed for shore. We could actually see them because they glowed red against the night sky. The targets were knocked out almost right away. But when that ammo dump exploded, I got a little concerned because I thought the Japs were shooting back at us! The guns got red hot and the next morning the rifling inside the barrels was still sticking out because it was still so hot and had expanded so much.

The *Massachusetts* was scheduled to sail back to the States for an overhaul when the war ended. But the captain wanted in on some of the glory so he sent some men in for the surrender ceremony in Tokyo Harbor. I applied to go but I was just a Ships Cook 1st Class, and 1st Class ranks weren't allowed to go. But then the captain was told that either the *Massachusetts* had to go home or another ship would be sent instead. He was no dummy and knew the crewmen wouldn't be happy if they found out we missed our chance to go home. So we sailed from Japan past the Aleutian Islands, and reached Bremerton, Washington, for our overhaul. I was there one month when I received a one-month leave. After that, we took her out on a shakedown cruise that ended up in San Francisco Harbor. There were six battleships tied up at the docks when we got there, and that was quite a sight!

I was supposed to be married aboard ship in San Francisco but Mary Wozney, who was one of our witnesses, suddenly couldn't be there. She was a WAVE at Hunter's Point Naval Base. So we later jumped in a car, drove to a USO up in the hills, and were married there.

I received my discharge at the Shoemaker Naval Center near Stockton, California, about 50 miles inland from San Francisco.

On March 2, 1944 the *News-Wave* published a letter written by Vitus to his parents, Mr. and Mrs. Roman Smieja. Prior to the war, he had worked in his father's meat market, and latter in this letter, he describes how much food his crew would be preparing the next few day:

Dear Folks:

Guess I'll get busy and drop you a few lines. I have been a very busy man the past week. I had four men under me and a working party of about 89 to take care of. Friday morning before I left for Los Angeles or Hawthorne, I or rather my men, unloaded three carloads of meat. One pork sausage, one corned beef and the other shrimps and clams. I left San Diego about five o'clock and got to Hawthorne at 9:30. Most of the men worked Friday night, but I spent all day Saturday and Sunday morning there. I left about three and was in San Diego at 7:45. Not bad. We've been having some terrible weather here. It just poured. Saturday night Hattie and Frank waited for the rain to stop until two o'clock Sunday morning. Finally we all stretched out on the floor and slept at Ida's They live in a two-room shack while their new home is being built. Oh yes, California is noted for its sunshine. Well, it's the only state where sunshine flows down along the road.

I know I have been lax at writing but I've been so terribly busy. I haven't gotten any mail myself for at least a week. I'm getting things straightened out so I'll feel more like writing from now on. I did have a heck of a time getting things lined up though. I do go out and drink a few bottles of beer occasionally, but I don't throw my money away. Shucks, one evening last week after I got through with work, I was really tired, but still couldn't go to bed, so I went to a place about two blocks away and had three bottles of Past Blue Ribbon beer, and gee, it really tasted good. I was so disgusted with my job, but I can see ahead now. Heck, when I come home I'll be able to handle a crew of men.

Thanks for sending those letters to me. I enjoyed reading them very much. About Clifford. Ha. Ha. He may have us all beat, but I'll take care of that later. Right now we've got a war to win, and after we win it I'll find myself something very special. By the way, don't you think our war news sounds very good? Our Navy is really doing a swell job and I'm proud to be a part of it. I really do think we'll win our war in the Pacific before we do in Germany. And I think I'll be in there doing my bit soon. Oh, not for a while yet, but it's coming. Things are looking very promising. I'll make my first class rating before then,

I hope.

Gee, I didn't know that "Ike" Kampa was working for you.

Here's today's break out: Bacon, 3,000 lbs., Clams, 1,272 lbs., Franks, 3,000 lbs., Pork Sausage, 3,400 lbs., Butter, 6,000 lbs., Ham, 15,499 lbs., cold meats, 1,896 lbs., beef hinds, 3,200 lbs. This stretches over our menu for about three days. We got about 45,000 pounds of fresh beef quarters this week. I'd like to show you the ice boxes. You'd be surprised, or I should say astonished!

Well, I guess I'll close for now. Don't worry and may God bless you all. I hope this finds you all healthy as I am.

So Long,
Vitus

Sources: Book (Karig, Harris, and Manson); Independence News-Wave

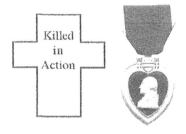

Killed in Action

JEROME J. SOBOTA
UNITED STATES NAVAL RESERVE

Jerome Sobota graduated from Independence High School in 1935. He received a degree from River Falls State Teacher's College (now the University of Wisconsin - River Falls) in 1940 and had been teaching for two years in Channing, Michigan, when he enlisted in the United States Naval Reserve in the fall of 1941. Following a three month V-7 training course at the New York City Naval Reserve Midshipman's School at Columbia University, Jerome was commissioned an Ensign, one of 753 in his class. Following a furlough home, he reported to Norfolk, Virginia, for amphibious training. He then was assigned duty aboard *LST-342* in the South Pacific.

LST's (Landing Ship, Tank) were slow and very difficult to maneuver. They were originally intended as second wave vessels for island invasions but they also became very useful in carrying cargo between Pacific bases.

According to Lieutenant Thomas B. Montgomery of South Carolina, in an interview with Will Oursler for the March 1944 issue of TRUE Magazine, it was a sunny day on a South Pacific island where LST-*342's* crew was busy loading materials to be transferred to another base forward. Among the ship's cargo was a significant amount of aviation gasoline and ammunition. Though slow-sailing ships such as LST's usually traveled in convoys in order to protect them better with warships, at the last minute *LST-342* was ordered to sail ahead as its cargo was needed badly. So it embarked alone, arriving later in the afternoon of July 18, 1943 at the Russell Islands.

After dark that same night, *LST-342* set sail for Rendova. It rained occasionally during the early night. Lieutenant Montgomery reported the crew was nervous as usual at this time because of the danger posed for the next several hours by Japanese submarines. Off New Georgia, Montgomery was at his conning post when he spotted a torpedo's wake heading for the ship on the port side. Before he could issue a warning, the torpedo from the Japanese submarine[1] struck the port side directly under the bridge, almost exactly on the crew's quarters. The initial explosion was quickly followed by another, louder explosion, and *LST-342* was cut in half completely. The officer's quarters, where Jerome would probably have been at that time, were in the stern half of the ship, and it sunk within seconds after having broken away.

---

[1] The Japanese submarine firing the torpedo was the *RO-106*. Just six days later, on July 24, 1943, *RO-106* reported to her headquarters that she had sighted enemy forces. *RO-106* was never heard from again, however.

43 men, all from the still floating forward part of the ship and including Lieutenant Montgomery, transferred to a raft where they remained for a day-and-a-half. By noon the next day, the forward floating half of *LST-342* was about five miles away from the raft when an American ship approached it. The ship failed to see the survivors in their raft, however, and they remained there for several more hours until they were spotted by a plane and subsequently rescued by another ship.

The forward half of *LST-342* was towed to a base and later used as a supply depot. But the stern half, with Ensign Sobota, was never seen again.

Also aboard *LST-342* at the time of the torpedo attack was famed artist Lieutenant Commander McClelland Barclay, who had requested duty in the war zone in order to sketch the American soldiers and sailors while carrying out their duies. He, too, was lost in this action, along with the many sketches he had done of the men of *LST-342*. Lieutenant Montgomery was the only surviving officer of the ship.

A Navy Department telegram was received by Jerome's mother, Mrs. Anton Sobota, on August 11, 1943, what would have been his 26th birthday, stating that he was missing in action and that no other information was available. An August 9, 1944, telegram, received by Mrs. Sobota from the Bureau of Naval Personnel on August 11, 1944, his 27th birthday, informed her that he was now presumed dead since no word otherwise had been received in the past year. The telegram stated:

> My dear Mrs. Sobota:
> The Bureau of Naval Personnel previously informed you that your son, Ensign Jerome Joseph Sobota, United States Naval Reserve, was being carried on the records of the Navy Department in the status of missing in action.
> In the early morning of 18 July 1943, the vessel in which your son was serving, the *USS LST-342*, was torpedoed in the Solomon Sea. The stern portion of the landing ship was blown off by the explosion and sank almost immediately. The part of the ship which did not sink was later towed to port. Most of the survivors remained aboard this section of the ship, and those in the water kept afloat by means of debris, life jackets or rafts until they were rescued during the afternoon. Weather conditions in the area included good visibility and a calm sea.
> In view of the immediate and subsequent searches made for the personnel after the action, and considering the length of time that has elapsed without any indication that your son survived, I am reluctantly forced to the conclusion that he is deceased. In compliance with Section 5 of Public Law 490, 77th Congress as amended, his death is presumed to have occurred on 19 July 1944, which is the day following the expiration of twelve months in the missing status.
> I extend to you my sincere sympathy in your great loss and hope you may find comfort in the knowledge that your son gave his life for his country, upholding the highest traditions of the Navy. The Navy shares in your sense of bereavement and has felt the loss of his service.
> > Sincerely yours,
> > Ralph A. Bard
> > Acting

On August 29, 1944, a memorial service was held for Ensign Jerome J. Sobota at Ss. Peter and Paul Catholic Church in Independence. At the cemetery, 12 members of Sura-Wiersgalla Post 186 conducted services, led by Chaplain M. A. Weimer, while a firing squad of eight from Camp McCoy assisted the Legion members. A Purple Heart was awarded posthumously to Ensign Jerome J. Sobota on that day, and presented to his mother.

Lieutenant Edmund J. Lyga, a good friend of Jerome's through high school and college, was aboard ship heading from Hawaii to Saipan when he ran into a mutual college friend who informed Ed of what had happened. Ed had not to that point known about the incident. He also told Ed he had received a letter from Jerome dated prior to his death stating Jerome had just given a ring to his girlfriend and that they were planning on being married after the war.

Left: Ensign Jerome J. Sobota following commissioning as a Naval
Reserve Ensign.
Right: Jerome with his fiance, Lorraine Voelker.

Sources: Mary Ann (Sobota) Olson, sister, personal papers; Independence News-Wave; Book (Karig, Harris, and
Manson)

A Quote From History. . .

"If not for her letters when I was in that jungle, I would have given up for sure."
      Everette "Blaze" Blaha
      United States Army
      From an interview, July 9, 1998.

ROMAN "BUTCH" A. SOBOTA
UNITED STATES ARMY AIR FORCE

Roman "Butch" Sobota was inducted into the service on April 10, 1943 and entered active service at Fort Sheridan, Illinois, on April 17 of that year. Following basic training, he went to Aerial Gunnery School in El Paso, Texas, and Pueblo, Colorado, during which time he was promoted to Sergeant. During this period, he also spent one month as an athletic instructor due to his personal athleticism and knowledge of team sports such as basketball, baseball, and football.

On October 22, 1944 Butch left the United States for England, arriving November 2, 1944, where he became a waist gunner on a B-24 Liberator bomber. He served with the 578th Bombardment Squadron, 392nd Heavy Bombardment Group, commanded by Colonel Lorin L. Johnson of Payson, Utah, a part of Second Bombardment Division, Eighth U. S. Air Force.[1] The Group's missions targeted Germany's war machinery, submarine and ship yards, airfields, aircraft factories, synthetic oil works, and the flying bomb sites, taking them over numerous cities including Berlin, Bremen, Friedrichshaven, Gotha, and Politz, among others, in Germany, Poland, Belgium, Holland, Norway, and France. The Group's 100th mission was in support of the Normandy D-Day invasion, and subsequently it flew other missions in support of the ground troops as they fought their way across the continent.

Sobota, Roman A.
36816224 370 44-15

On December 28, 1944, two months after Butch had arrived in England and less than one month prior to his 21st birthday, Field Order #558 described the 392nd Bomb Group's Mission #216. Briefings began at 5:45 A. M. that morning, and at 9:00 A. M., 29 aircraft began launching for the railroad marshalling yards at Kaiserslautern, Germany. Over target, 588 250- and 500-pound bombs were released and results were judged as fair. Approximately two minutes after releasing its bombs, Sgt. Sobota's aircraft was struck by German fighter aircraft and anti-aircraft fire, number two engine caught fire, and, though still under control, the aircraft dropped from formation. While losing altitude, number four engine also caught fire, and soon after the bomber exploded, at 12:42 P. M. and position 4925N-0755E, according to Group records. Prior to the explosion, however, six parachutes were observed to have opened, one of them carrying Butch Sobota.

After bailing out from his stricken aircraft, Butch was captured in the countryside near Muenchweiler, Germany. Years later he recalled he was relieved to have been

---

[1] Butch's aircraft was serial numbered 4-250623, added to the B-24 inventory on May 8, 1944, and flown to England on June 12, 1944. Its markings were "ECE," the "EC" being the indentification of the 578th Bomb Squadron and the second "E" being the individual aircraft's identification. It's pilot, 2nd Lieutenant R. E. Baetz, named the aircraft "Idiot's Delight."

captured by German soldiers as there were civilians approaching with pitchforks who appeared to be very angry and, he thought, might have killed him. In actuality, Adolf Hitler had ordered that any captured Allied fliers bombing the Fatherland should immediately be put to death by the civilian population. German Reichsminister Heinrich Himmler, in his radio broadcasts at that time, had not only been urging the German people to immediately kill any American airmen that they captured, but also issued orders for German soldiers not to interfer in these murders. Fortunately, Butch was captured by soldiers whose commanding officer was apparently questioning the Fuehrer's orders.

Butch spent the next five months until the end of the war in two German prisoner of war camps, first spending a short time in Dulag 1, then being transferred to Stalag Luft 1 near Barth, Germany, located on the Baltic coast. On May 1, 1945, Butch was liberated by the advancing Russian Army and found himself back in American hands one week later.

On June 21, 1945 Butch boarded ship and headed back to the United States where he received his separation and subsequent Honorable Discharge on November 3, 1945, at Lincoln Army Air Field, Lincoln, Nebraska.   Sgt. Sobota was awarded the American Theater Ribbon, European-African-Middle East Ribbon with one battle star, and the World War II Victory Medal.

Following his aircraft's failure to return from the December 28, 1944 mission, a Western Union telegram from the Adjutant General, Washington, D. C., was received by Butch's mother, Mrs. Helen Sobota, of Independence. It simply stated:

> The Secretary of War desires me to express his deep regret that your son Sergeant Roma A Sobota has been reported missing in action since Twenty Eight December over Germany if further details or other information are received you will be promptly notified.[2]

This was soon followed by another telegram stating:

> Report just received through the International Red Cross states that your son Sergeant Roman A Sobota is a prisoner of War of the German Government letter of information follows from Provost Marshal General.

A letter dated February 17, 1945 from Colonel Howard F. Bresee, Director, American Prisoner of War Information Bureau, Office of Provost Marshal General, Washington, D. C., was received by Mrs. Sobota, reading as follows:

> Dear Mrs. Sobota:
> 　　The Provost Marshal General has directed me to supplement the information you received recently from the Adjutant General concerning the above-named prisoner of war.
> 　　Information has been received which indicates that he is now interned as a prisoner of war by the German Government. The report received did not give his camp location. This conforms with the usual practice of the German Government not to report the address of a prisoner of war until he has been placed in a permanent camp. Past experience indicates that his camp address may not be reported to this office until one to three months have elapsed from the time he was first reported a prisoner of war.
> 　　Pending receipt of his permanent address, you may direct letter mail to him by following instructions in the inclosed mailing circular and by addressing his as illustrated above. One parcel label and two tobacco labels, with instructions for their use, will be forwarded, without application on your part, when his permanent location is reported.

On March 8, 1945 Mr. and Mrs. John A. Sobota received the following telegram:

> Following enemy propaganda broadcast from Germany has been intercepted. I'm in a German

---

2 All spelling and punctuation appear as found in the original telegrams and V-mail letter received by Sgt. Sobota's parents.

prisinor of war camp and am O.K. they treat me very good here so dont worry about me I'll be allright my present address is Stalag Luft I. You can send me a package of cookies but first contact the Red Cross tell everybody hello for me and please dont worry. your son Roman. Sargeant Roman A Sabotta 36816324.

Pending further confirmation this report does not establish his status as a prisoner of war stop Additional information received will be furnished stop.

The next day, March 9, 1945 a postcard was received by the Sobota's from the Prisoners of War Listening Post Association, Antrim, New Hampshire, stating that on March 6 at 11:00 P. M., a shortwave radio broadcast was received from Germany indicating that Sgt. Sobota was a Prisoner of War and being held at Stalag Luft I. The postcard then asked for donations to help defray costs of contacting relatives and loved ones of other POW's in this manner.

On May 28, 1945 a V-Mail from Sgt. Sobota was received by his parents. It was dated May 17, 1944, though the year was actually 1945. It stated:

Dear Mom,

Well we finally got evacuated from Germany and in France at a camp near Le Havre, and am waiting here to process, and ship home and that should take very long at the most a month, and its very probably that I will be home sooner than that. They treated us very good at this camp, and the food is excellent. I suppose they really celebrated at home when the war was over. I bet Ralph and Rich are happy the school is nearly over. I imagine the weather there is very nice its real swell over here. I forgot to tell you we were liberated by the Russians May 1st. You can't write to me cause I have no return address that's because we don't stay here long enough. Well I'll have to sign off for now and you can expect me home very soon.

Love, Butch

Ironically, on this same date Mrs. Sobota received a Western Union telegram stating,

The Secretary of War desires me to inform you that your Son Sgt Sobota Roman A returned to Military control date unreported.

His parents also received a phone call from the office of the Secretary of War telling them their son had been liberated by the Russians.

Following the war, and because he had been a prisoner of war, Butch was eligible for compensation under the War Claims Act of 1948. His original claim was for the period of December 28, 1944 to May 8, 1945, at a rate of $1.50 per day. However, the Claims Service of the War Claims Commission denied the period from May 2, 1945 to May 8, 1945, from the date he was liberated by the Russian Army through the date he was returned to American Military Control. The amount he was judged to have overclaimed was $7.00, which was deducted from the award by the War Claims Commission. "Therefore, the Treasury Department is being advised to issue to you a check for $180.50 . . ." for the five months Butch spent as a prisoner of war.

On Veteran's Day, 1990, through the efforts of Keith Johnson, Trempealeau County veteran's service officer, Roman "Butch" Sobota was presented with a special POW medal as authorized by an Act of Congress.

Of the ten men aboard his aircraft on December 28, 1944, only two survived the plane's being shot down, one them being Butch Sobota.
The crew of "Idiot's Delight":
2nd Lt. R. E. Baetz
2nd Lt. J. H. Hirshberg
2nd Lt. J. R. Merilli
2nd Lt. L. C. Farlow

Sgt. B. J. Davenport
Sgt. M. A. Scudder
Sgt. A. Kamenko
Sgt. A. C. Byars
Sgt. R. A. Sobota
Sgt. G. Schomberg (S-27) - mission photographer, observer

The officers of "Idiot's Delight," shot down over Germany on December 28, 1944. Of the ten men aboard, only two, including Butch Sobota, survived. From left to right:
   2nd Lt. J. H. Hirshberg, co-pilot
   2nd Lt. L. C. Farlow, bombardier
   2nd Lt. J. R. Merilli, navigator
   2nd Lt. R. E. Baetz, pilot

Sources: Ralph Sobota, brother; Colling's Foundation; George Michel; Book (Vickers)

EMIL SOBOTTA
UNITED STATES NAVY

    Emil Sobotta enlisted in the United States Navy in May 1929. He was only 17 years old at the time and had just completed his junior year in high school. By the time the attack on Pearl Harbor occurred, he had already spent 12 years in the Navy.

    Emil was assigned duty aboard the destroyer *U. S. S. Mayo* (DD-422), following his completion of training at a naval school in Los Angeles, California. He probably joined the crew of the *Mayo* at the time of her commissioning in September 1940 and helped ready the ship for

duty on the high seas. A ship of the Benson Class, *Mayo* was 348 feet long and carried a crew of 276 officers and men.

Following her shakedown cruise, *Mayo* joined the two battleships, two cruisers, and eight other destroyers of Task Force 19 that escorted a convoy carrying United States Marines to Iceland in July, 1941. The United States was already preparing, though slowly, for the possibility of becoming involved with the hostilities underway in Europe and saw the need for establishing a strong base in the North Atlantic. The 15,000 British Empire troops stationed in Iceland were needed in Africa, and with Nazi-occupied Norway only 530 nautical miles away, Iceland's parliament agreed to the Marines as part of a neutrality patrol to protect the important island. In August 1941, when President Franklin Roosevelt and British Prime Minister Winston Churchill met in the North Atlantic and agreed to the Atlantic Charter, *Mayo* was part of the protective force surrounding the two leaders, patrolling the waters off Argentia, Newfoundland.

When the United States formally entered World War II, *Mayo's* assignments were expanded to the protection of slow convoys heading from Boston to England. In January 1942 *Mayo* was at an assigned Mid-Ocean Meeting Point (MOMP), waiting for a convoy headed back to North America. A typically severe North Atlantic storm was in progress and visibility was low as she assumed her duty station alongside the merchant ships she was to help protect during the rest of their voyage. Suddenly, a British ship, *HMS Douglas*, crossed *Mayo's* bow and, though an "All Stop" was immediately ordered, nothing could prevent the two ships from colliding in the heavy seas. *Mayo's* bow was heavily damaged by the impact, with a number of officer's quarters being exposed to the sea. Her crew quickly sealed the bow section to prevent further danger, however, and once this was done and *Douglas* was under control, she was able to then escort the seriously listing *Douglas* to Reykjavik, Iceland, where the escort vessel was to be repaired. *Mayo* suffered only one casualty in the incident.

Mayo, on the other hand, sailed for the Boston Navy Yard, where a bow slated for a destroyer under construction was instead readied for her arrival. It was quickly welded in place and several armament modifications were made before she departed again for the North Atlantic to resume her duties.

By the summer of 1942, *Mayo* was being assigned screening duty for fast troop transports departing New York and delivering the first American soldiers to Great Britain in preparation for the upcoming Allied offensive in North Africa. It was in the midst of these escort missions that Emil was promoted to Chief Petty Officer on July 1, 1942. With the constant threat of German U-boats and the seemingly constant bad weather of the North Atlantic, the men of the *Mayo* were pushed to their limits in an effort to deliver the transports to England intact. One of *Mayo's* more heroic efforts occurred on September 3, 1942 when the *U. S. S. Wakefield* (AP-21) caught fire at sea and *Mayo* quickly moved alongside to rescue 247 survivors.

Mayo participated in the Allied invasion of North Africa by escorting troopships carrying reinforcements and protecting their landing on November 12, 1942, four days after D-Day. She then entered a period of training at the end of 1942 at Casco Bay, Maine, which interrupted her escort assignments for several months.

In August, 1943, *Mayo* joined Destroyer Squadron (DesRon) 7, part of the 8th Fleet operating in the Mediterranean Sea. When the assault on the beaches at Salerno, Italy, occurred in September, 1943, *Mayo* served as part of the Southern Attack Force, giving fire and antiaircraft support to the troops landing from the south bank of the River Sele eight miles to Agropoli. She then did the same with the landing at Anzio, Italy, beginning January 22, 1944.

On January 24, 1944, off Anzio, *Mayo* was rocked by a tremendous explosion that nearly tore the ship in two while killing seven and injuring 23 of her crew. Despite a huge hole at her waterline, she survived a tow to Naples where temporary repairs were made before she began a long tow back to the United States on March 3, 1944. She arrived at the New York Navy Yard on April 3, 1944, and remained there for the next four months. She then rejoined DesRon 7 and continued her convoy escort duty in the Atlantic before being ordered to the Pacific Theater, where she remained for the remainder of the war.

Following the incident off Anzio, Emil first sent a cablegram and then the following letter to his parents, Mr. and Mrs. Ignatz Sobotta, informing them of the explosion and the fact that he had not been injured. The letter appeared in the *News-Wave's* March 9, 1944, edition and, besides reassuring his parents of his safety once again, expressed his desire to return home to his wife Avery and son "Little" Emil:

Dearest Mother and Dad:

I know you must have received my cablegram by this time. I guess you were a little scared when you first got it, but I thought it would be better to send a cable letting you know that I was alright, because I know you'd worry yourself to death until you found out something.

Undoubtedly you've heard the news about the landings in the Anzio and Nettuno areas in Italy. We had quite an active part in the landing for about three days. I don't believe the Germans expected anything like that because there was hardly any resistance at all. After the Germans finally got wise on the second and third day things got a little hotter. There were quite a few air raids but they weren't very successful. They lost quite a few planes. This is about all I can tell you about this operation.

I still don't have any idea when I'll get back to the States, but I'm still hoping it will be for Easter and my birthday. I would like to be home for at least one Holiday - it will be seven months the fifth of March since we left the States. I sure do want to see Avery and Little Emil. He was six years old last month. I've only been with him once on his birthday; that was his first one. I guess he's getting to be quite a boy. I haven't been with him enough to realize how big he is getting to be. When I do get to go home, I stay just long enough to be acquainted and then it's time to leave. I'm still in hopes of getting thirty days furlough when we get back.

Well, folks, nothing more this time. I hope you're all in the best of health and didn't have a too cold winter. God Bless all of you.

Love, Emil

Another letter appearing in the April 6, 1944 *News-Wave* gave his parents more details regarding the incident at Anzio and also informed them of his transfer from the *U. S. S. Mayo*:

Comdesron 7
March 13, 1944
Dearest Mother and Dad:

I received your letter you wrote on the 15th of January yesterday, so it was just a couple of months late. I also got two letters from Clara, one from Pal and seven from Avery. It wasn't such a bad day; it was the first mail I'd received since about the middle of January.

I imagine you were kinda worried when you got my telegram. But I thought it was better to let you know I was alright than not to say anything at all. Our ship got hit but it didn't sink. Killed seven people and wounded about 35. I guess my luck is still holding out, or else God is looking over me. I thought maybe it would be in the papers before I could let you know that I was alright.

I'll bet it seemed funny to have a Christmas without any snow. I'll bet the children were disappointed. How did Santa Claus get there, on Dad's truck? Ha!!

I sure am glad that he got somebody to help him with the wood. Buying that forty with all that wood on it was a good investment.

I sure had planned on being home for Easter, but I don't believe I will be. I was transferred about two weeks ago and my old ship went back to the States and I was left over here, not very long I hope. I'm out of the danger area anyway, that's one good thing. I hope I never have to go up the front again. It's terrible!

How are Fred and Phyllis and the children? I hope they aren't angry with me for not writing but I just can't find time to write to everybody. You can show this letter to them, that will kill two birds with one stone.

Does Independence have a basketball team this year? How are they doing? They probably can't get the gas to travel.

Well, folks, nothing more to say this time so will close. I'll be 32 years old; the time sure goes by fast, except over here. A day seems like a week.

God Bless all of you.
> Your Loving Son,
> Emil

Emil did make it home sooner than he expected, visiting his wife, son, and parents, as well as his brother, Sergeant Ernest, whom he hadn't seen for several years, in Independence in mid-April, 1944. He was then ordered to report to Norfolk, Virginia, following this leave, but it is uncertain as to what he did for the remainder of the war. It was mentioned in the April 13, 1944 *News-Wave* that he was a Warrant Officer at that time and eligible for retirement from the Navy in five years. Emil eventually served, however, for 28 years in the United States Navy and retired as a Chief Warrant Officer in 1957.

Sources: Ernest Sobotta, brother; Independence News-Wave; Internet

ERNEST P. SOBOTTA
UNITED STATES ARMY

The following narrative is from an interview conducted with Ernie Sobotta on November 7, 1998 at his home in Independence, Wisconsin. By the time his military service had ended, Ernie had participated in the Northern France, Rhineland, and Central Europe campaigns and had been awarded the European-African-Middle Eastern Medal, American Theater Medal, two Overseas Service Bars, and Good Conduct Medal.

I was already in the National Guard unit in Arcadia, Wisconsin, when the war broke out. There was a rule at that time that said if you were in the National Guard for more than six years, you were put in Emergency Reserve, and therefore not draftable. But in November, 1942, the Emergency Reserve was eliminated so I was then eligible for the draft, and that happened on November 11 of that year. I was drafted at the same time as Marcel Skroch, who was known as "Whistle," and Pete Walek. Due to my Military Police training in the Arcadia Guard, I was sent to Camp Blanding, Florida, where I received more M. P. training as well as my basic training.

On July 27, 1943 I left for Algiers, North Africa, where I was stationed with Company B, 795th Military Police Battalion. I arrived in Algiers on August 19, 1943, and on that same day, the Germans bombed the port with about twelve bombers. Then that same night, Bob Hope and Francis Lankford put on a show for the troops stationed there. I and one other M. P. got to escort

Ernie Sobotta, top left, sitting on the jeep. The man on the right wearing the baseball cap is Pfc. Allen Sousa, son of famed music composer, John Phillip Sousa.

Left to Right:
Marcel "Whistle" Skroch, Pete Walek, and Ernie Sobotta.

them from the city of Algiers to the camp for the show. I remember Hope wearing a steel helmet when he came out on stage, playing up the bombing all he could. It was at this U. S. O. in Algiers where I ran into Jack Halama, too.

We began training almost immediately for landing in Italy. Our training involved landing craft. But after only one week, I was one of 32 men placed in a cadre and sent back to the States. While I was in the Army, I got a series of breaks that were just luck of the draw, and this was my first one because the rest of the M. P. battalion landed at Anzio and several were killed.

The ship on which I traveled back to the States was loaded with German prisoners of war that were being sent to camps in America. We landed at Camp Patrick Henry in Virginia and it wasn't long before I met up with Addison Hotchkiss in the camp's chow line. I remember he asked me what he could expect overseas and I told him it hadn't been too bad in the short time I had been in Africa and that you could trade a bar of soap or a chocolate bar for a bottle of champagne! From Virginia I was sent to Camp Blanding once again where we organized a new M. P. outfit. I was promoted to Corporal on January 23, 1944 and Sergeant on February 10, 1944.

209

After our new outfit had been trained, we were shipped to Scotland, arriving there on June 3, 1944. We were immediately sent by train to just south of London where we directed traffic at the beaches there in order to create what were really phony ship loadings revolving around the actual D-Day invasion. This was done so that if the invasion preparations were discovered, the feints would hopefully create at least a little confusion among the Germans as to where the real landing would take place.

Once the Normandy beachhead was secured, we crossed the English Channel and landed on Omaha Beach. We were then attached to the 2nd Infantry Division, 9th U. S. Army, and followed the Division as it attacked toward Brest, France.[1] As the Division moved forward, we would move in as quickly as possible behind them and help secure the newly-won territory. We had four tanks and four scout cars in our unit and I was a scout car commander throughout my time in Europe. I always carried a Thompson sub-machine gun, which was a 14-pound weapon.

When Brest was taken, we were assigned to escort an intelligence detail to the captured German headquarters. I figured something was up with the men we were escorting because they had uniforms with no insignia on them. They were just wearing a plain private's uniform. Plus I remembered meeting one of them while I had been in England, and he was wearing civilian clothes there. So I figured they must be big-shots of some sort, probably of the civilian intelligence department. I suppose the reason for the uniform was because if they had been captured in civilian clothing, they could be shot as spies. But, anyway, we were right near the front lines here because the infantrymen were in foxholes and I remember one of them saying, "What the hell are M. P.'s doing up here?" We took those intelligence guys straight to the German headquarters and they went through everything. There they found something considered pretty important -- the German radio codes for the following month. For some reason, the Germans had failed to totally destroy them.

In Brest, the infantry captured a concrete bunker that held six German officers and two French women. The French freedom fighters recognized the women immediately and didn't waste any time cutting their hair off completely. This identified them as collaborators with the Germans.

Also in Brest, we once escorted a group of French doctors and other medical people to an underground transportation tunnel. The tunnel was about a quarter-of-a-mile long and during the bombings of Brest, civilians would take shelter there. Near the time the Germans surrendered in Brest, the tunnel was full of civilians and it was burned from both ends. I don't know if it was accidental or whether the Germans intentionally did this, but the doctors were being sent in to check it out. I'll tell you, it was a mess. They counted 600 bodies in there, and the stench was horrible.

After Brest was secured, there was a bit of a lull and we were sent to the area around Lorient. This is where the Germans had some of their massive concrete submarine pens located. The Germans and their subs were gone already but we did find large stores of food -- canned hams from Poland, lemons from South America. We loaded up the scout car with as much of this stuff as we could carry! The infantry was being relocated to the east at this time but we remained along the coast, staying in contact with the Navy and patrolling along the beach to the border with Spain. We picked up a few German stragglers here and there and cooperated with the French freedom fighters. Those French didn't have any sympathy for the Germans!

During this time, we went out picking up jerry cans, the gas cans used to fill tanks and other motorized vehicles as they moved forward. Patton was short of gasoline because there were no cans to transport it in. They had always been simply discarded when emptied.[2] So we stopped

---

[1] The Battle for Brest lasted more than three weeks. In the end, more than 30,000 Germans surrendered. However, the 2nd Infantry Division suffered 2,314 casualties, while the 29th and 8th Infantry Divisions combined counted more than 4,100 killed and wounded.

[2] It was about this time when Third Army's commander, General George S. Patton, said that if he were given the gasoline, his men could make a run to Berlin before the Germans knew what had happened. This didn't happen, but the lack of gasoline was only one of the reasons it didn't, the other being the decision to allow the Russians to take Berlin, a decision that angered Patton to no end.

in towns and picked up as many as we came across. Then they were loaded on trucks and sent to the front. Sometimes the town's mayors wanted some official proof of what we were doing, so I took a whiskey cork and cut notches into it to make a seal that was then affixed to a letter supposedly from our regional commanding officer. To the mayors, we were now "official" and they didn't object to what we were doing.

There was quite a large prison camp in this area, too. They had Senegalese troops, tall black Africans, guarding the prisoners in the camp. There were thousands of Germans held at this camp but there were no fences. It was just an open field. The Germans came to fear those Africans, though, because if they wandered too close to the camp border, the Senegalese didn't hesitate opening fire. The Germans learned quickly not to push the issue too much.

Our M. P. unit was involved in a lot of different activities while in Europe. We weren't always attached to the 2nd Infantry Division, and sometimes operated independently and were assigned to special duties. At one point we were stationed at Rennes, France, when we received orders -- two officers and six sergeants -- to get back to the French coast. I think it was Cherbourg. We were assigned to guard a train as it traveled across France. There were six boxcars and we slept in one of them. But the others were all locked up and we had orders not to allow anyone near them. The train traveled only at night and when it stopped, even the train's crew was kept away from it. It took one week to reach Verdun and when it got there, it went underground and disappeared. I often wondered what was on that train, whether it had parts for an atomic bomb or some other secret weapon. Whatever it was, though, there's no doubt it was top secret. We just went back to our unit at Rennes after that.

We were then ordered to Cologne, along the Rhine River. Here the Allies were preparing to cross into Germany. But before we went there, we got some leave so we hitched a ride with a train carrying POW's and spent a weekend in Paris. We were dirty and had our combat clothes on and some M. P.'s picked us up thinking we were AWOL, absent without leave from our unit. They took us to headquarters and, wouldn't you know it, Cornelius "Turny" Sobotta of Arcadia was there! He was 1st Sergeant of the 32nd M. P. Company! He cleaned up the mess with the M. P.'s who had picked us up, got us some new clothes, and we had a good time in Paris with the guys from Arcadia.

When we got to Cologne, we were stationed between the British divisions to our north and the American divisions to our south, and we kept in contact with both. Along the river nearby, the American soldiers discovered there was a brandy distillery, but there was an open field of 100 yards or more to cross before you could get to it. The Germans had their positions only 200 or 300 yards away across the river and they could easily see anyone crossing that field. But for some of our guys, the temptation was too much and suddenly you would see somebody running zig-zag across that field carrying an empty jerry can, and the Germans would open up with their machine guns. After a few minutes, he'd be running back, but this time the can was full!

We crossed the Rhine at Cologne. British troops had been dropped into Germany by gliders some time earlier and we saw a lot of busted up gliders on the other side of the river.

In Germany, we followed the infantry to the Elbe River, and then moved back to Munster. Later, I and six others were transferred to Bielefeld, which was about a half-day trip by truck. I was in Bielefeld when the war ended. It wasn't long and the Army was packing up troops to send to the Pacific, and this is where I got another big break. General Eisenhower ordered that any troops who had been in Africa would not be sent to the Pacific. I hadn't been in Africa long, but it was long enough, so I didn't have to go there. Instead, I was sent to Marseilles, France, where I waited for six weeks on the Riviera for my turn to go home. I left France on August 25, 1945 on the troopship *U. S. S. Marine Raven* and, whereas my first two trips across the Atlantic were on slow Liberty ships, this trip was fast, and I arrived back in New York on September 3, 1945. I then traveled to Fort Sheridan, Illinois, and then to Independence for R-and-R. All I did in Independence was wait for my call to report to Camp McCoy for discharge. I was discharged at Camp McCoy on November 11, 1945, exactly three years to the day of my entering active duty.

Source: Book (Stanton)

211

PAUL P. SOBOTTA
UNITED STATES NAVY

In December 1941 the United States Asiatic Fleet consisted of nothing more than the equivalent of a small task force led by three cruisers, two of which were light. Thirteen old destroyers, all built around 1917-18, were also part of this group, a group that was totally outmatched by the Japanese fleet.

Prior to the Japanese attack on Pearl Harbor, these thirteen destroyers, including the *U. S. S. Peary* aboard which Albert Skroch was serving, were combined into Destroyer Squadron 29 (Desdron 29). The destroyer tender *U. S. S. Black Hawk* was attached to Desdron 29, and aboard her was Paul Sobotta, who had joined the Navy in 1928 and served aboard the battleship *U. S. S. West Virginia* before being transferred to the *Black Hawk*.

Paul Sobotta, front, middle. From the look of the officer's uniform (right) this photo was probably taken some years early, possibly on board the battleship *U. S. S. West Virginia.*

The *U. S. S. Black Hawk* (AD-9), was built in 1918 and originally named the *S. S. Santa Catalina.* It had a displacement of 8,900 tons when fully loaded, measured 420 feet in length, had a top speed of 11 knots, and was armed with four 3-inch 50-caliber, two pair of 40-mm, and sixteen 20-mm machine guns. The mission of destroyer tenders was to provide a mobile base and repair facility, as well as supply fuel, ammunition, and other supplies to destroyers and destroyer escorts.

On December 6, 1941 the *Black Hawk* and four destroyers, probably the *Stewart*, *Edwards*, *Barker*, and *Bulmer*, were in the harbor at Balikpapan, Dutch Borneo. For some time, the British, already at war with the Japanese, and Americans in the region had been monitoring the movements of the Japanese fleet off the coast of Indo-China. When the Japanese seemed to vanish from the area, the British mistakenly believed an attack on the Malay Peninsula was about to take place. The five American ships were ordered to sail for Batavia, but the Dutch, aware of unidentified submarines lurking in the area, would not allow them to leave the harbor at Balikpapan as they did not want to open their anti-submarine booms after dark. With daylight, however, the destroyers and their tender did proceed to Singapore for refueling where they were then pressed into service searching for survivors of the *HMS Repulse* and *HMS Prince of Wales*, two grand British warships that had just been sunk by the Japanese.

Soon after the attack on Pearl Harbor, Allied naval forces in the region were put under the command of Dutch Rear Admiral Karel W. F. M. Doorman, who quickly began formulating plans to attack the Japanese. On February 1, 1942 a large enemy convoy was detected at Balikpapan, which by then was in Japanese hands, and it was believed the Japanese were poised to attack either the east coast of Borneo or the southern portion of the Celebes Islands. A force including the four destroyers *Black Hawk* was probably tending was sent to meet the Japanese as it sailed down Makassar Strait. Shortly before 10:00 A. M. on February 4, 1942, the first Japanese planes began their attack, causing severe damage to the American cruisers *Marblehead* and *Houston*. Over the next several days, a number of other Japanese convoys were spotted operating in the area, seemingly closing on Sumatra or Java. When a convoy was discovered near Banka Island on February 7, 1942, several ships were sent to intercept, but on February 14, 1942 this force was bombed repeatedly by the Japanese. The destroyers *Barker* and *Bulmer*, though not hit by bombs, were nonetheless shaken enough to warrant their withdrawel from the area.

It was at this time that the Allied command decided to get its few warships out of the Java Sea region where they were becoming easy prey for the Japanese, so a base was established at Exmouth Gulf, midway down Australia's west coast about 800 miles south of Bali. On February 20, 1942 the *Black Hawk* began escorting the crippled *Barker* and *Bulmer* toward Australia.

The Allied command was now reeling under the onslaught of the Japanese advance across the Pacific. Cruisers had been lost and badly damaged and only five of the original thirteen destroyers in Desdron 29 were still in battle condition. Albert Skroch's *U. S. S. Peary*, one of those thirteen, was sunk on February 19, 1942 with the loss of half her crew while attempting to protect an Australian hospital ship with a smokescreen .

Paul and Pauline Sobotta

In the first issue of the *News-Wave* following the attack on Pearl Harbor, published on December 11, 1941, it was reported that several men from Independence were in the military, including Paul Sobotta, and that "thoughts turn to those who are in the service either on land or sea." The May 14, 1942 edition reported that Paul's mother, Mrs. Anton Sobotta, had received her first letter from Paul since the December 7 attack on Pearl Harbor, assuring her he was all right and was somewhere at sea.

Following the completion of its escort mission of the two destroyers to Australia, the *Black Hawk* apparently sailed to Pearl Harbor, and then, it appears, to Alaska before arriving in San Francisco in January 1943. In late January, Paul, a Petty Officer Second Class, arrived in Independence to visit his wife, Pauline, and his mother, whom he had not seen in eight years.

In November 1944 the *Independence News-Wave* published a large, "Special Serviceman's Edition," which was sent to servicemen and women around the world.

213

Among many other things regarding Independence's soldiers and sailors, it contained several letters that had been received from servicemen in response to the town's efforts. One of these was from Paul aboard the *U. S. S. Black Hawk*:

Dear Editor:
It is with great pleasure that I am in position to express my appreciation for the kindness of which has been rendered towards the men and women in the service from Independence.
On December 12th I was more than pleased to understand that the old home town has come to undertake such a worthy cause in the preparation of a 24 page edition of the News-Wave.
And last, but not least, I want to thank the members of the general committee for their hardship of which I presume they have spent many hours and sleepless nights in making a good thing possible.

Unfortunately, no additional information regarding Paul Sobota's naval service during World War II was uncovered.

Source: Independence News-Wave; Internet

ADOLPH SONSALLA
UNITED STATES ARMY

Adolph entered the United States Army on August 26, 1942, and received his initial training at Camp Grant, Illinois. From there he was transferred to the 7th Division, later the 7th Infantry Division,[1] at Camp San Luis Obispo, California. The Division arrived at Fort Ord, California, on January 15, 1943 and departed the San Francisco Port of Embarkation on April 24, 1943.
Serving with the 432nd Medical Collecting Company, Adolph landed with the 7th Infantry Division on Attu Island in the Aleutians in May 1943. He was there only a few days when he had to be transported to San Francisco suffering from exposure, one of more than 1,800 men of Landing Force Attu who had to be evacuated due to cold- and disease-related conditions.[2] On June 17, 1943 the *News-Wave* published a letter from Adolph to his parents in which he described his experience in the "Battle of Attu." It was written from Letterman General Hospital in San Francisco:

June 8, 1943
Dearest Mother and Dad:
Well, here goes another letter. I don't know if you got the letter I wrote aboard ship. If you did, I hope you saved the morning papers. If you didn't I wish you would try and pick up all the stories on the Battle of Attu. I was in the front lines of that battle for five days. Then I had to leave the lines because I did not feel my feet about four days.
They were frozen blue. They were so bad that I was sent back to the States. I can walk on them

---

[1] The 7th Infantry Division suffered 1,948 men killed and 7,258 wounded, of which 386 died of their wounds, during its Aleutian Islands, Eastern Mandates, Leyte, and Ryukyus campaigns.

[2] The Battle of Attu was the first experience with combat cold injuries that the American Army had in World War II. Attu veterans suffering from exposure were studied closely by doctors which then led to wholesale changes in Army footgear, clothes, tents, bedrolls, and food. Though many soldiers suffered additionally from amputation due to their time on Attu, their experiences undoubtedly saved many lives, and limbs, during the next two years.

now, but they get very tired. The toes still pain a little and sometimes feel numb but they will be alright.

I will never forget what I went through. Those Japs are not the best shots. If they were I would not be writing this letter. I had plenty of close calls. Some of them made my blood run cold, but they never hit me. I hope to be seeing you soon.

Will close for now.

Your Loving Son,
Adolph

Adolph remained in Letterman General for a week, then was transferred to McCloskey General Hospital, Temple, Texas, where he remained for three months. After discharge from McCloskey, he spent three months at Fort Sam Houston, Texas, and a short time at Gienna General Hospital, Okemulgee, Oklahoma. From there, he reported to Camp Reynolds, Pennsylvania, and then to Camp Patrick Henry, Virginia, from where he was scheduled to leave for duty in the European Theater. His orders were changed, however, and he returned to Camp Reynolds, only to be transferred a week later to Camp Shanks, New York. Finally, he left for England in June 1944 where he remained for two months before crossing the English Channel to the continent.

On April 12, 1945, the *News-Wave* published a letter from him to Editor Glenn Kirkpatrick dated March 22, 1945. Written from Germany, and mindful that Adolph was a medic dealing with saving lives daily, it is a very touching letter that certainly aroused in the people of Independence a desire to do even more to help their sons overseas:

Dear Mr. Kirkpatrick:

Received the Special Servicemen's Edition of the News-Wave a few days back. Though it was a couple of months old I believe I spent some of the most enjoyable moments of my life reading it. I wish to thank you and all those who took part in making up the best morale booster I have yet to see over here.

I and everyone of the boys in service were proud to find the faces of our mothers in the picture of the Red Cross Workers, and each and every one of them may be justly proud of themselves for the part they play in saving the lives of our wounded over here.

Those of you who have given your blood for the wounded have also taken part in this great fight to save lives. I have watched this blood of yours flow into the veins of men that would surely die, giving them new life, and I thank God for people like you.

In closing I again thank each and every one of you for what you have done. With you behind us we cannot lose.

As Ever,
Adolph

As a surgical technician in evacuation hospitals, Adolph participated in the Aleutian Islands, Northern France, Ardennes-Alsace, Rhineland, and Central Europe campaigns during World War II. At the time of his discharge at Fort Sheridan, Illinois, on November 30, 1945, he was wearing the European-African-Middle Eastern Ribbon with four battle stars, Asiatic-Pacific Theater Ribbon with one battle star, three overseas service bars, the Combat Medical Badge, Good Conduct Medal, and World War II Victory Medal.

Sources: Nadine Sonsalla, wife; Independence News-Wave; Books (Stanton) (Garfield)

DREXEL A. SPRECHER
UNITED STATES ARMY

As a graduate of the University of Wisconsin, London School of Economics and Political Science, and Harvard Law School, Drexel Sprecher began his professional career as a trial attorney with the National Labor Relations Board in 1938. During the next four years, he tried cases involving disputes between labor and management in California, Ohio, West Virginia, and New York. In 1942, however, Drexel found himself in the United States Army as a private, as did so many other men following the bombing of Pearl Harbor.

Attached to the Army Inspector General's office, he was sent to England where he monitored the administrative operations of hundreds of service and supply units. In December 1942, he was transferred to Oran, Algeria, where, as a Warrant Officer, he managed similar duties. In the summer of 1943, General Dwight Eisenhower, commander of American forces in North Africa, noticed a group of German prisoners of war who were working in an Army installation, something quite contrary to existing rules of warfare. Eisenhower ordered an investigation and the task was given to Drexel's commanding officer, Colonel Tom Brand. Colonel Brand then turned the investigation over to Drexel, by then a Second Lieutenant, who began traveling to every American prisoner-of-war camp in North Africa to determine whether other breaches of international law were occurring. He found none.

For Christmas in 1944, the American Legion Post 186 in Independence raised money to purchase and send cartons of cigarettes to its sons serving in the military, a practice that would undoubtedly raise eyebrows today, but was more than acceptable -- in fact welcomed by many -- in the 1940's. Upon receiving his carton, Drexel sent the following letter to the *News-Wave*, which appeared in the February 17, 1944 edition:

> January 21, 1944
> Dear Friends:
>
> Yesterday I received two packages of Old Gold cigarettes from the American Legion Post, Independence, and was happy to know that you had remembered me. Although I am not much of a cigarette smoker, I can assure you that I will trade them for some other luxury in the hands of another soldier who prefers a greater number of cigarettes than our ration allows.
>
> I am still in Africa, though I have transferred to a more interesting type of work than inspections and I am now based in a larger and more attractive city. Of course all of us are anxious to get on to the continent as soon as possible, and the sooner I can get some Munich beer in place of North Africa heavy wines, the better I shall like it. In saying this I know I speak for thousands.
>
> Thanks again, and my best wishes to all of you. We'll be back with a victory such as you brought back in the not too distant future.
> Drex Sprecher

Returning to the United States in March 1944, he telephoned his parents, Mr. and Mrs. Walter Sprecher, in Independence, and informed them that he was in Washington, D. C., where he expected to remain for a few days before heading to his next assignment. Shortly after, however, Drexel and his wife, Lieutenant Eleanor Sprecher, arrived in Independence for a visit with his parents, who hosted a party for them attended by family and friends. Drexel then returned to Washington, D. C., and from there was sent to Algiers, Algeria, in North Africa where he was stationed for several months with the Office of Strategic Services (OSS) helping train nearly 20 anti-Nazi Germans to be spies. These secret agents then parachuted into Germany to gather information for use by the Allied armies.

In late 1944, Drexel returned to Washington, D. C., where he was assigned the task of settling labor strikes occurring in the midwest that involved war industries. During this time, he also recruited workers for the important armament industries that were supplying Allied armies in operation around the globe. It was then when he learned of the formation of the Office U. S.

Chief of Counsel for War Crimes, and took an action that would profoundly affect the rest of his life.

In March, 1935, as a student at the London School of Economics and Political Science, Drexel and a fellow student set out on a 3,000 mile, eight-week journey across the European continent, visiting Holland, Germany, Poland, Russia, Finland, Sweden, and Norway. It was his second trip to the continent, the first being just two months earlier in the company of the American counsel in Strasbourg, Germany, and Stewart W. Herman, future pastor of American Church in Berlin who would later write a book detailing the persecution of religion by the Nazis.

Beginning May 3, 1935, and for seven weekly editions through June, the *Independence News-Wave* published a remarkably insightful, very lengthy letter from Drexel, which offered the citizens of a rural west-central Wisconsin community a first-hand account of life half a world away. Though many Independence area residents or their immediate ancestors had emigrated from these same countries, conditions were now much different from the times they recalled. Drexel described the Peace Palace, the showpiece of The Hague in the Netherlands; the surprising taxation experienced by the Poles; and Stalinist Russia. He was permitted a pass to attend the May Day demonstration in Moscow's Red Square, which included a nearly six-hour parade of almost three million people. In Sweden, he was granted an extensive interview with Prime Minister Hansson, leader of the progressive Social Democratic Party. But it was Drexel's portrait of 1935 Germany that would describe to readers an unfolding drama destined to become the greatest tragedy of the century, and among the greatest in all history.

Besides having the opportunity to tour a huge, modernized iron and steel concern in Oberhausen, Drexel was able to see first-hand the Krupp steel works, the largest plant of its kind in the world, in Essen. He wrote about the hold the company had on its workers and Essen itself and questioned the effects the production efficiency exhibited at Krupp had on individual workers. He also speculated as to the role played by German industrialists in Adolf Hitler's rise to power.

When he visited Berlin, Drexel learned of the censorship and repression cast upon the press by the Nazi regime, as well as the blind, unwavering obedience being pledged by the populace to Adolf Hitler, all of which bothered Drexel immensely. Hitler had come to power only two years earlier, and though most people of the modern world still knew little about him or were not yet taking him seriously, the people of Germany who still believed in freedom were realizing the fear and uncertainty inherent to life under his Nazi Party.

While in Berlin, Drexel was able to view the famous film, *Triumph des Willens* (Triumph of the Will), which glorified the Nazi Party and practically deified Hitler. On April 10, 1935, he witnessed in person the wedding procession of Herman Goering to a German actress, led by Hitler himself who acknowledged the response of hundreds of thousands with the raised hand of the Nazi salute. As hundreds of military aircraft flew overhead, the huge parade passed by Drexel who "watched this spectacle behind a row of Storm Troopers lining Unter den Linden."

Of this event, he wrote to the people of Independence, "Here again the intensity of the crowd's worship sickened me. I could not help but think of the concentration camps where many former leaders of Germany are still imprisoned in unlivable conditions because they dared to think differently than this little man whom I saw passing in the car before me." But Drexel also described how he understood the German people being drawn to the diminuative former painter who was promising deliverance from the intolerable conditions set forth upon Germany by the Treaty of Versailles following World War I. He summarized how and under what pretexts Hitler came to power and stated, "I think that Hitler's power, barring his death or another war, is quite firmly entrenched for a long time to come." He also wrote, "It is now all too plainly true that . . . this Treaty contained within itself factors, which given time to develop, would promote severe economic distractions, on the one hand, and prepare the way for a future war on the other."

Drexel was equally critical of the communists of Russia in his letter, writing, "The communists are intolerant of that which they do not believe in, and those who have sought to promote their ideas outside the Communist Party have met with exile, prison, or death." He ended his treatise on Germany and Russia by stating, "To those who love democracy and freedom,

217

Russia and Germany offer two great and rather simple lessons. If by democratic means we do not wrestle power from the greedy hands of the big capitalists and the high financiers, then the two roads, Communism and Fascism, eventually become the alternatives; and at least for me, both of these are destructive of that freedom which gives life most meaning."

Through his letter, it is fair to say the readers of the *Independence News-Wave* in 1935 were given an unusual opportunity to learn a great deal about world affairs of the time. Drexel's observations of Nazi Germany and Stalin's Russia gave them a head start on the next six decades -- a vision of world war soon to come and the cold war that followed.

In 1999, Drexel published a book entitled *Inside the Nuremberg Trial: A Prosecutor's Comprehensive Account*. It is a massive work of more than 1,500 pages that took ten years to write. It vividly describes the proceedings of the first of thirteen war crimes trials held in Nuremberg, Germany, following the conclusion of World War II. The trial brought to the world stage the true story of what occurred in Europe at the hands of Adolf Hitler and his henchmen, detailing how Nazi leaders planned and carried out aggressive war against her neighbor countries and committed appalling crimes against their peoples. It also gave the world a new word, "genocide," the systematic extermination of racial and national groups, and stunned people around the world with the extent to which this horrible treatment of human beings was practiced.

The reason Drexel was most qualified to author this book was because he was there, in Nuremberg, serving as an assistant trial counsel charged with bringing evidence of individual and organizational responsibility for the lawless events perpetrated by the Nazi regime. Early in the book, he called his involvement with the Nuremberg Trials "a transforming experience in my life," and he has been an active advocate of a strong international tribunal dealing with war crimes ever since. And though the Nuremberg Trials have had an impact on international law, it has been not nearly as much as Drexel would have expected, or liked.

Drexel was a prosecutor of record in three of the 13 war crimes trials held at Nuremberg, and served in various capacities in all of them. In the first trial, which addressed the actions of leading Nazis such as Hermann Goering, Albert Speer, Rudolf Hess, and Joachim von Ribbentrop, and the roles played by seven organizations including the Leadership Corps of the Nazi Party, the Gestapo (Secret State Police), and SS (Schutzstaffeln), Drexel prepared the brief and collected evidence regarding the destruction of the free trade unions in Germany and the creation of the German Labor Front. As assistant trial counsel, he delivered the principle presentations regarding Baldur von Schirach, the Hitler Youth Leader, and Hans Fritzsche, the leading Nazi radio propagandist, a man Drexel described as "the main broadcaster of hate of the Propaganda Ministry." In the succeeding trials, he served as chief of several divisions of the Office U. S. Chief of Counsel for War Crimes, was eventually appointed Deputy Chief Counsel, and then acted as Editor-in-Chief of the 15 official volumes summarizing trials two through 13 and entitled, *Trials of War Criminals Before the Nuremberg Military Tribunals*. It was this last assignment as an employee of the War Crimes Branch, The Judge Advocate General, U. S. Army, that led Drexel to compile his detailed account of the first trial.

When, in June 1945, newspapers related the first report to President Truman regarding the formation of the Office U. S. Chief of Counsel for War Crimes, Drexel immediately decided he wanted to be a part of the prosecution staff that would expose Nazi crimes. He was a First Lieutenant at the time on duty in the mid-west, and soon arranged to meet with people in Washington, D. C., who would be able to help him win an appointment to the team. With an appointment in hand, he was soon reassigned to OSS again, which had already begun supplying documents to Justice Robert H. Jackson, U. S. Chief of Counsel for War Crimes, a U. S. Supreme Court Justice and friend of President Roosevelt's appointed to head the American prosecution team. Drexel submitted himself to a crash course in the German language while simultaneously studying substantial numbers of documents detailing the history of the Third Reich. One of the documents he read, an order issued by Reich Organization Leader of the Nazi Party, Dr. Robert Ley, formed the cornerstone of his brief regarding the destruction of the free trade unions and how the Nazis took over labor in Germany.

By early July, 1945, Drexel was asked by Colonel Robert G. Storey, chief of the Documentation Division and later Executive Trial Counsel of the American Delegation in Nuremberg, to assist him in gathering evidence in Europe. He flew to London that month where he met Justice Jackson who complimented him on his preliminary brief regarding labor. He then began his work of tracking down labor leaders who had survived the Nazis for the purpose of obtaining affidavits regarding their experiences.

Late in July, 1945, Drexel flew to Paris and began reviewing a large collection of files belonging to the defendant Alfred Rosenberg, referred to as the philosopher of the Nazi Party, who held a large number of positions and was a major player in the Party. Rosenberg had hidden his records in an abandoned castle near Bayreuth, Germany, but was observed doing so, and before long the documents were in American hands and revealing a wealth of detail regarding Nazi intentions and policies, including their plans to totally eliminate the Jews from "Greater German space." Assigned the task of uncovering evidence of aggressive war in Rosenberg's documents, Drexel quickly found detailed notes of Nazi collaboration with the Norwegian traitor Vidkun Quisling prior to the German occupation of Norway that were later used in the judgment against Rosenberg. They were also used in Norway's prosecution of Quisling, which resulted in his execution.

It was while reviewing Rosenberg's files in Paris that the extent of the Holocaust was revealed, and Drexel began realizing that the murders of the Jews, Gypsies, Slavs, and other ethnic and religious groups numbered in the millions.

When Drexel flew to Nuremberg in August, 1945, he saw below him a country utterly destroyed. He states in his book, "The large and medium-sized cities had been bombed into desolate ruins. There were unbelievable numbers of shattered buildings, jagged walls, and huge piles of rubble." Nuremberg itself seemed even more desolate with the eastern half of the city almost completely demolished. "A walk through the Old City was an experience never to be forgotten," he writes. "I recall no building that was unscathed." In noting the many decaying bodies still to be removed from under the debris, he said, "The Nuremberg Trial was held next to an area that every day reminded us of the horrors of war."

The American team arriving in Nuremberg that August was initially housed at the Grand Hotel, a facility favored by Nazi officials during the prewar Party rallies held in the city. In order to reach his fourth floor room, Drexel had to walk a wobbly wooden gangplank that traversed a large hole caused by an Allied bomb. It was not long before he visited the Palace of Justice, the huge building in which the Trial would take place. While passing through one of the offices in the Palace of Justice, Drexel spotted a poster bearing the signature of Reich Propaganda Minister Dr. Joseph Goebbels, and the declaration, "In everything that you do and do not do, that you say and keep unsaid, Remember that you are German!" Drexel removed the poster and kept it on his office desk, but added in its margin, "Captured by Lieutenant Sprecher in Nuremberg on 15 August 1945."

The first task in Nuremberg was to clean debris in order to provide office space for the members of the American team. For this purpose, Drexel supervised more than a dozen former *Waffen SS* members. He then directed the establishment of a central library for the storage of books and other documents important to the upcoming proceedings, an area of the Palace of Justice that became quite impressive in its proportions.

As preparations for the Trial grew in immensity and scope, many attorneys left Nuremberg, unable to keep up with the work load. The amount of evidence was becoming more and more difficult to stay abreast of, so Drexel suggested to his superior that a series of lectures or seminars be held after dinner in the Grand Hotel in order to keep everyone up to speed on the different assignments. He presented the second seminar on "Organizational Structure of the Nazi Party." Other lectures were presented by the likes of Thomas Dodd, later to become Executive Trial Counsel and even later United States Senator, and Justice Jackson, U. S. Chief of Counsel.

Most of the prospective defendants arrived in Nuremberg on August 12, 1945, two days before Drexel's arrival. Drexel's office on the third floor of the Palace of Justice overlooked the

219

prison courtyard which was visited daily by the defendants for their exercise. But the desire on the part of the American staff for a closer view of the prisoners resulted in a tour, something Drexel describes as "an unforgettable experience." Through peepholes, he was able to see the stark cells and view the prisoners from close range, though he found most averted their eyes from their visitors.

The September 27, 1945 issue of the *News-Wave* carried the news that Drexel's parents had recently received a letter from him informing them he had been promoted to Captain. A segment of his letter also described his office view and an incident that occurred during Hermann Goering's interrogation:

> I can look sideways out of my window here and see the jail section where our big criminals are held. Each of them parades in exercise for ten minutes each day beneath my window. One gets so he doesn't pay much attention to them. I sat in on interrogations of Goering, Keitel and Wolff the other day. When the interpreter said 'zinc' instead of 'tin,' Goering protested and I had to admit that Herman had a proper beef for once, so I interjected and cleared it up. These members of the Herrenvolk don't look so masterful when Colonel John Harlan Amen examines them.

On October 6, 1945 Drexel attended the pre-trial interrogation of the defendant Robert Ley, who had signed the order directing the destruction and take-over of the trade unions. During the interrogation, Ley stated, "I am still very proud of it," as Hitler had personally directed him to take those actions. Within days, however, Drexel had written to his parents of his displeasure with not being able to ask questions during the interrogation because of a strict separation of functions between the Interrogation Division and his Documentation Division. He felt that since he had prepared the questions for the interrogation, he was better suited to ask them due to his team's more extensive knowledge of Ley's writings.

For his assignment regarding the destruction of the labor unions, Drexel was able to locate and contact two former union leaders from whom he received first-hand accounts of their treatment at the hands of the Nazis. Both had survived imprisonment at the infamous Dachau concentration camp and from them was gathered information later used in presentations to the Tribunal. In September 1945 Drexel visited Dachau and saw for himself the conditions under which prisoners lived, and the crematoria which disposed of their corpses after they had been killed. All of his work to that point was rewarded in January 1946 when Colonel Wheeler, deputy director of the Documentation Division wrote a letter for Drexel's personal file stating his brief "reflected great credit on this Section, particularly as your brief was one of the first completed and was used as a model for other members of this Section and for other Sections in the preparation of all the trial briefs."

But much of Drexel's work regarding the defendant Ley and the labor unions came to naught when shortly after receiving his indictment, Ley committed suicide by hanging. Because Drexel had invested so much time in preparing a prosecution of Ley, this news was quite disappointing to him. Ley, "my defendant," as Drexel described him, would not sit in the dock at Nuremberg, nor would the Trial record fully expose his role in the Nazi regime.

The day following Ley's suicide, Drexel was called into the office of Colonel Robert Storey, chief of the Documentation Division and later president of the American Bar Association, and given a new assignment. He and his assistants were to develop the case on the individual responsibility of the defendant Hans Fritzsche, a man of which little was actually known. Drexel saw it as a challenge and immediately began working on the case.

Drexel wrote to his parents again on October 16, 1945 following the serving of the indictments to the prisoners, where he described some of his duties. "My last task has been to get out a list of decrees from the German Legal Register," he stated, "most of which will undoubtedly be used at the trial. It was quite a painstaking job and required more time than I had thought. I first had to get each decree assigned a document number, then get a request for translation approved, and then set up tables, year by year, with citation, short title and document number." It was painstaking work, no question, but something that had to be done if the Nuremberg Trial's legitimacy was to withstand the scrutiny of future generations.

On November 10, 1945, just ten days prior to the start of the Trial, Drexel wrote to his parents that he was attending a reception for Senator Claude Pepper, a member of the Senate Foreign Relations Committee who he described as "a good liberal whom I look forward to meeting." With this meeting began a friendship that lasted until Senator Pepper's death forty years later. At Nuremberg, Drexel met numerous times with the Senator, familiarizing him with the trial preparations. In 1949, when the State Department was wavering in its support for publication of the fifteen volumes concerning the twelve subsequent Nuremberg trials, for which Drexel had been Editor-in-Chief, Senator Pepper was instrumental in the necessary appropriations being made available.

On November 20, 1945, the most significant trial in the history of the free world began as the defendants were led into the courtroom crowded with officials of the four Tribunal nations -- England, France, Russia, and the United States -- as well as more than 80 dignitaries and 150 journalists from around the world, including such notable American journalists as William L. Shirer, Howard K. Smith, and Daniel De Luce. Drexel had been given a pass to the Visitors' Gallery by Colonel Storey, where he took his seat in the very last row. From there he carefully watched the defendants as they were led to their prearranged seats in the dock. In his book, he wrote of this time, "I can still remember that a strange emotion came over me. There, less than one hundred feet away, were gathering a score of the surviving leaders of the Hitler regime. Shortly their deeds would be exposed before the eyes and ears of the world. It seemed too good to be true." He wrote that none of the defendants showed "any brutal characteristic or any noticeable bestiality." In fact, he wrote, "Rosenberg looked a little bit like my own father, much like a typical mid-western businessman." At 10:00 A. M., the eight members of the Tribunal, two from each of the four signatory nations, entered the courtroom.

When Justice Jackson made the opening statement for the American Prosecution the next day, he described the three steps by which the Nazis took total control and power: 1) Controlling the working class; 2) Stifling the Catholic Church; and 3) Destroying the Jews. Drexel was especially proud of the fact that Jackson gave such prominence to his principal responsibility, that of controlling the working class by destroying the trade unions.

The December 20, 1945 *News-Wave* carried a letter Drexel had written to his parents regarding the first week of the Trial and another incident with Goering:

24 Nov 1945

Dearest Folks,

The first week of the trial is over. On the third day, most of the material I had worked on went in without any particular comment from defendants' lawyers. It was the first day on which evidence was introduced, so they had not quite caught their breath. Yesterday, the fourth day (second day for evidence), the defendants and the court were much more active and alert to the evidence submitted by the prosecution.

There was an amusing incident with Goering the other afternoon. I was sitting at the American prosecutors' table, listening with my earphones to the prosecutor in the German language (we have a four-way immediate-interpretation machine). Goering was taking profuse notes and in his vigor broke the lead on his pencil. I had been watching his reactions, so I noticed this, and proceeded to go from the prosecutors table to the defendant's box with a pencil and paper, gave it to a guard to hand to him. When the session was over, I was standing near the defendants' box talking to Sen. Claude Pepper. Goering was gesticulating behind my back and someone said he wanted to talk to me. When I turned, he pointed to the pencil and indicated by motion that he would like to keep the pencil with his notes. I nodded my head and the incident was over. Next day I noticed he still was using my blue pencil. Well, as Senator Pepper said, he is entitled to all the pencils and paper he needs to make his defense. He seems quite gay and vigorous, nods or shakes his head as the proof goes in, and has been rated as the most intelligent of the defendants, which prods his already big ego a good bit. He's a fearless fighter to the end, and even tho we feel him to be perhaps about the most culpable of the lot, most of us are glad to see his spunk. It will make a better trial.

Love, Son,

Drex

In his book, Drexel describes the pencil incident with Goering a bit differently, however, indicating there was a verbal exchange that occurred during the recess. Drexel had been assigned as Senator Pepper's escort during the first week of the trial. As Drexel and the Senator spoke between the prosecution table and defendants' dock, a guard approached Drexel and said, "Goering wishes to speak with you." As Drexel turned toward Goering, Goering bowed deeply and said "Danke viel mals. Danke viel mals." (Thank you very much. Thank you very much.). Drexel states that he immediately responded, "Bitte sehr. Bitte sehr." (You are quite welcome. You are quite welcome.). Apparently Senator Pepper was quite surprised by the exchange and said something like, "Well, I never expected to see anything like that! Are you allowed to speak to defendants in the dock?" Drexel replied by saying it probably was against the rules but that neither he nor the guard had thought about it at the time.

Following Jackson's opening statement, the American Prosecution began submitting evidence against "the Nazi conspirators," detailing the Party's organizational structure, how it built its military, how it planned aggression against neighboring countries, and how it occupied Austria in March. 1938. Then on November 27, 1945, a film was introduced and shown to the court that became a defining moment in the Trial. When the first concentration camps were liberated in early 1945, General Eisenhower viewed several of them and was astonished and appalled at what he saw. Besides forcing German civilians of nearby towns to see the camps for themselves, he ordered film documentation of the camps in all their horror and repulsiveness. The graphic film was shocking, even to several of the defendants. One broke into tears while another visibly shuddered when the Buchenwald crematorium was shown. Others turned their eyes away or hung their heads. The defendant Albert Speer later said that he was "all the more resolved to acknowledge a collective responsibility of the Party leadership. . ." while the defendant Wilhelm Keitel, the former Chief of the High Command of the Armed Forces, said, "When I see such things, I'm ashamed of being a German!" But he followed that statement with one accusing the SS of the atrocities that he ultimately was judged as being responsible for as well.

The Prosecution then presented its case regarding the invasions and occupations of nations, the use of concentration camps and forced labor, the persecution of the Jews and mass murders in the occupied Soviet Union, and the destruction of the Warsaw Ghetto, among other acts of oppression and exploitation. When presentations were made regarding atrocities and mass murder, Drexel often sat at the American Prosecution table, from where he could easily see the reactions of the defendants to the accusations being made. He states in his book, "As I looked at the dock I often wondered about the feelings of the defendants as these horrible revelations were made public. When now and then a defendant's gaze met mine, the defendant would quickly avert his eyes."

When Drexel had visited Warsaw, Poland, in April. 1935, he had met an American Jew who was traveling to visit his family in the Warsaw Ghetto. The man took him on several visits to the Ghetto and also showed him some of the tourist attractions of the city. He later lost track of this friend but as he learned more during the Trial about the destruction of the Warsaw Ghetto by the Nazis, Drexel "could not but know that the kind members of my friend's family had perished during the destruction of Warsaw or later upon being dispatched to the Treblinka Concentration Camp."

When the Tribunal adjourned for a ten day Christmas recess, many of the American team were suffering from fatigue and stress brought on by overwork. In an effort to raise spirits of the staff, Tribunal President Geoffrey Lawrence visited staff members from desk to desk, letting each know individually of the great work they were doing. Justice Jackson also had a nice surprise for more than 100 of his staff who did not have other plans for the recess. He arranged for Hermann Goering's former special train to take them to Berchtesgaden where Drexel and others were given a special tour of the "Eagle's Nest," Hitler's favorite mountain retreat.

Following the recess, Drexel returned to work in Nuremberg feeling the stress associated with needing to present two of the prosecution's cases before the Tribunal, that of proving the individual responsibility of the defendants Baldur von Schirach and Hans Fritzsche.

Schirach had been Hitler Youth Leader until 1940 when he was appointed Gauleiter of

222

Vienna, a position akin to governor of a territory. He was also a Reichsleiter (Reich Leader) of the Nazi Party. With Schirach indicted on two of the four counts of the Indictment, Drexel was charged with proving his guilt under the Conspiracy Count where he promoted "the accession to power of the Nazi conspirators," and the Count on Crimes against Humanity, particularly in regards to actions taken against the Jews.

Drexel addressed Schirach's power as Hitler Youth Leader, of "poisoning the minds of youth with Nazi ideology and preparing youth for aggressive war," in order to prove Schirach's absolute loyalty to Hitler. He also implicated Schirach in the deportation of tens of thousands of Jews from the Vienna region, as well as participating in the use of forced labor, through speeches he gave as Gauleiter of Vienna. Though found guilty of the Count on Crimes Against Humanity when the Judgement was handed down beginning September 30, 1946, Schirach was judged to have not participated in Hitler's plan for aggressive war as Youth Leader. He was sentenced to twenty years imprisonment in Spandau Prison in Berlin and was released in 1966.

By the time Drexel had been assigned the Fritzsche case in November 1945, numerous problems had already occurred, including errors in the Indictment. Hans Fritzsche had been head of the Radio Division of the Propaganda Ministry and was charged under three of the four counts -- Conspiracy, War Crimes, and Crimes against Humanity. He was relatively unknown to the Allies and was not high on their list of potential defendants. But the Russians, who had captured Fritzsche, presented what was called the "Fritzsche Confession," a document purported to be a summary of Fritzsche's interrogation by the Russians, and insisted on his prosecution.

The confession document was shaky at best in its validity. The conspiracy charge was weak and the confession contained nothing to prove his complicity in War Crimes or Crimes against Humanity. Drexel recommended to his superior, Colonel Wheeler, that either an emergency task force be formed to search for more evidence regarding Fritzsche or drop the War Crimes and Crimes against Humanity charges entirely. Knowing that dropping the charges would have created serious problems with the Russians, it was decided that Drexel would continue with preparations for his prosecution of Fritzsche.

Captain Drexel A. Sprecher presenting the case against Hans Fristzsche, head of the Radio Division of the Nazi Propaganda Ministry. Nuremberg War Crimes Trial, January 23, 1945.

223

Dignitaries frequently were present during Tribunal proceedings. When Drexel submitted the Fritzsche case on January 23, 1946, Secretary of War Robert P. Patterson and Lieutenant General Lucian Truscott were in attendance, causing a greater than usual stir among the court photographers. This was without doubt the most difficult of the individual cases to prosecute and upon his completion, both Colonel Storey, Executive Chief Counsel for the American Prosecution, and Sir David Maxwell-Fyfe, British Deputy Chief Prosecutor and future Lord Kilmuir, Lord Chancellor of Great Britain, congratulated Drexel on his efforts.

Following his presentation, Drexel suggested to Colonel John H. Amen, Chief of the Interrogation Division, that it might be best not to use the Fritzsche "confession" in the future. The American, British, and French teams agreed, but when the Russian Chief Prosecutor, General R. A. Rudenko, quoted from it during his cross-examination of Fritzsche, Fritzsche in a very agitated manner restated his position as to the circumstances surrounding his signing the statement.

The case against Hans Fritzsche was not strong enough in the eyes of the Tribunal and he was acquitted on all three counts. However, following the war, various documents were discovered that might have had an impact on the judgment had they been available at the time of the Trial. Reichminister Goebbels' diaries, for instance, included this entry made June 14, 1941, one week before the invasion of the Soviet Union, that would have impacted the conspiracy charge: "The imminent invasion (of the Soviet Union) is the talk of London now. Fritzsche reports to me on his efforts to keep the deception going."

As the Defense portion of the Trial got underway in 1946, Drexel was appointed Director of the Subsequent Proceedings Division for the Office, U. S. Chief of Counsel for War Crimes, a team whose duties included the accumulation of information for use in subsequent trials. When his team found and supplied a document to Thomas Dodd and Sir David Maxwell-Fyfe regarding the defendant Joachim von Ribbentrop's complicity in the horrific treatment of the Jews, it played a role in the French prosecutor's cross-examination of Ribbentrop and the eventual judgment that he had been an important part of Hitler's "final solution" regarding the Jews.

On September 30 - October 1, 1946, the Tribunal's final judgment regarding the criminality of 22 individuals and seven organizations was read. A day or two prior to this, Justice Jackson's office gave special passes to about a dozen staff members, including Drexel, inviting them to sit with him at the American Prosecution table during the reading of the Judgment. In his book, Drexel wrote of this opportunity, "As I joined this group I recalled where I had sat in the Courtroom on the opening day of the Trial -- near the back of the Visitors' Gallery."

Drexel's role in the twelve subsequent trials that brought to justice another 199 officials of the Nazi regime continued to grow with time. Following his Subsequent Proceedings Division appointment in 1946, he was also named Director of the Economics Division. In 1946, Drexel was discharged from the United States Army with the rank of Captain, but remained with the Office, U. S. Chief of Counsel for War Crimes as a civilian attorney. In 1947, Drexel served as Director of the I. G. Farben Trial Team. And little did he realize when he first arrived in Nuremberg in 1945 that nearly four years later, in April 1949, he would speak the last words of the Prosecution in the Nuremberg War Crimes Trials as Deputy Chief Counsel in the Ministries Case.

After serving as Director of the Publications Division from 1948-49, Drexel was employed by the War Crimes Branch, The Judge Advocate General, United States Army, when he was named Editor-in-Chief of the 15 official volumes entitled *Trials of War Criminals Before the Nuremberg Military Tribunals*, which detailed the 12 trials that followed the International Military Tribunal Trial. Following this, his career took him into both private and public endeavors. He entered private legal practice for several years, as well as owning and operating construction and development concerns. He served as counsel to the Salary Stabilization Board and as assistant administrator of the Small Defense Plants Administration. He served as Deputy Chairman of the Democratic National Committee from 1957-60 and as Associate Counsel for the Small Business Committee of the U. S. House of Representatives from 1956-57. He has been involved in management training and consulting as well as being Associate Professorial Lecturer at George Washington University, Washington, D. C.

His most significant contribution, however, may well prove to be his ten year journey writing *Inside the Nuremberg Trial -- A Prosecutor's Comprehensive Account*. Many men from Independence, when called into the service during World War II, found themselves in combat overseas. Drexel Sprecher, on the other hand, who believes that "so much in life is chance," was in the right place at the right time, and helped bring to justice those responsible for a most horrible period of the Twentieth Century.

While in Nuremberg in 1948, Drexel met his present wife of over 50 years, Virginia Lee Sprecher, and they now live in Chevy Chase, Maryland. His book, *Inside the Nuremberg Trial: A Prosecutor's Comprehensive Account*, was selected by CHOICE magazine as one of the year's Outstanding Academic Titles in October 1999.

Sources: Drexel Sprecher letter; Independence News-Wave; Book (Sprecher)

EDMUND A. SUCHLA
UNITED STATES NAVY

The following edited narrative was prepared following an interview with Edmund Suchla at his home in Independence on August 4, 1998.

I enlisted in the Navy on September 10, 1942 in Milwaukee and entered active duty that same day. First I tried to join the Army but they wouldn't take me because of a minor medical problem. Doc Polzer in Independence said, "Try the Navy," so I did, though I thought the Navy's standards were higher than the Army's. But the Navy said, "We'll fix you up to meet our standards," so I went to the Navy Hospital at Great Lakes Naval Station in Chicago for surgery. After one week there I was discharged, walked out of the hospital door, and right into basic training at Great Lakes. I was in the chow line at Navy Pier one day when I heard a familiar voice say, "Do you want some potatoes?" It was Ray Halama.

The crew of *Little Jo*. Edmund Suchla is in the front row, far right.

Following basic, I was shipped out to Whidbey Island, Washington, for gunnery training. Then from there I went to San Diego, California, where I was assigned to Bomb Squadron 108, or VB-108, which consisted of B-24 Liberators. We flew to Kaneohe Air Base on Oahu of the Hawaiian Islands where we stayed a couple weeks and underwent daily training flights. We then moved on to a base on a small island called Nukufetau,[1] and from there to the Marshall and Gilbert Islands. There we flew missions about every three days or so. We flew what was called "the pie," which was a triangle of three B-24's.

From the Marshall's I went home on a ten day leave. When I returned, we went to the big base on the Marianas. Tinian was our main base but we also spent some time on Saipan, Guam, and Iwo Jima. On Iwo I saw one of our fighters land and tear off its landing gear, then hit a solid wall at the end of the runway. I don't know how the pilot came out of it.

I was a waist gunner in Crew 8 and our Liberator was number 09, named *Little Jo*. We were on a photo mission one day when we were hit by Jap fighters. The sun was blinding me and I never saw the fighter coming in until it turned and I saw his red ball. Our fuel tanks were pretty shot up. We made it back to base okay, but had to take the plane to Hawaii for repairs. We had a week off there during that time, then returned to the Marianas.

Sometimes we flew "fighter cover," believe it or not. Our fighters didn't have enough range to escort the bombers all the way to target, so sometimes B-24's flew cover. This was done especially for photo missions over enemy territory.

During my second tour, the squadon was sent to the Solomon Islands and New Guinea. On the way, we stopped over on Tinian and I remember seeing an Army plane parked on the runway being worked on. It was the *Enola Gay*. From the Solomons we flew a modified B-24 that had a single tail, twin top turrents, and a bigger engine.

One time our plane was being worked by the ground crew and whenever this happened, one of the crew had to stand guard. I was on guard and couldn't go when the rest of my crew was sent out on a mission with another plane. They were shot down but all of them were picked up okay.

When the war ended, we eventually flew our planes home, arriving at a base somewhere in California. We stayed there overnight, then went downtown where we were checked out and I boarded a train to Minneapolis. I was discharged from the Navy on October 5, 1945 as an Aviation Machinist's Mate, 1st Class.

The Navy's VB-108 arrived in the Pacific in 1943, in time for the Gilbert Islands campaign. Led by daring pilots, the squadron became airborne in weather that grounded other planes, and perfected methods of flying at water and tree level, downwind, at top speed, and under enemy detection height. They then pulled up sharply to drop their bombs by eyesight from 150 feet. These bombing runs and their strafing missions took the Japanese by surprise as the Liberators were on target and gone often before the Japanese could react. When Ed was asked about this via telephone, he simply said, "We had some crazy pilots and it was scary flying with them sometimes."

According to a document provided by Ed's son, Allen, Edmund Suchla was awarded five Air Medals during his two tours of duty with VB-108. This decoration is for meritorious achievement while in flight, during combat or noncombat, for single acts or for continuous operations against an armed enemy. Additionally, the same document indicates he also was awarded the Distinguished Flying Cross, a decoration given to U. S. military personnel who show heroism or extraordinary achievement while participating in aerial flight.

---

[1] Nukufetau is in the Ellice Islands group, southeast of the Gilbert Islands.

Edmund Suchla, right, being
decorated with an Air Medal.

Sources: Allen Suchla, son; Book (Johnsen)

A Quote From History. . .

"I went over the side into the water. . ."
    Ben Gasatis
    United States Navy
    From a letter home describing the torpedoing of his
      ship, the *U. S. S. Chicago*, on March 2, 1943.

CLARENCE SURA
UNITED STATES NAVY

Clarence Sura enlisted in the United States Navy on August 6, 1935 and attended basic training at Great Lakes Naval Training Station, Illinois. For two full enlistments, Clarence served aboard the aircraft carrier *U. S. S. Saratoga* (CV-3). He re-enlisted a second time in September 1940 and was assigned duty aboard the heavy cruiser *U. S. S. San Francisco* (CA-38). The *San Francisco* was destined to become one of the most storied American warships of World War II as it participated in many major naval engagements of the war.

The *U. S. S. San Francisco* was commissioned on February 10, 1934 at the Mare Island Navy Yard, Vallejo, California. She was 588 feet long and carried a crew of 708 officers and men. Originally armed with nine 8-inch and eight 5-inch guns, as well as eight .50-caliber machine guns, she was additionally fitted with four 3-inch guns while at the Puget Sound Navy Yard, Washington, during the summer of 1940. It was while she was there that Clarence joined her crew. After work was completed at Puget Sound, *San Francisco* made several trips between the west coast of the United States and Hawaii between September 1940 and October 11, 1941, upon which time she entered the Pearl Harbor Navy Yard for an overhaul that was scheduled to be completed by December 25, 1941.

In dry dock at Pearl Harbor, work began on scraping and cleaning her heavily fouled bottom and completely dismantling and overhauling her engineering plant. During this time, the ammunition for her larger guns was removed and stored on land and her machine guns were overhauled. It was while she was in this location and condition, and with most of her crew ashore, that *San Francisco* began the morning of December 7, 1941.

The few men aboard her did their best with light machine guns and small arms, the only weapons operational, when the Japanese attacked Pearl Harbor. It was later learned that a Japanese two-man submarine had previously entered the harbor and mapped the American ships docked there, including what they believed to be the *San Francisco*. Though it has never been determined whether this information was reported to the Japanese fleet, the ship misidentified as the *San Francisco* by the sub's crew did appear to be heavily targeted by the Japanese planes. Fortunately for *San Francisco*, being in dry dock drew no attention from them as no damage was suffered during their attack.

With fear of another attack on Pearl rampant, *San Francisco* sailed one week later despite most repair plans not being completed. On December 16, 1941 she joined Task Force 16 and was sent to relieve the embattled American force on Wake Island. But when word was received that Wake had fallen, the task force instead proceeded to Midway Island, from where it then returned to Pearl.

In early April 1942 the editor of the *News-Wave*, Glenn Kirkpatrick, received a letter from Clarence in which he enclosed "the sum of two dollars for another year's subscription to the *News-Wave* which I enjoy very much." His letter then offered a brief description of the action he had seen since the morning of December 7, 1941:

> I was in the midst of the attack at Pearl Harbor on December 7, as the ship I now serve on was one of the unfortunate to be present, but no harm befell us. The attack was very unexpected and sudden, but the reaction of the sailors was amazing. No noise or confusion, but going to their posts quietly with a grim determination that bodes evil for the enemy.
>
> It was a pleasure and a privilege to be one of the many serving our country that morning. Since that December morning we have had another brush with the enemy, being attacked by 18 Japanese bombers which we repulsed by shooting 16 planes, with a possible 17th, with the loss of only two of our planes and one pilot, and no damage to any of the ships engaged. Unable to divulge place or time of attack.

Undoubtedly, the time of the encounter with the Japanese that he was unable to divulge was February 8, 1942, and the place was in the area of the Solomon Islands. The *San Francisco*, under the command of Captain Daniel J. Callaghan, was then part of Cruiser Division 6, Task Force 11, which had sailed for the Solomons in order to attack the large Japanese base at Rabaul and hopefully slow their buildup for a push on New Guinea. By this time, the Philippine Islands had been written off, and instead it was decided a stand would to be made in the area of New Guinea and New Britain. Task Force 11 was 225 miles from Rabaul when it was discovered by Japanese aircraft, however, and soon attacked. The Japanese fighters and bombers were met by aircraft from the *U. S. S. Lexington* (CV-2) led by naval aviator Lieutenant Commander John Thatch, who would later win fame during the "Battle of Midway." When the skies were finally cleared of enemy planes, the Americans had shot down at least 16 two-engine bombers plus two flying boats, with one bomber crashing only 75 yards behind *Lexington*. But with surprise lost in

228

regards to raiding Rabaul, the task force retired to safer waters rather than risk losing more of its remaining warships.

On April 22, 1942. *San Francisco* escorted a convoy to her namesake, San Francisco, California, and one month later escorted another convoy from the west coast carrying the 37th Division to the southwest Pacific. She was back at Pearl on June 29, 1942, and then escorted a convoy to the Fiji Islands from where she rendezvoused with the Solomon Islands Expeditionary Force which was scheduled to land troops on Guadalcanal, marking the first American offensive action in the Pacific Theater. As flagship of Rear Admiral Norman Scott, she covered Operation Watchtower at Guadalcanal throughout August. 1942. She returned to New Caledonia for refueling and adding other provisions and then sailed back to Guadalcanal on September 8, 1942, where she covered reinforcements landing on the island. Upon her arrival, *San Francisco*'s Task Force 18 joined Task Force 17, led by the carrier *U. S. S. Hornet* (CV-8), and Task Force 61, both of which were already in covering operations. On September 15, 1942, the carrier *U. S. S. Wasp* (CV-7) was torpedoed. As *San Francisco* and the cruiser *U. S. S. Salt Lake City* (CA-25) made preparations for towing *Wasp*, her fires went out of control. Survivors of the *Wasp* were transferred to destroyers and *Wasp* was torpedoed and sunk by the destroyer *U. S. S. Lansdowne* (DD-486) to prevent her from falling into enemy hands.

On September 23, 1942. *San Francisco* and five other cruisers and the destroyers of Destroyer Squadron 12 were designated as Task Force 64 under the command of Rear Admiral Scott aboard *San Francisco*. Early in October, 1942 the Navy learned of a Japanese naval force heading for Guadalcanal and Task Force 64 was sent to stop it. Near midnight of October 11, 1942, radar spotted the Japanese ships and minutes later the "Battle of Esperance" began. Within 30 minutes the fighting was over with the Japanese withdrawing after losing a cruiser and destroyer. Two American cruisers and two destroyers had been damaged with destroyer *U. S. S. Duncan* (DD-485) later sinking. But in this action, the American Navy had made an impression upon the Japanese -- it would and could stand up to them.

San Francisco resumed its support of the Guadalcanal operation on October 15, 1942. before departing with an escort for Espiritu Santo on October 20. That night, enemy submarines fired several torpedoes at the ships, one of which damaged the cruiser *U. S. S. Chester* (CA-27).

After Rear Admiral Scott transferred his flag to the cruiser *U. S. S. Atlanta* (CL-51) on October 28, 1942, newly promoted Rear Admiral Daniel Callaghan, *San Francisco*'s commanding officer at Pearl Harbor, returned and raised his flag as commander of Task Force 65. His ships then proceeded to again escort transports to Guadalcanal.

In late morning of November 10, 1942, Task Force 65 was spotted and shadowed by a Japanese reconnaissance aircraft, and two days later, following departure from the Guadalcanal area, was attacked by 21 Japanese planes. Shortly after 2:00 P. M., a Japanese plane dropped a torpedo which narrowly missed *San Francisco*. The enemy plane, however, damaged by anti-aircraft fire, then crashed into her control structure, killing 15 and wounding 29, with one sailor missing. Control aft, a command post aboard the ship, was also destroyed along with three 20-mm gun emplacements. One of its antiaircraft and radar centers was put out of commission, as well.

As wounded sailors were being transferred to a transport, an enemy naval force was reported approaching. The transports were quickly escorted out of the area and a battle force consisting of *San Francisco*, another heavy cruiser, three light cruisers, and eight destroyers returned to intercept the Japanese. The enemy force was spotted by radar at 1:25 A. M. on November 13, 1942, and twenty minutes later, *San Francisco* opened fire on a Japanese cruiser and destroyer while two Japanese battleships began pounding her. Two of *San Francisco*'s 5-inch gun batteries were put out of commission almost immediately, but she continued her fight -- a fight which soon became one for survival -- with only her main 5-inch battery of guns operational. Shortly after, the navigation bridge received a direct hit, killing or badly wounding all but one of the officers, including killing Rear Admiral Callaghan and *San Francisco's* Captain Cassin Young, a Wisconsin native.[1]

With the bridge destroyed and steering and engine control out of commission, the ship's control was given to Battle Two, its secondary control center. But almost immediately, Battle Two was put out of commission by a direct hit, and control of the ship was again lost. The conning tower then assumed control of the ship but when it, too, was hit, steering and engine control were lost for a third time. By now all communications aboard *San Francisco* were out, but for some reason, the Japanese at this point stopped firing at her. Her crew again gained control, and she was able to limp away.

Besides Callaghan and Young, 25 other men had been killed, 105 wounded, and seven were missing of whom three were later rescued. Though *San Francisco* had been hit 45 times by Japanese guns, the structural damage she received did not jeopardize her remaining afloat.

At around 10:00 A. M., medical personnel from the cruiser *U. S. S. Juneau* (CL-52) transferred aboard *San Francisco* to help treat the many wounded. An hour later, a torpedo was sighted, which *San Francisco* was able to avoid. However, it slammed into the nearby *Juneau*, causing a tremendous explosion which literally disintegrated the ship. When the smoke cleared, nothing was left of *Juneau*. Because of the condition of the ships in the group, and because the *Juneau* had been so utterly destroyed, the belief was no one could have possibly survived, so the remaining ships continued on their way to Espirtu Santo. Initially, as many as 120 sailors may have survived the blast, but by the time they were located and rescued, only 10 men of the *U. S. S. Juneau* remained. Aboard the ship had been the five Sullivan brothers of Iowa who had insisted upon serving together, and all five were lost.

For her gallantry during the "Battle of Guadalcanal," during which she bravely took on overwhelming Japanese forces, the *San Francisco* was awarded the Presidential Unit Citation, the highest recognition a naval unit can receive during battle. On December 11, 1942 she reached San Francisco, California, under her own power where repairs were made during the next two-and-a-half months.

She departed San Francisco once again on February 26, 1943 escorting a convoy to Noumea, New Caledonia. From there she sailed to Hawaii and then to the Aleutian Islands where she operated out of Adak for four-and-a-half months patrolling the region and aiding in the assault of Attu and Kiska in May and July 1943, respectively.

Early October 1943, found *San Francisco* arriving off Wake Island from Pearl Harbor where she conducted two raids on Japanese positions there. She returned to Pearl once again before sailing to participate in the invasions of Makin and Betis Islands. Then, on October 26, 1943, she headed to the Marshall Islands to aid in attacking the Japanese in the Kwajalein area as part of Task Group 50.1.[2] On December 4, 1943, Japanese aircraft attacked Task Group 50.1 and, though not struck by bombs or torpedoes, *San Francisco* suffered one killed and 22 wounded from strafing. Later that night, the carrier *Lexington* was torpedoed and the ships broke off and headed to Pearl Harbor.

With Task Force 52 on January 22, 1944, *San Francisco* returned to the Marshall Islands and sortied against Japanese positions in the Kwajalein area once again. This continued until February 8, 1944, when she sailed to Majuro to join the powerful fast carrier Task Force 58. On February 16, 1944 she screened the carriers as they launched aircraft against the huge Japanese base at Truk. Then, after escorting the damaged carrier *U. S. S. Intrepid* (CV-11) out of the area, *San Francisco* sailed for Hawaii with Task Group 58.2 on February 25, 1944.

---

[1] As captain of the *U. S. S. Vestal* during the attack on Pearl Harbor, Captain Young took personal command of an anti-aircraft gun. After being blown overboard by the explosion on the *U. S. S. Arizona*, he swam back to his ship and moved it safely away from the battleship. For his actions on December 7, 1941, Captain Cassin Young was awarded the Congressional Medal of Honor.

[2] A Task Group is a detachment of ships from a Task Force.

Following hasty refueling and resupply operations at Pearl, Task Group 58.2 quickly departed to the Western Carolines where its carrier aircraft hit enemy positions there on March 30 and April 1, 1944. Task Group 58.2 next went to New Guinea to support the Hollandia landing, then returned to the Carolines for another raid on Truk. Following this operation, *San Francisco* was detached with eight other cruisers for a raid on Satawan before rejoining Task Group 58.2 in the Marshalls in May 1944.

In the May 25, 1944. edition of the *News-Wave*, editor Kirkpatrick announced that Clarence Sura, Chief Watertender aboard the *U. S. S. San Francisco*, had again renewed his subscription. Kirkpatrick reported, "He says he has seen action in various parts of the Pacific, and has been in some tight and exciting spots, but (is) still up and around."

On June 10, 1944. *San Francisco* left Majuro with Task Group 53.15, the bombardment group for the invasion of the Marianas Islands. Beginning June 14, 1944, she fired on Tinian and then supported the landings on Saipan. Two days later she began shelling Guam but returned to Saipan when suspicion of an approaching Japanese force arose.

As suspicion grew into reality, the ships of Task Group 53.15 quickly positioned themselves between the Americans on Saipan and the Japanese naval vessels. In their attack, the enemy planes dropped bombs and torpedoes at the American ships, once straddling the *San Francisco* with bombs, but by 2:30 P. M. they had broken off their attack. *San Francisco* chased the Japanese force for a day before returning to the Saipan area to shield the transports and bombard Guam in preparation for the upcoming landing there. Following the assault of Guam, she supported Marine operations on the island until July 30, 1944, when she left the area bound for San Francisco via Eniwetok and Pearl for a much needed overhaul. She arrived in San Francisco to much fanfare on August 16, 1944, having traveled 120,000 miles since February 23, 1943, despite an increasing need for repair and overhaul. While there, she was awarded a second Presidential Unit Citation in recognition of her recent gallantry in action.

Following the *San Francisco's* arrival back in the States, Petty Officer and Chief Watertender Clarence Sura arrived in Independence for a 21-day stay with his mother. The *U. S. S. San Francisco* continued its historic journey through World War II in the Pacific on October 31,1944, next participating in actions on Luzon, Philippine Islands. She then rode out a typhoon, struck Japanese positions on Formosa, chased enemy ships in the South China Sea, and attacked positions in Indo-China. She spent considerable time in support of operations in the Ryukyus Islands, especially in the invasion of Okinawa. She was sailing toward the Philippines in mid-August 1945. when word reached her that Japan had surrendered. By then, the *U. S. S. San Francisco* had earned 17 battle stars.

But the *San Francisco* completed its tour of duty without Clarence, as he was next assigned to the new warship *U. S. S. Vella Gulf* (CVE-111), a 557-foot long escort carrier carrying a crew of 1,066 officers and men and 34 aircraft that had just been commissioned at Tacoma, Washington, on April 9, 1945. *Vella Gulf* arrived in San Diego, California, on May 4, 1945, where she received her Marine air group and conducted a shakedown cruise along the southern California coast. She then departed for Hawaii on June 17, 1945, arriving on June 25, where she conducted further training exercises in anticipation of combat.

Upon leaving Hawaii on July 9, 1945, *Vella Gulf* sailed to Eniwetok and then Guam where she launched her first air strikes against Rota and Pagan Islands. On August 6, 1945, she headed for Okinawa where, upon arrival on August 10, her crew learned of the Japanese surrender negotiations that were taking place. Many ships at anchor in Buckner Bay set off pyrotechnics in celebration and probable relief that an invasion of the Japanese homeland was not necessary.

It was in Buckner Bay where Clarence met with his youngest brother, Clifford, for the first time in nine years. His letter to his mother regarding this encounter was published in the *News-Wave* on August 23, 1945 along with a letter from Clifford, who described seeing his brother, Clarence (see Clifford's biography). Both expressed great joy in being reunited with his brother after so many years:

Dear Mother,

As I have a little spare time I will jot down a few lines to let you know I'm all right and hope that this finds you well and happy.

Lately we have had more good news: that Russia declared war against Japan, which I have no doubt but what it will help shorten this war a great deal.

Perhaps the best news is that after nine years I saw my brother, Cliff, for I have been on the trail since May and as we pushed westward and stopped along the island ports I kept a watchful eye for his ship. Well, yesterday, Friday, August 10, as we were in port, I checked with a signalman to see if his ship was in port. It was. I sent a message to him but he was already aboard my ship and it sure was great to see him after so many years.

He stayed aboard several hours and had dinner and we enjoyed a swell visit; talked over many things. He is not as tall or husky as I am, but is very tan and a little bald, but all in all he looks to be in the best of health.

As we won't be in this port where he is, I hope we can meet again and have a longer visit.

It was a swell visit and I was glad to see him after all these years. "Cap" sent you his love.

Your loving son,
Clarence

When *Vella Gulf* arrived back at Guam on August 15, 1945, her crew learned of the formal surrender of Japan. She then proceeded to Japan to participate in the initial occupation of the home islands, entering Tokyo Bay on September 10, 1945. She left Japanese waters on September 21, 1945, picked up 650 men at Okinawa for transport home and, after a short stop at Pearl Harbor, arrived in San Francisco on October 14, 1945. She then operated as a training ship for escort carrier personnel in Puget Sound through March, 1946.

It has not been determined how long Clarence remained in the United States Navy following the war. He had, however, seen and experienced as much as any serviceman from Independence and had the honor of serving aboard one of the greatest warships in the history of the United States Navy.

Source: Independence News-Wave; Internet

A Quote From History...

"We argue almost continually with these Texans about which is the best of the two states. I've seen pictures of the Texas girls and I still prefer Wisconsin."
  Vilas Briggs
  United States Marines
  From a letter home, June 1943

DOMINIC SURA
UNITED STATES ARMY

The following edited narrative was written following an interview with Dominic Sura at his home in Independence on August 3, 1998.

I went to Milwaukee for my physical examination for the Army. On September 2, 1942 I was officially inducted, after which I entered active duty at Fort Sheridan, Illinois. From there I traveled by train to Camp McQuaide, California, for two months of basic training. While there I met up with Art Kulig.

From Camp McQuaide I went to Fort Jackson near Columbia, South Carolina, for one or two months of infantry training. I was ready to ship out to Africa but my orders were changed and instead I was sent to Sandy Hook, New Jersey, where I was stationed with the big guns guarding New York City. While there we were given a one- or two-day pass one day, and then were told to get ready to move again. This time we went by train to Seattle, Washington, where we stayed for a couple weeks.

From Seattle, we were taken to Kodiak Island off Alaska. We were there for only a short while before traveling by boat to our station on little Shemya Island.[1]

We arrived on Kodiak sometime in late January 1944. I remember very well going out for a walk one Sunday -- I always carried a rifle when walking because of the big bears on the island. Well, on that Sunday one of those bears came after us and I had to shoot him! It wasn't much fun.

I put five bullets into him and he kept coming after us! He probably thought we were trespassing on his fishing territory.

On Shemya, I manned both 50-caliber machine gun and 90-mm gun positions. Those 90's were quite the gun! From the Shemya airfield, bombers were sent on missions against the Japanese on Kiska Island and also west to some of the Kurile Islands of Japan. The Japs would follow the bombers back and we were there to protect them. Sometimes the American planes would crash near us. If they could make land they were usually okay, but if they crashed in the water, the water would often tear them apart. The sea always seemed to be very rough.

When we first got to Shemya, we put up quonset huts that served as our quarters and operations. In summer it was often very foggy and in winter it was usually very windy. Sometimes it was so windy we had to walk leaning into the wind. If the wind let up suddenly, you would fall right over on your face! It wasn't really cold and we had good

---

[1] Shemya Island is approximately 30 miles east-southeast of Attu Island, at the western end of the Aleutian Islands. The Japanese had actually invaded Kiska and Attu Islands in the Aleutians on June 3, 1942. After American forces recaptured Attu by May 29, 1943, an airfield was established on Shemya Island in order to launch air attacks against the heavily fortified Japanese base on Kiska. It was on Shemya where Dominic was stationed from late January 1944 through August 14, 1945.

clothes to protect us, but it wasn't a very nice place altogether.

I was supposed to take over a 50-caliber machine gun at one point when I also received a furlough to Prince Rupert, British Columbia. It was on that day that Japan surrendered. I left the Aleutians on August 14, 1945. and arrived back in the States on August 19, 1945. On January 1, 1946. I received my discharge at Camp McCoy, Wisconsin. By then I had the American Theater Service Medal, Asiatic-Pacific Theater Service Medal, Good Conduct Medal, and three Overseas Service Bars.

Source: Book (Garfield)

HENRY J. SURA
UNITED STATES ARMY

Henry Sura was inducted into the United States Army on June 17, 1942 and entered active service on June 29, 1942. at Fort Sheridan, Illinois. While in basic training, he qualified as an M-1 Rifle Marksman. He then was assigned to Company F, 351st Engineers General Service Regiment, whose first assignment was to construct a combat range at Fort Lewis, Washington.

When this assignment was completed, Henry and the 351st Engineers left the New York Port of Embarkation on July 17, 1943 and began arriving in England on July 27, 1943. While in England, the 351st Engineers was first given the task of constructing an advance repair depot for the Eighth Air Force at Walton. Following completion of this duty, it next was assigned the building of Supreme Allied Headquarters for General Eisenhower. During this time, the engineers themselves often had to occupy the air raid shelters they had constructed as the German air offensive over England was in full swing. With General Eisenhower moved in, Henry's unit next underwent training for three months at Port Cawl, Wales.

The 351st Engineers found itself crossing the English Channel and landing in France in August 1944. There they built hospitals and repaired railroads, bridges, and roads in the areas of Redon, Etampes, and Fontainbleau, France. In September 1944 the 351st moved into Paris where it continued its work in the same building and repair capacity.

In early December 1944. Henry's sister, Veronica, received a parcel from him in which she found a pair of French wooden slippers. In a note, he asked, "Do those shoes require a ration stamp?"

During the German Ardennes counteroffensive that began December 16, 1944, the 351st Engineers was given four hours notice and then rushed 250 miles to Luxembourg where it was attached to the 28th Infantry Division as an infantry unit for about a month. As the bulge collapsed and the Germans were being pushed back, it returned to Paris where it continued with its previous duties. The Regiment later moved to an area near Reims, France, where it helped construct the Assembly Area Command camps from which men were processed for their return to the United States.

During the normal operations of the Regiment, Henry carried out duties as a carpenter, participating in the Northern France, Rhineland, and Ardennes-Alsace campaigns during his tour in the European Theater of Operations. Following the war's end in Europe, Henry left the continent on August 5, 1945 and arrived at Camp Shanks, New York, on August 12, 1945.

Henry had earned the European-African-Middle Eastern Theater Service Medal, three overseas service bars, and Good Conduct Medal. He was separated from the Army with the rank of Technician Fourth Grade at the Camp McCoy, Wisconsin, Separation Center on October 16, 1945.

Sources: Dominic Sura, brother; Independence News-Wave; Book (Stanton)

LAWRENCE L. SURA
UNITED STATES ARMY

Lawrence Sura entered the United States Army on October 27, 1942, He was immediately sent to Camp White in Medford, Oregon, where the 91st Infantry Division[1] had been activated only two months earlier, for basic training. Following basic, Lawrence and the 91st Infantry participated in the IV Corps No. 1 Oregon Maneuvers in September 1943, upon completion of which it transferred on November 2, 1943 to Camp Adair near Corvallis, Oregon. Lawrence then was sent to the Yakima Artillery Range located at the Yakima Army Air Base, Yakima, Washington, for additional artillery-related training while the rest of the Division prepared for overseas shipment to the European Theater of Operations.

The 91st Infantry Division began staging at Camp Patrick Henry, Virginia, on March 30, 1944 and commenced departing the Hampton Roads Port of Embarkation on April 14, 1944 for North Africa. Lawrence, a machine gunner with the 346th Field Artillery Battalion's Service Battery, departed Hampton Roads on April 21, 1944, and upon arrival in North Africa began intensive amphibious training with his unit at Arzew Beach.

Lawrence's 346th Field Artillery Battalion landed at Anzio on May 27, 1944, and once the entire Division was ashore, a northward move was made so its infantry regiments could reinforce the attacks of other divisions. On July 13, 1944, the 91st Infantry Division initiated an attack of its own for the first time toward the Arno River. Its regiments quickly took several cities, including Ponsacco, Capannoli, Livorno, and Pisa, and on July 21-22, 1944, the Division found itself at the Arno River at Pontedera, Italy. After clearing that area of the enemy, the 91st Infantry was relieved on August 18, 1944 to undergo additional training near Certaldo, Italy.

On September 12, 1944 the 91st Infantry Division entered combat again as it attacked Mount Calvi, Monticelli, and Altuzzo, where enemy defenses marked the *Gothic Line*. The 346th Field Artillery Battalion, firing in support of the 362nd Infantry Regiment throughout its Italian campaign, aided in the taking of Mount Calvi, the Futa Pass, and St. Lucia by September 21, 1944. On October 14, 1944 Livergnano fell to the Division, after which the Division was relieved for rehabilitation. During its first five months in Italy, the 346th Field Artillery Battery had fired 126,000 shells from its 105-mm howitzers. In the assault of Futa Pass, 4,500 shells per day were fired.

---

[1] The 91st Infantry Division, known as "Powder River," suffered 1,400 killed and 6,748 wounded, of which 175 died, during its three campaigns in Italy.

The 91st Infantry Division relieved the 34th Infantry Division on February 13, 1945 in the Idice Valley area, from where it was later relieved itself on March 20,1945 in order to prepare for a new assault against the Germans. This attack began on April 5, 1945 in the 34th Infantry Division zone and progressed rapidly along Highway 65. Again, numerous pockets of resistance in cities and mountains were reduced and by April 24, 1945 the 91st Infantry found itself along the Po River at Sermide, Italy. Moving northeast, it then took Cerea and Legnano the next day, crossed the Brenta River on April 29, 1945, and found itself north of Venice on April 30. Three days later, all German forces in Italy surrendered.

Leaving Italy for home in late August, 1945, the bulk of the 91st Infantry Division arrived on September 10, 1945 at the Hampton Roads Port of Embarkation, but Lawrence and the 346th Field Artillery Battalion instead landed on that same date at the Boston Port of Embarkation . The Battalion then traveled to Camp Rucker, Alabama, where it was inactivated on September 15, 1945. Lawrence had participated in the Rome-Arno, North Apennines, and Po Valley campaigns, allowing him to wear three battle stars on his European-African-Middle Eastern Service Ribbon. He also earned two overseas bars, the American Theater Service Medal, and Good Conduct Medal. Additionally, the 346th Field Artillery Battalion's Service Battery was awarded the Meritorious Service Unit Plaque for its outstanding service and performance of duty while in combat in Italy.

No photo.
Source: Independence News-Wave; Book (Stanton)

LEONARD SURA
UNITED STATES ARMY

Leonard was inducted into the United States Army on August 26, 1942. He received his basic training at Camp Wheeler, Georgia, but also was stationed and trained at Fort Sheridan, Illinois; Camp Butner, North Carolina; and Camp Stoneman, California.

He left for overseas duty in the Southwest Pacific on January 23, 1943 and spent several days in New Zealand before traveling to Sydney, Australia, where he joined the 32nd Infantry Division[1] at Camp Cable. The 32nd Infantry had already participated in heavy fighting on New Guinea prior to Len's attachment to the Division and was then back in Australia for rehabilitation and additional training. The 32nd Infantry's efforts on New Guinea prevented the Japanese from taking control of the major island, from which an attack on Australia would have been their

1 The 32nd Infantry Division, the famed "Red Arrow Division" originally consisting of Wisconsin and Michigan National Guard units, lost 1,613 killed and 5,627 wounded, of which 372 died of their wounds, during its three Pacific Theater campaigns of World War II.

236

next logical step.

Following amphibious training at Newcastle, Australia, Leonard departed for Milne Bay, New Guinea, where the Allies had established a large base in anticipation of another major campaign, this time to drive the Japanese entirely from the island. As a member of a mortar unit, Leonard landed at Aitape, New Guinea, either with the 127th Infantry Regiment's initial assault on April 23, 1944, or with the reinforcing 126th Infantry Regiment that landed on May 4, 1944. Though the American troops encountered slight initial resistance, by June 1944 the fighting had become very bitter in the area of the Drinumor River. The area was not cleaned of enemy troops until late September 1944. On October 1, 1944 the 32nd Infantry Division left Aitape for Hollandia, New Guinea, where it immediately began preparations for the Philippine Islands campaign.

The 32nd Infantry Division landed on Leyte, Philippine Islands, on November 14, 1944, relieved the 24th Infantry Division, and began attacking toward Ormoc on November 16. Bloody battles were soon fought at places called Corkscrew Ridge and Breakneck Ridge, where the Division suffered many casualties. Following battles in the area of Limon through December, 1944, the 32nd Infantry participated in the "Battle of Kilay Ridge" from November 29-December 5, 1944, and then thwarted a Japanese counterattack along Highway 2 the night of December 13-14, 1944. On December 22, 1944 the 127th Infantry finally met up with the 1st Cavalry Division at Lonoy, effectively cutting the Japanese defenses on Leyte in half.

Landing at Lingayen Gulf on the island of Luzon, Philippines Islands, on January 27, 1945, the 32nd Infantry Division immediately began a drive towards the capital city of Manila. Ferocious battles occurred along the Villa Verde Trail for more than two weeks in February 1945 that involved numerous Japanese counterattacks. In March, battles were fought at Salacsac Pass and along the Arboredo and Ambayang Valleys. But by April 10, 1945, the Salacsac Pass was in American hands and mop-up operations had begun in the Villa Verde Trail area.

Following a few days of rest beginning June 4, 1945, the 32nd Infantry then continued with mop-up operations before relieving the 25th Infantry Division in the Sierra Madre Mountains of northern Luzon. It was clearing the region of Japanese at the time the war ended.

Leonard arrived back in the United States on October 30, 1945 wearing the Asiatic-Pacific Theater Ribbon with three battle stars, the Philippine Liberation Ribbon with one battle star, five overseas bars, the Combat Infantryman Badge, and Good Conduct Medal. At the time of his discharge from the Army at Camp McCoy, Wisconsin, he held the rank of Staff Sergeant.

Source: Independence News-Wave; Books (Stanton) (Prefer)

LEONARD L. SYLLA
UNITED STATES ARMY

Leonard Sylla was inducted into the United States Army on April 25, 1944 at Fort Sheridan, Illinois. He underwent basic training at Camp Hood, Texas, an infantry and tank destroyer replacement center, after which he was sent to Fort George G. Meade, Maryland, for overseas deployment. He shipped out on October 22, 1944 and arrived in England on November 4, 1944. From there he was assigned to Company G, 409th Infantry Regiment, 103rd Infantry Division, which had deployed to France just two weeks earlier.[1]

By the time Leonard entered the combat zone, the Division was in the Vosges Mountains and attacking in the St. Die, France, area. On December 2-4, 1944 it helped the 14th Armored

---

[1] The 103rd Infantry Division suffered 720 killed in action and 3,329 wounded, with 101 of those dying of their wounds.

Division take Selestat following vicious house-to-house fighting. It then crossed the Zintzel River at Griesbach on December 10, 1944 and crossed the Lauter River into Germany five days later.

On December 16, 1944 the Germans unleashed their Ardennes counteroffensive, which later became known to Americans as the "Battle of the Bulge." As the scope of this German attack became more apparent to the American command, the 103rd Infantry Division was sent to the Sarreguemines region of Germany, though the breakout never reached the sector. It was in this area that Leonard was reported missing in action on December 20, 1944. In fact, on that day he was wounded, for which he would later be awarded the Purple Heart.

According to the official history of the Division entitled *103rd Infantry Division: The Trail of the Cactus*, written by Harold Branton,[2] December 17, 1944 was a day of heavy clouds and falling mist during which heavy patroling took place in an effort to determine enemy positions and troop strength along the Seigfried Line, or *West Wall*, as Hitler called it. Despite the fact that the 103rd Infantry Division was out ahead of other Seventh U. S. Army units, an attack on *West Wall* fortifications had nevertheless been planned for December 18. The attack occurred on schedule and continued into the next day, December 19, 1944, when Len's Company G, along with Company B, encountered several pillboxes that were systematically blown up with 40- and 60-pound TNT satchel charges. One of these pillboxes in particular, which was steadily inflicting losses on the American units, was destroyed by Company G's platoon sergeant.

The morning of December 20, 1944, the day Leonard was wounded, the weather continued to be misty and visibility was poor throughout the area. Occasionally, snow was falling, making the scene more reminiscent of Christmas than an all-out battle. That morning, the Germans suddenly launched a counterattack that included tanks, followed by another that afternoon. In both instances, the men of the 409th Infantry Regiment held their ground and repulsed the attacks. Following these attacks, the Germans began shelling the 409th's positions with artillery and mortars, necessitating the withdrawal of small units from the trenches they had been occupying. German troops then reoccupied those trenches, and the battle for this ground continued for the rest of the day and into the night. According to Branton, "battle losses were great" that day, which included Leonard, who, as it turns out, was severely wounded and then initially listed as missing in action due to the shifting lines that day.

Nearly a month later, Leonard's parents, Mr. and Mrs. Thomas Sylla of Elk Creek, received word from the War Department that their son was missing in action. But shortly after that, they received another telegram from Washington, D. C., stating:

> Reference my telegram sixteen January and letter of eighteen January report now received states your son, Pvt. Leonard L. Sylla, was slightly wounded in action twenty December and is not missing in action as previously reported. Mail address follows direct from hospital with details.
> J. A. Ulic, Adjutant General.

While Len was hospitalized and being treated for his wounds that, according to his son, Michael, included the loss of part of a lung, his 103rd Infantry Division was moved to Reichshofen to relieve the 70th Infantry Division along the Sauer River. But it soon was withdrawn to the Moder River due to a German build-up in the area. Following heavy German attacks beginning January 22, 1945, the 103rd was pushed back past Rothbach. It then went on the offensive on March 15, 1945, driving through Reichshoffen, fighting the "Battle for Nieder Schlettenback" and the "Battle for Reisdorf" from March 18-21, 1945, mopping up west of the Rhine River, and relieving the 71st Infantry Division along the Rhine.

A subsequent offensive found the 103rd Infantry moving southeast of Stuttgart and reaching the Danube River northeast of Ulm on April 25, 1945. Following closely behind the 10th Armored Division, it took Landsberg, entered Lechbruck, and cleared Schongau by April 28, 1945. It then began negotiating for the surrender of Innsbruck, Austria, on May 2, 1945 and

---

2 Harold Branton was a replacement first lieutenant who joined Company G, 408th Infantry Regiment, the morning of December 17, 1944.

103rd INFANTRY DIVISION ATTACKS NORTHEAST IN ALSACE 10 - 24 DECEMBER 1944

Leonard Sylla. Through the gracious help of Mr. Cranston Rogers and Mr. F. A. Rogers (unrelated), both members of the 103rd Infantry Division during World War II, it has been determined where Len probably was wounded on December 20, 1944, and this is shown in the map above, published in the 103rd's official history, *103rd Infantry Division: The Trail of the Cactus*. If the reader looks along the Siegfried Line in the upper right hand quadrat of the map, the date "16 DEC" will be noted. Immediately above the "16" is a slight bulge in the 103rd's line. According to Division records in the possession of Mr. F. A. Rogers, this was the location of Len's Company G on December 20, 1944, as it was assaulting three German pillbox strongpoints on a hill along the Siegfried Line. In a telephone conversation, Mr. Rogers indicated to this writer that he remembers the incident well, and that Leonard Sylla's name appears in his battalion's "morning report" as a casualty.

accepted formal surrender of the city on May 4, 1945. Hostilities ceased for the 103rd Infantry Division on May 5, 1945 when German forces in southern Germany formally surrendered.

Leonard remained in Europe, hospitalized for as long as 11 months, until he shipped out for the United States on March 13, 1946. He arrived back in the States on March 23, 1946 and received his honorable discharge from the United States Army on March 30, 1946. Besides the Purple Heart for wounds received December 20, 1944, Leonard was awarded the Good Conduct Medal and the European-African-Middle Eastern Service Ribbon with three bronze battle stars for his participation in the Ardennes-Alsace, Rhineland, and Central Europe campaigns.

Sources: Mrs. Leonard Sylla; Michael Sylla, son; Cranston Rogers; F. A. Rogers; Books (Stanton) (Branton)

Died
on
Duty

RALPH SYLLA
UNITED STATES ARMY

Ralph Sylla, the son of Mr. and Mrs. Julius Sylla, was born on November 1, 1911 and enlisted in the United States Army on July 31, 1942. He was sent to Camp Barkeley near Abilene, Texas, which was an armored division camp and medical replacement training center. There, he was attached to the 32nd Medical Battalion. On September 25, 1942, Ralph became ill and was hospitalized in the camp where on October 17, 1942, at the age of 30, he died, becoming the first Independence resident to die while in the service during World War II.

When his parents received word of his death, they were told his body would arrive by train in Independence on October 22, 1942, so plans were made for a full military funeral at Ss. Peter and Paul's Catholic Church the next day. However, the family's pain was only heightened when Ralph's body did not arrive as scheduled. Soon after, they were informed there had been a mix-up and the body had been mistakenly returned to San Antonio, Texas. Finally, it arrived on October 28, 1942, and the funeral services were held on October 29.

The November 5, 1942 edition of the *News-Wave* carried a small "card of thanks" from the family of Ralph Sylla:

> We wish to thank everyone who in any way assisted us during our hour of sorrow, and the last rites for our son and brother, Pvt. Ralph Sylla. Especially do we thank Sura-Wiersgalla American Legion Post 186, Independence, the Rt. Rev. Msgr. L. J. Kufel, Lon F. Tubbs, and Raymond Pieterick.
> Mr/Mrs Julius Sylla and Children

No photo.
Source: Independence News-Wave

A Quote From History. . .

"He was the one who told me about a friend from Independence, Jerome Sobota. . ."
Ed J. Lyga
United States Army
From an interview, 1997, describing how an officer aboard a ship
heading to Saipan informed him of the death of one of his best friends, lost
in the torpedoeing and sinking by the Japanese of *LST-342*.

LON F. TUBBS, Jr.
UNITED STATES NAVY

The following narrative is taken from a letter received from Lon Tubbs regarding his military service during World War II.

My military experience is rather brief in comparison to some of the other guys from Independence.

I was inducted into the United States Navy in August 1944. I went through boot camp in San Diego where we lived since coming out to California in 1939. I was stationed at the North Island Naval Air Station, across the bay from San Diego. At the Naval Air Station, I was assigned to the fire department and was taught how to drive and work the controls on the Navy's first carbon dioxide remote controlled truck, which was used in responding to plane crashes. I was also promoted to Petty Officer 1st Class, as an aviation metalsmith. Having worked at Consolidated Aircraft, I had gained some knowledge of metals used in aircraft and was able to pass the tests required to get the Petty Officer's classification.

I received my honorable discharge in November 1945, the same day that Romelle Schneider Roosevelt gave birth to her first son, Jim.[1] I was eligible for early discharge because at that time we had three children, so I decided to get out of the Navy at that time.

---

[1] Romelle Schneider Roosevelt, sister of Lon's wife, Ruth Schneider Tubbs, and George Schneider, whose story can be found elsewhere in this document, was a nurse at the Mayo Clinic in Rochester, Minnesota, when in 1938, James Roosevelt, eldest son of President Franklin D. Roosevelt, was admitted for abdominal surgery. Romelle was assigned as his nurse and soon became his constant companion. Married in Beverly Hills, California, on April 14, 1941, they divorced in 1954.

No photo.

JOSEPH J. VOSS
UNITED STATES ARMY

Joe Voss joined the United States Army as a resident of Bloomer, Wisconsin, and has resided in Elk Creek north of Independence since shortly after the war where he operated the Elk Creek Store for many years. The following narrative is written from an interview with Joe at his Elk Creek home on July 10, 1998.

I was inducted into the Army on June 14, 1943 and I took a train to Camp Wolters in Texas for basic training. During basic we were given night problems now and then. One night, while on one of these problems, I was told to "keep walking," and I did -- right off a cliff! -- and I got banged up some. Following basic, I was sent to Fort Meade, Maryland, from where I boarded ship and went to Africa. I was in Company A, 143rd Infantry Regiment, 36th Infantry Division.[1] We stayed in Africa for a period of time but didn't do much except more training.

Then we invaded Italy. I was an ammo carrier and we went up into the mountains all the way to Pisa. From Italy we landed in Southern France on August 15, 1944. Here I was a mortar gunner and was wounded by a shell fragment in my arm on October 1, 1944. I was in the hospital for more than 60 days and finally left the hospital to return to duty on December 7. At first I couldn't get a ride back to my unit but finally was able to hitch along with a mail carrier. We got to an area of an old mill and we found ourselves with a large number of other Americans. When a battle broke out around us, we found ourselves surrounded and were forced to surrender. This was in France, about 15 miles from the German border.

After we surrendered, we were kept at a concentration camp for a time. Then we were put on a troop train by the Germans and taken to a prisoner of war camp near Moosberg, Germany, where I remained until liberated by American troops.

---

[1] By the end of the war, the 36th Infantry Division had suffered 3,131 killed and 13,191 wounded, of which 506 died of their wounds.

241

Joe Voss, Christmas 1943.

While I was in the POW camp, the British were bombing Munich almost every day, so every day a bunch of us were put on trucks and taken into the city and forced to repair the bomb damage.

In the POW camp, there were a lot of lice that were always on us. I got quite a few leg sores that never healed while I was there. When we were liberated by the American Army, we were taken to France and deloused several days in a row. Then we were put on a boat for England.

I was sent back to the States for rest and rehab at a camp near Miami Beach, Florida. I spent two or three months there, and it seemed the salty ocean water helped heal my leg sores. I still have scars today the size of a half-dollar from this.

Joe Voss earned his Rifle Marksman Badge on July 22, 1943 and his Combat Infantryman's Badge on May 2, 1944. His 36th Infantry Division landed in North Africa on April 13, 1943 and in Italy near Paestum on September 9, 1943. On September 20, 1943 the Division was placed in reserve after taking the Salerno Plain. By mid-November, it was back in action, relieving the 3rd Infantry Division. Joe's 143rd Infantry Regiment took part of Mt. Sammurco, after which it repulsed a vicious German counterattack. It then attacked San Pietro.

On January 20, 1944 the 143rd Infantry attacked across the Rapido River in front of Cassino but had to pull back two days later. The Division continued attacking in the Cassino area until March 12, 1944 when it was withdrawn for rehabilitation.

The Division landed in the Anzio Perimeter on May 22, 1944. After entering Rome on June 4, 1944 and traveling up Highway 2 as far as Piombino by June 26, 1944, it was pulled back to Paestum for training for the invasion of southern France.

The 36th Division assaulted southern France on August 15, 1944 in the area of Raphael and Frejus. It pushed up the Rhone River Valley, with the 143rd Infantry reaching the junction of the Drome and Rhone Rivers on August 30, 1944. By the third week of September, 1944 the Division was at the Vosges Mountains foothills. It was in this vicinity where Joe was wounded, for which he was awarded the Purple Heart.

The 36th Division continued its drive eastward, fighting the "Battle for Bruyeres" in mid-October 1944, and crossing the Meurthe River at St. Leonard and Clefcy on November 25, 1944. It drove on the Colmar Pocket in December, took up defensive positions in the Rohrweiler-Weyersheim area in mid-January 1945, and relieved the 101st Airborne Division on February 23, 1945. By March 24, 1945, the Division had reached the Rhine River at Leimersheim. When the fighting in Europe ended on May 7, 1945, it had reached the Kufstein area of Austria.

Joe was reported as missing in action on December 14, 1944. His mother and step-father in Bloomer, Wisconsin, were notified of this on January 10, 1945 by Western Union Telegram. Shortly after this, they received a telegram informing them of his prisoner-of-war status and that the following German radio broadcast had been received:

Dear Mother and Dad,

       I am a prisoner of war, in good health and being treated well. Contact the Red Cross for further information. Thank God, I am alive.

                 Your Loving Son,

                 Pvt. Joe J. Voss

In two days, his parents received 40 letters and cards from short-wave listeners all over the United States informing them of this broadcast.

Joe Voss participated in the Rome-Arno, Southern France, and Rhineland campaigns prior to his being captured. He was awarded the Purple Heart, European-African-Middle Eastern Service Medal with three bronze battle stars, Good Conduct Medal, and the World War II Victory Medal. On May 27, 1953, the War Claims Commission awarded Joe $205.50 "for inhumane treatment and/or compulsory labor" as a prisoner of war.

He was given his honorable discharge from the United States Army on November 3, 1945 at Camp Gordon Johnston, Florida.

Source: Joe Voss personal papers; Book (Stanton)

RAYMOND R. WARNER
UNITED STATES ARMY

When Ray Warner was inducted into the United States Army on September 16, 1943, little did he realize he would be involved in two very extraordinary events -- one in the Philippine Islands during the "Battle for Manila" and the other unfolding many years later back in Independence, Wisconsin.

It is unknown where Ray underwent basic training and whether he received any additional training before going overseas. But on June 8, 1944 he left Camp Anza, California, and sailed for the Southwest Pacific aboard the *U. S. S. Exchange*, arriving on June 29, 1944.

He landed first at Oro Bay, New Guinea, "when it was still a combat zone."[1] On October 2, 1944 he left Oro Bay as a private and joined the Cannon Troop of the 8th Cavalry Regiment, 1st Cavalry Division, on Los Negros Island in the Admiralty group of islands, located just north of New Guinea. There, following victory on the island, the 1st Cavalry Division was already preparing for the invasion of the Philippine Islands.

On October 20, 1944, most of the 1st Cavalry Division landed on Leyte, Philippine Islands, and two days later had reached Leyte's capital, Tacloban. Ray's 8th Cavalry, however, landed on the island of Samar on October 24, 1944, where it participated in mop-up operations and patrolling. By November 4, 1944 Ray had reached the town of Calbigo, where he remained at least through November 16, 1944. On November 8, 1944 he wrote a letter from Calbigo to his mother which was published in the *News-Wave* on November 30, 1944:

Dear Mother:

       Have time this evening for a few lines, so will try and finish this letter before it gets too dark. Right now we are camped on a hill, overlooking a small town which is pretty well run down because all the people left when the Japs took over. They re starting to come back down from the hills now that the Americans are here.

       There is a really old and beautiful church here that is supposed to be over 200 years old. The

---

[1] From a short journal kept by Ray while in the Pacific.

and talks good English. I had a long talk with him yesterday and he told me all the stories about the Jap atrocities upon the civilians. The priest that was there before him died just recently. He had been up in the hills with the guerillas and became ill and died.

How is everything back in the good old state of Wisconsin? I suppose the snow is starting to fall there by now. Wish I could see some snow again, but I guess it will be a while yet.

I'll close for now and don't worry about me.

All my love,

Ray

This was followed closely by a lively letter written November 23, 1944, in which Ray described in more detail some of his recent life on Leyte to Glenn Kirkpatrick of the *News-Wave*. One wonders whether Ray's parents read this for the first time in the newspaper:

Dear Mr. Kirkpatrick:

Just a few lines tonight to let you know of my change of address. I sure miss the News-Wave now as I haven't received any of the copies lately, but I've been on the move quite a bit so they might eventually catch up with me.

I'm in the Philippines now and landed here the first day of the invasion. It was a real show and gave me a thrill to watch the convoy land its troops and equipment on shore.

Things have been pretty tame yet, but I've been pretty scared a couple of times. One night we were camped on the top of a hill with a few of our troops a hundred yards below and to the front of us. About ten o'clock that night a party of Japs ran into the troops below us and then the firing started. In a little while one of the boys from the troop below us came running up and told us the Japs were coming. I was really scared and as they say in the army, I was really sweating it out. One of the Japs had a bugle and about that time he started to blow it and another one started yelling orders in Japanese. I sure thought a charge was coming and I sat in my fox hole with my rifle ready but I don't think I could have hit a thing because I was shaking like a leaf.

I've seen several good air battles and our boys really give those Jap Zeros a good going over. One of their bombers that was disabled seemed to be coming right down on top of us and I though for sure I saw my serial number on it, but it crashed into the bay about one hundred yards away from us.

I like the country here a lot better than that at New Guinea, but we still have plenty of rain. November, December and January are the rainy months and the rainfall averages between fifteen and twenty inches a month. They say that there are times when as much as one inch of water falls in an hour.

The people there are fairly well educated and are mostly small farmers. We buy bananas and coconuts from them in exchange for a few cigarettes. We are stationed in a small town now of about two thousand population. When we arrived here most of the people were back in the hills and the town was run down badly. When they heard the Americans were here they started to come back and now they are busy fixing up their homes again. The Japs really treated them roughly by the looks of things. There is a church here that is over two hundred years old. It is really beautiful and is built on the order of a Spanish mission. Most of the people are of Spanish descent and speak a mixture of Spanish and a dialog called tagalog.

Well, "Kirk," I'll have to close for now. Give my regards to all the folks back home. Hoping to hear from you soon, I remain

Ray

By January 8, 1945, 8th Cavalry had rejoined its Division on Leyte. The 1st Cavalry Division then landed on Luzon on January 27, 1945, from where Ray continued writing in his small journal. Though only a few entries were made, they offer proof nonetheless of Ray's having been involved in one of World War II's strangest, yet most heroic, incidents. The entries are presented here in their entirety and within the context of 1st Cavalry's actions over the next two weeks.

January 30. Landed on Luzon January 29 after a five day trip on a(n) LST from Leyte. We

244

left from near Tacloban and landed at Lingayen. The country is a lot different than either Leyte or Samar. Level land. I've seen some Guernsey cattle. The people seem to be a little darker. Getting ready for a raid on Manila. Just one squadron, the second, is going to hit it as a spearhead.

On January 30, 1945, just days after landing on Luzon, 1st Cavalry Division commander Major General Verne D. Mudge received orders from Sixth Army headquarters that stunned both him and his field commanders. Under the command of Brigadier General William C. Chase, the 1st Cavalry Brigade was to smash through the Japanese lines hell-bent for Manila in an all-out effort to rescue nearly 4,000 American men, women, and children who had been held prisoner by the Japanese at Santo Tomas University for more than three years.[2] Ray's 2nd Squadron was chosen as the spearhead of the spearhead.

The 700 men under Lieutenant Colonel Haskett "Hack" Conner learned of their mission just before midnight on January 31, 1945, and the prospect of a sixty-mile dash through Japanese-held territory to save the lives of so many American civilians sent a ripple of excitement through the men. The "Flying Column," as it became known through press accounts, readied their tanks, weapons carriers, jeeps, and other vehicles that were loaded with machine guns and cannon, and at midnight the 2nd Squadron moved forward. With the full knowledge that the route behind them would once again be closed by the Japanese as the column passed, the men traveled as quickly as road conditions and the enemy allowed. As the miles passed behind them, however, the "Flying Column" encountered stiffer and stiffer enemy resistance, and at times needed to halt completely in order to wipe out pockets of Japanese defenders. At near midnight of February 2, 1945 Colonel Conner halted the advance to give his tense, exhausted troops a much needed rest. They were just twelve miles from their objective when General Chase established his command post in a house in Baliuag, the very house the Japanese commander in the Philippines, General Yamashita, the famed "Tiger of Malaya," had used briefly as he evacuated Manila.[3]

The drive resumed in earnest before dawn on February 3, 1945 and soon reached the Novaliches Bridge, just eight miles north of Manila. The bridge was still standing, but if it was blown by the Japanese, the column would be halted here indefinitely and its efforts entirely wasted. The Japanese were heavily entrenched at the approach to the bridge and had the Americans pinned down when someone noticed a brightly burning fuse on the bridge, surely leading to explosives. The squadron's executive officer, Major James C. Gerhart, told a Navy bomb-disposal expert, Lieutenant James P. Sutton, to follow him, and in near-Hollywood fashion, they raced together onto the bridge and cut the fuse just before it reached what turned out to be four hundred pounds of TNT and three thousand pounds of picric acid, enough explosives to destroy the bridge several times over.

The American column quickly crossed the bridge and entered Manila early that evening, earning for the 1st Cavalry Division the honor of being "First in Manila."

The American internees at Santo Tomas already suspected that American troops were nearby when an American plane dropped a small bundle containing a note informing them, in

---

[2] Though no record is known to exist detailing the reason for this sudden order sending troops through Japanese lines, it is speculated Sixth Army headquarters had reason to believe the nearly 10,000 internees at Santo Tomas, Bilibid Prison, and several other locations, would be massacred by the Japanese before the front lines reached the area.

[3] General Tomoyuki Yamashita was one of Japan's most capable military commanders. He had won stunning victories in Malaya and Singapore, but for some reason, possibly jealousy over his sudden success and fame, he was sent to Manchuria by Premier Tojo, where his talents were basically wasted for several years. With Tojo removed from power, however, and the American invasion of the Philippines imminent, Tojo's successor, General Kuniaki Koiso, needed someone he could count on in Manila to direct the defense. He called on Yamashita, who took command there on October 10, 1944.

words that would be difficult for the Japanese to understand, that their release was imminent.[4]

Following a last firefight in a cemetery near Santo Tomas, the column finally reached its objective at approximately 9:00 P. M. on February 3, 1945. A tank of 1st Cavalry's 44th Tank Battalion, "Battlin' Basic," was the first to enter the compound, followed by another tank and then the troopers. What they found were 3,700 internees showing the effects of more than three years of malnutrition, disease, and physical abuse at the hands of their captors. But they were now liberated, thanks to the "Flying Column."

> February 3. Hit Manila tonight and what a nerve-wracking day this was. Ambushes all along the way. Lost a few men. Got into town about 7 in the evening. Snipers all over. Got to the internment camp at about 10. Really a happy bunch. About 3,800 we let go. Had to make a deal to let about 40 Jap soldiers go. They had about 200 internees in one of the buildings and we couldn't fire into the building for fear of hurting them. The Japs looked good and we led them out of town.

A firefight next broke out at the University's Education Building where a group of 63 Japanese, including the garrison commander, Lieutenant Colonel Toshio Hayashi, was holed up. When a liberated internee told the troopers that Hayashi was holding hostages with him, the firing into the building abruptly stopped, and in one of the most bizarre incidents of World War II in the Pacific, negotiations began with Hayashi.[5] Colonel Hayashi demanded that he and his men be allowed to leave the building with all weapons and under escort, and return to their own lines. Otherwise, he said, the hostages would all be killed. Following face-to-face negotiations between Lieutenant Colonel Charles E. Brady and Hayashi on February 4, 1945, General Chase and Hayashi agreed that if the hostages were left unharmed, the Japanese would be escorted safely through the lines, out of the city, and released, but while carrying only their personal light weapons.

> February 4. Met a couple of internees from Wisconsin.

With the agreement between General Chase and Hayashi, the Japanese emerged from the Education Building at 7:00 A. M. on February 5, 1945. They formed three columns, with American troops in single columns on either side carrying loaded weapons and orders to kill them all, but only if fired upon first. Following a route insisted upon by the Japanese and agreed to by the Americans during their negotiations, and with the battlefield enemies Colonel Brady and Colonel Hayashi side-by-side at the head of the column, they began their march through the front gate and out of Manila. When they finally reached a point past which Colonel Brady would not proceed, Hayashi snapped to attention and saluted him, eliciting an awkward return salute from the surprised Brady. As the Japanese soldiers filed past Colonel Brady, each in turn stopped and bowed to him. They then marched off past the Sampaloc Rotunda and down Aviles Street, which unbeknownst to the Japanese, was already in American hands. The Japanese column, still carrying weapons, marched directly into the American lines where Hayashi and several others were killed in the resulting firefight.

And thus ended the only known incident of negotiations between American and Japanese field commanders during World War II.

> February 11. Sitting in a hole along the R. R. track. Hope they get the Japs out soon. My nerves

---

[4] There are several accounts as to what the message actually said, one being "Roll out the barrel. There will be a hot time in the old town tonight." Another version is, "Roll out the barrel. Santa Claus is coming Monday or Tuesday."

[5] Hayashi was holding 267 hostages. The reason this incident is so bizarre is because Japanese commanders never negotiated during World War II, preferring to be killed or to commit suicide rather than "lose face" before their emperor and countrymen.

are sure shot.

This was Ray's last entry in his short, but interesting journal that ties him to a most unusual incident during the "Battle for Manila."

Mr. and Mrs. R. C. Warner received a letter written by their son, dated February 14, 1945, from the Philippine Islands where he describes some of the things that had happened to him, then tells his parents not to worry:

Dear Folks:

Well, I'm finally finding time to write you a much needed letter. This is the first chance I've have to write for some time as I've been pretty busy lately. I guess now I can be called a seasoned combat man as I guess I've seen all the horrors of war that can be imagined. I must have aged two years in the last two weeks. I suppose that you have read about the First Cavalry Division's latest move so you will know by that where I am. This is nice country around here but I can't seem to enjoy it under the circumstances.

Right now we are taking a few days rest, which believe me was needed by everybody. I never thought a fellow could keep going so long without stopping but something sure kept us going. I guess I did more praying the last two weeks than ever before in my life.

I got a few souvenirs of the Japs that I'll send home as soon as I get a chance to. The yellow guys are really meaner and crueler than I ever thought they could be, especially when they are cornered. Everyone should be killed. They don't seem to have a mind of their own and all they lack is a tail and then they would be an animal. I guess I've been mighty lucky so far and only hope it holds out. I and two other guys were down behind some tin and every time we moved a machine gun opened up on us. There was a wall behind us and we were all watching it because we could just see the line where the bullets were hitting over our heads, just like the thrillers you see in the movies.

Well, that's enough of that. Don't worry because its over now and maybe that will be the last of it for awhile. I had a letter from Rosemary today and she said that the camera was on its way. I sure hope it gets here soon as there are a lot of pictures I would like to send home.

Gee, I'd sure like to see the office now that its all fixed up. I can imagine that Edna is pretty proud of it. I sure hope that it can be kept up in good shape.

Well I'll close for now and don't worry.

Love,
Ray

The 1st Cavalry Division continued its drive through Manila, and then turned its attention to other regions of Luzon. By March 29, 1945 Ray's 8th Cavalry had taken Lipa and opened the Batangas-Calamba supply road leading into Manila. On June 26, 1945 the Division was relieved from the line and commenced intensive training exercises at Lucena in preparation for the invasion of Japan itself. Following Japan's surrender, however, the 1st Cavalry Division entered Japan as part of the Army of Occupation instead of as invaders, landing there on August 22, 1945.

Ray remained in Japan until September 4, 1945, but it is unknown where he spent the next three months. He arrived back in the United States on January 5, 1946 having participated in the Southern Philippines and Luzon campaigns. He was awarded the Asiatic-Pacific Theater Ribbon with two bronze battle stars, Philippine Liberation Ribbon with two bronze battle stars, Good Conduct Medal, Bronze Arrowhead, and World War II Victory Medal. He was separated from the Army on January 12, 1946.

Thirty Years Later

During the "Battle for Manila," Ray did what many American servicemen did -- he picked up several souvenirs. Among them were two Japanese battle flags, one of which was

247

still attached to its telescoping bamboo pole. Carried by a flagbearer as a unit marched from location to location, the flag also acted as a rallying point in battle charges. A third item Ray collected was a scarf, or "towel," as he later learned it was called, which was worn around the head by Japanese soldiers, sailors, and airmen as good luck charms. Called "sennin-bari" in Japanese, which translated to "one-thousand needles," they were made by first dying a rising sun in the middle of a white cloth. A thousand women then each added a stitch to the rising sun in red thread, one stitch at a time, and the completed towel was presented to the men as they left for the front. On Luzon, Ray removed a towel from a dead Japanese soldier and brought it home with him, often wondering what the inscription on it said.

In late 1974, an Independence native, Bob Edmundson, the son offormer 6th Armored Division tank commander, Jesse Edmundson, visited home with his new wife, Yashiko, a native of Japan. While talking with Ray's sons one evening, the topic of the towel was brought up, and when it was mentioned that Ray was curious as to what was written on it, Yashiko offered to translate for him. The next day, Bob and Yashiko visited the Warner residence where she was handed the towel, looked at it briefly, and immediately sat down, stunned. "I know who this man was," she told the Warner's. "This man's widow lives in my city, near my mother, and is my mother's best friend!"

Everyone, naturally, was astonished at Yashiko's pronouncement but the name of Kenichi Sumida was written on the scarf, which identified him as its owner. After further discussion, Ray offered that the scarf be returned to Sumida's widow, Hana Sumida, of Tokuyama City, Japan. Yashika made the arrangements by contacting her mother, who then contacted Mr. Mitsuteru Nakashima, Chief of Public Welfare, in Tokuyama City. On January 10, 1975, in a ceremony held at the city hall and with major Japanese television stations and newspapers covering the event, the sennin-bari of Kenichi Sumida was returned to his widow.

In a letter to Ray dated January 16, 1975, Yashiko wrote to inform him that the return of Sumida's towel to his widow was the subject of a major news story in Japan. She also sent articles from newspapers which stated that Sumida had been drafted and had joined the Japanese Navy on December 24, 1943, and was transferred to Luzon only five days later. His wife, Hana, received a last letter from him dated December 6, 1944. Yashiko also noted that after the war, in February 1948, Hana had received a letter from the government informing her that her husband had died in combat on Luzon on April 5, 1945. She then received a small white wooden box which to Buddhist's is intended to hold the remains of a deceased relative. But in the case of Kenichi Sumida, the box was empty as no remains of him were ever found.

In her letter to Ray, Yashiko said Hana still had hope that he might be alive and was asking whether Ray could remember any details of the event that had occurred in Manila. She explained to Ray how the towel was made and that Hana had only two days to complete it, so she had taken it into town and asked 1,000 people to add a stitch. She also said Mrs. Sumida never remarried but did adopt a baby girl following the war and had two grandchildren.

Another letter dated January 21, 1975 and written by Mitsuteru Nakashima, the chief of the Tokuyama City Public Welfare Office, was received shortly thereafter by Ray. "I can never thank you enough for your returning a valuable article," Nakshima stated. "The thing you returned is called "Sennin-Bari" in Japanese which means a "thousand needles. . . It had been said to be a charm for soldiers going to the front. . . Therefore, almost every Japanese soldier used to keep it with them during the war. . . The late Sumida went to the front on December 24, 1943, and his family received information in 1948 that he had been killed in action in some place (on) Luzon Island on April 5, 1945 and yet no articles. . . as well as his ruins (remains) weren't returned. . . I express my heartful thanks for your kindness on behalf of his family. . . and wish a good health and happiness."

Yashiko wrote another letter to Ray on January 22, 1975. It began, "I received a letter from Mrs. Sumida yesterday containing a letter for you. She asked me to translate and send it to you. She also enclosed a photo of Mr. Sumida, 37 years old at that time, hoping it will be of help to you to recall (the events in which Ray came into possession of Sumida's towel). . . I really hope that you can remember something for her."

Ray Warner. Photo taken while with
the Army of Occupation in Japan
following the war.

Mr. Kenichi Sumida, the subject
of a very bizarre story thirty years
after the war's end.

Mrs. Sumida's letter stated:

Dear Sir,
        My name is Hana, the wife of former Kenichi Sumida. I greatly appreciated your
kindness for sending me my husband's towel after 31 years. I have no words to express my
thankfulness to you.
        Although I heard that you forgot how you got the towel, could you please try to
remember anything, even a little bit again? I enclosed a photo of my husband and hope it
will be of help to you to recall the memory even if it's been a long time ago? I would be
very glad if you could give me any information.
        As I cannot write a letter in English, please allow me to use Japanese.
        Thank you very much for your kindness and I hope to hear from you soon.
            Sincerely,
            Hana Sumida

        Unfortunately, Ray could not recall the circumstances under which he came into
possession of Kenichi Sumida's towel, and Mrs. Sumida probably never did learn the fate
that befell her husband during World War II's "Battle for Manila."

Sources: Michael Warner, son; Ray Warner personal papers; Independence News-Wave; Books (Stanton)
(Connaughton, et al.)

CLARENCE JOSEPH "JACK" WEIER
UNITED STATES ARMY/ARMY AIR CORPS

The following narrative was prepared from a letter written by and received from Jack Weier in January, 1999. Jack spent one day short of three years in the Army Air Corps and Army during World War II. He participated in the Northern France campaign and was awarded the European-African-Middle Eastern Medal, American Campaign Medal, World War II Victory Medal, Good Conduct Medal, and Combat Infantry Badge.

My real name is Clarence Joseph Weier; I received my name "Jack" from my friends. My father, August Weier, was in Europe during World War I where he was subjected to mustard gas in France. When he returned home he contracted tuberculosis, a disease a lot of his buddies from the Independence area also suffered from. He died at the age of 31 when I was two years old. My friend's named me "Jack" because without a father at such a young age, I learned how to do many things other boys didn't have to do because they had a father they could rely on. Everybody asks me how I received the name and I guess it was because at an early age I became a sort of "jack of all trades."

I was drafted into the service in 1943. I left Independence on April 17, 1943, entering active service that same day with a lot of young men from our area. Butch Sobota was one of my friends that left with me that day.

We traveled by train to St. Petersburg, Florida, for basic training in the Air Force. We lived in hotels -- I think my place of residence was the Martha Washington Hotel. This, of course, was a real interesting experience, and my first time outside Wisconsin. Basic training was very difficult because it was a military experience with not much love and a lot of discipline, and I soon learned that it was up to me to get along with them since they weren't going to

---

A Quote From History...

"I later was selected as one of thirteen Chief Petty Officers to train qualified recruits to become the first black Naval officers."
    Bernie Isaacs
    United States Navy
    From a letter, 1998.

make an effort to get along with me. I learned that the only way to survive was to listen and do what I was told. If you fought them, you would always be in trouble. I was an athlete and in pretty good physical condition, so calesthentics, marching, obstacle courses, and nine-mile hikes did not put a lot of stress on my life. I just accepted it and did the very best I could, and I knew I would be okay. While I was in St. Petersburg, I ran into Roman Bautch, who was also from Independence.

K. P., or Kitchen Police, was always a dreaded experience. They would get you up at about 2:00 A. M., and even in Florida, 2:00 A. M. is a cold experience. We marched to the Savoy Hotel where they served a few thousand men. It was a long day! I think we pulled K. P. for a week at a time, and were always glad when it was over!

Following basic training, we were placed in some type of job, whatever the need was at the time, by our commander. I was placed in the Signal Corps to be trained as a radar operator. After receiving my radar training, I was sent to Long Island, New York, to a small peninsula near South Hampton. There we were stationed on a narrow slit of land in a large tent, operating radar and watching for any enemy aircraft that may approach the United States. We called in any aircraft that we detected approaching the coast to a hot line in New York City.

While at Long Island, I decided to apply for cadet training in the Air Force. I passed all the tests and was sent to Miami Beach, Florida, with intentions of becoming a bomber pilot. Of course, once again I was subjected to another cadet basic training exercise program, my second six-week basic training. I met all the requirements and was sent to Macon, Georgia, for pilot training, but after arriving there, instead of beginning pilot school, we didn't do anything for a month! Finally, one day we were notified that they didn't need any additional pilots and instead were going to be transferred to the 66th Infantry Division at Camp Rucker, Alabama, instead. We protested that, saying we were in the Air Force and should be placed in an Air Force unit, not infantry. I was a Private First Class at this time, as were most of us, so our complaints were ignored and off we went to the infantry. I'll never forget marching into Camp Rucker with our Air Force Cadet uniforms. The infantry soldiers were yelling out the windows saying, "We will get you junior birdmen bastards!" Going from the cadet program to the infantry like that was about as bad as anything that could happen to a young man!

At Camp Rucker we were informed we would receive six weeks of "infantry training." Can you believe it? It was my third basic training! I was placed in the 263rd Infantry Regiment of the 66th Infantry Division, the "Black Panther Division."[1] I was placed in Battalion Headquarters Company, which was filled with men from training programs called "ASTP," or Army Specialized Training Program. Most of the men had ratings of corporal, sergeant, and staff sergeant, and all were placed in rifle platoons. Needless to say, there would be no promotions in our outfit!

The training was extremely difficult. It was very physical with a nine-mile hike each week and a 25-mile hike monthly. Privileges were hard to come by in the 66th Division because there were thousands of men compared to the few hundred found in special service groups. We experienced several suicides by men jumping off the roof of barracks. Thirteen of us former cadets who had come from Macon began a program of regularly talking with the chaplain because of the fact that as cadets misplaced in the infantry, it was taking its toll on too many men. After a few months of this, we received an order from the War Department that we were being returned to the Air Force. When they finally started transferring us, they started alphabetically; needless to say there were two men remaining -- Weier and Williams -- when the 66th Infantry Division was alerted to go overseas. And that ended our chances of transferring back to the Air Force!

We were shipped to Fort Dix, New Jersey, and left for England in September, 1944. I sailed on the *U. S. S. LeJeune* and it took us 22 days to cross the Atlantic. Can you imagine 4,000 men on a ship with most of them becoming seasick? The smells in the holds were very depressing. We soon discovered that in the ladder trunks there was a dead space under the

---

[1] The 66th Infantry Division lost 795 killed during its time in the European Theater of Operations. Of these, 762 were lost when the troopship *S. S. Leopoldville* was torpedoed in the English Channel. Another 636 Panthermen of the 66th Infantry Division were wounded in action.

stairwell that five of us could sit in and play cards. We took turns reserving the place by getting up at 5:00 A. M. and sitting there until the rest were finished with breakfast. The air was fresh there because we were near topside. We played "hearts" every day.

After arriving at Dorchester, England, we awaited our departure to the ETO -- the European Theater of Operations -- just across the English Channel from England. It was the day before Christmas 1944 and we were expecting to celebrate Christmas in Dorchester when we were alerted, quickly loaded aboard ship, and shipped out. Most of our infantrymen boarded the S. S. *Leopoldville*. I was a truck driver so consequently I boarded an LST and sailed with our vehicles. To me, it seemed an LST was like a floating gymnasium. Once we set sail, however, we suddenly began to realize we were in enemy waters and you could feel the tension of not knowing what might happen next. We got across okay, unloaded our ship, and then heard we had lost one of our troopships.[2] Everything now was in turmoil and we had to kind of fend for ourselves. We and ten other vehicles found a large apple orchard and spent a week there scrounging for food and shelter; it was cold and the ground was snow-covered. Our outfit eventually was sent to the St. Nazaire-Lorient Sector of France where we relieved the 94th Infantry Division. When Patton marched through France, he had cut off about 100,000 German soldiers in this region and it was now our job to contain them. We began to realize that the 66th Division's original orders would have put us in the "Battle of the Bulge" but because of our disruption and loss of men crossing the Channel, we instead replaced the 94th Infantry Division and they went to the "Bulge." In a way, I guess we were lucky.

Our greatest danger in the St. Nazaire-Lorient area was from artillery barrages that could begin at any given moment. This became very nerve-wracking and caused constant tension and uncertainty. Most of the shelling seemed to take place during chow time for some reason. Our infantry had bunkers every 100 yards and my job was to supply ammo and wood to keep the men manning those bunkers armed and warm. It seems every time I took supplies to them, the German artillery began firing, and this was extremely nerve-wracking and, obviously, very dangerous.

When the war ended in Europe, we were sent to Marseilles, France, to stage soldiers for shipment to the Pacific Theater. When we completed that job, we were next sent to Austria, not far from Salzburg and Munich. There we were responsible for deactivating displaced Czechoslovakian soldiers. I was stationed in St. Johanna, Austria, not too far from Berchtesgarten, and met up with Bud Pieterick one day. At this time we just did our job and waited to accumulate enough points to go home. The desire to go home was tremendous. In fact, that's all one could think of. Finally, it happened in April 1946. I arrived at Fort Dix, New Jersey, was discharged from the Army there on April 16, 1946, and went home to Independence.

When Jack was stationed in St. Petersburg, Florida, he wrote a letter to his mother, Mrs. Rose Weier, describing his basic training and chances of additional future training. The *News-Wave* published the letter on May 13, 1943:

---

2 The *Leopoldville* was carrying 2,200 men of the 66th Infantry Division from Southhampton, England, to Cherbourg, France, to help stem the tide of the German's Ardennes Counteroffensive. Just five miles from Cherbourg, one torpedo fired from the German *U-Boat 486* slammed into the *Leopoldville* and killed as many as 300 men instantly. The Belgian crew manning the transport panicked, lowered a lifeboat and left the ship, which sank within minutes. A combination of rough seas, 48-degree water temperatures, and no one to radio for help doomed close to 500 more men. Because of the enormity of the disaster, the tragedy of the *Leopoldville*, like that of the *HMT Rohna* (see Addison Hotchkiss biography) a year earlier, was kept from the American public. Families were simply informed their sons and husbands had been killed in action. On April 12, 1945, the day President Franklin Roosevelt died, *U-486* was itself torpedoed by the British submarine *Tapir* as the German vessel was approaching its base at Bergen, Norway. An immense explosion blew the U-Boat to pieces and all crew members were killed.

Dear Mom:

Received your letter and am glad to know you are fine. So far I haven't much kick coming against the army, although we have a new sergeant who is kinda tough. There are 257 other men in our squad. Our regular sergeant is on furlough.

All the fellows are rather stiff from the exercises we have been getting. We do put in rather a full day -- get up at 5:30, go down for roll call at 5:45, then clean our rooms until 6:15 after which we go to breakfast. After breakfast we come back to our hotel and from there we leave for the drill field where we have calesthenics (exercises). Then we have a lecture, close order drill. About the toughest thing is the obstacle course. We will be plenty tough when we get out of here!

We were classified and my grades were satisfactory. I was interviewed and had my choice. I chose radio operator and mechanics as it will be advantageous to me after the war is over. My second choice was clerical work. I didn't know if I would make radio school so I took a clerical test also. I received a good score on that so it was put down as second choice. The next choice was aviation mechanics. We are stationed here at least six or more weeks.

The radio schools are located in Chicago and Madison, so I may have a good chance to be sent near home.

Say Mom, I sure could eat some of your cookies or candy. All the fellows in our room divide up whatever they get.

Will you send me Rudy Smieja's address. Also some of the other fellow's addresses -- Allie Kulig, Ed. Skroch, etc.

Boy, am I ever getting a sun tan. We take our shirts off every day for a couple of hours. When I get a better tan I'll have some pictures taken.

Well, there isn't much more to write so I'll close for now.

Your Loving Son,
Jack
P.S. How is the weather up there. Boy, it gets plenty warm here!

On February 1, 1945 Jack wrote a letter from "Somewhere in France" to the *News-Wave*, thanking everyone for the "Special Serviceman's Edition" that he had received. It was published on February 2, 1945:

Dear Friends:

Received the special edition of the Independence News-Wave a few weeks ago. Due to the terrific flow of mail it arrived a little late, but no matter how late it might have been it still was a happy surprise. I enjoyed reading it. While looking at all the old familiar scenes and familiar faces so very much, I decided to drop a little note thanking you for all the hard work involved. It must have been an enormous job, but it was well worth the effort because I am sure it reminded us GI's of many pleasant memories of home so many miles away.

It's really great knowing that the folks back home are still thinking of us and knowing that they are willing to do all they can to perhaps take our mind off things for a few moments helps make us realize we are going through all this for a good cause. I can't begin to imagine what it would be like to watch the boys come home, one by one, and see their loved ones faces lighten up. There will also be tears, am very sorry, but deep down in their heart they, too will be happy that all this suffering is over.

Thanking you again for a grand job, by a grand group of people from the city of Independence.

Guess when that happy day arrives "Old Joe" and the boys will have to find a better means than the push cart.

Sincerely yours,
Jack Weier

Jack's mother received a letter from her son written from La Baule, France, and dated May 19, 1945, about two weeks after Germany's surrender. It also appeared in the *News-Wave*:

Dearest Mom and Sister:

253

Am very sorry I haven't been writing as regularly as usual but we really have been busy - mostly with moving.

We are feeling the after effects of the war now, and believe me its great. For instance, nobody reads my mail anymore except the person to whom I send it. In other words we do not have any unit censor any more. We can say anything but discuss troop movements.

We finally came into St. Nazaire and what a strange feeling it was to drive right on through the German lines that we have been defending so long. The French people really cheered us when we came through. They threw roses at us and shouted "Fini Lau Gau" (War is finished).

We were stationed at Budpost in England. We moved from there Christmas Day. Guess you know one of our ships was sunk. It was really a shock to all of us and I couldn't believe it. I lost a few of my Cadet buddies and the fella from home as you already know.[3] That was not a very nice Christmas. We were supposed to go to Belgium, but losing all those men changed our plans, so New Year's Eve we moved up in line in Temple - between Fay de Bee and Temple to be exact. It is a place about 20 miles from Nantes, the largest city.

We were shelled quite heavily but fortunately no one was hurt seriously. So that was another holiday! On or about three months later we were finally given a rest and Easter Sunday we moved to Plormel in the Lorient sector. Then a few days later, moved back because the Krauts were giving the outfit trouble.

About the third month, we were in line just before we were relieved. We received a heavy shelling from the Krauts. We were putting up barb wire when all of this took place. Lt. Regio from Montana (he heard of Uncle Joe) was killed by shrapnel. One of the fellows was in the same fox hole and didn't get a scratch. It was my job as driver to pick him up and haul him back. Golly, it gave me an awful feeling. That's all over now, thank God. Now I shall tell you where I am.

I just came up from the lower floor after riding a motor cycle, one that we picked up - previously used by a Kraut. We have a grand time running around in it.

We sleep in beautiful hotels right on the beach. There are no lights yet, so am writing by candle light.

St. Nazaire was bombed very heavily. In fact, there is hardly a building left standing. That is where the famous pig pens are. I saw them, and Holy Mackerel, they are built for good. All along the coast the Krauts constructed a wall about 10 feet high and about 6 feet thick to prevent an invasion. Everything is very heavily mined and booby-trapped, but the Krauts are slowly removing them. Ha! Ha!

Well, Mom, it is really getting late so I must close for now. Don't worry about me. I'm really feeling wonderful. One of the fellows left on discharge today. Lucky man!

Send me candy or anything good to eat.

Love Always,
Jack

Jack remained in Germany with the Army of Occupation following the war. The July 19, 1945 *News-Wave* carried a brief report stating Jack had informed his mother that he had met up with Alphonse Symiczek, serving with the Army engineers, on a street in a small French town, and at first didn't recognize him.

On October 15, 1945 he wrote a letter to his mother in which he described a deer hunt he had been on. The ritual the guide went through after bagging the deer that Jack didn't understand at the time is part of the hunting tradition that had been practiced for many generations in Germany, and still is today. The letter was published on November 1, 1945:

Dearest Mother and Sis:
It was Saturday night I started a letter but didn't finish it. We were planning to go hunting Sunday. We did, and had a good trip.

We had a swell hunting trip. Four of us left Sunday morning at two o'clock. We had two

---

3 The "fella from home" who lost his life in the *Leopoldville* disaster was Pfc. Ernest M. Moen of Company A, 264th Infantry Regiment. Moen was from Whitehall, Wisconsin.

German Forest Rangers for guides. We went about 19 miles by truck then split up. Stanley and I and Leo, the guide, went one direction and Paul and Will went the other way. I never knew those mountains were so steep. We were up about 9,000 feet on top of high ridge where we could see the valley and opposite sidehill. We sat and watched the deer for almost an hour. We saw five of them but were out of range. We then walked up another grade and I spotted a buck. I shot him but didn't kill him outright. I broke his front leg. Leo has a wonderful dog so we trailed him for a couple of miles way down to the bottom of the mountain. We found him pretty sick and tired in a mountain stream. I shot him in the neck to finish him off. He had eight points and was a big son of a gun.

The guide broke off a piece of evergreeen and stuck it in his mouth. I don't know why. I couldn't speak German well enough to find out. Then he broke off another little piece and put some blood on it from the wound and shook my hand and put it in my hat. I was really proud. Wished I could have had my camera. Leo said he would take the head and mount it for me. He is going to bring it in within four days. We dressed him and washed him out in the stream.

We started off again, this time to get Stan one. We walked through the valley and up there on the top of another mountain Leo spotted a mountain goat. We were off again to another 9,000 foot climb. We edged up within range, about 300 yards, then Stan shot him. He hit him in the spine, so we got him. Leo did the same thing with the evergreen. We dressed him and dragged him to the bottom and once again we were at the bottom we took him to where my prize was and left them there so we could come and get them with the truck. It was pretty late, so we started back to where the truck was to meet us. Leo kept looking up the mountain. Stan and I were so tired we we were praying he wouldn't spot any more deer. He did, but we told him we were too tired so we went back to see what Rose and Wall got. We saw them but they didn't have a buck. We built a fire and did our hunting trip all over. The truck came and we took him to the Mess Sgt. He was tickled pink because there were plenty of steaks there. We skinned him and put him in the ice box. I want to get the hide tanned and perhaps have something made from it.

It was a wonderful trip. We have everybody talking hunting now.

Well, Mom, guess I'll close for now.

Your loving son,

Jack

Sources: Books (Stanton) (Andrade) (Wessman)

A Quote From History. . .

"Those of you who have given your blood for the wounded have also taken part in this great fight to save lives. I have watched this blood of yours flow into the veins of men that would surely die, giving them new life, and I thank God for people like you. . . With you behind us, we cannot lose."

Adolph Sonsalla
United States Army
From a letter to the *Independence News-Wave* dated March 22, 1945, from Germany in which Adolph, a medic, thanks the people of Independence on behalf of wounded American soldiers.

RAYMOND WEIER
UNITED STATES ARMY

The following edited narration was prepared following an interview with Raymond Weier at his Independence home on June 24, 1998.

I was drafted on May 15, 1942. I went to Milwaukee and from there to Fort Sheridan, Illinois. The next six months I spent in basic training at Camp Shelby, Mississippi. Here I met up with Len Kern of Independence. He later went to Officer's Candidate School and eventually ended up a Major, I believe.

First, I was in the 85th Division, but after awhile I became part of a cadre that was to form a new division. Two first lieutenants, four second lieutenants, six staff sergeants, and one first sergeant, along with other men, were sent to Camp Claiborne, Louisiana, where we helped form the 103rd Infantry Division, known as the "Cactus Division."[1] One of the first lieutenants was promoted to captain and became a company commander while the other first lieutenant became assistant company commander. The second lieutenants were all promoted to first lieutenant and became platoon leaders. I was one of the staff sergeants and took over as a mess sergeant. After nine months of division training we were sent to Camp Howze in Texas.

From Camp Howze, we traveled to New Jersey for overseas shipment, and left for Europe in September 1944.[2] There were 19 ships in the convoy with between 150,000 and 200,000 troops in all. I was one of 4,000 of the 410th Infantry Regiment aboard the *U. S. S. General J. R. Brooke*. It took 19 days to cross the Atlantic and we hit two hurricanes. The biggest problem during those storms was trying to keep from hitting another ship. I remember one sailor saying, "This tub won't take much more!" On board we slept in bunks that were four high.

When we reached Marseilles, France, we landed as if we were part of a beach invasion, going over the side of the ship on ropes while carrying full field packs. Once we made land, we walked about 10 miles. Then we pitched our pup tents and stayed there for two weeks. After that we went by truck to the Austrian border where we had troops in action within a few days.[3]

The 103rd attacked through the Hardt and Vosges Mountains, part of the Alps in Austria, and it was in the Hardt's where we had our first encounter with the enemy. We were up against German SS and regular troops, and they were tough! I was a quarter-of-a-mile from the front and could hear the shells. Lieutenant White was in charge of the jeeps and also in charge of finding out where to take the food we prepared each day. One of the first nights we were there he told us, "Don't go to sleep and keep your carbine ready." The Germans were really pounding our guys with artillery emplaced on the mountain sides. The company for which I was a cook, Company B, was getting hit especially hard. They sent a runner named Hubbard back to get the cooks to report to the lines but he was captured by the Germans. As it turned out, of the 200 men in the company that started in this action, only 26 men were left. Two or three officers were killed and all the others wounded. The whole company was replaced because of this.

One thing our guys learned early was that enemy snipers liked to use church towers in towns as their sniping positions. This was so deadly to our men that when we entered towns, the first thing our guys did was blow the church towers.

I was in the 410th Regiment, and as a company cook for Company B, I was usually one-

<hr>

1 Ray was one of 210 officers and 1,446 enlisted men selected from the 85th Infantry Division to help bring the 103rd Infantry Division, formally a National Guard unit, to active duty status in late 1942. By the time the war ended, the 103th Infantry Division had lost 720 men killed in action and 3,329 wounded, of which 101 died from their wounds.

2 The 103rd actually boarded ship on October 5, 1944, and departed the following day.

3 The 103rd left by truck and train from Marseilles on November 1, 1944 with its destination Docelle, France, where it became a part of Lieutenant General Alexander Patch's Seventh U. S. Army.

quarter to one-half mile from the front when it was stationary and had to take hot food to the infantrymen in the line every day. We prepared the food in mermite cans which kept the food hot for 12 hours. The cans were then loaded on a truck, a driver and I got in a jeep, and off we went. Usually I had a .45 in my lap and a carbine next to me for the trip. We served 180-200 men in the company every day and I delivered to Company B all the way through to the end.

Our Division commander, General Haffner, had been a banker in Chicago before the war, and I don't think he really knew what he was doing. In six weeks we lost what seemed like half our division! We were pulled back to be reorganized, still as the 103rd Infantry Division, and General Haffner was relieved of command. He was replaced by General McAuliffe, the already-famous commander of the 101st Airborne's defense of Bastogne. One day I had to pull my jeep over because there was a line of vehicles coming towards me. The first vehicle stopped and a guy asked me, "Sergeant, what's going on around here?" I responded, "Hell if I know." They simply drove on and the guy with me said, "Do you know who you were talking to?" Well, I did then! It was General McAuliffe!

At this time we were south of where the "Battle of the Bulge" took place and our unit was engaged in steady fighting as the Germans were attacking. We were in the "Battle of Bitche," or as we called it, "the Battle of the Bitch," against tough SS troops.[4] But we pushed them back. From then on it seemed our troops were moving steadily and more quickly.

With the Germans on the run, we only had C-rations or K-rations for the troops. We were just moving so fast now. One day I was told, "Ray, make some doughnuts for them." I said, "I don't know. We need about a thousand." But we did it, took them to the lines, and the men lined up when they saw we had doughnuts and coffee for them.

One day I got to talk a little with a Major in the German army who had surrendered. He was an Austrian, actually. He told me, "When we saw the first American vehicle, we knew we had lost the war."

I also remember once seeing two dead Germans in a field we were passing. We passed by them for more than a week and I was thinking, "When are they going to bury those soldiers?"

The turning point for the Seventh Army, which we became part of in March, 1945, was when we caught the Germans retreating through a mountain pass. There were a lot of them, more than a division. We just destroyed them and the American bulldozers simply pushed all that equipment off to the side so our troops could pass.

Finally we reached Innsbruck. The city is surrounded by mountains and we couldn't get in because the Germans had their guns positioned on the mountainsides. The local people showed us a passage around the positions, however, and we were able to take all the guns out. Then we entered Innsbruck. It was such a beautiful city. We were there when the Germans surrendered.

I remember another city in Austria called Kingsbury, I believe. We had to take it three times and it was completely destroyed, except for the church tower.

After the war was over, I was transferred from the 103rd to the 26th Division. I was placed in a chemical mortar battalion to support infantry, training for the invasion of Japan. Then the Pacific War ended and I helped organize troops to send home. I was single so there were a lot of others ahead of me for a trip home. Finally I left Le Havre, France, the first week of February, 1946.

---

4 This German attack bagan late on December 31, 1944. and was aimed at eventually taking Rohrbach in the eastern Sarre Valley. The SS troops described by Ray were actually the crack *17th SS Panzer Grenadier Division*, one of three German divisions involved in what has become known as the "Bitche Salient." Though an indentation was made into American lines, the German attack was halted within a few days.

No photo.
Sources: Books (Stanton) (Branton)

Come On America! It's 1944!

THIS is what we've been working for all along. This is the year to hit and *hurt* the enemy. This is the time when everything you do counts double. If we all get together and do *all* we can, we'll be over this hurdle and well on our way to complete and crushing victory.

No question about the men in uniform—they'll go "all out." But can we count on *you* to back them *all the way?* Your quota is where you work—you've got to buy your War Bonds and then buy more, until every last loose cent you have is *fighting*. Tough? Of course, it's tough—unless it is a sacrifice you're simply not doing your share!

Make the sacrifice now—buy *more* than the extra $100 Bond your country counts on you for—winning the war is worth *any* sacrifice you make. Besides, you aren't *giving*, you're *lending* to America! You'll get back every dollar you invest in War Bonds, with interest.

An extra $100 War Bond now is the minimum for everybody—can't we count on *you* for *more?*

This sticker in your window means you have bought 4th War Loan securities.

Let's All BACK THE ATTACK!
— SPONSORED BY —
THE INDEPENDENCE NEWS-WAVE

While the young men and women of Independence were away fighting the war, the people on the "home front" did their part to support them. This full-page ad for the 4th War Loan appeared in the December 27, 1943 edition of the *Independence News-Wave.*

Glimpses of 174 Other Veterans
of
World War II
from the
Independence, Wisconsin, Area

Despite a complete review issue-by-issue of the *Independence News-Wave* from 1941 through 1946, and a search for veterans and relatives of veterans, very few details were found regarding the participation of many of Independence's veterans in World War II. Many families did not deliver much information to the newspaper, a source that provided so many clues as to the travels and experiences of the veterans. Many veterans themselves simply returned home following their discharge to no fanfare and no fuss whatsoever other than that from their families. They felt they had done their job like everyone else and it was time to find a new source of employment and just get on with their lives. And many simply did not want to discuss it.

As stated in the Introduction to this document, all of these men and women played an important role in winning World War II, whether that role was on the front lines or behind a desk in the States. So all of their stories, regardless of how trivial they may seem when compared to those of others, are important pieces of history. This writer did, however, uncover small bits of information regarding a large number of veterans, all of it gleaned from newspaper articles published during and immediately following the war years, and from this, at least a glimpse of their participation in World War II is available. It is very unfortunate, however, that so much has seemingly and undoubtedly been lost.

In their honor and memory, the information as reported in the *Independence News-Wave* is presented here. Dated references may be directly stated or noted in parenthesis. All dated references are from the *News-Wave* unless otherwise noted.

A Quote From History. . .

"There was an amusing incident with Goering the other afternoon."
    Drexel Sprecher
    United States Army
    Letter to parents, November 24, 1945, while an assistant prosecutor
      at the Nuremberg War Crimes Trial.

ANDERSON, ALFRED

Alfred entered service with the United States Army on May 15, 1942, received his initial training at Camp Shelby, Mississippi, and attended cook's school at Gainesville, Georgia, for three months. He was then stationed at Camp Stewart, Georgia, for a year-and-a-half, after which he was admitted to a hospital. He received his discharge at Finney General Hospital, Thomasville, Georgia, on September 27, 1945. (November 15, 1945)

ANDERSON, GOODWIN

Goodwin served in the Army Quartermaster Corps and spent one year in the Pacific Theater.

ANDERSON, VERNON L.

Vernon, at age 18, joined the United States Navy. On November 2, 1944 it was reported he had been selected to attend a specialty school at the Amphibious Fireman Naval Training School, University of Illinois, Urbana, Illinois. Selection to the school was based on results of training aptitude tests administered to all recruits. An article regarding written by Glenn Kirkpatrick this noted, "Folks here are glad to know that he is making good in his work for he was known to be one that would not shirk his duties at any time."

Several weeks later, on December 7, 1944, it was announced that Vernon had graduated from the Amphibious Fireman school, where he also studied the use, operation, and maintenance of diesel engines, as well as basic shop practices and electrical fundamentals. He then was awaiting orders to a naval sea or shore station.

On November 15, 1945 it was reported Vernon was an Electrician First Class and believed to be at Pearl Harbor.

ANDRE, LA VERN

La Vern was reported to be a Seaman Second Class in the United States Navy at the end of the war.

BAUTCH, ANSELM

With the Army Air Corps, Anselm was stationed for a time in Walla Walla, Washington, before being transferred to a training school at Springfield, Illinois. He visited home in early October 1942 (October 14, 1942). At the time he received another furlough in March 1943 (March 18, 1943), he was stationed at a base in Pyote, Texas. Shortly after, he embarked for duty in England, and on June 10, 1943 it was reported the *News-Wave* had received a V-Mail from him in which he was quoted as stating, "The country here where I am is a lot like back home, and the people are very nice to us." Anselm was attached to an 8th Air Force bomber squadron while in England.

In January 1944 Anselm was contacted by his brothers Edmund and Adelbert, both also stationed in England, who had come across one another at a service center in London. Anselm's commanding officer gave him leave so he could meet with them, which turned out to be a fateful event as his brother Adelbert soon left for the main continent where he was killed in action. This meeting is best described in Edmund's biography found elsewhere in this document. A photo of the three brothers taken during their meeting in England can also be found there.

Anselm returned to the United States aboard the *Queen Elizabeth* in mid-August 1945.

Photo with brothers: Page 12

260

BAUTCH, EVERETT

Everett entered the United States Army in October 1944. He was home on furlough in early March 1945 before reporting to Fort George G. Meade, Maryland, for shipment to the European Theater. (March 15, 1945)

BAUTCH, GEORGE V.

George was inducted into the United States Army on May 23, 1945 as part of Trempealeau County's May quota that year.

BAUTCH, HERMAN

Herman was a private in the Army Air Corps at the end of 1944 (December 28, 1944). He was stationed then with Headquarter's Squadron at the air base at Santa Barbara, California.

BAUTCH, LARRY P.

Larry was a Private First Class in the Army Air Corp as of late 1943 (January 25, 1944). He was a supply clerk with the 361st Fighter Group, 8th Air Force, a group of P-51 Mustang fighter aircraft initially stationed in England. It appears the 361st Fighter Group may have later relocated to the main continent.

On V-E Day, all 150,000 men and women of 8th Air Force received a message from its commanding officer, the famous Lt. General James H. Doolittle, congratulating them for the "magnificent job you have done."

Larry was discharged on November 16, 1945 at Camp McCoy, Wisconsin.

BERGERSON, HAROLD T.

Harold was a Private First Class serving with the 7th Marines, 1st Marine Division during World War II.

BIDNEY, HOMER O.

Homer entered the United States Army on September 12, 1942. He attended basic training at Camp Robinson, Arkansas, and also received training at Camp Shelby, Mississippi, and Fort William Henry Harrison, Montana. He left the States for the Southwest Pacific on October 25, 1943 and was with a Quartermaster Truck Company on Guadalcanal for at least a major portion of his 16 months in the Theater. At one point, Homer was a Technical Sergeant Fifth Grade and a mechanic in the lubrication department of his unit.

It was reported on January 11, 1945 that while on Guadalcanal, Homer met up with Corporal Clarence Mlynek. The story had it they were both there for some time already -- Homer for a year -- and though they were billeted only a thousand feet apart, had never met. They had even attended the same movies at the same times, never knowing the other was on the island.

Homer was home on leave in April 1945. A September 21, 1944 report stated he had earned the Good Conduct Medal and at war's end wore the Asiatic-Pacific Theater Ribbon, as well.

BIDNEY, SPENCER

Spencer joined an undetermined branch of the military but due to medical problems, received an honorable medical discharge.

BRIGGS, ROBERT "Bob" E.

Bob's family, former residents of Independence, moved to Ettrick several years prior to World War II.

A Private First Class attached to a field hospital "somewhere in India," he wrote an insightful letter regarding life there, parts of which were published on February 24, 1944:

> One senses the contrast between the incredibly wealthy class and the sad and pitiful poverty stricken group. One sees richly dressed, highly ornamented women who haunt the gayer spots of the city, and then one sees the lowly, diseased, ill-clad, ignorant "untouchables" as the beggars are called. One becomes nauseated at the sight of gaping wounds and running sores.
>
> Religion is the center of every native's life. Here there are about 256,000,000 Hindus, followers of Brahma, and some 97,250,000 Moslems who follow Mohammed. Religious group ceremony is unheard of and religion is a purely personal devotion. The natives pray individually on prayer rugs, and during the prayer go through many a bow and contortion in veneration of their god. When one has been to the temple to pray, he has upon leaving, various markings put upon his forehead in red ashes.
>
> The greatest nuisance to the traveling public are the sacred cows. There are millions of them in India and they are permitted to go everywhere. No Hindu will kill a cow, and the animals are a sorry looking sort. There isn't fodder for them, nor pasturage and they are mighty thin and gaunt. Many of them appear to be dying of fatigue and starvation.
>
> There are about 100 different languages and dialects common here, but 24 of them most used by the people.

Following receipt of the "Special Serviceman's Edition" of the *News-Wave*, Bob sent a letter dated January 1, 1945 to Glenn Kirkpatrick, the "erstwhile" editor of the paper, thanking him for the efforts made on behalf of service men and women everywhere. By that time, Bob was a Sergeant and at a field hospital "somewhere in China." Again, he offers a glimpse of things he saw in China:

> Dear Mr. Kirkpatrick:
>
> Greatly inspired by the "Special Serviceman's Edition of the News-Wave," I want to take this opportuniity to let all the people of the "little metropolis" of Independence know, through this erstwhile editor, that their idea for a boost of morale of the lonely "G-I" was first rate. Although I've been away from the town for a number of years, my thoughts often revert to days when I called it my home. In the many pages of the edition were pictures of men and women who have been close to us all, such notables as Myron Olson, Martin Wiemer and Harvey Abend, plus all the other businessmen whose years of service to the community has endeared them all to our hearts. So to you all, I say "thanks," and I'm sure every boy and girl in the service will manifest their appreciation likewise.

A Quote From History. . .

"It's great, if you have what it takes."
Glenn Hendrickson
United States Navy
Describing Navy life, May 1943.

China is quite a country. Her antiquity, her social customs, her people have changed very little. Still today the old Confucious temples rise majestically in every village and city; the statues ornate in their glittering gold with buring fire pots of incense before them. Conjested towns and cities effervesce with the clinging and clanging of Chinese temple bells, noisy children and shouting merchants. It's like stepping from a picture book to step into China, but now here as elsewhere, the war and the monotony of it all makes one a bit weary. But we carry on amid the fray to aid our Allies technically and skillfully in the great field of medicine with the one hope in mind that 1945 will see us home with our loved ones. Such is China - "the land of the dragon and the Lotus-blossom."

Every kind wish and best regards to you, and all, who have been so interested in the men and women in the service of their country. I should appreciate hearing from you all at your convenience.

As always,
Bob Briggs

BRIGGS, VILAS

Vilas was employed by the *News-Wave* prior to joining the United States Marines in January 1943 (March 4, 1943). In June 1943 he was training at a camp at San Diego, California, and sent the following letter to Glenn Kirkpatrick at the newspaper, who published it on June 24, 1943. In it, he describes California weather, Texas girls, and some of his training:

Dear Kirk:

I received the paper the other day and was certainly glad to get it.

This is my last day here at the Base, as tomorrow we go to the Range which is about 14 miles from here.

I like it here and am getting along fine. The only thing I don't like is this blasted California weather. I caught a cold the first night I was here and still have it. It is cold here at night and hot during the day time. It rained today for the first time since I've been here.

We go to the movies just about every other night and on Saturday nights there are boxing matches. One of the boys from 438 boxed last Saturday but he got a lickin'. Of course, he was from Texas!

There are 17 Wisconsin boys in our platoon and there are four of us in one tent. We argue almost continually with these Texans about which is the best of the two states. I've seen pictures of the Texan girls and I still prefer Wisconsin.

This last week we have been pretty busy getting ready for the range. They have been trying to teach us everything we can hold before we go to the range.

Yesterday we went on parade and had to march with sixty-pound transport packs and boy, they were heavy, and it was so hot!

The food is good and there is plenty of it. You can go back for as much as you want, but with this cold I don't sem to eat very much although I have gained a little weight.

Boy, I sure do appreciate those letters from home and so do the rest of the boys. You should see them rush when they have mail call. Everyone seems to want to be the first one there.

Well, I'll have to close now 'cause we have to fall out pretty soon.

Yours truly,
Vilas

By August 1943 Vilas found himself stationed in Norman, Oklahoma, a Private First Class attending Aviation Ordnance School. From there, he wrote a letter to the *News-Wave*, dated August 4, 1943, that Kirkpatrick published on August 12:

Dear Kirk:

Here's a note to tell you my new address. I am going to Aviation Ordnance school which is here at Norman, Oklahoma. I am at least a little closer to home now. I like it better here than in California, even if it is just as hot, if not hotter.

I am going to be here 14 weeks and maybe 16. Here I will learn about guns and gunnery. Then probably if I am good enough I will be sent on to gunnery school.

I have been promoted to Pfc. and that means about four bucks a month extra. After finishing school, if I am still in the class, 85% of the boys will get a corporal's rating.

Tomorrow we are to be the honor guard for a man who is getting the purple heart. Then Saturday the base is getting is regimental clothes and I will have to parade. There are a bunch of women stationed here, but of course that is a restricted area for us.

So long, and say hello to everybody.

Vilas

A third letter, dated February 15, 1945, was published one week later. Since there is only a one week lag between the dates, it is possible the letter was written while overseas and then simply mailed upon his return to the states, though this cannot, of course, be confirmed:

Dear Kirk:

I guess its about time I wrote and thanked you for the Servicemen's edition of the News Wave. It sure was wonderful. It made me a little homesick to look at the pictures of the old familiar places, but it did plenty of good. I'm waiting patiently for the day when I can walk down those streets again.

I got a letter from Blaze Blaha (Ed. - Everette) today. He is in the Philippines now. I guess he is really in over there.

I hope we will be back in another couple of months, at least I'm hoping so. That is the day I have been waiting for for almost two years now. So here's hoping its soon.

I'll have to close for now as its time for lights out. So long and tell Eileen (Ed. - Eileen Kirkpatrick, Glenn's daughter) hello for me.

Bye Now,
Vilas

By this time, Vilas had apparently been in the Pacific Theater for some time. But he did return to the States shortly after, following which he was married to Betty June Beal of Seminole, Oklahoma, on June 11, 1945 in Memphis, Tennessee (June 21, 1945). After attending school in Memphis, he reported to a camp at Mojave, California, from where he believed he would leave for overseas once again.

BRINK, REV. NEWELL V.

Reverend Brink was the very popular and well-liked pastor of the Independence Methodist Church, as well as that of the Whitehall Methodist Church. Appointed to the post in 1942, he and his family moved to Independence where he quickly became involved with the community, including directing the Boy Scout Troop in town. He had attempted enlisting in the Navy in May, 1945 but was told he had failed due to a vision defect.

On July 16, 1945, however, he was informed that he was to report to Great Lakes Naval Station, Chicago, Illinois, for induction. He did this on Friday, July 20, 1945, then returned to Independence on Saturday to fulfill his congregational duties the next day. That Sunday evening, he left for Williamsburg, Virginia, and entered training at the College of William and Mary. After three months there, he expected as many as nine months of duty in the states before becoming eligible for overseas duty (July 26, 1945).

On August 2, 1945 an announcement was made of an auction to be held at the Brink residence on August 4 due to Rev. Brink's call to service as a Naval Chaplain. On August 5 his wife and two children were to leave for West Union, Iowa, where they would reside with Rev. Brink's mother while he was in the service.

264

BROWSKOWSKI, BEN

Ben served with the United States Army in the European Theater. He was a Corporal when he returned home in July 1945.

BROWSKOWSKI, ROY B.

Roy served in the United States Army from 1941-1947. A member of the 7th Armored Division, he participated in the "Battle of the Bulge." He was discharged with the rank of Staff Sergeant.

BURT, OAKLEY, W.

Oakley was a Private First Class in the United States Army during World War II.

COOKE, GERALD

The July 12, 1945 edition of the *News-Wave* stated Gerald was an Army Staff Sergeant and serving in the European Theater of Operations.

DAHL, ELMO

Elmo was born in Independence on May 13, 1913 and grew up on a farm in Borst Valley. His parents, Mr. and Mrs. Bennie Dahl, later moved the family to Pleasantville, Wisconsin.

In July 1944 his parents were informed their son, Private First Class Elmo Dahl, was killed in action in Europeon June 11, 1944. He was the first Trempealeau County resident reported killed following the D-Day invasion of June 6, 1944.

Elmo was inducted into the United States Army on December 18, 1942 and trained at Camp Wolters, Texas. He left with an infantry division for the European Theater on January 11, 1944. His parents had last heard from him on May 25, 1944. He was survived by his parents and five brothers, one of whom was also serving in the infantry and last reported in England. (July 27, 1944)

A Quote From History. . .

". . . when a General says to do something, you'd better do it! I think they shot you if you didn't!"
   Adolph Nogosek
   United States Army Air Corps
   From an interview, August 2, 1998, describing how General Ralph
   Cousins countered his wishes to be sent overseas.

DEJNO, ALPHONSE

Alphonse Dejno with his mother, Mrs. John Dejno.

Alphonse entered the United States Army in April 1941. In March of the following year, he was stationed at Fort Leonard Wood, Missouri, where he spent about two years (April 2, 1942). Alphonse was one of only four of 36 who passed a rigorous exam at Fort Leonard Wood, following which he transferred into the Army Air Corps and was promoted to Sergeant (February 11, 1943). He then transferred to Washington, D. C., where he awaited shipment overseas.

Arriving in England in November 1943, Alphonse served as an engineering clerk with the 447th Bomb Group, Eighth Air Force. Following D-Day, most of the 447th's missions were coordinated with Allied ground offensives. The group also participated in the famous England-to-Africa shuttle bombing attack on the Messerschmitt factories at Regensburg, Germany.

Alphonse's duties included keeping accurate records of all B-17 Flying Fortress' in his squadron so that an engineering officer could tell at a glance whether a plane needed an inspection, engine change, or other maintenance (May 10, 1945).

He was discharged in late October 1945. (November 1, 1945)

ELLIFSON, ARCHIE

A Fireman First Class in the United States Navy, Archie participated in five campaigns in the Pacific Theater of Operations. He earned five battle stars, including one for the Ryukyus campaign (Okinawa). He enjoyed a leave in August 1945, following which he expected to return to the Pacific region for further duty with the Navy (August 23, 1945).

ELLIFSON, EDNER

Edner was a United States Army Staff Sergeant by war's end (September 27, 1945). By then he had been in the service for 36 months, serving 18 months with the 91st Infantry Division in Italy.

ERICKSON, GORDON

Gordon's family moved to Eau Claire sometime prior to the war. On December 28, 1944 it was reported he had been "slightly wounded" in France and subsequently hospitalized in England.

ERTEL, WAINWRIGHT

Wayne was a Tech Sergeant who served with the Army Air Corps.

FELLENZ, MILLARD

In November, 1942, Millard was a Naval recruit undergoing training at Great Lakes Naval Training Station, Illinois. From there he mailed a card, postmarked November 8, 1942, to his friend, Ray Warner. His return address identified him as part of "CO 1553 21st REG. 31st BAT.

> Dear Ray,
>   Haven't had time to write a letter as yet so am dropping this card to say hello. So far Navy life is really swell. I already had 3 shots & a baldy. Will write a letter soon.
>   Pal, Dutch   (Source: Ray Warner personal papers)

By November, 1944, Millard was stationed at Norfolk Naval Base, Virginia, and holding a rating of Specialist Second Class.

FILLA, GEORGE

George served in the United States Army. On April 15, 1943, it was reported he would be returning to Fort Fisher, North Carolina, upon completion of a two week furlough spent at home. Upon his return there, he was expecting to be promoted to Staff Sergeant.

FILLA, PETER JACOB

On August 26, 1943, the *News-Wave* reported that 37-year-old Peter had received a permanent appointment as Chief Pharmacist Mate at the U. S. Naval Air Station in Richmond, Florida, a lighter-than-air base. Prior to this, he had served on a battleship, cruiser, and destroyer in the Atlantic Fleet, as well as serving on convoy duty in anti-submarine service. It was reported he also had served five-and-a-half years in the Army before joining the Navy.

FJELD, ELMO

Elmo was 22 when he and his younger brother, Ernest, joined the United States Army. He served in the Pacific Theater of Operations.

FJELD, ERNEST

The Fjeld's moved to the Whitehall-Blair area prior to World War II. In a *News-Wave* article of March 19, 1942, he and his brother, Elmo, were recalled as "just little tots" when they had lived in Independence. Ernest enlisted in the United States Army in 1942 at the age of 18.

He arrived overseas in November, 1944, a switchboard operator in headquarters telephone central of a combat communications unit in the Netherlands East Indies. While there, he was promoted to corporal (March 22, 1945). He was a member of an organization known as the "Triple Wingers," whose job it was to provide and maintain vital communications between the headquarters of Brigadier General P. H. Prentiss' Troop Carrier Command and their forward air fields. General Prentiss' forward detachments aided 5th Air Force Troop Carriers by hauling freight, dropping supplies, evacuating wounded, and transporting essential personnel to and from the front..

GAMROTH, BENEDICT

Bennie served with the 806th Engineer Aviation Battalion as a Sergeant. He left the Portland Port of Embarkation on April 26, 1944, arriving in Hawaii on May 3, 1944. Six weeks following the landing on Saipan, on July 31, 1944, the 806th arrived on the island. Bennie's unit later landed on Ie Shima on June 1, 1945 and Okinawa the next day during the Ryukyus campaign. Later, at least by September 1945, he was a truck driver with the Army's 3759th Quartermaster Truck Company, on Luzon, Philippine Islands. On September 20, 1945 he was reported to have been overseas for six months and wearing the Asiatic-Pacific Theater Ribbon with two campaign stars and the Philippine Liberation Ribbon. He had also been stationed on New Guinea for a time before being transferred to Luzon.

GAMROTH, CLARENCE J.

Clarence was a Private in the United States Army during World War II.

GASATIS, JOHN

December 7, 1941 found John Gasatis in Marine basic training at San Diego, California (December 11, 1941). In early October 1943 he spent a furlough in Independence, having already served in the Aleutian and Solomon Islands (October 7, 1943). He then spent about a year stateside during which time he married Barbara Chavez of Albuquerque, New Mexico, on August 7, 1944 (August 24, 1944).

On March 18, 1943 a short letter was published by the *News-Wave* that John had mailed to his mother. In it, he mentions hearing of the sinking of his brother Ben's ship, the *U. S. S. Chicago*:

> I received your letter today and was glad to hear from you. I am glad that you are all well, and as for myself, I am in the best of health. I go through the same work day after day, so I can't kick. As for the food, it is the best one can get out here.
>
> I heard the USS Chicago went down. Well, it was too bad. Did you hear anything from Ben?
>
> Well, this is the next day. I got another letter today from you. You said there is a lot of snow out there. Well, I wish I were there to enjoy it. Out here we have no snow, so I guess we'll have to make the best of it.
>
> Guess I will have to end this, because I can't think of anything more to write.

John also served in the Korean War, attaining the rank of Master Sergeant.

A Quote From History. . .

"That's my sister!"
    George Schneider
    United States Marines
    Aboard a hospital ship and scheduled to have a leg amputated
        following being wounded on Iwo Jima. It was George's
        response after the doctor said his best nurse at the Mayo Clinic
        was named "Schneider." The doctor saved George's leg.

GIEROK, CHARLES A.

On Janaury 18, 1945 it was reported Charles had grown up in Travers Valley and then moved to Winona, Minnesota, to find work. He entered the United States Army on May 9, 1944 and attended basic training at Camp Fannin, Texas. Following a furlough, he was then sent to Camp George G. Meade, Maryland, on October 10, 1944, from where he was shipped to the European Theater of Operations. He spent time in England and Scotland before crossing the channel to France. As a Private in the infantry, Charles was wounded in December 1944 in either Belgium or Germany, for which he was awarded the Purple Heart.

In a letter to his sister, Mrs. John Fueling, dated December 25, 1944, he stated that he was in England and doing fine. He also asked about his brother, Ignatius, who had been wounded in the Pacific.

GIEROK, IGNATIUS

Ignatius was a private in the Army, and was wounded in the Pacific Theater in September 1944. He was hospitalized following this on the Hawaiian Islands.

GUNDERSON, ARNOLD

Arnold was a Private First Class at the war's end. He was in the Pacific Theater for two years, including Leyte. Upon his return home, he spent some time in a military hospital in Battle Creek, Michigan, for unknown reasons.

A Quote From History. . .

"He pulled back his covers to show me his missing leg."
    Ralph Jonietz
    United States Army
    From a letter, 1998, describing his meeting up with a friend in an
      evacuation hospital in France.

GUNEM, HELMER R.

Helmer was a Private in the United States Army, serving with the 1633 Service Command Unit.

HALAMA, HILLARY "Jack"

Hillary "Jack" Halama entered the service on Janaury 9, 1942, and following basic training was sent to the European Theater of Operations in August 1942. A member of the Army Air Corps, he spent time in England, Ireland, Wales, and Scotland before transferring to North Africa where he spent the next 18 months supporting air operations in the North Africa and Tunisian campaigns. He next was sent to Italy where he participated in that campaign until its conclusion.

An athlete in high school in Independence, Sergeant Hillary spent his leisure time in Italy engaged in basketball through programs established at Army Air Corps Service Command Depots. These recreation programs were believed to help relieve the stress suffered by combat personnel.

On his European-African-Middle Eastern Service Ribbon, Hillary wore three stars signifying his participation in three campaigns. He also earned the Good Conduct Medal, among other awards.

In May, 1945 Hillary arrived at the Army Air Corps Redistribution Station No. 4 at Santa Ana Army Air Base, California. At this station, Army Air Corps men who had experienced combat received complete medical examinations and underwent classification interviews before being reassigned to stations in the United States. (May 31, 1945)

HALAMA, RAYMOND B.

On November 5, 1942 it was reported that Ray and Joseph Libowski were among a group of 18 from Trempealeau County who had enlisted in the Navy as members of the "token crew" of the *U. S. S. Wisconsin*, a battleship that was then in the early stages of construction.

The August 2, 1945 *News-Wave* reported Ray was a Petty Officer Second Class, and stationed at Boca Chica, Florida.

HANSEN, GEORGE R.

George served in the United States Army. On April 30, 1942 he was reported to be a Private who had just arrived at the Armored Force Training Center at Fort Knox, Kentucky.

A Quote From History. . .

"Sir, would you like a little bit off the top today?"
　　　Jesse Edmundson
　　　United States Army
　　　Tank Commander and personal barber to balding Major General Robert
　　　　W. Grow, 6th Armored Division, Commanding. Date unknown,
　　　　quoted by Marge Edmundson, wife.

HENDRICKSON, ARDELL

Ardell, apparently a guitarist, was with the United States Army and served in the Pacific. In June 1945 he wrote two letters to his parents, both of which were published in the July 19, 1945 *News-Wave*:

> Note: It has been brought to this writer's attention that Ardell Hendrickson and Ardell Melby are the same person. See page 291 of Volume I for an additional "glimpse" into Ardell's World War II service.

June 7, 1945
Luzon, P. I. (ed. - Philippine Islands)
Dear Mother:

I really don't have much in mind to write about tonight, but thought I would drop you a few lines. How is everybody. I am just swell and hope you all are the same. Well, mom, I finally bought a guitar and am I ever in a bad shape as I have no strings. I'm going to send a request to you for some. Say, would you please gather up about three sets or more and send them as soon as possible as I'm anxious to hear what my guitar sounds like. It is Philippino made and cost me $50.00. Say, be sure and wrap them good, even a small tin box or wooden box, and send it air mail so I'll be sure to get them.

I made another rating. I am now a Third Class Motor Mack (Ed. - Machinist) which of course means 12 bucks more a month. It all helps. Well, mom, will close for now, hoping you do this for me as soon as possible.

Love, Ardell

June 30, 1945
Luzon, P. I.
Dear Mother:

Well mom, I haven't heard from you for quite a while, but thought you maybe have been very busy, being you mentioned you had quite a little back work to catch up with.

How are you all back home? Swell, I hope. I am just fine.

Oh, say, mom, I had a thrill of my life last night. As Gunderson and I were sitting singing and playing away on my guitar, I heard someone yell out, "Well, hello there, Ardell, you son of a gun. How are you?" Right then for a moment I was stumped because no one ever calls a person here by his first name. So I turned around and there was Ernest Fjeld. Boy, mom, I can't tell you how much better I felt after seeimg him. It was as if I had just arrived in the States. He's just like always. Same old Ernest. Monday night it rained something awful, so we stayed in my tent and shot the breeze. Such as our post war plans and the times we used to have and we planned to go out last night. We did, and did we ever have a swell time. You know just to be with an old friend is pleasure over here.

Well, mom there isn't much now. Oh, yes, Ernest is stationed about a half mile from here so we can see each other every night if we wish. He works tonight, however. We have plans for Sunday to go to Manila.

I must close for now. Hope to hear from you soon and also receive some guitar strings. May God be with you all. Bye now.

Love, Ardell

HENDRICKSON, LEROY

LeRoy enlisted in the Navy in March 1944 and attended basic training at Great Lakes Naval Station, Chicago, Illinois. Following basic, he was transferred to Camp Endicott in Davesville, Rhode Island. This was then followed by duty at the Ammunition Storage Depot, Clatskanie, Oregon; the Naval Base at Port Hueneme, California; and the Naval Repair Base, San Diego, California. He was discharged at Great Lakes Naval Station in June 1946.

About three months after his discharge, LeRoy was killed in an auto accident on his 23rd birthday. Following the funeral at Chimney Rock Church, Trempealeau County American Legion Chaplain Louie Luhrson of Mondovi, Wisconsin, conducted a cemetery service. The escort consisted entirely of Legionnaires from Independence, and the firing squad and color escort was commanded by Leonard Kern. After the flag was presented to LeRoy's family, taps was played

by Alan Hanson. (September 12, 1946)

HUNT, KENNETH

Kenneth was a former resident of Silver Fox Ridge whose family moved to Eau Claire, Wisconsin. He served five years in the Army Air Corps, 16 months of which were spent in the China-Burma-India Theater. He was a tail gunner on a B-29 bomber and flew 35 missions during which he was credited with shooting down two Japanese aircraft. A Sergeant at the end of the war, he was decorated with the Distinguished Flying Cross, Air Medal with three oak leaf clusters, Asiatic-Pacific Theater Ribbon with four battle stars, and a Distinguished Unit Citation. (August 30, 1945)

HUTCHINS, EARL

Earl joined the United States Army on October 13, 1942 and was trained as a rifleman with the 91st Infantry Division at Camp White and Camp Adair, Oregon. He later was transferred to the 70th Infantry Division before ending up serving at Camp McCain, Mississippi, a German and Italian prisoner of war camp. He was discharged as a Corporal at Fort Sheridan, Illinois, on September 26, 1945. (October 11, 1945)

ISAACS, JEROME

Jerome was a former resident of Independence who was held as a prisoner of war by Germany. Before learning of his POW status, his mother, Mrs. Hannah Issacs, had previously received a telegram from the War Department in December, 1944, stating he had been missing in action since December 4, 1944. (April 12, 1945)

JAHR, ROBERT O.

Bob served with the United States Army after being inducted on July 13, 1945. He attained the rank of Technician Fifth Class before being discharged.

JASZEWSKI, ANDREW

Andy was a Staff Sergeant in the United States Army in September, 1943. He was stationed at Camp Adair, Oregon, when he received a disability discharge and returned to Independence. (September 30, 1943)

JASZEWSKI, ROMAN

Roman served in the United States Army during World War II. In August, 1942, he sent a card to the *News-Wave*, his former employer, informing Glenn Kirkpatrick that his address was Barracks T1575, Co. A, 28th Signal Training Battalion, Camp Crowder, Missouri. He also wrote:

Finally got settled in the army and like it fine. Arrived here after two weeks training at Ft. Sheridan, and will be given 17 additional weeks in teletype maintenance and repair work. Following this will have a chance to take officer's training as I rated high enough in the tests to qualify for it.

Stationed in the United States throughout the war while serving in the Signal Service, Roman wrote long letters to Kirkpatrick. In the following letter, published December 31, 1942, he tells of meeting film star-turned-soldier Tom Brown:

Dear Glenn and staff:
It is nearing midnight so this will of necessity be short and sweet.

I've thought of you often, but as day by day my time is increasingly limited by added duties, I find myself with a pressing lack of it. So much so that even my family has felt a greater lapse of time between letters than is usual.

I am about through with teletype school which will qualify me for a Technician's rating worth a Staff Sgt's pay as soon as I'm assigned to a tactical unit. I have charge of my barracks now, a platoon of 40 men. It really is a lot of fun mixed with "headaches." I don't know which outweighs the other.

Had a chat with Tom Brown of film fame this noon at Service Club No. 2. He arrived at Camp Crowder only recently. He's a very polite and likeable fellow, not a bit undemocratic. He likes army life and is not at all out of place here.

So far I've enjoyed this first part of a winter season in the south. This was the first time a crust froze on the surface of the ground (though) not sufficiently solid to support a man's weight. Grass in company area lawns is still a bright green. This is a part of the country that is warm when a south wind blows and cools off with a northerly blast. No snow has remained on the ground although about half an inch has fallen so far this winter.

Together with the enclosed renewal go my heartiest best wishes for a happy and most prosperous New Year for the News-Wave and its personnel.
Sincerely yours,
Roman J.

In a letter dated February 16, 1943 and published February 25, 1943, Roman described some of the historic sights he had visited while stationed in Washington, D. C.:

Dear Glenn and All:
As time goes swiftly by I often think of all my good friends back home. One would not think that were true if he were to judge by the volume of my outgoing mail. But believe me it's true. Lately it seems that after a hard day's work, during the week, I'm perfectly content to do a little "bunk fatigue" after my daily letter is written. When a weekend comes, there's Washington with all its historic attractions which just cannot be missed, that takes up all of my time and often leaves me with none to write letters on at all.

In the short time we've been here, almost a month now, we've been quarantined twice for measles. Each time it included the weekend which didn't please us at all. On the Sundays that we were free, a few buddies and I would board a bus and go to town to view some of the very interesting things to be seen here. First of all of course came a ride through the city to view the Capital, Washington Monument, Lincoln Memorial, the White House, and the various departmental buildings.

A visit to the Smithsonian Institute with its many scattered buildings seemed to be the next in importance for me. In the Industrial Arts building we saw everything from meteors, rubber trees, textiles, synthetics, plastics, etc., to Wright's first successful airplane, the Spirit of St. Louis (Lindberg's plane), the Winnie Mae, some of the first gliders, World War planes, old locomotives and automobiles, and the all plastic, transparent, 1940 Pontiac sedan, a real wonder of the modern engineering.

One of the most inspiring visits for me was that through the house where Lincoln died. Across the street from this is Ford's theater where the shooting took place. In the home everything is arranged as it was on the night of the assassination. The deathbed looks very much like a modern bed of our own day. In fact the whole place looks much like many still to be seen to this day. This would seem to make one

273

realize the relative "newness" of this nation.

 The theatre has been made into a "house of memories." There are to be seen Boothe's personal belongings. He carried, at the time of the infamous crime, not only half an arsenal consisiting of two identical pistols, a couple of knives, a rifle, and belt; but also camping equipment and a very interesting diary. This shows he was prepared for a "hunting." In a very neat and readable hand writing he wrote of his feeling before and after the killing. These feelings indicate he was aware of the magnitude of the act he was about to commit and that he regretted the step but thought it an absolute necessity. He was sure that the death of Lincoln would stamp out all he stood for. What seemed most important to me in that diary is the fact that so many of us today feel that if Hitler, Mussolini, and Hirohito were done away with all the world's wounds would suddenly halt. How far this is from the truth can be measured by the little Boothe accomplished by killing a president of the U. S. These rats, of course, cannot be classed with the noble Lincoln. It is merely a comparison I'm making, you understand. I rather think of them as the gatherings of pus that accumulate on a human body sick with loathsome smallpox. They are the symtoms and after effects of a seriously ailing European continent. This of course, excludes Japan because they always copy things, either good or bad, from Europe and America. They have no mind of their own.

 Enough of such boresome rambling. I may say here that the Knights of Columbus have done much to make my stay here more like home. My traveling card makes me "one of the boys." I have access to the club rooms in their four story building, the brothers are a swell bunch from all walks of life. Sunday evenings there is a banquet for service men, Waacs, Waves, and Marines in the basement. These are provided by the brotherhood, assisted by the ladies of the National Catholic Community service. They serve an average of 500 diners each Sunday evening. There's dancing from 6 to 11 p. m. on the first and third floors each having a good orchestra. Really this city is a service man's paradise. Oh yes, the famous Stage Door Canteen, with Washington's elite serving as hostesses is another attraction. Eleanor Roosevelt use to grace the place with her presence occasionally but autograph hunting soldiers must have tired her out. She hasn't been there since I've been here. The place takes its name from the building that houses it. It's an old theatre building with the stage and balonies still unaltered except for removal of seats and fitting it's terraces with tables. Stage shows, eating and dancing are its main features of entertainment.

 This perhaps sounds like I live in town more than out here but really I saw all this on but three trips to town. We haven't been paid in two months so you see I couldn't

 Living costs around here for the civilian population are staggering, yet some things, especially men's clothing can be bought here more reasonable than around home.

 The weather has been grand here all winter. Yesterday and today were coldest by far. The temperature dropped to a low of 7 degrees above zero. We have no snow.

 Wonderful how much a person can write without revealing any military secrets. I wouldn't have believed it.

  Roman

Roman was transferred to Seattle, Washington, sometime in the first half of 1943. He wrote a letter to Glenn Kirkpatrick on June 17, 1943 regarding his new duties:

Dear Glenn:

 Just a year ago, at this time of year, I was seeing before me the very possibility of a military career. To be sure, at that time I was certain that that career would be of no more than a year's duration. How wrong my calcualtions were is demonstrated in events which have occurred in the 18 months since Pearl Harbor. I am well convinced that we are now only in the beginning of the conflict.

 Aside from anxiety and yearning for those I love back home, I find myself quite happy in the Army so far.

 Most recent thrills Uncle Sam has provided will be noted by the change of address incident to a trip across the continent from coast to coast. I'm still with the 2nd Signal Service Battalion and will be for the duration. They have "farmed me out" to the Detachment of 2nd Signal located in the Federal Bldg. here in Seattle.

 The Alaska Communication System cares for our personal well being in exchange for our services.

Our office is staffed with the finest group of commissioned and non-commissioned officers I've ever met. My only hope is that I can stay here with them for a long time. This is almost beyond my wildest dreams because I have a lot of traveling in all directions coming to me in connection with my work. The nature of this work I'd like very much to tell you but at this time that is impossible for reasons of military security.

Being able to live in a private home with expenses paid and more freedom than I've ever had in the army so far is wonderful.

Beyond the foregoing, news is limited here. Write when you have a moment to spare. I always enjoy your letters. I realize your time is well taken up, but I'd sincerely appreciate even a short note now and then.

I hope that all is well with both of you as to health and that God in His Goodness is providing the utmost for your happiness.

Thank you heartily for faithfully sending the paper in the past. Besides bringing me welcome news from friends and relatives at home, it gives me a feeling of just pride to compare its workmanship with others that reach my desk. I still haven't dismissed from my mind the idea that some day I might own a small paper of my own, hence the interest in makeup.

Love,
Roman

In March 1944, Roman was transferred to San Francisco. Again he wrote to Glenn Kirkpatrick, informing him of that and also describing the West Coast sights he and his wife had experienced. Dated March 21, 1944, the *News-Wave* published it on April 6, 1944:

Dear Glenn:

No word has been exchanged betweeen us in some time. Have often wondered how you and Eileen were getting along. A good reviver of correspondence is always a change of address. It will now be Sgt. R. J., 1245 Wallen Ave., San Francisco, Cal. The change of title was effective October 1, 1943, the address just changed yesterday.

Dot and I were very fortunate in being able to drive by car from Seattle here. We took three days to make the trip. The last day (Sunday) we took our time along the Redwood highway getting many breathtaking scenic thrills.

As most everyone does who travels that route, we drove by the world's tallest tree, a super-mast rising 364 ft. into the air. Next we got a picture of our car in the huge tree through which has been gouged a passage wide and high enough to drive through.

Our first view of the Pacific at Crescent City, California, gave us another burst of rapture.

We had seen Puget Sound at various points in the state of Washington which is in direct connection with that body of water, but this was our first view of the main body of water. I can see how Balboa must have felt when he first set eyes on it.

The weather was most beautiful all the way. We started from Seattle at 7:30 a. m. on Friday of last week, making Roseburg, Oregon, by night where we were fortunate in getting a cute "doll house" of a modern cabin. The first day was our best as to distance covered, 400 miles. We wanted to arrive here by afternoon of Sunday and still have time to do a little loafing in the Redwood section. All worked out very well.

An impressive sight for the last 100 miles was the unbroken chain of vineyards covering millions of acres. These are farmed by Italians in a meticulous manner. Many wineries dot the landscape every few miles. Many of them are known the world over for their fine products.

W have been fortunate in finding a place to live in this war inflated city. At present we are occupying a hotel room until remodeling is completed in the house in which we have secured a furnished room. There we will have a cozy room with brand new furniture.

Haven't been on an army post for about a year. Must get acclimated all over again. I am living off the post even now and will continue to do so, I hope. Our new office is located at the Presidio of San Francisco, truly the most beautiful Army post I have ever seen. Some parts of it are even quaint, others most modern. The Presidio was established by the Spaniards before the Revolution and was an active fortification in 1776. Many things around here testify to that fact.

Guess I must get out of here and go home to my wife.

God's blessing to you. Greet all our friends, too, please.

Sincerely,

Roman J.

Roman's last published letter to the *News-Wave* during the war was written after receipt of the "Special Serviceman's Edition" of November 30, 1944, and appeared in the paper on January 4, 1945:

Dear Glenn and Gang:

Must take this opportunity to congratulate all on the fine job you did on the Servicemen's Edition of the Independence News-Wave. It really is a job to be righteously proud in presenting. It must have caused an ocean of extra work.

Each and every man and woman in the service will deeply appreciate receiving a copy of that little token of greeting. Almost two years have passed since I last visited that good old home town. You have no idea how good it is to glance through the pages at those many faces which were so great a part of our boyhood. One doesn't realize himself how he misses all of them until such an occasion as this arises. I know that to all of those in faraway places a pang of homesickness will cling as they repeatedly pick up that best of all material Christmas gifts this season. However, the pleasure they will derive from it will outweigh their anxiety to return home by many times.

Our sincere thanks to each and everyone who in any way assisted in making the Edition the great success it is.

Now for a little news from the home front. We have a rare combination of home and fighting front in this war. In fact it divides itself between two addresss, Presidio of San Francisco and 317 12th Avenue. The latter is a cozy, roomy apartment. A permanent guest has arrived for that too, in the person of Thomas Michael Jaszewski, the new heavy weight member of the family. He weighed 6 lbs. 3 ounces at birth.

Fall is the most beautiful time of the year here, the warmest, too. Believe it or not it is warmer here now at around 65 degrees above zero as a maximum, and around 40 degrees above minimum each day, than it is in July and August when a constant is maintained in the middle fifties. Besides it's sunny almost every day now, whereas most of the summer is dark and foggy.

Wanted to tell you that at last I'm doing what the army trained me so long for. After a year at office work at a desk of my own and with my old gang all overseas but two besides myself, they left me here as a repair man on thirty units of various Teletype equipment. Most of it runs non-stop twenty-four hours a day too. I love my new work, stayed with the same outfit but was put in a different branch and have a "boost" on the way.

Wishing you the best this holiday season has in store, and a Happy and Prosperous New Year.

Romy, Dot and Tommy

A Quote From History...

"Biak was a tough one."
  Bennie Kloss
  United States Army
  Describing action of his 205th Field Artillery Battalion in
    May-June 1944.

JELEN, CODDY

Coddy completed his boot training at Great Lakes Naval Station, Chicago, Illinois, in May 1945 and was being sent to San Diego for further assignment with the Navy.

JELEN, ROMAN S.

Roman, a Private in the United States Army, wrote his parents that he was confined to a hospital in Palm Springs, California, following four months on Guadalcanal. (July 15, 1943) On August 12, 1943, it was reported he was home on a furlough after which he would undergo a physical exam and be reclassified. The reason for his hospitalization was not identified.

Roman Jelen, left, with Joseph "Chester" Mlynek, center, and Bernie Kulig, right.

JOHNSON, DAVID

David entered service with the United States Army on March 16, 1943. He served with a special Air Transport Command unit of the Army Air Corps in China and Central Burma. When discharged on March 14, 1946, he was a Private First Class and had earned the American Theater Service Medal, Asiatic-Pacific Theater Ribbon with three battle stars, and Good Conduct Medal. (March 21, 1946)

David's wife, Corporal Edith, also served with the Army Air Corps. (March 8, 1945)

JOHNSON, ERLING

In early March 1945 Erling was a Seaman Second Class serving with the Navy Air Corps in Pensacola, Florida. (March 8, 1945)

JOHNSON, KERMIT

Kermit was a medical military policeman serving at Torney General Hospital, Palm Springs, California, in early March 1945. (March 8, 1945)

JOHNSON, ORVILLE G.

Orville earned the American Theater and Asiatic-Pacific Theater Ribbons while serving in the Navy during World War II. About the time the war ended, he was promoted to Quartermaster Third Class while serving aboard a destroyer in the Pacific.

JONIETZ, RAYMOND J.

Ray joined the Army in the early summer of 1945. Following a furlough, which he spent at home, he was to report to San Francisco for further assignment (August 2, 1945).

KAMPA, BENNIE J.

Bennie was overseas with the Army when he wrote a letter to Glenn Kirkpatrick at the *News-Wave* on July 20, 1943. Published on August 12, 1943, it informed Kirkpatrick of his change of address:

Dear Mr. Kirkpatrick:

Must drop you a few lines to give my right APO number which is now 508, Care Postmaster, New York, N.Y. I have been getting the paper so far until I got transferred, and it was very interesting for me to read about my good old friends who are working hard at home trying to keep us rolling to win this war.

I am getting along fine. I try to do my best, and I like army life. I get plenty to eat, and a place to sleep -- what more would a person want. Of course I have to work pretty hard, but I do not believe there is anyone who isn't working right now. This war keeps everybody on the ball.

The last paper I received was April 22, but it takes quite a while for the mail to reach us when the APO isn't right.

Regards to all my friends,
Bennie J. Kampa

As a Corporal in late February 1945, he wrote again to the *News-Wave*, a portion of which was published on March 15, 1945:

I sure appreciate reading about the goings on back in my home town. I have been transferred so much in the past, and I sure had plenty of rough going, but it seems like I'm use to it already. I've been serving overseas now for over two years with eight months of that time in France. Have had a chance to visit a few of these cities and find it a good experience, but have been getting it the hard way. The other boys get their share of it here. Best regards to all my friends of Independence and to those who are reading your paper.

KAMPA, DOMINIC

Dominic was a Private First Class in the 39th Military Police Company. On April 26, 1945 it was reported he had landed at Lingayen Gulf on the island of Luzon, Philippine Islands, on D-Day, January 27, 1945. Through much of the battle, he operated at or near the front lines and was involved in the effort to free the capital city of Manila. By this time he had been overseas for two years, being stationed at New Caledonia, Guadalcanal, and Bougainville before reaching Luzon. He wore the Good Conduct Medal and Asiatic-Pacific Theater Ribbon with one battle star, this for his participation in the Luzon campaign, and was also awarded the Philippine Liberation Ribbon with one battle star. It was reported the 39th Military Police was the "oldest MP organization in the Pacific."

Dominic received his discharge in November 1945 (November 22, 1945). He may have served in the Army of Occupation as it is stated that he saw Tokyo following Japan's surrender.

KAMPA, EDWARD

One week after the bombing of Pearl Harbor, Ed arrived home and announced he was enlisting. The next day he left for Great Lakes Naval Training Station, Chicago, Illinois.

Ed was a Naval electrician. He was sent to Hawaii and from there to Johnson Island, southwest of Hawaii, where he spent most of his tour of duty at a naval radio station. (Roy Kampa, brother)

After arriving back in San Diego on his way home, he telephoned his mother, Mrs. Mike Kampa, on December 8, a day after her birthday, and told her he would be home soon. The next day, his mother received a surprise birthday telegram. (December 13, 1945)

KAMPA, GEORGE

George served with a Naval air unit during World War II. He held the rating of Aviation Machinists Mate Third Class in May 1945.

A Quote From History. . .

"Jesus, I don't ever want to see that again! There were box cars with bodies loaded like cordwood!"
    Ray Pieterick
    United States Army
    From an interview, July 9, 1998, describing the liberation of
        Hurlach Lager No. 4 concentration camp.

KAMPA, LAWRENCE M.

Lawrence was a Mess Sergeant with the Army and was stationed in Brazil when he wrote the following letter to Glenn Kirkpatrick at the *News-Wave*. Dated January 9, 1944, it was published January 20, 1944:

Hi Kirk:

Just a line or two from this part of the world to let you know that the News-Wave arrives safely. I am one of the many men in this great Army that the rookie dreads to come in contact with from the day he is called to the day he leaves. We go by the title of Mess Sgt., but we are seldom called that. Even if we are hard boiled, broiled, fried or otherwise, we still enjoy reading a paper from home and more so after spending over a year without one.

While reading the paper I noticed that the rationing did not affect the News-Wave the least bit, it is still the same as it was the day I left home. Of course the credit for this can only go to you, Kirk, and your staff. So keep up the good work and some day after this is over, we hope to see you and the people of Independence in a better and more peaceful world.

Just one of the Boys,
S/Sgt. Lawrence M. Kampa

The foster son of Mr. and Mrs. August A. Mish, Lawrence had deep feelings for Mrs. Mish, the only mother he had ever known. She received a letter from him from Brazil just prior to Mother's Day 1944 in which he included a poem expressing his thoughts:

I lay awake nights thinking of my Mother that I knew
    Because my real mother's years were limited to so few.
The almighty God placed me into yours hands to raise
    So I don't know anyone in this world that deserves more praise.
Mother, you did a good job with a punk like me,
    So I pray that God with his own eyes will see
The best days of your life you spent just toiling for me.
    Mother I hope I am forgiven for some of the rules I broke,
Because as a youngster, I thought some of them were a joke.
    But as I grow older, I could begin to realize,
That Mother's rules meant more to me than I could see with my own eyes.
    So, Mother, now that I am so very far away,
I can still see you as I saw you that first day.
    And I pray that the good Lord will keep you that way,
Until I get back, because this time I know I will stay.

On June 14, 1945 it was reported Lawrence had married Miss Rose Marsolek, Independence, in Milwaukee on June 6. He was stationed at the time at Carlisle Barracks, Pennsylvania.

KAMPA, PAUL E.

Paul entered service with the United States Army on December 30, 1941. At some point he transferred to the Army Air Corps before going overseas in June, 1942, and spending two years in Iceland as a "slum burner," as he described himself in a letter to Glenn Kirkpatrick dated July 25, 1943 and published on August 5, 1943:

Dear Mr. Kirkpatrick:

Just a line to let you know that I am fine and enjoy reading the News-Wave very much. It certainly is nice to read about what's going on back home.

I am stationed somewhere in Iceland. We have here with us several boys from Wisconsin. In fact, some from every state in the union in my outfit and I'll still say they've never been in Heaven until they've come to Wisconsin. As for my job I'm an army cook, in other words a "slum burner." I enjoy my work very much. The food is good and we get plenty to eat.

By the way, Kirk, would you plese change the A.P.O. No. on my address from 860 to 610? I just haven't much time at the present, so I suppose I'll have to sign off. Give my regards to all back home and keep smiling and the world will smile with you.

Sincerely,

Pfc. Paul E. Kampa

P. S. - Please write.

On March 2, 1944 a note from Paul was published thanking the American Legion for the cigarettes sent to him. He reported the weather in Iceland wasn't too bad, that "We have a bit of snow and sometimes the sun shines two hours a day."

From Iceland, Paul was sent to England for several months and then crossed over to France.

In December 1944 he received a furlough home on the rotation of personnel plan. He indicated he had grown accustomed to Iceland, found England an interesting country, and believed Paris was the most beautiful city he had ever seen. He had mastered some of the French language, enough to get around, and found some customs there to be "quaint."

Following his furlough, Paul reported to the air base at Santa Ana, California, where he was to await reassignment. In late November 1944 he was promoted to Tech Sergeant. (December 28, 1944)

KERN, LEONARD

Len enlisted in the United States Army on May 15, 1942 and was immediately sent to Camp Shelby, Mississippi, to join the newly formed 85th Division (later the 85th Infantry Division). Assigned to the Signal Corps of the 339th Infantry Regiment, he attended Radio School for several weeks. He then left Camp Shelby after he was accepted to Officer's Candidate School at Fort Benning, Georgia. He graduated from OCS and was commissioned a 2nd Lieutenant on February 15, 1943.

Len spent approximately the next two years stationed at Indiantown Gap Military Reservation, Pennsylvania, a 17,000 acre Army training center. While there, he was promoted to Captain and then soon after sent overseas where he served as a stevedore officer and in the Transportation Corps as a Movement Officer. While a Movement Officer, he was in command of a port company of 226 enlisted men and five officers with the task of loading and unloading ships.

Len was separated from the Army on April 12, 1946 at Camp McCoy, Wisconsin.

Source: Phyllis Kern, wife.

A Quote From History. . .

"We lost 24 of 25 tanks that day and a lot of good guys were killed or captured. I ran all night to get out of there."
Paul Pampuch
United States Army
From an interview, October 10, 1998, describing action during the Battle for Metz, France.

KILNESS, HOMER

A Technical Sergeant in the United States Army, Homer served with the 135th Medical Battalion as a mess sergeant. He had been in New Guinea for eight months before traveling to Australia. The March 25, 1943 *News-Wave* indicated he had written to his parents and sent numerous souvenirs home, including a grass skirt, beads strung by natives, sea shells, other trinkets, and many snapshots.

On March 22, 1945 Homer was reported to be a Technical Sergeant Fourth Grade and back in the states at the Army Ground and Service Forces Redistribution Station in Miami Beach, Florida, where he was awaiting reassignment. He had served 35 months as a cook in the Southwest Pacific Theater and had been awarded the Asiatic-Pacific Theater Ribbon with five battle stars, plus was allowed to wear the Distinguished Unit Citation bar. He joined the United States Army on April 8, 1941.

KLIMEK, CLIFFORD

Clifford, the fourth son of Mr. and Mrs. Simon Klimek, was inducted in Milwaukee, Wisconsin, in mid-September 1945. Following induction, he traveled to Fort Sheridan, Illinois, for active duty. (September 27, 1945)

KLIMEK, JOSEPH

Joe entered the Army Air Force in May 1945, it appears (July 12, 1945). He was stationed at Sheppard Field, Texas, where he was undergoing training as a ground crew member. In September 1945 he was reported to be home on furlough. (September 27, 1945).

KLIMEK, PETER

Peter was inducted into the United States Army in May 1945. While at Camp Ellis, Illinois, he received a medical discharge after which he returned to Independence. (August 23, 1945)

KLOSS, JOSEPH F.

A *News-Wave* article early in 1942 reported the Associated Press had listed 107 Wisconsin men who had been recently wounded in action. Among them was Private Joseph F. Kloss. The article stated his mother had been informed of his having been wounded but no other details were provided then, nor was any other information reported in future editions of the paper.

KLOVE, BENNIE A.

Bennie served with the 497th U. S. Army Hospital Platoon. He was discharged December 23, 1945 at Fort Sheridan, Illinois.

KLOVE, WILLIAM

William was a Technician Fourth Grade in the United States Army by August 1945 and had served 42 months prior to that time with Battery B, 209th Anti-Aircraft Automatic Weapons

Battalion. He had been in Australia, New Guinea, New Britain, and the Philippine Islands. (August 23, 1945)

The 209th was originally designated as the Separate Coast Artillery Battalion Anti-Aircraft Automatic Weapons (2nd Battalion, 94th Coast Artillery). As such, it arrived in Australia on May 15, 1943 and New Guinea on May 19, 1943. Redesignated on October 5, 1944 as the 209th AAA Automatic Weapons Battalion, his unit arrived in the Philippines on January 8, 1945, where it was credited with having participated in the Luzon campaign. In New Guinea, the 209th Coast Artillery -- which consisted of the 2nd Battalion, 94th Coast Artillery Regiment, in which William served -- participated in the Papau campaign.

Source: Book (Stanton)

KUKA, ROMAN

Roman was a Private in the United States Army stationed at Fort Sheridan, Illinois, in June, 1945.

KULIG, ADOLPH P.

Adolph was a Seaman First Class with the United States Navy during World War II.

KUPKA, ALEX P.

Alex was drafted into the United States Army on September 26, 1941. He completed basic training at Camp Livingston, Louisiana, and received further training in Florida. Following a furlough spent at home, he left from Virginia on September 21, 1943 bound for England. He later saw action in France, Belgium, and Germany.

In January 1945 Alex's mother, Mrs. Margaret Kupka, received word from the War Department that her son had been "slightly wounded" on December 17, 1944, for which he was subsequently awarded the Purple Heart. A Private First Class, he was serving with the 130 CML Processing Company as an artillery gun crewman at the time. (January 18, 1945)

Alex was discharged from the Army in December 1945 at the General Hospital in Hot Springs, Arkansas, following three years, three months in the service. He spent one year, nine months overseas. (December 27, 1945)

KWOSEK, FRANK M.

Frank served in the Army's 37th Infantry Division in the Southwest Pacific. He was a 30 year old private when he earned his Combat Infantryman's Badge for his role in helping defeat Japanese attacks on Hill 129 on Bougainville. He spent at least 26 months overseas. (November 9, 1944)

The *News-Wave* reported on November 9, 1944, that Frank had been on the Fiji Islands, New Hebrides, and Guadalcanal, as well as Bougainville. (Ed. -This may be only partially correct as the 37th, which had been on the Fiji's and Guadalcanal, was on New Georgia rather than the New Hebrides as reported in the newspaper.)

The 37th Infantry Division underwent intensive training exercises when it landed on the Fiji Islands on June 11, 1942. It then relocated to Guadalcanal for additional training before landing on New Georgia in the Solomon Islands. On October 18, 1942 Frank wrote a letter to his mother, probably from Guadalcanal, which was published on November 4, 1943:

Dear Mother:

Just a few lines to let you know that I am well.

I finally saw Irvin Sather yesterday. Was he surprised to see me? Took me a half day to find him. He came to camp with me and stayed for the show. I took him back after the show. It was sure nice Marcus sent his address to me. Tell Marcus I saw Irvin and thank him for the address.

What is dad doing now. Tell him hello from me. Will write to him later.

I get all the letters you and the girls send.

I am still driving a jeep and still a boat ride from the Fiji Islands.

Well, I don't know of any more to write, so hope this finds you and Dad well.

With love,

Frank

The 37th Infantry Division landed on Bougainville between November 8-19, 1943 where it relieved the Marines there. During March 1944 the Division repulsed eight Japanese division-strength attacks, these probably the attacks mentioned in the November 9, 1944 article. (Book: Stanton)

KWOSEK, MARCUS

As of November 1944, Marcus was an Army private serving with a field artillery unit stationed in California.

LEQUE, LYLE A.

Lyle was a Private First Class with the United States Army when the war ended. He had served in the Pacific Theater.

LIBOWSKI, EDWARD

In December 1944 Edward was stationed in Oshkosh, Wisconsin. At that time, he wrote a short letter to the *News-Wave* regarding the "Special Serviceman's Edition:"

Dear Kirk:

I am a little late in sending my remittance for the News-Wave as we have been rather busy here.

I did want to write earlier and tell you how much I enjoyed the special edition that you put out. It was the best that I have ever seen and you and the people at home are to be congratulated on the good job. I hope that there will be more like that in the future. After reading the paper I was a bit homesick. There are so many new names that I realize that it has been many years since I left there.

Seasons best wishes to you and yours.

Edward Libowski

LIBOWSKI, PAUL

Paul served in the United States Navy. The June 7, 1945 *News-Wave* reported he was home on convalescent leave following surgery at a Naval Hospital in California. It also stated he had served 10 months at sea and had participated in "several major battles in the South Pacific."

In February 1946 Paul was serving aboard the battleship *U. S. S. Wisconsin* (BB-64). He was discharged on April 15, 1946. (February 21, 1946)

MACIOSEK, EVERETT

Everett served in the United States Navy, apparently aboard ship in the Pacific Theater (January 18, 1945), though he makes mention of tents in letters mailed home. On April 8, 1943 a letter was published in the *News-Wave* indicating he was at Great Lakes Naval Station in Chicago. In it, he described his housekeeping routine:

Dear Mother:

Just a few lines to let you know where I am at. I am at Great Lakes. Was separated from the other boys.

Received the letter, also the box for Easter. Thank you very much. Some of the fellows helped me eat it. I suppose you are wondering what I am doing. I guess every mother does.

Cleaning the barracks is about the toughest job we have to do. We have to wash our own clothes and we have to keep the deck clean with steel wool.

The food is not exactly like yours at home, but its satisfactory, so why should I complain.

It is rather hard to get up in the morning, especially if you have guard duty for four hours. We must be in our bunk at 9:30. It may seem kinda early to you but its a treat for us. We have movies every Monday, Wednesday and Friday nights. That is pretty nice for those who have time to go.

Boy, is it raining out now! I don't think I will do any drilling this afternoon as we had enough of it this morning.

Well, I will sign off as I have a lot of work to do yet. Closing with best regards.

Your son,
Everett

By March 1944 Everett was a Seaman Second Class, stationed at Monterey, California. Another letter home appeared in the March 16, 1944 edition of the *News-Wave*:

Dear Mom:

Have a little spare time so will drop you a few lines. Must let you know that we got here to California March 2. We traveled three days. It certainly was a long ways to go, and now I must say something about California.

The weather here is just like in Wisconsin in summer and the trees and everthing is nice and green. I had some oranges right from the orange tree. One can see lots of different kinds of fruit trees, but many aren't bearing fruit right now so it doesn't look as pretty as in summer.

On the way we stopped nine hours at Los Angeles. I had a few beers there. Sure is beautiful to see the pretty flowers, buildings, etc. Wish you could see the interesting things. I will have lots to tell you when I come home. The name of the town where I am at is Monterey. Its right along the coast. I can see the ocean from my barracks. I am a long ways from home.

How is everything at home? Hope alright. Tell Irene and Roy I will write later as I am very busy now. Well, I believe that's all I can say as we are going out on a hike soon. Closing with best regards to all the relatives and friends at Independence. Good bye.

Your son,
Everett

In a letter to his mother dated December 26, 1944, Everett described his Christmas, some of the fish he was seeing in the waters of the Pacific, and a brief meeting with his good friend, Dominic Sluga. Published on January 18, 1945, he also makes mention of some unknown event that sounds quite tramatic:

Dear Mom,

Will try and answer your letter which I received. I wasn't getting mail for some time, but one day I received 15 letters, so I hope I will be able to answer them.

I met Dominic Sluga. We spent a half day together. He was going to the Philippines but I can't say where I am. We both were very glad to see each other. I wish I could tell you the reasons why you didn't hear from me so long, but I hope I won't have to go through that again.

Well, it's day after Christmas (I mean out here). I suppose out there you people are waiting for Santa to come. You see we are a day ahead of folks back there. How did you spend Christmas? Write and tell me about it. It made me feel blue to think it was Christmas. We had turkey for chow. I received both of your packages and everthing was very good. I didn't have a game yet with those cards. I also received a Christmas package from Milwaukee where I worked. I thank you very much.

We see lots of big fish out here, like those sharks, Baracuta (Ed. - barracuda), and so forth. Are they ever big!

Now I suppose you would like to know what I am busy with. Well, my buddy and I are building another tent and what a job! I must tell you I bought a film, and you know what it cost me? Three dollars and fifty cents and for developing it cost 35-cents a picture. Try and send some butterscotch or carmel candy. Would they taste good!

Well, I will close for tonight. Would like to answer some other letters. Goodbye, mother, and write soon.

Love,
Everett

On July 3, 1945, Seaman First Class Everett wrote a letter home from the South Pacific that was published on July 26, 1945. It was introduced on the front page of the *News-Wave* with the byline "Everett Maciosek, Seaman First Class, Catches Shark." Editor Kirkpatrick than stated that fishing had been a hobby of Everett's when he was home and that he was writing about catching a 200 pound shark, and "that is no fish story:"

Dear Mom,

I promised to write as soon as I had the pictures developed. The ones of the shark. So here goes. This letter may sound based on fish but I know you are anxious to know how I got it out of the water. One night I saw a lot of fish jumping out, so I thought I would try my luck but I caught only one about 11 inches long, so I didn't want to throw the fish away. I thought I would leave the line set over night. Well, in the morning I got up at five o'clock, as usual, for work and the first thing I did I went to check on my line. I couldn't see the cork but it was docked so I paid little attention to it. Not until I went on the raft and saw the line was tight did I start to pull and so did the shark. And, boy, Mom, I wish you could have seen me. It wouldn't have been bad if I were not alone, but so early in the morning almost all of the fellows were asleep. I hollered for help but no one came so I tried to get it out alone and you bet I did. But it sure was a fight. It so happened that I had a big rope on the raft and I made a ship knot in it with one hand and fought the shark with the other. Then I put the rope around the shark the first time and it got away and the same the next two times, but the fourth time I put it around the body and the two front fins and hung on to it. He was tired by that time so at last he gave up and I pulled his head above the raft and the rest of the body stayed in the water. Then I tied the rope down to the raft, and left him that way for about three hours. Later after I let him free he was still alive, but not much any more.

I was late for work on account of playing out the shark for one hour and 45 minutes but didn't get put on "report" because I told the story to the one in charge of me first and he thought I was telling a fish story but I took him down to the tent and proved my statement. He let me go. About half an hour later the whole island of men was looking at the big catch.

This fishing really reminded me of fishing in the good U. S. A.

The size of the line I used that morning was 95 pound test. The same as that used by carpenters. My hook was once again as large as the ones I used back home for pickerel. The enclosed picture was taken just below my tent along the beach. Oh, yes, I must tell you the weight of this shark was 200 pounds, length was eight feet and three inches. And that tells the fish story.

I should like to have some of the fishermen back home learn of my interesting experience. It may be hard for you to believe but its true just the way I wrote it.

How is everyone around Independence? We are fine and busy. Will be moving soon so, should you not hear from me, do not worry.

Wish I could run across Dominic Sluga again. Tell Irene and Roy hello from me and don't forget

Everett Maciosek. Photo at right shows the shark
he caught that is described in his letter of July 3, 1945.

about my new address. It is getting late so will close with best regards to all.
>Love,
>Everett

Everett was discharged on December 14, 1945 with the rank of SSML, Third Class -- and one big fish!

MALONEY, CALVIN

Calvin served with the 804th Medical Air Evacuation Squadron of the Army Air Corps' 5th Air Force. He entered the service in March, 1943. and was stationed at Kearns Field, Utah, and Bowman Field, Kentucky, before going overseas. During his 21 months in the Pacific stationed on New Guinea, Leyte, and Okinawa, the 804th evacuated 100,000 wounded and ill soldiers. Calvin was decorated with the Air Medal with cluster and the 804th was presented with a Distinguished Unit Citation. (January 24, 1946)

After spending 10 weeks in Japan with the Army of Occupation, Calvin arrived back in the United States and received his discharge at Fort Lewis, Washington, on December 6, 1945. with the rank of Tech Sergeant, Third Grade. When he returned to his home in Bruce Valley, he brought with him kimonos for his mother and other relatives, as well as chopsticks, which the News-Wave reported "he had learned to use with skill."

On June 15, 1944, Calvin wrote a letter from New Guinea to his parents that was published on July 27, 1944:

Dear Folks:

Was swell to get your letter of the twenty-fifth before we left. Glad you got the address, but this letter has a new one and I'll try to write it plain so you can read it.

Yes, we're starting all over again, and what a place to start.

Tonight it looks as though we should have a beautiful sunset. It's clear except for the dust, and that usually makes a pretty sunset. Speaking of dust, this is the only place I've seen that has Utah beat. It's so thick one darn near has to cut it.

To get back to our situation. It isn't bad, course it's a stony place with a lot of tall grass, but they've got a bulldozer in tonight leveling off a place for the tents. The best part of it is that there's a rocky stream running along the edge of camp and there are lots of deep spots in it that are swell for bathing. It's clear and not muddy and we sure need a good place to bathe with all the dust there is around here.

We've got seven fellows in our tent. We'll only have four when we get our place built up, but we've got quite a bit of room even with seven guys and their stuff in here.

Had jungle rations for breakfast, powdered milk which we made some chocolate out of, then some sort of breakfast food which was filling but awfully sweet.

We're really on the beam. Have lights and all. We're sorta lucky as the electrician is in our tent. We've got a driver. The rest of us contribute our bit so we usually have about the most up to date lodgings in camp. Its okay only it attracts a crowd and we hate to be rude and run the guys out.

They brought up some mail today. Got one from Curt and one from Wilma. Really makes a fella feel good to get mail. I imagine you know what I mean.

I must close now.

Love
"Cal"

On September 24, 1944 Calvin wrote a letter from New Guinea that was published on October 26, 1944:

Dear Olive and Curt:

About time you say, and so do I. I have some fifty odd letters to answer so you see I've got a job. This one I'm answering tonight happened before I left, but I didn't get home the couple of days before we took off for the big city so you have been waiting all this time for the answer to your letter.

First of all the furlough is all over, and how we know. Just no more than get back hardly for we were up early and at it.

Now before I forget it, I sent a package home. I'd like to have made it all individual but it was better to have it shipped as one. It isn't very much but it's about the best we could do. It's awfully hard to get nice souvenirs there. It will probably get there before Christmas, but I will let you open it before if you will promise to be real good.

No, I'm not going to settle in Australia. Yes, it's nice; people are friendly. Sydney is a very nice city. They made wonderful beer or so the other fellas said but I did find out I can drink as much milk as ever, even gained about five pounds while I was there, and that's not bad.

We'd like to have driven the people wild, I guess, but they should be used to these jungle happy nephews of Uncle Sam. Anyway, we really got service. Our eating headquarters were Hotel Adams and Australia. At each one the gang had a special table and waitress. I should say the same one each time, and I do mean we got service. Even got steaks when no one else did. Sure, we had to talk. Sometimes I think we gave 'em headaches but we were having a good time and they got tipped for their trouble. The girls, well as a group they aren't as pretty as those in the states. One reason the men don't seem to expect so much of them as we do. I don't suppose the girls in the states would admit that they care what the men think but it makes a difference both ways. The general dress there is much sloppier than in the states. I don't see why it should be; I imagine they enjoy life as much as we do.

Here I was going to get a lot written tonight and one of the guys has been in talking so guess I'll have to sign off and get some sleep. I'll try to do better next time.

Love,
Cal

288

In June 1945 Calvin's mother received a letter from the office of 5th Air Force's commander, General George C. Kenney, informing her the Calvin had been awarded the Air Medal. It was published on June 28, 1945:

Headquarters, Allied Air Forces, Southwest Pacific Area
Office of the Cammander

Mrs. George Maloney
Independence, Wisconsin

Dear Mrs. Maloney:

Recently your son, Tech. 3rd Grade Calvin G. Maloney, was decorated with the Air Medal. It was an award made in recognition of courageous service to his combat organization, his fellow American airmen, his country, his home and to you.

He was cited for meritorious achievement while participating in aerial flights in the Southwest Pacific Area from May 29, 1944 to January 15, 1945.

Your son took part in sustained operational flight missions during which hostile contact was probable and expected. These flights included bombing missions against enemy installations, shipping and supply bases, and aided considerably in the recent successes in this theatre.

Almost every hour of every day your son, and the sons of other American mothers, are doing just such things as that here in the Southwest Pacific.

Theirs is a very real and very tangible contribution to victory and to peace.

I would like to tell you how genuinely proud I am to have men such as your son in my command and how gratified I am to know that young Americans with such courage and resourcefulness are fighting our country's battles againt the aggressor nations.

You, Mrs. Maloney, have every reason to share that pride and gratification.

Sincerely,
George C. Kenney
General, United States Army, Commander

While Calvin was stationed in Japan as part of the Army of Occupation, he wrote a letter to his siblings, Olive and Curt, on November 15, 1945. (December 6, 1945) It appeared in the *News-Wave* on December 6, 1945. In it, he described scenes of post-war life in Japan as well as expressed his anticipation of a trip home:

Dear Olive and Curt:

It's time I was dropping you a line or two -- been ages since I wrote. I hope next time I can put on "at sea" or Seattle heading, which brings me to the fact that you'd better not write me any more as I won't be here to get it. It may be another week before I leave. I don't know exactly but I'm in the high point group now and I hope there will be a boat in before long.

The Jap people had been pretty well scared about what they thought we would do to them. The first month we were here they kept pretty clear of our installations -- even used to get off from trains when we got on; now they feel quite different. Almost a little arrogant. Certainly not afraid. Of course that is only true in the towns. If we happen into the coutnry or outlying towns they still back for cover when the Americans show up. At other places the kids come out begging for candy. We haven't felt very liberal toward them like we did the Philippinoes.

The Jap trains are apt to fall apart any time. They are run almost entirely by teen-age boys and girls. The P. W.'s told us about it and I thought they were kidding but I found out they weren't. At that the service is very good.

Speaking of purebred stock, another kid and I were out bicycling around the country the other day and stopped by a University experiment farm. It was cold and, of course, we had hot tea. Then one of the guys showed us around. They had some nice looking chickens though they certainly have a poor method of raising the young ones. There were two hundred about a week old and the only heat was a couple of clucks.

Their cows were thoroughbred holsteins but the stuff looked two thirds starved. They did have a nice looking three-year old sire.

The horses were some beat up nags that should have gone to the foxes months ago. I don't wonder, the stuff they fed 'em. Hay for cows was chopped rice straw nearly as white as the paper on which I'm writing and something they call ground corn but which really looked like ground cobs. I didn't see anything else around. They were collecting garbage from the army mess hall for the pigs so they didn't look bad but the sheep, I felt sorry for them. The poor things were only about half grown and so thin they could hardly stand up. Their bones even stuck out through quite a heavy coat of wool. They must have been on a starvation diet a long time.

It's a cold rainy day in Japan and I've written about enough, so I'll be seeing you some day.
Love,
Cal

MARSOLEK, ERNEST E.

Ernest joined the United States Army on January 9, 1942, and received his initial training at Cheyenne, Wyoming, and Oklahoma City, Oklahoma. He left for North Africa on January 13, 1943, where he served with the Army Air Corps on detached service. Later, while still in North Africa, Ernest served with the 34th Infantry Division as a truck driver. Besides serving in North Africa, he also was stationed on Sicily and Corsica. During his two years, nine months in the service, he earned the Northern Defense Service Ribbon, one service stripe, five overseas bars, and the Good Conduct Medal.

Ernest returned to the United States on October 4, 1945 and was discharged at Camp Grant, Illinois, on October 15, 1945, as a Private First Class. (January 3, 1946)

The January 3, 1946, edition of the *News-Wave* reported he suffered three bouts of malaria while in North Africa, which, surprisingly, was quite common in that desert region.

MARSOLEK, GEORGE P.

It appears George entered the service in late 1940 or early 1941. As a Sergeant with the Army Air Corps, he graduated from a technical school at Chanute Field in Rantoul, Illinois, around January 1, 1942. (January 15, 1942) By June, 1942, he was a Staff Sergeant and aircraft mechanic and was stationed at Hamilton Field, California, with the the 49th Fighter Squadron. (June 11, 1942)

In December 1942 his parents received a cablegram from George, then a Technical Sergeant, stating that he had arrived safely in North Africa. His parents indicated his widely-spaced letters seem to come from different parts of the world. (December 24, 1942)

In the June 8, 1944 issue of the *News-Wave*, it was reported George was home on furlough from Italy, having previously been in England and North Africa. He spent two years overseas.

MARSOLEK, JOHN P.

John served as a Private First Class in the United States Army during World War II. He also served in the Korean War.

MARSOLEK, RUFUS

In December, 1943 Rufus was a Petty Officer Second Class in the United States Navy and stationed at Fort Dix, New Jersey. (December 23, 1943) The November 2, 1944, edition of the *News-Wave* reported he had joined the recently formed Seabees in October, 1943, and was sent to

North Africa in February 1944. There he was stationed with a Construction Battalion Maintenance Unit and was a motor machinist with the rank of M MOM, Second Class. At one point he sent to the *News-Wave* a long poem (not written by Rufus) entitled "Africa," which described how the Seabees were glad to be helping but couldn't wait to get home. After 19 months in North Africa, he was sent home due to the serious illness of his mother.

MARSOLEK, VALENTINE
Valentine served as a Private in the United States Army.

MATCHEY, RAYMOND A.
Ray served as a Private First Class with the Army Air Corps' 16th Bomb Group.

MATTSON, ELROY
Elroy, his brother and mother, had moved to Eau Claire from the Chimney Rock area. Elroy was a Private First Class in the United States Army, serving about two-and-a-half years. He was stationed in the Philippines at one point, only 30 miles from his brother, Lyle, also stationed there, but both were unaware of their proximity to one another.

MATTSON, LYLE
Lyle was a cook with the rank of Sergeant in the United States Army during World War II. He was stationed on the Philippine Islands at one point.

MAULE, ALBERT J.
Albert joined the United States Army in October 1942. He served with the 361st Infantry Regiment, 91st Infantry Division, which distinguished itself through three campaigns in Italy. (January 11, 1945) He was awarded his Combat Infantryman's Badge in Italy while a Staff Sergeant. He later was decorated with the Bronze Star for "heroic achievement in action." At the time of his discharge from the service, Albert was a Technical Sergeant. (February 15, 1945)

MAULE, CLARENCE
An article in the December 23, 1943 *News-Wave* reported Clarence was a Fireman, Third Class, aboard a Navy cruiser in the Southwest Pacific. From there, he sent home a 10-yen piece, "which is worth about $20 in Japan but only 80 cents here." He wrote he had gotten it from a Marine. It is known that he spent time stationed in New Zealand.

Clarence was reported home on furlough in early January 1944. He had entered the service in May 1943. (January 13, 1944)

MELBY, ARDELL G.
Ardell served with a construction unit, possibly in the Seabees, in the Pacific Theater. A letter to the *News-Wave*, published August 2, 1945 best describes some of his travels and duties:

Dear Friends:

I have been overseas for quite some time and miss the old home town very much. It will be a great day when we'll all again be home. A fellow doesn't realize how much his friends and family and such mean to him, until he has to leave them.

I left the states with C. B. M. U. 606. The majority of the men in the unit are on their second tour of overseas duty, having previously served with various Construction Battalions.

The record of our unit has been both unique and enviable. The attributes of willingness, skill and cooperation have been demonstrated time and time again by all hands.

Abourd our transport, the U. S. S. Sarasota, a large percentage of us were called upon to complete unfinished work in communications, carpentering, electricity, ship-fitting and boiler room installations.

We stopped at a number of islands before we reached New Guinea, which we thought was our final destination.

We left New Guinea on various LST's bound for the Philippines. On arrival during the invasion in January and the events immediately following will always remain a part of my memories. Lying out in the Gulf watching the ships shell the beaches, waiting to go ashore ourselves, watching the night artillery fire, finally hitting the beach and soon thereafter being subject to Jap air raids and artillery, all blended together giving most of us our first taste of war in progress.

Then came our move to the site where we erected a complete 2,000 man camp in two week's time only to find we had a higher priority job ahead of us -- the erection of a Naval camp. Thus began the long overland move hampered by rough, muddy, bombed-out roads and the thought that we had been allowed only twelve days to place the new camp in operation. Together we turned what was nothing but a rugged, dusty field of wrecked Jap planes, dugouts and bomb craters into a 2,500 man temporary tent camp in the allotted time.

We were all justly proud of the congratulatory dispatch from Admiral Wagnen for the job we had done so well.

Now, that temporary camp has completely disappeared and a permanent camp with all modern conveniences has taken its place -- all because of our efforts and initiative under adverse conditions.

Things are very quiet here, now, and we laugh at the hardships of only a few months ago. What is and has been on our mind for so long is to get rid of this mess as soon as possible and return to the land we love.

Yours truly,
Ardell G. Melby

Note: It has been brought to this writer's attention that Ardell Melby and Ardell Hendrickson are the same person. See page 271 of Volume I for an additional "glimpse" into Ardell's World War II service.

MISCH, ALBERT J.

Albert was a former resident of Independence whose family moved to Arcadia. On July 5, 1945 the *News-Wave* stated Albert was one of the machinists involved with the reconditioning of B-17's for possible relocation from England to the Pacific Theater. While at an aerial depot near Bury St. Edmunds, Suffolk, England, he had invented and manufactured a number of time-saving devices which aided in speeding up the repairs of the bombers, and for this he was awarded the Bronze Star.

A Quote From History. . .

"Thank God there is such a thing as the Red Cross."
T. George Smick
United States Army
Letter to parents, January 11, 1944, while a POW at Stalag 3B.

MLYNEK, CLARENCE

Clarence served with the United States Army's 217th Signal Corps. Drafted on June 17, 1942, he left the States in 1943 for the Pacific Theater where he was stationed on the Society, Figi, and New Hebrides Islands. In October 1944 he was on Guadalcanal where he performed office clerical duties. A *News-Wave* article of November 2, 1944, described some of the leisure-time activities Clarence participated in while on Guadalcanal, which included taking part in sporting events organized by the men stationed there. He also spent a great deal of time in the hobby shop there where he and other men created many articles made from salvaged flags, bayonets, hand grenades, and other pieces of equipment the Japanese had left behind. The article states he had "turned out some very clever bookends, smoking sets, bracelets, crucifix sets, and a number of other souvenirs," as well as "bracelets from left over parts of the Jap planes that were shot down." He also sent home Fijian and Japanese money and two grass skirts that "are being treasured as a novelty by his sisters."

From a copy of the 217th Signal Corps' bulletin, "The Palm Reader," the *News-Wave* printed an excerpt regarding Clarence's role in his unit's baseball team: "We beat the Pile Driving Engineers by a merry tune of 5-1. With Mlynek and Ferlisi sharing the offensive spotlight, the Depot Demons hit pay dirt in five of the nine frames. . . Mlynek, the little man with the big bat, accounted for our lone marker in the second frame by blasting a home run to deep center field. . ."

Along with the bulletin, Clarence enclosed a letter to his parents dated October 15, 1944 from which several paragraphs were published in the newspaper article of November 2:

> It's Sunday morning and here I'm at work today. I was in church this morning, for I never miss that. It's my Sunday to work, so I'll have a little time to catch up on my letter writing. I have quite a few to write. Margaret wrote and told me that she has been out on the farm for a week. Also said that her folks had an auction, but Uncle Matt bought the farm back. Well, mom, how is everything around home this fine fall day? I sure would like to be there now with the pheasant season on. I bet Uncle Tom is out hunting. They say the ducks are very good this year. A buddy of mine got a letter from his wife and she says this year there are plenty of ducks and pheasants. His wife is a great hunter. She's from St. Cloud.
>
> Has Aunt Martha moved into town yet? I suppose Alfred is still driving truck for Uncle Pete. How is dad making out this year? If you see Alfred, ask him why the heck he doesn't write. I haven't heard from Rudy for quite some time. I suppose he is out on the field somewhere. He sure has a good job. Hope he can keep it.
>
> I am glad to hear that you received the book ends and elephants. How did you like the pictures of the natives that I have sent? Also the Japanese money? It will be something to remember these bastards anyway. I will want to forget that I ever was down this way. Yesterday we got an issue of beer again. It sure is good to have a bottle once in a while, but they raised the prices on us. This beer is not as good as the beer back home. It's like drinking water with a little coloring in it. Well, mom, I guess I'll have to be closing for this time. May God bless you and protect you all.
>
> Your loving son,
> Clarence

In the January 11, 1945 *News-Wave*, it was reported the John Mlynek's had been informed by their son that he had come across Private Homer Bidney of Independence while on Guadalcanal. They had both been on the island for a year, billeted only 1000 feet apart and attending the same movies at the same time, but had never met before. At this time, Clarence held the rank of Corporal.

MLYNEK, EDWARD

Edward entered the United States Army on July 17, 1941, and received training at Camp Lee, Virginia, and Fort Bragg, North Carolina. On March 2, 1942, he departed for the Pacific Theater of Operations where he spent two years serving in a medical unit in Australia, New

Guinea, and Luzon, Philippine Islands. He arrived back in the States on August 2, 1945 wearing seven overseas bars, the Asiatic-Pacific Theater Ribbon with one battle star, the Philippine Liberation Ribbon with one star, and the Good Conduct Medal. (August 23, 1945)

MLYNEK, RUDY

In February 1945 Rudy was a Corporal in the United States Army. On the 24th of that month, he wrote a letter to his parents that was published on March 22, 1945 in the *News-Wave*:

Somewhere in India
February 24, 1945
Dear Mom, Dad and Sisters:
Well, I've finally reached my destination which is somewhere in India. If nothing else, Mom, have them check the watch completely and then return it to me. If you can get some kind of pipe, please send that too, because I can't get one here.
We were issued eight cans of beer yesterday and also eight cans today, and is it ever good!
What I've seen of the country coming here, I wouldn't care for any of it. But I do believe it will pass for a few days, even months. In fact, it will have to do.
I've started the work for which I was trained in the states. Yesterday I was working in the Officer's Mess Halls doing a little K. P.
It's better late than never, but I want to wish Dad a Happy Birthday and more to come.
I must close for now. May God bless you and keep you in the best of health.
Your loving son,
Rudy

MORCHINEK, EDWARD D.

Edward served as a Private in the United States Army. He was attached to Company C, 744 Military Police Battalion. In December 1942 he was reported stationed in Georgia. (December 24, 1942) On June 14, 1943 he was stationed in Yuma, Arizona, from where he wrote a letter to his brother, Frank, that was published on July 1, 1943:

Dear Brother:
Received your letter yesterday and was glad to hear from you. I am now in Arizona, stationed on a desert. It is hot as hell here and when a fellow walks he sinks ankle-deep in sand. I am with the automotive group. All we do is stop all government vehicles and check up on them and see in what condition they are in. It is a snap. All I do is flag them down and the other boys check them. Last week we didn't do a thing for we ran short of forms.
We drive two jeeps. We can go any place we want to when off duty. Last week we went to Old Mexico. Stayed there Saturday and Sunday. Attended a bull fight which cost us 75-cents in Mexican money. The whiskey is cheap there, 30-cents a pint and we pay 40-cents a shot and 25-cents a bottle of beer in the states.
I received a couple letters from "Sinker" and he says he doesn't hear from you folks at all. Well, there is no more news so will close. Best of luck to you all.
Edward

MORCHINEK, NICK

Nick was stationed in San Diego in December 1942, probably (though not confirmed) with the Navy.

MORCHINEK, ROMAN R.

Roman served as a Private First Class in the United States Army, entering the service around April 1942. Two letters, dated April 12, 1943 and May 16, 1943, were published in the *News-Wave* on April 15, 1943, and May 27, 1943, respectively. The first was sent to G. L. Kirkpatrick at the newspaper:

Dear Kirk:

As I am moving to a different camp I thought I would let you know and have my paper sent to me on a new address. I sure enjoy reading it and the news that's going on around home. I am o. k. and hope that you and all my friends back home are the same.

I am writing this letter while I am moving on the train. I started on the trip from Fort Lewis Saturday afternoon, April 10, and today it is the 12th, somewhere in Utah. I will get to my new camp sometime tomorrow morning, the 13th. Went through some nice cities while on my trip, such as Portland, Oregon; Shoshone and Pocatello, Idaho; Salt Lake City, Utah; and a lot more them that I don't remember.

Have one more state to cross which is Nevada before I will reach my new camp in California. I am traveling all the way on the Union Pacific, going the round about way on account of the railroads being so busy transporting troops nowadays. We've got our kitchen right with us, also the P. X., so we can buy our cigarettes and candy at any time.

Guess I will close as it is kinda hard to write while the train is moving. Hoping I will be getting the paper right along with the best regards to all around Independence.

Roman R. Morchinek

His second published letter was written from Los Angeles, California, and sent to his brother, Joseph:

Dear Brother:

Just a few lines to let you know that I received your letter the other day and was glad to hear from you. I am feeling fine and hope these few lines will find you the same.

The weather is about the same, hot and dry wind blowing almost every day and dusty. A fellow can't open his eyes from dust. I suppose the weather is nice back home right now and everything is in bloom. I received a letter from Sophia the other day and she said Archie Hanke was killed in Ohio. Was sorry to hear that.

Will you go to the News-Wave office with my change of address? I am out here on the desert and do not know what's going on. I miss the News-Wave and would appreciate your giving him my new address.

I am up for reclassification on account of my age as I'm unable to take the infantry anymore. I don't know when or where I will be transferred but will let you know later. I haven't heard anything from Fred lately or John either. The last time I heard from Fred was at Easter when I received a card. I wrote him but haven't heard since.

Guess I will close for this time.

Your brother,
Roman

NORLYN, ALFRED E.

Alfred served with the United States Army during World War II.

PALKOWSKI, JOHN

In March 1945 John was a Corporal serving with the United States Army in Germany. On March 17, 1945 he wrote the following letter thanking the people of Independence for the

"Special Serviceman's Edition" of the *News-Wave* he had received. The letter was published in the April 5, 1945 edition:

Dear Sir:

I want to thank you very much for sending me a copy of your 24-page edition. Although it arrived here yesterday, I enjoyed reading it. By the looks of the pictures in your paper the old home town hasn't changed a bit. It sure was good to see the old town even on paper. It really boosted my morale.

I also want to thank the folks in the vicinity of Independence and the Legion and Auxiliary for their kindness.

Give all the people and friends my regards and I hope to see you all in the old places again.

One of the gang,

Johnny

PAMPUCH, ROMAN P.

Roman Pampuch enlisted in the United States Army on November 5, 1942 in Milwaukee, Wisconsin. Where he underwent basic training is unknown as is the location of any additional training he may have received. He was trained as a truck driver and mechanic, however, and also earned a marksman's badge in the use of the 30-caliber Model 1903 Springfield rifle. On September 29, 1944 Roman left the United States with the 22nd Truck Battalion where he was assigned to the Service Company, and arrived in the European Theater of

Operations on October 12, 1944. As a Technician 5th Class, Roman drove 2-1/2 ton GMC trucks as well as performed maintenance work on the vehicles of his battalion.

Roman remained in this capacity through the end of the war in Europe, participating in the Ardennes, Rhineland, and Central Europe campaigns. Near the end of the war he was promoted to Staff Sergeant and placed in charge of the trucks and supplies of the battalion. On April 1, 1945 Roman was wounded in action near Wandershausen, Germany, though the details of this incident are not known. He did, however, apparently spend several weeks at the 182nd General Hospital in Europe, where he was awarded the Purple Heart on April 25, 1945. On May 4, 1945 Roman left Europe bound for the United States, arriving there on May 15, 1945. He was separated from the Army at Fort Leonard Wood, Missouri, on October 21, 1945. In addition to the Purple Heart, Roman was awarded the European-African-Middle Eastern Theater Campaign Ribbon with four bronze battle stars, one Overseas Bar, and the Good Conduct Medal.

PAPE, ELMER F.

Elmer was a Private First Class serving in an Army artillery unit in the Pacific Theater. (October 11, 1945) On March 15, 1945 it was reported in the *News-Wave* that he was in the Philippines.

PARAZINSKI, LOUIS

Louis served in the United States Army. After two-and-a-half years, most of which was spent in a North Carolina camp, Louis received an honorable medical discharge. (January 25, 1945)

PIETERICK, EUGENE

Gene Pieterick graduated from Independence High School in May 1945 and was drafted shortly afterward. At the time he entered active duty, he already had two brothers, Ray and Gerald ("Bud"), serving in Europe. Gene went to Aberdeen Proving Grounds, Maryland, for basic training, then was given additional training in clerical procedures.

Following that training period, he boarded ship and landed in Le Havre, France. By this time the war was over in Europe, but a great deal had to be done in managing the occupation army and beginning the rebuilding process. From Le Havre, Gene was transported to Frankfurt, Germany, where he was to be stationed. He was in Frankfurt only a short time, however, when he received orders reassigning him to the Eschwege Ordnance School in Eschwege, Germany, located close to the Russian zone of occupation. He was assigned to the Ordnance Center there where he performed clerical duties.

Gene completed his tour in Europe in early 1947, whereupon he returned to the States and was discharged from the Army. (Personal letter)

Photo: Page 149

PYKA, RALPH

Ralph served in the United States Army during World War II. According to a letter sent to the American Legion Post 186 in Independence, written on January 19, 1944, he had been in North Africa and was then in Italy. The letter was in response to the Legion's sending cigarettes to the boys overseas and it was published in the *News-Wave* on February 17, 1944:

Hello Boys:

Well, I was surprised to see a carton of cigarettes from you boys. I sure did appreciate them from you boys. Thanks a lot for them.

How are things going around good old Independence now days? There are days that I wish I was there with you boys. I cannot tell you where I am in Italy. But I can tell you where I was in Africa. I was at Casablanca, Port Lyoutey, Oran, Rabat, Side ble Abbes, Mostagnemen, Bizerte, Tunis, and when you went to town down there it was hell. They are so unclean that a man even did not care to go to town. Those Arabs are hell. I don't want to see no part of Africa no more. These people are a lot cleaner and they wash our clothes, but they are high on their price.

We get shelled and bombed and get strafed by planes and that is hell. We got fox holes 4 or 5 feet deep.

Yours truly,
Ralph

REBARCHEK, HERMAN H.

The July 26, 1945 *News-Wave* reported Herman, an Army Private, had graduated from the track vehicles chassis course at Ordnance School, Aberdeen Proving Grounds, Maryland.

RECK, EDWARD

Edward had moved from Independence to Cudahy, Wisconsin, in 1937. He entered the United States Army in mid-1942 and served in the infantry with the 28th Infantry Division. He went overseas and spent time in England and Wales before crossing to the continent. The 28th Infantry entered combat on July 30, 1944 in the hedgerow country near St. Lo, France, and participated in the Normandy, Northern France, Rhineland, Ardennes-Alsace, and Central Europe campaigns. As a Technical Sergeant, Edward saw action throughout from Normandy to the heart of Germany and participated in two of the most famous battles of World War II, the "Battle for the Huertgen Forest" and the "Battle of the Bulge" (see Edward J. Maule biography for more 28th Infantry Division details).

At some point, Edward was wounded, after which he spent five months, six days in a hospital. Besides the Purple Heart, he had earned four campaign stars (Ed. - He may have been hospitalized during one of the 28th's five campaigns), the Combat Infantryman's Badge, and Good Conduct Medal.

Edward wrote the following letter to the *News-Wave* on April 7, 1945 from Germany, thanking and complimenting Independence for the "Special Serviceman's Edition" that he had received and describing some of his activities overseas. It was published on June 14, 1945:

> Hi You Folks:
>
> Don't know if you remember me or not, but I must write you this letter and compliment you on a fine edition of the Special Edition of the News-Wave for the boys in service. It's been some time now since I last paid good old Independence a visit, and in your paper I am able to keep up with the good old town very satisfactorily and read the news of the boys who are scattered over the globe. Most of all I was very pleased to be able to follow the basketball team which did so splendidly this year and last. I can brag about good old Independence and proud to do so, even if I have been away from it now eight years or so.
>
> Many changes have taken place I notice, all for the good, which shows the people of Independence are very well up in the world with the rest of the communities, and are taking no back seats from anyone. Keep up the good work.
>
> I have been receiving your weekly edition quite regularly, but due to some change, want you to send it to a different address. I myself now have been in close to three years. Of these three years, 19 months have (been) spent overseas in the following countries: Wales, England, Scotland, France, Belgium, Luxemburg, and Germany. A tour of the countries the hard way as an infantry man, all except Scotland where I enjoyed a seven-day leave.
>
> I was in a hospital for five months and six days, and just returned not too long ago, and am glad to be back with the old boys, those that are still left. Changes do occur often. I have not run into anyone from Independence as yet -- looked hard too. I did run into a fellow from my new home town, Cudahy, three of them overseas. It sure was good to see them, so you can imagine how I would feel to meet a boy from Independence.
>
> I did meet, however, the former Evelyn Filla's brother-in-law over here. He is in the same battalion as I once was -- in my company. Knew him well. He is Lt. Beggs.
>
> Guess I better close for this time hoping this letter finds you all in the best of health and enjoying the spring season for it sure is a lively one over here. Keep up the good work.
>
> Bye,
> Eddie

The *News-Wave* reported on August 9, 1945 that Edward, then a Staff Sergeant, was on his way home. Following a furlough spent with his parents, who lived in Arcadia, Wisconsin, he was discharged from the United States Army on September 19, 1945.

RECK, RUDOLPH C.

Rudy attained the rank of Tech 5 with the United States Army during World War II. He served with the 156th General Hospital.

RECK, VINCENT

Vincent served in the military during World War II, but it is not clear as to the branch. His letter from Iran of November 16, 1943 to his wife and daughter was published on December 9, 1943. It offers a glimpse of life in the Middle East at the time:

Dear Dorothy and Susan:

I received your letter dated October 26th several days ago and was certainly glad to hear from you. I'm getting along fine and in the best of health.

Well, it's getting much cooler now and several weeks ago we moved into our new winter quarters which are much nicer than the tents that we were living in. They are made of brick, coated with mud, and more suitable for the rainy season that starts the first of December and rains continuously for about two months.

How is Susie? I certainly would like to see her and of course you too. But I imagine that will be impossible until after this war is over, and the way this war is going it won't last much longer, and then I can come home.

Last week we had a terrible dust storm which lasted about all day. The dust was so thick we couldn't see ten feet ahead. Most of the men wore goggles. It hasn't rained since we came here so you can imagine how dry it is.

This afternoon the men who were off duty played baseball. We don't have very much amusement here. We have shows every other night, but the shows are very old, the latest one I saw was "Stagedoor Canteen." It was very good. They dedicated our new recreations building last week. When the rainy season starts they will have the shows inside. Now they are outside. All the towns are out of bounds because there is too much disease and they're not worth while going to anyhow. We do have a lot of fun with the natives. They are very interesting people.

In one of the nearby cities the natives were doing some construction work. They were given wheelbarrows to push cement in. They didn't know how to use them so they took the wheels off and carried the bed full of cement on their heads. They always do their work the hard way, carrying everything on their heads. In another nearby town the natives wash the streets with small brushes on their hands and knees, carrying the water in five gallon pails. Can you imagine that?

The men wear long dresses about down to their ankles, most of which are ragged and filthy dirty. Both the men and women go barefooted, now and then they wear shoes. They also wear rags around their heads.

Well, I can't think of any more to write, so I'll say so long, honey, and answer soon.

Vincent

A Quote From History . . .

"A guy near me was killed by a direct hit from a mortar. That was my first taste of combat."

Clarence Sluga
United States Army
From an interview, June 23, 1998, describing the "Battle of the Bulge" when, on his first day in the lines, 27 of the 38 men in his unit were killed or wounded.

RESLER, EVERETT

Everett served in the United States Army. On August 3, 1944, he wrote a letter to Independence resident Charlie Pieterick, in part describing where he was stationed along with news of others from town. The letter was published on August 24, 1944:

Hello Charlie:

Received your letter of July 31 today. Have time so am answering it right away. I'm still in good health and getting along all right. Hope this letter finds you the same back in Independence.

Some of our censor restrictions have been lifted lately so now I can tell you just where I am at and where I've been in Iran. I'm stationed at Luarry Camp near Ahwoz, Iran. A town with a population of about 10,000. It's dirty and filthy as hell. I've heard tell that as much of the town is underground as above. I've also been in Andimick, Karramshakr, Guum and Teheran. Teheran is the capital and by far the nicest town in Iran. In fact, it's the Paris of the Middle East. Arthur Kulig, Vince Reck, and Getts (Clara Maule's husband) are stationed at Khrammashakr, Iran. Haven't seen them yet.

I heard from Ed. Maule a couple of days back. He's still in England. Says he isn't seeing so many of the fellows from around home. I guess they're either on the front, or training some place. He also wrote that his brother Al., and Pete Mish are over in Italy now. I imagine they are seeing action.

You asked if I saw or am seeing any action. So far, Charlie, I haven't been within a thousand miles of a battlefront. I can be grateful to the Lord for that. I'm not in a hurry to get on the front either.

My brother Ed. is in New Caledonia now. He doesn't like it there any too well. Says there's too much rain and mud to suit him. Maybe he'd like in a lot better on a desert where the sun shines daily and the thermometer hits 120 degrees in the shade and 170 degrees out in the sun. So far in nearly two years I've seen rain only six times so you can see why I'd appreciate a little rain.

Well, Charlie, how was the Fourth back home? I imagine everybody had a swell time. I sure would have liked to have been there to drink my quota of Calverts and soda. Over here there is no good liquor of any kind and we only get five cans of U. S. beer every 10 days. Boy, when I get back I'll sure have a lot of catching up to do. Believe me there will be a lot of stories to tell too. Everybody will have a different tale to tell.

Yes Charlie, by the time we get back from this war a lot of the old faces will be gone. An awful lot of them have passed on already and we still aren't home. A lot of young fellows won't return either. That's too bad. Just because some crazy maniac thought he could conquer the world.

The folks wrote that they had a swell time on their vacaiton, but it wasn't long enough. I guess everybody who gets a vacation feels the same way. When the folks were in Independence dad looked over my Ford and ran it. He said it was still in good shape. It better be because I expect to make plenty of use of it when I get back. I hope that's pretty darn soon too.

Well, the war news sure sounds good lately. Especially on the Russian front. They're really going to town. I guess they are making good use of American war materials. Hope they can bring it to an End soon.

That's all I can think of, so I will close. May God bless and protect you and your family.

Your Old Pal,
Evy Resler

P. S. Greet some of my old friends for me if you see them.

RESLER, LEONARD

Len was an Army Private First Class when he arrived on the Hawaiian Islands on June 26, 1945.

ROMBALSKI, GEORGE M.

George served in the United States Army, spending his overseas time in Iceland. He was stationed there when his mother died and came home for a short time before returning to Iceland once again. He received his discharge on June 5, 1945. (July 5, 1945)

The *News-Wave* received many responses from service men and women around the world regarding its "Special Serviceman's Edition" of November 30, 1944. George's letter, from "Somewhere in Iceland," was published December 28, 1944:

Dear Mr. Kirkpatrick:

It is with mixed feelings of surprise and extreme pleasure that I take this opportunity to thank you for the copy of the Servicemen's Edition of the News-Wave, which arrived today.

Realizing the extra effort you, and the kindly folks of Independence and vicinity, have put in to make this special edition possible, one can more readily appreciate the true meaning of friendship. The warm hearted sentiments of those back home will certainly help to make this Christmas Season much more pleasant.

It is certainly evidence of unswerving loyalty and devotion, and a bond that should draw us all closer together after this war.

Though the Army is doing everything possible to make things more pleasant on Christmas Day, it is the warm grip of hands across the seas that adds the final touch of home and makes things the more easily bearable.

In the same warm hearted spirit of peace on earth to men of good will, may I extend my greetings of the Season to you, and the many loyal friends back home.

Thanking you all again for a pleasant surprise indeed.

George M. Rombalski

ROMBALSKI, JOSEPH P.

Joe was a Staff Sergeant with the Army's 320th Engineer Combat Battalion, 95th Infantry Division, in the European Theater. On December 14, 1944 an article released by the 95th Infantry Division described how he and another engineer "saw a pair of German 88-gun shells with their address written on, but evidently with postage due." Apparently Joe and his partner were tapping into a telephone line when the building they were in came under enemy fire.

"They thought the first shell was a mortar," the article read, "but learned the score when shell No. 2 geysered mud in the yard. When the third shell sailed through an open window of the room adjoining their third-floor observation post, only to clump harmlessly on the floor, Rombalski and Sicafus ran for the stairs, dragging wire and phone behind them.

"Numbers 4 and 5 followed in the next second, ripping off a house-corner in one instance and proving a second dud through another third-story window in the other, barely ticking jagged window-glass as it entered. Whole glass in either window might have meant explosion.

"As the engineers crawled away, the 88-gunner seemed still on their beam, dropping a few more near-misses close to their escape route. But the midwesterners hugged a hedge and crawled away safely."

In a letter dated March 3, 1945 from Germany, Staff Sergeant Rombalski informed his sister, Mrs. Bert Kulig, of his chance meeting with Sergeant Bennie Kulig, that being the first time he had come across anyone from home. The letter was published March 29, 1945:

Dear Sis:

Received your V-Mail today and want to answer now that I have the time and am in the mood. I'm allowed to say now that we are in the 9th Army and if you check my last letter, you ought to have a good idea where we are. I am glad to hear that there is some improvement in mom's health as I was wondering if she was any better.

Sure am relieved to hear that Geo. is getting that much time off as that makes it easier for mom. I sure wish that I could be there for the supper Monica and George are having at your house. Maybe if all goes well it shouldn't be too long before this all ends and a lot of us are allowed to come back before the Pacific war is over.

As chance would have it you mentioned that there might be a possibility of seeing Bennie Kulig

301

somewhere up here. That's just what happened as I got to see him the other day in a town not so far away from here. We just happened to go to the same shower unit at the same time. I didn't recognize him at first, but he came right up and said "hello." We had quite a talk together before I had to go. He's a lot stouter and grown out since I saw him in 1940. He has made a name for himself and more power to him. In fact, he is the only one that I've ever met from home and there are a lot of them here somewhere, but they are hard to run into.

This is a Heinie typewriter and the key board is partly different from the ones in the States. Hard to get used to; so far I haven't found the period or anything to punctuate with. How is Peter? Haven't heard from him for some time. I suppose Bert and Marcel are getting ready for spring's seeding.

Best regards to mom and the rest. Guess I'll close and may God bless you all.

With love,
Joe

A short article in the July 12, 1945 *News-Wave* said the *Milwaukee Journal* had carried a photo on July 9, 1945 of the troop transport *Marine Dragon* which had brought men home from the European Theater, docking at Piermont, New York, on July 5. Joe Rombalski was identified in the photo.

ROMBALSKI, ROMAN R.

Roman was a Tech Sergeant and served with the Army Air Corps' 786th Base Unit.

ROMBALSKI, ROY R.

Roy was a Corporal serving with Battery A, 517th Field Artillery Battalion, a unit comprised of 155-mm truck-drawn guns, in the Pacific Theater of Operations. The 517th landed on Bougainville on November 10, 1944 and Luzon, Philippine Islands, on January 14, 1945. It was awarded a battle star for its participation in the Luzon campaign. [Book (Stanton)]

ROSKOS, RALPH

Ralph was a Private in the United States Army and stationed at Camp Joseph T. Robinson in June 1945.

RUNKEL, JOHN W.

A pre-war resident of Independence, John was promoted to First Lieutenant at Cherry Point Marine Corps Air Station in July 1944. He joined the United States Marines in early 1943 and became a Naval Aviator on July 14, 1944 at Corpus Christi, Texas. Following his promotion he was assigned duty as assistant flight officer and pilot for the Ninth Marine Aircraft Wing at Cherry Point. (August 10, 1944)

RUNKEL, WILLIAM "Billy"

Billy was a pre-war resident of Independence. In July 1943, he was commissioned a Lieutenant in the United States Marines. A pilot, he later flew an aircraft from Camp LeJuene, North Carolina, to New York aboard which was Marine and Independence native Captain Ben V. Schneider, Jr. (July 29, 1943) He spent time in the Pacific where, in a letter to his sister, Miss Katherine Runkel, he reported they were "striking the Japanese" and that he "was just one of the fortunate ones to escape injury at all times." (September 20, 1945)

RUSTAD, OLIVER E.

Oliver was a Private in the United States Army at the time an article was published on January 25, 1945 regarding souvenirs he had sent home to his mother. The box Mrs. Ole Howland received contained a camoflaged German parachute, made of silk and apparently not washable, with its production date of "18 January 1943" imprinted on it. A canteen also was included, which was described as "typical," with a plastic filler, enameled tinned cup fitted over it, and leather straps. The items were displayed at Garthus Store for a while and apparently attracted considerable attention from the home folks. The American Legion Post 186 also displayed the articles at its January 22, 1945 dance.

Oliver was serving at the time with an ambulance company "along the front lines in Germany."

SATHER, EDWIN

Edwin was a Private serving with the 108th Field Artillery Battalion, 28th Infantry Division, during World War II, and saw action in several campaigns in the European Theater of Operations.

SATHER, ERVIN

Ervin was a Private First Class in the United States Army. Inducted in January 1942, he served overseas for 23 months with a quartermaster truck company of the 13th Army Air Force Service Command. (May 10, 1945) His unit had been commended for "superior performance in the transporting of men and supplies and equipment at an advanced air base," and he was wearing the Asiatic-Pacific Theater Ribbon with two battle stars and the Good Conduct Medal.

In October 1944 he wrote a letter to his mother from the Netherlands West Indies that the *News-Wave* published on November 9, 1944. While asking about his brother, Norval, he didn't know that Norval was at the time quite ill and hospitalized in England:

Dear Mom:
Well at last I found time to answer your letter. Under certain circumstances I just couldn't do it before this. How are you and everyone else at home? Just fine I hope. I'm still O. K. and feel fine. I wrote Vivian a letter today, too. I suppose it is getting pretty cold there now. Have you had any snow yet? I had a wonderful trip here. I came here by air. Have you heard from Norval lately? I haven't heard a thing. Maybe it is because he's a Master Sergeant now. Getting stuck-up. Well, Mom, I guess I had better sign off and hope I hear from you soon.
Love,
Ervin

A Quote From History. . .

"Hell if I know."
Ray Weier
United States Army
From an interview, June 24, 1998. This was Ray's response to the question, "Sergeant, what's going on around here?" posed by famed Brigadier General Anthony McAuliffe, newly-appointed commander of the 103rd Infantry Division.

SATHER, ODIN H.

Tech Sergeant Fifth Grade Odin Sather, formerly of Independence and living in Mondovi, Wisconsin, with his family prior to World War II, was inducted into the United States Army on March 22, 1945. He received his basic training at Fort McClellen near Anniston, Alabama, an infantry replacement training center, which was followed by a month's duty at Camp Adair, Oregon. On September 22, 1945 Odin left the United States for Okinawa where he served with the 152nd Engineer Combat Battalion until November 3, 1945. He then left the 152nd Engineers and was sent to Korea where he remained for two months. On January 3, 1946 he sailed for the United States, arriving in Tacoma, Washington, on January 17, 1946. Three days later he traveled to Camp McCoy, Wisconsin, where he was discharged on January 24, 1946.

During his short time in the Army, Odin earned the Asiatic-Pacific Theater Service Medal, Good Conduct Medal, and the Expert Infantryman Badge. (February 28, 1946)

SATHER, OTIS

Otis joined the United States Army on May 15, 1942 and received training at Camp Claiborne, Louisiana. He left for the European Theater on August 5, 1942 and, after arriving in England on August 17, 1942, was stationed at various air bases with the 332nd Engineer General Service Regiment. On June 24, 1944 his unit crossed the English Channel to France where it constructed railroad lines, and then crossed into Belgium on December 13, 1944. About this time, Otis was transferred to the 3482nd Ordnance Company which was engaged in moving supplies from the rear area to the front lines.

Otis left Antwerp, Belgium, for the United States on November 13, 1945, arriving in New York on November 29. He then traveled to Fort Sheridan, Illinois, where he received his discharge with the rank of Tech Sergeant Fifth Grade on December 4, 1945. On his European-African-Middle Eastern Theater Ribbon was one battle star for his participation in the Rhineland campaign, plus he wore six overseas service bars, one service stripe, the Good Conduct Medal, and World War II Victory Medal. (January 3, 1946) [Book (Stanton)]

SCHNEIDER, CLEMENTS

Clements served in the Army Air Corps. At one point he was reported to hold the rank of Corporal. (article, unknown date)

SCHNEIDER, HUBERT

Hubert served with the 103rd Engineer Combat Battalion (August 9, 1945), 28th Infantry Division. In June 1944 he was wounded and spent three-and-a-half months in the hospital. (October 12, 1944) He later got to see Paris, France, as well as further action with his unit. He arrived back in the States with his unit and was reported to have been in Camp McCoy on August 9, 1945 for redeployment.

SCHNEIDER, JOHN J.

John was a Private stationed at Camp Chaffee, Arkansas, when he received a disability discharge from the Army. (October 14, 1943)

SCHNEIDER, Dr. O. M.

Mark was a Medical Doctor who had interned at Charity Hospital in Shreveport, Louisiana. He was commissioned an Army Lieutenant in November 1944 and then graduated from the Medical Field Service School, Carlisle Barracks, Pennsylvania, which qualified him for field duty as a Medical Corps officer. (January 4, 1945) From there, he went to Dallas, Texas. He and his wife arrived in Independence from Camp Livingston, Louisiana, in early May 1945, from where he was next to report to Camp Beale, California, for overseas duty in the Pacific Theater. (May 17, 1945)

He served with the 49th General Hospital in Manila, Philippine Islands, through the end of the war. He then was transferred to Tokyo, Japan, with the Army of Occupation where he was promoted to Captain in late-1945 or early-1946. (January 17, 1946)

SEVERSON, OMAR A.

The August 2, 1945 *News-Wave* reported Omar was a Private serving with the 338th Infantry Regiment, 85th Infantry Division, a unit that distinguished itself in three Italian campaigns. It was reported he had earned a Combat Infantryman's Badge for action against the enemy in Italy.

SIEFERT, ANDREW

Andrew served with a heavy automotive equipment company of the 302nd Depot Repair Squadron, a unit responsible for maintenance of combat aircraft. He was inducted on October 13, 1942 and was stationed at Camp White, Oregon, until leaving for overseas on April 12, 1944. First landing in North Africa, he found himself leaving there within a few days for Italy, and was subsequently stationed near Naples for the duration of his time in Italy.

The July 12, 1945 *News-Wave* carried a story announcing that Andrew's 302nd Depot Repair Squadron had been awarded the Meritorious Service Unit Plaque. Its commanding officer, Captain Robert E. Keane, commended all the officers and enlisted men for "superior performance of duty in the accomplishment of exceptionally difficult tasks in the Mediterranean Theater from June 1944 to Dec 1944." By early 1945 the unit was busy preparing aircraft for redeployment to the Pacific Theater of Operations.

Besides the unit award, Andrew also earned the European-Africa-Middle East Ribbon with battle stars for the Rome-Arno and Northern Appenines campaigns, three overseas service bars, one service stripe, the Good Conduct Medal, American Theater Ribbon, and Victory Medal.

He returned home aboard the aircraft carrier *U. S. S. Randolf* in late November 1945 and was discharged at Fort Sheridan, Illinois, on December 6, 1945. (January 3, 1946)

SIEFERT, PETER

Pete entered the United States Army on July 17, 1941 and trained at Camp Lee, Virginia. He was a Private First Class when he left for the Southwest Pacific Theater on January 23, 1942. Stationed with the 4th General Hospital Detachment Medical Department, he spent 36 months overseas, including time in Australia and participating in campaigns on New Guinea and the Philippines. He earned four battle stars, the Good Conduct Medal, American Defense Medal, and Asiatic-Pacific and Philippine Liberation ribbons. He also was awarded a Purple Heart for wounds received on Wee Wak, New Guinea. (July 19, 1945) A February 1, 1945 *News-Wave* article indicated that Pete, a Corporal, was home on the rotation of personnel plan. He was discharged on July 6, 1945.

SKROCH, CLARENCE

Clarence served with the Army's 30th Infantry Division in the European Theater, landing at Normandy on D-Day plus four. The 30th Infantry spearheaded the St. Lo breakout and eventually moved through Northern France, Belgium, and Holland before entering the *West Wall* (Siegfried Line) to encircle the key city of Aachen, Germany.

On December 17, 1944 the 30th Infantry was rushed south to stop the German Ardennes Counteroffensive (the "Battle of the Bulge"). It saw bitter fighting in the Stavelot-Malmedy sector, scene of the infamous Malmedy Massacre where a German SS unit executed a large number of American prisoners-of-war. It then helped stop the German Army's attempt at reaching its main objective of the Counteroffensive, the taking of Belgium ports and dividing of Allies forces. Stunned SS Panzer troops taken prisoner referred to the men of the 30th Infantry Division as "Roosevelt's SS."

On March 24, 1945 the 30th Infantry led the 9th U. S. Army's assault across the Rhine River. It then covered another 200 miles to the Elbe River at Magdeburg, Germany, where it met with the Russian Army.

Clarence held the European-African-Middle Eastern Ribbon with battle stars, the Good Conduct Medal, and a Distinguished Unit Citation, the highest award given a unit for its conduct in battle. (newspaper article, unknown source and date)

SKROCH, EDMUND G.

Edmund served with the United States Navy in the Pacific, spending a year stationed at Samar Island, Philippine Islands.

SKROCH, ERNEST J.

Ernest was an Army Lieutenant stationed at Camp Barkeley, Texas, in November 1944 when his brother, Everett, forwarded a copy of the "Special Serviceman's Edition" of the *News-Wave* to him. A short note to Glenn Kirkpatrick later appeared in the December 28, 1944 edition:

Dear Editor:

A copy of your servicemen's edition was forwarded to me here at Camp Barkeley by my brother Everett who is stationed at Waco.

Frankly, it seemed like renewing old acquaintants. I enjoyed it thoroughly.

My very best wishes for a Merry Christmas to all of you!

Lt. Ernest J. Skroch

A Quote From History. . .

"Most of our infantrymen boarded the *S. S. Leopoldville.*"
Jack Weier
United States Army
From a letter, January 1999, describing the sinking of the one of the ships carrying his 66th Infantry Division to France. Leopoldville was sunk by a German torpedo, resulting in the loss of 800 men.

SKROCH, EVERETT

In November 1944, Everett was stationed at Waco, Texas.

SKROCH, MARCEL

Unfortunately, no information regarding Marcel's World War II service came to light during this writer's research.

SLABY, GEORGE

George entered the United States Army in February 1945 and trained at Camp Robinson, Arkansas. He left for the Southwest Pacific in August 1945. There he was assigned to Company D, 126th Infantry Regiment, 32nd Infantry Division in the Philippines. He later served in the Army of Occupation on the Japanese home island of Kyushu. (February 14, 1946)

SLABY, MARCEL M.

On December 11, 1941 Marcel was reported to be stationed with the Army infantry at Dutch Harbor in the Aleutian Islands. He had enlisted in February 1941. He was a Sergeant when he visited his parents around Christmas in 1943. (January 1, 1943) In February, he was reported stationed at Camp White, Oregon. (February 24, 1944)

SLABY, ROMAN J.

Roman served as a Private, First Class in the United States Army.

SLUGA, DOMINIC

Dominic entered the United States Army in 1942. Following his initial training, he was sent to the Pacific Theater in mid-1943 where he served on Bougainville for at least 16 months. (November 30, 1944) On February 3, 1944 the *News-Wave* reported Private Dominic had lost his hearing entirely in one ear and partially in the other due to combat in the South Pacific. The youngest of the four Sluga brothers in the service during World War II also served in Japan with the Army of Occupation as a Private First Class. (January 3, 1946)

SLUGA, FRANK

Frank joined the United States Army in 1941. He served with the 176th Engineer General Service Regiment in the Alaska Defense Command. On June 17, 1942 the 176th departed the Seattle Port of Embarkation, arriving in Bethel, Alaska, on July 13, 1942. The Regiment was stationed in the interior of Alaska, and Frank remained there with his unit until August 1944, at which time he received a furlough and returned to Independence. His brother, Raymond, also served in the 176th, and when Frank was granted his furlough, it was the first time since entering the service that he had been separated from Ray. Following his leave, Frank returned to Seattle, Washington, to where his unit returned on December 2, 1944. (November 30, 1944; Book: Stanton)

Frank was discharged from the Army in December, 1945, as a Technical Sergeant Fourth Class. (January 3, 1946)

A Quote From History. . .

"One of them hit near us and killed 65 of our troops."
    John Lucente
    United States Army
    From an interview, November 8, 1998, describing a V-2 rocket.

SLUGA, RAYMOND

Ray joined the United States Army in February, 1942, and received his training at Camp Robinson, Arkansas, and Camp Bowie, Texas, He joined the 176th Engineer General Service Regiment, the same unit his brother, Frank, served in, at Camp Bowie. Ray was in Company C. The 176th left the Seattle Port of Embarkation on June 17, 1942 and arrived in Bethel, Alaska, on July 13, 1942. The Regiment then remained in the interior of Alaska serving with the Alaska Defense Command until November 25, 1944, at which time it began returning to Seattle, Washington. [Book (Stanton)]

Ray returned to the states on December 15, 1944. Following a furlough, he reported to Fort Belvoir, Virginia, where his Company C was redesignated as the 3187th Engineer Base Equipment Company. The 3187th then traveled to Fort Lewis, Washington, and was aboard ship bound for the Pacific Theater when the war was declared ended. He then disembarked, and remained at Fort Lewis where he received his discharge on October 8, 1945 with the rank of Technical Sergeant Fourth Class. He had been awarded the Asiatic-Pacific Theater Ribbon and Good Conduct Medal. (January 3, 1946)

The same article of January 3, 1946, regarding the Sluga brothers said "He (Ray) found Alaska very bleak and chilly but was busy constructing roads, airports, and buildings of all kinds. Sluga said the Eskimos of the region where he was stationed lived on a low plane of existence. Their homes were crude shelters made of whatever kind of lumber or materials they could find. Large families were cramped into small shacks and disease such as tuberculosis was prevalent."

SMIEJA, RAYMOND

Ray left Independence for Fort Sheridan, Illinois, on July 27, 1944. From there he went to Sheppard Field, Texas, to begin V-5 training in the United States Army Air Corps. (July 27, 1944) In July 1945 he transferred from Boca Raton, Florida, to Chanute Field, Illinois, where he attended an aeronautics school. (August 2, 1945)

Ray, as so many servicemen did, expressed his thanks for the "Special Serviceman's Edition" of the *News-Wave* in a short letter to Glenn Kirkpatrick that was published on December 28, 1944:

Dear Mr. Kirkpatrick:
        I want to thank you very much for the swell paper you sent to all of us in the service. I know everyone else enjoyed it as much as I did. Thanks again!
        Kind remembrance and sincere wishes for Christmas Cheer and New Year Happiness.
                Ray Smieja

In August 1945 Ray received a two day leave from Chanute Field, Illinois, but instead of traveling home in an inconvenient train, he hitchhiked.

SOBOTTA, CLIFFORD B.

Clifford served with an Army anti-aircraft artillery unit that landed in North Africa for a short time before seeing action in Italy and France. Late February 1944 found him in the Cassino area of Italy where he could see the famous Abbey from which the Germans were able to temporarily halt the Allied advance and causing numerous Allied casualties. A Private First Class, he spent 34 months overseas before receivng a 30-day furlough during which time he visited relatives in the Independence area. (February 22, 1945)

While in Italy, Clifford wrote the following letter to his sister, Mrs. Clifford Kampa. Dated March 24, 1944, it was published the following April 20:

Dear Sis:
        Received your letter dated February 22 and so, having a change of address, decided to let you know.
        Moved up a ways lately, and February 28 was in the Cassino area. We could look across the river and see the town and the Abbey. It is really a sight to see.
        Yes, sis, I got the News-Wave, and about seven or eight little packages. Also got all the Christmas packages.
        I guess it will be quite some time before we get furloughs from here. Hope they do send us home soon tho'. It is pretty hard to find anything to write about around here. Everything is censored and what you'd like to say you can't. The fellows on the other side keep us pretty busy and we don't have much time for writing. Will write more after we leave here. Some of the things I've seen since I've been in Italy are really interesting. Will have a lot to tell you when I do get home.
        Sis, when we left England we landed in Africa. Left Oran and went to Telegrma near Constantine. Have been to Constantine on pass a few times. Not such a lovely city as it was once. Left here to go to Algiers. There I had some good times. Two weeks after we got there they had two raids, and we got three planes. We moved closer to the harbor and got into another raid. They dropped flares and you could read a paper in our gun pit. The flares were a good four miles away. We left there and went back to Oran for awhile before coming over here. Can't write about this part of the war as yet, but will some day when they give the okay.
        Closing now with love and best wishes from
                Chip
        P. S. Say hello to Ma and Pa

SOKOLOSKY, HENRY

Henry was a Private in the United States Army in May 1945 when he was sent to Fort George G. Meade, Maryland, for further assignment.

SOLFEST, SIDNEY

Sidney received his initial Army training at Camp Shelby, Mississippi. As an Army Private First Class, he then spent two years on the Aleutian Islands where he was stationed with Bob Skroch and Glen Insteness. (June 15, 1944) From there, he sent a letter to the American Legion in Independence thanking them for the cigarettes he had received from them at Christmas. Dated January 4, 1944 from "Somewhere in the Aleutians," it was published on February 17, 1944:

> Dear Sirs:
>
> I received the cigarettes which you sent this evening, and am thanking you very much for the gift.
>
> Saw by the News-Wave there are quite a few men from in and around Independence in the service at this time. Bob Skroch and I are still together, and have been ever since we got in the Army. He gets the News-Wave, so we keep pretty well up on the news from around home.
>
> The war news is beginning to look brighter every day, so here's hoping we may see you all in the near future.
>
> Sincerely,
> Sidney O. Solfest.

SONSALLA, ROMAN A.

Roman was a Seaman Second Class in the United States Navy in the summer of 1945.

SOSALLA, RUDOLPH

Rudy served in the Army a total of four years, eight months. He was an Army Air Corps mechanic stationed in England for a period of time and then later crossed onto the continent following the D-Day invasion where he was "slightly wounded" on September 8, 1944 in France. His wounds required hospitalization and he was awarded the Purple Heart. (October 5, 1944)

In October 1944 Mr. and Mrs. Louis Schoenberger, managers of the Hotel Independence, received a letter from Rudy, written from a hospital in Paris. It was published September 25, 1944:

> Hello Everyone:
>
> Just a few words to let you know that I haven't forgotten you folks. I sure hope that you're all happy and well.
>
> I was wounded on the 8th of this month. Just a slight thigh wound, just above the knee. I'm getting along swell. The last few days I've been up and round already. I guess in a few more days I'll be as good as new again.
>
> This hospital is located in Paris. A beautiful place. I only wish I could take a few days off and look the city over. I came to this hospital by plane.
>
> I've been thinking all day how I wish I could be at your place having a drink and talking about different things. I guess this will be all.
>
> Here's hoping this bit of scribbling finds you all okay. I'll try and write more again soon.
>
> Friend,
> Rudy

The August 16, 1945 *News-Wave* stated that Private First Class Sosalla had arrived home August 22, 1945 from the European Theater, and that following a furlough with his parents, would be reporting to a camp in Texas for reassignment.

SOSALLA, DOMINIC

Dominic served with the Army's 30th Infantry Division in the European Theater of Operations. A Private, he returned home in August 1945 where, following furlough, he was to report for redeployment. (August 30, 1945)

SPRECHER, ROBERT J.

Bob, an accomplished musician, had enlisted in June 1942 as an Aviation Cadet after which he discontinued his schooling because he thought he would be called to active duty within a short time. When that didn't happen, he joined Ty Tyson and His Band, a combo well known by Independence residents. In December 1942 he was still playing with them, having performed in many theaters throughout the southern states. (December 24, 1942) While home visiting his parents for Christmas in 1942, he finally was called to active duty and ordered to report to Tennessee for training.

By August 1943 Bob was trained as an aerial gunner in the Army Air Force. He had completed his training in both ground and bomber operation of .30- and .50-caliber machine guns at the Army Air Force's Flexible Gunnery School, Tydall Field, Florida. (August 19, 1943)

On November 2, 1944 the *News-Wave* contained an article from an Eighth Air Force B-24 Liberator Station in England in which Bob's 2nd Bombardment Division was cited by Major General William E. Kepner, commanding, "for distinguished and outstanding performance of duty" during its recently completed 100 combat missions. Bob was reported to be serving as a Special Service Clerk with the Division.

STEFFENSON, ALBERT

Albert served in the United States Army and spent 23 months in the Aleutian Islands. In January 1945 he was a Corporal and stationed at Camp Hood, Texas, where he was receiving additional infantry training. By May 1945 Albert was reported to be a Staff Sergeant and "training rookies" at Camp Hood. (May 24, 1945)

STEFFENSON, CLAYTON

Clayton served with Headquarters Company, 361st Infantry Division, 91st Infantry Division, after receiving his preliminary training at Camp White and Camp Adair, Oregon. On October 19, 1944 the *News-Wave* reported he had recently been wounded in the arm, requiring hospitalization. On January 18, 1945 a short article stated his parents, Mr. and Mrs. August Steffenson of the Chimney Rock area, had received his Purple Heart. They also indicated their son had been wounded twice, once in August in the right arm, then again on November 2, 1944, when he was hit in the jaw. He had returned to his unit, however, shortly after receiving this second wound.

On September 13, 1945 the *News-Wave* reported Clayton, a Private First Class, was home on furlough. Besides his Purple Heart, it was reported he was wearing three battle stars on his European-Africa-Middle Eastern Theater Ribbon.

STRATMAN, JOSEPH

Joe was a teacher in Independence for two years prior to World War II. He was not forgotten upon his leaving, however, as he, too, received a copy of the "Special Servicman's Edition" of the *News-Wave*. Editor Kirkpatrick printed a letter from him on December 28, 1944:

Dear Mr. Kirkpatrick:

I recently received a very pleasant surprise in the form of the Christmas edition of the Independence News-Wave. Mrs. Stratman and I read it page for page and column for column. Seeing all those familiar faces looking up at us was like a visit with each and everyone we knew, but haven't seen for so long. I read over forty names on your honor roll whom I had as students when I taught there. I was very interested in the picture of the band. Your director is to be commended on her fine showing.

I have been in the Navy since August 25 (Ed. - 1944). The training is excellent, but it is hard to break home ties. I met Pete Skroch down here one day. It did seem so good to see someone I knew, and Independence folks have always held a very special place with us. We had two very happy years there, and are looking forward to a visit there at our first opportunity.

Thanks again for the paper, and I wish you a very happy holiday season.

Joe Stratman

SURA, BENEDICT

Benedict entered the service, branch unknown, in April 1942.

SURA, CHANCY J.

Chancy, one of four sons of Mr. and Mrs. Andrew C. Sura to serve during World War II, was a Private First Class when he graduated December 23, 1943 from a B-24 Liberator bomber mechanics school at Keesler Field in Biloxi, Mississippi. (December 23, 1943) At the time, it had not yet been determined whether he would then report to a factory school for further specialized mechanics training or to one of the Army Air Force's Training Command's flexible gunnery schools where he would be trained as an aerial gunner. On October 26, 1944 it was reported Chancy was home on furlough from Fort Port Field, Mississippi, where he was stationed at the time.

SURA, CHESTER

Chester received his military training in Mississippi around March 1945. Following his initial training, he was stationed in Greensboro, North Carolina, as a Private First Class. (August 23, 1945)

SURA, CLIFFORD

Clifford joined the United States Navy in 1936, several months after his brother, Clarence. At the time of the Japanese attack on Pearl Harbor on December 7, 1941, he was reported to be in the Canal Zone area serving aboard the *U. S. S. Mallard* (ASR-4), a 187-foot submarine rescue vessel that had been converted from minesweeper AM-44. (December 11, 1941)

By the end of the war in the Pacific, he was aboard *YMS-467*, a motor minesweeper used for inshore sweeping prior to amphibious assaults. He was one of five officers and 29 crew aboard the 136-foot vessel that had a top speed of 13 knots and carried one 50-caliber and one 20-mm machine guns. At that time, Clifford held the rank of Chief Boatswain's Mate.

On August 10, 1945 Clifford and his brother, Clarence, aboard the *U. S. S. Vella Gulf*, chanced to meet in the South Pacific, the first time they had seen each other in nine years. Both soon wrote letters home to their mother, Mrs. Paul Sura, and the letters were published simultaneously on August 23, 1945. In his letter, Clifford describes the surprise he felt finding *Vella Gulf* anchored near his *YMS-467* the morning of August 10 and the time the brothers spent together:

Dear Mother,

 I know you will be surprised when you receive this letter for I wrote to you the day before.

 It is said that surprises come one after the other. Well, I've another one for you now. You remember I mentioned receiving a letter from brother Clarence, saying he was on his way out here. Well, imagine my surprise when I looked out over the side the morning of the 10th and saw his ship anchored just a little way off from us. At first I thought I was seeing things, but it was his ship all right.

 My captain said it would be all right for me to go over to see him and I was on his ship and talking to him within 15 minutes. I stayed with him from about 10 a. m. until 3 p. m. He sure had a lot to tell me. Seems as though he did all the talking. He sure was glad to see me and was trying to get in touch with my ship when I found him. I stayed aboard with him for the noon meal and the rest of the time he showed me around and we talked. He showed me a few pictures he had and also told me about the nice time he had at home on his last leave. Also told of having visited at the Tubbs home in San Diego. I didn't get to see them when I was there.

 They came in here the night of the ninth, I saw him on the 10th and right now it is two p. m. of the 11th and I see they are heading out. He told me where to. Don't worry for they are heading back, not out. He expects to be back in the states again shortly.

 I sure hope we can get back home together soon. As I sit here, now, he is out of sight. He sure did look good.

 Did you hear the news the night of the 10th? About the war being over? By the time you receive this letter the war will probably really be over.

 Write again soon. May God bless and keep you well and happy for me.

  Your ever loving son,
  Clifford

SURA, PETER

 Peter was reported to be training at an Army camp in Mississippi in the October 26, 1944 *News-Wave*. He later served as a Private First Class with the 78th Infantry Division in the European Theater where he was wounded in Germany on March 4, 1945. His parents, Mr. and Mrs. Andrew Sura, received a War Department telegram on March 19, 1945 informing them he had been awarded the Purple Heart. Two days later, another telegram arrived stating that Peter's left hand had been badly shattered. (March 29, 1945)

SYGULLA, ADOLPH R.

 Adolph attained the rank of Tech Sergeant Fourth Grade while serving in the United States Army during World War II.

SYGULLA, ALEX

 A short note in the December 31, 1942 *News-Wave* appeared as follows:

 Who likes Army life? Private First Class Alex Sygulla hasn't told anyone here for a long time, but his relatives have been told that he really finds life interesting at Guadalcanal.

SYGULLA, SIMON R.

Simon served in the United States Coast Guard late in World War II. In June 1945 he was stationed at Curtis Bay, Maryland, and prior to that in Beaufort, South Carolina.

SYLLA, JOHN P.

John served in the United States Navy during World War II.

SYLLA, PAUL

Paul was a Seaman First Class in the United States Navy in May 1945.

SYMICZEK, ERNEST F.

On May 24, 1945 it was reported Ernest was a Private First Class in the Army Air Force. He had received his aerial gunner's wings at the AAF Flexible Gunnery School, Tyndall Field, Florida, which was the largest training school of its kind. Trained in the use of .30- and .50-caliber machine guns, Ernest was then qualified to become a combat bomber crewman.

THEISEN, JOHN C.

John served in the United States Army during World War II.

TORSON, JOHN

John was a Seaman First Class in May 1945 when he graduated from a Naval radio training school in Madison, Wisconsin. From there he went to Shoemaker, California, to be assigned further duties. At the war's end, John was a Seaman, Second Class.

ULBERG, LESTER C.

On March 30, 1944 a *News-Wave* article reported that Corporal Lester Ulberg and Corporal Adelbert Bautch, "two well-known boys, now in service, have a 'secret weapon' which they are quite certain will do away with anything that Hitler can use to overcome their strength. These are the weapons: Their own endurance and inventivenes, coupled with the intense training they are getting. Both boys are infantrymen, and the item was reported through headquarters of the European Theater of Operations."

On April 25, 1945 an article stated Lester, then a Staff Sergeant, was home following seven months as a prisoner of war in the European Theater. It said he entered the United States Army on April 8, 1941 and completed basic training in Michigan. He then was sent overseas in early 1942 and was in France when captured by the Germans in September 1944. He was to spend two months home before reporting for reassignment.

WALETZKE, ERNEST E.

Ernest was a Private in the United States Army during World War II.

WALSKE, Dr. B. R.

Doctor Walske, a native of Arcadia, Wisconsin, moved to Independence in December 1938, where he established his medical practice. He was called into the service as a Lieutenant in the Medical Corps on February 5, 1941. In December, 1941, he was promoted to Captain.

He was first stationed at Camp Grant, Illinois, but then was transferred to Fitzsimmons General Hospital in Denver, Colorado, where he remained until transferring back to Camp Grant in March 1942. On November 12, 1942 Dr. Walske was reported to have been promoted to the rank of Major and serving as chief of surgery and orthopedics at the Camp Grant station hospital.

Doctor Walske had graduated second in his class of 64 from Marquette University's School of Medicine. (newspaper article, unknown source and date)

WARNER, MALCOLM F.

Malcolm was a Yeoman First Class in the United States Navy during World War II.

WIENCH, HERMAN

The *News-Wave* reported on August 23, 1945 that Herman was a Private stationed at Fort Sheridan, Illinois, and had recently arrived home on leave.

WILCZEK, JOSEPH A.

Joe served in the United States Army during World War II. He was also a veteran of World War I.

WINSAND, ORVILLE M.

On March 15, 1945 the *News-Wave* stated Orville had been promoted to Staff Sergeant and was serving with the 66th Infantry Division in France where it had 60,000 Germans trapped in the St. Nazaire and Lorient areas.

WITT, LYLE F.

Lyle was a Tech Sergeant in the United States Army during World War II.

WOYCHIK, ROMAN J.

Roman entered service with the United States Army on November 27, 1941, and received his basic training at Camp Grant, Illinois. Following basic, he was transferred to the Army Flying School in Enid, Oklahoma, where he served as a pharmicist in the station hospital pharmacy for 16 months before being transferred to Atlanta, Georgia, for three months of special training. (September 17, 1942) Following that, he was transferred as a Staff Sergeant to the 32nd Medical Depot Company at Fort Knox, Kentucky, from where he left for overseas duty in March, 1944. He reached England on Easter Sunday, 1944. While at sea, Roman wrote a letter to his parents informing them he actually liked traveling by ship -- can it be surmised he didn't experience that scourge of most landlubber troops, seasickness? This and a second letter, which described his first impressions of England, were both published on April 27, 1944:

April 7, 1944
Dear Folks:

I am writing this letter somewhere at sea. Quite an unusual place for me to be.

I sort of enjoy being out at sea but living conditions aren't a bit comfortable. We live in a mess hall and eat twice a day. At night I spread a blanket on the floor, cover with my overcoat and use the life jacket for a pillow. It's just a way to pass the time and realize how good a hard bed would feel. Last night I improved things a little for myself. I slept on a table. Try it sometime!

Yesterday I discovered a La Crosse resident in our midst. He's a musician and played several times at Independence dances. An unusual place to meet a local man.

Roman

Easter Sunday
Dear Folks:

I am now somewhere in England. In spite of some of the inconveniences we all experienced during the transit, I personally got a kick out of it all. It really was quite an unusual experience for me.

What do I think of England? I must say that here is the most picturesque scenery I have ever seen. I took a walk out into the country this morning and actually admired everything that I have seen. What I have seen of this country so far it is much more than I have expected. Certain things out here impress me greatly.

This Easter is one that I will never forget. Never in my life have I conceived of spending Easter in a foreign land.

You need not worry about me. I'm well taken care of, and happy as can be under the circumstances. Notice that my APO has changed.

Roman

In July 1944, Roman crossed the English Channel to Normandy where he served as a pharmicist with the 3rd U. S. Army. The following letter, dated November 10, 1944, was received by Roman's parents, Mr. and Mrs. Paul F. Woychik, and published on December 7, 1944. It briefly describes his duties and some of the sites of Paris, in addition to reflecting on the reasons for such a terrible conflict as he had seen in Europe:

Dear Folks:

It's 9:30 and I have just finished working. I am now operating a pharmacy and the place keeps my assistants and I quite busy at times. Today we were especially rushed. I also have two prisoners (Germans) working for me.

Most of my work consists of manufacturing various concoctions. We don't think of making any less than five gallons of cough syrup at a time. Business is good out here.

One of my best days in France was the one spent in Paris. I was quite impressed by Paris. I purchased perfume, rode their subways, saw Eiffel Tower, walked through the Arc de Triomphe where the tomb of the unknown soldier is located. In passing the tomb men tip their hats and servicemen salute. My fascination reached the peak when I entered Notre Dame Cathedral. I recall admiring a picture while in grade school but then it never entered my mind that some day I would cross its threshold. There I purchased a crucifix, the best of all souvenirs in my possession.

Today I had an occasion to speak with a Polish refugee. Three years ago the Germans killed his 62 year old father and then deported his mother and him to Germany to work. About three months ago he escaped from the Germans and remained two weeks in the woods with his infirm mother until surrounding area was liberated. He is only one of a multitude. Hearing that kind of story makes one ask only one question: "How do I ever dare to utter a complaint?"

God must have a reason to permit the world to be afflicted with such an anguish. We scorn the enemy but why not admit our own defects also. Seeing people rummaging through our garbage cans makes one wonder if Hitler is the only guilty one. There is a lot to think over when you're among people elsewhere.

I am enclosing a picture taken during my first week in France. The orchard in the background looks peaceful but its there where I slept four nights in a foxhole. However, I consider myself fortunate to have spent only that much time that way. Since then I have always had a cot, and at one place, a real bed

to sleep on. Anyway I'm glad I didn't miss this.
                    Yours,
                    Roman

On January 31, 1945 Staff Sergeant Woychik wrote another letter to his parents in which he described the parts of France he had recently visited. Published March 15, 1945, it is part religious culture and part powdered eggs!

Dear Folks:
        This is the last day of the first month of this year and once again I have been paid with Francs. Sometimes I wonder how long this foreign money business is to continue. Optimists last summer thought that it would have been over by Christmas.
        I guess you realize by now that I have crossed most of France and probably wonder what I think of it. France is a land unlike any I've ever seen. Along the highways, at the approaches to towns, villages or hamlets, at the road forks, and in many streets within the towns, stand Crucifixes from 15 to 25 feet in height. Usually the Crucifix is enclosed in a beautifully fenced-in garden, landscaped with a profusion of evergreens and flower beds. In most instances the cross is of concrete, stone or marble, and it faces the traffic going into town. Wherever we go, He is already there.
        The French are a deeply religious people and have built great churches and cathedrals. At present we attend Holy Mass celebrated by an American Chaplain, in a famous cathedral.
        The most sacriligious violation that I have ever witnessed is the use of a beautiful church, an ancient structure, by the Germans for storage purposes. Its magnificent spire attracted me from a distance and I could hardly believe my eyes when I encountered such gruesome disorder.
        This winter is the real McCoy in contrast to my three previous ones south of the Mason and Dixon line. The temperature is milder than that of Wisconsin so I can boast about enduring my coldest winter at home. I have no desire of breaking that record in a foxhole.
        Oh, what about all those warm sleeping bags they write about in the papers? Yes, those powdered eggs were cracked up to be so delicious! Have you heard of a GI overseas recommending a dry milk plant for the Army-Navy Production Flag? Please pass me the Independence Creamery butter and let's change the subject.
        The day I shall arrive home, don't be surprised if I request fresh fried eggs for lunch and a quart of fresh cold milk. By the way, you had better warn Harold not to display any dehydrated foods when the GI's

Roman Woychik. This photo was taken while he was stationed in France.

start coming home or the fish and turtles in the Trempealeau River will be terribly annoyed. Then, drop in next door and inform Harvey to abandon his plans about that dehydrated pop because there will be an abundance of water after the war, for it is so rigidly conserved now.

I believe I have indulged quite adequately in nonsense this evening and its past my time to hit the sack (GI bed). Due to security reasons the news around here is our headache and soldiers do not write about scandal lest it should worry the taxpayer excessively.

Yours,
Roman

A V-Mail letter dated March 8, 1945. and printed March 29, 1945. mentioned an award Roman had received for his work in the Medical Corps in France. His Certificate of Merit stated:

This Certificate of Merit is awarded to Staff Sergeant Roman J. Woychik in recognition of conspicuously meritorious and outstanding performance of military duty.

Staff Sergeant Woychik's meritorious service in the organization and direction of the pharmacy section of this unit reflects just credit upon his ability and devotion to duty.

(Signed) John Tenholm, Major
Com. 32nd Medical Depot Co.

WOZNEY, ROMAN

Roman spent eight months training with an armored division at Camp Chaffee, Arkansas. On September 2, 1943 he was reported home following a disability discharge.

ZIMMERMAN, DOMINIC P.

Dominic served with Company A, 147th Infantry Regiment, a non-division unit. He entered the United States Army on August 13, 1942. and completed basic training at Camp Wolters, Texas. He left the United States for the South Pacific on February 23, 1943, where he joined the 147th Infantry either on Guadalcanal about the time that battle ended or on the New Hebrides or Samoa where the 147th was relocated in mid-May 1943. following the "Battle for Guadalcanal." [June 21, 1945; Book (Stanton)]

The 147th went back to Guadalcanal in April 1944 but after only four days was sent for garrison duties on the Emirau St. Matthias Islands. It remained there until returning to Guadalcanal on July 3, 1944. It later was assigned to the New Caledonia Garrison Command on September 1, 1944 and the South Pacific Base Command on New Caledonia on February 28, 1945. It then served with the Pacific Ocean Area Command beginning March 15, 1945. before arriving on Iwo Jima on March 21, 1945. where it assumed security and, on April 4, 1945, garrison duties.

On June 25, 1945 the 147th was assigned to the Pacific Base Command. Five days later, its 1st Battalion, of which Dominic's Company A was a part, was sent to Tinian as an occupational force. It remained here through the end of the war in the Pacific. [Book (Stanton)]

An article published June 21, 1945. referred to a letter his parents at Route 2, Eleva, had received from their son (Dominic was listed in the Honor Roll of Service men and women in the November 30, 1944. issue of the *News-Wave*). In it, he described how he and two others of Company A -- Richard Urice, Carrigansville, Maryland, and John Burnett, Loveland, Ohio -- had picked up pieces of six enemy trucks and built a working vehicle. The *News-Wave* stated the "only U. S. parts on her are a bunch of tire patches and a sealed beam fair frame and chassis and a somewhat delapidated motor. It showed signs of battle as bullet holes were noticeable throughout." They had added to the original truck the wheels, tires, radiator, carburetor, distributor, steering wheel, dashboard, generator, horn, battery, and hydraulic brakes, among other parts. "Practically every day we went on combat patrols, and almost always we'd come back with something for our truck," Dominic wrote. "We did it nearly all on our own time. It was a lot of work, but we enjoyed it." Their main concern at that time was how they would get it back to the States, however.

This probably took place on Iwo Jima just prior to the 147th's being sent to Tinian.

The Women of Independence, Wisconsin, Who Served During World War II

A surprisingly large number of women from Independence served during World War II, in a variety of capacities. Several of them, like their male counterparts, experienced things beyond what anyone should be expected to endure. They gave up their homes, their friends, and their way of life, and participated in their own ways in the signal event of the Twentieth Century. They, too, made history, and are remembered here for their contributions.

ELEANOR A. DEJNO
UNITED STATES ARMY NURSES CORPS

Eleanor graduated from Independence High School in 1937 and entered the St. Francis (Aurora, Illinois) Hospital School of Nursing that fall. She graduated in June, 1940, and enlisted in the Army Nurses Corps. As a Second Lieutenant, she was transferred to the Station Hospital at Fort Bragg, North Carolina, remaining there for two years, and then to Northinton General Hospital, Tuscaloosa, Alabama. On December 2, 1943, she was assigned duty overseas and sent to England. As of November 1944 she was stationed in Belgium.

MARY DEJNO
UNITED STATES NAVY NURSING CORPS RESERVE

Mary graduated from Independence High School in 1928, entered St. Francis Hospital School of Nursing in La Crosse, Wisconsin, and graduated from there as a registered nurse in June 1932. After working in Arizona for three years, she applied for admission to the Navy Nurses Corps. She transferred to San Bernadino, California, from where she was called to the Naval Hospital at Balboa Park in San Diego, California. She was serving there as of November 1944.

EILEEN KIRKPATRICK
UNITED STATES NAVY

Eileen was the daughter of Mr. and Mrs. Glenn Kirkpatrick, publisher of the *Independence News-Wave*. After passing her physical examination in Milwaukee, Wisconsin, on June 22, 1945, she left with Mary Margaret Wozney for training at Hunter College, New York. A WAVE, she completed an eight-week course at the United States Naval training School, The Bronx, New York, after which she was assigned duty at the Naval Air Station in Jacksonville, Florida. There she served as a linotype operator, her civilian occupation.

On July 26, 1945, her father, News-Wave publisher G. L. Kirkpatrick, placed the following article on the front page of the newspaper, entitled "Dad Pays Tribute To A Daughter:"

This week's issue of the News-Wave is printed without the assistance of Eileen, daughter of G. L. Kirkpatrick, the publisher. Yes, that's news, for during the past ten years Eileen has been an important cog

Three of the four Dejno sisters, daughters of Mr. and
Mrs. John Dejno, who served during World War II.
Top left: Eleanor
Top right: Mary
Right: Patricia
A biography and photo of the fourth sister, Verna
(Veronica), can be found elsewhere in Volume I.

in the wheels of the publication of the News-Wave.

Finishing high school in 1934 she chose to take up work in her father's print shop. She has been a constant employee ever since, up to publication of last week's News-Wave when she washed the ink off her hands, hung up her apron and departed from familiar pressroom and office scenes to do a hitch for Uncle Sam. She's in the WAVES. And Dad is just a bit proud of that fact, even though he loses his best helper and best pal.

Through the years Eileen has mastered the joys and sorrows of publishing a country newspaper and has become profoundly efficient. Not only was she an expert linotype operator, but she could take over in any department of the business and carry on in a commendable manner.

Twice during recent years when her father was confined to a hospital for long periods, she carried on with the business and carry on in a commendable manner.

The name Eileen has been closely connected with the News-Wave during her decade of service here.

To Dad, her absence at the office is keenly felt, and in the home it is touching, for since her mother's death in 1943 she has kept the home a home, so you see when Eileen left, Dad sorta had to endure a double dose of absenteeism.

There's considerable personal pride in writing the above, and somehow we wanted to do it before an occasion might call for a black heading and black border.

Dad

Eileen held the rank of Seaman First Class.

CAROLINE KLOSS
UNITED STATES WOMEN'S ARMY CORPS

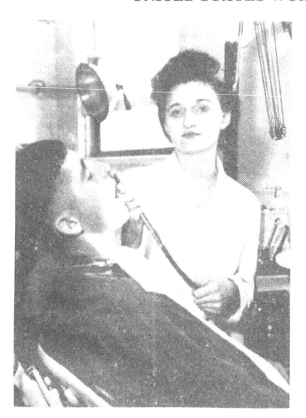

Caroline Kloss enlisted and entered active military active service on October 25, 1943 in Milwaukee, Wisconsin. She was sent to Daytona Beach, Florida, for Women's Army Corps (WAC) basic training, a six week program. She was then transferred to Fort Sheridan, Illinois, where she was assigned and trained as a dental technician. Working in the Regional Hospital dental clinic, Caroline assisted the dental officer. Among her duties, she sterilized and laid out instruments and medical supplies, mixed cement and amalgam for fillings, developed X-rays, charted the diagnosis of cases, and kept appointment books.

In a letter received from Caroline relating this information, she ended by stating, "It was interesting work but also sad to see all those young soldiers going overseas to fight that nasty war and knowing that they all wouldn't be coming back."

Caroline was separated from the Army on February 16, 1946.

Caroline Kloss on duty as a dental technician at Fort Sheridan, Illinois.

322

MARTHA MARSOLEK
UNITED STATES ARMY NURSES CORPS

Martha graduated from St. Joseph's School of Nursing, Marshfield, Wisconsin, in 1944. She joined the Army Nurses Corps in July, 1944, and trained at Camp McCoy, Wisconsin. A Lieutenant in August. 1945, she was expecting duty overseas.

On September 3, 1946, while stationed in Japan, First Lieutenant Martha Marsolek drowned in an auto-related accident in Yokohama, Japan. At the time, she was serving with the 1453 Air Force Medical Air Evacuation Squadron. Her brother, Private First Class John Marsolek left Korea and returned to San Francisco, from which point he accompanied her body to Independence.

CAROLYN MATCHEY
UNITED STATES ARMY NURSES CORPS

Carolyn entered St. Francis Hospital School of Nursing in La Crosse, Wisconsin, following her graduation from Independence High School in 1934. In January. 1942 she became the first woman from Trempealeau County to enlist in the military, and following her initial training, she was commissioned a Second Lieutenant. She then was stationed at Letterman (also reported as "Lademan") General Hospital in San Francisco, California. (November 4, 1943; November 25, 1943)

By November 1944 she had been transferred to England where she was put in charge of a surgical ward at the 83rd General Hospital in Wales. Her duties included responsibility for the administration and management of a ward of 28 wounded combat soldiers who were receiving routine medical and personal care. (December 14, 1944) In the April 26, 1945 edition of the *News-Wave*, it was reported Carolyn had been promoted to First Lieutenant, the rank she held at the time of her discharge in 1945. There is an indication she may have gone into France following the Normandy invasion of June 1944, though the following letter to her parents published in the *News-Wave* on November 30, 1944 was apparently written from Wales:

Dearest Mom and All:

How is everything with you? I hope everything is fine.

I am going to have five days leave and I think I will take a trip to London.

What do you hear from Laddie? I have never heard from him.

The weather has been cool and rainy here lately. It also is getting dark earlier.

What's the news back home? There is nothing new here. What is Dominic doing and how are Dad and Verna?

Will write again.

As ever,

Carol

ESTHER M. SKROCH
UNITED STATES ARMY NURSES CORPS

Esther graduated from St. Francis Hospital School of Nursing, La Crosse, Wisconsin, in the fall of 1939. While a nursing staff member at Columbia Hospital, Milwaukee, Wisconsin, she received her commission as a Second Lieutenant in the Army Nurses Corps. She was the first "Independence girl," as the *News-Wave* put in on May 6, 1943, to enlist in the service. In May 1943 she was assigned to Lovell General Hospital, Ayers, Massachucetts, from where, after three weeks there, she was sent to England.

Arriving in Bristol, England, Esther was assigned duty with the 298th General Hospital. On D-Day plus 30, the 298th was the first General Hospital to cross the English Channel to France, landing on Utah Beach. An article published in the *News-Wave* on October 11, 1945, stated Esther landed on Utah Beach by LST (Landing Ship, Tank) about midnight and immediately traveled to Cherbourg where her unit took over a French Marine hospital. The hospital consisted of three wings, one of which contained wounded German prisoners of war. In the article, Esther indicated the combat clothing the nurses were required to wear during the landing and subsequent move to Cherbourg were "anything but comfortable."

The 298th later moved to Liege, Belgium, where it received and cared for soldiers wounded during the German Ardennes counteroffensive, known better to Americans as the "Battle of the Bulge."

Throughout her time in the Nurses Corps, Esther served with Lieutenant Phyllis Boland of Arcadia, Wisconsin, and Lieutenant Margaret Walker, who following the war married Walt Baecker of Waumandee, Wisconsin, and moved to Independence. At the time of her discharge around October 1, 1945, following 29 months in the service, Esther was wearing the European-African-Middle Eastern Ribbon with three battle stars and a Meritorious Unit Citation for outstanding service against the enemy.

PRAKSEDA SKROCH
UNITED STATES ARMY NURSES CORPS

After graduating from Independence High School and the St. Francis Hospital School of Nursing in La Crosse, Wisconsin, Prakseda worked for several years on the staff at St. Francis and then three years in Milwaukee as an industrial nurse. She enlisted in the Army Nurses Corps in early February, 1945 and was commissioned a Second Lieutenant. In July 1945 she was stationed near Whitehorse, Yukon Territories, Canada.

IRENE SYLLA
UNITED STATES NAVY NURSES CORPS

Irene entered the St. Francis Hospital School of Nursing, La Crosse, Wisconsin, in the fall of 1937, from where she graduated in 1941. She remained on the staff there until enlisting in the Navy Nursing Corps on September 21, 1943. As an Ensign, she was stationed with a Naval Hospital in Corona, California, in late 1944. However, a *News-Wave* article on December 14, 1944 stated she was then receiving her mail through the Navy fleet post office out of San Francisco, California.

AUDREY LUCILLE TORGERSON
UNITED STATES NAVY

Audrey joined the United States Navy in November, 1944 and received her recruit training at the Naval Training School at Hunter College, The Bronx, New York. She later received yeoman training involving office and clerical work at the Naval Training School in Stillwater, Oklahoma . By July 1945 Audrey was stationed at the Fleet Home Town News Center, Chicago, Illinois, the arm of the Navy where news and photos of men and women serving around the world was sent for editing and distribution to their home towns. There, she worked in the media section where distribution was determined.

Audrey was later sent to the Naval Personnel Separation Center in Toledo, Ohio, where she performed office duties. From there she was transferred to the Washington, D. C., Naval Barracks where she remained until her discharge in April 1946 with the rank of Seaman First Class.

IANTHE WIEMER
UNITED STATES WOMEN'S AIR CORPS

Ianthe enlisted in the WACS in April 1944 and completed her basic training at Fort Oglethorpe, Georgia. From there, she was transferred to Grenier Field, New Hampshire, where she was as of November 1944 with the rank of Private.

While stationed at Grenier Field, Ianthe wrote a letter on December 8, 1944 to the *News-Wave* regarding the "Special Serviceman's Edition" of November 30, 1944:

Dear Independence Friends:

I want to express my thanks along with others in the service for the grand contributions you all have made in the Christmas edition of the News-Wave, and especially to the American Legion and American Legion Auxilliary for sponsoring such a project.

I didn't get my paper during the day as I usually do because I was in Boston on a three day pass, but that evening when I got back to the barracks I made myself comfortable, settled myself on my bunk, and opened the News-Wave. Lo and behold all the familiar faces and places began to appear along with all the good wishes, and I must confess I had a small feeling of homesickness for a few minutes.

I suppose the folks have told you that I am enjoying my life in the WAC and wish more than once that I had gotten in sooner. Grenier Field is a very pretty place. Our barracks are located right among the trees, so to speak. In fact, we walk through the woods along a stone bordered, and now, leaf cluttered path to the mess hall. We also have a lake in full view from our windows. A small stream winds its way around the field. It is pretty now. What must it be like in the spring of the year.

In return for your thoughts of all of us at this time I wish all of you, young and old, the Best Christmas and New Year that you have ever known and my prayers will go up with yours in the hope that this war will soon be over.

Ianthe Wiemer

MARY MARGARET WOZNEY
UNITED STATES NAVY

Mary Margaret passed her physical examination for acceptance into the WAVES on June 22, 1945 at the same time as Eileen Kirkpatrick. She completed an eight-week course at the U. S. Naval Training School, The Bronx, New York, and then was sent to San Francisco, California, for further duties.

Following is a list of other women from Independence known to have joined military nursing services during World War II:

ANDERSON, JOYCE
Joyce graduated from Independence High School in 1943 and entered Marquette University College of Nursing that summer. After completing three semesters at Marquette, she joined the United States Nurses Cadet Corps, after which she began her pre-clinical work. She was scheduled to receive her cap in February 1945.

BAUTCH, ESTHER
Esther entered Cadet Nurses Corps in the fall of 1944 while a student at St. Francis School of Nursing, La Crosse, Wisconsin.

BAUTCH, MARTINA
Martina graduated from Independence High School in 1942 and entered City College at Los Angeles, California. She enlisted in the Cadet Nurses Corps at a Hollywood, California, hospital in September 1944.

DEJNO, PATRICIA
Patricia graduated from Independence High School in 1943 and in August of that year entered the St. Charles Hospital School of Nursing in Aurora, Illinois. Several months later she joined the Cadet Nurses Corps.

Photo: Page 321

HARTNAGEL, ANGELINE
A 1943 graduate of Independence High School, Angeline entered the Ancker Hospital School for Nurses in St. Paul, Minnesota, where she immediately joined the Nurses Cadet Corps.

JAHR, VERNE
Verne graduated from Independence High School in 1942, following which she worked for one year in Milwaukee, Wisconsin. On September, 20, 1943 she entered the nurses training program at Lutheran Hospital in Moline, Illinois. In October 1943 she joined the Cadet Nurses Corps, and on May 5, 1944 completed her probationary work and received her nurses cap.

KULIG, PATRICIA

A May 1942 graduate of Independence High School, Patricia entered Mercy Hospital School of Nursing in Oshkosh, Wisconsin as a Cadet Nurse in June, 1944.

SYGULLA, PAULINE

Pauline graduated from Independence High School in 1944. She entered the St. Francis School of Nursing, La Crosse, Wisconsin, as an Army Cadet Nurse that fall.

TUBBS, JANET

A June 1943 graduate of Independence High School, Janet entered nurses training that fall at the Luther School of Nursing, Eau Claire, Wisconsin. One month after entering Luther, she joined the Army Nurses Cadet Corps. She received her nurses cap in March 1944.

A Quote From History. . .

"Anyone who has never been in combat can never imagine what those boys went through, as well as what the medical personnel caring for them experienced. War is a horrible, horrible thing."
Marge (Walker) Baecker
United States Army Nursing Corps
From an interview, August 4, 1998.

BIBLIOGRAPHY

Books

The following books were sources for biographical and background information regarding units, actions, and campaigns. Any books used as primary sources are identified with the individual biographies.

Andrade, Allan. *S. S. Leopoldville Disaster: December 24, 1944.* New York: The Tern Book Company, 1997.

Appleman, Roy E., James M. Burns, Russell A. Gugeler, and John Stevens. *Okinawa: The Last Battle.* Washington, D. C.: The Center of Military History, 1991.

Arnold, James and Roberta Wiener. *Operation Overlord: Utah Beach and the U. S. Airborne Divisions, 6 June 1944.* Braceborough, UK: Ravelin, Ltd., 1994.

Astor, Gerald. *Operation Iceberg: The Invasion and Conquest of Okinawa in World War II.* New York: Dell Publishing, 1995.

Astor, Gerald. *Crisis in the Pacific: The Battles for the Philippine Islands by The Men Who Fought Them.* New York: Donald I. Fine Books, 1996.

Bonn, Keith E. *When the Odds Were Even: The Vosges Mountains Campaign, October 1944 - January 1945.* Novato, CA: Presidio Press, 1994.

Bowman, Martin W. *The U. S. Eighth Air Force in Camera.* Phoenix Mill, UK: Sutton Publishing, Ltd., 1997.

Boyne, Walter J. *Clash of Titans: World War II at Sea.* New York: Touchstone, 1997.

Boyne, Walter J. *Clash of Wings: World War II in the Air.* New York: Touchstone, 1997.

Branton, Harold M. *103rd Infantry Division: The Trail of the Cactus.* Paducah, KY: Turner Publishing, 1996.

Breuer, William B. *Retaking the Philippines.* New York: St. Martin's Press, 1986.

Cannon, M. Hamlin. *Leyte: The Return to the Philippines.* Washington, D. C.: The Center of Military History, United States Army, 1954.

Carlisle, John M. *Red Arrow Men: Stories About the 32nd Division on the Villa Verde.* Nashville, TN: The Battery Press, n. d.

Center of Military History, The, United States Army. *The War Against Japan.* Washington, D. C.: Brassey's, 1994.

Connaughton, Richard, John Pimlott, and Duncan Anderson. *The Battle For Manila.* Novato, CA: Presidio Press, 1995.

Cortesi, Lawrence. *Pacific Siege.* New York: Kensington Publishing Group, 1984.

Craig, Berry. *76th Infantry Division: Onaway.* Paducah, KY: Turner Publishing, 1992.

Crowl, Philip A. *Campaign in the Marianas.* Washington, D. C.: The Center of Military History, United States Army, 1960.

Crowl, Philip A. and Edmund G. Love. *Seizure of the Gilberts and Marshalls.* Washington, D. C.: The Center of Military History, United States Army, 1953.

Department of the Army Historical Division. *Utah Beach to Cherbourg.* Nashville, TN: The Battery Press, 1984.

Eichelberger, Lt. Gen. Robert L. *Our Jungle Road To Tokyo.* Nashville, TN: The Battery Press, n. d.

Feifer, George. *Tennozan: The Battle of Okinawa and the Atomic Bomb.* Boston: Houghton, Mifflin Company, 1992.

Fifth Division Historical Section, The. *The Fifth Infantry Division in the ETO.* Nashville, TN: The Battery Press, n. d.

Flanagan, Lt. Gen. E. M., Jr. *Corregidor: The Rock Force Assault.* Novato, CA: Presidio Press, 1988.

Frank, Richard B. *Guadalcanal.* New York: Penguin Books, 1990.

Gailey, Harry A. *"Howlin' Mad" vs. the Army: Conflict in Command, Saipan, 1944.* Novato, CA: Presidio Press, 1986.

Gailey, Harry A. *The War in the Pacific: From Pearl Harbor to Tokyo Bay.* Novato, CA: Presidio Press, 1997.

Garfield, Brian. *The Thousand-Mile War: World War II in Alaska and the Aleutians.* Fairbanks, AK: University of Alaska Press, 1995.

Gaul, Roland. *The Battle of the Bulge in Luxembourg: The Southern Flank, December 1944 - January 1945, Vol. II The Americans.* Atglen, PA: Schiffer Publishing, 1995.

Green, Michael. *Patton's Tank Drive: D-Day to Victory.* Osceola, WI: Motorbooks International, 1995.

Hoffman, Major Carl W. *Saipan: The Beginning of the End.* Nashville: The Battery Press, 1988.

Johnsen, Frederick A. *B-24 Liberator.* Osceola, WI: Motorbooks International, 1993.

Karig, Commander Walter, Lieutenant Earl Burton and Lieutenant Stephen L. Freeland. *Battle Report: The Atlantic War.* New York: Farrar and Rinehart, 1946.

Karig, Captain Walter, Lieutenant Commander Russell L. Harris and Lieutenant Commander Frank A. Manson. *Battle Report: The End of An Empire.* New York: Rinehart and Company, 1948.

Karig, Captain Walter, Lieutenant Commander Russell L. Harris and Lieutenant Commander Frank A. Manson. *Battle Report: Victory in the Pacific.* New York: Rinehart and Company, 1949.

Karig, Commander Walter and Lieutenant Welbourn Kelley. *Battle Report: Pearl Harbor to Coral Sea.* New York: Farrar and Rinehart, 1944.

Karig, Captain Walter and Commander Eric Purdon. *Battle Report: Pacific War: Middle Phase.* New York: Rinehart and Co., 1947.

Love, Captain Edmund G. *The 27th Infantry Division in World War II.* Nashville: The Battery Press, 1982.

MacDonald, Charles B. *The Last Offensive.* Washington, D. C.: The Center of Military History, 1973.

MacDonald, Charles B. *A Time For Trumpets: The Untold Story of the Battle of the Bulge.* New York: William Morrow and Company, 1985.

Miller, Edward G. *A Dark and Bloody Ground: The Hurtgen Forest and the Roer River Dams, 1944-45.* College Station, TX: Texas A & M Press, 1994.

Miller, Jr., John. *Guadalcanal: The First Offensive.* Washington, D. C.: The Center of Military History, United States Army, 1949.

Milner, Samuel. *Victory in Papua.* Washington, D. C.: The Center of Military History, United States Army, 1957.

Morison, Samuel Eliot. *The Two-Ocean War.* Boston: Little, Brown and Company, 1963.

Nichols, Jr., Major Chas. S. and Henry I. Shaw, Jr. *Okinawa: Victory in the Pacific.* Nashville: The Battery Press, 1989.

Prefer, Nathan. *MacArthur's New Guinea Campaign: March-April 1944.* Conshohocken, PA: Combined Books, 1995.

Robbins, Major Robert A. *The 91st Infantry Division in World War II.* Nashville: The Battery Press, 1999.

Smith, Robert Ross. *The Approach to the Philippines.* Washington, D. C.: The Center of Military History, United States Army, 1953.

Spector, Ronald H. *Eagle Against the Sun.* New York: The Free Press, 1985.

Sprecher, Drexel A. *Inside the Nuremberg Trial: A Prosecutor's Comprehensive Account,* 2 vol. Lanham, MD: University Press of America, 1999.

St. John, Philip A. *Hell on Wheels: Second Armored Division.* Paducah, KY: Turner

Publishing, 1991.

St. John, Philip A. *Fourth Infantry Division: Steadfast and Loyal.* Paducah, KY: Turner
    Publishing, 1994.

Stanton, Shelby L. *World War II Order of Battle.* New York: Galahad Books, 1991.

Starr, Lt. Col. Chester G. *From Salerno to the Alps: A History of the Fifth Army, 1943-1945.*
    Nashville: The Battery Press, 1986.

van der Vat, Dan. *The Pacific Campaign: The U. S. - Japanese Naval War, 1941-1945.* New
    York: Touchstone, 1991.

VFW Magazine, ed. *Faces of Victory: Europe: Liberating a Continent.* Kansas City, MO:
    Addax Publishing Group, 1995.

Vickers, Col. Robert E., Jr. *The Liberators From Wendling.* Manhatten, KS: Sunflower
    University Press, 1977.

Walkowiak, Thomas F. *Destroyer Escorts of World War II.* Missoula, MT: Pictorial Histories
    Publishing, 1987.

Wessman, Siinto S. *The 66th Infantry Division in World War II.* Nashville, TN: The Battery
    Press, n. d.

Whitaker, W. Denis and Shelagy Whitaker. *Rhineland: The Battle to End the War.* New York:
    St. Martin's Press,1989.

Yahara, Colonel Hiromichi. *The Battle for Okinawa.* New York: John Wiley and Sons, 1995.
    _____. *The Legacy of Merrill's Marauders.* Paducah, KY: Turner Publishing, 1987.

Additional Recommended Reading

While conducting this study of the veterans of Independence, Wisconsin, this writer read a number of books
not directly related to the biographies he was compiling. Of these, the following offer great insights into
what the soldiers on the front lines and those in training were experiencing, as well as that of the civilians
on the home front.

Ambrose, Stephen E. *Band of Brothers: E Company, 506th Regiment, 101st Airborne, From
    Normandy to Hitler's Eagle's Nest.* New York: Touchstone, 1993.

Ambrose, Stephen E. *Citizen Soldiers: The U. S. Army from the Normandy Beaches to the
    Bulge to the Surrender of Germany, June 7, 1944 - May 7, 1945.* New York: Simon and
    Schuster, 1997.

Ambrose, Stephen E. *D-Day, June 6, 1944: The Climactic Battle of World War II.* New York:
    Touchstone, 1994.

Ambrose, Stephen E. *The Victors: Eisenhower and His Boys: The Men of World War II.* New
    York: Simon and Schuster, 1998.

Bradley, James and Ron Powers. *Flags of Our Fathers.* New York: Bantam Books, 2000.

Brokaw, Tom. *The Greatest Generation.* New York: Random House, 1998.

Brokaw, Tom. *The Greatest Generation Speaks.* New York: Random House, 1999.

Norman, Elizabeth M. *We Band of Angels: The Untold Story of American Nurses Trapped on
    Bataan by the Japanese.* New York: Random House, 1999.

Stillwell, Paul, ed. *The Golden Thirteen: Recollections of the First Black Naval Officers.*
    Annapolis, MD: Naval Institute Press, 1993.

Internet Sources

Much information regarding ship histories was located through the internet. For the most part, these ship histories originally appeared in the following series of books:

Dictionary of American Fighting Ships. Several volumes. Several dates. Navy Department, Office of the Chief of Naval Operations, Naval History Division: Washington, D. C.

These histories not only provided an accurate historical timeline for the ships but also, in so doing, in most instances allowed this writer to place Independence's sailors aboard ship during specific periods of time. The writer has taken the liberty of listing the site addresses in their general form as most sites contained information on multiple ships and were accessed at numerous times. Sites that were a major source of information regarding particular ships have those ships listed below them.

http://www.uss-salem.org/danfs/
- U. S. S. Robert I. Paine (DE-578)
- U. S. S. Algorma (ATO-34)
- U. S. S. Ticonderoga (CV-14)
- U. S. S. Belleau Wood ((CVL-24)
- U. S. S. Chicago (CA-29)
- U. S. S. Ashland (LSD-1)
- U. S. S. Duluth (CL-87)
- U. S. S. San Francisco (CA-38)
- U. S. S. Peary (DD-226)
- U. S. S. Perch (SS-313)
- U. S. S. Mayo (DD-422)

http://metalab.unc.edu/hyperwar/USN/ships/
- U. S. S. Vella Gulf (CVE-111)
- U. S. S. Idaho (BB-42)

http://metalab.unc.edu/pub/academic/history/marshall/military/USN/
- U. S. S. Independence (CV-22)

http://www.navsource.org/Naval/Register/
- U. S. S. Aylwin (DD-355)

http://sunsite.unc.edu/hyperwar/USN/ships/
- U. S. S. Duluth (CL-87)

http://members.aol.com/oldfungi/cvl24his.html
- U. S. S. Belleau Wood (CVL-24)

http://www.geocities.com/Pentagon/Barracks/1041/collision_mayo.html
- U. S. S. Mayo (DD-422)

The internet was the source of information regarding other biographies, as well, in particular unit histories. These addresses are listed in their entirety:

http://www.execpec.com/~brouchou/
- 8th Air Force, 392nd Bomb Group (H)

Additional Recommended Internet Sites

There are several outstanding internet sites regarding World War II that would be of interest to family members of veterans. They are listed here, with addresses current as of December 1999:

In Memory of World War II
Includes many histories of those who served, plus a place to deposit stories you may have recorded.
http://members.tripd.com/~Memory_WWII/

The Institute on World War II and the Human Experience
A museum established at Florida State University for the purpose of preserving stories and artifacts regarding World War II.
http://www.fsu.edu/~ww2/

Dad's War
A web site established in honor of the author's father, this site has many, many links to other World War II related websites. A wealth of information is available here.
http://members.aol.com/dadswar/index.htm

WAE Message Board
Here, one can ask a question or answer those posed by others. Numbers of people daily appear here searching for a veteran, seeking clarification of an event, or requesting other help regarding the people and events of World War II. Post your own question or message.
-- To post a question or message:
http://wae.com/qmsgs.html
-- To go directly to the message board:
http://wae.com/discus/messages/board-topics.html

National World War II Memorial
Find out about the progress of this long-overdue memorial to the veterans of World War II.
http://wwiimemorial.com/

Index
of
Independence Names

Abend, Harvey, 262
Anderson, Alfred, 260
Anderson, Goodwin, 260
Anderson, Joyce, 326
Anderson, Vernon C., 260
Andre, LaVern, 260
Austin, Waldo, 3-5

Baecker, Margaret "Marge" (Walker), 5-6, 324
Baecker, Philip, 9
Baecker, Walter, 5, 7-9, 92
Bautch, Adelbert A., 10-12, 13, 15, 260, 314, 342
Bautch, Anselm, 12, 13, 260
Bautch, Edmund, 12-13, 260
Bautch, Ernest P., 15-17
Bautch, Esther, 326
Bautch, Everett "Icky", 66, 261
Bautch, M/M Frank, 17
Bautch, George V., 261
Bautch, Herman, 32, 189, 261
Bautch, M/M John C., 16
Bautch, Larry P., 261
Bautch, Martina, 326
Bautch, M/M Paul, 10, 12, 13
Bautch, Roman T., 17-18, 250
Benjamin, Miss, 148
Bergerson, Harold T., 261
Bidney, Ernest, 163
Bidney, Homer, 163, 261, 293
Bidney, Spencer, 262
Birkeland, Rev. O. G., 28, 162, 163
Bisek, Mrs. Agnes, 20, 22, 23
Bisek, Alphonse, 21s
Bisek, Benedict, 18, 19, 20, 23
Bisek, Emil, 18, 19, 20, 23
Bisek, Frank, 20-21, 23
Bisek, John, 20
Bisek, Louis, 18, 22-23
Bisek, Miss Martha, 19

Blaha, Everette "Blaze", 23-26, 103, 127, 264
Briggs, Robert "Bob" E., 262-263
Briggs, Vilas, 101, 232, 263-264
Brink, Rev. Newell V., 264
Browskowski, Ben, 265
Browskowski, Roy, 265
Burt, Oakley, W., 265

Carlson, M/M Carl "Charley", 27, 28
Carlson, Clarice, 28
Carlson, Hiram, 28
Carlson, Owen, 27-29
Cilley, Gordon D., 29-31
Cilley, M/M William H., 30, 164
Cooke, Gerald, 265
Cripps, Charles, 32
Cripps, Maureen, 32
Cripps, Peggy, 32
Cripps, M/M Ralph, 31
Cripps, Ruth, 32
Cripps, Sammy, 32
Cripps, Willis R., 31-32, 164-165

Dahl, Mrs. Bennie, 265
Dahl, Elmo, 265
Dejno, Alphonse, 32, 266
Dejno, Eleanor, 32, 320, 321
Dejno, John, 32
Dejno, M/M John, 32, 266, 321
Dejno, Mary, 32, 320, 321
Dejno, Patricia, 32, 321, 326
Dejno, Verna "Veronica", 32-33, 321

Ellifson, Archie, 266
Ellifson, Edner, 266
Edmundson, Bob, 248
Edmundson, Jesse, 31, 33-36, 270
Edmundson, Marge, 33, 34-35, 270
Erickson, Gordon, 266

Ertel, Wainwright, 266

Fellenz, Albert, 34
Fellenz, Millard, 267
Filla, Evelyn, 298
Filla, George, 267
Filla, Peter Jacob, 267
Fjeld, Elmo, 267
Fjeld, Ernest, 267, 271
Fueling, Mrs. John, 269

Gamroth, Mrs. Anna, 39
Gamroth, Bennie, 40, 266-267
Gamroth, Clara, 39-40
Gamroth, Clarence, 125, 268
Gamroth, Henry "Hank", 36-41
Gamroth, Mary, 38
Gamroth, Roland, 39
Garthus, Miss Lillian, 162
Gasatis, M/M August, 43
Gasatis, Ben, 42-45, 227, 267
Gasatis, John, 268
Getts, Clara (Maule), 300
Gierok, Charles A., 269
Gierok, Ignatius, 269
Girtman, Mrs. Broadus (Alpha), 28
Gunderson, Arnold, 269
Gunderson, Donald, 162
Gunem, Helmer R., 270
Gunem, Lester, 32, 45-46, 189

Halama, M/M Aloysie, 94
Halama, Hillary "Jack", 31, 136, 163, 189, 209
    270,
Halama, Larry, 137
Halama, Ray, 225, 270
Hanson, Alan, 28, 162, 271
Hanson, George R., 270
Hartnagel, Angeline, 326
Helgeson, Henry, 28, 163
Hendrickson, Ardell, 271
Hendrickson, Glen F., 46-49, 262
Hendrickson, LeRoy, 271-272
Hendrickson, M/M Ole, 47

Higgins, Miss, 148
Hogue, Miss, 148
Hotchkiss, Addison, 50-51, 74, 209
Howland, M/M Ole (Emma), 161, 163
Hunt, Kenneth, 271
Hutchins, Earl, 32, 189, 272

Insteness, Glenn, 52, 310
Isaacs, Bernie, 53-55, 250
Isaacs, Mrs. Hannah, 272
Isaacs, Jerome, 272

Jahr, Robert O., 272
Jahr, Verne, 326
Jaszewski, Andrew, 272
Jaszewski, John J., 55-57
Jaszewski, Joseph "Jazzy" J., 58-62
Jaszewski, Marie, 62
Jaszewski, Nicholas B., 56, 63-65
Jaszewski, Roman, 272-276
Jelen, Coddy, 277
Jelen, Roman S., 277
Johnson, David, 277
Johnson, Erling, 277
Johnson, Kermit, 277
Johnson, Orville, G., 278
Johnson, Elizabeth, 189s
Jonietz, Ralph J., 66-68, 161, 269, 347
Jonietz, Raymond J., 278

Kampa, Bennie J., 21, 278
Kampa, Mrs. Clifford, 309
Kampa, Dominic, 144, 278-279
Kampa, Edward, 279
Kampa, George, 279
Kampa, "Ike", 199
Kampa, Lawrence "Laury", 68-69
Kampa, Lawrence M., 280
Kampa, Louis P., 69-70, 185
Kampa, Mrs. Mike, 279
Kampa, Paul E., 280-281
Kampa, Roy, 279s
Karasch, Apolinary "A. J.", 70-72
Karasch, M/M John, 70

Karasch, Vincent, 32, 73, 189
Kern, Leonard, 256, 271, 281
Kern, Phyllis, 281
Killian, Eugene, 51, 73-74
Kilness, Homer, 282
Kirkpatrick, Eileen, 264, 275, 320, 322
Kirkpatrick, Glenn "Kirk", 5, 26, 44, 48, 55, 56,
    67, 100, 101, 104, 105, 143, 215, 228, 231
    244, 262, 263-264, 272-276, 278, 280-281,
    284, 286, 295, 301, 306, 309, 312, 320
Klick, Raymond, 74-76
Klick, Mrs. Ray, 76s
Klimek, Clifford, 81, 282
Klimek, George, 81
Klimek, Joseph, 282
Klimek, Peter, 282
Klimek, Ralph, 76-81
Klimek, M/M Simon, 282
Klink, Clifford, 144
Kloss, Alex E., 25, 82-83
Kloss, Bennie, 83-85, 97, 276
Kloss, Caroline, 322
Kloss, Donnie, 83s
Kloss, Joseph F., 282
Klove, Bennie A., 282
Klove, William, 282-283
Knudtson, George, 34
Kufel, Msgr. L. J., 12, 23, 188, 189, 240
Kuka, Roman "Cookie", 73, 283
Kulig, Adolph P., 283
Kulig, Alphonse "Al", 85-88, 171, 253
Kulig, Arthur "Art" A., 88-92, 233, 300
Kulig, Benedict "Bennie", 6, 95, 15n, 16, 32,
    92-96, 136, 189, 301
Kulig, Bernard "Bernie" J., 96-97, 277
Kulig, Clifford, 94, 95
Kulig, Edward J., 97-98
Kulig, Joseph and Petronella, 89
Kulig, Patricia, 327
Kulig, Ralph, 91
Kupka, Alex P., 283
Kupka, Mrs. Margaret, 283
Kwosek, Frank M., 283-284
Kwosek, Marcus, 284

Lee, Audrey (Cilley), 31s
Leque, Mrs. Arthur (Millie), 99
Leque, Carl "Ole", 98-100, 174
Leque, Lyle, 99, 284
Libowski, Edward, 284
Libowski, Joseph, 9, 100-106, 269
Libowski, Paul, 284
Lucente, John, 106-107, 308
Lyga, Edmund J., 21, 32, 81, 86, 87, 89, 107-
    114, 189, 200, 240

Maciosek, Everett, 285-287
Maloney, Calvin, 287-290
Maloney, Curt, 288-289
Maloney, Olive, 288-289
Markham, George F., 114, 115-121, 122, 123
Markham, Attorney and Mrs. John A., 116, 123
Markham, Richard "Dick", 87, 115, 116, 119,
    121-123
Marsolek, Ernest, 189, 290
Marsolek, George P., 290
Marsolek, John P., 290, 323
Marsolek, Marcel "Zeke" M., 124-129
Marsolek, Martha, 323
Marsolek, Michael, 32, 130-131, 189
Marsolek, Rose, 280
Marsolek, Rufus, 290-291
Marsolek, Valentine, 291
Matchey, Carolyn, 323
Matchey, Ladislaus "Laddie", 131-133, 323
Matchey, Raymond A., 291
Mattson, Elroy, 291
Mattson, Lyle, 291
Maule, Albert, 291
Maule, Clarence, 104, 291
Maule, Edward, 93, 94, 133-134
Maule, Mrs. Peter (Mary), 41
Melby, Ardell G., 291-292
Meyer, Dr., 34
Misch, Albert J., 292
Misch, Henry, 144
Mish, M/M August, 280
Mish, M/M Frank, 136
Mish, Marc, 34

Mish, Peter P., 134-136
Mlynek, Clarence, 124, 261, 293
Mlynek, Edward, 293-294
Mlynek, Joseph "Chester" C., 94, 136-137, 277
Mlynek, Rudy, 294
Morchinek, Edward D., 294
Morchinek, Frank, 294
Morchinek, Nick, 294
Morchinek, Roman R., 295

Nogosek, Adolph A., 137-139, 265
Nogosek, Simon, 139
Norlyn, Alfred E., 295

Olson, Afner H., 139-140
Olson, Mary Ann (Sobota), 201
Olson, Myron, 262

Palkowski, John, 295-296
Pampuch, Marcel, 140-141
Pampuch, Paul, 142-144, 281
Pampuch, Mrs. Paul, 141
Pampuch, Roman P., 296
Pape, Allen C., 144-145
Pape, Elmer F., 296
Parazynski, Louis, 297
Passon, Adolph, 31
Pientok, Alfred, 31, 163
Pientok, LaVerne, 32, 189
Pieterick, Alfred, 146, 149, 151
Pieterick, Bob, 148s
Pieterick, M/M Charles "Charlie", 146, 149, 300
Pieterick, Eugene "Gene", 146, 149, 151, 163,
    297
Pieterick, Gerald "Bud" J., 32, 145-149, 150,
    151, 185, 189, 252
Pieterick, Raymond, 145, 146, 147, 149-160,
    163, 240, 279
Polzer, Doc, 225
Prokop, Carrie (Kulig), 88, 90, 91, 92
Prokop, Frank, 88, 90, 91
Przybylski, Rev. Francis, 12, 23, 188
Pyka, Ralph, 297

Rebarchek, Herman, 297
Reck, Edward, 298
Reck, Rudolph C., 299
Reck, Vincent, 90, 299, 300
Resler, Ed, 300
Resler, Everett, 300
Resler, Leonard, 300
Ressel, M/M Clemence, 161
Ressel, Stanley A., 67, 160-161
Rombalski, George M., 300-301
Rombalski, Joseph P., 301-302
Rombalski, Roman R., 302
Rombalski, Roy R., 302
Roskos, Ralph, 302
Runkel, John W., 302
Runkel, William "Billy", 302
Rustad, Glen H., 91, 161-163
Rustad, Leone, 162
Rustad, Myron, 162
Rustad, Oliver, 31, 162, 303
Rustad, Walter, 162

Sather, Edwin, 303
Sather, Ervin, 31, 164, 303
Sather, George R., 163-164
Sather, M/M Helmer, 31, 164
Sather, Irwin, 283
Sather, Norval, 164-165, 303
Sather, Odin H., 304
Sather, Oscar W., 166-167
Sather, Otis, 304
Sather, Peter L., 164
Schneider, Mrs. Agnes, 171
Schneider, Ben V., Jr., 124, 167-169
Schneider, Clements (Clemence), 101, 304
Schneider, George, 170-171, 268
Schneider, Mrs. George (Fran), 171
Schneider, Hubert, 304
Schneider, John J., 304
Schneider, Dr. O. M., 305
Schoenberger, M/M Louis, 310
Severson, Omar A., 305
Siefert, Andrew, 305
Siefert, Peter, 305

Skroch, Adrian, 172-173
Skroch, Albert, 173-174, 212, 213
Skroch, Bernice, 180s
Skroch, Bill, 180
Skroch, Clarence, 306
Skroch, Edward G., 85, 306
Skroch, Edward I., 175-176, 253
Skroch, Ernest J., 306
Skroch, Esther, 6, 324
Skroch, Dr. Eugene E., 177-178
Skroch, Everett, 306, 307
Skroch, M/M John C., 174
Skroch, Marcel, 208, 209, 307
Skroch, Peter, 180-183, 312
Skroch, Prakseda, 324
Skroch, Sally, 172
Skroch, Simon "Bob" R., 51, 178-180, 310
Slaby, George, 307
Slaby, Marcel M., 307
Slaby, Peter, 183-184
Slaby, Roman, 31, 189, 307
Sluga, Betty Lou, 189
Sluga, Bobby, 189
Sluga, Clarence, 57, 145-146, 184-187, 189, 299
Sluga, Delores, 189
Sluga, Dominic, 285, 286, 307-308
Sluga, M/M Eddie, 187, 188
Sluga, Elizabeth, 187, 188, 180
Sluga, Frank, 144, 308
Sluga, George, 189
Sluga, Gerald, 189
Sluga, Ralph R., 187-189
Sluga, Raymond, 144, 308
Sluga, Romelle, 189
Smick, Jeffrey, 190s, 195s
Smick, Louis and Anna, 191
Smick, Thomas George, 189, 191-195, 292
Smieja, Diane, 162
Smieja, Gary, 197s
Smieja, Ray, 32, 189, 309
Smieja, M/M Roman, 196, 198
Smieja, Rudolph "Rudy" R., 31, 195-197, 253
Smieja, Sarah, 91, 161, 162
Smieja, Vitus, 31, 85, 163, 195, 197-199

Smieja, Wilfred, 196
Sobota, Mrs. Anton, 200, 213
Sobota, Jerome, 110, 162, 199-201
Sobota, John and Helen, 203-204
Sobota, Ralph, 73, 205
Sobota, Roman "Butch" A., 202-205, 250
Sobotta, Clifford B., 309
Sobotta, Emil, 205-208
Sobotta, Ernest, 163, 167, 208-211
Sobotta, M/M Ignatz, 207
Sobotta, Paul P., 212-214
Sokolosky, Henry, 310
Solfest, Sidney, 51, 310
Sonsalla, Adolph, 214-215, 255
Sonsalla, Nadine, 215s
Sonsalla, Roman A., 310
Sosalla, Dominic, 311
Sosalla, Rudy, 310-311, 342
Sprecher, Drexel, 216-225
Sprecher, Robert J., 311
Sprecher, M/M Walter A., 216
Steffenson, Albert, 311
Steffenson, Clayton, 311
Stratman, Joseph, 312
Suchla, Allen, 227s
Suchla, Edmund A., 225-227
Sura, M/M Andrew C., 312, 313
Sura, Benedict, 312
Sura, Chancey J., 312
Sura, Chester, 312
Sura, Clarence, 227-232, 312-313
Sura, Clifford, 231-232, 312-313
Sura, Dominic, 32, 233-234, 235s
Sura, Henry, 136, 234-235
Sura, Lawrence, 235-236
Sura, Leonard, 237-239
Sura, Mrs. Paul, 313
Sura, Peter, 313
Sura, Veronica, 234
Sygulla, Adolph R., 313
Sygulla, Alex, 313
Sygulla, Pauline, 327
Sygulla, Simon R., 314
Sylla, Irene, 324

Sylla, John P., 189, 314
Sylla, M/M Julius, 240
Sylla, Leonard, 161, 237-239
Sylla, Mrs. Leonard, 239s
Sylla, Michael, 238, 239s
Sylla, Paul, 314
Sylla, Ralph, 240
Sylla, M/M Thomas, 238
Symiczek, Alphonse, 254
Symiczek, Ernest F., 314
Symiczek, Ollie, 96

Theisen, John C., 314
Torgerson, Audrey, 325
Torson, John, 314
Tubbs, Janet, 327
Tubbs, Lon F., Jr., 240-241
Tubbs, Lon F., Sr., 34, 192-193

Ulberg, Lester, 11, 314

Voss, Joseph J., 241-243

Walek, Pete, 208, 209
Waletske, Ernest E., 314
Walske, Dr. B. R., 315
Warner, Malcolm F., 315
Warner, Michael, 249s
Warner, Raymond, 180, 243-249, 267
Warner, M/M R. C., 247
Weier, Clarence "Jack", 51, 181, 250-255, 306
Weier, Raymond, 256-257, 303
Weier, Rose, 252
Wiemer, Ianthe, 325
Wiemer, Martin A., 200, 262
Wiench, Herman, 315
Wilczek, Joseph A., 315
Wiltsey, Dallas, 31
Winsand, Orville M., 315
Witt, Lyle F., 315
Woychik, M/M Paul, 316
Woychik, Roman J., 315-318
Wozney, Mary Margaret, 197, 320, 326
Wozney, Roman, 318

Zimmerman, Dominic P., 318-319

Added At A Later Date:

Bautch Brothers (photo), 365
Bisek Frank (photo), 364
Gamroth, George R., 359
Isaacs, Jerome, 351
Jonietz, Ralph (photo), 345
Klimek, Ralph (photo), 346
Kuka, Joseph E., 359
Olson, Elmer Lester, 340
Pampuch, Alfred, 347
Pape, Earl, 360
Sluga, Clarence (photo), 363
Sobota, Roman "Butch", 365
Stendahl, Ivan C., 360
Sylla, John P., 361
Thalacker, Lloyd, 362
Weier, Raymond (photo), 350
Wicka, Robert, 342
Wilczek, Joseph A., 363

Biographies and Photos Added At a Later Date

ELMER LESTER OLSON
UNITED STATES ARMY

The following narrative was prepared following an interview with Lester at his Independence home on March 19, 2000. Lester was originally from the Strum, Wisconsin, area and moved to Independence following the war.

I entered the Army on, I believe, April 7, 1941, and went to Fort Custer, Michigan, for basic training. There I joined the 5th Division[1] and went with them on maneuvers in Tennesee and Louisiana. I was in the same company of the 2nd Infantry Regiment as Dominic Smick and once we traveled home together on furlough. Others from around home that were in the 5th Division were Adelbert Bautch, Joe Johnson of Pigeon Falls, Lester Melsness, and Rudy Sosalla. I saw them occasionally but they were in different companies.

In April 1942 we left Michigan for Fort Dix, New Jersey, and then from there left by ship to Iceland. I was aboard the *S. S. Menargo*.

Iceland was an interesting place; I was there for 12 or 13 months, I remember. During the summer, there was no real night; it only turned dusk due to the long days. We put blankets over our windows in order to sleep. We also had outside latrines with pails and the one detail nobody wanted was the "honey bucket" detail, cleaning the pails.

In Iceland, we patrolled in the mountains. I was trained as a machine gunner, and our machine guns were dug into the ground with very little showing. Once a German plane was shot down and the pilot captured.

There was snow there in the summer and it was really windy during winter. One guy went to Reykjavik for supplies one day and was blown off the truck; he ended up with a fractured skull. Another guy, a smaller guy, had to be led to the mess hall now and then because of the winds.

In Reykjavik, there was a restaurant that served pony steaks. The people raised a lot of ponies and sheep; I couldn't eat the mutton.

In 1943 I was part of a cadre sent back to the States. We went to Fort Leonard Wood,

---

[1] The 5th Infantry Division eventually participated in five campaigns in the European Theater. It suffered 2,298 men killed and 9,549 wounded in action. 358 died from their wounds.

Missouri, to form the 75th Infantry Division.[2] We participated in several training maneuvers before leaving for Camp Shanks, New York, in October or November of 1944. From there, we shipped out to South Wales where we stayed in a camp for a while. Then we crossed the channel to Le Havre on December 13, 1944, just before the Battle of the Bulge. The Le Havre area was blown to hell. We slept in tents in a pasture and it always seemed to be raining, which made it hard to stay dry.

One day our company commander told us, "Boys, I have some bad news. We're being sent to relieve the 106th at the Bulge." This was because they were all shot up so we figured we were in for a fight. We traveled to Belgium by truck and went right into action. A young guy, maybe 19 years old, got killed shortly after we got there.

We fought through Nancy, France, and into the Colmar area. When we reached the Rhine we were pulled back into Belgium for a rest. We later tried to cross the Rhine River twice but the Germans managed to blow our pontoon bridges both times with artillery. When we finally did manage to cross, at H-Hour there was a heavy artillery bombardment by the Allies and the sky was reddish from the firing. When we got to the other side, the Germans began surrendering; there were a lot of older guys by then in the German lines.

We then fought through Germany but didn't go to Berlin; instead we were told to just wait and that's what we were doing when the war ended. After V-E day, I went to St. Vieth, Germany, for a few days. I believe it was here where a colonel had orders to take German ammunition off railroad flatcars and destroy it. Right after I had breakfast one day, there was a hell of an explosion. It turned out a guy had crawled into a truck and stepped on a land mine. The driver was killed along with others. It was a mess.

Later I was sent back to France, where I stayed for several months. There were four or five guys together in tents and we built a wet and dry canteen and mess. An officer and I were in charge of the wet canteen. We hired Frenchmen to take care of the beer but they gave it away in trade for stuff they wanted. Then we got German displaced persons from the stockade and they took care of the wet canteen real good. If beer was left over, the lieutenant said the Germans could have some, but not too much.

We went to an open air theater for movies.

Then in November 1945, I left for Marseilles, France, from where I left for home. I came out on the point system. Guys without enough points were sent to Japan but I think that was all over before they got there. I landed at Camp Patrick Henry, Virginia, on November 23 and then traveled to Fort Sheridan, Illinois, where I was discharged on November 28. I was a Technician Fifth Grade when I left the Army.

During my time in Europe, I served as a machine gunner with H Company, the heavy weapons company, of the 290th Infantry Regiment of the 75th Infantry Division. I took part in the Ardennes-Alsace, Rhineland, and Central Europe campaigns with the 75th, so had three bronze battle stars on my European-African-Middle Eastern Theater Ribbon. I also was given an American Defense Service Medal, Victory Medal, and Good Conduct Medal. I ended up with five overseas service bars and one service stripe. I could operate and make minor repairs on carbines, pistols, the M-1, 30-caliber machine gun, 81mm mortar, and bazooka.

I got to see Paris once while on leave from the front lines, and also Brussels. Belgium was a nice, clean country and a lot of people there spoke English. I remember, too, that the French always wanted cigarettes and candy.

Reykjavik, Iceland, was a nice place, too. They always had natural hot water from the volcano nearby. I never saw any flies in Iceland, either. Fishermen would go out in boats and then come back and clean their fish in a guts factory. Fish guts were all over after they cleaned the fish and hauled them down the street. But I never saw any flies.

I even managed to learn some Icelandic; I guess we had to. One thing I learned is pronounced, "eta egoskeet." It means, "Stop or I'll shoot!"

---

2 The 75th Infantry Division lost 817 men killed and 3,314 wounded, with 111 of these dying from their wounds, during its three European Theater campaigns.

I saw some buzz bombs during the war and they would scare us. We could hear them, but when the motor stopped we knew it was coming down somewhere. Another thing I didn't like were the "screaming mimi's." I don't know for sure what they were -- I think rockets -- but they really scared people, too.

ROBERT WICKA
UNITED STATES ARMY

The following narrative was prepared following an interview with Bob Wicka on March 19, 2000 at his Hunt's Valley home in rural Independence. Bob was born in Minnesota and lived in the Dodge, Wisconsin, area prior to the war. He moved to his Hunt's Valley farm in 1957.

I was inducted into the United States Army on June 16, 1943 and entered active service on June 30 that same year. I was sent to Camp Ellis, Illinois, for basic training. About that time the 1303rd Engineer General Service Regiment was being formed at Camp Ellis, so a lot of new recruits, including myself, were attached to it. I was put in E Company. Following basic and further training, I was given a one-week leave to go home, after which I reported back to Camp Ellis. We then packed everything up and left for Camp Myles Standish, Massachusetts, from where we embarked from the Boston Port of Embarkation on March 21, 1944 aboard the *S. S. Argentina*. We landed in Scotland on April 4 and traveled to England.

In England, we didn't train at all, but they sure put us to work! We laid cement and wood slabs to store bombs for the coming invasion of Europe, and also built a hospital to house the wounded that would be brought back. We saw an awful lot of cement. I drove a truck, a 6x6 dump truck.

We didn't go over on D-Day but did help load the invasion troops. Our job was to help the 101st Airborne get their equipment aboard planes.

One bad thing that happened during this loading was when a jumpmaster forgot something, jumped off his plane, and a grenade went off. It killed 10 or 11 guys. I didn't actually see this but some of my buddies did and they had to pick up the pieces. They were just sick.

On July 24, 1944 the 1303rd landed across Omaha Beach in Normandy. Our first night there was real quiet and it didn't sound much like a war. But then the Germans began bombing us.

We went all the way through France and into Luxembourg. The Germans had blown all the bridges as they retreated and it was the job of engineer units to rebuild them. I didn't see much of actual battles but a few times we received orders to build a bridge and the town hadn't been taken yet. We built a lot of Bailey bridges; these were made of steel and built on land and then pulled across the river.

We also built some prisoner-of-war camps. Sometime here, Captain Watkins -- we called him "Smokey" because he always had a cigar -- was injured real badly when a cement mixer fell on him. He was a good commander; I liked him a lot.

At Toul, France, there was a chateau, like an old-time castle, on a steep hill. We moved in and used it as a headquarters. There was an American Indian in our unit and one day he went into town and had a few drinks. I picked him up and as I was driving up the hill he fell out of the back of the truck. We had two Indians in the unit; they were hell of nice guys. The guy who fell out of the truck was a good buddy of mine.

We built several bridges over the Moselle River, one of them at Toul. But high water took that bridge out. Fortunately, it wasn't being used at the time.

In mid-December 1944, when the Germans began their Ardennes Counteroffensive -- the Battle of the Bulge -- we were south of Nancy, France. General Patton, our overall commander, ordered us to Esch, Luxembourg, where the breakthrough was, in support of XII Corps. We drove at night with no lights, and that was a scary deal. I was driving a weapons carrier by then and often had officers with me. On this night run, Captain Cook was riding with me; he was giving directions while I drove. I drove the Captain much of the time.

At Christmas, everyone received a copy of the prayer Patton had handed out, and the sky cleared. At that time we were in the area of Bastogne where the 101st Airborne was trapped. We were told to prepare to assume infantry duties in an emergency and had orders to stop the enemy at all costs. The biggest weapon E Company had was a bazooka, so we kind of lucked out there that the Germans didn't advance on us.

It was so cold at this time. My job was to ___ed the ements to rotate men in the line; I was driving all night. Finally I fell asleep, ___ing the w__ad frozen feet and hands. They were sore and discolored, so they were ___ ern Franc ___ uys I began driving again. Years later I had four toes amputated; ___ as ___ha___ years.

As the Germans were pushed bac___ into Germany and just kept moving with Third Army. We built a bridge at Trier be___ the Rhine River. Here, too, the old bridge had been blown by the Germans. But we ___ could use the old supports for the bridge we were going to build. One day I took Captain Cook to check the old bridge area and German artillery began shelling us. I told the Captain I'd move the truck and no sooner did I do this and a shell hit where the truck had been.

We had special boats brought in to build this bridge -- it ended up being 1,865 feet long! We'd drive the truck loaded with cement onto the boat and the truck would then dump the cement onto the bridge.

When this bridge was completed, the Red Ball Express had a two-lane bridge over the Rhine.[1] That was our biggest project and it took so much materiel. I believe it took 17 days to put up. General Patton even came to congratulate us for this work. We thought a lot of Patton. Another company, F, I believe, built the "General Patton Bridge" over the Rhine as well.

One of the guys I remember well from our company was Archie Lucks. One time on guard duty, another guy approached him and Archie says, "Halt! Who goes there?" The other guy hit the deck and began shooting at Archie! The Captain asked what was going on and Archie told him, "Don't worry, sir, he's shooting at me!"

The last bridge we built was over the Danube River. Here, Archie fell off the bridge and drowned. Another guy jumped in to save him but just couldn't reach him. I guess Archie didn't have much luck.

One day I took a 9mm handgun off a prisoner. He was a rookie, no doubt, and the way I could tell was because the gun wasn't cleaned. It was cocked and loaded but still had cosmoline in it. I also picked up a beautiful three-barrel hunting gun that I put in a box and sent home.

On V-E Day, we moved into Passau, Austria, after the German surrender. They kept us working and the guys were mad about this. Our unit uncovered 100 executed POW's; we made the civilians bury them.

We then moved on to Marseilles, France, and thought we were going home. Some of us went by train but I drove a truck there. I found out after the war that at a depot where I gassed up, another Wicka -- a cousin from Dodge, Wisconsin -- stopped in shortly after. The guy in charge told him, "There was another Wicka just in here."

On June 23, 1945, we left France aboard the *S. S. General Pope*. When we arrived in Panama, we began wondering whether we were actually going home. As luck would have it, we got "shanghied" to the Pacific Theater because we didn't have enough points. We arrived in the Philippines on July 28, 1945, where we prepared for the invasion of Japan. In the Philippines, my truck had five battle stars on it from our time in Europe, and as we drove around, everyone would stop and salute because they thought a general was in the truck!

---

[1] The "Red Ball Express" consisted of the seemingly unending stream of trucks delivering supplies to the advancing American army. Marked with a big red ball, these trucks were given priority both to and from the front over their established route.

We lucked out when the atomic bomb was dropped on Japan; we were ready to invade with the first waves.

On August 28, 1945 I left the Philippines for Japan, where I arrived on September 14 in Yokohama. We soon left for Tokyo where we moved into a stadium built in 1940. We had a good home there -- swimming pool and all. Then we fixed up the roof and inside of General MacArthur's headquarters. I had a photo taken of me on top of the roof.

That 10 mile stretch from Yokohama to Tokyo was so completely destroyed. They had dropped a lot of incendiary bombs here.

Early in December 1945 I left Japan for the USA, and landed in Seattle, Washington, on Christmas Day. Our engineers regiment, call███ "Eager Beavers" by General Patton, had the record for most traveled unit in the Army du██████. We had covered 32,000 miles in all. I had five battle stars for the Normandy, North█████ ████nnes-Alsace, Rhineland, and Central Europe campaigns. On January 5, 1946 I wa███ ███ ██m the Army at Camp McCoy, Wisconsin, with the rank of Technician 5th G███.

Left: Bob Wicka
Right: Bob on the roof of General MacArthur's headquarters in Tokyo.

344

A bridge built by Bob Wicka's 1303rd Engineer General Service Regiment.

Ralph Jonietz. This photo was received shortly after initial publication of "A Small Town Goes To War." Awarded a Purple Heart and Bronze Star, Ralph's written history can be found on page 66 of this volume.

Ralph Klimek was a member of the 5307th Composite Unit (Provisional), a unit that gained fame during World War II as "Merrill's Marauders." On page 81 of this document, it is suggested that Ralph probably was a member of the 1st Battalion, but it has now been verified that he served with the 2nd Battalion. On April 9, 1944 the 2nd Battalion was rescued after having been surrounded by the Japanese for two weeks. On that day, an Easter Sunday service was conducted in the jungle of Burma and this photo was taken, clearly showing Ralph standing immediately to the left of the bent sapling on the left side of the photo. (Photo and identification courtesy of Merrill's Marauders Association)

Staff Sergeant ALFRED PAMPUCH
UNITED STATES ARMY AIR CORPS

The following narrative was prepared from an interview conducted with Alfred Pampuch at his home in Independence, Wisconsin, on October 26, 2002.

I joined the Army Air Corps on February 9, 1942 as a draftee, right after my 22nd birthday. I spent one week at the air base near Chicago, and then was sent to Shepard Field, Texas, for six weeks of basic training. The base was filling up with recruits for air training so I was soon sent to the Casey Jones School of Aeronautics in New Jersey. This was a school for aircraft mechanics and I was there from mid-March 1942 until August 10, 1942.

Next, I spent four weeks at the air base at Montgomery, Alabama, and then was sent to the base at Vincennes, Indiana. This was a flight training school and for the next two years I helped maintain the Cessna's and fighter planes used in training the pilots.

After I got orders to go overseas, I went to Charlotte, North Carolina, for a week, and then to New York. From there, I went to Bermuda and the Azores. We were pretty lucky on the flight from Bermuda to the Azores. It was so overcast that the pilot couldn't see the island. Finally he just dropped the plane down to sea level and there it was! Aboard the plane, the crew chief was keeping good records of our fuel consumption the whole time. I guess they were compiling records under all different conditions so they could be as efficient as possible.

Next we flew to Casablanca in North Africa. From Casablanca, I went to Tripoli, then Cairo for one night, Tehran, Iran, and then to Karachi, India, where I remained for a week. After leaving Karachi, I saw the Taj Mahal from the air before landing at a base up river from Calcutta. It was a large base – actually it was two bases, Tasgon and Kermatola – from where supplies were going to be flown over the "hump." I was one of the first to arrive at the base.

Supplies came up river to the bases, were loaded on C-47's and C-46's, and then flown over the hump to supply the Chinese. When we arrived, it was a British base and the landing strips were hard surfaced.

Airplanes were loaded in revetments, areas actually dug into the ground with protection on both sides. If the Japanese did send in their planes, they'd have to hit it just right to get at our planes. Once our planes were loaded with supplies, they taxied out and took off immediately. Planes flew day and night – we would check them out and clear them, they would be loaded, and they took off. Sometimes we were up at two and three in the morning if planes needed work.

Some of the planes that took off from our base were lost in Three Sisters Peaks, the worst part of the flight over the "hump." I remember one survivor of a crash walked out; it took him three weeks to reach the coast. There was usually a four- or five-man crew aboard the transports.

B-29's landed a couple times later in the war. I didn't work on these, however. The ground just shook when they took off. It seemed like there was always a delay on getting parts for those planes, so there was a lot of down time.

Fighter pilots also landed once in a while at our base. Sometimes they operated out of there.

One day, when I was working in the revetment, I saw a plane take off, drop back down and crash into the stump field at the end of the runway. It blew all to hell. The pilot actually lived through it, even though he went through the windshield. I don't know whether he survived long, though, because he was burned pretty badly.

I was caught in only one air raid in all the time I was in India, but the British airmen took care of that. When the Japs came to bomb us, the British drove them off pretty easily. It was the only incident I had with the enemy.

Our lodging was pretty simple. When we got to the base, we put up tents in rows. The flaps were always tied up due to the heat. During the monsoon season, it rained a lot. Our cloths would mildew pretty easily and we just ended up throwing them out when we left after the war. We wore raincoats and Frank Buck hats when we went to mess, but we usually got wet anyway. Because of the heat, the water was always warm, so we dug a well in order to have cool water for showers.

We had natives cut a lot of bamboo for us, splitting and stripping the bark. Then we would make mats of bamboo strips, put long grass on top, and put it on the roofs of the buildings. It really worked good because there wouldn't be any leaks.

Our bunks were made with bamboo posts four inches thick with a bamboo strip mattress stretched across. The mattress would stretch after a time and we would have to retighten it on the posts.

A lot of guys got sick with jungle rot because of all the heat and humidity. I still get a red rash on my chest from it. And talk about ants! I never saw so many different kinds! They would make a trail right up the bedpost, through the mosquito net, down the post on the other side, and on to the next bed. They were biters and would give you a tough time now and then.

There was lots of malaria, too, and they gave us quinine to prevent it as best they could. Every day at mess, there would be a sergeant at the door handing out the pills with a glass of water. "I want to see you swallow it," he would tell everyone.

I had a tooth filled at the base one time. The drill was powered with a foot pump, and you can bet that felt pretty good!

The base wasn't really close to town. When we did go to town, though, there were always cows in the streets; they were sacred so could do what they wanted. It wasn't clean, that's for sure! The people wore clothes only around their privates and the kids were usually naked. The British sure kept those people poor.

I don't know whether sending all that stuff to the Chinese paid off or not. An awful lot of the supplies they were supposed to get ended up on the black market. A lot of supplies went down the Burma Road, too, but, I think it was all stolen for the black market! A guy could buy all kinds of stuff on the black market. But when it was time to go home, there was a big shakedown and some officers were caught with eighty- and ninety thousand dollars!

One of the best times was when the war ended and the guys started cooking with booze. Some natives brought in a bunch of large bananas and other wild fruit. A couple of guys from Tennessee who worked in the kitchen got some of the stainless steel pots and kettles and set up a still. They made some pretty good moonshine. Even the officers tasted it! But so much sampling occurred that there was little of the booze left to put in reserve!

Another thing that happened at the end of the war was some big shipments of beer were coming in and being stockpiled. This was probably being brought in in advance of the invasion of Japan. But then the war ended and all this beer was just piling up. Well, one guy got smart. He made three trips with a truck and brought in 90 cases. It only cost him 60-cents a case. The cases had sawdust in them to help keep the bottles from breaking, so the sawdust was put in a hole in the ground, the hole was filled with ice, and we had cold beer! We had a couple of good weeks there! It was something like the TV show "MASH"!

When the war ended and we were ready to ship home, all of our tools were destroyed – cut in half – and thrown in the marshes. The people were so poor, I still can't understand why we couldn't have just given the tools to them. Their life expectancy at that time was only 27 years.

I was able to go home on points and was supposed to leave on one of the first flights on October 15, 1945. But some officers bumped me off two days in a row. I had to keep checking my bedding in and out each day because of this.

Finally, I got out. I flew to Karachi, stayed there from October 20 to New Year's Eve, and then boarded a boat that was to go through the Mediterranean Sea but ended up doing the Pacific run around India. We stopped at Singapore, which was quite a sight from the sea. They wouldn't let us get off the ship, though, because no doubt they would have had trouble rounding us all up again. You can't leave these army guys go, you know!

From Singapore, we headed to Guam, Wake Island, and then straight to Pearl Harbor in Honolulu where I had my first warm shower in six weeks! There was still a lot of damage visible at Pearl Harbor from the Japanese attack.

The ship stayed in Hawaii only two days, just long enough to reload drinking water, I think. Altogether, it took 31 days to get to Seattle from Karachi. In Seattle, we went to a few bars and there was beer there from all over the United States. Again, this was all being stockpiled for the invasion of Japan that never happened. We even found Arcadia Beer there!

From Seattle, I went to Camp McCoy where I was discharged on February 5, 1946, and from there I went straight to Independence. I was in the service just four days short of four years and was given the Asiatic-Pacific Theater Medal with three campaign

Stars, the Victory Medal, and Good Conduct Medal. I made my first three stripes in the states and staff sergeant while in India.

It was interesting, but it doesn't seem like I did a hell of a lot. The government sent me half way around the world by air and the other half by boat. But I did get to see the Pyramids in Egypt from the air.

Raymond Weier, 103rd Infantry Division. Ray's oral history can be found on page 256 of this document.

JEROME ISAACS
UNITED STATES ARMY

This record of Jerome Isaacs' World War II service is based upon an interview conducted on March 10, 2007, in the Los Angeles, California, Public Library.

I was born on January 25, 1919, in Independence, Wisconsin. I had four brothers and two sisters -- Ethel, Bernard, George, Saul, Harold, and Mae.

I graduated from high school in 1937, was out for two years, and then went to the University of Wisconsin. My father died on October 19, 1934, when I was 15. He had a general store in a town of about 860 people when he died. My mother was the strongest person I ever knew in my life. With seven children, the thing I remember most was that I never saw her cry. We had a rugged life after my father died; we never had much money and were just scraping by. But she would say, "Never think of yourself as poor. Just think of yourself as without money. If you think of yourself as poor, you're going to lose your ambition." I thought of that a lot over my life.

When I got out of high school, there was nothing to do in that small town. I went to Milwaukee, Wisconsin, which was a fairly large city. My sister was living there. A clerk who had worked for my dad said I could live with him until I found a job. Things were pretty rough.

I got a job at Thompson's Cafeteria -- I don't know if they're in business anymore -- bussing dishes. I lived with Alex Marsolek. But every day I'd come home and he'd ask me if I found a job, and I had to tell him I didn't. So, I finally decided I had to move out. I got myself a room and then got a job stocking groceries. One day I walked into the Pfister Hotel and asked Steve Pilsen, the head porter, if I could get a job. He said he'd try me out as a bellboy, so for over a year, that's what I did. I made good money there. I got tips and a small salary, and when they had conventions and meetings, you made pretty good money.

In my early days, I looked like a Greek god! That's what my wife called me! Then, when I reached 60, she said I looked like a goddamned Greek!

After a year or year-and-a-half in Milwaukee, I had enough and went back to

Jerome Isaacs

Independence. Then I went to the University of Wisconsin. I was at Lake Delavan, Wisconsin, for the weekend when I heard of Pearl Harbor. I thought it was a radio program; I didn't realize it was a war.

I was starting my third year at the university when I got drafted. I wanted to go into the service. My friends were in and I felt it was my obligation. People were pretty patriotic.

I had to take a physical. I had poor eyes all my life and didn't have good vision, but I got in to the Army alright. I went to Fort Bragg, North Carolina, for basic infantry training. It was tough! We were up at five in the morning and had breakfast at six. I think we went out to the exercise field before breakfast. Then we came back to eat and after that went to classes. We did a lot of hiking to get in physical shape. After what I went through, I think I and many others came out alive because of the physical shape we were in.

We missed out on going with the National Guard to New York City to welcome troops coming back. Instead, we went to Fort Sill, Oklahoma, for training in artillery. From there we shipped out to Camp Howze, Texas, and then to New Jersey and overseas.[1] We sailed overseas on the *U.S.S. Monticello* and they had Navy ships guarding the troopships. The trip was uneventful.

The thing was, the troopship had triple decks to sleep. To get in bed, you would grab a hold of the next bed and slide in sideways. We used salt water for showers; you can't soap yourself in it because there are no suds. I was on F deck. This was low in the ship. At night, they told us goodnight. "By the way, if we're hit by a torpedo, we'll be closing off F deck." That was a goodnight!

We landed in Oran, in the Mediterranean but didn't get off the boat. Then we crossed the Mediterranean to Marseilles, France.[2]

Every day we got to go up to the top deck for fresh air. One day I sat next to a guy in our outfit – an ex-truck driver, not to tall, and all muscle – and he was bragging about how many Germans he was going to kill. He had enough muscles to kill a lot of them!

When we got off the boat at Marseilles, we went to bivouac. German planes were flying over day and night and bombing near there, but not where we were. This guy, the truck driver, cracked up and they sent him out and we never saw him again. The guys who bragged about the danger were usually the most vulnerable, I think.

I figured this out – everybody was afraid, especially when you could see the enemy. If you saw someone ahead of you turn and run, the whole

The *U. S. S. Monticello* (AP-61), which carried Jerome to the European Theater of Operations. Prior to and after the war, it was known as the Italian cruise ship *Conte Grande*.

---

[1] Elements of the 103rd Infantry Division, to which Jerome was assigned, left for overseas on October 6, 1944.
[2] The *U. S. S. Monticello* arrived in Marseilles, France, on October 20, 1944.

damned gang would run!

Well, when we got to Marseilles, we went into bivouac. They had cleared the area because it had been mined by the Germans. They had piled the mines up by a tree and a mess truck backed up against it, and nine or twelve people got killed from the mines! They laid them out in front of us; that wasn't a pleasant welcome!

When I got overseas, I was put in the 382nd Field Artillery.[3] "We're going to make you a forward observer," they said, and I told them, "I don't have 20/20 vision." Then they said, "That's okay, we'll put you up there where you won't miss anything!" This all happened when we were in the combat area.

We were in France at Selestat and we soon relieved the 3rd Infantry Division.[4] A division is about 12,500 men and they only had stragglers coming back. That scared the hell out of us!

We crossed the Rhine River and into combat.[5] Our first day in combat, our guns were in place, and they gave us a jeep – three of us forward observers – and we went up to the front lines. As a forward observer, you have to get out in front.

I'll tell you how we worked. We used precision firing, which is when the target, observer, and guns are in a straight line. Not much azimuth is used in precision firing. They would just fire over our heads and we would only adjust the range.

To line up the guns, they send you out at night with a pole with a pin light on it. You go out a distance – I don't think it was 500 yards – and at the guns they see the pin light. When you're out there alone, though, the German patrols are going by and you can hear them. When you're out there alone, a guy can come up and stab you in the back. That was the worst duty I had, I think.

Anyway, the guns zero in on the pin light and that's the reference point whether to go left or right. Then you give commands, "battery adjust, shell HE, charge five, fuse six" and so forth. I can't remember all the commands. Then you gave them the azimuth to move the guns left or right.

We took turns carrying radios. They were about 50 pounds. I got a Bronze Star just before I was taken prisoner. We were precision firing our one-oh-five (105-mm) howitzers. When in your position on top of a hill, you try not to give your position away because the Germans had the top of hills zeroed in just like we did. So, the Germans started firing at the top of this hill and their airbursts were hitting the trees. We tried to dig in but the ground was so hard and we couldn't dig. So, everybody took off, but I stayed because we were precision firing. Our 105-mm howitzers didn't carry to the Germans, who were quite a ways down in the valley, so I called in two-forty (240-mm) howitzers, which had a longer range. I took off with the radio and the Germans were still firing at the top of this hill. After a while, I was dragging the radio by the aerial but when I got down the hill the radio was still working. So, I got a Bronze Star.

105's would fire 5,000 or 5,500 feet, I think. They were the most practical guns. When the Germans fired at us and we'd get airbursts, you'd really have to do something

---

[3] The 382nd Field Artillery Battalion, 103rd Infantry Division, consisted of 105-mm truck-drawn howitzers.

[4] The 103rd Infantry Division relieved the 3rd Infantry Division on November 8-9, 1944.

[5] The 103rd Infantry Division actually crossed the Lauter River, a 30-mile-long tributary of the Rhine, into Germany on December 15, 1944.

about that – dig in or get out!   Shrapnel splattered like an umbrella coming down on us. It was dangerous and a helmet didn't help too much with this.

I got hit when we crossed the Rhine. That was December 1944. We were in a house, about 113 of us. We were to take a town and the plan was to surround it and attack. We were the first to get to our location. When we looked out the windows we could see the Germans coming across the field. Infantry had set up machine guns and were firing at them, but one of the Germans came up to the door and fired a grenade. The general who was with us got hit in the legs and it almost took his legs off. They didn't get us out of the house and we didn't know if the others had arrived in their three positions. I was in the basement, laying against the wall, and the Germans stuck a muzzle of a big gun, like a one-oh-five, through a basement window and the whole house came down. A beam came out of a wall and hit the side of my body and made it numb. It hit me on the helmet, shoulder, and side.

I thought they shot off the side of my body. I just lay there and it took me a while to realize I was still alive. I don't know if I said a prayer for being alive, or what. That's when we surrendered. We carried the general out and he was taken away. I don't know if he lived or not.

That was the closest I came.

We got out of the house and the Germans lined us up. I was told to go back to the house and say "hande hoch!" or "hands up" to have others come out of the house. I did what they said because I thought they would shoot me if I didn't. Nobody came out, though. They must have gotten out the other side of the house and across the little river that was there.

When I was taken prisoner, I threw away my dogtags because I was Jewish. All the Jewish people did that. Now I think they don't put a guy's religion on the tags.

The Germans knew everything. Their intelligence was excellent. When I was taken prisoner, they picked the forward observers right out of the line, and I don't know how the hell they did that! They put us in a prison, each of us alone in a cell. I don't know what town that was in. All we had was a bucket and a little food. Then they gave us some Phillip Morris cigarettes. I didn't smoke so I didn't take any.

Then at midnight, they'd take you out to interrogate you. When they questioned you, you were only supposed to give your name, rank, and serial number. You have quite a bit of fear – we were afraid – and you're in there alone and something would happen, so you probably gave little bits of information you shouldn't have. They didn't question us in the cell. They took me into a room with an officer and a guard. The officer was sitting at a desk with a P-38, a pistol, and he was rolling a cartridge in his fingers. By the time they questioned us, they knew our whole route, where we landed in Oran and Marseilles. They knew everything.

Then we started marching with the other prisoners. 800 miles, we walked. Shortly after this was the Battle of the Bulge.

We were filthy. We took showers with ice cold water and put our uniform back on. There were no towels or nothing like that.

I remember one place we stopped. It was a prison with bars in the cells. I think they still kept the forward observers in separate cells. I know I was in a separate cell. I had pneumonia again. I thought I was just getting a bad cold. They gave us something to drink in a tin can and I put a note in the tin can and threw it across the room trying to get it through the bars. It fell down and a guard picked it up. That was the first time I tried that. There was an officer's compound across from where the guard was patrolling and when I tried it again, the can went all the way across. Then they took me out of there and got me some medicine.

It was around Christmas time when they put us on boxcars. But we weren't going anywhere. The engineer just moved the train back and forth and back and forth. I remember I yelled, "Why are you punishing me like this? I'm Jewish? I don't celebrate Christmas!"

I remember not many guys got sick. Like I said, we were in pretty good shape. One time, they closed the door to the boxcar and the guard had his rifle leaning against it. Well, the gun fell, went off, and it killed one of the prisoners. They just threw him off the boxcar and that was the end of him.

Our guards were older and they were pretty kind people, like old grandfathers. They were more lenient. The more dangerous ones were younger – the guys that when growing up were put in military schools or were snipers. They were dangerous people. They would have probably killed a lot of Americans if they were guards. But the older people knew what the war was all about because they had seen one before – World War I.

We were told to get out of the boxcars then and we started walking again. We walked in ranks and they had mounted guards. We would pick up, like, I think it was rhubarb, in the fields and chew on it. They didn't want you to do it but if you saw it, you picked it up because you were hungry.

At night, we would sleep outside. It was cold and icy. The way you'd sleep was you lay on your back with your legs spread out and another soldier would sleep between your legs. You'd keep warm that way from body heat. But when you had to get up and pee, everybody hollered! But that's the way you kind of kept warm. There were no blankets; we didn't carry anything, either.

They gave us grass soup. They'd give you a bowl, you'd take a sip, and pass it on. We sometimes got Red Cross boxes. The boxes would have cigarettes – you can't eat those and I didn't smoke – sandwiches, candy, and so forth. Non-perishable things. We were generally fed better than you'd expect, under the circumstances. You know we walked a lot so under the circumstances, there was only so much they could do. The food was pretty lousy, though.

We could sign up to escape, too. I signed up with another guy. We would get out of the compound and go to the Russian or French compound and try to trade cigarettes for food. So, we got out one night and went into another barracks, and the beds were so close only one body could go down the aisle. It was raining that night and I guess the lightning put out the lights while we were talking to – I don't know if it was a Russian or French soldier – to trade cigarettes for food.

Here we see a guard coming up that aisle with a rifle and all. The aisles were pretty long. We waited until he got close to us and we knocked him down and ran over him and ran outside the barracks. I went out one end and I thought the other prisoner was back of me. But I looked around and he wasn't there. So, I stopped. Well, he went out the other door. The guard got up and yelled "hande hoch!". There was a fence there and

I don't know how the hell I got over that fence. I think I just put my hands on the top and threw myself over and started running. I got back to the compound and the other prisoner got back, too! But that scared the hell out of me. I shouldn't have stopped and waited for him.

Someone was in charge of escapes. They gave us scissors to cut the wire of the fence and if you remembered where you went out, you went back to that spot to get in again. I think we went out twice. I remember we were on a train once, and you can tell a G.I. by his haircut and clothes, and we got caught. Someone identified us. But, like I said, the guards weren't too cruel. They were more lenient and wouldn't kill you.

At our final camp, there was a Russian compound and an American compound and, I think, an Italian compound. The Germans kept moving us and pushing us ahead of the Russians, who were advancing to attack Berlin. This camp was about 37 miles from Berlin, as I recall. The Russians herded German cattle to the compounds because they were going to find Russian prisoners there. They were cooking steaks and all but their stomachs couldn't handle it and a lot of them died from overeating. They were wheeling them out of there because they ate too much. But, they didn't know about these things at the time.

It was at this camp where we went to the control of the American army. We were taken to Hildershide, Germany, where we got on a plane to Le Havre, on the north coast of France. I weighed 105 pounds – I was 165 pounds when I went into the Army. It didn't take long to gain my weight back to 150 or 155 pounds, though. I didn't eat much after I got out until the hospital in Hildershide. They moved us pretty fast once we were out of the camp.

This photo of Jerome was taken in a training camp in the United States, probably at either Fort Sill, Oklahoma, or Camp Howze, Texas, prior to his going overseas.

357

In the POW camp, a lot of American prisoners made radios out of tin cans and we got most of the news over the British Broadcasting system from those tin can radios. This was towards the end of the war. For instance, we knew when President Roosevelt died and a lot of other news. I don't know how the hell they made radios out of tin cans, though. I think there's a museum back east where they have a lot of gadgets made by the prisoners of war.

I remember when we were in a town and the Germans were on one side of the street and we were on the other. There were houses and shops – maybe it was a main street – and if someone across the street showed themselves, they'd be fired at. Anyway, there had to be a guard outside so the back of the house we were in would be covered. The front was always covered.

So, they put me out there in the back one night. It was sort of a lean-to that I was in and a German soldier came walking on the other side of the wall from where I was. We were both armed. I don't think he knew I was on the other side so nothing happened.

I never fired my carbine once while I was in the war area. Forward observers always carried carbines. But I never fired mine when up ahead of the artillery because that would give away your position.

I'll tell you something. I don't know how to explain fear. You get so tired sometimes, you're not fearful. You can't think about fear all the time. When the situation gets bad, the fear gets worse. If you're in a bad situation, you feel like your hair is standing up on your head.

I remember one time in combat a German patrol walked right through us American soldiers. Nobody did anything. They were talking German and we were all quiet. They went right through us and maybe they knew we were there, but nothing happened. It was pitch black out that night, and I had bad eyes, but I could still see them. But nothing happened.

I was given the Bronze Star, two Purple Hearts, and the Good Conduct Medal. One of the Purple Hearts was for frozen feet. I don't know why they gave it to me for that. I think I went in to get some socks or something from the supply department and had frozen feet.

When I was there, I was always so fatigued and didn't think about things too much. Because of the fatigue, when you see things, it doesn't hurt you too much. You don't retain what you saw because there are always other duties. You're always busy. Then after you get out you realize the magnitude of it all. When I got home, my mother and everybody thought I had changed. But I didn't think I had changed. But you've got to rationalize things in life or otherwise you'll go nuts, you know? You know a lot of things are important but you shouldn't exaggerate their importance.

I'm anti-war now. It bothers me that so many volunteers for the military are young people with no skills. But maybe I'll enlist again and I can come back for another interview!

358

GAMROTH, GEORGE R.

      Seaman 2/c George Gamroth enlisted in the United States Navy on February 2, 1944 while in high school, and entered active service on July 1, 1944. Following basic training, he entered the Navy's V-12 aviation training program, which he attended in Michigan, Illinois, and Iowa. With the war's end, he was released to inactive duty and eventually separated from the Navy on April 23, 1946.

KUKA, JOSEPH E.

      Joe entered the Army on May 31, 1944. He spent two-and-a-half years in the European Theater during World War II where he participated in the Rhineland and Central Europe campaigns with the 42nd Infantry Division.

      Following World War II, Joe remained in the Army until he retired after 20 years of service on June 30, 1964. He attained the rank of Warrant Officer.

PAPE, EARL

Earl entered the Army on May 15, 1942. He arrived in Europe on December 25, 1944 and served with Company M, 335th Infantry, 84th Infantry Division, as a Private. He participated in the Rhineland and Central Europe campaigns and was awarded the American Theater Service Medal, Good Conduct Medal, and European-African-Middle Eastern Medal. Earl was discharged in late February 1946.

Earl brought home many photographs, some taken by himself personally, while others were "liberated." The photo to the left is one he found. On the back, Earl had written, "Here is Hitler with his body guards. They are of no help to him anymore. People think that Hitler left Germany."

The back of the photo below has the inscription, "We had are (sic) fun along with action. We couldn't let the Germans have all the beer." Earl identified himself on the left, pouring the barrel.

Earl also personally took photos of concentration camps he had seen, including Buchenwald.. Several photos were very graphic in their content.

STENDAHL, IVAN C

Ivan was a native of Whitehall and made his post-war home in Independence. He entered the United States Army on January 14, 1943 and served in the Signal Detachment Service Company. He spent one year beginning in January 1945 in Alaska and was separated from the Army on February 23, 1946. A Tech 4 at war's end, Ivan wore the American Theater Service Medal and Good Conduct Medal.

SYLLA, JOHN P.

John enlisted in the United States Navy and entered service on July 16, 1943. During World War II, he served aboard *USS LCS(L)-70* ("Landing Craft Support, Large", called the "Mighty Midgets" by the men who served aboard them) in the Asiatic-Pacific Theater. Upon his discharge in June 1946, he was awarded the American Defense Medal, Asiatic-Pacific Theater Medal with one battle star, and World War II Victory Medal.

John re-entered the Naval Reserve in 1952 and served until June 1958. During this time, he served aboard the *USS Menard (APA-201)* and at the San Diego Naval Station.

John was a Ship's Cook, Third Class.

THALACKER, LLOYD

Lloyd entered the United States Army on July 27, 1942 and served in the Medical Detachment of the 3rd Field Artillery Observation Battalion. The battalion left New York on January 2, 1944 and arrived in England on January 10, 1944. It entered France on July 17, 1944 and was in Salzburg, Austria, at war's end.

Lloyd participated in four campaigns with the 3rd Field Artillery Observation Battalion – Normandy, Northern France, Rhineland, and Central Europe. The battalion arrived back in New York on November 29, 1945 and Lloyd was discharged on December 5, 1945. He attained the rank of Staff Sergeant.

WILCZEK, JOSEPH A.
World War I -- World War II

Joe Wilczek has the rare distinction of having served in both World War I and World War II. He was a Private assigned to the 161st Depot Brigade, 353rd Infantry, 89th Division, and served in Europe during World War I. He reenlisted in the Army Air Corps in the early days of World War II at the age of 45. In April 1943 he was discharged "to accept employment in an essential industry."

Clarence Sluga

The Bautch Brothers (l to r) – Edmund, Anselm, Adelbert. Adelbert was killed in action in Europe shortly after this photo was taken.

Frank Bisek – in the photo below, Frank is on the far right. Frank also had three brothers in the service during World War II – Benedict, Emil, and Louis (killed in action on Luzon).

364

The crew of *Idiot's Delight*, shot down on December 28, 1944 following a raid on Kaiserslautern, Germany. Best identification is as follows: Top Row (l to r): 2/Lt Jack Hirshberg, 2/LT Leland Farlow, 2/LT James Merrill, 2/LT Robert Baetz. Middle Row (l to r): Sgt Allen Byars, Sgt Bobby Davenport, unknown. Front Row (l to r): unknown, Sgt Alexander Kamenko, Sgt Roman "Butch" Sobota. Sobota and Farlow were the only survivors when the B-24 exploded after being hit by flak. The two unidentified in the photo are Sgt Eugene Lambert and Sgt Monroe Scudder. On the mission in which the aircraft was lost, Lambert was not aboard. Instead, a voice interceptor, S/Sgt Guenther Schaumberg, was aboard, and killed.

Ignatius Gierok, wounded in action in Europe. Ignatius' brother, Charles, was also wounded in action in Europe.

Ben Gamroth

Calvin Maloney, far right